Fundamentals of Law Office Management: Systems, Procedures, and Ethics

Fourth Edition

DELMAR CENGAGE Learning

Options.
Over 300 products in every area of the law: textbooks, online courses, CD-ROMs, reference books, companion websites, and more – helping you succeed in the classroom and on the job.

Support.
We offer unparalleled, practical support: robust instructor and student supplements to ensure the best learning experience, custom publishing to meet your unique needs, and other benefits such as Delmar Cengage Learning's Student Achievement Award. And our sales representatives are always ready to provide you with dependable service.

Feedback.
As always, we want to hear from you! Your feedback is our best resource for improving the quality of our products. Contact your sales representative or write us at the address below if you have any comments about our materials or if you have a product proposal.

Accounting and Financials for the Law Office • Administrative Law • Alternative Dispute Resolution • Bankruptcy Business Organizations/Corporations • Careers and Employment • Civil Litigation and Procedure • CLA Exam Preparation • Computer Applications in the Law Office • Constitutional Law • Contract Law • Court Reporting Criminal Law and Procedure • Document Preparation • Elder Law • Employment Law • Environmental Law • Ethics Evidence Law • Family Law • Health Care Law • Immigration Law • Intellectual Property • Internships Interviewing and Investigation • Introduction to Law • Introduction to Paralegalism • Juvenile Law • Law Office Management • Law Office Procedures • Legal Nurse Consulting • Legal Research, Writing, and Analysis • Legal Terminology • Legal Transcription • Media and Entertainment Law • Medical Malpractice Law Product Liability • Real Estate Law • Reference Materials • Social Security • Sports Law • Torts and Personal Injury Law • Wills, Trusts, and Estate Administration • Workers' Compensation Law

---

DELMAR CENGAGE Learning
5 Maxwell Drive
Clifton Park, New York 12065-2919

For additional information, find us online at:
www.delmar.cengage.com

Fundamentals of
Law Office Management:
Systems, Procedures,
and Ethics

Fourth Edition

Pamela Everett Nollkamper
Fullerton College

DELMAR
CENGAGE Learning

Australia • Brazil • Japan • Korea • Mexico • Singapore • Spain • United Kingdom • United States

DELMAR
CENGAGE Learning

**Fundamentals of Law Office Management:
Systems, Procedures, and Ethics,
Fourth Edition**
Pamela Everett Nollkamper

Vice President, Career and Professional
Editorial: **Dave Garza**

Director of Learning Solutions: **Sandy Clark**

Acquisitions Editor: **Shelley Esposito**

Managing Editor: **Larry Main**

Product Manager: **Melissa Riveglia**

Editorial Assistant: **Lyss Zaza**

Vice President, Career and Professional
Marketing: **Jennifer McAvey**

Marketing Director: **Debbie Yarnell**

Marketing Coordinator: **Jonathan Sheehan**

Production Director: **Wendy Troeger**

Production Manager: **Mark Bernard**

Senior Content Project Manager: **Betty Dickson**

Art Director: **Joy Kocsis**

Technology Project Manager: **Tom Smith**

Production Technology Analyst: **Thomas Stover**

For product information and technology assistance, contact us at
Professional & Career Group Customer Support, 1-800-648-7450

For permission to use material from this text or product,
submit all requests online at **cengage.com/permissions**
Further permissions questions can be e-mailed to
permissionrequest@cengage.com

Library of Congress Control Number: 2007941011

ISBN-13: 978-1-4283-1928-8

ISBN-10: 1-4283-1928-X

Delmar
5 Maxwell Drive
Clifton Park, NY 12065-2919
USA

Cengage Learning products are represented in Canada by Nelson Education, Ltd.

For your lifelong learning solutions, visit **delmar.cengage.com**

Visit our corporate website at **cengage.com**

Notice to the Reader
Publisher does not warrant or guarantee any of the products described herein or perform any independent analysis in connection with any of the product information contained herein. Publisher does not assume, and expressly disclaims, any obligation to obtain and include information other than that provided to it by the manufacturer. The reader is expressly warned to consider and adopt all safety precautions that might be indicated by the activities described herein and to avoid all potential hazards. By following the instructions contained herein, the reader willingly assumes all risks in connection with such instructions. The reader is notified that this text is an educational tool, not a practice book. Since the law in constant change, no rule or statement of law in this book should be relied upon for any service to any client. The reader should always refer to standard legal sources for the current rule or law. If legal advice or other expert assistance is required, the services of the appropriate professional should be sought. The publisher makes no representations or warranties of any kind, including but not limited to, the warranties of fitness for particular purpose or merchantability, nor are any such representations implied with respect to the material set forth herein, and the publisher takes no responsibility with respect to such material. The publisher shall not be liable for any special, consequential, or exemplary damages resulting, in whole or part, from the readers' use of, or reliance upon, this material.

Printed in Canada
1 2 3 4 5 X X X 12 11 10 09 08

Dedication

This text is dedicated to my mother, IRENE T. BUNNELL, whose love and memory
are an inspiration to me.

Preface

A law office is an exciting place to work. It provides employees with a stimulating environment that is rich with opportunities to learn and grow. It is a world that speaks its own language, has its own systems, and contains elements that are not found in other offices. Like other industries, law is a business; but it conducts its business differently from other industries. Without proper education in the business of law in general, students are not prepared for a career in law. Students must have knowledge of the business of law, know how a law office functions, and understand the legal world.

Learning law is a difficult task. There is much to learn to prepare a student for a successful legal career. In addition to substantive and technical courses, knowledge of the business of law is important to understand how the substantive material is delivered to a client. Nonsubstantive subjects, such as cultural elements of an office, are important to learn so that one feels comfortable in a legal environment. These elements are just as important as the mechanics of doing the job.

Fundamentals of Law Office Management: Systems, Procedures, and Ethics, Fourth Edition, is directed to students who choose a legal career, whether as a manager, paralegal, secretary, or attorney. It will inform the student how a law office is managed rather than how to manage a law office. Therefore, students who have no management aspirations, as well as those who have management goals, will find that this text contains vital information.

Organizations of the Text

Law Office Management: Systems, Procedures, and Ethics, Fourth Edition, has three goals and is organized in three sections to accomplish those goals:

Section 1. *To provide knowledge of the industry.* Chapters 1 through 5—The Legal Marketplace, The Legal Team, Personnel Relations, The Attorney-Client Relationship, and Paralegal Ethics and Client Relations—provide an overview of the legal industry. These chapters explain the parameters and policies of the business of law, and provide a strong foundation upon which to build a legal career. The information contained in these chapters is essential to understanding why law firms conduct business differently from other industries.

Section 2. *To provide knowledge of how a law office functions.* Chapters 6 through 10—Legal Fees, Timekeeping, Billing and Financial Management, Managing the Client Funds Trust Account, and Technology in the Law Office—introduce students to the functions and procedures common to a law office environment. Understanding how legal offices function will make students' transition into legal employment easier.

Section 3. *To provide essential skills.* Chapters 11 through 14—Law Office Systems, Docket Control Systems, File and Records Management, and Law Library Organization and Management—provide students with essential skills they will use throughout their legal career.

The text is organized to accommodate a 16-week semester course, although it is also conducive to a shorter schedule. The chapters are placed so that they may be assigned in sequential order to give the student requisite information to continue on with the subsequent chapters.

Features

The text has many features to contribute to a student's learning experience, including:

- Chapter objectives at the beginning of each chapter. These objectives highlight the main concepts of the chapter and provide a preview of what is to come.

They act as a checklist for the student to review after the chapter is read to make sure all of the concepts were learned.

- Key words emphasized in four ways. First, new terms are highlighted in bold print within the chapter. Second, each new term is defined in the margin adjacent to the paragraph in which it is found. This helps students learn the definitions at the time the material is read and increases comprehension of the material. Third, a list of key terms is included at the end of each chapter. Fourth, a comprehensive glossary is found at the end of the text.
- Exhibits to illustrate concepts throughout the text. Photographs, charts, and diagrams provide visual reinforcement of the material.
- Ethics Alerts call attention to important ethical information. An Ethics Alert symbol appears in the margin next to the coverage of an ethical principle. In addition, the pertinent material is italicized within the body of the chapter.
- Professional Profiles of people working in the field. This feature, which appears in various chapters, allows a student to see how the chapter material relates to individuals and communicates another's viewpoint about the topic.
- Technology section that lists the various technology. New technology and tried-and-true older technology used in the everyday systems and procedures of a law office, such as timekeeping, billing, and docket control, is included in each applicable chapter. While it is not the intent of the course to give specific instruction on software, the section illustrates how technology increases the efficiency of a particular process. It also illustrates how technology is incorporated into various law office systems.
- Cybersites section. The Cybersites section at the end of each chapter lists websites that pertain to the chapter material. This feature will be very useful to instructors as well as students. Students can gain additional information about the subject matter by researching the topic on the Internet. Instructors can assign Internet research assignments using the Cybersites material. Since websites change often, the author cannot guarantee the reliability of all websites listed in this section.
- Of Interest sidebars. There are many Of Interest sidebars that enhance the chapter material by giving illustrations or tips pertaining to the chapter material.
- Chapter Illustrations. This section reinforces the chapter material in a real-world context. The section follows one law firm, Black, White & Greene, from its formation (Chapter 1) through its growth.

Students are introduced to the firm's employees and follow them throughout the book as they apply the concepts in the chapter. The characters experience the everyday problems and successes that average law office personnel experience. The story format will amuse students, as well as reinforce the material in the chapter. The story approach to the material will give students a different perspective of the material and will illustrate how an average small firm is managed. This section can also be used for class discussion.

- Self Test. This feature, at the end of each chapter, makes purchasing a separate study guide unnecessary. The self test is a list of questions about the chapter material. Students can test their comprehension of the material by answering the questions and comparing their answers with the correct answers found in Appendix A. The questions are comprehensive and cover all of the material in each chapter.
- A summary at the end of each chapter. The summary highlights and summarizes the main points in the chapter. It is not a substitute for reading the chapter, but it helps students study for exams.
- Chapter Review questions at the end of each chapter. These questions review the main points of the chapter and test the students' comprehension of the material. These questions can be assigned as homework or used for class discussion. Answers to these questions are found in the Instructor's Manual.
- Examples for Discussion at the end of each chapter. These examples stimulate class discussions and can also be used for group projects. These examples bring the chapter contents to life by illustrating how issues, technology, and situations must be addressed in a law office. Suggested responses are found in the Instructor's Manual.
- Assignments at the end of each chapter. Some are easily completed and others require more effort. Most are individual assignments but can also be used for group assignments. Suggested answers are found in the Instructor's Manual.
- Appendices containing material that will help students understand the text. The Appendices contain reference material that is useful during the course, as well as on the job, such as a list of associations for paralegals and managers, and the codes of ethics for the National Paralegal Associations.
- A CD that contains additional material for the student. The material on the CD supplements the chapter material and aids to further help the student understand the material. The CD is frequently referenced in the text to remind students that additional information is readily available.

Changes in the Fourth Edition

This fourth edition has been prepared to further the text's goals. Course material has been updated, outdated material has been deleted, and new exhibits, photos, and illustrations have been added. The text is more user-friendly, and this makes the material more fun to learn. It has been completely overhauled while keeping its original continuity and organization.

A goal of the fourth edition is to keep the material as comprehensive as the third edition without increasing its size. Some of the material has been transferred to the accompanying CD to reduce the size of the book. The Tech Tips sidebar has been removed to further this goal.

Supplement Package and Ancillary Materials

The fourth edition is accompanied by a support package that will assist students in learning and aid instructors in teaching.

Instructor's Manual

The Instructor's Manual includes teaching tips, suggestions for class discussions, answers to Chapter Review and Discussion questions, and lecture outlines. The Instructor's Manual consists of the following sections:

1. Section 1 is an outline of each chapter. This outline will assist the instructor in planning lecture material. Incorporated in Section 1 is a guide to the PowerPoint slides that accompany the Instructor's Manual. It directs the instructor where to use each slide, and gives specific instructions on how to present each slide. Each PowerPoint slide has been prepared to deliver the material in a dynamic manner to grab the students' attention.

2. Section 2 is a list of key words and their definitions. This list will aid the instructor in planning lecture material.

3. Section 3 contains the answers to the chapter review questions found at the end of each chapter.

4. Section 4 includes the answers to the discussion questions found at the end of each chapter. It provides the instructor with suggestions on where to direct the discussion questions.

5. Section 5 includes answers to the assignments at the end of each chapter.

6. Section 6 contains teaching pointers and suggestions and includes group assignments and activities.

7. A test bank that consists of multiple choice, true/false, and short answer questions is included in the Instructor's Manual. Instructors may use all, or some, of the questions as they see fit.

Student CD-ROM

The new accompanying CD-ROM provides additional material to help students master the important concepts in the course. This CD-ROM includes Chapter Outlines, Chapter Objectives, Key Terms, and Chapter Questions.

Instructor's eResource CD-ROM

The new e-Resource component provides instructors with all the tools they need in one convenient CD-ROM. Instructors will find that this resource provides them with a turnkey solution to help them teach by making available PowerPoint® slides for each chapter, a Computerized Test Bank, and an electronic version of the Instructor's Manual.

All these instructor materials are also posted on our website, in the Online Resources section.

WebTUTOR on WebCT and BlackBoard

The WebTutor™ supplement to accompany *Fundamentals of Law Office Management: Systems, Procedures, and Ethics,* Fourth Edition, allows you, as the instructor, to take learning beyond the classroom. This Online Courseware is designed to complement the text and benefit students and instructors alike by helping to better manage your time, prepare for exams, organize your notes, and more. WebTutor™ allows you to extend your reach beyond the classroom.

Online Companion™

The Online Companion™ provides students with additional support materials in the form of reality-based examples, review questions, and relevant terminology.

The Online Companion™ can be found at <http://www.paralegal.delmar.cengage.com> in the Online Companion™ section of the website.

Web Page

Come visit our website at <http://www.paralegal.delmar.cengage.com> where you will find valuable information such as hot links and sample materials to download, as well as other Delmar Cengage Learning products.

Please note that the internet resources are of a time-sensitive nature and URL addresses may often change or be deleted.

Acknowledgments

Many thanks to the staff at Delmar who contributed to this text. Also, a heartfelt "thank you" to Jennifer Scroggins, my assistant, who worked hard on many aspects of this project.

My appreciation is also extended to the reviewers of the text, who offered their suggestions and comments. The effort required for a book review is substantial and certainly appreciated. I seriously considered each and every comment and suggestion and implemented most of them. The reviewers' contributions make this edition a great text—**thank you very much.**

Reviewers of the Fourth Edition:
Konnie Kustron
Eastern Michigan University
Ypsilanti, MI

Kathleen Reade
University of Toledo
Toledo, OH

Last, but certainly not least, thanks to my family whose love, understanding, and support of wife, mom, grandma, and sister make life beautiful and hard work worth the effort.

To the Student

After teaching this class for over 25 years, I've heard many comments and opinions from my students. They told me of their desires for this course and what material is useful to them. I appreciate all their comments and sincerely hope to continue receiving them.

Many students have told me that the material in this text made their transition into their new legal career easier—and that is the goal of this text. If this text helps you understand the legal world better, then it has succeeded in reaching its goals. I'd like to hear from you. Let me know what you like, and don't like, about this text. Just drop me an e-mail from our website.

You've made a wise decision to pursue a legal career. It will challenge and exhilarate you, as well as satisfy your personal and professional goals. Sincere best wishes in your studies and career development.

Pamela Everett Nollkamper

Contents

Chapter 4: The Attorney-Client Relationship   116

Chapter 6: Legal Fees 205

Chapter 8: Billing and Financial Management 274

Chapter 14: Law Library Organization and Management   489

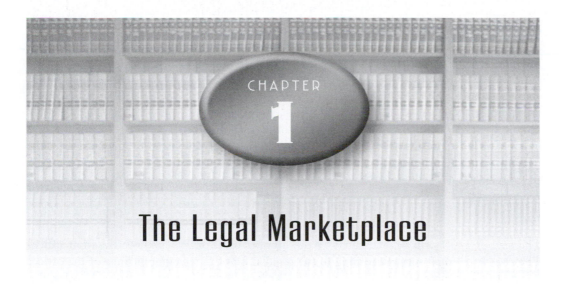

CHAPTER 1

The Legal Marketplace

OBJECTIVES

After completion of this chapter, the student should be able to do the following:

- Describe the structure and organization of small, medium, and large firms.
- Explain the autocratic, democratic, managing partner, committee, and combination management styles.
- Discuss the differences between a sole proprietorship, partnership, professional corporation, limited liability company, boutique firm, office-sharing association, and legal clinic.
- Discuss the differences between corporate legal departments, private companies, and government agencies.
- Identify the changes that have affected the legal marketplace.

INTRODUCTION

Most employers of paralegals are attorneys. Both paralegals and attorneys are professionals whose talents and personalities are as diverse as their numbers. They work in many different types of law offices: small firms, large firms, corporate legal departments, legal clinics, government agencies, and specialized boutique firms. All of these offices have similarities, yet they are different. Each law office has its own structure, organization, and combination of personalities.

The purpose of this chapter is to provide an overview of the different types of law office settings and discuss the various management styles. Comments from paralegals working in the various types of law offices will give an idea of the diversity of law offices. This chapter will supply the foundation for a more in-depth discussion of elements that are common among all law offices and provide a familiarity with the diversity of the legal marketplace.

This chapter describes the structure and organization of law firms. Then, it examines the three categories of the marketplace in which attorneys practice law: private law firms, private industry, and government agencies. Finally, it discusses the changing marketplace of law firms. Throughout the chapter, we will explore paralegal opportunities in the legal marketplace.

STRUCTURE AND ORGANIZATION

For a law office, the term *structure* refers to many parts combined to form a whole. *Organization* refers to the management of each part so that all parts function as one unit. The structure and organization of a law office depend on the needs and desires of its attorneys, especially the senior attorneys who own the firm. These components are subject to change. Variables such as the economy and the changing needs of society influence a law office's structure and organization. A paralegal must be flexible to accommodate organizational changes.

The structure and organization of a law office are determined by four characteristics: size, specialty, management style, and form.

Size

The size of a law office is measured by the number of attorneys employed by that office. The size differential varies according to the population of the geographic area of the office. For example, in large metropolitan areas, such as New York, Chicago, and Los Angeles, the average size of law firms is larger, so the size differential is larger. The size differential for a highly populated area follows:

Small office: 1 to 50 attorneys

Medium office: 51 to 250 attorneys

Large office: 251 or more attorneys

Mega-firm: 1,000 or more attorneys

In areas of average to large populations, the size differential is somewhat smaller.

Small office: 1 to 35 attorneys

Medium office: 36 to 249 attorneys

Large office: 250 or more attorneys

In rural areas with smaller populations, the size differential is smaller yet.

Small office: 1 to 15 attorneys

Medium office: 16 to 60 attorneys

Large office: 60 or more attorneys

The number of branch offices a firm has also determines its size. For example, a large law firm with 300 attorneys may have those attorneys disbursed in several branch offices. A branch office may employ only three to four attorneys, thereby making it a small office. However, the size of a law firm is calculated by the total number of attorneys employed by the firm, including the attorneys in all of its branch offices.

SMALL FIRM   Small firms are the preferred setting for practicing law for most lawyers in the United States. The average size of a small firm is three to four attorneys. A small firm may be less formal and less structured. Most of a small firm's clientele are individuals.

MEDIUM FIRM   The size of a medium firm depends on the area of the United States in which it is located. Medium firms tend to attract entrepreneurial clients who are cost conscious.

LARGE FIRM   Four traditional types of large law firms exist: local, regional, national, and international. A local firm is located in one geographic area with no branch offices. A regional firm has branch offices within a specific region. A national firm has branch offices within the United States. An international firm has branch offices in other countries as well as in the United States.

Large firms are formal and highly structured. They employ many types of support personnel and, for the most part, service large corporate clients. Most large firms have branch offices in major American cities to meet the needs of their corporate clients that conduct business in other areas of the country.

MEGA-FIRM   Mega-firms employ one thousand or more attorneys and have branch offices all over the world. They have a high ratio of support staff per attorney.

mega-firm
A firm that employs more than 1,000 attorneys and has branch offices throughout the world.

Of Interest . . .

MEGA-FIRMS

Four of the six largest firms in the world are based in London in the United Kingdom. In 2006, the largest law firm in the world was the British firm Clifford Chance, which had revenue of US $2.039 billion. It has 27 offices in 20 countries, with its headquarters in London. Clifford Chance employs 3,857 fee-earning lawyers and 3,620 support staff. It is a limited liability partnership and was voted Law Firm of the Year in 2006.

Law firm stereotypes have followed general preconceptions. Large law firms are seen as competitive, impersonal, high paying, and prestigious, with gradual opportunity for client contact and real responsibility for cases. Smaller law firms are seen as family-oriented, low-paying, and personal with mentor opportunities available.

Although these stereotypes may contain a grain of truth, these descriptions are just broad generalizations. Law firms are as varied as the attorneys who practice in them. Small firm "sweat shops" exist where the partners seem only to care about their share of the profits, as do large firms that place family, community, and social obligations high on their list of priorities. Medium-sized firms may have characteristics of both large and small firms. It is important to look beyond the common stereotypes before deciding the size of law firm that fits your career goals.

Specialties

As society has become more complex, law has become more complex. Thousands of new laws are passed each year, and it has become increasingly difficult for attorneys to keep abreast of the many changes. This has forced attorneys to specialize in a particular area of law.

In 1971, California became the first state to adopt a pilot specialization program. In 1979, the American Bar Association (ABA) adopted the Model Plan of Specialization. By 1990, 13 states had plans to recognize legal specialties. The trend for state regulation of specialties arose because of an increase in lawyer advertising (see Chapter 4).

The transition to specialization in law is analogous to that in the medical profession. Before World War II, doctors and lawyers were "general family practitioners." They took care of all the legal and medical needs of a family from birth to death. Now, however, the complexities of law and medicine have made general practice unfeasible for the welfare of the client and the patient.

The areas of law in which a firm's attorneys specialize help determine the firm's clientele and its need for staff, equipment, and materials. For example, a criminal attorney does not need a plush office in which to greet clients since he will probably meet with clients in jail. A business law specialist, who offers clients a wide range of services, will need a tax department, corporate department, litigation department, labor relations department, and contract department. The firm must have a large support staff and a sophisticated computer system. A professional office environment is necessary to greet business clients and conduct conferences.

There are hundreds of legal specialties, and the list continues to grow with the needs of society. There is a specialty area for each area of law, and as we discover and develop new areas, law is created to cover them. For example, as we venture into space, law will be created to govern space. As we explore the vast resources of our oceans, law will be created to govern oceans. As technology advances, law must advance with it. The most recent specialty areas include gay law and law involving toxic mold. In 2008, disaster law became a new specialty in response to the hurricane Katrina disaster. Technology and the Internet opened up many new specialty areas. Among them are **cybercrimes** and **cybertorts**. As more people enter cyberspace, laws are needed to govern their behavior.

Lawyers may become certified in certain specialty areas. A number of states have developed programs for the recognition of legal specialties. In some states, attorneys whose law practice consists of a particular area of law can designate themselves a specialist. In other states, the state bar monitors a certified specialist program. To become certified, an attorney must pass a specialty exam in addition to the bar exam in order to be a certified specialist.

In 1993, the ABA adopted a set of voluntary national standards, along with a process to accredit specialist certification programs. The standards were designed to establish criteria for granting specialist certification and to provide state bar associations with a basis for approving programs. Some states have adopted the ABA's guidelines and others have not. As of 2007, there are 47 specialties offered by state and private programs.

cybercrimes
Crimes committed on the Internet, including hacking and fraud.

cybertort
Actions or damages resulting from libelous material posted on the Internet. Also included is posting material that is protected by copyright or trademarks, such as magazines and photos.

1. Administrative law
2. Admiralty and maritime law
3. Alternative dispute resolution law
4. Animal rights law
5. Antitrust law
6. Appellate law
7. Aviation law
8. Banking law
9. Bankruptcy law
10. Business law
11. Child and juvenile welfare law
12. City, county government law
13. Communications law
14. Constitutional law
15. Construction law
16. Consumer law
17. Corporate law
18. Criminal law
19. Disability law
20. DUI defense law
21. Education law
22. Elder law
23. Employment and labor law
24. Entertainment/sports law
25. Environmental law
26. Estate planning law
27. Family law
28. Federal Indian law
29. Franchise and distribution law
30. Health care law
31. Insurance law
32. Immigration law
33. Intellectual property law
34. International law
35. Military law
36. Municipal law
37. Natural resources law
38. Oil, gas, and mineral law
39. Patent law
40. Professional liability, accounting, medial, and legal law
41. Real estate law
42. Securities law
43. Space law
44. Tax law
45. Tort law
46. Trial advocacy
47. Workers' comp law

Although certification requirements vary under different programs, a lawyer must accomplish a minimum of five tasks to become a certified specialist. The lawyer must

1. provide specific evidence of extensive practice in the specialty area.
2. be a member in good standing of one or more state bar associations.
3. take a written exam in the specialty area.

4. demonstrate completion of at least 36 hours of specialty continuing legal education every 3 years.

5. become recertified at least every 5 years and be subject to revocation of certification if the program's requirements are not met.

According to a census conducted by the ABA Standing Committee on Specialization in 2006, there are more than 32,714 legal specialists in the United States. The largest specialty area is civil trial advocacy (24 percent). Criminal law and family law are second (9 percent), followed by personal injury law and estates (8 percent). New specialty areas, such as elder law, increased tremendously. Most of the certified lawyers are certified by 10 states, with the vast majority found in California, Florida, and Texas.

Attorney specialties fluctuate according to outside factors such as the economy, legal trends, and social concerns. For example, in the late 1980s, attorneys specializing in employee retirement programs were in the most demand. In the early 1990s, environmental attorneys were in the most demand. When the recession hit in the mid-1990s, bankruptcy specialists were in the highest demand. As the recession subsided, corporate and transactional specialties were prominent. At the millennium, technology skyrocketed, which transferred the demand from corporate to intellectual property and patent specialists. Elder law is becoming a popular specialty as baby boomers age.

Specialists tend to earn more than nonspecialists or general practitioners. They charge more for their services because they handle more complex cases and are considered experts in the area. "Specializing makes life easier," says John Shea, a personal injury specialist in Richmond, Virginia. "You build up a body of knowledge so you can do things efficiently. It's very difficult, if not impossible, to do a lot of things well." Lawyers in small towns and rural areas find it very difficult to specialize because the community demands a variety of legal services. Other general practitioners do not specialize because they prefer the diversity that general practice provides.

Paralegals specialize in the same areas as attorneys. Paralegal specialist programs are offered by the national paralegal associations, some state paralegal associations, and a few state bar associations. Both paralegal and attorney specialist programs are optional.

Management Styles

One very important aspect of the practice of law is not taught to attorneys in most law schools: managing their business. Consequently, many law firms have suffered from poor office management, which has resulted in reduced profits, increased attorney discipline proceedings, and office disorganization. These problems are reflected in dissatisfied clients.

Since the early 1970s, attorneys have realized the importance of effective management. Before this, attorneys ran their businesses by "panic management," which, unfortunately, still exists today.

A law office's environment is referred to as its **culture,** which includes such intangible elements as sharing work assignments, recognition, autonomy, responsibility, attitudes toward the community and family, and social atmosphere.

Culture is unique to each law office. It is usually defined as "the way things are around here." Culture can be analogous to a human personality. It is not only the presence or absence of certain traits, but how those traits interact with each other. Culture is comprised of beliefs and assumptions held by individual members of an organization. A person's beliefs are formed by what they are told, and reinforced by what they observe. Firms where common beliefs and assumptions are widely held with deep conviction are said to have a strong culture. A weaker culture exists when there is less uniformity of beliefs and assumptions. Generally, firms with a strong culture are more profitable than those with a weaker culture because uniformity of beliefs and assumptions results in a more unified and coordinated effort. An element of a firm's culture is its management style.

culture
The working environment of a law firm, consisting of intangible elements such as the social environment, employee relationships, and attitudes.

Of Interest . . .

OLDEST LAW FIRMS

Fifteen Oldest Law Firms in the United States

DATE	NAME	STATE
1792	Cadwalader, Wickersham & Taft	New York
1794	Dabney & Dabney	Mississippi
1806	Emmet, Marvin & Marvin	New York
1809	Guste, Barnett & Shushan	Louisiana
1813	Cooper, Erving, Savage, Nolan & Heller	New York
1817	Hodgson, Russ, Andrews, Woods & Goodyear	New York
1818	Tillinghast, Licht & Semonoff	Rhode Island
1819	Emison, Doolittle, Kolb & Rosllgen	Indiana
1819	R. M. Blanchford, now Cravath, Swaine & Moore	New York
1820	Smith, Taliaferro, Purvis & Boothe	Louisiana
1820	Magavern, Magavern & Grimm	New York
1822	Fletcher, Tilton & Whipple	Pennsylvania
1826	Potter, Anderson & Corroon	Delaware
1843	Arter Hadden	Ohio
1845	Foley & Lardner	Wisconsin

Two distinct managerial areas are addressed by any law firm: administrative (financial, office systems, and so forth) and governance (associates, client relations, personnel, marketing, and the like). The combination of approaches used in these two areas is the management style of the firm. Attorneys, growing tired of chaos, have developed five management styles that are used in most law firms in the United States: autocratic, democratic, managing partner, committee, and combination.

autocratic
Relating to government by one person with unlimited power.

AUTOCRATIC   In an **autocratic** form of management, one person makes all the decisions for the firm. This style is most often found in small offices with one employing attorney. In small offices with more than one attorney, the autocrat is usually the attorney who formed the law firm or manages the major clients of the firm. However, an autocrat is also found in larger offices.

An autocrat in a small office makes all the decisions for the firm, and a secretary, paralegal, or both help implement the decisions. In a larger office, an autocrat makes all the decisions, and an office manager implements them. Small firms with strong leadership have prospered under this type of management. Successful autocrats gain the respect of their associates and usually ask for their input before making major decisions. Like any good leader, they can motivate their staff and associates and delegate responsibility well.

Some autocrats have poor management skills and do not request input from their staff when making decisions. They become tyrants who intimidate staff and clients. An autocratic management style combined with poor leadership skills causes low employee morale and reduces productivity.

Despite the authoritarian nature of this type of management, it is generally effective in getting things done. An autocrat is usually a "born boss" and gladly accepts management responsibility. Strong leadership is an essential element of the success of prosperous law firms.

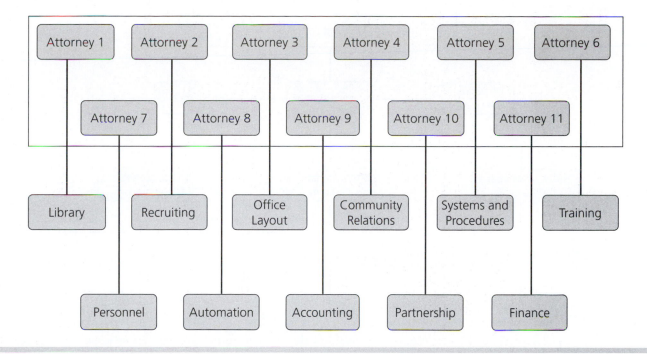

EXHIBIT 1–1   Democratic Organizational Chart

DEMOCRATIC   There are two types of the democratic form of governance: those in which all attorneys in the firm have a vote on management policy and those in which only owners of the law firm have a vote in management policy.

In small offices with fewer than 15 attorneys, usually all attorneys participate in the firm's management. In larger offices, only owners participate in making management decisions.

Actual management duties are accomplished in a democratic management style: In a large firm, the decisions of the firm are delegated to a **legal administrator,** who accomplishes the task or delegates it to an appropriate person. The administrator is a full-time administrator whose only duty is to implement the decisions of the attorneys. In a small firm, a part-time manager/paralegal whose management duties are shared with paralegal duties implements the decisions.

In a smaller firm, each attorney is assigned an area of management, such as equipment procurement, personnel relations, or billing. Each attorney then performs management duties with the assistance of a secretary, paralegal, or both. This form of democratic management style is shown in Exhibit 1–1.

Since people hold many opinions as to how a firm should be managed, complete agreement on a topic is rare in this type of management style. Unless a senior partner or another leader takes control of this group, a consensus of opinion is difficult to reach. Consequently, action is delayed because decisions are delayed. In addition, some attorneys have neither the desire nor the skill to handle management functions. Some attorneys in this management style view their participation in management as a burden, taking time away from their cases and resulting in lower billing for the firm. Generally, this style of management is ineffective and expensive for a firm.

MANAGING PARTNER   In the managing partner style of management, one of the owners of a firm is designated the managing partner, and is responsible for managing the firm. In smaller firms, a managing partner manages a firm in addition to practicing law. This person delegates duties to a paralegal, secretary, or office manager to carry out the decisions. The delegated person is a part-time office manager in addition to being responsible for other duties.

In medium firms, the managing partner spends more time on management duties but is encouraged to continue to practice law so as not to lose legal skills, therefore contributing to the firm's income. The average managing partner spends about 40 percent of his or her time practicing law. The managing partner often has an **office manager,** legal administrator, or

legal administrator
Experienced manager who is hired to manage a law firm. Has the authority of a managing partner.

office manager
A person hired to assist a managing partner or legal administrator with management functions of a firm.

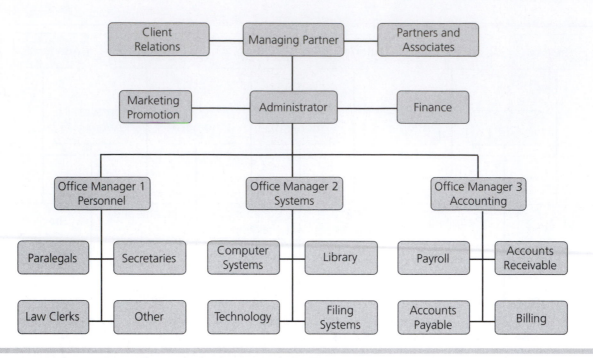

EXHIBIT 1–2   Managing Partner Organizational Chart for a Large Firm

both to assist in the firm's management responsibilities. The managing partner is the head of the firm and often is a senior attorney of the firm.

In large firms, a managing partner may devote all his or her time to management functions and employ an administrator and perhaps many office managers to manage individual areas of a firm, as shown in Exhibit 1–2. These management professionals have no duties other than management functions.

The managing partner style of management is the style most commonly used in law offices. A managing partner with the necessary management and leadership skills is an effective manager. This person must be capable of delegating day-to-day decisions to others while maintaining control. This style of management is closely related to the autocratic style, especially in a small firm.

COMMITTEE   Some firms rely on a committee structure for management. This management style is normally found in large firms. Committees form when the firm cannot agree on a leader or when no strong person emerges after the founder retires.

The terms of committee membership are generally limited, and members rotate from committee to committee to participate in the various areas of management. Management committees generally consist of five to seven members and may comprise senior partners only, a mixture of senior and junior partners, a mixture of partners and associates, or a mixture of partners, associate office managers, and paralegals (see Exhibit 1–3).

A firm may have various committees, the most common of which follow:

Associate personnel (including legal assistants)

Automation and technology

Client relations

Community relations

Compensation

Employee training

Equipment and supplies

Finance and accounting

Marketing

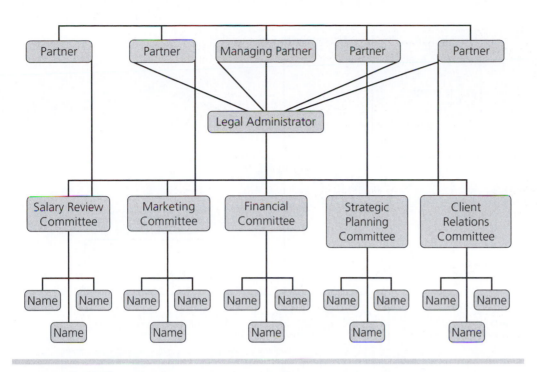

EXHIBIT 1–3   Committee Organization Chart—Large Firm

Office facilities and furnishings
Office space and layout
Partnership matters
Recruiting
Strategic planning
Support personnel
Systems and procedures

An **executive committee** composed of heads of the various management committees coordinates the activities of the committees, as shown in Exhibit 1–4. In medium to large firms, a legal administrator helps coordinate the various committees and is responsible for implementing the decisions. In large offices, the administrator delegates responsibilities to an office manager or managers and sits on each committee.

executive committee
A committee comprising the heads of the various committees in a law firm.

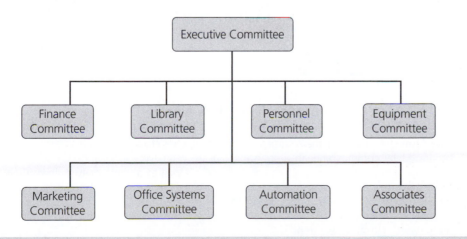

EXHIBIT 1–4   Executive Committee Organizational Chart

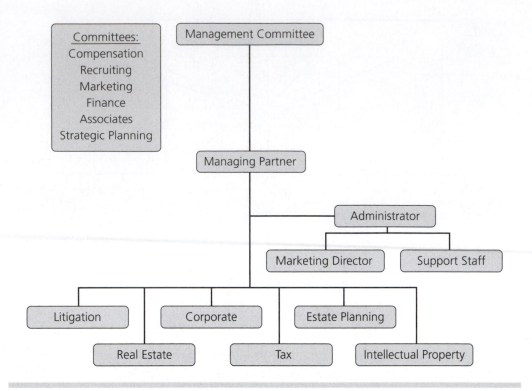

EXHIBIT 1–5   Combination Organization Chart—Large Firm

Many problems may occur with this type of structure. It has been said that a committee is composed of the unwilling, picked from the unqualified, to do the unnecessary. Closely related committees may duplicate efforts. Attending committee meetings may be difficult for some attorneys, especially trial attorneys. Some committee members may be weak because of no management training or knowledge of the subject area. An example is when the committee members take time to educate themselves about technology. Adding this extra step causes delays in the decision process. In addition, committee work requires the use of the firm's greatest asset: the time of its attorneys. Committees are normally ineffective, especially in times of change.

COMBINATION   A combination management style is one that uses two or more management styles at the same time, such as managing partner and committee or democratic and committee (see Exhibit 1–5).

TRENDS

LAW FIRM NAMES

Law firms are changing their names. Names that consist of the owners' last names separated by commas and an ampersand (&) are often very long and cumbersome. Firms are dropping the commas and ampersand, as well as a name or two, from their names. For example, Pierce, Atwood, Scribner, Allen, Smith & Lancaster is now Pierce Atwood. When Thompson & Mitchell merged with Coburn & Croft, the new name did not become Thompson, Mitchell, Coburn & Croft; it is Thompson Coburn. Receptionists are pleased with this new trend.

Forms of Management

Management takes two forms: centralized and decentralized. Having a centralized form of management means that an entire law firm is managed from one source, whether by autocratic, democratic, managing partner, or committee style of management. Having a decentralized form of management means that a law firm is managed in segments, or in many areas. For example, in a decentralized form of management, branch offices may have their own management structure and may not rely on a parent firm for management direction. Each branch may have a different management style, with one managed by committee and another managed by a managing partner.

In a large law firm, each department, identified by areas of law, may manage itself in an **autonomous,** or independent, manner. In this form of decentralized management, the managing partner of each department sits on an executive committee to make decisions involving the whole firm and is solely responsible for management decisions of the department.

autonomous
Being self-governing, independent, and subject to its own methods of management.

PRIVATE LAW FIRMS

Almost two-thirds of all lawyers work in private law firms. Private law firms are small, medium, large, or mega-firms and are organized into seven different business structures: sole proprietorships, partnerships, professional corporations, limited liability companies, boutique firms, office-sharing associations, and legal clinics.

Sole Proprietorships

The term **sole proprietorship** means that a law firm is owned by one attorney. A sole proprietorship is usually a small office; however, it may employ 30 attorneys, making it a medium law firm in some areas of the United States. Most sole proprietorships are managed by the autocratic management style.

A sole proprietor who employs no other attorneys is a **sole practitioner.** Sole practitioners who do not specialize in a particular area of law are **general practitioners.**

The American Bar Association estimates that almost half of all attorneys in private practice are sole practitioners. A new attorney who has just graduated from law school is most likely to be a general practitioner. The cost of opening a law office is very high, and because of financial concerns, a new attorney will accept almost any type of case. A new lawyer is also developing a client base, so it is important to work for as many clients as possible. As a new attorney's client base, skill, and reputation increase, more opportunities for specialization present themselves. Most attorneys who live in rural areas and small towns are general practitioners because the needs of the community require more general legal services. The five most common specialties for sole proprietors are family law, real estate, torts and personal injury, criminal defense, and probate and estate planning.

Some sole practitioners work only for attorneys, not for clients. They are called **contract attorneys,** or temporary lawyers. They work for temporary agencies much in the same way as do temporary support staff personnel. The temporary agency contracts them out to law firms and corporate legal departments to work on a project basis. The project may last a few days or many months. This form of sole practice is gaining popularity both with the lawyers and with the firms for which they work.

Most contract attorneys are recent bar admittees. However, experienced, reputable attorneys are choosing contract work over the more traditional employment for various reasons. Some lost their jobs to corporate downsizing, whereas others recently relocated to new areas, had babies, or decided that the partnership track was not for them. A large portion of contract attorneys, about 25 percent by some estimates, are sole practitioners who accept contract work to compensate for slow periods in their own business.

sole proprietorship
A business that has one individual owner who operates the firm. A sole proprietor may employ other attorneys.

sole practitioner
An attorney who practices law alone. A sole practitioner does not employ other attorneys.

general practitioner
An attorney who does not specialize but accepts cases in all areas of law.

contract attorney
An attorney who works for law firms on an assignment basis or as an independent contractor.

Contract attorneys are subject to the same canons of ethics as their employing firms. The ethical issues faced by contract attorneys are addressed in ABA Formal Opinion 88-356, which defines a temporary lawyer as a lawyer engaged by a firm for a limited period of time, either directly or through a lawyer placement agency. They are bound by the same rules of confidentiality, conflict of interest, disclosure, and fee sharing, as described in Chapter 4.

PROFESSIONAL PROFILE 1

Linda J. Metcalf, paralegal, works for Roger W. Moister, Jr., a sole proprietor in Atlanta, Georgia. The office specializes in bankruptcy, and Roger is also a bankruptcy trustee. The office also handles civil litigation matters. When asked about the structure of her office, Linda states:

"I am the office. I do everything here. I manage the office and am responsible for everything except for reconciling bank statements. In addition to my paralegal duties, which consist of completing all bankruptcy documents and monitoring the litigation cases in bankruptcy adversary proceedings, I have a lot of client contact."

"My job is always different. Each day brings a new challenge. There is never a dull moment. I worked for a large company for 20 years, and I like a small firm much better. I am appreciated here, and I learn more with a variety of work."

"There is a lot of pressure in a small office. We have many cases. My salary may be lower than it would be in other firms, but my bonuses are better. I do not get paid for overtime, but I receive compensatory time off. I like the small atmosphere and team concept of my job. I also like the control I have with my management responsibilities."

Law firms are realizing that they can utilize the talent and skill of a contract attorney at a fraction of the cost of an employee and realize the following benefits from using contract attorneys:

- An opportunity to try out potential hires
- Less administrative work
- Ability for small firms to accept bigger cases without hiring additional personnel
- Staff attorneys relieved from mundane work
- Positions covered for attorneys who are out on sick leave or on vacation
- Reduced employee costs, such as benefits and employee-related expenses

Contract attorneys realize the following benefits from accepting temporary assignments:

- Sole practitioners able to supplement their practice
- Affords a lawyer the time needed to find the right job or to pursue other endeavors, such as continuing education
- Flexible hours for lawyers who juggle work and family
- Work as little or as much as they would like
- Ease of relocation to a new area
- More control over work schedules

A sole proprietor may change the type of organization as time goes by. A sole proprietor may promote an associate to ownership status, thereby evolving the firm into a partnership. A sole proprietor may also incorporate a business and turn it into a professional corporation or form a limited liability company.

A TYPICAL SOLE PRACTITIONER   The office of Eric Norby consists of one attorney, one secretary, and one paralegal. The management style of the firm is autocratic, and the paralegal, Cindy Upcraft, assists Eric in the management duties. In addition to her paralegal duties, Cindy is responsible for billing, accounts receivable, and accounts payable. She also does some light bookkeeping to prepare records for the accountant.

Eric does family law, estate planning, probate, criminal, and landlord-tenant work. Cindy handles most of the day-to-day maintenance of cases under Eric's supervision, from an initial client interview to the close of a case. The firm uses a freelance probate paralegal to handle the probate cases. Since the office is small, the probate paralegal works out of her home and bills the firm hourly for her time.

Cindy is busy with paralegal and management functions, so she relies heavily on the legal secretary, Carol Vinnecomb. Carol is very experienced in wills and family law matters and prepares the necessary paperwork under the direction of the paralegal and the attorney. She is responsible for all clerical functions and also for receptionist duties and greeting clients who come into the office.

Everyone in the office works very hard. Cindy works a lot of overtime and, on occasion, weekends. She is underpaid for her skills and knows she could make more money in a larger firm. However, she likes the family atmosphere of a small office and the close client contact.

PROFESSIONAL PROFILE 2

Jeanne M. O'Neill, a certified paralegal **(CLA),** works for a sole proprietor, Jeffrey Mazor, in Florida. She supervises the paralegals in her office and has other administrative functions. Her office has one major client, a very large bank in her area. The firm does a variety of work for the bank, including forfeiture and seizure, bankruptcy, and collections. She states:

"I am exposed to more variety of work when working for a small firm. I have more responsibility and work independently. I have more control over the cases. If I do a good job, my boss will reward me with a bonus. This would not happen in a large firm where bonuses are structured and approved by the governing body."

"I like the close family atmosphere. We don't have as many benefits and 'comforts' in a small firm, but we do have a very good, high-quality computer system. My attorney and the office are very organized. Anyone in the office can answer a client's question if the attorney is out—*as long as it does not require giving legal advice.* The structure of our office allows maximum productivity for the firm. Since we are very experienced paralegals in our firm, the attorney just supervises our work. The advantages far outweigh the disadvantages."

CLA
Certified legal assistant. A certification that is granted after a paralegal passes an exam given by the National Association of Legal Assistants.

Partnerships

A partnership is a law firm formed by two or more attorneys. Attorneys work cooperatively on cases that are taken in by the firm, and the partners share in the profits. Three classes of attorneys work in a partnership: partners, associates, and nontraditional attorneys, such as contract attorneys, as more specifically discussed in Chapter 2.

Choosing a partner is an important decision. A potential partner must be dependable, reliable, and trustworthy. Each partner in a firm is liable for the decisions and conduct of other partners. If one partner obligates a firm, all partners are liable for the obligation. If one partner commits fraud or is unethical, the other partners are also liable.

A TYPICAL PARTNERSHIP   The law firm of Goldes, Levin & Strong is composed of six full partners, three junior partners, ten associates, nineteen secretaries, thirteen paralegals, seven law clerks, and one legal administrator. The firm also employs one receptionist, one full-time bookkeeper, one case manager, and five file clerks.

The business is run by a managing partner, Helane Strong. Helane is a senior partner because she was one of the founders of the firm. She was chosen to be the managing partner because of her management background before she became an attorney. Helane devotes 80 percent of her time to management duties; she spends the remaining 20 percent on tax work. The administrator is responsible for the day-to-day management of the firm and reports directly to Helane.

The firm specializes in business organizations and works for business clients. It has four departments: business litigation, tax, corporate, and contracts. Each department has at least one partner. Seven attorneys make up the business litigation department; three attorneys, including Helane, work in the tax department; five attorneys form the corporate department; and four attorneys are in the contracts department.

The firm employs one secretary for each attorney and one paralegal for every two attorneys, except in the litigation department, which employs one paralegal for each attorney. The law clerks are organized in a pool and work for all the attorneys as needed.

PROFESSIONAL PROFILE 3

Sandra Allen is a litigation specialist with the medium-size firm of Ramey, Flock, Jeffers, Crawford, Harper & Collins, a defense firm in Tyler, Texas. Its clients are mainly insurance companies. Sandra's duties are focused on discovery matters, collections, and the evaluation of medical records. She also assists the attorneys in jury selection. Of her job, she states:

"I enjoy the structured environment of this firm. It is well managed by a professional legal administrator and has very clear written policies for the entire firm. The office manager acts as a liaison between the attorneys and support staff. It is a prestigious firm where everyone knows each other."

"Some senior attorneys in this firm have a difficult time delegating responsibility to a paralegal. My duties are rather routine. I am not given as much responsibility as I would like. All and all, though, I like working here."

The firm is managed by a combination style: managing partner and management committee. It has one management committee composed of all six partners. The managing partner, Helane, is the chairman of the management committee. The committee meets once each month, at which time decisions are made. Helane carries out the decisions of the committee and delegates tasks to the administrator.

The administrator is directly responsible for all personnel, all systems, and the general functioning of the firm. He is also responsible for ensuring that all timekeeping records are turned in so that clients may be billed in a timely manner. If a personnel dispute occurs, the administrator attempts to resolve it. If it is a problem the administrator cannot resolve, he asks for Helane's assistance.

All the paralegals in the firm specialize in one of four areas of law: business litigation, tax, corporate, and contracts. The secretaries also specialize. The firm has a sophisticated computer system. Each secretary, paralegal, legal administrator, and attorney has a computer. The computers are linked by a network so that each person has access to all departments of the firm.

The employees are satisfied with their compensation, which is comparable to that provided by other firms in the area. Most of the paralegals enjoy working as a specialist. Others, however, find the work too repetitive and would like more variety.

Professional Corporations

A law firm or an individual lawyer who wishes to incorporate will form a professional corporation. A professional corporation is different from a general corporation in that all its shareholders must be of the same profession. Doctors own professional medical corporations, and lawyers own professional legal corporations. Attorneys purchase shares in a professional corporation as they would in a public corporation. The number of shares an attorney owns determines the attorney's ownership percentage in a corporation.

All attorneys employed by a professional corporation, including the shareholders, are employees of the corporation and receive a salary for their work. In addition, the shareholders receive **dividends** according to the profitability of the corporation and the number of shares they own. A professional corporation may have one shareholder or many shareholders.

The organization of a professional corporation is like that of other, nonprofessional, corporations (see Exhibit 1–6). The corporation is considered a separate entity. Therefore, shareholders are not personally responsible for the corporation's debts. The shareholders elect a board of directors by voting their shares. The board of directors is the policy-making

dividend
A payment according to the profitability of a firm and the number of shares of stock owned by an attorney.

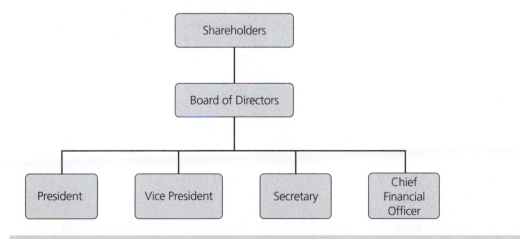

EXHIBIT 1–6 Professional Corporation Organizational Chart

body of the corporation, and it elects officers: president, vice president, secretary, and treasurer. The officers are responsible for the day-to-day management of the corporation. A shareholder may be a director and an officer.

Attorneys incorporate because they receive certain tax advantages, mainly pension benefits. Many attorneys prefer to be incorporated because of the reduced liability they are offered as shareholders. For example, in a partnership, if partner Sam Smith purchased a $300,000 computer system for his partnership, each partner would be liable for the debt if the firm could not pay for the equipment. In a professional corporation, only the corporation would be responsible for the debt.

P.C.
Professional corporation.

Some firms organized as professional corporations may themselves consist of professional corporations. For example, Anderson & Kopecki, Professional Corporation (**P.C.**), employs Randall Anderson, P.C., an individual who is a professional corporation, and Sharon Kopecki, P.C., another individual who is a professional corporation. The firm pays the individual professional corporations for the services of the attorneys. The attorneys are paid a salary from their own corporation.

A sole practitioner may be a professional corporation. The sole practitioner would be the only shareholder as well as a director and an officer. All sizes of firms may incorporate and become a professional corporation.

PROFESSIONAL PROFILE 5

Deborah Ebert is a senior litigation paralegal and paralegal administrator for the Newport Beach, California, branch office of Latham & Watkins, a large professional corporation of approximately 413 attorneys. The firm is managed committee style, and Deborah serves on a management committee. Her tenure on the committee is for 2 years. Each committee has a representative from each branch office, but not all have a paralegal representative.

"I really enjoy my administrative functions," states Deborah. "However, my time spent on administrative functions is not calculated in my annual billing requirement of 1,600 hours. I must work extra hours to fulfill my billing requirements. It is all worth it at bonus time because those extra hours and management functions are calculated into my bonuses."

"I enjoy the team approach in this office. You have more support in a large firm than a smaller firm. There are always people available to help you if you should get in a bind. In this firm, we have paralegal assistants to help us. I share a secretary with another paralegal, and we have floater secretaries (secretaries not assigned to a permanent job) to fill in any gaps. All our secretaries are well trained."

"There are opportunities here that are not available in a smaller firm. We are trendsetters in our paralegal program, which provides a career ladder and advancement opportunities for our paralegals. Another advantage of working for a large, prestigious firm is the respect and recognition one receives from all aspects of the legal community."

"When I worked in a smaller firm, I had more variety of duties. I used to calendar dates in the smaller firm, but I do not have to do that here. I also did more legal research in the smaller firm. Here, we have law clerks and associates who do most of the research. Also, there were more opportunities to assist the attorney at trial in a smaller firm."

A TYPICAL PROFESSIONAL CORPORATION   Major, Pierce & Saunders is a large, international, professional corporation that employs 740 attorneys—246 of whom are individual professional corporations—in 14 offices around the world. It has 287 shareholders. The shareholders elect ten members to serve on a board of directors. The board of directors elects four officers—president, vice president, secretary, and treasurer—who are responsible for the day-to-day management of the firm.

The corporation has a centralized form of management that is organized into five groups: administration, policy, financial, marketing, and operations. Each group comprises many committees. For example, the financial group encompasses a compensation committee and an investment committee. The members of the compensation committee determine compensation and benefits for employees as well as a bonus structure. The investment committee determines how to invest the firm's funds and monitor its retirement program.

The firm employs seven legal administrators, one of whom is the chief legal administrator. The chief legal administrator is like the corporate chief operating officer. This person serves on all committees and is responsible for implementing the committees' decisions. The corporation also employs 20 office managers who work under the direction of the legal administrators. Each branch office has an office manager, and the larger branches have a legal administrator. The administrator or office manager in each branch reports to corporate headquarters and must submit monthly reports and time records. Corporate headquarters handles all the billing for the branch offices.

In addition to hundreds of support staff, this firm employs other nonlawyer specialists: accountants, information systems specialists to manage the firm's computer system, librarians to manage the various libraries, communications specialists to manage the telephone systems, human resource managers to manage personnel, and marketing managers to handle marketing activities.

PROFESSIONAL PROFILE 6

Jean Evers works for the large firm of Poyner & Spruill in Raleigh, North Carolina. Poyner & Spruill is a regional firm of approximately 120 attorneys. The firm has many specialty areas. Jean specializes in environmental law.

"The best thing about working for a large firm is the ability to specialize," states Jean. "You can concentrate on a project more intensely. In a small firm, you bounce from project to project and work on a project in bits and pieces. Since environmental law is a fairly new area, I have been able to watch the law evolve in this area."

"Large firms have more support staff available. In the smaller firm, I did filing, copying, and clerical work. All those functions are done by other people here. There is higher technology here, which is a big help. I am paid more money and have better benefits, including retirement, which was not available in the small firm. I also feel that my status as a paralegal is higher in a large firm."

Corporate headquarters is the largest of the branches. All major decision makers for the firm are located here. The corporation has a very sophisticated computer system. Each branch office is linked to the computer system so that the branch can have access to information contained at corporate headquarters.

The firm is highly departmentalized. Corporate headquarters has 14 departments, as follows:

Tax	Admiralty and maritime
Family law	General litigation
Contracts	Estate planning, trusts, and probate
Bankruptcy	Real property
Commercial litigation	Corporate
Patents, trademarks, and copyrights	Labor tort
Environmental	International

The branch offices do not have all of these departments. Each branch office has different departments and specialties according to the needs of the clients. For example, the Hong Kong office was formed primarily to help one of the firm's major corporate clients establish a manufacturing plant there. That branch office consists of a contracts department, a corporate department, and a labor department.

The paralegals in this firm are highly specialized. Some of them like highly specialized work, and others do not. Some say the work is too repetitive. However, they are all among the highest paid paralegals in their area and have a lot of employee benefits, including retirement benefits after they have been with the firm for 5 years.

Some paralegals thrive on the politics and bureaucracy of this large firm, and others do not. Some feel the red tape is burdensome. Some complain that the firm is too large for them to feel "connected," or part of a family.

Limited Liability Company

limited liability company
A company formed to shield its owners and their assets from liability arising from the misconduct of other owners or employees.

The early to mid-1990s saw the creation of a new legal form of organization—the **limited liability company** (LLC). It was created under state law, and each state has its own requirements for an LLC. However, a few states will not allow a law firm to form an LLC. This prohibition stems from an ethics rule that forbids lawyers from limiting their liability to clients. Exact titles for this form of organization may vary from state to state. For example, a Pennsylvania LLC for professionals is a "Restricted Professional Company." In other states, a professional limited liability company is known as such and has the letters "PLLC" after its name.

An LLC is owned by its members. They are analogous to partners in a partnership or shareholders in a corporation, depending on how the business is managed. An LLC may be managed by its members (owners) or by selected managers. A member will more closely resemble a shareholder if the LLC uses a manager, because the member will not participate in management. If the LLC does not use a manager, then the member will closely resemble a partner because the member will have a direct say in the decision making of the company. A member's ownership of an LLC is represented by his or her interests, just as partners have an interest in a partnership and shareholders own stock in a corporation.

There are three primary differences between an LLC and a partnership:

1. Avoidance of personal liability, plus a limitation on general and commercial liability to one's investment in the LLC
2. A need to file articles of organization and, in some jurisdictions, to have an operating agreement
3. Opportunity to be taxed as a partnership (like a Subchapter S corporation) but without the size limitations placed on a Subchapter S corporation.

LLCs offer numerous advantages: pass-through taxation, limited liability, and flexible management and ownership structure. The main advantage of an LLC is that members are not liable for the misdeeds of other members. In the 1980s, the law firm of Kaye Scholer, a partnership, became liable for $41 million in government claims for its involvement in the Lincoln Savings scandal. The firm's insurance paid only half of the claims. The remainder had to be paid by the firm's 109 partners.

Many law firms are structuring their businesses as an LLC to take advantage of its flexibility. In Texas and Florida, nearly every major law firm is organized as an LLC. However, some firms are reluctant to change to an LLC because they feel it sends a message to clients that they don't stand behind their work or that they distrust the work of their fellow partners.

Boutique Firms

The trend toward specialization brought a new type of law firm in the 1980s: the boutique firm. A **boutique** firm is a small firm in which attorneys specialize in only one or possibly two areas of law. These firms are replacing the small general practice that assisted the public in various areas of law and are normally found in highly populated areas. A boutique firm may be a sole proprietorship, partnership, professional corporation or LLC.

Examples of the specialties of a boutique firm are government contracts, domestic law, taxes, intellectual property, labor law, patent law, and workers' compensation.

A TYPICAL BOUTIQUE FIRM   The law firm of Ellingboe, Rialto, Loh & Young is a professional corporation that employs four attorneys. All four attorneys are shareholders of the corporation. The attorneys specialize in estate planning and probate: Nancy Ellingboe specializes in estate and gift tax, Ernest Rialto in trust administration, Pete Loh in wills, and Alexandria Young in probate. The firm employs four paralegals, four secretaries, an office manager, and a receptionist. One secretary and one paralegal are assigned to each attorney.

The firm has a committee style of management, with all four attorneys on the executive committee and each attorney responsible for one of four areas of management: financial, personnel, administrative systems, and community relations. The office manager carries out the decisions of the executive committee and works with all the attorneys for the general management of the firm.

The library in the firm is very small and consists of only the books needed for estate planning and probate. The firm has a state-of-the-art computer system with the latest applicable software, which enables the staff to prepare documents in a few minutes. The firm has streamlined its systems to increase the volume of work. It has a good reputation in the legal community. In addition to high salaries, the staff enjoys many benefits.

boutique
A law firm that offers services in one area of law only.

Office-Sharing Associations

Changes in the economy, law, technology, and the practice of law in general have made sole practice too expensive for most lawyers. Higher capital contributions are required for the office equipment, a library, furniture, and supplies required to start a business. In addition, the costs of office space and employee wages have skyrocketed. Attorneys are forced to devise alternative methods of practice to maximize their profit margin. Office-sharing associations, also called legal associations, are a popular alternative.

Two types of office-sharing arrangements are used: the suite concept and the firm concept.

SUITE CONCEPT   The suite concept developed in the 1970s. With this arrangement, one attorney, group of attorneys, or management company leases out an entire floor of an office building and builds individual offices in various sizes. The suite is decorated and equipped with a law library, a conference room, a copier and fax equipment, a telephone system, a receptionist area, and other law office essentials. The individual offices are subleased—either furnished or unfurnished—to lawyers whose rent proportionately pays the costs of the operation and of the general upkeep of the suite. The attorneys pay each time they use the fax machine or the copier, and these costs are added to their monthly bill.

A suite usually offers secretarial or paralegal services or both on an as-needed basis, thereby cutting employee costs. If an attorney employs a secretary and a paralegal, additional space can be rented for them.

A suite is usually elegantly decorated and gives the impression of a large, prosperous firm. Management functions are the responsibility of a suite owner, with no input from the tenants. The attorneys have the benefits of a larger firm—networking and referrals from other lawyers—while maintaining the autonomy of a sole practice.

FIRM CONCEPT In the firm concept, an attorney rents an office that is vacant in an established firm. The renting attorney may arrange to do work for the law firm in lieu of paying rent. The renting attorney has the use of the firm's receptionist services and other facilities. Arrangements are made for use of the firm's support staff services, or the attorney may rent additional space for a secretary and a paralegal.

This type of arrangement allows a young lawyer to begin the practice of law without high start-up costs. It is also used as a "trial marriage" if a firm is considering hiring an attorney. The attorney and the firm can see whether they are compatible without making any commitments to each other.

The obvious disadvantage to this type of arrangement is that a renting attorney is subject to the needs of a law firm. If the firm grows and needs an extra office, the renting attorney must move. In addition, if the attorney is very busy, the attorney may find it a burden to do the firm's work for payment of rent.

A TYPICAL OFFICE-SHARING ASSOCIATION When Tony Florentine passed the bar exam, he desired to practice law as a sole practitioner and to specialize in family law. He had limited funds to start his practice, so he rented an office in a suite of 22 other sole practitioners. The owner of the suite is also a practicing attorney in the suite.

The suite is spacious, with a large, very plush reception area. It has a law library with all the books and periodicals Tony needs. It also has a secretarial service to service attorneys who have no staff. Tony utilizes the secretarial service, so he has no need for a full-time secretary.

Since he is a new attorney, he also works on other types of cases in addition to family law. He advises other attorneys in the suite of his desire to specialize and asks them to refer all the family law matters they do not want to him. In return, he will refer cases he does not want or is not qualified to handle to them.

Tony is happy with the arrangement, although he has had some difficulty with the secretarial service. He once needed some work done immediately to take to court for a hearing, but the secretarial service was too busy with other attorneys' work to drop everything for him. Consequently, he was not prepared for his court hearing. Since then, he has hired a part-time secretary who also does some paralegal work.

He also has a problem with Sally Whitefeather, one of the receptionists. She does not answer his calls promptly and hangs up on his clients. At times, he does not get important messages left by clients. Tony complained about this to the suite owner, who indicated he would remedy the situation. However, Sally has continued in her poor work habits, and Tony is upset because he can do nothing to remedy the situation.

Tony has practiced in the suite for 2 years, which has been enough time for his practice to grow considerably. He has become associated with two other sole practitioners who are leaving the suite to form a partnership. They have asked Tony to come with them and join their firm as a full partner. In this partnership, Tony will be able to practice family law exclusively, and he is glad to accept their offer.

Legal Clinics

legal clinic
Legal offices formed for the purpose of providing low-income people with free or low-cost legal services.

Legal clinics are legal offices formed for the purpose of providing low-income people with free or low-cost legal services. They are established to provide equal access to justice for the poor who cannot afford a traditional attorney.

Legal clinics are established by:

- Federal government programs
- State government programs
- County and local government programs

- Churches
- Bar associations
- Law schools
- Private organizations

Low-income and **indigent** people are typical clients of a legal clinic. Seventy-five percent of the clients are mothers with children. Although some legal clinics may take litigation cases, most of their cases are family issues, landlord-tenant, immigration, public benefits, and contracts. A legal clinic usually has neither the resources nor the time to take a complex litigation case. Legal clinics are tax exempt, nonprofit organizations.

Legal clinics are located in poor areas, and some have several branch clinics throughout a large metropolitan area. For example, Chicago Legal Clinic, Inc. has four neighborhood offices to serve its clients. Legal clinics sponsored by law schools are found on the college campus. Some legal clinics will go directly to the client by visiting nursing homes, homeless shelters, and churches.

Legal clinics receive funding from federal and state grants, private contributions, and fund-raising events. They rely on volunteer services from local attorneys, paralegals, and others. Most legal clinics have paid positions, but cannot afford to pay all personnel. The clinic's director is normally a paid position.

Clinics sponsored by law schools use law students to provide service to their clients. The students, who must be certified, represent clients from beginning to end, including appearances in federal court and administrative agencies. Some states will allow certified student interns to represent indigent clients in state court. An attorney, normally a faculty member, supervises the students and cases.

Congress created the Legal Services Corporation (LSC) in 1974 to provide equal access to justice to all citizens. Whereas, indigent people accused of crimes have access to a public defender for free legal representation, indigent people involved in civil disputes may receive free legal service through legal aid offices. Each year, the federal government gives money to the LSC, which grants the money to local programs. The size of the grant is based on the number of people living in poverty in a particular area. On average, LSC provides about half the budget of the programs it funds.

A TYPICAL LEGAL CLINIC   Neighborhood Legal Services is a legal clinic based in Dallas, Texas. It is funded by the Legal Services Corporation, Dallas Bar Association, Texas Women Lawyers Association, and private contributions. Monica Valentino is the director, who oversees 2 staff attorneys, 30 volunteer attorneys, 5 staff paralegals, and 22 volunteers from the Dallas Paralegal Association. All staff and volunteers must be bilingual.

Neighborhood Legal Services has three offices throughout the Dallas area. Each office has one staff attorney to supervise the cases. It represents clients in such matters as dissolution of marriage, wills, probate, landlord-tenant disputes, minor civil matters, and public benefits assistance.

Since the office does a high volume of cases, appointments for clients are limited to one-half hour. Clients who work during the day may request an evening or weekend appointment. When clients come into the office, they are given an information sheet to complete. This sheet is then given to the paralegal who interviews the client.

When a file is opened, the case is given to a paralegal who prepares the documents for the attorney's review and signature. The attorney reviews the documents and makes changes or signs the documents. The paralegals handle the day-to-day maintenance of a case.

One weekend a month, Monica will take three paralegals to nursing homes and elder centers in the area to help senior citizens with their legal needs. Monica is also responsible for obtaining volunteers. The employees at Neighborhood Legal Services are not paid much, but receive personal satisfaction that they are helping people in need.

indigent
Poor or needy.

PRIVATE INDUSTRY

Private industry includes companies formed for purposes other than providing legal services and consists of all sizes of businesses: small, medium, and large. A company often employs its own attorneys. A private industry legal department is located within the company that employs it. It is most often called an in-house legal department and has one client: the company.

Private industry uses two types of legal departments: corporate legal departments for very large corporations and legal departments for smaller private companies.

Corporate Legal Departments

preventative law
Legal information designed to avoid legal problems before they occur.

outside counsel
A private law firm retained to do legal work for a corporation.

in-house counsel
An attorney who is an employee of a corporation and works in the corporation's legal department.

Legal and business issues have increased a corporation's legal demands. To meet these demands, corporations hire their own attorneys to meet their legal needs and to practice **preventative law,** or law designed to avoid legal problems. With attorneys monitoring a project from its inception, the possibility of legal problems in the future is reduced. At the same time, corporations were under pressure to reduce costs. These issues forced corporations to handle more matters in-house and to monitor the activities of **outside counsel** closely. Attorneys who are employed by the corporation are known as **in-house counsel.**

PROFESSIONAL PROFILE 7

Jennifer Sawyer, CLA, a trademark paralegal at the corporate headquarters of Tupperware, International, in Miami, Florida, is experienced in real estate, litigation, and intellectual property, specializing in defense work. For Tupperware, she monitors trademarks, submits new trademarks for research, handles all trademark and copyright infringements, and monitors litigation. She states:

"Working for a corporate legal department is great because you only have one client. I have worked for many private law firms in general practice, and I like specialized work better than general practice. I also don't work much overtime, [as] I used to do in a private firm. The salary and benefits are better in a corporate legal department."

A corporate legal department functions as a part of the whole corporation around the projects of the corporation, as shown in Exhibit 1–7. For example, an automobile manufacturing company introducing a new line of automobiles requires the contribution of each department of the company. Sales and marketing work on the automobile's promotion, personnel hires additional staff as necessary, engineering is responsible for designing the automobile, manufacturing is responsible for producing the automobile, legal is responsible for contracts with dealers to sell the automobile and for any patent requirements, and the executive department supervises all departments.

The type of business a corporation is in influences the legal needs of the corporation. A manufacturing corporation has a greater need for a large patent department than does a service corporation. A chemical corporation has a greater need for environmental attorneys than does a banking corporation.

general counsel
An attorney in charge of a corporate legal department; often an officer of the corporation.

The head attorney in a corporate legal department is called a **general counsel.** Frequently, the general counsel is also an officer of the corporation, usually a corporate secretary or vice president. A general counsel reports directly to the president of the corporation. Increasingly,

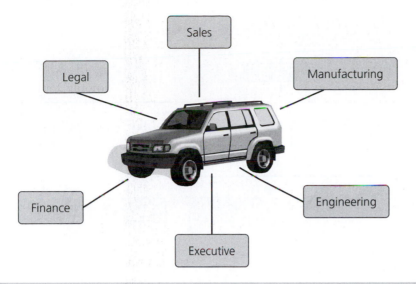

EXHIBIT 1–7   The Corporate Legal Department Functions as a Part of the Corporation around the Projects of the Corporation

a general counsel is responsible for the legal requirements of the corporation, such as minutes, stock transfers, and state filing requirements.

Corporate legal departments have both centralized and decentralized forms of organization. Most corporate legal departments are centralized. Centralized legal departments are located in corporate headquarters and provide legal services for all a company's departments and locations. All attorneys can be found in the legal department under the authority of a general counsel. This form of organization is shown in Exhibit 1–8.

PROFESSIONAL PROFILE 8

Marie Smith, CLA, is a corporate paralegal for US West Communications in Salt Lake City, Utah. She is the custodian of records for her company and responds to subpoenas and telephone records requests. She is involved in a variety of legal work, including criminal investigations, workers' compensation, and labor disputes. She testifies as the custodian of records on behalf of her company and represents the company in employment hearings. She also reviews and tracks legislation for the company. Of her work, she states:

"My company is very supportive of continuing education. They will pay for courses and seminars and let us off to attend them. We also have the very latest in technology, which makes my job easier."

"We receive no overtime pay. Sometimes the bureaucracy of a large company can be a hassle. Once, I needed a particular form, and I had to order a form to order another form to get the form I needed. You learn to work within the constraints of the red tape, though."

In a decentralized form of organization, corporate headquarters consists of a general counsel and a few attorneys. Other attorneys are disbursed among the various departments of the corporation and function independently of the general counsel. For example, a labor attorney works in the personnel department, a patent attorney in manufacturing and engineering, and a collection attorney in sales.

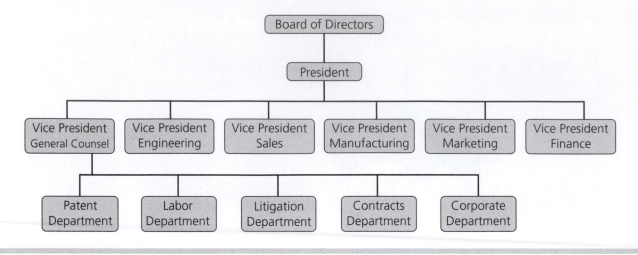

EXHIBIT 1–8 Corporate Legal Department Organizational Chart

The management style of a corporate legal department must conform to the management style of the whole corporation. Therefore, a legal department is not autonomous in its management decisions. For example, if it is necessary for a legal department to hire additional personnel, the decision must be approved by the personnel department in most corporations. The personnel department will then take over the hiring process and be responsible for finding qualified applicants.

The concerns of a corporate legal department are different from those of traditional law firms. For example, public relations and attracting clients are not concerns to a corporate attorney. Corporate legal departments must prepare and adhere to department budgets, which are subject to management approval outside a legal department.

Corporate legal departments are small, medium, or large. The size of a legal department depends on how much legal work is done in-house. A corporate legal department that handles a corporation's litigation will have a large litigation staff. Corporate legal departments that handle corporate secretary functions and patents only and send all other work to outside counsel have a smaller staff.

A TYPICAL CORPORATE LEGAL DEPARTMENT ABC Corporation manufactures computer circuit boards used in the airline industry. The legal department at ABC is small, consisting of one general counsel, one office administrator, twelve attorneys, six paralegals, ten secretaries, one file clerk, and one case manager.

The general counsel does not practice law; he interacts with other departments of the corporation and delegates assignments to the attorneys. Three attorneys are patent attorneys, three are corporate attorneys, one is a labor specialist, three are litigation attorneys, and two are contract attorneys. Two of the paralegals are patent paralegals, two are corporate paralegals, and two handle warranty disputes for the corporation. Each attorney is assigned a secretary, except the patent attorneys who share the services of one secretary.

The corporation has a contract with Major, Pierce & Saunders, a very large international law firm, to handle all its litigation. Major, Pierce employs attorneys who practice in all areas of law. It also has branch offices in many major cities in the United States, which is convenient for ABC.

ABC has a lot of litigation since its circuit boards are used in airplanes of all sizes all over the country. If injuries are sustained because an airplane malfunctioned in an area where the circuit board is located, ABC is sued. ABC's litigation attorneys monitor outside counsel's management of the litigation cases. They are apprised of each step in every case. The attorneys at Major, Pierce receive direction and authority from ABC's litigation attorneys.

Other areas of ABC's legal department also use the services of outside law firms. If the corporate or contract attorneys should get behind, they will ask for assistance from outside counsel.

The office manager is responsible for the general management of the department and reports to the general counsel. She spends 33 percent of her time on budgeting and accounting, 20 percent on personnel administration, 20 percent on practice support and office systems, 15 percent on information support systems, and 12 percent on other management functions.

The paralegals enjoy their company benefits and are treated as professionals by other employees of the corporation. They seldom work overtime or weekends, and they have good salaries. People who used to work as paralegals in the legal department have been promoted to management positions in other departments of the corporation.

Private Industry

Private industry includes smaller companies formed to provide nonlegal services or products to the public and services directly to law firms. The legal needs of these companies are more targeted than those of large corporations. For example, a real estate company would employ its own real estate attorney and paralegal to handle real estate contracts and closings. A small company that specializes in franchise work would employ a legal staff to handle franchise contracts and transactions.

PROFESSIONAL PROFILE 9

Debbie Dee, a paralegal in Durham, North Carolina, works for Lawyers Title Insurance Corporation of North Carolina. She manages the office, responds to title problems, and performs underwriting functions. She hires and trains paralegals who work for the company. Of her job, she states:

"Opportunities in the title insurance industry are challenging. I have a lot of autonomy. The company is reputable, and I work in a good atmosphere."

"The company is structured differently than a private law firm. Most law firms are run by attorneys like a small business. This company is managed like a large corporation, which gives paralegals more room for advancement. I make good money and have very good benefits."

Private companies, although smaller than large corporations, have the same structure as a corporation. Management decisions are made not by the attorneys but by company management—unless an attorney is part of the management of a company. Unlike an attorney in a corporate legal department, one in a private company may not be an officer or a manager of the company.

Some private companies are also divided into departments. The departments are fewer and smaller than those in a large corporation. As in a large corporation, each department functions together around projects of the company.

Paralegals have successfully used their paralegal training for careers in private companies and obtained the following positions:

- Insurance underwriter
- Law firm administrator
- Recruiting coordinator

- Law firm marketing specialist
- Rehabilitation counselor
- Corporate personnel director
- Consultant
- Commercial arbitrator
- Sales representative
- Legal software trainer
- Law librarian
- Investigator
- Real estate broker
- Litigation consultant
- Civil rights analyst
- Corporate bond department manager
- Employee benefits manager
- Association manager
- Writer
- Teacher
- Career counselor
- Politician
- Sales marketer
- Negotiator
- Convention marketer
- Editor
- Environment specialist
- Stockbroker
- Paralegal program director
- Computer-related positions

SELF-EMPLOYED PARALEGAL SERVICES   Paralegals are also forming their own private companies. They are independent contractors and are self-employed. There are two types of self-employed paralegals: **freelance** (or contract) **paralegals** and independent paralegals. Freelance paralegal services offer their services to attorneys, and independent paralegals offer their services to the public.

freelance paralegal
Contracts his or her services out to law offices and works under the supervision of an attorney.

contract basis
Working as an independent contractor on a per case or assignment basis. The person is not an employee of the firm.

FREELANCE PARALEGAL SERVICES   Freelance paralegal services are offered to attorneys on a **contract basis.** A freelance paralegal is not an employee of a firm but works for the firm on an independent contractor basis. Attorneys have increased the use of freelance paralegal services since the early 1980s to control high employee costs.

A variety of paralegal services are available in the United States. The organizations offering these services range from companies with one paralegal to firms that have many paralegals and employ attorneys. Most freelance paralegals specialize in one area of law. The most common specialty areas are litigation, corporate, real estate, and probate. A freelance paralegal may work in an attorney's office, work out of the home, or rent an office.

A specialty area that is popular for freelancers is a paralegal service that provides computerized litigation support. A law firm that does not have sophisticated computer capabilities or the staff to handle a complex litigation case may contract with a service to computerize the many documents, thereby saving thousands of dollars on new equipment and additional staff. The scope and sophistication of computer services offered by paralegal firms runs the gamut from coding data entry to building specialized databases and storing data on in-house mainframes.

Freelance paralegal services are sole proprietorships, partnerships, corporations, and LLCs. Most freelance paralegal services are sole proprietorships consisting of one paralegal. If the paralegal service incorporates, it may not incorporate as a professional corporation but may incorporate as a general corporation or limited liability company.

Freelancing offers paralegals versatility in scheduling work around family obligations. Before starting a career as a freelance paralegal, one should have at least 3 to 5 years experience in a law office setting; a diploma or certificate from a paralegal program alone is not sufficient. Most attorneys utilizing the services of freelance paralegals are new sole practitioners. They are not experienced enough to supervise a new paralegal adequately. Freelancing is not the way to receive on-the-job training. Freelancing also entails risk since there is no steady income, and clients may be slow to pay for services. It is highly recommended that freelancing be given careful consideration and be entered into only when you are experienced and feel very comfortable with your skill level.

PROFESSIONAL PROFILE 10

Alice Penny is the owner of Paralegal Services of North Carolina, Raleigh, North Carolina. She employs six people: one office manager and five paralegals. Her company does land title research; public document filing, search, and retrieval; real property foreclosure; estate administration; background investigations; and corporate work. Alice started her company in 1988 after more than 30 years' legal experience.

Alice began accepting outside work while still employed by a large firm in Raleigh. She moonlighted in order to test the market for freelance paralegals and to build a clientele before she quit her job. Of her company, she states:

"I started my own business to be my own boss. But then I found out that being one's own boss is a myth. I have many bosses. My clients are my bosses. I have found that the stress level is higher with your own business. I have to wear all of the hats: management, marketing, promotion, advertising, administrator, and do the paralegal work. I have all of the headaches of running a business. On the other hand, having your own business is exciting and rewarding, in spite of the hard work."

INDEPENDENT PARALEGAL SERVICES   **Independent paralegal** services offer their services directly to the public. Most have their own offices. While the legality of this form of paralegal service is controversial, the number of independent paralegal businesses is growing every day. It is important for paralegal students to understand the difference between a freelance paralegal service and an independent paralegal service.

Many independent paralegals do business as legal-typing or form-preparation services that offer clerical help and forms on a variety of basic or routine cases, such as bankruptcy, uncontested divorces, and landlord-tenant matters. Some independent paralegals work for nonprofit organizations, such as women's shelters. They charge less than attorneys. *Independent paralegals cannot give legal advice or represent clients in court,* but they can help people complete their own paperwork and represent themselves. Despite their limitations, independent paralegals are carving out a niche among consumers who want to handle their own legal problems. A more in-depth discussion of this issue is found in Chapter 5.

independent paralegal
A person who does law-related work for the general public without the supervision of an attorney.

ETHICS ALERT

Attorney Service and Nonprofit Companies

Many companies offer services to legal offices. Companies that offer essential services include service of process, messenger, court filings, preparation of demonstrative evidence, corporate record checking and retrieval, courier services, and investigations. Law book and legal periodical companies need legal editors and knowledgeable salespeople. Companies that produce legal software use educated paralegals to develop the software, sell the software, and train people on how to use the software. Bonding companies are used by law firms in many different types of cases. A paralegal familiar with the legal process can be very successful in an attorney service company.

Private companies vary in their organization and structure. Some are small companies, while others are large corporations. Most companies offer their employees opportunities for advancement and increases in salary.

Nonprofit, charitable organizations also employ attorneys and paralegals. Organizations such as the American Association of Retired Persons (AARP) and religious organizations such as Catholic Charities offer legal services to members of their particular group. While nonprofit organizations cannot afford to pay top wages, many paralegals have found the work challenging and rewarding.

A TYPICAL PRIVATE COMPANY   Sandy Varella just graduated from paralegal school. She is a single mother who has been employed by a computer company for many years and is used to a good salary. When she began looking for a job as a paralegal, she was discouraged to discover that law firms would not pay her very much as a paralegal trainee. It would be difficult for her to take a cut in pay to pursue her goal of being a paralegal.

She was just about to give up her dream when she read an ad in the newspaper that read, "Paralegal position. Computer experience essential." She got the job and went to work for International Computer Manufacturing Company (ICM).

ICM manufactures computers and software for business and industry. It has five departments: retail, medical, legal, grocery, and education. Sandy works in the legal department, which consists of two computer marketing consultants, two computer programmers, two attorneys, and one paralegal (Sandy).

The department develops software for law offices. It has software for computerized litigation support, timekeeping systems, spreadsheets, billing, and word processing. The attorneys develop the functions of the software. Sandy's job is to go into the offices of the company's customers and train the staff to use the software. She gives seminars on the various ways the software can be used in a legal office. Her computer background and paralegal education made her a perfect candidate for the job.

Sandy is thrilled with her new position. She is considered an expert in her field and enjoys meeting people. Her hours are flexible, so she can be home when her children get home from school. She did not have to take a cut in pay—she makes more money than she did before.

GOVERNMENT AGENCIES

Paralegals work in four main areas of government offices. They may work with:

1. Chief government lawyers; for example, attorneys general and corporation counsel
2. General counsel of individual agencies
3. Individual agencies; for example, enforcement departments and civil rights divisions
4. Individual legislators, individual legislative committees, legislative counsel, or legislative drafting offices

Government agencies vary in their administration systems, as do private law firms. Some organizations are more complex than others, and agencies have diverse legal needs as well as

SERIES	DESCRIPTION OF GROUP
GS-000	Miscellaneous
GS-100	Social science, psychology, and welfare
GS-200	Personnel management and industrial relations
GS-300	General administrative, clerical, and office services
GS-400	Biological science group
GS-500	Accounting and budget
GS-600	Medical, hospital, dental, and pubic health
GS-700	Veterinary medical science
GS-800	Engineering and architecture
GS-900	Legal and kindred
GS-1000	Information and arts
GS-1100	Business and industry
GS-1200	Copyright, patent, and trademark
GS-1300	Physical science
GS-1400	Library and archives
GS-1500	Mathematics and statistics
GS-1600	Equipment, facilities, and services
GS-1700	Education
GS-1800	Investigation
GS-1900	Quality assurance, inspection, and grading
GS-2000	Supply group
GS-2100	Transportation

EXHIBIT 1–9   Federal Government General Schedule Occupational Structure

organizational size, structure, power base, and so on. An agency's need for paralegals varies with these elements.

Four types of government agencies employ paralegals: federal, state, county, and city.

Federal Agencies

The federal government is the largest employer in the United States. At the time of this writing, Uncle Sam employs almost 3 million workers and hires 300,000 new employees each year to replace retiring or terminating employees. The government classifies workers into groups that fall within an occupational structure. There are 22 occupational groups that include 441 different occupations. They are classified under the General Schedule, GS-000 through GS 2100 (see Exhibit 1–9). Each group is further subdivided into subgroups that have their own numerical code.

The government's existing classification system includes an occupational structure that groups similar jobs together. The Wage Grade Trades and Labor Schedule offers an additional 36 occupational groups (WG-2500 through WG-9000). GS-900, entitled the Legal and Kindred Group, is where paralegals are placed. There are 15 grades within each group and 10 steps within each grade as shown on Exhibit 1–10. Pay steps are earned on the basis of length of employment and the employee's work performance.

The federal government uses a two-tiered approach for paralegals: legal clerk/technician and paralegal specialist. A legal clerk/technician position is a stepping-stone to a paralegal specialist position. It is mainly clerical but involves some basic paralegal duties. The salary level of a legal clerk starts at GS-4 and usually does not go beyond GS-9.

A paralegal specialist is classified under GS-950 within that series. A paralegal specialist can start as low as GS-5 and go as high as GS-15. According to the *Handbook of*

SALARY TABLE 2008-GS

INCORPORATING THE 2.50% GENERAL SCHEDULE INCREASE

EFFECTIVE JANUARY 2008

Annual Rates by Grade and Step

GRADE	STEP 1	STEP 2	STEP 3	STEP 4	STEP 5	STEP 6	STEP 7	STEP 8	STEP 9	STEP 10	WITHIN GRADE AMOUNTS
1	$ 17,046	$ 17,615	$ 18,182	$ 18,746	$ 19,313	$ 19,646	$ 20,206	$ 20,771	$ 20,793	$ 21,324	VARIES
2	19,165	19,621	20,255	20,793	21,025	21,643	22,261	22,879	23,497	24,115	VARIES
3	20,911	21,608	22,305	23,002	23,699	24,396	25,093	25,790	26,487	27,184	697
4	23,475	24,258	25,041	25,824	26,607	27,390	28,173	28,956	29,739	30,522	783
5	26,264	27,139	28,014	28,889	29,764	30,639	31,514	32,389	33,264	34,139	875
6	29,276	30,252	31,228	32,204	33,180	34,156	35,132	36,108	37,084	38,060	976
7	32,534	33,618	34,702	35,786	36,870	37,954	39,038	40,122	41,206	42,290	1,084
8	36,030	37,231	38,432	39,633	40,834	42,035	43,236	44,437	45,638	46,839	1,201
9	39,795	41,122	42,449	43,776	45,103	46,430	47,757	49,084	50,411	51,738	1,327
10	43,824	45,285	46,746	48,207	49,668	51,129	52,590	54,051	55,512	56,973	1,461
11	48,148	49,753	51,358	52,963	54,568	56,173	57,778	59,383	60,988	62,593	1,605
12	57,709	59,633	61,557	63,481	65,405	67,329	69,253	71,177	73,101	75,025	1,924
13	68,625	70,913	73,201	75,489	77,777	80,065	82,353	84,641	86,929	89,217	2,288
14	81,093	83,796	86,499	89,202	91,905	94,608	97,311	100,014	102,717	105,420	2,703
15	95,390	98,570	101,750	104,930	108,110	111,290	114,470	117,650	120,830	124,010	3,180

EXHIBIT 1–10 General Schedule Salary Structure

Note: GS pay is adjusted geographically to account for higher costs of living. Pay for position's outside the United States are 10–25 percent higher. (**Note:** the General Schedule is adjusted periodically. This schedule is current as of January, 2008.

Occupational Groups and Families published by the federal government, a paralegal specialist performs the following duties:

> The specialists analyze the legal impact of legislative developments and administrative and judicial decisions, opinions, determinations, and rulings on agency programs; conduct research for the preparation of legal opinions on matters of interest to the agency; perform substantive legal analysis of requests for information under the provisions of various acts; or perform other similar legal support functions that require discretion and independent judgment in the application of a specialized knowledge of laws, precedent decisions, regulations, agency policies and practices, and judicial or administrative proceedings. Such knowledge is less than that represented by graduation from a recognized law school, and may have been gained from formalized, professionally instructed agency or educational institution training or from professionally supervised on-the-job training. While the paramount knowledge requirements of this series are legal, some positions also require a practical knowledge of subject matter areas related to the agency's substantive programs.

According to William P. Statsky in *Essentials of Paralegalism*, the following federal agencies employ the largest number of paralegal specialists:

- Department of Health and Human Services
- Department of Justice
- Court system
- Department of Treasury
- Department of Transportation
- Department of Labor
- Department of Interior
- U.S. Air Force

The main selling points of federal employment are job security and benefits. In addition, federal employment is generally not affected by fluctuations in the economy as are other areas of the legal marketplace. However, political changes can influence staffing levels. Each presidential administration may have different public policy priorities that result in greater levels of federal employment in some programs and declines in others. Layoffs have occurred but are generally uncommon. The federal government offers 140 law-related careers for the paralegal (*Paralegal Reporter*, National Federation of Paralegal Associations, 1998).

A paralegal specialist in the federal government usually specializes in one particular area of law. Often, a paralegal in this position becomes as familiar with a particular area of law as the attorneys in the office, if not more so. As attorneys come and go in the government, a paralegal becomes the ongoing foundation of many government law offices.

Since deficit reduction, lawyers are still employed, but some positions are being filled by paralegals. For example, the Bureau of Prisons, an agency of the Department of Justice, has a program in which a paralegal is placed in almost every federal prison in positions that were once filled by lawyers.

Paralegals in government have more autonomy than paralegals in private law firms. According to federal standards, a paralegal may or may not be supervised by an attorney. Paralegal specialist is considered a professional position, guaranteeing career mobility and tenure. In addition, paralegals employed by the federal government may represent their agency before federal administrative tribunals.

State Agencies

State government agencies function like federal government agencies except they report to state government officials rather than federal government officials. The opportunities for employment in state government continue to increase. State attorney general offices employ many paralegals.

County Agencies

County government provides many legal services for its constituents. Among the employment opportunities at the county level are positions in the offices of county counsel, who represent a county when the county is sued; district attorneys; public defenders; public administrators; and court clerks. The governing body of county governments is the county supervisors.

Most often, paralegals employed by county governing offices are not assigned to a particular attorney but are organized in pools, working for many attorneys on an assignment basis. Most counties have structured review procedures and periodic pay raise schedules.

City Agencies

Legal offices in city government include a city attorney's office and other governing offices. A city attorney represents a city if the city is sued, and handles other matters as well. Each city structures its city attorney's office differently. For example, some city attorneys are appointed by a city counsel, and some are elected by the people. Some city attorneys handle criminal cases, and others handle only civil cases, leaving the criminal cases to a district attorney.

Larger cities employ many attorneys, and others employ only one attorney to monitor the work of outside council, much like a corporate legal department. Smaller cities may not have a city attorney but engage the services of a private law firm to represent their interests.

THE CHANGING MARKETPLACE

What does the future hold for the legal marketplace? One cannot predict, but one thing is certain—change. Technological innovation is the catalyst for those changes.

Technology will change the way legal professionals perform research, file documents, and communicate with clients. The Internet will play an important role in the delivery of legal services. Legal professionals will continue their education through online courses and distance education.

Multidisciplinary Practice

A **multidisciplinary practice** (MDP) is a firm that employs professionals from nonlegal disciplines to offer its clients nonlegal services in addition to legal services. Services such as accounting, medical consulting, and lobbyists are offered to large corporate clients in hopes of satisfying all their business needs. The structure of a multidisciplinary practice is highly controversial. The ABA, and most state bar associations, has ethical rules that prohibit nonlawyers from participating in the ownership of a law firm. It is felt that it compromises an attorney's ability to exercise independent legal judgment and interferes with the attorney-client relationship. In addition, it is an established ethical rule that lawyers may not split legal fees with a nonlawyer. Therefore, lawyers cannot enter into a partnership with a nonlawyer, so they must hire these professionals as employees or on a contract basis. Firms have circumvented these legal rules by establishing multidisciplinary firms in other countries that do not have rules prohibiting this type of practice.

New York is the first state to change its rules to allow MDPs. The new rule change is called "Cooperative Business Arrangements Between Lawyers and Nonlegal Professionals." Under the rules, nonlegal professionals cannot direct professional judgment, share legal fees, or compromise lawyer-client confidentiality. Nonlegal professionals must meet court approval for their type of service and professional qualifications. Other state bar associations are reviewing the possibility of allowing MDPs. The trend toward multidisciplinary practice will increase as the state bar associations relax their rules concerning them.

multidisciplinary practice
A lawyer and a member of another profession practice together to provide both legal and nonlegal services to a client.

Nonlegal Subsidiaries

A **nonlegal subsidiary** is a company that is owned by a law firm but provides nonlegal services. Law firms and individual attorneys are opening separate, nonlegal businesses that utilize their legal expertise, such as the following:

- Management consulting
- Specialized newsletter publication
- Environmental consulting
- Seminars
- International trade consulting
- Publishing
- Professional association formulation
- Public relations
- Government contracting
- Personnel relations

nonlegal subsidiary
A company that is owned by a law firm but provides nonlegal services.

EXHIBIT 1–11 Example of Legal Subsidiary (*Reprinted with Permission of Corporate Creations.*)

For example, a mid-Atlantic law firm found that it was doing a lot of research for human resource vice presidents, so it formed an association for human resource vice presidents. For a fee, it offers seminars, a newsletter, consultations, and special research services. This business is managed by nonlawyer personnel and has been lucrative for the firm (see Exhibit 1–11).

Law Firm Structure and Organization

Law firms are becoming more global and establishing offices in other countries. There is an increase in international law firms. As law firms grow, merge with other firms, or form multidisciplinary practices, their leadership and management will take on a corporate look. The managing partner will be replaced by a corporate CEO whose only responsibility is to manage the firm. Firms will gravitate toward professional management and multitier partnership levels.

Legal Insurance Plans

Traditional law firms, especially smaller firms, are becoming more involved with prepaid group legal services. Almost all the states ethically permit lawyers to participate in a plan of this type.

A prepaid group legal plan operates just like a medical insurance plan. Large insurance companies already offer such plans to large employers, such as General Motors and Chrysler Motor Corporation. Each employee pays a monthly fee for legal insurance. When an employee needs a lawyer, the insurance company contributes to the legal fees.

SUMMARY

Most employers of paralegals are attorneys. The structure and organization of a law office depends on the needs and desires of its attorneys, especially senior attorneys who own the firm.

The structure and organization of a law office are determined by four characteristics: size, specialty, management style, and form. The marketplace in which attorneys practice law is divided into three categories: private law firms, private industry, and government agencies.

The size of a law office is measured by the number of attorneys it employs. Small firms are still the preferred way to practice law for most lawyers in the United States. Four sizes of law firms exist: small, medium, large, and mega-firm. Four types of large law firms exist: local, regional, national, and international.

As society has become more complex, law has become more complex. This has forced attorneys to specialize in a particular area of law. The transition to specialization in law is analogous to specialization in the medical profession.

A firm's structure and the areas of law in which its attorneys specialize determine the firm's clientele and its need for staff, equipment, and materials. Numerous attorney specialties exist in the United States, and a number of states have developed plans for the recognition of legal specialties.

Two distinct managerial areas are addressed in any law firm: administrative (financial, office systems, and so on) and governance (associates, client relations, personnel, marketing, and so on). The combination of approaches used in these two areas is the management style of the firm.

Attorneys have developed five management styles that are used in most law firms in the United States: autocratic, democratic, managing partner, committee, and combination.

Two forms of management are defined: centralized and decentralized. In a centralized form of management, an entire law firm is managed from one source, whether by autocratic, democratic, managing partner, or committee style. In a decentralized form of management, an office is managed in segments, or in many areas.

Private law firms are organized into seven different business structures: sole proprietorship, partnership, professional corporation, limited liability company, boutique firm, office-sharing association, and legal clinic.

Private industry consists of all types of businesses: small, medium, and large. Two types of legal departments are identified: corporate legal departments for very large corporations and legal departments for smaller, private companies.

Freelance paralegal services are offered to attorneys on a contract basis. A variety of freelance paralegal services are available in the United States. Numerous private companies also provide support services for attorneys.

Four types of government agencies employ paralegals: federal, state, county, and local.

Technological innovation is the catalyst for future changes in the delivery of legal services. Technology will change the way legal professionals perform research, file documents, and communicate with clients. A multidisciplinary practice is a firm that employs nonlegal professionals from other disciplines to offer its clients nonlegal services, such as accounting, in addition to legal services. The trend toward multidisciplinary practice will increase. Law firms and individual attorneys are opening separate, nonlegal businesses, known as nonlegal subsidiaries, which utilize their legal expertise.

There is a trend that shows an increase in international law firms. As law firms grow, merge with other firms, or form multidisciplinary practices, their leadership and management will take on a corporate look. Traditional law firms, especially smaller firms, are becoming more involved with prepaid group legal services. The needs of society and the individual client have changed since the days of the family lawyer.

CHAPTER ILLUSTRATION

Robert Black and Dennis White are new attorneys who were classmates in law school. Dennis wants to practice general litigation, family, and criminal law. Robert is interested in specializing in intellectual property. When they graduated from law school, Dennis wanted to start his own business but could not afford to purchase the necessary supplies and equipment to establish his own office, so he rented an office in an office-sharing facility.

This law suite is equipped with a law library, secretarial service, receptionist service, and fax and copying services. Dennis's rent gives him access to the suite amenities. There are about 20 lawyers in the suite who practice in various areas of law, mostly general practice. Each of the 20 lawyers in the suite is a sole practitioner. Some have their own secretaries, and others use the secretarial service. Dennis is pleased with the office-sharing arrangement.

Robert pounded the pavement for a job in intellectual property in corporate legal departments but was unsuccessful. He started doing some general practice work to help him get by. Dennis convinced him to establish his practice in the office suite. Dennis told him that an attorney in his suite was looking for a contract attorney who did intellectual property work and suggested that he may also get referrals from other attorneys. Robert joined the office and works on intellectual property cases and general litigation cases.

After a couple of years, their clientele had increased so that both men were very busy attorneys. They found that their practices were too busy to rely on the secretarial service, so they hired a secretary, Tricia Bunnell, to work for both of them.

After a year, their businesses had outgrown the law suite. They were ready to establish their own practice and agreed to practice law together. Dennis found an office in a new professional building and rented it. They discussed the form of their business. They discussed the advantages and disadvantages of a partnership and corporation. They wanted neither the liability of a partnership nor the structure of a corporation. They agreed that a professional limited liability company (PLLC) would be the right form of business for them.

Each agreed to contribute $25,000 to get the business started. Robert's friend, Grant Greene, a tax specialist who worked for the IRS, was looking for a new job and wanted to join in the business. However, Grant had no money to contribute to the start-up endeavor. Grant became a junior partner, owning 10 percent of the firm. When Grant could pay his contribution of $25,000, he would be promoted to full partner. Therefore, Robert owned 45 percent, Dennis 45 percent, and Grant 10 percent. Since Robert had management experience, the partners agreed that he would be the managing partner.

On the first day of May, their law firm opened. They celebrated as they hung out their shingle "Law Firm of Black, White & Greene, PLLC."

CHAPTER REVIEW

1. What are the four things that determine the structure and organization of a law office?
2. What has forced attorneys to specialize?
3. What are the five management styles used in most law firms?
4. What is the difference between centralized and decentralized management?
5. What is the most common management style of a private law firm?
6. What are the three classes of attorneys found in a partnership?
7. How does a legal clinic differ from a private law firm?
8. What is outside counsel?
9. What is the head attorney in a corporate legal department called?
10. What is the management style of a corporate legal department?
11. What are the two managerial areas found in a law firm?
12. What is the difference between a freelance paralegal and an independent paralegal?
13. What is the federal government's General Schedule?
14. What is a nonlegal subsidiary?
15. What is a multidisciplinary practice?

EXAMPLES FOR DISCUSSION

1. THE BOOKS ARE IN THE SAFE

It all came apart in less than a year: a booming products liability boutique headed by an ex-partner from a big firm—the scion of one of Maryland's most prominent legal families, an author, and a lecturer—in partnership with two of his old buddies, one a law school classmate.

Attorney Edward S. Digges of Annapolis, Maryland, left Baltimore's Piper & Maybury in 1984 and set up his own firm with David A. Levin and James T. Wharton. David and James were busy lawyering. Edward was the managing partner, who took on all the onerous administrative tasks—billings, for example.

In February 1989, client Dresser Industries sued the firm, charging that Edward had overbilled it by more than $2 million. His busy partners now found the time to demand to see the books, only to be told they were in the safe and not available. The next month, though, they saw the books and came to the conclusion that Edward had cheated them out of $1 million in compensation. They forced Edward out of the firm.

By September, Dresser won a motion for summary judgment, a determination of issues without a trial, against David and James for $3.1 million in damages for the overbillings, in part because expert witnesses testified that the two partners failed to come up with a mechanism that would have allowed them to oversee Edward's billings.

In January 1990, Edward pleaded guilty in federal court to fraud. He was sentenced to 30 months in prison, fined $30,000, and ordered to pay $1 million in restitution. (Reprinted with permission from *The National Law Journal,* April 23, 1990, p. 29.)

a. What went wrong with this partnership?

b. Why did David and James, rather than Edward, have to pay the client $3.1 million?

c. How could this situation have been avoided?

d. If you were involved in a partnership, what steps would you take so that this situation would not happen to you?

2. MANAGEMENT STYLES

Of the five management styles discussed in this chapter:

a. Which management style(s) have you experienced?

b. Which style do you think is the best for the following:

- Small firm
- Medium firm
- Large firm
- Mega-firm

c. What are the reason(s) for your choice?

ASSIGNMENTS

1. Interview two sole proprietors in your area. What are the differences between the two? Write a report comparing the following:

a. Years of experience

b. Income level

c. Office structure

d. Management style

e. Type of clientele

f. Number of hours worked each week

g. Office setup and staff

2. Before you enrolled in this class, did you have an idea of your "ideal" place of employment? Do you know what your employment needs are? If not, take a minute to think about it. To determine your needs, consider the following:

   a. Do you need to be in a luxurious, prestigious environment?

   b. Do routine tasks bore you?

   c. Do you enjoy interacting with many people or do you prefer to work alone?

   d. Would you be happy doing research in a law library all day?

   e. Do you enjoy working with high technology?

   f. Do people with serious problems upset you?

   g. Do you work well under pressure?

   h. Are you flexible?

   i. Are you an organized person?

   j. Would working more than 40 hours a week bother you?

   k. What are your talents?

   l. Do you desire to travel in your work?

   m. What are your strengths?

   n. What are your weaknesses?

   Write your answers to the above questions on a piece of paper and put it in a safe place to review later. Be candid with yourself. In what type of environment do you need to work to reach your maximum potential? When you have completed your paralegal training, review this assignment and make any changes you feel appropriate. This list will help you in your future job search.

3. Based on the information in this chapter, describe the law office that will satisfy your employment needs. Describe the "ideal" law office in which you would like to work. Describe your expectations. Keep the description of your ideal office in a safe place and review it after you have completed your paralegal training. When you start looking for a job, concentrate your efforts on offices that come close to your description.

4. Research the websites of the law firms listed in the Cybersites section. Pick one firm and answer the following questions:

   a. What are the specialties of the firm?

   b. Does the website list the attorneys in the firm? If so, what are their qualifications?

   c. Does the site have links to other websites? If so, which ones?

   d. Does the website list the firm's philosophy or mission statement? If so, what is it?

   e. Does the website offer reference material for legal research?

   f. Does the firm offer a newsletter? If so, download and print it.

   g. Does the firm have a nonlegal subsidiary? If so, name it.

   h. What did you find especially interesting about the website?

5. Does your state formally recognize legal specialties? If so, which specialties? Research this area and report on the following:

   a. What are the qualifications of an attorney to be a specialist?

   b. What are the requirements for certification?

   c. What are the areas of specialties?

   d. What is the duration of certification?

6. Research the five management styles in terms of structure, organization, behavior techniques, and policies. Prepare a report of your findings and conclude with your opinion of the most effective and ineffective management styles.

7. Compare centralized and decentralized forms of management. In what cases would a decentralized form of management be effective? Ineffective? In what cases would a centralized form of management be effective? Ineffective?

8. Contact an insurance company that offers prepaid group legal insurance, and ask for a copy of a policy. Review the policy and write a report answering the following questions:
   a. What are the services offered?
   b. What are the requirements?
   c. What are the costs?
   d. How many people are enrolled in the plan?

9. Compare a corporate legal department with a traditional law firm. What are the differences? What are the similarities?

SELF TEST

How well did you grasp the material in the chapter? Test yourself by answering the following questions. Check your answers against the answers in Appendix A.

1. What four things determine the structure and organization of a law office?
2. How is the size of a law office measured?
3. What factor determines the size differential of law offices?
4. In what size firm do the majority of lawyers prefer to practice?
5. What are the four types of large law firms?
6. What is a mega-firm?
7. What has forced attorneys to specialize?
8. How do specialty areas affect a law firm?
9. What is a law office's culture?
10. What are the five management styles used in the majority of law firms today?
11. What is an autocratic form of governance?
12. What are the two types of democratic governance?
13. What is a legal administrator?
14. What is an office manager?
15. What is the most common management style?
16. Why is the managing partner encouraged to practice law in addition to management duties?
17. What is an executive committee composed of?
18. What is combination management style?
19. What are the two forms of management?
20. What is a sole proprietor?
21. What is a general practitioner?
22. What are the five most common specialties for sole proprietors?
23. What is a contract attorney?
24. What are the three classes of attorneys that work in a partnership?
25. Who may own shares in a professional legal corporation?
26. What is the function of the board of directors of a professional corporation?
27. What is an LLC?
28. What is a boutique firm?
29. What are the two types of office-sharing arrangements?
30. What motivates an attorney to seek an office-sharing arrangement?

31. What is a legal clinic?
32. How is a legal clinic funded?
33. What type of cases do legal clinics take?
34. What is an outside counsel?
35. What is preventative law?
36. How does a corporate legal department function?
37. What is the head attorney in a corporate legal department called?
38. What is an in-house counsel?
39. What are some areas in private industry in which legal assistants have utilized their paralegal training?
40. What is a freelance paralegal service?
41. What is an independent paralegal?
42. Where do freelance paralegals work?
43. How many years of experience should a paralegal have before they freelance?
44. What four types of government agencies employ paralegals?
45. What federal agencies are the largest employers of paralegals?
46. What is the General Schedule?
47. What is a legal clerk?
48. What are some examples of paralegal employment opportunities in county government?
49. Under what classification on the General Schedule of Occupational Classification do paralegals fall?
50. What is a multidisciplinary law practice?
51. What is a nonlegal subsidiary?
52. Describe prepaid legal insurance plans.

Key Words

autocratic	executive committee	mega-firm
autonomous	freelance paralegal	multidisciplinary practice
boutique	general counsel	nonlegal subsidiary
CLA	general practitioner	office manager
contract attorney	independent paralegal	outside counsel
contract basis	indigent	P.C.
culture	in-house counsel	preventative law
cybercrime	legal administrator	sole practitioner
cybertort	legal clinic	sole proprietorship
dividend	limited liability company	

 # Cybersites

Need more information about law firms? Check out the following websites.

MEGA FIRMS

Baker & McKenzie—<*http://www.bakerandmckenzie.com*> Mega international firm with more than 3,200 attorneys.

Jones, Day, Reavis & Pogue—<*http://www.jonesday.com*> Mega international firm with more than 1,800 attorneys.

LARGE FIRMS

Anderson Kill & Olick—<*http://www.andersonkill.com*> Regional East Coast Law firm of 150+ attorneys. Has newsletter page and description of branch offices. Has nonlegal subsidiaries in insurance services.

Baker, Donelson, Bearman & Caldwell—<*http://www.bakerdonelson.com*> Large international firm located in the Southeast with 450+ attorneys. Established in 1888.

Arent Fox Kintner & Kahn, PLLC—<*http://www.arentfox.com*> Firm has 300+ attorneys. Site contains firm brochure and many other features, including a publication about their paralegals.

Crowell & Moring LLP—<*http://www.crowellmoring.com*> Firm has 270+ attorneys. Site contains pro bono area, a description of its culture, and information regarding its nonlegal subsidiary C&M International, Ltd.

Pierce Atwood—<*http://www.pierceatwood.com*> East Coast law firm with 100+ attorneys. Has client relations and technology pages. Describes its nonlegal subsidiary, Pierce Atwood Consulting.

Lex Mundi—<*http://www.lexmundi.org*> An international association of private law firms.

MEDIUM FIRMS

Schuyler, Roche & Zwirner, PC—<*http://www.srzlaw.com*> Firm with 45+ attorneys. Site has news page.

Heller Ehrman—<*http://www.hellerehrman.com*> Firm with 100+ lawyers. Specialists in representing deal-intensive technology companies and venture capital banking firms in Silicon Valley, California.

Moye White, LLP—<*http://www.mgovg.com*> Voted best medium-sized firm specializing in business, litigation, and real estate.

Banner & Witcoff—<*http://www.bannerwitcoff.com*> Medium-sized national firm with 80+ attorneys specializing in intellectual property. Good reference site.

BOUTIQUE FIRMS

Kapilan Meyers Rosen & Louik, PC—<*http://www.kmrlmedmal.com*> Medical malpractice and personal injury law firm. Employs six attorneys and two doctors. Newsletter is online.

Birch, Steward, Kolasch & Birch, LLP—<*http://www.bskb.com*> Law firm that specializes in intellectual property. They have an extranet on their site.

The Tax Prophet—<*http:www.taxprophet.com*> Sole practitioner who specializes in tax matters.

Timothy W. Tuttle & Associates—<*http://www.tuttlefirm.com*> Specializes in tax and accounting.

SMALL FIRMS

Law Offices of Seth J. Arnowitz—<*http://www.ctattorney.com*> Sole practitioner who specializes in real estate litigation.

Clifford Law Offices—<*http://www.cliffordlaw.com*> Small firm of three attorneys. Take a tour of their office, winner of the ABA office design award.

Robb & Robb, LLC—<*http://www.robbrobb.com*> Husband and wife team specializing in personal injury. High-profile media cases.

FOREIGN FIRMS

Chan Robles & Associates—<*http://www.chanrobles.com*> International firm in the Philippines. Office is open 24 hours a day to accommodate international clients. Site contains links to many international legal databases and many links to various governmental agencies. Firm has many nonlegal subsidiaries, including a consulting company, CPA firm, collection firm, training services, and publishing company.

Clifford Chance—<*http://www.cliffordchance.com*> The largest mega-firm in the world by revenue ($2.039 billion in 2006). It employs more than 3,600 attorneys and was named Law Firm of the Year. Located in London with offices throughout the world. Originated in 1802.

FREELANCE PARALEGALS ON THE WEB

Patricia Durham—<*http://www.pwdurham.net*>
Freelance Paralegal Network—<*http://www.freelanceparalegal.com*>
Full Service Legal Support, LLC—<*http://www.fullservicesupport.com*>
Moyer Paralegal Services—<*http://www.moyerparalegal.com*>

INDEPENDENT PARALEGALS ON THE WEB

Independent Document Preparation Services—<*http//:www.divorce-me.com*>
Paralegal Plus—<*http://www.paralegal-plus.com*>
Arizona Association of Paralegals—<*http://www.azaip.com*>
Attorney Alternative—<*http://www.attorneyalternative.org*>

FEDERAL JOBS ON THE WEB

For a listing of available job opportunities with the federal government, check out the following websites:
Federal Job Search—<*http://www.federaljobsearch.com*>
Federal Jobs Digest—<*http://www.jobsfed.com*>
Office of Personnel Management—<*http://www.opm.gov*>
Federal Jobs Central—<*http://www.fedjobs.com*>
HRS Federal Job Search—<*http://www.hrsjobs.com*>
Government Jobs—<*http://www.govtjobs.com*>

 Student CD-ROM
For additional materials, please go to the CD in this book.

 Online Companion™
For additional resources, please go to http://www.paralegal.delmar.cengage.com

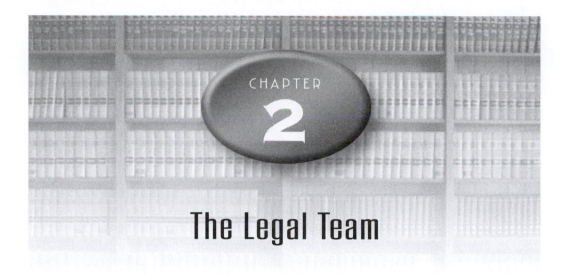

CHAPTER 2

The Legal Team

OBJECTIVES

After completion of this chapter, the student should be able to do the following:

- Describe the titles, functions, and duties of each member of a legal team.
- Describe the functions and differences of the different categories of attorneys in a law firm.
- Describe the history, present position, and responsibilities of a law office administrator and a law office manager.
- Explain the difference between an office administrator and an office manager.
- Identify the various types of managers in a large firm.
- Describe tiered paralegal assistant programs.
- Explain how different law office staff members contribute to a legal team.
- Describe the types of outside services and consultants contracted by a law office and how they contribute to the delivery of legal services.
- List the many employment opportunities for a person with a paralegal education.

INTRODUCTION

The purpose of this chapter is to introduce the various types of personnel that work in the legal marketplace and to briefly describe their job duties. It is important to understand how the legal team functions together and to illustrate how legal professionals interact with other staff. Although no two law offices are alike and employees' duties may vary, a general description of the duties of law office staff will be very helpful to a new paralegal to understand fully each member's contribution to the legal team.

After a brief history of law office personnel, this chapter will discuss the various types of personnel in a law office and their responsibilities. Personnel will be dealt with according to size and type of firm. The various services law firms use will also be covered. After completing this chapter, you should understand the components of a dynamic legal team.

HISTORICAL PERSPECTIVE

In the 1940s and 1950s, a legal team consisted of an attorney and a secretary. The management duties of a law firm were the responsibility of both and most often were not given high priority. In the 1960s, the American Bar Association (ABA) determined that attorneys' incomes were below those of other professionals. To discover the reason, the ABA conducted a survey that compared attorneys' businesses with those of other professionals and found that attorneys' lack of attention to law office management resulted in their decreased incomes. The survey also revealed that other professionals employed assistants and delegated routine work to their assistants. The ABA found that lawyers' incomes would increase if their efficiency increased. Therefore, the paralegal and legal administrator professions were born.

The advent of the paralegal and legal administrator roles changed the traditional law firm. By delegating routine tasks to paralegals and management duties to legal administrators, lawyers could realize greater efficiency and increased incomes. Attorneys, however, were slow to recognize the full benefits of these new positions.

A 1963 Prentice Hall survey of 311 Missouri attorneys revealed that 63 percent would not use the services of nonlawyer assistants. Of the 37 percent who would use those services, approximately 66 percent would hire nonlawyer assistants part time for clerical functions.

It took only 5 years for part of this attitude to change. In surveys conducted in 1968, 60 percent of attorneys indicated they would hire nonlawyer assistants. However, the majority would hire them only for clerical functions. Many lawyers resisted delegating legal tasks to nonlawyers.

Despite the resistance of attorneys, the paralegal profession flourished. In addition to economics and efficiency, four elements contributed to its growth.

- *Promotion by Bar Associations.* The ABA established the Special Committee on Lay Assistants for Lawyers in 1968. This committee encouraged employment of paralegals. The ABA adopted a formal definition of a paralegal and guidelines for using paralegal services (see the "Paralegal" section later in this chapter). State bar association committees for law office economics extensively promoted the use of paralegal services. Today, many state bar associations have paralegal divisions or committees.
- *Growth of Paralegal Education.* Many paralegal educational programs emerged, training qualified paralegals. These paralegals demonstrated their skills and capabilities to attorneys while on the job.
- *Organization of Paralegals and Managers.* Paralegals and law office managers organized nationally and locally. These organizations worked hard to educate attorneys on the benefits of employing nonlawyer assistants. (Appendix B lists national and state associations for paralegals and related associations.)
- *Restructuring of Other Professions.* Other professions, such as the medical, dental, architectural, and teaching professions, realized the benefits of employing assistants and demonstrated these benefits by increased incomes and efficiency.

Today, paralegals, legal administrators, and law office managers are recognized as essential members of a legal team.

LEGAL TEAM MEMBERS

A law firm's need for staff varies according to the size and specialty of the firm. For example, a general practitioner would need a staff with skills in various areas of law. A boutique firm would need a staff with skills in its specialty. A large law firm would need more management personnel than a small law firm.

A person with a paralegal education and experience has management opportunities in a law office. Many law firms promote their legal secretaries and paralegals to management positions instead of hiring outside people. This trend is especially true of small and medium law offices. Paralegals are enhancing their paralegal education with management courses, with the goal of managing a law office or becoming a paralegal manager.

Certain types of legal personnel can be found in each law office: attorney, legal administrator or office manager, paralegal, law clerk, secretary, and receptionist. One person may fill more than one position. For example, a paralegal may also be an office manager or law clerk, and a secretary may also be the receptionist.

Attorney

The attorney is the captain of a legal team. The number of attorneys in the United States reached one million in the year 2000. In 2007, there were 1,116,967 lawyers in the United States; one for every 300 people or 36 percent of the total population. By contrast, Japan has one lawyer for every 10,000 people. Twenty-four percent of attorneys in the United States are women. In 2010, it is expected that 40 percent of the nation's lawyers will be women.

Four categories of attorneys exist: rainmakers, owners, associates, and nontraditional.

RAINMAKERS   **Rainmakers** are known as such because they bring in the clients that provide the firm with work. Rainmakers are often very active in community organizations and bar associations. They are usually senior members of the firm. Some rainmakers serve on clients' boards of directors. Because of their outside civic activities, they may have a lower annual billable hour requirement than other attorneys in the firm—that is, the firm does not require them to bill as many hours to clients (see Chapter 7).

Owners, whether sole proprietors, partners, or shareholders, maintain client relations and train associates. They are responsible to the clients and supervise associates. Owners are more likely to be rainmakers than are other attorneys.

rainmaker
An attorney responsible for client development for a firm.

Of Interest . . .

WHAT DO THE LETTERS AFTER THE ATTORNEY'S NAME MEAN?

JD—Juris Doctor: Granted to a person on graduation of law school if the graduate has a bachelor's degree

LLB—Bachelor of laws: Granted to a person on graduation of law school if the graduate does not have a bachelor's degree

LLM—Master of laws: Granted to a person who has a JD and who successfully completes graduate course work in an area of law

Esq.—Esquire: Used for attorneys as a title of respect, such as "Honorable" is used for judges

OWNERS   Owners of a partnership are not considered firm employees who are entitled to a salary. They are paid out of firm profits according to the percentage of the firm they own, as shown in Exhibit 2–1. In addition, partners contribute money to a partnership endeavor and pool their money to capitalize the business. The percentage of a firm that a partner owns depends on the category of the partner. Some law firms have multiple classes of partner, but most firms have two categories: full partner and junior partner (see Exhibit 2–1).

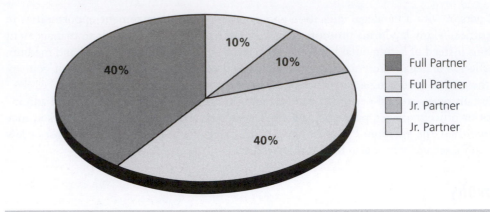

EXHIBIT 2–1 Firm Ownership by Partner Level

equity partner
A partner who is entitled to a portion of the firm's profits and is responsible for a portion of the firm's losses.

nonequity partner
A partner who is not entitled to a portion of the profits and is not responsible for a portion of the losses of a firm.

A full partner, also known as an **equity partner,** has an equal voice in management policies and shares equally in the profits of the law firm. Within the class of full partner is the senior partner. A senior partner is usually a firm's founder, has more seniority than other partners, or controls the cases of the majority of clients.

Junior partners are newly admitted to a partnership and generally have little input in the direction of the firm. In some firms, the term **nonequity partner,** or special partner, is used to indicate the noncapital position of a junior partner. They are entitled to a smaller portion of the profits. An attorney will remain a junior partner for a certain amount of time until promoted to full partnership.

One advantage of junior partnership status is that a junior partner is not required to contribute money into the partnership to equal the contribution ratio of the other full partners. The time spent as a junior partner gives an attorney an opportunity to save for a partnership contribution.

ASSOCIATES   Associate attorneys are employees of a firm and are not entitled to a percentage of the firm's profits. They are paid a salary for their work. Associates do much of the work and often have a higher annual billable requirement than partners (see Chapter 7). Associates may be eligible for partnership in a firm when they have been employed by the firm for a certain length of time.

Before the 1940s, associates were employed for as long as 20 years before they were eligible for partnership. During the 1970s and 1980s, the average length of time an attorney had to be employed to reach the goal of partnership was 5 to 7 years. Figures compiled by the National Association of Law Placement indicate that, during that period, the average length of time required before associates were considered for partnership status was 6.7 years in firms of 25 or more lawyers. However, since 1990, the length of time has increased, and some firms are reevaluating whether associates should be promoted at all.

Because of business constraints and competition in the marketplace, firms are promoting fewer associates to partnership status. They are finding that it is important to **leverage** an associate to the fullest extent possible. Leveraging is making a profit on the work of others. Studies have shown that the higher the ratio of associates to partner, the higher a partner's income. Therefore, it is not profitable for partners to promote associates in most cases.

leverage
The ability to make money from the work of others.

leverage ratio
A formula used to identify the number of income-producing employees per owner.

A **leverage ratio** is a formula used to identify the number of leveraged income earners per partner. If a sole proprietor employs one associate, the ratio is 1:1. If a sole proprietor employs three associates, the ratio is 1:3. Paralegals are also income producers for a law firm. Since they do not generate as high an income as an associate, their ratio is calculated at one-half of that of an associate, or .5. In other words, it takes two paralegals to equal one associate in a leverage ratio. Therefore, if a sole practitioner employs two associates and two paralegals, the ratio is 1:3. If a partnership of two attorneys employs five associates and two paralegals, the ratio is 1:3, as shown here:

$$5 + (2 \times .5)/2 \text{ partners} = \text{Ratio } 1:3$$

According to recent analyses of the 2006–2007 *NALP Directory of Legal Employers* published by the Association for Legal Career Professionals, the national average ratio of lawyers to partners is just over 2.19 (1:2.19). On average, larger law firms leverage their partners with associates and other income producers to a greater degree than do smaller firms. Leverage rates are also higher in the most heavily populated areas of the country.

Some firms have a limit on the number of associates they will promote to partner. A firm with seven or eight senior associates may promote only two or three to junior or full partner in order to maintain leverage. The remaining senior associates may become **permanent associates.** They receive a salary and fringe benefits but are not entitled to share in the firm's profits and have no possibility of partnership.

There are four classes of associates: senior associate, associate, junior associate, and nontraditional associate. Senior associates and associates supervise junior associates. Junior associates assist senior associates. A junior associate is usually a new attorney with little experience. Junior associates are analogous to an apprentice who must go through a period of training before advancing in the profession.

NONTRADITIONAL   Law firms may use the services of a **staff attorney.** A staff attorney is neither a partner nor an associate but is hired as a permanent employee with no possibility of advancement within a firm. Recently, firms have created 44 separate classifications for firm lawyers that are neither partner nor associate. Among these classifications are counsel, affiliated attorney, special counsel, contract attorney, and advisory counsel (usually used for retired partners). The use of nontraditional attorneys is increasing as the potential for new partners is decreasing.

An **of-counsel** refers to a semiretired former partner or an attorney who is affiliated with a firm on a part-time basis. An attorney who is well known may also be of-counsel to a law firm to help attract clients to the firm. In this capacity, the of-counsel attorney would be considered a rainmaker. An of-counsel attorney may be an employee of the firm or paid as a consultant only. Most of-counsel positions are not **equity** positions, which means that they are not entitled to a share of the firm's profits.

Law firms have established a variety of arrangements for their of-counsel positions. This has resulted in some confusion regarding the exact role of the of-counsel. The ABA, in its Model Code, defined an of-counsel as "A lawyer . . . [who] has a continuing relationship with the lawyer or law firm other than as a partner or associate." This definition allows for a variety of functions, and law firms apply the of-counsel designation for various reasons. The of-counsel position carries no clearly defined job description or duties, but the ABA opined that the relationship must be more than a casual relationship. The of-counsel attorney must be involved with the firm's cases and day-to-day affairs, as well as be available for consultation and advice on a regular basis.

Legal Administrator

A legal administrator manages the business of a law firm. Some legal administrators have a law degree, but most have a master's of business administration **(MBA)** degree. A legal administrator's compensation is related to experience, size of firm, and geographic location.

Legal administrators have also been called office managers. However, the two are different. A legal administrator is responsible for making major business decisions for a firm. An office manager is under the direction of a legal administrator or a managing partner and does not have the authority of the administrator. Three major differences distinguish a legal administrator and an office manager.

1. An administrator attends all partnership or committee meetings, although the administrator has no right to vote on issues.

---

permanent associate
An employed attorney who is not eligible for a partnership in, or ownership of, a firm.

staff attorney
An employee of a law firm who has no advancement opportunities.

of-counsel
An attorney affiliated with a firm on a part-time basis.

equity
A right of ownership in a firm, entitling the holder to a portion of the profits.

MBA
Master's of business administration degree.

2. An administrator has the authority to hire and discharge staff personnel and administer salaries within approved guidelines.

3. An administrator has the authority to make major purchases of furniture and equipment and to make financial decisions for a firm.

Before the legal administrator profession existed, secretaries acted as office managers and were asked to assume management functions under the direction of a managing attorney. In the late 1960s, the legal administrator profession emerged to assume management functions. Most office managers were promoted from legal secretary positions and had the status just above support staff but below associate. Most were hired to take over accounting and personnel functions and were regarded as administrative assistants to a managing partner.

Eventually, firms reviewed the amount of time managing partners devoted to management duties and determined that they would make more money if managing partners spent that time on billable matters. Management functions could be performed by an administrator at less cost to a firm. Therefore, the legal administrator position evolved to assume the duties of a managing partner, and some administrators are now partner-level employees, advising owners on key operational decisions.

ROLE OF ADMINISTRATOR IN A LARGE FIRM   A legal administrator in a large firm is an experienced business executive, enjoying the same status and compensation as an attorney. A legal administrator may be referred to as a chief operating officer or executive director. In most cases, however, an administrator is under the direction of a managing partner or executive committee.

Most senior legal administrators come from outside the legal profession. They have advanced degrees and years of senior management-level experience. They are expert delegators and have strong leadership skills.

ROLE OF ADMINISTRATOR IN A SMALL FIRM   In a small firm, a legal administrator has the same responsibilities but on a smaller scale. Most often, the administrator's authority is not as great as in a large firm. This person may have other duties in addition to management responsibilities, such as paralegal or accounting work, and often has the title of office manager under the direction of the managing attorney. Owners of small firms are more autocratic and are possessive of the decision-making process.

While an administrator's areas of responsibility are similar in large and small firms, a small-firm administrator does not have the resources of a large-firm administrator. For example, while a large-firm administrator has information specialists on staff, a small-firm one needs to be familiar with the available technology. In addition, small-firm administrators are responsible for training new personnel, whereas large-firm ones delegate training to an employee or office manager.

The management areas for which an administrator has responsibility are divided into eight categories:

1. Financial management
2. Personnel management
3. Systems management
4. Facilities management
5. General management
6. Practice management
7. Marketing
8. Leadership

Whether a legal administrator performs all these functions or delegates them to an office manager or managers depends on the size of the firm and the amount of authority given the legal administrator by the attorneys in the firm. The managing attorney or attorneys may not be willing to release some responsibilities to an administrator and may keep some for themselves. How an individual law firm accomplishes administrative tasks depends on the policies of the firm.

Law Office Manager

A law office manager works under the direction of a legal administrator or managing partner. In a small firm, an office manager performs all management functions. In a large firm, specialized office managers perform specific management functions under the supervision of a legal administrator, as shown in Exhibit 2–2. Each manager's duties vary according to the needs of the firm, as shown in Exhibit 2–3.

FINANCIAL MANAGER   A financial manager, usually a certified public accountant **(CPA),** is responsible for the various financial aspects of a firm. Duties consist of handling billing and collections, payroll, accounts payable, and investments.

CPA
Certified public accountant.

PERSONNEL MANAGER   A personnel manager is responsible for managing the various aspects of a firm's human resources. This manager's duties include these six tasks:

1. Manage employee benefits
2. Monitor vacation and sick leave
3. Establish promotion and salary increase guidelines
4. Hire and fire employees
5. Interview prospective new employees
6. Develop personnel policies and procedures

ADMINISTRATIVE MANAGER   An administrative manager is responsible for systems management. This person develops and maintains systems used in various areas of a firm. This manager's duties include these five tasks:

1. Manage file maintenance systems (see Chapter 12)
2. Manage general office systems such as calendaring and tickler systems (see Chapter 10)
3. Manage substantive systems (see Chapter 9)
4. Write procedures for each system (see Chapter 9)
5. Change systems as the need arises

FACILITIES MANAGER   A facilities manager is responsible for managing the facilities of a firm, which include the office property, grounds, and structure. For employees to be productive, the office area must have enough space for all employees, be organized, and be

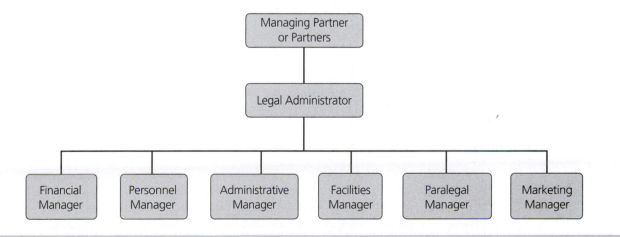

EXHIBIT 2–2   Hierarchy of Managing Partner, Legal Administrator, and Office Managers

---

LEGAL ADMINISTRATOR

Legal administrator wanted for growing law firm of 25 attorneys. Previous law firm management experience necessary. Bachelor's degree in business required; MBA a plus. Must have excellent organizational, communication, and training skills. Must be knowledgeable of computer systems and law firm accounting methods. Firm located in financial district. Excellent salary and benefits. Send résumé and cover letter to Bunnell, Shuran and Kehl, P.O. Box 245, San Francisco, CA 94104.

MARKETING MANAGER

Large New York international law firm of Bristol, Snell, Procunier & Valentino has opening for marketing manager to coordinate the firm's public relations and client development program. Must have five years of marketing experience and have strong writing and communication skills. Must be detail oriented to coordinate seminars, produce newsletter, and coordinate client surveys. Excellent salary, benefits, and working environment. Please send cover letter and résumé to Legal Administrator, Bristol, Snell, Procunier & Valentino, 111 Eighth Avenue, New York, NY 10001.

OFFICE MANAGER

Office manager needed for corporate legal department of large, Fortune 500 company. The ideal candidate will have at least two years of management experience in budget development, personnel management, and training. Must have a bachelor's degree. Professional position that reports to general counsel. Must be a self-starter and computer literate. Send résumé and cover letter to Dept. of Human Resources, ABC Corporation, 9000 Corporate Way, Chicago, IL.

MANAGEMENT

Seeking innovative manager to oversee general management of small law firm specializing in family law. Must have knowledge of employment and labor laws and have previous management experience, preferably in a law firm. Send résumé and salary history to 5507 Longview, Paradise, CA 95969.

EXHIBIT 2–3   Requirements for a Law Office Manager Vary Depending on the Firm's Needs

structured in a manner that encourages productivity. The duties of a facilities manager include these six tasks:

1. Supervise parking conditions for employees and clients
2. Plan the office area to accommodate current and future employees and maximize the use of space (includes assessing needs; deciding where to locate the library, conference rooms, copy center, and receptionist; and ensuring accessibility to the various centers for the employees)
3. Supervise security systems for the premises
4. Supervise cleaning services for the premises
5. Plan employee safety in case of a disaster
6. Plan records preservation in case of a disaster

MARKETING MANAGER   A marketing manager is responsible for marketing and advertising. Marketing is one of the "nonlaw" activities that take place in a law firm. Marketing activities constitute 8 percent of a firm's workload, because marketing ensures a steady flow of clients. A chief marketing officer, a person whose time is devoted to marketing, used to be found in large firms only. However, medium firms are realizing the benefit of a full-time marketing manager.

TRENDS

THE CERTIFIED LEGAL MANAGER

The Association of Legal Administrators developed a voluntary certification program for managing partners, legal administrators, and office managers. The program requires the applicant to meet certain qualification requirements, pass an exam, and accumulate continuing education credits. The exam consists of four areas: financial management, human resources management, legal industry, and office management systems. Those who pass the exam receive the designation of certified legal manager (CLM).

Marketing managers are often recruited from the private sector and most do not have a law degree. Marketing managers employed by very large firms are executive-level employees, such as the legal administrator. Seasoned marketing directors are scarce and often demand partner-sized salaries. The duties of a marketing manager include these nine tasks:

1. Prepare and analyze client surveys to determine firm strengths and weaknesses (see Chapter 4)
2. Direct the firm in defining a target market
3. Direct advertising activities
4. Direct promotional activities, such as client seminars and entertainment
5. Prepare a firm newsletter and brochure (see Chapter 4)
6. Direct public relations activities, such as press releases
7. Monitor the public's perception of the firm
8. Prepare a marketing plan
9. Monitor and update a website and electronic advertising

For more information on law firm marketing, contact the National Law Firm Marketing Association (see Appendix B).

PROFESSIONAL PROFILE 1

Diane Mortenson, owner of Direct Legal Management, is a marketing consultant for law firms. She started out in the legal field as a paralegal and worked as a paralegal for many years before obtaining her master's degree in management and pursuing a career in management. Of her responsibilities, Diane states:

"Marketing consultants are responsible for a number of areas. We set up and monitor seminars and workshops for clients and produce a firm newsletter. We establish and maintain databases and circulate client surveys. We also train and assist the attorneys in client development and help them with client relations, particularly in the area of client communication. One of our major duties is setting up a marketing plan to attract the firm's target market and develop marketing materials." She said that law firm marketing professionals are needed especially for large international law firms that establish a presence in another country. "A marketing professional who knows the needs and trends of a particular country is extremely valuable." She said that law firm marketing is not just for large firms. Smaller firms, especially boutiques, benefit greatly from the services of a law firm marketing specialist.

PARALEGAL MANAGER   A paralegal manager is found in offices with many paralegals and is generally a senior paralegal with many years of experience. A paralegal manager is responsible for supervising paralegals and may also do paralegal work, as shown in Exhibit 2–4.

There is no specific educational background or experience required to become a paralegal manager. The typical paralegal manager is college educated, has a paralegal certificate, and has experience working as a paralegal. Statistics for 2007 state that approximately two-thirds of all paralegal managers have a bachelor's degree and over half have a paralegal certificate. While it is not absolutely necessary to have been a paralegal in order to become a manager, it clearly is the career path most often traveled. Of the paralegal managers who responded to a 2007 International Paralegal Management Association survey on educational criteria, more than 90 percent indicated they had previously worked

---

What does it take to be a good paralegal manager? There are a number of qualities absolutely essential for a good paralegal manager.

1. *The Ability to Work under Pressure.* Paralegal managers receive pressure from legal assistants as well as from attorneys. This is a position where the individual is literally caught in the middle and sits on a fence determining, on a case-by-case basis, which side of the fence to jump to.

2. *Analytical Skills.* The ability to gather facts from two disputing sides (usually an attorney and a paralegal) and to make sense from these facts is essential. It's helpful to have highly tuned mind reading skills as it seems no one actually communicates verbally—there is just an incredible amount of mind reading going on.

3. *Quality Writing and Speaking Skills.* In order to train legal assistants well, a paralegal manager must be able to communicate verbally as well as in writing.

4. *Practical/Common Sense.* A legal assistant manager must have the ability to take fiction and turn it into reality.

5. *Adaptable Personality.* A paralegal manager must take on multiple personalities in order to deal with the quiet, sensitive individual as well as the boisterous, high-strung individual.

6. *High Productivity.* A legal assistant manager is expected not only to take care of the hiring, firing, training, financial accounting, and space considerations but is frequently also expected to do some kind of legal work and to produce it in a very reliable fashion.

7. *Superior Organizational Skills.* The ability to keep training, hiring, and most important, vacation schedules in order!

8. A good legal assistant manager must also be *assertive* and *aggressive,* remembering there is a fine line between these two. One must tread this as if walking a tightrope.

9. *Patience.* Patience is a virtue that a legal assistant manager must have and instill in the legal assistants as well as the attorneys. In the legal profession, there is no room for impatience as everyone suffers.

10. *Attention to Detail.* The legal assistant manager must pay close attention to detail and catch *all* mistakes coming from *all* directions. It is like being a mother—you make everything work, and people just expect it.

11. *The Ability to Handle Three Things at Once.* I like to refer to this as "multipurpose programming," whereby multiple jobs can be done in one fell swoop.

12. *A Sense of Humor.* Last but not least, without a sense of humor, a paralegal manager surely would not survive more than five minutes.

EXHIBIT 2–4   Profile of a Paralegal Manager *(Reprinted with permission from Legal Assistant Today. Copyright 1998, James Publishing, Inc. For subscription information, call 800-394-2626.)*

as a paralegal, and more than 40 percent had specialized in litigation. Among the duties of a paralegal manager are these 11 tasks:

1. Direct the personnel matters of paralegals and act as a **liaison** between paralegals and firm management

2. Supervise paralegals

3. Coordinate the paralegal workload and assign responsibilities

4. Train paralegals

5. Verify that paralegal duties are performed in accordance with an attorney's instructions and act as a liaison between paralegals and attorneys

6. Evaluate paralegals' performance (see Chapter 3)

7. Oversee the firm's paralegal program

8. Establish policies and guidelines relating to the effective use of paralegal services

9. Recruit, interview, and hire new paralegals

10. Conduct orientation and training sessions for new paralegals

11. Maintain personnel records for paralegals

liaison
A person responsible for communication between groups; a spokesperson.

For more information about legal administrators and paralegal managers, contact the Association for Legal Administrators, the International Paralegal Management Association, and the National Association for Law Firm Marketing (see Appendix B).

PROFESSIONAL PROFILE 2

While **Donna Barr** no longer calls herself a paralegal, she firmly states that without her paralegal background she could not perform in the position she now holds. Barr has been a real estate paralegal, office services supervisor, and paralegal manager for a major law firm. An attorney for whom Barr worked suggested to the archdiocese that (1) hiring an in-house paralegal to manage its properties would be more cost-effective than its traditional policy of hiring outside counsel, and (2) he knew an excellent paralegal to be the first to hold the position.

For the past 5 years, Barr has used her knowledge of real estate law and the managerial skills she gained as a paralegal to manage the archdiocese's properties and work with outside counsel. She continues to support the paralegal profession by teaching real estate law, introduction to the profession, and law office administration in the paralegal studies program at the Community College of Aurora.

Paralegal

What is a paralegal? What is the difference between a legal assistant and a paralegal? There is a difference of opinion as to the meanings of the two terms. In some areas of the country, a legal assistant is an entry-level paralegal or a paralegal's assistant. In the Midwest, a legal assistant is a new title for a legal secretary. In other areas, the term *legal assistant* refers to the person, whereas *paralegal* describes the person's work. For example, a legal assistant does paralegal work. In at least one state, Massachusetts, a legal assistant is an attorney who assists a district attorney. Elsewhere, there is no difference. National paralegal associations take the stand that the two terms are synonymous. However, the trend is to use the term *paralegal* instead of *legal assistant*.

According to a My Opinion Survey conducted by the *Legal Assistant Today* magazine in 2006, 94 percent of the respondents said that the term "paralegal" denotes a higher professional status than "legal assistant" because a paralegal is held to higher educational and professional standards. "Too many administrative assistants and legal secretaries are using the legal assistant title," said Cindy Geib, a 14-year paralegal.

There is no definition of a paralegal that is accepted throughout the legal community. Many states have developed definitions of a paralegal, whether through case law, state legislatures, or state bar associations. In addition, the various national, state, and local paralegal associations developed their own definitions of a paralegal.

In 1997, the American Bar Association defined a legal assistant as follows:

> A legal assistant or paralegal is a person, qualified by education, training or work experience who is employed or retained by a lawyer, law office, corporation, governmental agency or other entity and who performs specifically delegated substantive legal work for which a lawyer is responsible.

In 2002, the National Federation of Paralegal Associations (NFPA) amended its definition to exclude the term *legal assistant* from its definition, as follows:

> A Paralegal is a person, qualified through education, training or work experience to perform substantive legal work that requires knowledge of legal concepts and is customarily, but not exclusively, performed by a lawyer. This person may be retained or employed by a lawyer, law office, governmental agency or other entity or may be authorized by administrative, statutory or court authority to perform this work. Substantive shall mean work requiring recognition, evaluation, organization, analysis, and communication of relevant facts and legal concepts.

The following definition was adopted by the American Association for Paralegal Education in 1998:

> Paralegals perform substantive and procedural legal work as authorized by law, which work, in the absence of the paralegal, would be performed by an attorney. Paralegals have knowledge of the law gained through education, or education and work experience which qualifies them to perform legal work. Paralegals adhere to recognized ethical standards and rules of professional responsibility.

In July, 2001, National Association of Legal Assistants (NALA) members voted to adopt the ABA's definition as its own. The International Paralegal Management Association, formerly Legal Assistant Management Association, did the same in 2002. Other paralegal associations have adopted the ABA's definition.

Of Interest . . .

CERTIFICATION VERSUS NONCERTIFICATION

As of September, 2007, NALA certified 14,344 paralegals (the majority of which are in Florida) and 1,126 certified specialists in the United States. Not all paralegals agree that certification is essential for career growth. It is debatable among paralegals whether certification enhances a paralegal's employability and professional status. What paralegals are saying . . .

PRO CERTIFICATION

"I think legal assistants should be certified—it looks better."

"The exam should be taken for no other reason than for yourself. Do I understand my profession? Am I on top of what is going on? Use it to sell yourself and your knowledge as a paralegal."

"Passing an exam is one way to tell the world that you know your stuff."

Of Interest . . . (Cont.)

CON CERTIFICATION

"I have been a paralegal for 17 years. What will a certification exam do for me? All I know is that NALA or NFPA will make more money off me."

"The profession's love of rules and egotistic recognition is damaging to the future of many of its practitioners. Certification overkill!"

"Certified paralegals don't make more money than uncertified paralegals, so what's the point?"

Source: *Legal Assistant Today,* September, 1998.

In 2007, *Legal Assistant Today* did a survey of their readers as to their titles. The magazine reported that 58.2 percent identified themselves as paralegals, and 16.8 percent identified themselves as legal assistants. The remainder had other titles, such as senior paralegal/legal assistant, and paralegal/legal assistant manager. The majority of the respondents (79.7 percent) indicated that they preferred the paralegal title. Many respondents indicated that the paralegal title seemed to denote a higher professional status.

These broad definitions allow attorneys, legal administrators, and paralegal managers to define a paralegal's role in their particular law office. Since they delegate tasks to the paralegal, they determine the paralegal's level of responsibility. They also define an employee's job description, which establishes the difference between a legal assistant and a paralegal.

EDUCATION According to the 2007 *Legal Assistant Today* National Salary Survey, 47.4 percent of its respondents have a bachelor's degree, 6.9 percent have a master's degree, 24.1 percent have an associate's degree, and 20.3 percent have no degree. The higher the paralegal's education, the higher his or her salary.

In the early 1980s, the American Association for Paralegal Education (AAfPE) was organized (see Appendix B). This association has contributed much to the success of the paralegal profession. Educators and employers agree that a paralegal's education is of utmost importance. The days when a paralegal without a paralegal education or advanced degree could receive on-the-job training are over. According to the 2007 *Legal Assistant Today* Salary Survey, 72 percent of the respondents had a paralegal certificate. It also stated that most employers (50.5 percent) required one. Just 16.1 percent of paralegal employers had no educational requirement.

According to a resolution passed by AAfPE, paralegals are qualified to do entry-level work with a college degree (associate's or bachelor's) and a paralegal credential. The bases for the resolution follow:

- Formal education is more learner-friendly than on-the-job training from busy attorneys.
- Those without an education will now find it more difficult to move forward as paralegals.
- More respect will be accorded to paralegals, as a distinct profession, working with attorneys as part of the legal services delivery team. Paralegals will receive more respect and recognition.

A paralegal who meets certain qualifications can be certified through either the NFPA, by taking its Paralegal Advanced Competency Exam (PACE) exam (established 1996), or the NALA, by taking its CLA/CP exam (established 1976). A paralegal may also be certified through the American Alliance of Paralegals. Each certification is voluntary. According to the 2007 *Legal Assistant Today* Salary Survey, 5.5 percent of respondents held the NFPA's Registered Paralegal certification and earned an average of $59,289, while 14.8 percent of respondents passed NALA's CLA/CP exam and reported an average salary of $57,149.

Only 1.7 percent hold NALA's Advanced Certified Paralegal certification for an average salary of $44,800. AAPI certified 0.4 percent of respondents with an average salary of $52,000. There were 4.2 percent of respondents who held state certification with an average salary of $55,929.

The PACE developed by NFPA is a 4-hour, computer-generated test. Those paralegals who complete the exam may use the term *Registered Paralegal* (RP) after their names. The exam contains two stages, identified as tiers. Tier I consists of general and ethics questions. Tier II consists of specialty sections.

The requirements for the PACE exam are:

- An associate's degree in paralegal studies obtained from an institutionally accredited school, and/or ABA approved paralegal education program; and six (6) years substantive paralegal experience; OR
- A bachelor's degree in any course of study obtained from an institutionally accredited school and three (3) years of substantive paralegal experience; OR
- A bachelor's degree and completion of a paralegal program with an institutionally accredited school, which may be embodied in a bachelor's degree; and two (2) years substantive paralegal experience; OR
- Four (4) years substantive paralegal experience on or before December 31, 2000.

To maintain the RP credential, 12 hours of continuing legal or specialty education is required every 2 years, with at least 1 hour in legal ethics. All profits received from the exam program are donated to the "Foundation for the Advancement of the Paralegal Profession," an independent foundation, to further the entire paralegal profession.

The Certified Legal Assistant examination developed by NALA is a two-day comprehensive examination based on federal law and procedure. The major subject areas of the examination follow:

- Communications
- Ethics
- Legal Research
- Human Relations and Interviewing Techniques
- Judgment and Analytical Ability
- Legal Terminology
- Substantive Law—This section consists of five mini-examinations covering the American Legal System and four of the following areas:

  – Administrative Law
  – Bankruptcy
  – Business Organizations/Corporations
  – Contracts
  – Family Law
  – Criminal Law and Procedure
  – Litigation
  – Probate and Estate Planning
  – Real Estate

To be eligible for the CLA/CP examination, a paralegal must meet one of the following requirements:

1. Graduation from a paralegal program that is one of the following:
   - Approved by the ABA
   - An associate's degree program
   - A post-baccalaureate certificate program in paralegal studies
   - A bachelor's degree program in paralegal studies

- A paralegal program that consists of a minimum of 60 semester hours of which at least 15 semester hours are substantive legal courses
2. A bachelor's degree in any field plus 1 year's experience as a paralegal. Successful completion of at least 15 semester hours of substantive paralegal courses is considered equivalent to 1 year's experience as a paralegal.
3. A high school diploma or equivalent plus 7 years' experience as a paralegal under the supervision of a member of the bar, plus evidence of a minimum of 20 hours of continuing legal education credit to have been completed within a 2-year period prior to the examination date.

CLA Specialty Examinations (CLAS) are available in bankruptcy, civil litigation, corporate/business law, criminal law and procedure, intellectual property, probate and estates, and real estate. An advanced paralegal certification (ACP) is also available.

A paralegal who passes the CLA/CP exam may put the acronym CLA (Certified Legal Assistant) or CP (Certified Paralegal) after his or her name. There is no difference between the CLA and CP designations. CP is used for those who prefer the term "paralegal" to "legal assistant." The CLA/CP credential is awarded for a period of 5 years. To maintain Certified Legal Assistant status, paralegals must submit proof of completion of a minimum of 50 hours of continuing legal education programs or individual study programs.

To qualify for the American Alliance of Paralegals' certification, a candidate must have one of the following:

- A bachelor's or advanced degree
- An associate's degree in paralegal studies from an ABA approved paralegal program
- A certificate from an ABA approved paralegal program

The certification status is renewed every 2 years after completion of 18 hours of continuing education, with 2 hours in legal ethics.

SPECIALIZATION Paralegals specialize in the same areas as attorneys. Since a course in all the various specialties cannot be found in paralegal educational programs, they have learned their specialties on the job by working for a specialist. Others have taken a class in some of the more popular specialties. Today, paralegals are realizing the advantages of specializing in two, and perhaps three, areas to increase their marketability. Specialty exams are available from the NFPA and the NALA in some specialty areas.

The specialty with the highest number of paralegals is litigation. Litigation courses are taught in paralegal programs, and many other specialties involve the litigation process.

TRENDS

PRO BONO ACTIVITIES FOR PARALEGALS

Paralegals contribute to the community by volunteering their time and expertise in the following pro bono activities:
- Help an attorney work on a case for an indigent client
- Assist the local bar association's volunteer legal services program
- Assist the elderly in obtaining Social Security as authorized by law
- Represent children in court through a court appointed Special Advocates as authorized by law
- Participate on paralegal advisory boards of a local college to ensure quality education
- Volunteer as a Small Claims Advisor for small claims court
- Tutor a paralegal student
- Volunteer at local shelters
- Serve on the board of directors of local agencies, such as the YWCA of Hospice Homes

EMPLOYER	PERCENTAGE
Private Law Firms	69
Insurance Company	2
Government/Private Sector	8
Self Employed	2
Health – Medical	1
Bank	1
Corporate Legal Department	14
Court System	1
Nonprofit Corporation or Assn.	1

EXHIBIT 2–5 Where Do Paralegals Work? *(2004 National Utilization and Compensation Survey, National Association of Legal Assistants, Tulsa, Oklahoma. Reprinted with permission. Inquiries should be directed to NALA, 919-587-6928 or www.nala.org.)*

According to the 2007 *Legal Assistant Today* National Salary Survey, 46.7 percent of its respondents worked in litigation. The next largest group, 23.1 percent, worked in personal injury law, and 21.3 percent specialized in probate, trusts, and estates. The highest paid specialty was securities (3.0 percent) with an average salary of almost $69,600.

Specializing will increase a paralegal's salary. According to a survey conducted by *Legal Assistant Today* in 2007, the areas of specialization that have the largest salaries are product liability, securities, and civil rights. Paralegals practicing in workers' compensation and family law were paid the least.

PARALEGAL RESPONSIBILITIES BY FIRM STRUCTURE Paralegals work in private law firms, corporate legal departments, private industry, and the government. Private law firms are the largest employer of paralegals. According to the NALA 2004 National Utilization and Compensation Survey Report, Paralegal employers are as shown in Exhibit 2–5.

The average law office employs one paralegal for every three or four attorneys. There is no fixed goal with respect to the ratio of attorneys to paralegals, and the number varies according to the size of the firm. Some areas of law are paralegal intensive (litigation), and some are not (criminal).

A paralegal in a small firm has different duties and responsibilities than a paralegal in a large firm. In a small firm, the paralegal may have duties in addition to paralegal work, such as office management and clerical work. This paralegal may also work in a number of areas of law as demanded by the employer. In a large firm, a paralegal's duties are more narrow and structured. A large firm, having more resources than a small firm, allows a paralegal to specialize and focus his or her concentration on a few duties and areas of expertise. Office managers handle the management, secretaries handle the clerical work, and file and calendar clerks handle filing and calendaring. In a small firm, the attorney supervises the paralegal. In a large firm, the paralegal may have many supervisors: the paralegal manager, legal administrator, supervising attorney, and managing partner.

Another area of difference is upward mobility. In a small firm, paralegals have fewer opportunities to advance than in larger organizations. Few small firms develop levels for their paralegal employees. Corporate legal departments offer their paralegals advancement opportunities inside and outside of the legal department. Large firms create paralegal programs that have levels, or tiers, according to the paralegal's education, experience, and seniority.

The late 1980s saw the beginning of tiered paralegal programs in law offices. A tiered paralegal program provides upward mobility for a paralegal by establishing categories of paralegal positions. An inexperienced paralegal would start at step (or level) one and move up the paralegal ladder to higher positions with greater responsibility and pay. For example,

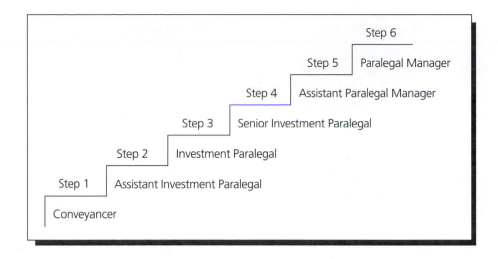

EXHIBIT 2–6   Main Street Insurance Company's Tiered Paralegal Program

paralegals in the legal department of the 3M company are placed on one of four levels: legal aid, legal assistant, advanced legal assistant, and senior legal assistant. Main Street Insurance Company has six steps, as shown in Exhibit 2–6. Promotions are based on demonstrated abilities.

Paralegals perform substantive and clerical tasks. The smaller the firm, the more likely the paralegal will do some clerical work. However, it is considered an inefficient use of a paralegal's time to have them perform clerical tasks because clerical duties are normally considered firm overhead and not billed to the client. According to a survey conducted by *Legal Assistant Today* in 2003, 33.5 percent of responding paralegals performed clerical duties more than substantive duties. According to the NALA 2004 National Utilization and Compensation Survey, 39 percent of its respondents handled their own clerical duties.

SALARY AND BENEFITS   Salaries vary by geographic area. On a national scale, the average salary for 2007 was $51,771, a 1.4 percent increase from 2005 (*Legal Assistant Today*, March, 2007). According to the 2007 *Legal Assistant Today* National Salary Survey, paralegals in corporate legal departments were paid higher salaries than paralegals in private law firms or government positions. Paralegals in private law firms with over 100 attorneys earned the highest salaries. Just over 66 percent (66.1) of respondents received a bonus, the average of which was $2,962. Paralegals employed by private law firms (79.2 percent) were more likely to receive a bonus, the average of which was $3,224. Twenty-nine percent of government offices offered their paralegals a bonus, the average of which was $505; and 57.5 percent of corporate legal departments offered their paralegals a bonus, the average of which was $4,354. The highest bonus reported was $24,000.

Most paralegals are satisfied with their pay. The 2007 *Legal Assistant Today* National Salary Survey asked its respondents if they felt they were fairly paid. Sixty-three percent of the respondents said yes. Of the total respondents in each category, the following felt they were fairly paid:

- 64.5 percent of those who worked in private law firms
- 58.8 percent of those who worked in the government
- 75 percent of those who worked in corporate legal departments

Benefits vary greatly by employer. Generally, large firms and corporate legal departments offer their employees a better benefits package than small firms or small private industry companies. Results of various surveys of the legal profession indicate that benefits are declining. As legal offices become more cost conscious, benefits are normally the first

BENEFIT	PERCENTAGE
Profit Sharing	27.8
Retirement Plan	82.6
Association Dues Paid	59.1
Health Insurance	81
Parking Paid	32.1
Life Insurance	62
Child Care	2.5
Dental Insurance	61.2
Flex Schedule	38
Vision Insurance	39.2
Paid Vacation	85.2
Cell Phone	9.7
Gym Membership	12.7

EXHIBIT 2–7 Employee Benefits in Law Firms *(As seen in the March/April 2007 issue of* Legal Assistant Today. *Copyright 2007, James Publishing, Inc. Reprinted courtesy of* Legal Assistant Today. *For subscription information call 800-394–2626, or visit <www.legalassistanttoday.com>.)*

area in which to cut costs. The benefits reported in the *Legal Assistant Today* 2007 National Annual Survey are shown in Exhibit 2–7.

For more information regarding the paralegal profession, contact a national or local paralegal association (see Appendix B and Cybersites).

Law Clerk

A law clerk is a law student, usually in the second or third year of law school, who typically works for a law firm on a part-time basis. Clerking supplements a law student's education.

Some firms have elaborate programs to attract the best law students from the best law schools. They want to establish a relationship with a student so that the student will consider being employed by that firm on graduation.

A law clerk's duties are performing legal research, writing memorandums of law, and preparing case briefs. Some third- or fourth-year law students may also draft legal documents. Paralegals also do research, write memorandums, and draft legal documents. A law clerk is distinguished from a paralegal by the following:

- Law clerks are normally temporary employees of a firm.
- A clerk's time may or may not be billed to a client.
- Law clerks will usually not make a career out of clerking.
- Law clerks generally work part time while attending law school.

★ Legal Secretary

Prior to 1980, the traditional legal secretary was responsible for all clerical tasks, some paralegal work, and some management duties. This "supersecretary" was an attorney's right arm. In the 1990s, a legal secretary was responsible for clerical tasks. Today, legal secretaries are technology specialists and are given more responsibility. The new millennium introduced a change in the secretary's job title from legal secretary to administrative assistant and, in some cases, legal assistant. Many of today's paralegals started their legal careers in the role of legal secretary.

Of the 4.1 million secretarial positions in 2004, just 272,000 were legal secretaries, and that number is expected to decline further in the next decade. People are leaving the legal secretarial profession and there are few new legal secretaries stepping up to replace them. Some feel that the position does not carry the same prestige as the paralegal position, so they are becoming paralegals. Legal secretaries are in great demand. It is this great demand, along with technological advances, that has caused legal offices to redefine the legal secretary's role.

The typical duties of a legal secretary are clerical in nature. However, the secretary's role is evolving into one that gives more responsibility and client contact. These new responsibilities create a new position outside the box of traditional secretarial duties. Thus, legal secretaries have searched for a title that reflects this change in position. Secretaries now use titles such as Legal Assistant, Administrative Assistant, and Client Service Coordinator.

As attorneys become computer literate, their need for secretarial assistance decreases. For example, one large firm hired 53 new attorneys in an 18-month period without hiring an additional secretary. It is not uncommon for a secretary to support three or four attorneys, paralegals, or both. A firm strives for a ratio of one secretary for three attorneys. This places pressure on secretaries and lawyers to increase efficiency to reduce rush assignments.

PROFESSIONAL PROFILE 3

Maureen Schell has been a legal secretary for 15 years. She started by working as a secretary for Sears and was promoted to the legal department, where the lawyers specialized in labor and employment law. She found it very interesting. Her 15-year career took her to various departments, a very large international law firm, and now a medium-sized firm, Milbank, Tweed, Hadley & McCoy, in Los Angeles. She states:

"When I went to a law firm, I was very surprised at the difference. There is a hierarchy in a law firm that was not found in the legal department. The first law firm I worked for was a very strict, traditional firm. I worked for two corporate attorneys. When I went to work for Milbank, I had to learn to do things differently. They have different policies here. They are not as strict as my other firm. I think it is because the attorneys are young and are bringing new ideas to the firm."

Maureen works for three attorneys in the real estate section of the firm. Two of her bosses are under the age of 32 and are computer literate. They produce their own correspondence and documents. Only the older attorneys dictate to their secretaries. She feels that it is because of her bosses' computer literacy that she is able to handle the work of three attorneys.

Maureen makes a very good salary. She has good benefits, including retirement. She receives a Christmas bonus plus an annual bonus based on the firm's profitability. She is evaluated once a year.

"I like my work. This is a good firm with good people. They have good management, and all the employees pull together as a team. My bosses trust me and have confidence in my abilities. I feel appreciated. The only thing I dislike about the job is that sometimes I have to work under pressure. I can handle pressure, but there are times when it becomes just too much when three attorneys need their work done immediately. Communication is the key to success in a busy law office."

The National Association of Legal Professionals (NALS), formerly the National Association of Legal Secretaries, offers two voluntary certifying exams for legal secretaries. The Accredited Legal Secretary (ALS) is an entry-level certification that requires a candidate to pass a one-day exam. The Professional Legal Secretary (PLS) is an advanced certification that requires a candidate to pass a two-day exam.

For more information about the legal secretarial profession, contact the National Association of Legal Professionals (see Appendix B and Cybersites).

Receptionist

A receptionist is responsible for answering the telephone and greeting clients. This person is often a client's first contact with a law firm. The manner in which the client is greeted sets the stage for the attorney-client relationship. It is important that the client's first experience be a positive one. The importance of this position cannot be overstated.

A receptionist's duties vary according to the size and the structure of a firm. In a large firm, a receptionist may have no other duties than to answer the telephone. In a smaller firm, a receptionist may have additional duties.

The receptionist, being the first contact with a law firm, should be knowledgeable about such things as what seminars the firm is planning, how client disputes are solved, and who practices what kinds of law and for what clients. It is important for law firms to realize that 99 percent of their business starts with a telephone call to a receptionist.

As telephone systems have become automated, the need for a receptionist has declined. In the future, this position will be absorbed by technology. Although law firms will need a person to greet clients as they come into the office, an administrative assistant will soon fill this position.

Other Personnel

Other law office personnel are found in law offices according to the size, specialty, and need of those offices. Large law firms need specialized personnel to handle specific areas. Small firms combine responsibilities and duties. The following sections describe the types of personnel that can be found in a law office setting.

LAW LIBRARIAN A librarian manages the most valuable tool in a law office: information. Law librarians are also known as information resource managers or information systems directors. In addition to maintaining a library, they have a thorough knowledge of research manuals, **legal databases,** and **nonlegal databases.** They also assist attorneys and paralegals in their research projects. Some librarians have a law degree or a paralegal degree, but most have a master's degree in library science (MLS).

The role of a law librarian continues to change with the information explosion of the twenty-first century. As information becomes more abundant and accessible, a manager is needed to handle it. It is vital that information is current and up-to-date, especially changes in the law. The librarian may supervise library staff and have other management responsibilities. Law librarians do legal research projects, which are billed to the client. Some librarians are responsible for the firm's conflict of interest checking systems (see Chapter 13).

Some librarians, particularly those in small- to medium-sized firms, have additional duties outside a library, such as managing paralegal or secretarial staff. Librarians may also manage a firm's central filing area. In small- and medium-sized firms, paralegals and experienced legal secretaries act as librarians. It is a common practice for librarians to assist attorneys and associates with research projects. Law firms normally bill the client for the librarian's research services. A librarian's billing rate is from $80 to $180 per hour and is normally based on the rate charged for senior paralegals. Paralegals are excellent candidates for the librarian position.

CALENDAR CLERK A calendar clerk keeps track of all court hearings, depositions, and other important dates for a law firm. This clerk works closely with all staff and also keeps track of the statute of limitations on cases.

PROOFREADER A proofreader reviews documents for typographical, grammatical, and syntactical errors. A proofreader also compares versions of contracts and highlights areas of change. A proofreader is normally found in large law firms.

PARALEGAL AIDE An aide, clerk, or paralegal assistant helps a paralegal with such functions as finding files and documents, photocopying, and performing general file maintenance. An

---

legal database
An organized collection of statutes, case law, administrative rulings, and legal memorandums.

nonlegal database
An organized collection of nonlegal information such as medical information, business statistics, and the like.

aide may be an intern who is studying to be a paralegal and works for a firm on a part-time basis. In some areas of the country, a paralegal aide is known as a legal assistant. The type of experience gained in this position is very valuable for paralegal students.

INFORMATION SYSTEMS MANAGER   An information systems manager is responsible for the computer system and technology of an office. Some large firms also employ a functional manager and technical specialists to meet their computer needs. A functional manager is in charge of a specific application area. Technical specialists are responsible for training and for the maintenance of various systems. Other terms for an information systems manager include database administrator, systems specialist, and information resource manager. Large firms employ information systems managers on a full-time basis. Other firms hire consultants for this function.

LEGISLATIVE ANALYST   A legislative analyst tracks legislation that affects clients. This person has access to legal databases that monitor all types of legislation: federal, state, and administrative hearings. This information helps attorneys keep abreast of the rapid changes in the law. In addition, an attorney may alert business clients of legislation that would affect their enterprise. Legislative analysts are normally found in corporate legal departments. They track legislation and laws that affect the corporation's area of business. Many paralegals are finding the legislative analyst position an attractive position to pursue.

INVESTIGATOR   An investigator examines cases and interviews witnesses. Many large firms and small boutiques that handle criminal matters employ their own investigator. Other firms use the services of outside investigator firms.

MESSENGER   A messenger, also called a courier or a runner, runs errands for a firm. Typical duties include delivering documents, filing documents with a court, and serving summonses. Most firms bill a client for the services of their messenger.

PROCESS SERVER   A process server is responsible for **service of process.** This person may work sporadic hours in order to "catch" an elusive defendant. Most firms bill a client for the services of a process server. A firm's investigator and messenger may also serve documents. Many firms contract with an outside firm for service of process.

> **service of process**
> The personal delivery of summonses, complaints, or other legal documents to a defendant or respondent.

RECRUITER   A recruiter seeks out new attorneys and law clerks. Some very large firms employ full-time recruiters. Other firms use outside recruiter firms. Some firms give their legal administrator recruitment responsibilities.

CASE COORDINATOR   A case coordinator has responsibility for the successful management of a case, usually a complex litigation case. This person will determine staffing needs; develop a strategy, timetables, and responsibilities; and supervise a project. A case coordinator will keep clients and attorneys apprised of progress. Litigation paralegals are often case coordinators.

CLERK   A clerk handles clerical or administrative assignments according to the needs of a supervisor. This person's responsibilities include numbering and indexing documents, creating file folders, and preparing bindings, trial exhibits, and trial notebooks. Clerks often work under the supervision of a paralegal. A firm may bill a client for a clerk's time.

ACCOUNTANT   Most large and many medium-sized firms employ their own full-time accountant. Smaller firms use outside accountant services. The duties of a law firm accountant include handling accounts receivable, accounts payable, and collections; balancing a checkbook; and preparing financial statements.

BILLING CLERK   A billing clerk assists an accountant or financial manager with a firm's billing. This person prepares the bills and monitors each client's ledger card or account summary. Large firms may employ many billing clerks. In smaller firms, an office manager or secretary performs this function.

FILE CLERK   A file clerk works in a firm's file room and is responsible for maintaining the firm's filing. This person opens and closes files and files documents. Large firms may employ many file clerks. In smaller firms, a secretary performs this function.

PHOTOCOPY CLERK   A photocopy clerk is responsible for photocopying a firm's documents. A full-time photocopy clerk is found only in large firms. In smaller firms, secretaries and paralegals are responsible for their own photocopying needs.

Outsourcing

outsourcing
A firm's use of outside services for support functions.

A firm's need for support staff is being replaced by **outsourcing,** which is the use of outside companies for support staff functions, such as copy center, facilities management, and mail room services. An outside service will install its own equipment and employees to manage, for example, a firm's photocopy and mail room centers. When a law firm has overflow work, an outside company uses its own off-site facilities to accommodate the overload. Outsourcing is spreading to other major areas of the firm, such as information management, records management, and even legal research and law libraries. The trend to outsource began with downsizing and cost-cutting policies. According to a recent survey, the respondents indicated that they received greater cost-efficiency with their outsourced functions. Larger firms report greater use of outsourcing services.

ATTORNEY SERVICE   An attorney service picks up documents from a law firm and files them with a court for a monthly charge. This service also provides service of process functions. In addition, some attorney services prepare subpoenas and notices. Most law firms use an attorney service instead of employing their own process servers.

COMPUTERIZED LITIGATION SUPPORT SERVICE   For firms with limited computer capabilities, a computerized litigation support service will organize and computerize documents in complex cases. Many of these services are owned and operated by experienced paralegals. Small firms that do not have the resources to handle a complex litigation case find that they can accept such a case with the assistance of these services.

PARALEGAL SERVICE   Firms use outside paralegal services for assistance with rush assignments or with overloads. In addition, they use freelance paralegals to do deposition summaries and other paralegal duties on an ongoing basis. Attorneys also use specialized paralegal services, such as probate or bankruptcy, to expand their services without expanding their facilities. Freelance paralegal service is a growing market for experienced paralegals (see Chapter 5).

EMPLOYMENT AGENCY   Most firms have an ongoing relationship with employment agencies for temporary staffing and employee recruitment. Temporary workers are paid by an employment agency instead of a law firm. In the past, employment agencies were called when an employee was sick or on vacation or for general backup work. With the trend to outsource clerical functions, temporary employees are working steadily in law firms. Firms are utilizing temporary clerical workers, or temps, instead of employing their own because doing so is more cost-effective. Firms are also using the services of temporary employment agencies for attorneys (see nontraditional attorneys on page 47).

PHOTOCOPY SERVICE   A photocopy service copies records in large photocopy projects. Often, a service accepts large photocopy projects from a firm. This service saves the firm money in purchasing additional photocopy equipment and hiring additional staff.

BONDING COMPANY   Bonding companies provide bonds for litigation cases, probate cases, notary needs, or other requirements. Most firms have an ongoing relationship with one or two bonding companies.

RECORDS SEARCH COMPANY   Records search companies search records in any secretary of state's office to give an attorney the information required. They also file documents and register companies in the various secretary of state offices. Some records search companies can search other types of records in the various states.

CONSULTANTS   Law firms use myriad consultants. Consultants assist law firms with management advice, intrafirm training, and **expert witness** testimony. The specialties of a law firm determine its need for specialized consultants. Consultants are also used to assist attorneys in evaluating cases. Donohue Rajkowski was the first law firm in the state of Minnesota to hire a full-time salaried consultant. The consultant works in the area of personal injury and health-related litigation and interprets medical information and claims.

Consultants may be employed by a firm or used by a firm on an as-needed basis. Most large- and medium-sized firms use the services of some sort of consultant for marketing. Consultants are also used extensively as expert witnesses for trials.

The following is a sample list of consultants used by attorneys:

Accountants	Computer experts
Public relations experts	Environmental experts
Engineers	Actuaries
Financial planners	Legal search consultants
Nurses and doctors	Investment bankers
Accident reconstructionists	Scientists
Lobbyists	Psychologists
Metallurgical experts	Economists

Law firm employees and outside services function together as a team to give a client the best possible representation. An attorney cannot represent a client adequately without the expertise of the rest of the team. Most often, a client will see a receptionist, a secretary, and a paralegal before seeing an attorney. A client's first impression of a firm starts with the support staff. The support staff is just as essential as an attorney to good client relations.

Side note:
expert witness
A person who testifies at trial on the basis of professional expertise.

SUMMARY

In the 1940s and 1950s, legal personnel consisted of an attorney and a secretary. The advent of technology and the paralegal and legal administrator roles changed the traditional law firm. Paralegals and legal administrators have gained prominence and they are now recognized as essential members of a legal team.

A law firm's need for staff varies according to its size and specialty. Certain types of legal personnel can be found in most law offices: attorneys, legal administrators or office managers, paralegals, law clerks, secretaries, and receptionists. Other law office personnel are found in law offices according to size, specialty, and need. In addition to the services of their own personnel, law firms use the services of a number of outside firms and consultants.

CHAPTER ILLUSTRATION

When Black, White & Greene opened its doors, the secretary who worked for them in the office suite, Tricia Bunnell, went with them. She was the secretary for all three attorneys and also helped Robert Black, the managing partner, with management duties. She soon found the workload too heavy.

The firm hired a secretary to work for Dennis White. Sandy Stinson was an experienced secretary who had worked for a very large firm in the area. She had extensive experience and a background in litigation and intellectual property, which was just what Dennis needed to help him with a large business litigation case he was working on. The case involved a business owned by the mayor of the city and received a lot of media coverage.

After the trial, Dennis received a very favorable outcome for his client. The firm received a lot of media attention that made the firm highly visible in the marketplace. Soon the telephone rang off the hook with new clients, and the three attorneys were having difficulty meeting the demand.

After a partnership meeting, the attorneys decided that they needed a paralegal to help with the increased workload. They contacted the local paralegal association and placed an ad for a paralegal in the association's newsletter. Before long, they had many résumés from qualified paralegals. They chose Milton Nollkamper, a paralegal with a bachelor's degree in business and an associate arts degree in paralegal studies from Fullerton College. Milton had litigation experience and also worked as a trademark and intellectual property paralegal for Nissan Motor Corporation. He was perfect for the job.

The firm's litigation practice continued to grow. Grant was able to save enough money to make a full financial contribution to the partnership and received the status of full partner. The firm wondered whether its existing staff could handle the workload. They decided to retain the services of a freelance paralegal service that specialized in litigation management and a contract attorney to assist in the litigation cases. The firm found it necessary to invest in new computer equipment and additional office space to accommodate the additional staff.

Soon the workload increased to the point that they needed an additional attorney. Patrizia Boen just graduated from law school after working many years as a paralegal. She could step right into the litigation cases but needed support staff to help her. The firm could not justify hiring a secretary and a paralegal, so it hired Melvin Goldberg, a paralegal, who performed secretarial functions for Patrizia. He also worked for Grant. Tricia assisted Robert in his management duties and was promoted to office manager in addition to her secretarial duties. The firm now consisted of the following staff:

Robert Black, managing partner
Dennis White, senior partner
Grant Greene, junior partner, now full partner
Patrizia Boen, associate attorney
Tricia Bunnell, secretary/office manager
Sandra Stinson, secretary to Dennis White
Milton Nollkamper, paralegal
Melvin Goldberg, paralegal/secretary to Patrizia Boen

The firm outsourced the following services:

Litigation Services, freelance paralegal service
George Templeton, contract attorney

In addition, the firm used the services of Speedy Attorney Service and All-in-One Process Service. The firm also outsourced its large photocopy projects to Compex Corporation.

The partners are pleased with the growth of the firm and are working hard. Generally, their clients are satisfied with the firm's services.

CHAPTER REVIEW

1. What elements contributed to the use of the services of nonlawyer assistants?
2. What are the differences between an office manager and a legal administrator?
3. What is the difference between the responsibilities of an administrator in a large firm and those of an administrator in a small firm?
4. What two variables dictate the scope of an administrator's responsibilities?
5. What are a paralegal manager's responsibilities?

6. In what type of legal office do most paralegals work?

7. What is a tiered paralegal program?

8. What are the differences between a law clerk and a paralegal?

9. What is outsourcing?

10. What is a nontraditional attorney?

EXAMPLES FOR DISCUSSION

1. I WANT OUT

A New York attorney stated, "As I become more exposed to the adversarial system, the more I hate it. I work at a large, well-respected firm where no one engages in low-ball [deceptive] tactics. Unfortunately, some opposing counsels do not operate as my firm does. I am beginning to reconsider whether I want to be a lawyer because of the unpleasant encounters with ruthless, dishonest, and manipulative attorneys who accuse me of 'bad faith' and 'delay tactics' when there is no foundation for such accusations. I am a relatively new attorney, and if this is what practicing law is all about, I want out. If it weren't for this unpleasant aspect of the profession, I would love being a lawyer."

1. Describe a scenario that might have caused these comments.

2. If you were the manager of this firm, how would you respond to this attorney's comments?

3. What advice would you give this attorney?

4. What are some possible solutions to this attorney's problem?

2. DEFINITION

Three national organizations have defined a paralegal. The definitions are found on page 54. Compare the definitions, note the similarities and differences, and answer the following questions:

1. What are the similarities?

2. What are the differences?

3. Are the differences significant? If so, how?

4. How do the differences affect the profession as a whole?

3. THE NEW PARALEGAL

Brenda Starr, a legal secretary, had been employed by Ray Shuran, a sole practitioner, for many years. Starr was Shuran's right arm. She performed management duties, secretarial duties, and some paralegal duties. He was extremely busy, and she worked late and most weekends. Shuran was concerned that Starr had too much work to do, so he employed a part-time law clerk to do research assignments. When the law clerk quit to pursue her own law practice, Shuran hired a paralegal to do research and the paralegal work currently assumed by Starr.

When the new paralegal came to work, Starr automatically resented his presence. She resented that the paralegal was doing work that Starr used to do. She had a difficult time letting go of some of her responsibilities. When the paralegal requested clerical services, Starr would reluctantly provide them only if Shuran's work was completed. This conflict caused real tension in the office.

1. What is the reason for this conflict?

2. What could Shuran do to remedy the situation?

3. If you were the new paralegal, how would you handle the problem?

4. If you were Starr, how would you handle the problem?

5. How could this conflict have been prevented?

ASSIGNMENTS

1. Most paralegals have chosen to be a paralegal as their second career and have had experience in another area of business or industry. Some paralegals have experience as legal secretaries, and others have no legal experience. Many paralegals have been able to apply their past experience to their present position as a paralegal. You have unique qualities to bring to the paralegal profession. You have skills and talents you have learned in your past experience, even if you have not had experience in the business or legal world. It is time for you to access your talents and abilities, and apply them to your future goals. On a sheet of paper, write down talents, abilities, and skills you have gained in the past. If you have no business experience, list the abilities and skills you have learned at home, church, or in a community organization. You will need them to answer the next question.

2. Chapter 2 contains a description of the duties of the various types of legal personnel. It also contains options for your paralegal education. How many of your talents and abilities could apply to members of the legal team other than a paralegal? Consider outside services and consultants. What other options are open to you?

3. List all members of the legal team of Black, White & Greene described in the Chapter Illustration section of Chapter 2. After you name each member, insert a description of their duties in the law firm and describe how they fit into the legal team.

4. Interview any one of the following persons. Ask the interviewee to describe his job and actual job duties. Report your findings to your class, and compare them with those reported by other students. Do the functions and duties of the positions reported differ?
   a. Attorney
   b. Legal administrator
   c. Paralegal
   d. Legal secretary
   e. Law clerk
   f. Receptionist
   g. File clerk
   h. Messenger
   i. Calendar clerk

5. Contact two or three offices in your area that have a tiered paralegal program and answer the following questions about each:
   a. How many steps does the program have?
   b. What is the title of each step?
   c. What are the qualifications for each step?
   d. How does one advance?
   e. What is the compensation for each step? Compare the programs. Which one do you think is the best? Why?

6. Look in the telephone book and list all the types of businesses under "Attorney Services." What different services are offered attorneys?

7. List all the job opportunities a paralegal education offers. Consider outside attorney service companies, consultants, and law office personnel other than paralegal. What areas interest you? What additional training or education would you need to pursue a career in these areas?

8. The law firm of Smith, Jones & Brown has three partners, six associates, and six paralegals. Calculate the leverage ratio as illustrated on page 46.

9. Access the Internet sites found in the Cybersites section. Choose ten sites and prepare a report about what each site offers the paralegal student.

10. Access the Internet sites found in the paralegal Cybersites section. Find the area that discusses paralegal salaries and benefits. Compare your findings with the paralegal salaries and benefits discussed in this chapter. Have they increased? Decreased?

SELF TEST

How well did you grasp the material in the chapter? Test yourself by answering the following questions, and check your answers against the answers in Appendix A.

1. The advent of what two professions changed the traditional law firm?
2. For what reasons were the paralegal and legal administrator professions developed?
3. How have paralegals and legal administrators increased a lawyer's efficiency?
4. What factors have contributed to the growth of the paralegal profession?
5. What determines a firm's need for personnel?
6. What are the four categories of attorneys?
7. What do rainmakers do?
8. What do associates do?
9. What is leveraging?
10. What is a leverage ratio?
11. What is a permanent associate?
12. What is a staff attorney?
13. What does the term *of-counsel* mean?
14. What do legal administrators do?
15. What is the significant difference between an office manager and an administrator?
16. What are the three major differences between an administrator and an office manager?
17. What is the status of a legal administrator in a large firm?
18. What are some other terms used for a legal administrator?
19. What is the difference between the responsibilities of an administrator in a large firm and an administrator in a small firm?
20. What are the eight main areas of an administrator's responsibilities?
21. What two factors dictate an administrator's responsibilities?
22. What other types of office managers are there?
23. What are a paralegal manager's responsibilities?
24. What is a tiered paralegal program?
25. How does a paralegal advance in a tiered paralegal program?
26. In what area do the majority of paralegals specialize?
27. What is a law clerk?
28. Why do some firms have elaborate programs for their law clerks?
29. What do law clerks do?
30. What are the differences between a law clerk and paralegal?
31. What do legal secretaries do?
32. What do receptionists do?
33. What do law librarians do?
34. What do investigators do?
35. What do messengers do?
36. What do recruiters do?

37. What do process servers do?
38. What do case coordinators do?
39. What is outsourcing?
40. What does an attorney service do?
41. What do paralegal services do?

Key Words

CPA	leverage ratio	outsourcing
equity	liaison	permanent associates
equity partner	MBA	rainmaker
expert witness	nonequity partner	service of process
legal database	nonlegal database	staff attorney
leverage	of-counsel	

 # Cybersites

THE ATTORNEY PROFESSION

American Bar Association—<*http://www.abanet.org*>
Martinedale Hubbel Corp.—<*http://www.martindale.com*>
West Legal Directory—<*http://www.wld.com*>
Hiros Gamos—<*http://www.hg.org*>

THE PARALEGAL PROFESSION

National Federation of Paralegal Associations—<*http://www.paralegals.org*>
National Association for Legal Assistants—<*http://www.nala.org*>
American Association for Paralegal Education—<*http://www.aafpe.org*>
Association for Legal Career Professionals—<*http://www.nalp.org*>
American Alliance of Paralegals, Inc. —<*http://www.aapipara.org*>
Legal Assistant Today—<*http://www.legalassistanttoday.com*>
National Paralegal Association—<*http://www.nationalparalegal.org*>

LEGAL ADMINISTRATOR PROFESSION

International Paralegal Management Association—
    <*http://www.paralegalmanagement.org*>
Association for Legal Administrators—<*http://www.alanet.org/home.html*>

LEGAL SECRETARIAL PROFESSION

National Association for Legal Professionals (formerly National Association of
    Legal Secretaries)—<*http://www.nals.org*>
Legal Secretaries International—<*http://www.legalsecretaries.org*>
Legal Secretary Careers—<*http://www.legalsecretarycareers.com*>

LAW LIBRARIAN PROFESSION

American Association of Law Libraries —<*http://www.aallnet.org*>
Library Law Blog—<*http://blog.librarylaw.com*>
Northern California Association of Law Libraries—<*http://www.nocall.org*>

LAW CLERKS

Federal Law Clerks Society—<*http://www.fedlawclerks.com*>

OUTSOURCING

The Outsourcing Institute—<*http://www.outsourcing.com*>
Outsourcing.Org—<*http://www.outsourcing.org*>

 Student CD-ROM
For additional materials, please go to the CD in this book.

 Online Companion™
For additional resources, please go to http://www.paralegal.delmar.cengage.com

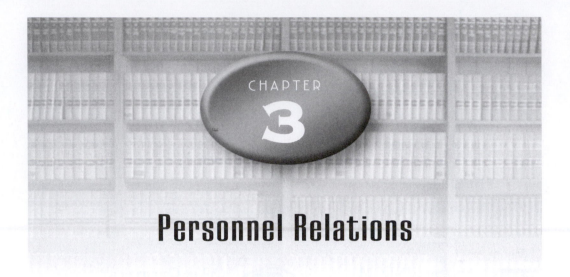

CHAPTER

3

Personnel Relations

OBJECTIVES

After completion of this chapter, the student should be able to do the following:

- Explain the objectives of law office management.
- Discuss employee motivation.
- Describe the management role.
- Identify the necessary skills and functions for effective management.
- List the various considerations in hiring the right employee.
- Identify appropriate interview questions.
- Outline the evaluation process.
- Discuss paralegal compensation and the laws affecting compensation.
- Explain the difference between an exempt employee and a nonexempt employee and how a paralegal qualifies for exempt status.
- Discuss the elements of the team approach and working as a team to benefit a client.

INTRODUCTION

For a legal team to function at its peak, it must be managed effectively so that each team member contributes his maximum potential. Many elements contribute to effective personnel management.

A law firm's personnel are its most important resource—and the most expensive. Most people find either great satisfaction or dissatisfaction in their work. Finding the right place to work is essential to personal character building, self-esteem, and overall happiness in life. People spend one-third of their lives at work, so it is important that they choose a positive working environment that meets their needs.

Whether an office is a pleasant or unpleasant place to work is the responsibility of both the employees and management. Management is responsible for developing an environment where employees can grow personally and professionally. Employees are responsible for contributing their skills and talents to the organization. Everyone involved with the organization, including clients, benefits when employees are happy with their work.

Management's personnel policies greatly affect a firm's environment. Employees' relationships to management also affect a firm's environment. How management and employees interact with each other influences a firm's environment. This chapter is devoted to describing the perspectives of both management and employees.

First, this chapter will look at employee relations from management's perspective. It will discuss the many duties and responsibilities a manager has in relation to personnel and various methods of ensuring positive personnel relations. Second, the chapter will look at employee relations from an employee's perspective. It will discuss what employees can expect from management and their responsibilities to an employer. Finally, the chapter will combine both perspectives and discuss how management and employees work together as a team for the benefit of the organization, employees, and clients.

MANAGEMENT OBJECTIVES AND EMPLOYEE RELATIONS

Management is defined by Peter Drucker, a prominent management consultant, as "the method of using available resources to achieve desired goals" (*The Practice of Management*, published by Harper and Morners, 1954). Just as a conductor directs members of an orchestra to produce beautiful music, a manager directs employees to work in harmony together to achieve a firm's goals. If one member of an orchestra is playing an instrument incorrectly or is missing, the desired outcome is affected. In the same way, if one member of a legal team does not contribute to a firm, services to a client are affected.

Managers work with and through other people to achieve a firm's goals. A manager cannot perform all aspects of a business, just as an orchestra leader cannot play all the instruments in an orchestra. According to Drucker, a manager's performance can be measured by two characteristics: efficiency and effectiveness. *Efficiency* is doing things right, and *effectiveness* is doing the right thing. The most important characteristic is effectiveness, which includes choosing appropriate objectives and the methods to reach those objectives. For a positive employment environment to exist, a manager must be effective. Good personnel relations are a test of effective management.

Each employee must have a clear understanding of his or her position on a legal team and of how his or her position relates to achieving the goals of a firm. Before this understanding can be attained, employees must clearly comprehend a firm's objectives.

Objectives are the purpose of a firm—the reasons for its existence. The goals and objectives of a firm are the reasons for management decisions and policies. Effective management guarantees success in achieving a firm's goals. Ineffective management guarantees failure in achieving a firm's goals.

Although law firms differ in structure and management style, most have basically the same three main objectives.

1. Provide quality legal services to the client
2. Provide growth and profit for the firm
3. Provide growth and satisfaction for the employees

A government agency may have different objectives. Although some government agencies are required to produce enough income to make themselves profitable for the government, others operate within a budget set by the government as a service to the people. An example of a government agency's objectives is as follows:

1. Provide quality legal services to the government or people
2. Operate within the budget set by the government
3. Provide growth and satisfaction for the employees

Since a corporate legal department has one client—the corporation—its goal is to keep legal expenses low and within a budget. An example of a corporate legal department's objectives follows:

1. Provide quality legal services to the corporation
2. Keep outside legal costs low, and operate within the budget set by the corporation
3. Provide growth and satisfaction for the employees

Providing growth and satisfaction for employees is an objective of each type of legal office. Since people are the most important resource of a firm, each person's productivity must be maximized. The methods used to maximize employee productivity have been set forth in various management theories. Managers are responsible for implementing those theories. They are also responsible for carrying out five managerial functions, as set forth in "Functions of a Personnel Manager."

The Manager's Role in Personnel Relations

A personnel manager is responsible for all aspects of personnel relations. In large firms, a manager in charge of personnel may report to an administrator. In smaller firms, an administrator or manager is directly responsible for personnel relations. In firms with no administrator or manager, a managing attorney is responsible for personnel.

A manager's role is influenced by external and internal conditions. External conditions consist of economic conditions, government regulations, and laws. Internal conditions include the nature and structure of a firm, nature of the work, and nature of the employees.

EXTERNAL CONDITIONS Changes in our economy directly affect the personnel policies of any organization. The decisions to hire additional staff, lay off staff, or grant a bonus or raise are influenced by the economy. In addition, many government regulations and laws influence personnel relations. More laws are being passed each day in this area, and court decisions also establish laws by which employers must abide. A manager must be knowledgeable of all laws and keep abreast of court decisions relating to personnel issues. Since laws relating to personnel relations are changing each day, a manager and a firm must be flexible to change personnel policy if the law should mandate it.

INTERNAL CONDITIONS Internal conditions include the nature of a firm, nature of the work, and nature of the firm's employees. Several elements make up the nature of a firm, such as objectives, strategies, structure, and size. A small boutique firm will have different personnel needs than a mega-firm. The specialty of a firm, or the nature of the work, influences management's staffing requirements. The nature of the employees includes whether employees work independently or in groups.

Functions of a Personnel Manager

A personnel manager, or a law office manager responsible for personnel relations, has five functions: planning, controlling, organizing, leading, and staffing.

PLANNING Human resource planning covers all areas of the human resource field. Before managers can control, organize, lead, or staff, they must make plans that define the purpose and direction of a firm. This process is called **forecasting** and includes strategic planning and long-range planning for a firm. Forecasting involves anticipating a firm's future need for personnel and making plans accordingly.

forecasting
Planning for the future by anticipating future events.

Human resource planning is divided into four areas:

1. Establishing human resource objectives
2. Assessing current human resource conditions
3. Designing and evaluating human resource activities
4. Monitoring and evaluating the results of activities

human resource audit
A determination of the strengths and weaknesses of current employees.

Another aspect of planning is conducting a **human resource audit.** An audit assesses the strengths and weaknesses of current employees and helps a manager develop training plans.

Planning also includes deciding what needs to be done, when it needs to be done, how it needs to be done, and who will do it. Managers integrate human resources into a firm's plans by developing a human resource plan that supports the firm's goals and objectives.

The goal of human resource planning is to develop personnel policies and programs that will achieve a firm's objectives. The ultimate objective of a human resource plan is to maximize a firm's effectiveness by maximizing employee effectiveness and productivity.

CONTROLLING   Controlling is the process of ensuring that actions conform to plans. Since implementing plans requires action, controlling actions is the next managerial function. Controlling cannot take place unless a plan exists, and a plan has little chance of success unless activities are controlled and efforts are made to monitor its progress. Control has three main elements:

1. Establishing standards of performance
2. Measuring current performance and comparing it against established standards
3. Taking action to correct performance that does not meet established standards

Controlling includes evaluating activities. For activities to be evaluated, standards must be set. If standards are set too high for employees to meet, employee frustration develops; if they are set too low, employees will not be challenged in their work. Standards must be realistic, attainable, and challenging.

Adherence to a budget is a common method of measurement. If a plan is proceeding within budgeted amounts, it is considered a good plan. If not, some changes need to be made to the plan or the budget. Other methods of measurement include employee evaluations and questionnaires.

Action taken to correct performance that does not meet established standards might include offering training programs for existing employees, firing an employee, or restructuring a work group.

When making personnel policies to control employees, managers must consider the needs of the employees. When management makes policies that disregard the personal needs of employees, it is **win-lose management.** Win-lose management has eight consequences:

1. The atmosphere in an office becomes competitive and hostile.
2. Time and energy are diverted from the main issues.
3. Creativity, sensitivity, and empathy are eliminated from an office environment.
4. Authority conflicts become more frequent and bitter.
5. Important organizational decisions are increasingly made by an isolated, elitist group.
6. New ideas are discouraged.
7. Deadlocks are created, and decisions are delayed.
8. Nonaggressive people are discouraged from participation.

win-lose management
A form of personnel control in which the policies of management are directed totally to profits and disregards employee needs.

ORGANIZING   The organizing function requires a manager to coordinate the resources of a firm to maximize productivity and effectiveness. The more integrated the work of a law firm, the more effective the firm will be in delivering legal services to a client. The more organized the work, the more productive the firm. The more productive the firm, the more profitable the firm.

Different firms have different organizing objectives. For example, a large firm may be organized into several departments, with various subgroups working within each department, whereas a small firm may have only one or two specialties that require organization on a smaller scale. One firm may have one paralegal for every four attorneys, whereas another firm may have one paralegal for each attorney. Management's responsibility is to organize a firm in a manner that will be effective for the firm and will allow the firm to accomplish its goals.

LEADING   A firm must have strong leadership if it is to maximize productivity and effectiveness. Employees look to firm leadership for direction.

Leading involves working directly with people. It includes determining what is to be accomplished and how to accomplish it. This requires a manager to assume three roles—interpersonal, informational, and decisional—as shown in Exhibit 3–1. The manner in which these three roles are delivered determines an organization's level of leadership.

INTERPERSONAL	INFORMATIONAL	DECISIONAL
Figurehead	Monitor	Entrepreneur
Leader	Disseminator	Conflict resolver
Liaison	Spokesperson	Negotiator
Motivator	Investigator	Resource allocator

EXHIBIT 3–1   Leadership Roles

The title of manager does not give a person the essential leadership skills to manage people. Results of an employee relations test indicated that many managers are not doing what many experts feel should be done to ensure good employee-employer relations.

- Almost 50 percent of the managers who took the test did not understand that people repeat behavior that is rewarded.
- Almost 70 percent did not believe that finding a mutually satisfactory solution to a problem is a way to handle a grievance.
- Almost 50 percent did not understand that improving quality will reduce operating costs.

What is the difference between managing and leading? This question has been the topic of much research and analysis. The U.S. military has spent a lot of time analyzing leadership and distinguishes between the two by simply saying "People are led, things are managed." However, many disagree with this simplistic conclusion by observing that people are, indeed, managed. Marcus Buckingham and Curt Coffman, in their book *First, Break All the Rules*, say that the most important difference between managers and leaders is one of focus. Managing is focusing retrospectively, being reactive. Leading is focusing forward, being proactive.

Ideal managers recognize two things about their job. First, they realize that a business is not a democracy. Management is not elected by popular vote; it is placed in power by an arbitrary

Of Interest . . .

MOVING THE ORGANIZATION FROM MANAGEMENT TO LEADERSHIP

MANAGEMENT	LEADERSHIP
Communicate direction	Create enthusiasm for goals
Achieve compliance	Achieve commitment
Explain decisions	Make decisions by input and consensus
Direct	Delegate
Solve problems for others	Solve problems through others
Control risk	Manage risk
Maintain individual performance	Improve group performance
Empower others	Work with others in the "trenches"
Ad hoc training	Develop skill sets
Manage the work	Manage communication
Correct the work	Provide feedback
Monitor the quality of work	Improve the quality of work

SOURCE: Adapted from Altman Weil Report to Legal Management, October 2001. Reprinted with permission.

decision of a small group of people who are in positions of power. The people who appoint managers expect them to act like leaders. Certain decisions are made by managers alone; managers cannot delegate those decisions, and they cannot abdicate their position of responsibility.

Second, ideal managers know that people need to grow, to contribute, and to assume power up to their level of ability. Effective managers have responsibility for decisions, but they pass on decisions that can be handled by capable people under them. They set high standards and demand excellent and consistent performance. They also recognize their subordinates' right to question and share in decision making about things that affect them. They know they can get superior results from a person as long as that person has some say in how, where, and when an effort is applied.

Leadership includes the ability to motivate employees to reach their maximum potential. A law office that motivates employees gives employees an opportunity for growth by assigning tasks with adequate responsibility and direction. Strong leaders make people feel like they are great, so they will strive to do work that lives up to that expectation.

Employees' contributions must be acknowledged to encourage them in their work. Kenneth H. Blanchard, in his book *One Minute Manager,* mentions the importance of praising employees for a job well done. A good leader takes advantage of every opportunity to acknowledge employees for doing a good job, meeting a deadline, or showing enthusiasm for a project.

Of Interest . . .

LEADERSHIP CHECKLIST

- Am I sincerely interested in people? How do I show it?
- Am I a good listener?
- Do I look for opportunities to sincerely compliment others?
- Is my speech free of sarcasm or prejudice?
- Do I seek the opinions of others?
- Do I enjoy giving credit to others?
- Am I earnestly enthusiastic in my speech?
- Am I trustworthy and confident?
- Do I interrupt others when they are talking?
- Do I tend to argue?
- Do I give unsolicited advice?
- Do I criticize others openly?
- Do I attempt to look good by making others look bad?
- Am I too positive?
- Do I tend to exaggerate?
- Does my voice sound threatening?
- Do I attempt to impress others by using large and unusual words?
- Do I use the pronoun "I" too much?
- Do my stories tend to reflect too much credit on me?
- Do I tend to brag about my achievements?
- Do I enjoy proving others wrong?

STAFFING   Staffing includes such duties as recruitment, screening, interviewing, testing, hiring, firing, job analysis, job description, and personnel record keeping. Successful staffing ensures that the right people are hired for the right jobs.

Staffing is the most important function of a manager. It is important for the success of the firm to employ the right employees. Employees impress clients; a client who is not satisfied

FUNCTION	COST
Recruitment and interview—manager's time, 10 hours	$ 700
Follow-up interviews—attorney's time, 2 hours	$ 800
First-day initial orientation—manager's time, 4 hours	$ 280
First-day orientation—attorney's time, 2 hours	$ 800
Ineffective time—new paralegal's time, the equivalent of two weeks' salary	$ 3,200
Reduction in efficiency—attorney's time, 2 weeks at 20% reduction	$ 6,400
Training—senior paralegal's time, 3 days	$ 1,680
Payroll taxes and benefits during ineffective time, 30%	$ 4,158
Total	**$18,018**

Manager's time calculated at $70 per hour.

Attorney's time calculated at $400 per hour.

Senior paralegal's time calculated at $70 per hour.

New paralegal's time calculated at $40 per hour.

EXHIBIT 3–2   Typical Cost of Hiring a New Paralegal—Per Employee

with an employee can be dissatisfied with the entire firm. Good client relations require the involvement of all staff members. An employee with a poor attitude or other personal problems can negatively affect a firm's environment and damage the firm.

Hiring employees is expensive. In addition, a firm with a high turnover rate is not operating at 100 percent efficiency. Studies have shown that an attorney with a new paralegal is 20 percent less efficient. It takes at least 3 months for a new employee to be productive. During that training period, other employees are filling in or important tasks are not getting done. An example of the average cost of hiring a new paralegal is shown in Exhibit 3–2.

The Hiring Process

The hiring process consists of four steps: planning, recruiting, selecting, and training.

PLANNING   The first step in planning a position is to determine whether the position should be filled at all. At this time, the external and internal conditions of a firm are examined. If the economic environment is not stable, it may be possible to restructure or eliminate the position. If it is a necessary position, management must decide whether to hire a new person or to promote from within the firm.

Promoting from within a firm offers many advantages, including the following:

- The selection cost of hiring a new employee is eliminated.
- The loss in productivity is reduced because the employee already knows the structure and procedures of the firm.
- Promotions encourage employee loyalty.
- A promoted employee receives recognition, which increases employee morale.

Promoting within a firm also has disadvantages. Among the most common is the difficulty of making a transition from one position to another. A legal secretary who is promoted to paralegal after completing her paralegal education is often still viewed as a secretary by other employees. A paralegal who is promoted to manager is often still viewed as a paralegal and has difficulty assuming a position of authority.

If no viable candidates are available from within a firm, candidates are recruited from outside the firm. Before a manager is ready to recruit candidates, the position must be carefully detailed in a position description that includes a hiring specification of the ideal

---

Law Offices of Black, White & Greene

Position Description
Litigation Paralegal

Department: *Litigation*   Supervising Attorney: *Dennis White*
Hours: *8:30 to 5:00*   Level: *Grade P-2—$34,000–$48,000 per yr.*
Overtime Required: *Some*   Nonexempt position

Brief Position Summary: *Assistant to litigation attorney specializing in business litigation. Heavy trial and discovery work.*

Major Duties: *Draft and answer discovery documents including interrogatories and production of documents. Prepare client for depositions, assist attorney in depositions, and summarize depositions. Legal research and memoranda of law. Draft motions and other litigation documents. Trial preparation and trial notebooks. Organization of documents and files. Document deadline control.*

Recurring Duties: *Interview witnesses and investigation.*

People Contact: *Heavy. Clients, opposing counsel, witnesses.*

Work Group: *Dennis White, Esq., Grant Greene, Esq., Sandra Stinson, Sec., Melvin Goldberg, Sec., and Milton Nollkamper, Paralegal.*

Skills: *Good writing and communication skills. Good organizational skills. Computer skills with knowledge of WordPerfect, WestLaw, Timekeeping software, and database management.*

Education: *Bachelor's degree and paralegal certificate. Bachelor's degree may be substituted for substantial experience.*

Experience: *Minimum of 3 years recent litigation experience. At least 1 year experience in complex litigation.*

Other Requirements: *Ability to speak Spanish a plus. Detail oriented.*

_____   _____
Tricia Bunnell, Manager   Approved: Robert Black, Esq.

EXHIBIT 3–3   Position Description

candidate. The **position description** contains the title, duties, and responsibilities for that position; an example is shown in Exhibit 3–3. The **hiring specifications** identify the education, experience, skills, and capabilities required.

Before a position description can be prepared, a law office manager must have a clear understanding of the position and the necessary qualifications of the prospective employee. The manager must know all aspects of the position, including the temperament and expectations of the supervising attorney. An exit interview with the outgoing employee is helpful to gain a clear understanding of a position. An interview with the supervising attorney is also important to understand the attorney's expectations.

Several questions need to be answered before a position description can be prepared.

- To what area of the law or specific tasks will this employee be assigned?
- Will this employee have contact with clients? If so, what are desirable qualities for positive client contact?
- What specific training should the employee possess?
- What specific experience should the employee possess?
- If a former employee is being replaced, what strengths and weaknesses of the former employee contributed to a marginal, adequate, or superior job performance?
- What necessary skills are required?
- What special requirements are required by the attorney for whom the employee will work?
- What are the minimum and maximum salaries paid for this position?
- What is the minimum educational requirement?

position description
A document that describes the duties and responsibilities of a position.

hiring specifications
The requirements for a position.

When preparing a position description, a manager must give careful thought to establishing requirements for the position. Requirements must be reasonable and must relate to the position. If a candidate is required to have 7 years' computer experience, the manager must be able to show why 3 years' experience is not enough.

RECRUITING Many avenues of recruitment are open; among them are employment agencies, newspaper advertising, paralegal associations, and word of mouth. Whatever the route chosen, the recruitment process must meet employment guidelines set by federal and state governments.

The federal government has established staffing guidelines in various legislative acts, including the Fair Labor Standards Act of 1938, the National Labor Standards Act, and many other acts that are discussed in the Federal Employment Laws document that is on the accompanying CD.

Of Interest . . .

VIDEO RÉSUMÉS

Numerous online listers, such as Jobster, CareerBuilder, HireVue, and others, have launched sites featuring video résumés. Recent studies show that many employers are open to the concept of video résumés. According to the 2007 Video Résumé Survey by career publisher Vault, Inc., 89 percent of employers surveyed indicated that they would watch a video résumé if it were offered to them. The survey also found that only 17 percent had actually watched a video résumé.

Lawyers are not supportive of video résumés. In fact, lawyers are warning their clients that video résumés can open the possibility for a slew of discrimination claims. They are advising their clients to reject all video résumés. Lawyers' main concern with video résumés is that they reveal information about a person's race, sex, disability, and age; all details that could produce a discrimination lawsuit.

The Equal Employment Opportunity Commission is not opposed to using video résumés. Their use is not against the law. However, the EEOC has expressed concern that video résumés may contribute to hiring discrimination. The EEOC stated that it is the responsibility of the hiring party not to discriminate at any point during the hiring process.

In addition, individual states have their own employment and compensation laws. Unlike traditional conflict-of-law problems in which federal laws supersede state laws, in matters concerning employment, the prevailing law is the law that sets the highest standard. Although a manager will probably not know all state and federal employment laws in detail, she or he must be familiar with employment guidelines imposed by those laws.

A firm's employment application must comply with federal and state guidelines. Questions on the application that pertain to an applicant's age, sex, race, height, or weight violate federal regulations. Necessary information, such as date of birth, can be obtained after an applicant is formally hired.

Legal offices use various methods to recruit employees.

• Legal placement firms
• Referrals from employees and associates
• Newspaper ads
• College recruiting
• Professional association job placement services
• Internet career centers

Many paralegals begin their career by working for a legal temporary (temp) agency. This offers many benefits to the new paralegal. Going into different law offices gives the new paralegal an opportunity to see how the various offices are managed and gives them experience with various types of assignments. Firms often have an ongoing relationship with a temp agency, and when they find a temporary employee that fits, they can hire that employee when the need arises. The firm benefits because they are familiar with the skills of the temp employee, and the training time is shortened. The new employee benefits because he or she is familiar with the firm and its employees.

SELECTING   A manager needs to understand that an applicant is probably nervous during an interview (see Exhibit 3–4). At the beginning of an interview, a manager should make every effort to calm an applicant. Casual conversation is one method of giving an applicant an opportunity to relax.

The next step is for a manager to describe the position in detail. Profiles of the supervising attorney and of those in the work group are helpful. An applicant should also be informed of the requirements of the position.

The last part of an interview is for a manager to find out as much as possible about a job candidate. This involves asking questions.

The most important area in which to guard against federal law violations is interviewing. *To be sure not to discriminate in terms of race, color, religion, sex, or national origin, an interviewer must carefully structure interview questions to comply with the law.* This process can be difficult. To comply with federal guidelines, follow the recommendations given in Exhibit 3–5.

If all the do's and don'ts in Exhibit 3–5 seem rather complicated, a manager can apply the **ouch formula** to interview questions. *Ouch* is an acronym for proper interview questions. Questions must be **o**bjective, **u**niform, and **c**onsistent, and they must **h**ave job relatedness.

An objective question solicits information that is verifiable or measurable. Examples of objective questions follow:

ouch formula
A acronym for proper interview questions.

- Do you have paralegal training?
- What is your educational background?
- Who was your previous employer?
- Who was your supervisor at your previous employer?
- Do you have experience in bankruptcy?

EXHIBIT 3–4   Law Firm Manager and Paralegal in an Employment Interview

CATEGORY	IT IS LAWFUL TO	IT IS UNLAWFUL TO
Sex	restrict employment to one sex if it can be proven that the position requires an employee of a certain sex.	ask an applicant's sex. Physical labor does not justify excluding women.
Race or color	ask about distinguishing physical characteristics, such as scars.	ask an applicant's race, or skin, eye, or hair color, or height or weight questions if they are not relevant to the job.
Address	ask an applicant's address and how long the applicant has lived at current and previous addresses.	ask about foreign addresses that would indicate national origin; ask for the name or relationship of a person with whom an applicant resides; ask whether an applicant owns or rents a home.
Birthplace	request that an applicant produce a birth certificate or other proof of U.S. citizenship after employment.	ask for an applicant's birthplace or the birthplace of an applicant's spouse, parents, or other relatives; ask any questions that indicate religion or customs.
Military record	ask about education and experience in the service as they relate to the job.	ask type of discharge.
Photograph	ask for a photograph after hiring for identification purposes.	request a photograph before hiring, either on the application or after the interview. If desired, request that an applicant submit one at her option.
Citizenship	ask whether an applicant is a U.S. citizen and, if the applicant is hired, request that she or he submit proof.	ask in what country an applicant maintains citizenship; ask whether an applicant's parents or spouse is a U.S. citizen.
Ancestry or national origin	ask what language an applicant reads, speaks, or writes fluently.	ask questions pertaining to an applicant's lineage, ancestry, birthplace, or native language; ask about an applicant's parents' or spouse's national origin.
Car	ask whether an applicant would have any transportation problems if hired.	ask whether an applicant owns a car, unless the applicant must have a car to do the job.

EXHIBIT 3–5   The Do's and Don'ts of Interviewing

All questions must be uniform in application. In other words, they must apply to female as well as male applicants. They must apply to older as well as younger applicants and to minority as well as nonminority applicants. The questions must be asked of all applicants, regardless of sex, age, or background.

Questions must be consistent among applicants. If a manager asks one applicant one set of questions and another applicant another set of questions, the manager is not being consistent. Although each question does not have to be verbatim every time it is asked, its purpose for gaining information must be the same for all applicants.

Questions must have job relatedness. If an employee does not need a car for the position—as one might if the position were that of messenger—all questions regarding vehicle ownership would be inappropriate. If a paralegal will have secretarial assistance, some questions regarding secretarial skills may be inappropriate.

During the interview, a manager should look for certain characteristics. Although exceptions exist, a manager can spot "danger signals" that alert him or her to potential problems with an applicant. Asking an **open question** that requires a narrative answer is a good method to obtain information. A manager can learn a lot about an applicant by listening carefully. Some danger signs to look for are the following:

open question
A question that requires a narrative answer and cannot be answered yes or no.

- *Job Hopping.* If an applicant's previous working experiences have been short, the applicant may be a job hopper. A manager can expect that the applicant will do the same with this position and not remain employed for more than a year. Having many employers in a relatively short period of time may indicate that an applicant is dissatisfied easily.

CATEGORY	IT IS LAWFUL TO	IT IS UNLAWFUL TO
Education	ask about an applicant's academic or professional education; ask what school an applicant attended.	ask about a school's national, racial, or religious affiliation; ask how an applicant acquired a foreign language.
Experience	ask about an applicant's work experience and which countries the applicant has visited.	
Conviction and court records	ask about convictions that relate to an applicant's fitness to *perform* a particular job.	ask about arrests; ask about convictions that are not related to a job function and responsibilities.
Relatives	ask for the names of an applicant's relatives already employed by the firm; ask for the names and addresses of a minor's parents or guardian.	ask for the names or addresses of an adult applicant's relatives.
Emergency	ask for the names of *persons* to notify in case of an emergency.	ask for the names of *relatives* to notify in case of an emergency.
Organizations	ask about an applicant's membership in an organization if the organization's name or character does not reveal the applicant's race, religion, color, or ancestry.	ask an applicant to list all the organizations and lodges to which she or he belongs.
Credit rating		ask any questions about an applicant's credit rating, charge accounts, or other related information.
References	ask who referred an applicant to the firm; ask for the names of people willing to give professional or character references.	require an applicant to submit a religious reference.
Union	state the firm's philosophy on unionization.	ask questions about an applicant's feelings toward unions; ask about prior union activity or membership.
Miscellaneous	notify an applicant that any misstatement or omission of facts may be cause for dismissal.	

EXHIBIT 3–5 *Continued*

- *Long Commute.* An applicant's address on an application form will indicate the applicant's area of residence. If it is far from the office, the applicant will spend a lot of time commuting. Although some people do not mind a long commute, others grow tired of it, especially in populated areas with congested traffic, and employees tend to seek employment closer to home after a while.

- *Poor Health.* Although a manager may not ask applicants whether they are healthy, a sharp eye can see whether an applicant is having health problems. It is important to hire a healthy person. Frequent absences due to health problems can be disruptive to a firm. In addition, employee absence is expensive for a law firm.

- *Improper Termination Notice to Previous Employer.* If an applicant did not give proper notice to a former employer, this may be an indication that the applicant left abruptly, leaving the employer in a difficult position. The applicant might do the same in new employment. If an applicant is still employed, a desire to give proper notice is a good sign that the applicant accepts responsibility.

- *Questionable Reasons for Leaving Previous Employment.* Why did an applicant leave previous employment? If an applicant says she left because she was not given responsibility and challenging work, this answer indicates that the applicant is a self-starter who desires to increase skills. A danger signal is if an applicant had personality conflicts with previous coworkers. This information alerts a manager that the applicant may have problems working with others. However, other problems, such as sexual harassment, may have caused the applicant to leave previous employment. Flexibility in judgment is required in this area.

- *Negative Relationship with Previous Employer.* Watch for indications of a negative relationship with a previous employer. If an applicant had a poor relationship with a previous employer, it could be an indication that the applicant resists direction or is upset easily.

After an interview, a manager will choose the most desirable candidates and call them back for additional interviews and interviews with the supervising attorney. Some firms administer tests to determine an applicant's knowledge, grammar skills, and computer skills.

Often, the selection process is difficult, especially when many desirable candidates apply for a position. Personality and how well a candidate "fits" with a firm are considered. An applicant's references and previous employers must be checked before the successful candidate is chosen. Often, management will use a rating sheet, such as the one shown in Exhibit 3–6, when making the final decision.

When a selection is made, all applicants are notified by letter and thanked for applying for the position. The finalists' applications are kept in case another opening occurs or the selected employee does not work out. Many firms put new employees on a 60- or 90-day probation period. This is a good policy to ensure that the right person was hired for the right job.

Of Interest . . .

THE MOST COMMONLY ASKED INTERVIEW QUESTIONS

1. Why should we hire you rather than someone else?
2. Can you work under deadlines and pressure?
3. What kind of salary are you worth?
4. How long would it take you to make a contribution to our firm?
5. How long would you stay with our firm?
6. Why do you want to work for us?
7. Tell us about yourself.
8. What do you think of your last boss?
9. How would you describe your own personality?
10. What is your outstanding strength?
11. What is your greatest weakness?
12. Do you consider yourself dependable? Why?
13. What are your long- and short-term goals?
14. What is your opinion of the company for which you last worked?
15. Can you manage people?
16. What interests you the least about the available position?
17. What interests you the most about the available position?
18. Why did you leave your last job?
19. What did you like least about your last job?
20. What salary range are you looking for?
21. What are your three biggest accomplishments?
22. What would you do if . . .?
23. In what type of position are you most interested?
24. What jobs have you had, how were they obtained, and why did you leave?
25. What do you know about our firm?

APPLICANT EVALUATION FORM

4 = Superior   3 = Qualified   2 = Marginal   1 = Unqualified

Applicants	TRAINING			SKILLS						PERSONAL			OTHER		TOTAL
	Bachelor's Degree	Paralegal Certificate	Experience	Computer Skills	Westlaw/Lexis	Writing	Management experience	Substantive area 1	Substantive area 2	Appearance	Demeanor	Communication	Organization skills	Follow Instructions	
1. Mary Edwards	4	3	3	3	1	3	1	4	1	3	2	2	3	2	31
2. Bob Fulton	4	3	1	2	1	2	2	2	1	3	3	2	2	3	31
3. Linda Wall	4	4	4	3	3	3	3	4	3	3	4	3	4	3	48
4. Marleen Granger		4	4	4	3	2	1	3	3	3	3	3	3	3	39
5.															
6.															
7.															
8.															

Date: 4-12-xx   Manager: Benita Fowler   Recommendation: Linda Wall

EXHIBIT 3-6   Applicant Rating Sheet

ORIENTATION AND TRAINING When a new employee is hired, the orientation begins. It is management's responsibility to provide the necessary training for a new employee. Orientation involves training on the policies and philosophies of the organization, as well as specific training for the position. Effective orientation and training involve contributions from the administrative staff, the supervising attorney or supervisor with whom the new employee will work, the person who formerly held the position if still employed, contemporaries in similar positions in the firm, and specialized training from vendors or suppliers of various software and equipment.

A firm's policy and procedures manual is a valuable tool to train new employees. A written manual is vital for a complete understanding of the workplace and a basic understanding of how the firm functions. Many firms spend a lot of time keeping their manuals up-to-date. Some firms, particularly small firms, do not have a policy and procedures manual or only have a manual that is not current. Updating a busy small firm's policy manual is not given the high priority it deserves. The Law Practice Management Section of the American Bar Association published *Law Office Policy and Procedures Manual* to aid firms in creating a manual. To give you an idea of how a manual is organized, its table of contents is as follows:

- Introduction
- Departments and Committees
- Organization, Management, and Administration
- Support Personnel and Their Functions
- Office Policies
- Personnel Policies and Benefits
- Preparation of Correspondence, Memoranda, and Legal Documents
- Office Security and Emergency Procedures
- Financial Management
- File System
- Technology
- Communications Systems
- Duplication Services
- Equipment, Maintenance, and Supplies
- Library
- Travel
- Miscellaneous Guidelines

It takes time for a new employee to become familiar with employees, surroundings, systems, and policies. A common complaint of law office personnel is that training was inadequate, especially in a busy law office. With adequate training, however, an employee can function at 100 percent productivity in about 3 months.

EMPLOYEE OBJECTIVES AND MANAGEMENT RELATIONS

Good management-employee relations require a joint effort. Managers expect employees to do their jobs in an efficient and productive manner. Employee expectations can be best described in the **CEMEC principle.** CEMEC is an acronym that stands for **c**ommunication, **e**ducation, **m**otivation, **e**valuation, and **c**ompensation.

CEMEC principle
An acronym to describe employee expectations.

Communication

Effective communication is an essential ingredient in the success of any endeavor—personal or business. Communication involves body language, tone of voice, listening, and speaking.

The first communication an employee has with a firm is usually the employment interview. During the interview, it is management's responsibility to communicate the position to an applicant. An applicant must have a firm understanding of the position so that she or he can accept or reject the position. Often management does not adequately communicate essential aspects of a position, such as attorney expectations, firm policy, and responsibilities. Time constraints often interfere with a manager's ability to adequately describe a position. It is common for a paralegal to accept a position only to discover that the position is quite different from what she or he expected.

Communication between a paralegal and a supervising attorney is crucial. It is the attorney's responsibility to adequately communicate an assignment. However, it is the paralegal's responsibility to give the attorney feedback on the communication. For example, if an area of the communication is not clear to the paralegal, the paralegal must clarify the communication. If the paralegal does not do this, the attorney will assume that the communication was clear and fully understood. The same principle applies to all members of the legal team.

Communicating with fellow employees is an essential part of every position within a law office. Every communication should be carefully phrased so that no one is offended or embarrassed by it. An improper remark, spoken in jest, could have damaging results for an employee and, indirectly, a firm.

Each member of a legal team must promote open communication by doing the following:

- Accepting responsibility for his ideas and feelings
- Being open to the ideas and feelings of others
- Experimenting with new ideas
- Helping others to be open with their ideas and feelings by exhibiting a nonjudgmental attitude

Openness, honesty, and integrity create an atmosphere for open communication. Fear is the inhibiting element of open communication: fear of rejection, fear of looking stupid, or fear of loss of respect by coworkers. Each team member's contribution is valuable, but only when it is shared with others.

Of Interest . . .

NONVERBAL COMMUNICATION

What is your body language communicating at a job interview?

Direct eye contact: Self-confident, assertive
Firm handshake: Friendly, sincere
Avoiding direct eye contact: Cold, evasive, indifferent, insecure
Shaking head: Disagreeing, shocked, disbelieving
Yawning: Bored
Patting on back: Encouraging, congratulatory, consoling
Scratching the head: Bewildered, disbelieving
Smiling: Contented, understanding, encouraging
Biting the lip: Nervous, fearful, anxious
Tapping feet: Nervous
Folding arms: Angry, disapproving, disagreeing
Raising eyebrows: Disbelieving, surprised

Narrowing eyes: Disagreeing, resentful, angry
Flaring nostrils: Angry, frustrated
Wringing hands: Nervous, anxious, fearful
Leaning forward: Attentive, interested
Slouching in seat: Bored, relaxed
Sitting on edge of seat: Anxious, nervous, apprehensive
Shifting in seat: Restless, bored, nervous, apprehensive
Hunching over: Insecure, passive
Erect posture: Self-confident, assertive

Education

When a paralegal is hired by a law office, a period of training will ensue. It is unrealistic to expect a new employee—even an experienced paralegal—to "hit the ground running" in a new position. It is up to a law firm to give employees a certain level of competency by providing on-the-job training. Often, a new paralegal will be trained by the person he or she is replacing. If this is not possible, a senior paralegal or paralegal manager will train the new employee. Sometimes, a firm will place a new employee with an experienced employee in the same capacity; the experienced employee will guide and train the new employee. This is called the **buddy system.**

buddy system
A system of putting two employees together for training purposes.

The buddy system has many advantages. It brings employees together to promote friendships and gives a new employee someone at the firm with whom he is familiar. This facilitates the new employee's integration into the firm. It also trains the new employee from the perspective of a peer.

The buddy system also has disadvantages. Often, a veteran paralegal who is training a new paralegal falls behind on work and perceives training as an inconvenience. Or the veteran paralegal may not have the same duties as the new paralegal, thus making the training inadequate.

Mentoring is a successful method of paralegal training. A mentor is an experienced paralegal or attorney from whom a new paralegal can learn. Mentoring is not a structured training program but occurs during the course of employment. All new paralegals should have a mentor.

Motivation

Motivation is vital, yet it cannot be measured. Motivation can only be assumed to exist by observing performance and behavior. Abraham Maslow, a prominent management theorist, opined that one person cannot motivate another; personal motivation must come from within an individual. Therefore, management cannot motivate an employee. However, management can provide employees with a working environment that is conducive to personal motivation. In the proper working environment, employees can be motivated to do their best. A positive working environment is one where employees are recognized for their achievements, have adequate responsibility, are creative, and have advancement opportunities.

WORKING CONDITIONS Working conditions have a major effect on overall job satisfaction. Poor working conditions increase turnover and decrease efficiency. Good working conditions decrease turnover and increase efficiency.

Good working conditions include the following:

- *Policy.* Reasonable office policies fully set forth in an office manual, with grievance procedures and an appeal process established and explained

- *Health and Safety*. Good lighting and a clean, comfortable environment with regulated heating and air conditioning
- *Tools*. Updated tools and equipment, including technology

Poor working conditions include these:

- *Policy*. Strict and unreasonable office policies that are neither documented nor enforced, with no grievance procedures or appeal process established
- *Health and Safety*. Poor lighting and a dirty, messy environment with unreliable heating and air conditioning
- *Tools*. Outdated tools and equipment, including technology

The field of **ergonomics** is defining acceptable and unacceptable standards for employees' health and safety. Ergonomic concerns include office furniture, computers, and equipment that maximize employee health and safety. It is an employer's responsibility to provide ergonomically acceptable equipment—such as computer glare screens and keyboard stands—because the employer is responsible for an employee's health problems acquired at work.

ergonomics
An area of science concerned with health issues in the workplace.

Good working conditions also include an environment that is conducive to positive working relationships and free from personality conflicts and sexual harassment problems.

SEXUAL HARASSMENT Every person has a right to pursue a career free from sexual harassment and suggestive remarks. According to the National Association for Female Executives, 77 percent of the women it surveyed felt that sexual harassment was a problem. Fifty-three percent had been sexually harassed or knew of someone who had been sexually harassed. Sixty-four percent of those sexually harassed did not report the incident. Of the 36 percent who reported the incident, 52 percent said it was not resolved to their satisfaction.

T R E N D S

PREPARING A RÉSUMÉ TO BE READ BY A COMPUTER

As technology is performing more functions for management, many candidates are preparing a résumé that is read by the company's computer system. Some companies may want two versions of your résumé: one for management to read and one for the computer to read. Prepare your résumé so it maximizes the computer's ability to "read" your résumé by preparing it according to the following tips:

- Use white paper printed on one side only.
- Submit an original, not a photocopy. Laser printed is preferable.
- Do not fold or staple.
- Use standard fonts such as Times New Roman, Palatino, Arial, or Helvetica in 10 to 14 point type (12 is preferable—avoid Times 10 point).
- Don't condense spacing between letters.
- Use bold or all caps for section headings only.
- Avoid italics, underline, and shadows.
- Avoid lines, graphics, and boxes.
- Do not use a two-column format.
- Place your name at the top on its own line.
- List your phone number on its own line.
- Do not center headings—put them flush left.
- Use key words that coincide with the position advertisements.

Tip: When faxing your résumé, set the fax to "fine mode." The recipient will get a better quality copy.

Government agencies have issued guidelines intended to interpret employment laws as they pertain to sexual harassment. Federal guidelines have established that sexual harassment is a violation of title VII of the Civil Rights Act. These guidelines hold that an employer is responsible for the actions of its employees and define sexual harassment as follows:

> Unwelcome sexual advances, requests for sexual favors, and other verbal or physical conduct of a sexual nature constitute sexual harassment when (1) submission to such conduct is made either explicitly or implicitly a term or condition of an individual's employment, (2) submission to or rejection of such conduct by an individual is used as the basis for employment decisions affecting such individual, or (3) such conduct has the purpose or effect of substantially interfering with an individual's work performance or creating an intimidating, hostile, or offensive working environment.

Sexual harassment can take many forms, can be either verbal or nonverbal, and is often difficult to recognize. It is highly subjective. What is offensive to one person may not be offensive to another. Any instances of sexual harassment, or suspected sexual harassment, must be immediately reported to management.

Most employers have established policies concerning sexual harassment and written policies that define sexual harassment. The written policies describe the type of conduct an employer considers unacceptable. Most policies are contained in an employee handbook.

Evaluation

informal evaluation
A procedure by which an employee's work is evaluated verbally. It occurs in an informal manner.

formal evaluation
A procedure by which an employee's work performance is evaluated and rated in writing. It occurs annually or bi-annually.

Two types of evaluation take place: informal and formal. **Informal evaluation** occurs daily when employees' mistakes are corrected or employees are told they did a good job on a project. **Formal evaluation** occurs once or twice a year. A formal evaluation is in writing, followed by a performance interview with the employee and evaluators.

The purpose of a formal performance interview is to do the following:

- Discuss openly and candidly how an employee's performance meets an employer's requirements
- Make suggestions on how to correct weaknesses
- Follow up after a time period to report on the progress being made, giving any additional suggestions that might help
- Discuss an employee's professional development
- Set goals for the following year
- Access an employee's professional goals
- Give an employee suggestions on how to enhance professional development

Of Interest . . .

TIPS FOR THE FORMAL EVALUATION

1. Problems arise if a performance evaluation is not based upon common agreement on what primary duties will be rated and how they will be measured. The evaluation session will start with a lack of mutual agreement concerning the performance management process, which will affect the evaluation's outcome.

2. Both the supervisor and employee must adequately prepare for the evaluation session. If the employee has kept good records of his or her accomplishments, the performance evaluation meeting will be easier. The supervisor prepares for the evaluation by gaining feedback from clients and coworkers about the employee's performance.

Of Interest . . . (Cont.)

3. Don't allow the evaluation discussion to be one-sided. If you believe the supervisor's comments to be unfair or wrong, be sure to bring them to his or her attention.

4. If there is a disagreement on an issue, a communication problem could arise if the supervisor tends to turn to power or avoidance modes rather than working with the employee to reach a mutual understanding about the issue.

5. End the meeting on a positive and amicable note.

6. At the end of the evaluation, make a record of the areas discussed, plans, and commitments made and follow up accordingly.

7. Evaluate how you handled the discussion. Could you have communicated your position better? If so, how?

Often, an employee's raise and bonus are based on the review process. Goals set at these sessions state what an employee would like to achieve in the next year. At the next annual performance interview, achievement of these goals is discussed.

Employers rate employees using a performance review sheet, such as the one shown in Exhibit 3–7. This sheet identifies several areas of performance that are important to the position and the firm. Each area is discussed, and the employee is asked to sign the performance review and is given a copy of the review. A copy of the review becomes a permanent part of the employee's personnel file.

Some of the areas considered in the performance evaluation are the following:

- Client relations
- Punctuality
- Dependability
- Communication skills
- Leadership capabilities
- Initiative
- Work habits
- Willing to work overtime
- Skills rating
- Job performance

Most firms go to great lengths to ensure that performance evaluations are objective. However, whenever one person evaluates the performance of another, a certain amount of subjective judgment is involved. What one supervising attorney considers superior may be only satisfactory to another. A performance interview is the setting in which to discuss any disagreements a paralegal may have with an evaluation.

A common complaint paralegals have with law firm management is the lack of formal evaluation procedures. A paralegal's supervising attorney must participate in or provide the evaluation. Some attorneys are uncomfortable with evaluating an assistant. They are afraid they will upset the employee, wonder if they are correct in their evaluation, and worry that the evaluation is a legal document that could be used against them in a legal proceeding. When all is going well, there's a temptation to adopt an "if it isn't broke, don't fix it" attitude, particularly if the attorney is busy with other, more pressing matters.

If a paralegal is not satisfied with a performance evaluation after a thorough discussion with the evaluator or evaluators, she or he should immediately take steps to resolve the

Law Offices of Black, White & Greene

Performance Evaluation

Name: Title:
Employee No.   Date:

Rating Factors

5 = Outstanding: Exceptional performance; demonstrates rare ability
4 = Excellent: High-quality performance; above standard
3 = Good: Consistently meets job requirements; excellent in some areas
2 = Satisfactory: Meets job requirements; requires supervision for some tasks
1 = Needs Improvement: Occasionally below standards; close supervision req'd
0 = Unsatisfactory: Unacceptable; fails to meet minimum job requirements

Performance Objectives   **Achieved**   **Not Achieved**

1.
2.

DESCRIPTION	RATING	DESCRIPTION	RATING
Quantity of Work		Attitude	
Quality of Work		Oral Communication	
Problem Analysis		Written Communication	
Decision Making		Staff Development	
Planning and Organization		Job Knowledge	
Skills		Collaboration & Teamwork	
Innovation		Responsive to Change	
Initiative		Persuasiveness	
Persistence		Leadership	
Ability to Work with Others		Client service	
Judgment		Job Enthusiasm	

Overall Performance

☐   ☐   ☐   ☐   ☐   ☐
Unsatisfactory   Needs Improvement   Satisfactory   Good   Excellent   Outstanding

Strengths

Weaknesses

Employee Comments (attach extra sheet if necessary)

Goals for next year
1.
2.
3.
All items recorded on this form have been discussed and are understood between us.

_____   _____
Employee signature   Date

_____   _____
Supervising attorney signature   Date

_____   _____
Management signature   Date

EXHIBIT 3–7 Performance Evaluation Form

problem. Since performance evaluations are a permanent part of one's record, one should be assertive in resolving the problem. The paralegal should contact the firm's administrator to determine what steps can be taken to remedy the situation. Firms often have an appeal process available to employees.

The evaluation process is an opportunity for employers to communicate their satisfaction, or dissatisfaction, with an employee. It is also an opportunity for employees to understand their strengths and weaknesses. Without this knowledge, an employee's efforts at improvement may be misdirected or nonexistent.

Of Interest . . .

PERFORMANCE EVALUATION DO'S AND DON'TS

Don't rely on attorneys to remember all the great things you did during the year. Prepare a one-page memo outlining your accomplishments and submit this to your supervisors before the review process begins.

Don't wait for the review to get feedback on your performance. Ask for input from the attorneys every time you complete a project and record their comments on a performance log.

Don't focus solely on your needs during the review. Ask about the needs of the firm. Consider your relationship with your employer as that of a partnership and make it clear to the reviewer that you understand such needs as cost-cutting, efficiency, and increased billable hours. Stay focused on why the firm is the business in the first place.

Don't be afraid to toot your own horn. Nobody knows what you have been doing better than you do. Be mentally prepared to discuss your accomplishments and the reasons that you deserve more responsibility. Keep a log of your accomplishments.

Don't assume that you know what is expected of you. Ask what the expectations are of each new assignment so that you can adjust your performance to meet explicit needs. Understand the expectations of the job.

Don't wait until the review to talk about a raise. Often, salary decisions have already been made at this point. Research what paralegals in your community are being paid and discuss this information with your supervisor before the review process begins. This kind of objective data is more convincing than an emotional appeal for more money.

Compensation

For employees to be satisfied with their work, they must be compensated adequately. Although many experts in the field have said that money is not a motivator in employee productivity, money contributes to employees' overall satisfaction with their work. Employees cannot give their best effort to a firm when their morale is low because of personal financial problems.

Employees should be satisfied with their wages at the time employment is accepted. If an employee accepts a low salary, anticipating high raises and bonuses, the employee is doing her- or himself and the profession a disservice.

Before a position is accepted, a paralegal should contact a local paralegal association and ask for a salary survey. Most local paralegal associations have salary information for paralegals based on education, experience, and specialty.

Generally, a new paralegal should not accept anything less than the average salary in the appropriate category. If a paralegal accepts a low salary, it will reflect on the next salary survey and bring the average down. This will affect all paralegals in the area. Accepting a low base salary will also influence a paralegal's future earning power because raises, and sometimes bonuses, are based on that salary. A paralegal's total compensation consists of salary, raises, bonuses, and benefits.

BASIC SALARY STRUCTURE   A good compensation plan is a goal of a firm. To establish a basic compensation structure, firms consider the following:

- *Marketplace.* What other firms in the area pay their employees
- *Job Analysis.* Study of the activities, duties, and responsibilities of a job
- *Job Description.* Detailed description of a job and the skills required to perform it
- *Job Evaluation.* Determination that establishes the value of a job and puts a monetary value on the job

Often, a firm may assign points to each function and skill required for a job, and then assign a monetary value to each point. In a position with a salary range—$32,000 to $45,000, for example—an employee with a low point value would be entitled to the lower salary, an employee with a high point value would be entitled to the higher salary, and an employee with an average point value would be entitled to a salary in the middle of the range. Exhibit 3–8 shows a sample form for assigning point values and salary equivalents.

RAISES AND BONUSES   Raises are based on the consumer price index and on merit, base salary, incentive, firm profitability, and/or the supervisor's discretion. Bonuses are based on the market, merit, base salary, tenure, incentive, billable hours, and/or firm profitability. Exhibit 3–9 shows the results of the 2007 salary survey conducted by *Legal Assistant Today* as to raises and bonuses.

Raises are usually given as a percentage of the base pay. When calculating raises, the **consumer price index** may be considered. If the consumer price index indicates that the cost of living rose 3 percent during the year, a raise will usually include a 3 percent cost-of-living increase in addition to a percentage increase based on merit, tenure, or incentive. According to a 2007 salary survey conducted by *Legal Assistant Today*, the average raise for a paralegal was $3,282 for a private law firm, $4,220 for a government office, and $3,575 for a corporate legal department. A raise is rarely over 15 percent of the base salary.

Merit raises and bonuses acknowledge above-average quality and quantity of work. Studies have shown that merit raises, properly given, will raise productivity 50 to 90 percent and efficiency 50 to 125 percent. Over 25 percent (25.8) of the respondents to the *Legal Assistant Today* 2007 survey received a bonus based on merit.

consumer price index
An index that determines the annual increase in the cost of living.

FUNCTIONS AND SKILLS	MAXIMUM POINTS	TOTAL POINTS
Education	10	
General experience	10	
Related experience	10	
Responsibility	10	
Supervisory responsibility	10	
Management responsibility	10	
Client contact	10	
Ability to travel	10	
Coordinating responsibility	10	
Training responsibility	10	
Total	100	

Note: 0–30 = Grade 1; 31–60 = Grade 2; 61–80 = Grade 3; 81–100 = Grade 4

EXHIBIT 3–8 Sample Point Values and Salary Structure

FACTOR	RAISES	BONUSES
Total number of billable hours	9.6%	12.3%
Market	10.7%	1.3%
Tenure (years of service)	13.5%	19.4%
Percentage of salary	19.7%	14.2%
Firm's profitability	21.9%	45.2%
Employer's discretion	52.8%	56.1%
Merit	—	25.8%

EXHIBIT 3–9 Factors Upon Which Raises and Bonuses Are Based *(As seen in the March/April 2007 issue of* Legal Assistant Today. *Copyright 2007 James Publishing, Inc. Reprinted courtesy of* Legal Assistant Today. *For subscription information call 800-394-2626, or visit <http://www.legalassistanttoday.com>.)*

Some administrators feel that merit raises and bonuses weaken employee morale because some employees will receive a higher raise or bonus than others. To eliminate this problem, some firms give employees a bonus based on base salary. Each employee, regardless of merit, will receive the same bonus according to his or her classification of employment. For example, attorneys receive 8 percent of their base salary, paralegals receive 5 percent of their base salary, and secretaries receive 3 percent of their base salary. Studies have shown that although this will eliminate employee dissension over bonuses, it does not encourage employees to work harder.

Raises and bonuses are based on tenure when an employee is rewarded for longevity with a firm. Incentive raises and bonuses are given when an employee reaches a goal set by the firm. According to the 2007 salary survey conducted by *Legal Assistant Today*, 69.5 percent of respondents received a bonus. Corporate legal departments paid the highest average bonus. A breakdown of average bonus by type is shown in Exhibit 3–9.

Not all law firms offer bonuses to their employees. Statistics show that employees in large firms receive lower bonuses than those in small firms. The average bonus according to firm size is reported by the 2007 *Legal Assistant Today* salary survey as follows:

Firms with 1 attorney—$2,335

Firms with 2–5 attorneys—$2,864

Firms with 6–10 attorneys—$4,999

Firms with 11–25 attorneys—$1,978

Firms with 26–50 attorneys—$2,308

Firms with 51–100 attorneys—$5,445

Firms with more than 100 attorneys—$3,983

Firms have various methods of determining raises and bonuses. Some use performance evaluations on which to base salary increases. A large firm may form a committee to evaluate salary increases and performance reviews to determine salary increases and bonuses. In a small firm, a managing partner or senior partner may determine salary increases and bonuses.

BENEFITS Studies indicate that companies with good benefits enjoy a higher degree of employee loyalty. As medical expenses increase and the cost of medical insurance skyrockets, firms with good medical benefits have more solid employee relationships. Employees of firms with few or no benefits are leaving to join firms with benefits. Some benefits, such as retirement plans, are contingent on longevity with a firm and encourage employees to stay with the firm.

Benefit plans vary with the size of a firm. Small firms and sole practitioner offices tend to offer fewer benefits. The cost of benefits is often too high for small firms to afford.

Large firms and corporate legal departments usually have better benefit packages that are more likely to include employee retirement and savings plans. Some large firms offer other benefits, such as health club memberships, company cars, flex-time, and work-from-home opportunities. In addition, most firms (65 percent) will pay for continuing education and membership dues in professional associations (60 percent).

Some firms offer their employees some innovative benefits, such as job sharing and flex-time, telecommuting, wellness programs, personal family counseling, tuition reimbursement, travel discounts, theater passes, store discounts, urgent family care, free legal services, and a massage on company time. The benefits reported in the *Legal Assistant Today* 2007 National Salary Survey Report are shown in Exhibit 2-7 in Chapter 2.

When calculating compensation, always include benefits in the total. A firm with few benefits may offer a higher salary, but when benefits are included, the total compensation may be greater with an office offering a lower salary and a good benefits package.

To ensure a satisfied and motivated staff, each decision affecting an employee's compensation must be made in a fair and objective manner. Firms go to great lengths to protect objectivity in their compensation standards.

LAWS AFFECTING COMPENSATION　The federal government has passed laws that establish minimum wage and overtime requirements, and prohibit wage discrimination. The Federal Labor Standards Act **(FLSA)** designates the parameters within which an employee may be designated exempt or nonexempt.

FLSA
Federal Labor Standards Act.

exempt
A professional status that exempts an employee from overtime compensation.

nonexempt
A nonprofessional status that requires payment of overtime.

EXEMPT AND NONEXEMPT STATUS　**Exempt** (professional) and **nonexempt** (nonprofessional) refer to minimum wage and overtime requirements.

Employees who are exempt are paid an annual or monthly salary and are not entitled to overtime compensation. Employees who are nonexempt are paid by the hour and are entitled to overtime compensation for all hours worked in excess of 40 hours a week. Even though an employer may inform a nonexempt employee of his yearly "salary," that employee is actually paid by the hour. In return for X hours of work a year, the employer will pay the employee X dollars. If an employer docks the pay of a "salaried" employee who comes in late, leaves early, or must take time off for personal needs, the employee is not a salaried employee in the true sense of the word. A true salary is paid to exempt employees only.

The FLSA sets the standards of who may be exempt employees. Exempt employees are categorized into specific categories, three of which may apply to paralegals: executive exemption, professional exemption, and administrative exemption. Whether an employee is exempt depends on whether the employee meets certain criteria in each category. According to the Labor Department's guidelines, "professionals must perform work requiring knowledge of an advanced type in a field of science or learning customarily acquired by a prolonged course of specialized intellectual instruction and study." A prolonged course of study has been defined as "at least a baccalaureate degree or its equivalent." In addition, an employee must do work requiring consistent exercise of discretion and judgment.

In 2005, The Department of Labor issued two Wage and Hour Letter Opinions that specifically addressed the duties of paralegals. They state that paralegals are considered nonexempt professional employees because, in the Department's opinion, an advanced academic degree is not a standard prerequisite for entry into the field. Although many paralegals possess 4-year advanced degrees, most paralegal programs are 2-year associate degree programs. However, the professional exemption is available for paralegals who possess advanced degrees in other professional fields and apply that knowledge in the performance of their duties. For example, if a law firm hires a CPA as a paralegal to provide expert accounting services in business cases, that paralegal would qualify for a professional exemption. A description of FLSA requirements for exempt status and the two opinion letters from the Department of Labor described in this paragraph are included in a document entitled "FLSA" in Chapter 5's documents on the accompanying CD.

The *Legal Assistant Today* magazine's 2007 salary survey states that 43 percent of its respondents have exempt status. The exempt and nonexempt status of paralegals is an issue that has been long debated. The issue was brought before the U.S. District Court for a determination when the Department of Labor (DOL) sued the Dallas law firm of Page & Addison for classifying their paralegals exempt and refusing to pay overtime (*Department of Labor v. Page & Addison,* U.S. District Court for the Northern District of Texas, No. 3:91-CV-3655-P). It was the Department of Labor's opinion that a paralegal is a production worker and, therefore, did not qualify for exempt status. It was Page & Addison's opinion that the paralegal's work is substantive and, therefore, qualifies for exempt status. The jury agreed with Page & Addison that paralegals should have exempt status. The Department of Labor appealed this decision, but (for unknown reasons) abandoned its appeal with prejudice. This decision may trigger additional litigation to exempt paralegals from overtime on a case-by-case basis because a decision from the U.S. District Court, Northern District of Texas, may have no effect upon paralegals in other parts of the country. Regardless of the court's ruling, the DOL considers paralegals as a class nonexempt from the FLSA.

This controversy has caused law firms to think carefully about classifying their paralegals. Some firms are placing their junior paralegals in the nonexempt status and their senior paralegals in exempt status. The reasoning behind the difference is that the senior paralegal performs more management functions than a junior paralegal, and the junior paralegal requires more supervision.

Some paralegals do not want to be exempt because they want to be compensated for overtime. They say that the higher wage paid exempt paralegals is not high enough to compensate them for all the extra hours required. Others, even those who make more money with nonexempt status, prefer the prestige exempt status brings them. In any event, this issue has a tremendous impact on individual paralegals. According to the *NALA's 2004 National Utilization and Compensation Survey Report,* 26 percent of the respondents reported that they worked overtime almost every day; 27 percent worked overtime at least one a week; 19 percent worked overtime at least once a month; and 27 percent rarely or never worked overtime. Of the paralegals who worked overtime, 22 percent received comp time off, 38 percent were paid, and 37 percent were not compensated for overtime.

Don't let this controversy confuse you. Paralegals are certainly professional. A paralegal's level of professionalism has nothing to do with their exempt or nonexempt classification. The work is challenging, and the rewards are great.

THE TEAM APPROACH

Many different concepts have been proposed for integrating management and employees for an effective organization. Many theories and approaches have been developed, as well as techniques, to maximize a firm's productivity. A popular approach applied in many law firms and private industry is the **team approach.**

The basic theory behind the team approach is that by aligning an organization's needs with the needs of its employees the organization will benefit from the employees' personal motivation, energy, and drive, as well as benefit employees by being a vehicle for achieving their personal goals.

Studies have shown that the team approach plays an important role in the personal satisfaction of employees, success of an enterprise, and good service to a client. To have a successful team, all members must function together. As on a good football team, individual contributions to a work team are dimmed when the contributions of other team members are considered. It is important that all team members feel that they belong to the team and are recognized for their contribution.

Legal Assistant Today, in its search for the best law firm, asked its readers to nominate the best firm to work for and to indicate what made the firm so desirable. The paralegals who

team approach
A management theory in which management and employees work together for the benefit of an organization.

responded to the survey were mainly from small firms. They responded that respect and a professional attitude were very important to them. One respondent said, "Paralegals [in this firm] are treated fairly, respectfully, and as professionals. We are recognized and utilized as valuable assets to the firm." Another wrote, "Each partner is concerned with the career development and potential of each legal assistant. They develop you as an individual and a team player and encourage our professional growth."

One method of the team approach consists of the five Cs: each member of the paralegal team must exhibit **c**ommitment and **c**ompetency, receive **c**onstructive feedback, be allowed **c**reativity, and show **c**ooperation.

Commitment

Building a strong team in a law office involves a commitment to the objectives of a firm. Each member of a football team knows the objective of the team and has the same goal: to win football games. Each team member makes an individual contribution to achieving the goal. Likewise, each member of a legal team should have the same objectives: (1) provide quality legal services to the client, (2) contribute to the profitability of the firm, and (3) derive personal satisfaction and growth from work.

A commitment to a firm is not made on one's first day of employment. Making this commitment requires trust in an organization and in its people. Once an individual can trust the motives of an organization—know that the organization will support her or him in achieving individual as well as company goals—a sense of loyalty develops. For this sense of loyalty to build, employees must know that they are an integral part of a team and in control of their own destiny within an organization. Then, a sense of belonging to the organization exists, and a positive sense of self-esteem develops.

Competency

To be part of a dynamic team, each employee must be competent. Employees rely on one another. Since employees are responsible for different aspects of a project, it is important that team members have confidence in the contribution of other team members. If one member's contribution has to be redone or is substandard, it affects the entire project and the contribution of other team members. Incompetent employees will affect a firm's environment by creating dissent and inefficiency.

Graduating from paralegal school will not make a paralegal competent—but it will give a paralegal the tools to begin the journey to competency. Education, experience, on-the-job training, and continuing education are the keys to competency.

EDUCATION AND EXPERIENCE   When paralegals graduate from paralegal school, their paralegal education has just begun. Once paralegal skills are learned, paralegals are constantly upgrading those skills with on-the-job experience. Studies have shown that it takes 3 years to learn a job completely. Does that mean that it will take 3 years to be competent? No. *Webster's New Collegiate Dictionary* defines *competent* as "having requisite or adequate ability or qualities." Each day a paralegal works, something new is learned. Competency is always increasing.

ON-THE-JOB TRAINING   Training is closely related to other personnel activities. For example, planning identifies a firm's needs. These needs can be filled either by hiring new personnel or by increasing the skills of current employees through training. One purpose of a formal evaluation is to identify any problem areas. When a problem area is identified, it can be eliminated by proper training.

On-the-job training is effective because it concentrates on subject areas relevant to a job. Many paralegal programs offer an internship course that allows students to demonstrate their skills and receive exposure to the real legal world. A student observes an experienced paralegal, who has learned the tricks of the trade, and, therefore, benefits directly. The experienced paralegal is a role model for the student and can illustrate how a task relates to other tasks. In a classroom, it is difficult to get a real-life feel for the subject matter.

Many large firms conduct their own training programs. Firms that do not offer formal training programs encourage workers to attend seminars and continuing education programs sponsored by legal organizations. Most firms will pay for, and give, employees the requisite time off to attend a seminar.

CONTINUING PARALEGAL EDUCATION The law is always changing and evolving. Law and its procedures that are learned this year and next year will change and will have to be relearned. Continuing legal education is essential to keep abreast of the changes in the law and procedures. A paralegal must be flexible with the law and be willing to devote time to continuing legal education.

Most law firms and legal offices will pay for an employee's continuing education if it pertains to the job. Some firms have a policy of paying for all continuing education because they feel it will benefit the firm in the long run by increasing competency levels. Some firms and paralegal departments will even reimburse employees for expenses incurred to obtain an advanced degree or college education.

Constructive Feedback

Giving constructive feedback is closely related to communicating effectively and is essential for successful employer-employee relationships. A paralegal who works hard on a project needs to know whether the work satisfies a supervising attorney. If areas did not meet the attorney's expectations, the paralegal needs to know about them. If areas exceeded the attorney's expectations, the paralegal needs to know about them. Constructive feedback motivates people to reach personal goals and improve their work. This allows each employee to grow in her or his chosen field. Unfortunately, constructive feedback is often overlooked in a busy law office and frequently must be requested.

A paralegal should be prepared for possible negative feedback, often called **constructive criticism.** Many people avoid giving negative feedback for fear that they will damage an employee's morale. Actually, usually so little positive feedback is given in a law office that negative feedback is perceived as a drastic event rather than as a challenge in a series of positive feedback events. Constructive criticism, although sometimes disturbing, is essential to improving job performance.

constructive criticism
A negative performance evaluation that is given for the purpose of providing instruction and direction.

Employment evaluations and reviews are part of the feedback process. Evaluation is the process that appraises performance. It should occur often—preferably after a paralegal completes a project. Being deprived of this feedback results in the loss of an opportunity to learn and grow.

Constructive feedback also includes praise and recognition for a job well done. Employees who receive little recognition for their work begin to lose the motivation to work hard and do their best on a project.

Each member of a legal team must be kept apprised of the status of a case. Just as a football player must have knowledge of the plays of a game, employees must know what is going on before they feel like an integral part of a team. As captain of the legal team, an attorney is responsible for keeping staff apprised and giving adequate instructions when assigning work.

Creativity

For a person to grow, a job must provide an opportunity for creativity. Opportunities for creativity are great when company procedures are flexible, all team members interact as peers, and decision making involves all team players. A person who is given the responsibility to complete a project in a manner consistent with her competency level is given an opportunity to be creative. Everyone has the ability to be creative.

Research has proven that one need not have a high intelligence quotient (IQ) to be creative. Creativity is encouraged by increasing activities that exercise the following attributes:

- *Open Mind*. Willingness to change one's viewpoint and approaches and try new things and experiences.
- *Curiosity*. Spirit of inquiry; realization that one has much to learn; an enjoyment of learning
- *Ability to Concentrate*. Ability to delve below the surface of situations; willingness to apply energy and efforts to solve problems; enjoyment of working on complex problems; willingness to spend considerable time alone thinking
- *Persistence*. Willingness to keep working on a problem until a satisfactory solution is found; patience in working out solutions
- *Confidence*. Willingness to risk being ridiculed by others for unconventional ideas and approaches; optimism and enthusiasm about finding and implementing solutions to problems
- *Cooperation*. Ability to work productively with others to define problems, formulate solutions, and implement action plans; flexibility in adapting to the reality of situations

The essence of creativity is identifying a need and meeting it in an original and effective way. An element inherent in all legal cases is a problem or issue. A lawyer's job is to solve problems and resolve issues to the satisfaction of a client. A paralegal's job is to help a lawyer find effective solutions. Examples of being creative in a legal case include applying the law in a unique manner, persuading a jury in an imaginative manner, and developing a system to make a law office run more smoothly.

A creative person is also a critical thinker. A critical thinker questions "facts" and will not be satisfied until all information is known. A critical thinker obtains a complete understanding of a situation and more easily produces a creative solution for a client.

Many paralegals are afraid to assert their creativity for fear it will be rejected by others. A good place to start asserting creativity is to develop solutions to problems or develop a system to make a project easier. For example, Cheryl Miller is a paralegal who spends a lot of time going through files to obtain information. She wanted an easier way to gather the information, so she developed a case flow cover sheet that listed all the documents in a file (see Chapter 12). She uses the cover sheet in all the files she reviews. When the office manager saw how efficient the system was, every paralegal was required to complete a case flow cover sheet for their files. Cheryl's creativity ultimately saved the firm money.

Cooperation

Cooperation is essential for the success of a solid team. Interacting with other employees is essential in any job. Service to a client, being one of an employee's goals, requires flexibility in work habits. Occasionally, it is necessary to step outside the boundaries of a position to help a coworker.

Cooperation is not always easy to attain. In a legal environment, it is easy to be abrupt to a coworker. The nature of legal work is stressful, and stressful working conditions express themselves in personality conflicts. Stress reduction should be a goal of all team members.

PERSONALITY CONFLICTS Like personal relationships, business relationships are subject to strain from time to time. On a whole, the business of law is more stressful than many other industries because of constant deadlines and the immediate needs of clients. A legal team is under more pressure to perform quality work in less time as clients become more fee-sensitive.

Each person has her or his own personality traits and style of handling stress. Good management understands the personalities of lawyers and support staff and must be careful to match the right support staff to the right lawyer. A mismatch can have disastrous effects on staff and on the productivity of a firm. For example, some secretaries and paralegals can handle—and even thrive on—working for an aggressive and disagreeable lawyer, whereas others work well with a soft-spoken, pleasant attorney.

Stress affects every member of a team, from an attorney to a messenger. The ability to get along with people is a particular challenge in a law office environment. A harried employee may make a sharp comment to another employee—not because of a personality conflict, but because of stress. The second employee, being sensitive, may take the comment personally, feeling that it was a direct attack. Consequently, the relationship of these two people may begin to deteriorate, eventually affecting the entire working environment of the firm.

Of Interest . . .

TEN STEPS TO CONFLICT RESOLUTION

1. Listen more. Talk less. It helps you understand the other person's point of view.
2. Ask when you want something. Making demands only makes things worse.
3. Focus on the problem, not the person. It's the only way to solve a disagreement.
4. Always deal with the problem at hand. Never bring up old issues or resentments.
5. Take responsibility for your part in the conflict. Your view may not be completely right either.
6. Express your feelings without blaming the other person. Blame never solves anything.
7. Always talk things out. Never use physical force to express your anger.
8. Choose your words carefully. Once a word is spoken, it cannot be taken back.
9. Look for a solution that is agreeable to both parties. If one person isn't satisfied, the problem isn't solved.
10. Step back and put the problem in perspective. Remember . . . a problem you have today may not seem so bad tomorrow.

SOURCE: Reprinted with permission of @Law, a NALS publication, 2002.

Conflicts are a source of personal and organizational malfunction. Most personality conflicts are a result of lack of communication. An effort should always be made to improve a conflicting situation before terminating employment. People citing a personality conflict as the reason for leaving prior employment are looked on with suspicion by potential employers. The key to success in dealing with personality conflicts is communicating and addressing issues directly to the offending person.

CONSTANT DEADLINES   One source of stress for paralegals is meeting constant deadlines. Deadlines and time constraints are inherent in the practice of law. Paralegals are often under pressure to complete a task before a deadline. Therefore, time management skills are essential for a paralegal. Often, time management skills are acquired by experience. Many organizations provide time management seminars and help employees acquire necessary time management skills.

UNETHICAL BEHAVIOR   Another source of conflict for a paralegal is to observe unethical behavior. Whether the perpetrator is an attorney or a paralegal, the circumstance puts a paralegal in a compromising position. The unethical act must be corrected, and the paralegal must exercise tact and good judgment in this situation. The paralegal may bring the problem to the attention of the perpetrator and strongly suggest that the situation be corrected, or the paralegal

What to Do about an Illegal Activity

The law firm's policy manual should contain a written statement prohibiting termination or other retribution for paralegals who blow the whistle on attorneys committing ethical violations or criminal acts. The firm's top management, including the paralegal manager, should communicate this policy on a regular basis to the paralegal staff.

The policy manual should also outline the following steps for Paralegals who either spot such activity, or who are asked to commit acts which they consider unethical or illegal:

- Speak first to the attorney. Is the act really illegal, or are there mitigating circumstances of which you are not aware?
- If the attorney does not address these concerns adequately, report the problem to the paralegal manager, who should approach the firm's ethics committee or managing partner.
- If the firm does not take the action the issue requires, report the activity to the ethics committee of the state bar association.

EXHIBIT 3–10   What to Do about an Illegal Activity *(Copyright 1993 by James Publishing, Inc. Reprinted with permission from* Legal Assistant Today.*)*

ETHICS ALERT

may bring the problem to management's attention and let management handle the problem. *Whichever option is chosen, the paralegal must not allow any unethical behavior to pass unnoticed or unreported.* Exhibit 3–10 lists some suggestions for handling knowledge of an illegal activity.

There are many different methods of reducing stress. Experts in this area recommend stress reduction activities to sustain health. Exhibit 3–11 provides some suggestions for reducing stress.

Ten Rs to Reduce Stress

1. *Relaxation.* Take 10 minutes out of the day to sit quietly, take deep breaths, and relax all the muscles in your body.
2. *Release.* Release worries and concerns. Eighty percent of what we worry about never happens, 15 percent of our worries are beyond our control, and 5 percent are within our control.
3. *Recreation.* Take the time to have fun and to exercise.
4. *Refuse.* Practice ways of saying no to tasks that will overburden you. Avoid feeling overloaded with work and feeling guilty about saying no. Make realistic demands on yourself.
5. *Reorganize.* Get rid of unnecessary clutter and low-priority projects. List high-priority projects and complete them first.
6. *Reevaluate.* Reevaluate all your projects. Are they all as urgent as you think? Set new priorities and prepare project lists in order of priority.
7. *Refocus.* Refocus in a positive direction. Choose to see situations positively instead of negatively.
8. *Recuperate.* Get plenty of rest and take care of yourself.
9. *Reduce standards.* Often, we place high demands on ourselves. Must we always be right? Allow yourself some room to be wrong and forgive yourself for mistakes.
10. *Recognize.* Be aware of stress signals such as sore eyes, stiff neck, and rapid heartbeat. Then retreat to a place where you can relax.

EXHIBIT 3–11   Ten Rs to Reduce Stress

CONCLUSION

Personnel relations can mean success or failure for a firm. The cost of replacing employees is very high. Employees of a small office may have more independence than employees of a large office, but small firms have reported problems usually not found in a large law office—for example, small legal clinics have more employment disputes than other firms.

A firm that loses a member of its team is disrupted until a replacement can be found. Firms with high **attrition** rates suffer from constant disorganization when an employee's position is vacant. Studies have shown that it takes an employee at least 2 or 3 months to become a productive member of a team. During the time of vacancy and training, someone's job is not getting done, and this affects the whole team. Chaos and confusion dominate the team, which is reflected in poor service to a client. Imagine a football team trying to play a game with half of its fullbacks missing.

A firm's environment is never static; it is in constant transition. The dynamics of a firm's environment ebb and flow at the direction of the team members. Each person is responsible for his own contribution to a firm's environment. A positive firm environment consists of positive employees—those with the team spirit, a high degree of motivation, confidence, and the five Cs.

attrition
A reduction in workforce due to death, termination, retirement, or resignation.

TRENDS

WHY DO EMPLOYEES LEAVE?

The *Harvard Business Review* suggests the following are reasons people leave their jobs:

- Job content
- Inadequate level of responsibility
- Negative company culture
- Disputes with colleagues
- Inadequate salary
- No management effort to motivate them
- Lifestyle/work/family concerns
- No communication or input on issues
- Lack of resources or support
- Lack of recognition
- Do not identify with the organization
- No team commitment or involvement
- Work is not fun anymore
- Lack of equity
- Don't feel appreciated
- No pride in the work product
- No prospects for promotion or growth
- Incompetent management
- Poor working conditions
- Inadequate salary and benefits

SUMMARY

Management is defined by Peter Drucker as "the method of using available resources to achieve desired goals." Managers work with and through other people to achieve a firm's goals. Good personnel relations are a test of effective management.

Although law firms differ in structure and management style, most firms have basically the same objectives. Many of a government agency's and corporate legal department's objectives may be different than a law firm's, but growth and satisfaction for employees is an objective of each type of legal office.

The manager is responsible for all aspects of personnel relations. The manager's role is influenced by external and internal conditions. External conditions include economic conditions, government regulations, and laws. Internal conditions include the nature and structure of a firm, the nature of the work, and the nature of the employees.

A personnel manager has five functions: planning, controlling, organizing, leading, and staffing. The goal of human resource planning is to develop personnel policies that will achieve a firm's objectives. Controlling is the process of ensuring that actions conform to plans. The organizing function requires a manager to coordinate the resources of a firm to maximize productivity and effectiveness. Leading involves determining what is to be accomplished and how to accomplish it. Staffing includes such duties as recruitment, screening, interviewing, testing, hiring, firing, job analysis, job description, and personnel record keeping.

The hiring process consists of four steps: planning, recruiting, selecting, and training. The manager must complete a position description for the position that includes hiring specifications. Before a position description can be prepared, the manager must have a clear understanding of the position and the necessary qualifications of the prospective employee.

The government has established employment guidelines in various legislative acts. In addition, individual states have their own employment laws and guidelines. The firm's employment application must comply with federal and state guidelines. The most important area to guard against federal law violations is the interviewing process. A manager may apply the ouch formula to interview questions to remain within interviewing requirements.

There are certain characteristics a manager looks for when interviewing a prospective employee. They are job hopping, long commute to work, poor health, improper termination notice to a previous employer, reasons for leaving, and a poor relationship with a previous employer. Management often uses an applicant evaluation form when making a final decision.

Good management-employee relations require a joint effort. Employee expectations can be best described in the CEMEC principle, which consists of communication, education, motivation, evaluation, and compensation.

Working conditions have a major effect on motivation and overall job satisfaction. The emerging field of ergonomics is defining acceptable and unacceptable standards for employees' health and safety. Good working conditions also include an environment that is conducive to positive working relationships free from personality conflicts and sexual harassment problems.

Two types of evaluation take place: informal and formal. Informal evaluation occurs daily when employees' mistakes are corrected or they are told they did a good job on a project. Formal evaluation occurs once or twice a year in a performance review.

For employees to be satisfied with their work, they must be compensated adequately. A good compensation plan is a goal of a firm. Often, a firm may assign points to each function and skill required for a job and then assign a monetary value to each point.

The federal government has passed laws that establish minimum wages and overtime requirements, and prohibit wage discrimination. The FLSA designates the parameters within which an employee may be designated exempt or nonexempt. The terms *exempt* (professional) and *nonexempt* (nonprofessional) refer to minimum wage and overtime requirements.

Many different concepts have been proposed for integrating management and employees for an effective organization. A popular approach applied in many law firms and private industry is the team approach. The basic theory behind the team approach is that by aligning an organization's needs with the needs of its employees, the organization will benefit from the employees' personal motivation, energy, and drive; as well as benefit employes by being a vehicle for achieving their personal goals.

Studies have shown that the team approach plays an important role in the personal satisfaction of employees, success of an enterprise, and good service to a client. One method of the team approach consists of the five Cs: each member of a legal team must exhibit commitment, competency, constructive feedback, creativity, and cooperation.

Personnel relations can mean the success or failure of a firm. A firm that loses a member of its team is disrupted until a replacement can be found. A firm's personnel relations affect its environment. For this reason, a firm's environment is never static; it is in constant transition.

CHAPTER ILLUSTRATION

Robert Black is the managing partner for Black, White & Greene. Tricia Bunnell is his assistant and has gained the title of office manager. Robert asked Tricia to develop human resource policies and procedures for the firm. In order to do this, she must conduct a human resource audit of the firm's existing staff to determine whether the staff should be restructured to increase productivity and to plan for the future needs of the firm.

She began by asking each employee to list and describe each area of her or his job and to rate the frequency of each task. When she received the reports, she found the following:

- Some employees' tasks could be delegated to a subordinate employee.
- Some employees were not adequately trained to complete certain tasks.
- Some employees were overloaded with work, while others were underutilized.
- Secretaries were spending too much time filing and copying documents, causing them to fall behind on their secretarial work.

After discussing the findings with Robert, they developed the following plan:

1. Hire a file clerk.
2. Paralegals were to delegate their clerical functions, such as file maintenance, to the secretaries.
3. The complex litigation paralegals were to receive training in handling complex litigation.
4. The senior paralegal was to delegate all deposition summaries to the junior paralegal.
5. Each employee would be evaluated once a year.

GOAL 1 To accomplish goal 1, Tricia prepared a position description for the file clerk position. After a discussion with the secretaries who were currently performing the function, she determined the major duties and requirements for the position and included all the main areas in a position description, as shown in Exhibit 3–3. After Robert and the secretaries reviewed the position description, Tricia began the recruiting process by placing an ad in the classifieds section of the local newspaper. She also called the local college and submitted the position with the paralegal program director.

The first day, Tricia received about 15 résumés, the second day 25, and the third day 13. She then eliminated all résumés with typos or grammatical errors to arrive at 25 résumés worthy of consideration. Of those résumés, some applicants did not have the requisite background, some were overqualified, and others were underqualified. Two applicants appeared to be job hoppers. After eliminating those candidates, she arrived at 10 qualified applicants for the position. She wrote all the rejected applicants a letter, thanking them for their interest; and she set appointments for the qualified applicants.

Before her first appointment arrived, Tricia developed her interview questions. She formulated them using the ouch formula and made sure that each question complied with the law. She also developed an applicant rating sheet like the one shown in Exhibit 3–6. She and Robert interviewed the applicants and compared their ratings. There were two applicants who were tied for first place: Lori Smith and Kay Bowen. They were called back for a second interview. Kay Bowen received the most points after the second interview and was hired as the firm's file clerk.

On Kay's first day of work, Tricia conducted her orientation. She introduced her to all the members of the firm and described the firm's policies and procedures. For her training on filing procedures, Tricia used the buddy system and delegated the training to Sandra, the most experienced secretary in the firm.

GOAL 2   With Kay performing the filing for the firm, the secretaries were now ready to maintain the files and keep them current for the paralegals. This task involved maintaining the status worksheets and categorizing documents. The secretaries required training on the correct method of file maintenance. The most logical person to train the secretaries was the most experienced paralegal, Milton, who developed a training program for the secretaries and delivered the training.

GOAL 3   Specialized training was required to make sure the complex litigation paralegals were knowledgeable about all areas of managing a complex litigation file. Since Milton was a member of the local paralegal association, he received information on all their educational programs. A workshop on complex litigation was being presented in 3 weeks, so the firm paid for him to participate. Tricia told him to watch for all workshops pertaining to complex litigation and encouraged him to attend them.

GOAL 4   The junior paralegal, Melvin, was given the responsibility to summarize depositions. To ensure that he had the proper training, he signed up for a refresher course in trial preparation at the local college. To assist Melvin, the firm also contracted the services of Depo Sum, a paralegal service that specialized in deposition summaries. Tricia spoke with the owner of Depo Sum, who agreed to come to the firm to supplement Melvin's training for deposition summaries.

GOAL 5   Prior to the human resource audit, the firm had no policy for evaluating its employees. This was one area of concern for the employees who requested a formal evaluation process. After a discussion with Robert and the other attorneys in the firm, it was determined that the attorneys were the most qualified to evaluate their staff. However, most of the attorneys expressed concern about the process because they had little or no experience in the evaluation process. It was important that the attorneys receive training in this area before developing a formal plan.

The firm contacted a human resources consultant to educate the attorneys on the process. The consultant agreed to train the attorneys and the staff on the process. The consultant also developed an evaluation form for the firm like the one shown in Exhibit 3–7. While this was very expensive for the firm, the firm felt that it was extremely important that the evaluations be as objective as possible to maintain employee morale.

The evaluations were scheduled for the employment anniversary of each employee. When Melvin was evaluated, he was dissatisfied with his rating. He felt that he should have been given a higher rating. Sandra was marked down on her evaluation because she had a tardiness problem. While her performance was excellent in many areas, her tardiness imposed undue hardship on other employees. She was admonished and encouraged to be punctual. Dennis White, her boss, gave her a formal warning about her tardiness. Sandra agreed to be punctual and was convinced that her performance evaluation would improve when she resolved her punctuality problem. Milton's evaluation was so good that he now wants a raise.

Part of each employee's evaluation is to set goals for the year. Goals included improving on areas of performance and learning new skills. While some employees were dissatisfied with areas of the evaluation, for the most part they were very pleased with the process. With the exception of Melvin, the employees felt that the evaluations were fair.

With reference to compensation, the employees, except Milton, felt that they were fairly compensated. With the evaluations completed, the firm can now consider raises and bonuses for the employees.

The human resources audit took the firm 1 year to complete and implement. While it was being developed, the firm contracted with a temp agency for a temporary secretary to fill Tricia's position while she worked on the audit. Now that the audit is completed, Tricia can assume her secretarial duties. Robert has other plans, however. He decided to make Tricia a full-time office manager to handle the management of the law firm. She accepted. The temporary secretary, Pam Cody, was offered the position as a full-time employee, and she accepted. Tricia was happy with her promotion.

The audit was a time-consuming and expensive program. However, the firm was rewarded for its hard work and commitment by creating a culture that is positive and cohesive. The employees work together as a team and are included in management's policy development.

CHAPTER REVIEW

1. Describe the internal and external conditions that affect a firm's management.
2. What are the five functions of a personnel manager? Which is the most important?
3. What are the three main goals of a law firm?
4. What are the three main elements of control?
5. What are the three roles of a leader?
6. What are the four steps of the hiring process?
7. What is the ouch formula?
8. What danger signals do managers look for in an interview?
9. What is the CEMEC principle?
10. What are the reasons for conducting a performance evaluation? What are some of the areas of performance considered?
11. What issues are considered when establishing a compensation plan?
12. What is the difference between an exempt employee and a nonexempt employee?
13. What is the team approach?
14. What are the five Cs of the team approach?

EXAMPLES FOR DISCUSSION

1. **IRON FIST MANAGEMENT STYLE**

   The Paralegal Department of the Federal Contracts Agency is a government agency consisting of five attorneys, three paralegals, and five secretaries. The office manager is known for managing the department with an iron fist. She is a retired accountant, committed to staying within the budget of the agency and earning recognition for reducing costs. She thinks that if very strict rules are implemented, productivity will increase and the department's reputation will increase.

   When Sam Weeks was hired as a paralegal for the department, the office manager gave him a three-page memo of rules. The memo stated:

   ### Notice to Employees
   1. Nothing will be placed on the top of the desk except essential working tools (no pictures, plants, etc.).
   2. Desk drawers must be neat and tidy at all times and subject to unannounced inspections.
   3. All tardiness (even 5 minutes) will be deducted from pay.

4. No personal telephone calls will be allowed except in extreme emergencies. Each employee's phone is equipped with a monitoring device that monitors all calls. Personal calls will be deducted from the paycheck for both time and charges.

5. Breaks are permitted only for attending to bathroom duties.

6. Absolutely no personal conversation with other employees will be permitted. All conversation must be work related.

7. Errors in work will not be permitted and will be monitored.

8. All supplies must be accounted for. When a pen runs out of ink, it may be turned in for a new pen. No pens will be issued unless accompanied by a used pen. This applies to scissors, staplers, hole-punchers, highlighters, etcetera.

Thank you for your attention to these policies.
The Management.

1. What goal of the firm is the office manager overlooking?
2. What management function is missing with this office manager?
3. What leadership qualities are missing with this manager?
4. Would you like to work for this agency? Why or why not?

2. CAROLYN'S BAD DAY

Carolyn Albers, a real estate paralegal, knew the trial date of the Twin Lakes real estate case was quickly approaching. She also knew that she needed to complete a summary-of-events project before the trial. Since the case was complicated, she needed instruction from her boss, Michael Varisco.

Michael is extremely busy. He is always in a meeting, in court, or with clients. Whenever Carolyn tried to talk to him, he was always too busy. Carolyn wrote him e-mails and slipped hand-written notes under his door. They were never acknowledged.

After repeated attempts, Carolyn went by Michael's office and found him on the telephone. She went in his office to wait until he got off the phone. When he hung up, Carolyn requested instruction on the events summary for the Twin Lakes case.

"You mean you haven't started that yet?" said Michael.

"I've been waiting for your instructions," said Carolyn.

"Just do a summary of the events that occurred from the purchase of the property to foreclosure. You don't need to include Rick Everett's participation or Jennifer Hemstreet's participation. Be sure to include all activities of all the brokers and salespeople. Check the deposition for information," said Michael as he picked up his briefcase and left for court.

Carolyn returned to her office and sat down in her chair. She thought about what Michael had said: Do not include the activities of Rick Everett or Jennifer Hemstreet but include the activities of all salespeople and brokers. "But Rick Everett was a broker acting in the capacity of a salesman in one aspect of this case," thought Carolyn. "Is he confused? Am I confused? What do I do with Everett? Include him? I'll check the deposition. But . . . what deposition? There are 17 depositions in this case! Which one did he mean? I guess I'd better review them all."

Carolyn, unsure of Michael's instructions and unable to meet with him again, reviewed all the depositions and could not find the answer to her question. She decided to be safe and include Rick Everett in the broker and salesperson categories. Time was running out. This extra work caused Carolyn to work late each night. The Friday before the trial, she was not finished with the summary, so she came into the office on Saturday and Sunday to complete it. She finally finished the project Sunday evening and put it on Michael's desk.

Carolyn arrived at the office early on Monday morning to make sure Michael was ready for trial. Michael was not there early but came in at his usual 9:30 a.m. When Carolyn asked him about the trial that morning, Michael said, "I'm not going to trial on the Twin Lakes real estate case. We settled the case last Wednesday."

Carolyn was furious! This was not the first time this had happened. She immediately set an appointment with the administrator to request a change in supervising attorneys.

1. What were the consequences of Michael's lack of communication?
2. Take a guess at approximately how many hours Carolyn unnecessarily worked on the project. Carolyn's billable rate is $90 an hour. How much money did Michael's actions cost the firm?
3. Carolyn has requested a transfer, but no opening exists for her in any other area of the firm. Carolyn has threatened to quit the firm. If you were the administrator, what would you do to resolve the problem?
4. If you were Carolyn, what would you do?
5. What areas of the team concept are missing here?

3. THE BIG BONUS

A management policy of Noguchi & Black is that all employees keep all compensation matters confidential. No one knows how much another employee makes or the amount of his raise or bonus.

Noguchi & Black establishes bonuses based on billable hours. Each paralegal is required to bill 1,500 hours a year for wages. If a paralegal bills more than 1,500 hours a year, that paralegal is rewarded with a bonus according to the number of excess hours billed.

Larry Esteban heard through the grapevine that Elizabeth Rinehart received a very large bonus because of the hundreds of hours of overtime she worked. Larry felt that was strange since it was common knowledge that Elizabeth refused to work overtime. She was never in the office on the weekends Larry was in. Elizabeth was always too busy to help another paralegal. She appeared to be the last person that should be given a large bonus.

1. What could be the problem here?
2. What elements could have contributed to Elizabeth's bonus?
3. What are the consequences of this problem?
4. How could the problem be avoided?
5. If you were the administrator, what would you do to solve the problem?

4. EVALUATION, PLEASE!

Adam Knight is a litigation paralegal for the corporate legal department of Reysack Corporation. His boss, Mary Micheau, asked him to do a research memorandum on a case involving contributory negligence. Adam was excited about the project because it was the first time he had researched this area of law and he was interested in the subject. He worked very hard on the project, reading all the cases he could find on it. He proudly turned in the project before the deadline.

A week went by without Mary mentioning the memorandum. Adam knew the trial was approaching and was anxious to find out whether the memorandum helped the client. He decided he would ask Mary about it when she got back from court in the afternoon. Before she returned, however, Adam noticed that Stuart Kline, the other litigation paralegal, was in the library doing research and had Adam's memorandum in front of him.

When Adam asked Stuart what he was doing, Stuart replied, "Oh . . . I'm doing research on contributory negligence for Mary."

"But I did that already," said Adam. "Yes, but . . . Mary said that you completely missed the point and asked me to do it over."

Adam was shocked. He was embarrassed and humiliated in front of a coworker and felt sure that Stuart thought he did inferior work.

1. What were the consequences of Mary's lack of constructive feedback?
2. What should Mary have done?
3. Imagine that you are Mary and have trouble giving constructive criticism. What do you say to Adam?

4. If you were the office manager, how would you resolve the situation?

5. What area or areas of the team concept are missing?

5. THE DEPOSITION DILEMMA

Polly Ferraro is a paralegal with the large firm of Major, Ingles & Hernandez. Her boss, Franklin Rush, informed her that his case was going to trial next Thursday and a few depositions had to be summarized before the trial. She said she would be happy to summarize them but was shocked to see a stack of 95 depositions brought into her office.

Perplexed and worried that she could not complete the assignment, Polly immediately started to summarize the depositions. While doing so, she overheard a conversation between Mike Gekeler and Marilyn Ling, two other paralegals. Mike told Marilyn that he had completed his work and had nothing to do.

Polly hurried into Mike's office, where he was reading a magazine with his feet up on his very empty, very clean desk. She told him of the predicament she was in and asked him to help her with the depositions.

"Summarize depositions? No way! I hate to summarize depositions. I'm a corporate paralegal, Polly, not a litigation paralegal," stated Mike smugly. "I told myself I was through summarizing depositions, and I meant it. No, I won't help you with them."

1. What might be the consequences of Mike's lack of cooperation?

2. How might Mike's response ultimately affect the firm and the client?

3. If you were Polly, what would you do?

4. If you were the office manager, what would you do?

5. What area or areas of the team concept are missing?

6. THE DEMISE OF SHEA & GOULD

Shea & Gould, a prominent New York law firm of 230 attorneys, was formed in the early 1960s by William A. Shea, a prominent attorney. Shea Stadium was named after him for his efforts in forming the Mets baseball team. His firm enjoyed a prestigious clientele and was very prosperous.

Problems emerged at his firm in 1985 when he retired as managing partner and there was no one available with the leadership skills necessary to lead the firm. An executive committee was responsible for management decisions that were implemented by various managing partners who lacked the necessary skills to lead the firm. The business was decentralized and diversified.

Dissention among the partners grew, and the firm's structure was chaotic. Although the firm remained profitable, the partners and employees were dissatisfied with the firm's compensation program. Employees were leaving in droves. One partner was quoted as saying, "The firm has no economic problems, no serious debt. What it lacks is a social fabric, harmony as a unit."

A management consultant was retained to create a better compensation structure and a more structured firm government, but it was too late. The firm's intellectual property department defected to join another firm and took $20 million in business with them. Panic set in, and the firm could not recover. It finally dissolved and closed its doors forever. One partner summed it up this way: "A law firm has to exist for more reasons than just making money. Otherwise, you just keep selling out to the highest bidder."

1. What was missing from this firm's governance?

2. What should have been done to stop its demise?

3. What aspects of the CEMEC principle are missing here?

4. What aspects of leadership are missing here?

ASSIGNMENTS

1. For each of the following situations, taken from *Law Office Economics and Management Manual,* answer the following questions:

   1. Which of the five Cs are present or missing, if any?
   2. If you were the manager of the firm where the situation exists, what would you do to solve the problem?
   3. With what management function is the situation associated?

   SITUATION 1: "Sometimes policies set by law firms can be infuriating! In our office, we have a policy of not replacing equipment until it is completely worn out. In my opinion (which is never asked for, incidentally) this is false economy. There are many breakdowns, especially in dictating equipment and computers—causing errors and lost time, and costing far more than any money the policy might save. This doesn't count the frustration that comes from retyping copy that has been erased from the computer!"

   SITUATION 2: "At one time, I was asked to train an individual for a job equal to or better than mine. I did my very best, taking every opportunity to explain, illustrate, and guide him through all the details of his job. But he didn't listen to me. Then, that fateful day came when he really goofed! A procedure he should have followed was ignored. The error came to the attention of my boss. My boss came directly to me and criticized me for not training the new man properly. Can you imagine that? After all the years of faithful service I've given to the firm, my boss had to show me so little respect and confidence!"

   SITUATION 3: "I have been with our firm for many years. My boss has given me much responsibility, and I feel challenged by the work I have to do. However, my title is still secretary. Clients or other people coming into the office can't recognize me from anyone else by my title. Even on the telephone, people refuse to talk to me as soon as they discover that I am a secretary. I am sure I could be of much more service to the firm if my title described what I do—office manager or administrative assistant or something like that. It would also give me a feeling that I am progressing within the firm and my profession."

   SITUATION 4: "In my work experience, I have been fortunate to have a boss believe that individuals can accept responsibility if it is given properly. She recognized that there are many things in the firm that I can do as well as or better than she or any of the lawyers. So she patiently taught me what to do—and as soon as she saw that I could do it on my own, the job became my responsibility, and I incorporated it into my routine. Because of this trust on her part, I feel greatly motivated and very loyal to her and to the firm."

   SITUATION 5: "For the past 8 years, I have worked for and with numerous lawyers and countless law students. I think the biggest dissatisfaction I experienced is the lack of organization on the part of these people. As a paralegal, I could help organize the office in many ways and relieve the burden of a lawyer. But somehow, this responsibility is not shared. The lawyers feel that their training somehow includes office organization—but no one would ever notice it! They are overburdened with paperwork, visiting clients, and telephone calls. We could help them so much if they would only let us. One doesn't have to have a law degree to organize an office—or to do much of the paperwork and telephoning that is necessary. They just have to show a little confidence in us. Instead, they blame us for errors that come from their poor management."

   SITUATION 6: "I am quite certain that the most satisfying experience that I have had in the paralegal profession has not been working with other people but the extra responsibility given me on occasion. Occasionally, I am given the opportunity to sit down with a yellow pad and see what I can work out on this matter or that. Sometimes, my solutions are accepted with few changes. This makes me feel good—useful to the firm. Also, I am given opportunities to get away from the stale routine of work by traveling out of the city and the state for my firm, taking care of other company business."

SITUATION 7: "I am a former legal secretary. I enjoy being associated with a profession that helps people in desperate need. This aspect is satisfying and rewarding. But I have always wanted to be closer to the cases, to talk to the people involved, and to know more about the cases I was working on. Finally, the dull routine of typing, filing, and mailing got to me, so I went to paralegal school. After graduation, I expected more challenging assignments, but they never came. The lawyers in my firm still see me as a secretary—not a paralegal."

SITUATION 8: "Where can I go? I was hired as a paralegal 9 years ago, and I'm still doing much the same work as when I was hired. New paralegals come into the firm and do much the same work I am doing—and for the same pay. I have no future but to summarize depositions for the rest of my working life. It is a pretty bleak outlook!"

SITUATION 9: "I began working in law offices over 30 years ago. I was really excited about my job and the people I worked for. It wasn't long until I discovered that there were many things in the office that were off limits to me. I was to do only as I was told and nothing more. There are many courses I could have taken at the university and special courses elsewhere to make myself more valuable to the firm. But the firm did not encourage continuing legal education and would not pay for any courses. Even though I wanted to better myself to benefit the firm, I knew it would be of no use."

2. Talk to two or three of your friends about the environment at their work. Are your friends motivated? If so, why? If not, why not?

3. On the evaluation form shown in Exhibit 3–7, evaluate your boss. If you are not working, evaluate a parent or spouse. Would you recommend this person for a raise?

4. Conduct a human resource audit at your place of employment or home. Are employees or family members 100 percent productive? If not, why not? Could some positions be eliminated or restructured to save money? If so, how? Write a report to your instructor detailing your recommendations for improvement.

5. Prepare a position description for your position at work. If you are not working, prepare a position description for your duties at home or in a club. Ask your supervisor, parent, or club leader as well as your coworkers what their concept of your position is. Do their understandings of your position correspond to yours? What are the differences, if any?

Source: Reprinted with permission from *Law Office Economics & Management Manual* Vol. 1, Published by Clark Boardman Callaghan, 155 Pfingsten Road, Deerfield, IL 60015.

SELF TEST

How well did you grasp the material in the chapter? Test yourself by answering the following questions and check your answers against the answers found in Appendix A.

1. What is a law firm's most important resource?
2. Why is finding the right place to work important?
3. What two characteristics are a measure of effective management?
4. What are the three main objectives for a law firm?
5. What are the three objectives of a government office?

6. What are the three main objectives of a corporate legal department?
7. What are the external conditions that influence management?
8. What are the internal conditions that influence management?
9. What are the five functions of a personnel manager?
10. What is forecasting?
11. What are the four areas of human resource planning?
12. What is the goal of human resource planning?
13. What is the controlling process?
14. What are the three main elements of control?
15. What happens if management's standards are set too high?
16. What happens if management's standards are set too low?
17. What are the consequences of win-lose management?
18. What is the organization function?
19. What is the leadership function?
20. What is the staffing function?
21. What are the four steps in the hiring process?
22. What are four advantages of promoting from within the firm?
23. How are prospective employees recruited?
24. What questions on employment applications violate federal regulations?
25. What is the ouch formula?
26. What is one method to calm an applicant during an interview?
27. What are some danger signs a manager should look for when interviewing an applicant?
28. What is the CEMEC principle?
29. What is the inhibiting factor of open communication?
30. What is the buddy system?
31. What is a mentor?
32. What two things do poor working conditions produce?
33. What two things do good working conditions produce?
34. Good working conditions consist of three things. What are they?
35. What are the two types of evaluation?
36. What is formal evaluation?
37. What is informal evaluation?
38. What are some of the areas considered in a formal performance evaluation?
39. What should a paralegal do if she or he is unhappy with the formal performance evaluation?
40. What four things do firms consider when establishing a compensation structure?
41. What are raises based on?
42. What are bonuses based on?
43. What is often considered when calculating raises?
44. What do merit raises and bonuses acknowledge?
45. What is a raise or bonus based on tenure?
46. What type of firm usually offers fewer benefits?
47. What does FLSA stand for?
48. What does FLSA do?
49. What does *exempt* mean?

50. What does *nonexempt* mean?
51. What is the basic theory behind the team approach?
52. Studies have shown that the team approach plays an important role in what three things?
53. What are the five Cs of the team approach?
54. What are the three things to which each employee should be committed?
55. Making a commitment requires trust in two things. What are they?
56. What are the keys to competency?
57. Why is continuing legal education important?
58. What attributes increase creativity?
59. Why is the legal business more stressful than other businesses?
60. What is the basis of most personality conflicts?
61. If a paralegal observes unethical behavior, how should the paralegal handle the problem?

Key Words

attrition	FLSA	open question
buddy system	forecasting	ouch formula
CEMEC principle	formal evaluation	position description
constructive criticism	hiring specification	team approach
consumer price index	human resource audit	win-lose management
ergonomics	informal evaluation	
exempt	nonexempt	

 # Cybersites

JOB SEARCH WEBSITES

There are numerous sites to help you with your job search. Some sites are free, while others charge a fee to access résumés or post jobs.

Careers—<*http://www.careers.org*> Contains links to hundreds of career-oriented sites.

Jobtrak—<*http://www.monstertrak.monster.com*> Database of job opportunities for students. In its Search Tips section, it provides information on how to conduct an effective job search, networking, business protocol, letters, résumés, and personality tests.

Monster Board—<*http://www.monster.com*> Contains job listings for U.S. and international jobs in all fields. In its career center, it offers information on résumés, relocation services, employer job posting, and seminar notices.

Career Path—<*http://www.careerpath.com*> Contains a database that can search job listings posted in all the major newspapers. Résumé postings. This site was voted the number-one job site by Media Matrix.

NFPA—<*http://www. Paralegals.org*> In the career center, NFPA posts job openings for paralegals in the United States. Offers information on salary, résumé writing, opportunities, and career advancement.

JobBank USA—<*http://www.jobbankusa.com*>

Career Builder—<*http://www.careerbuilder.com*>

Job Web—<*http://www.jobweb.com*>

Job Guide on the Internet—<*http://www.dbm.com*> Making a transition to a new career.

Student CD-ROM
For additional materials, please go to the CD in this book.

Online Companion™
For additional resources, please go to http://www.paralegal.delmar.cengage.com

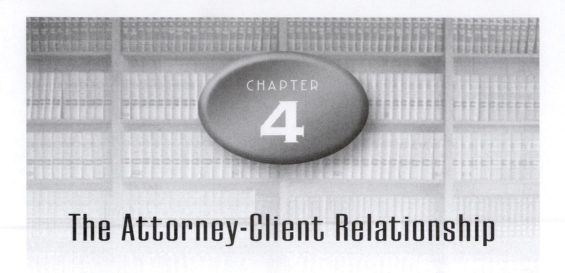

CHAPTER 4

The Attorney-Client Relationship

OBJECTIVES

After completion of this chapter, the student should be able to do the following:

- Describe the variables affecting client relations.
- Explain a bar association's involvement in client relations.
- Discuss a lawyer's ethical responsibilities to a client.
- Explain what clients expect from their lawyers.
- Describe the various methods lawyers use to attract clients.
- Describe the difference between public relations and advertising.
- Identify when an attorney-client relationship begins and ends.
- Define confidentiality, the attorney-client privilege, and the attorney work-product doctrine.
- Check for conflicts or potential conflicts.
- Identify the various types of discipline that may be imposed on lawyers.

INTRODUCTION

Law firms would not exist without clients, just as other businesses would not exist without customers. Since the legal business has become more competitive, attracting and retaining clients has become a major part of it—requiring the efforts of each member of a legal team.

Often, a client's first exposure to a law firm is through one of the firm's employees, usually a receptionist, secretary, or paralegal. A client's first impression of a firm—formed within the first three minutes—is often dependent on interaction with employees. An unfriendly receptionist greeting a potential client in an unprofessional manner influences whether the client will retain the firm. If clients do not retain the firm, the firm will cease to exist.

An attorney-client relationship is personal. Establishing rapport with a client so that the client will trust a firm is an essential element of this relationship. Although an attorney has the ultimate responsibility to maintain an attorney-client relationship, the attorney's employees play a major role in positive—or negative—attorney-client relationships. Actually, the relationship is between a client and a legal team. Paralegals have a direct responsibility to participate in an attorney-client relationship.

Paralegals are not ultimately responsible for an attorney-client relationship. However, for paralegals to have a complete understanding of how a law office functions, they must understand this vital area of law office management. They must understand the boundaries within which a lawyer must function because a paralegal must also function within those boundaries. For a paralegal to spot potential ethics problems, she or he must have knowledge of the parameters of an attorney-client relationship.

As explained in Chapter 3, one goal of a law firm is to provide quality legal services to a client. Another goal is to ensure the firm's profitability. The attorney-client relationship is directly related to these goals. Positive attorney-client relationships are rewards for quality legal services. Satisfied clients pay their bills and recommend others to a firm, which ensures the firm's profitability.

The purpose of this chapter is to provide an overview of the unique relationship between a client and a legal team. First, this chapter will discuss the variables that affect an attorney-client relationship, including the roles of a bar association, an attorney, a paralegal, and a client. Second, it will describe the various methods firms use to obtain clients. Third, it will examine the five major elements of an attorney-client relationship—the five Cs. Finally, the chapter will review attorney discipline—the consequences of not adhering to ethical guidelines concerning an attorney-client relationship. Throughout, the chapter will present ethical guidelines concerning an attorney-client relationship.

VARIABLES AFFECTING CLIENT RELATIONS

Before the 1970s, lawyers enjoyed fairly stable relationships with their clients. Most firms had an ongoing relationship with their clients that lasted for many years. This guaranteed a secure client base for a firm, and a client was guaranteed legal services from attorneys who understood the client's business and legal needs. During this time, the demand for lawyers exceeded the supply of lawyers. Because of this, law firms were managed to satisfy lawyers' needs.

Since the 1970s, however, certain variables have affected the traditional attorney-client relationship. Firms that previously rendered services to an ongoing and stable clientele found that relationship threatened by economics, a demand for varied specialties, marketing, and business management changes. For law firms to succeed in the new millennium, they must be managed to satisfy clients' needs.

The economic flux of the United States has caused changes in the economics of the practice of law and business in general. Higher overhead, technology, and equipment costs have raised the price of legal services to the point that the average middle-class person cannot afford them. Large corporations, in an attempt to reduce their legal costs, have hired their own in-house attorneys, decreasing the demand for outside legal services. Law has become more complex, which has expanded the need for legal specialties. Increased government regulations have burdened businesses, which has caused them to turn to legal specialists for assistance.

To add to these pressures, the number of lawyers in the United States continues to increase. A client now has many choices of lawyers, and the supply of lawyers exceeds the demand. Young, more aggressive lawyers with impressive skills have caught the eye of many clients. This has caused traditional law firms to enter an area once forbidden for established, sophisticated firms: marketing and advertising.

Another change that occurred in the three decades leading up to the early 2000s is the development of laws that define, govern, and protect a client. An attorney is now bound by rules that have been established by legislatures and bar associations that set parameters and guidelines for an attorney-client relationship and provide for remedies if a client is damaged by an attorney.

Role of Bar Associations

Attorney-client relationships, as well as other areas of a lawyer's role in society, are governed by state bar associations. Every state bar association has adopted a code of professional responsibility by which every lawyer in that state must abide. This code governs an attorney's conduct in various areas, including an attorney-client relationship. The code of professional responsibility provides a **joint venture** approach to the attorney-client relationship and provides a model by which the responsibilities in any representation are allocated between the attorney and the client.

joint venture
A grouping of two or more persons for a common goal.

The American Bar Association (ABA) adopted rules of ethics known as the Model Code of Professional Responsibility (Model Code). Originally adopted in 1908 as the Canon of Professional Ethics, it was last amended in 2002. In 1983, this code was replaced by the Model Rules of Professional Conduct (Model Rules). A lawyer's professional responsibility to clients is described in the ABA's Model Rules as well as in statutory and case law. These rules act as a framework to guide an attorney in the role of lawyer.

The ABA is a voluntary national organization. Because a lawyer does not have to belong, the ABA has no authority to bind a lawyer to its rules. However, many individual state bar associations have adopted the ABA's rules as their code of professional responsibility. In addition, federal, state, and local courts in all jurisdictions look to the Model Rules for guidance in resolving lawyer malpractice cases and determining disciplinary actions.

compulsory organization
An organization to which all persons of the same class must belong.

Many state bar associations are **compulsory organizations.** For these organizations, every lawyer in the state must belong to the association and abide by its code of ethics. Each state bar association adopts its own code of ethics. Some state bar associations have adopted the ABA's Model Rules entirely, without changes. Other states have adopted the Model Rules in part, making amendments as they see fit. And other states have established their own ethical rules, using the ABA's Model Rules as a guide. Always check an individual state's rules before relying on the ABA's Model Rules.

Role of the Lawyer

Lawyers are clients' representatives, officers of the legal system, and public citizens having special responsibilities for the quality of justice. As a client's representative, a lawyer performs three functions—the three As: advisor, advocate, and agent.

ADVISOR   As an advisor to a client, a lawyer will do five things:

1. Exercise independent judgment for the client
2. Be candid no matter how unpleasant the advice may be
3. Discourage illegal or fraudulent conduct
4. Inform the client of adverse consequences
5. Apprise the client of the proposed course of action

Model Rule 2.1 states:

> In representing a client, a lawyer shall exercise independent professional judgment and render candid advice. In rendering advice, a lawyer may refer not only to law, but to other considerations such as moral, economic, social and political factors that may be relevant to the client's situation.

The client sets the objective of an attorney-client relationship and makes the ultimate decisions. For the client to do so intelligently, the lawyer must inform the client of the relevant facts and issues and advise the client of the law regarding those facts and issues. A lawyer may be disciplined if she or he is negligent in advising a client of all relevant issues of the case.

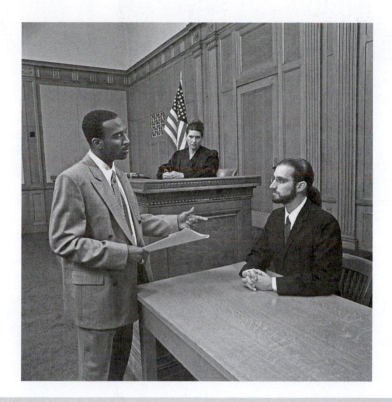

EXHIBIT 4–1   An Advocate Represents Clients in Court (Courtsey Artville Stock Images)

ADVOCATE   As a client's advocate, a lawyer will carry out three obligations:

1. Represent the client before a court or tribunal, as shown in Exhibit 4–1
2. Make reasonable efforts to expedite litigation consistent with the interest of the client
3. Not bring a claim that has no basis in fact, to harass another

Rule 3.1 of the Model Rules states:

> A lawyer shall not bring or defend a proceeding or assert or controvert an issue therein, unless there is a basis in law and fact for so doing that is not frivolous, which includes a good faith argument for an extension, modification or reversal of existing law. A lawyer for the defendant in a criminal proceeding or the respondent in a proceeding that could result in incarceration, may nevertheless so defend the proceeding as to require that every element of the case be established.

An advocate has a duty to use legal procedure and substantive law to the fullest benefit of a client. However, an advocate also has a duty to society and the legal system. An attorney also must act in the best interests of society and uphold the integrity of the legal system.

An advocate has an obligation to reject frivolous cases that take up a court's time and resources. A case is considered frivolous if an action is taken primarily to harass a person or to injure another maliciously. An example of a malicious action commenced to harass or injure another is a domestic case in which a woman consistently drags her former husband into court every 2 or 3 months seeking an increase in child support, when a need for the increase cannot be supported by the facts.

Of Interest . . .

CASE WAS FRIVOLOUS

A Pennsylvania man was fired by U.S. Steel in 1968. He felt the firing was unjustified and sued U.S. Steel for wrongful termination. He lost the case in 1971, but continued his feud with U.S. Steel for 28 years—until 1999. When he realized that his battle with U.S. Steel was futile, he blamed God for not bringing him justice in his dispute with U.S. Steel and sued Him.

The complaint alleged "God was the sovereign ruler of the universe and took no corrective action against the leaders of U.S. Steel for their extremely serious wrong, which ruined my life." It also complained that God failed to restore his youth and grant him the guitar-playing ability of famous guitarists. God also failed to resurrect his mother and pet pigeon. The plaintiff argued that if God failed to appear in court, He must lose by default.

In addition to God, the complaint listed other defendants including former presidents Ronald Reagan and George Bush, several television networks, all 50 states, every single American, the Federal Communications Commission, all federal judges, and the 100th through 105th congresses. The plaintiff represented himself and appeared in pro per.

U.S. District Judge Norman Mordue found the lawsuit frivolous.

A matter is also considered frivolous if a lawyer is unable to make a good-faith argument for a change in existing law. If a lawyer believes that a law or court ruling is wrong, the lawyer may challenge that law through the courts. If the challenge has no merit, the proceeding is considered frivolous.

The Model Rules has nine rules that relate to a lawyer's role as advocate (rules 3.1 through 3.9). In addition to the above, the rules impose the following duties upon the advocate:

- Expedite litigation in the interests of the client
- Be truthful to the court or tribunal
- Be fair and honest to the opposing party and do nothing to obstruct his or her case
- May not engage in conduct intended to disrupt a court
- Make no statement to the media that will be prejudicial to the proceeding
- May not be an advocate in a case in which the attorney is a witness
- A prosecutor may not prosecute a criminal matter that is not supported by probable cause
- Must adhere to disclosure requirements when representing a client in an administrative hearing or legislative body

AGENT   As a client's agent, a lawyer will perform four duties:

1. Seek results advantageous to the client while being honest and fair with others
2. Be a spokesperson for the client
3. Negotiate on the client's behalf
4. Abide by the client's decisions after informing the client of the issues of the case and the ramifications of the client's decision; a lawyer shall take such action on behalf of the client as is impliedly authorized to carry out the representation

Model Rule 1.2(a) states:

> A lawyer shall abide by a client's decisions concerning the objectives of representation and . . . shall consult with the client as to the means by which they are to be pursued. A lawyer may take such action on behalf of the client as is impliedly authorized to carry out the representation. A lawyer shall abide by a client's decision whether to settle a matter. In a criminal case, the lawyer shall abide by the client's decision, after consultation with the lawyer, as to a plea to be entered, whether to waive jury trial and whether the client will testify.

It is generally agreed that a lawyer has ultimate authority and responsibility to control the procedural elements and tactics of a client's case. However, when it comes to a settlement or binding a client to any provision of a contract, the client must consent. Lawyers have been disciplined for making decisions beyond their authority, against their client's wishes, and prejudicial to their client's interests. The extent of a lawyer's authority to bind a client is set forth in state statutes. States differ on this subject.

Role of the Paralegal

The attorney is ultimately responsible for an attorney-client relationship. The client may sue the attorney if a breach occurs in the attorney-client relationship. If a paralegal participates in a breach of an attorney-client relationship or violates any ethical rule, the attorney will be disciplined since the attorney is responsible for the paralegal's actions.

Paralegals are not bound by the rules of professional conduct of state bar associations. They are, however, considered lawyers' agents. As such, *every paralegal is ethically obligated to comply with the state bar association code of professional responsibility*. Therefore, paralegals must be familiar with the code of professional responsibility of the state, as well as the ABA's Model Rules.

ETHICS ALERT

Role of the Client

Clients' perceptions of the quality of legal services they receive are based on several factors. At a conference of the American Marketing Association, three professors reported the results of their study of how business executives evaluate outside legal counsel. The 341 respondents were chief executive officers (CEOs) or general counsels of large corporations. This survey indicated that the following were important to these CEOs, listed in order of importance:

- Results obtained from a firm's work
- Counsel and advice
- Expertise in a specific area
- Personal interest taken in a client's legal matters
- Quality of a written product
- Keeping a client informed of a firm's progress

Pay their bill to attorney

Of course, clients' opinions will vary by industry and individual. Another survey was taken of 65 CEOs of large Chicago companies. The following results were important to those CEOs, in order of importance:

- A compatible personality
- Proven experience in a particular issue
- Evidence of giving clients proper attention
- Accessibility
- Understanding a client's priorities

The four items clients generally want most from attorneys are commitment, integrity, commentary, and fairness in fees. Clients have listed commitment to their case as the most important element of an attorney-client relationship. Surveys have shown that clients are not as interested in results as they are in an attorney's zeal in representing them. Most important is that an attorney show an interest in a client's case and in the client as a person.

Surveys show that cost is not an important criterion when clients evaluate legal counsel. A busy Washington, DC, lawyer, overwhelmed with work, decided to raise her fees so that she could take on less work without losing money. After she raised her fees, her workload did not decrease but continued to increase.

Clients want lawyers who will help them meet their business or personal goals. To do this, a lawyer must take a personal interest in a client and the client's business. Often, a busy lawyer with a heavy trial schedule does not have the time to take a personal interest in clients. Paralegals can help lawyers by conveying to clients a message that a firm is interested in them.

Law firms and businesses in general focus on customer service and satisfaction as a major element of their company policy. Law firms have found that despite brilliant legal work done on the client's behalf, some clients were dissatisfied with the service because it lacked that "personal" touch. According to Milton W. Zwicker in his article ("What Clients Really Want from Their Lawyers,") clients want the following 10 traits in their lawyers:

1. Really listen to what the client has to say.
2. Ask the client what the client thinks about the subject.
3. Do not belittle or reject the client's concerns.
4. Treat the client like a person, not a file.
5. Speak to the client, not "at" the client.
6. Tell the client how much the legal services will cost.
7. Be available when the client needs the attorney.
8. Do not brag about past successes; rather, show the client expertise.
9. Keep the client informed.
10. Let the client know that the legal team cares about the client's case.

CULTIVATING CLIENTS

Satisfied clients are the best source of new clients for a firm. In general, 50 percent of new clients come from the recommendations of existing and former clients, 30 percent come from the recommendations of people who are not clients but would be if the occasion should arise (friends, associates, relatives), and 20 percent come from marketing activities.

netvertising
Advertising services on the Internet.

Marketing activities consist of client surveys, advertising, **netvertising,** and other promotional activities.

Marketing Activities

A firm's marketing activities are stated in a marketing plan. This plan is an essential element of successful client cultivation. It analyzes several variables that affect a firm's practice, such as external and internal conditions. The beginning of the planning stage includes gathering information about a firm, a firm's clients, and a firm's employees. This requires asking who, what, when, where, and why questions. A client questionnaire is often sent to clients to determine their perception of a firm. Once all the necessary information is gathered, marketing strategies are developed and placed into the plan.

Client Questionnaire
Black, White & Greene LLC
1212 Main St.
Anytown, IL

Thank you very much for consulting our office regarding your legal problem. We appreciate your trust and confidence. We are interested in improving our legal services and would appreciate your assisting us by completing this questionnaire. Your response will be confidential. Please use the following measurements: 5 = extraordinary, 4 = excellent, 3 = good, 2 = fair, 1 = poor.

1. Did you feel our office personnel were friendly and treated you courteously?
2. Why did you select our office originally?
3. Did our office keep you adequately informed regarding your legal matter? If not, do you have any suggestions for improving this area?
4. What was the nature of the legal work we did for you?
5. Did you feel the lawyer spent sufficient time with you on your legal matter?
6. Did you feel that sufficient attention and time were devoted to your legal matter?
7. Were your telephone inquiries answered to your satisfaction?
8. Were you satisfied with your dealings with the office staff?
9. Do you feel that our fee for services was reasonable for the work performed?
10. We would appreciate any comments that you might have that will help us improve our service to our clients. Please use the reverse side of this sheet if necessary.

THANK YOU very much for your time and courtesy in completing this questionnaire.

EXHIBIT 4–2 Sample Client Survey

Marketing is one of the top "non-law" activities that take place in an average week. On average, practicing law takes up 63 percent of a lawyer's week, managing the business takes up 14 percent of the week, and marketing activities take up 8 percent of the week. The majority of marketing responsibility lies with a partner, unless the firm has its own marketing director.

CLIENT SURVEYS As client satisfaction becomes increasingly important to law firms, client surveys are conducted on a regular basis to assess client satisfaction and identify areas of future need. Client surveys are gaining popularity as an essential element of a marketing strategy for law firms. An example of a client survey appears in Exhibit 4-2.

A marketing manager analyzes the information from client surveys to determine a firm's strengths, weaknesses, opportunities, and roadblocks. This is called **positioning** a firm. A position statement includes a description of a firm's position in the legal community as it relates to competitive firms and resources.

A firm then establishes a **target market** for its strategic plan. A target market is a group the firm wants to attract as clients. After an analysis of a firm's position, a marketing plan directed to the target market is developed.

MARKETING STRATEGIES Average attorneys have little or no education in marketing strategies and find themselves dealing in a foreign area when asked to prepare a marketing plan for a firm. Most attorneys do not want to be involved in marketing activities. Attorneys, feeling unfamiliar in this area, are hiring professional marketing people to handle marketing strategies for a firm (see Chapter 2). The emergence of this new professional for law firms has a promising future as attorney marketing becomes an integral part of law firm management. Law firm marketing directors have various titles, including director of client services, director of communications and business development, and economic development director.

positioning
Determining a firm's strengths and weaknesses in relation to those of other firms in the community.

target market
A group of people a firm wants as clients.

Law firms use various methods to attract clients. Marketing personnel go to great lengths to position a law firm to a specific target market. Once a target market has been determined, a firm's efforts and money are directed toward attracting those clients to the firm. Methods for attracting clients to the firm include advertising in print, radio, television, and the Internet; publishing law firm newsletters and brochures; sponsoring seminars; and providing leadership for community organizations.

Advertising

"All business entrusted to us will be attended to with promptness and fidelity." The year was 1853, and this ad appeared in the *Iroquois Journal*. It was placed by a young attorney, Abraham Lincoln, and his partner. In addition to newspaper advertising, Lincoln wrote letters soliciting business from the railroads, the wealthiest clients in Illinois in the 1800s. Such advertising was common at that time in the United States.

In 1908, the ABA adopted the first national standards for ethical conduct governing lawyers titled the Canons of Professional Ethics. These canons were patterned after the first code of ethics for lawyers, adopted by the Alabama Bar Association in 1887. Canon 27 banned lawyer advertising, including solicitation. The canons were adopted by individual states to control the conduct of lawyers and their marketing efforts. This was done to avoid "extravagant, artful, self-laudatory brashness" that could mislead laypersons and cause public distrust of the legal system. It was assumed that every lawyer had an established clientele that would spread the word of the lawyer's skill and abilities, thereby making advertising unnecessary. It was considered demeaning of the profession to advertise. It was also believed that advertisements had a negative effect on society. For example, the ABA felt that advertising divorce services might encourage the breakdown of the family unit.

In the 1970s, public interest groups and groups of lawyers began to question the validity of the advertising ban relative to the Sherman Antitrust Act and the free-speech guarantees of the First and Fourteenth Amendments to the U.S. Constitution.

"Do you need a lawyer? Legal services at very reasonable fees." The year was 1976, and this ad appeared in the *Arizona Republic*. It was placed by two young attorneys, Van O'Steen and John Bates, who opened a legal clinic in Phoenix. They were trying to attract the middle- to below-average income client in need of legal assistance, as shown in Exhibit 4–3.

The ad resulted in disciplinary action by the Arizona State Bar Association against the two Phoenix attorneys to suspend them from practicing law. The case, *Bates v. State Bar of Arizona*, 433 U.S. 350 (1977), was heard by the U.S. Supreme Court, which ruled that the ban on lawyer advertising was a violation of First Amendment guarantees of lawyers' right to advertise. The Court further found that the advertising restriction on lawyers was a restraint of trade. Justice Harry A. Blackmun wrote for the majority and declared that the First Amendment guaranteed lawyers the right to advertise. The primary dissenter was former Chief Justice Warren E. Burger, who was appalled at the prospect of his colleagues being involved in a price war. He insisted that "the public needs protection from the unscrupulous and incompetent practitioner anxious to prey on the uninformed." Justice Burger, until his retirement in 1986, continued to discourage lawyer advertising. In a speech made at a convention of the ABA in 1985, Justice Burger said, "My advice to the public is never, never, never, under any circumstances, engage the services of a lawyer who advertises." He went on to label advertising as pure shysterism and to say that he would dig ditches before advertising.

After the *Bates* decision, the ABA was faced with a dilemma. The *Bates* decision established a lawyer's right to advertise but did not address what type of advertising was appropriate. It quickly went to work to establish the ABA Task Force on Advertising (currently the ABA Commission on Lawyer Advertising), which conducted public hearings within 6 weeks of the *Bates* decision. It recommended two alternative amendments to the Model Code of Professional Responsibility to allow attorney advertising. Although it recognized that it could not prohibit attorney advertising, its goal was to impose strict regulations. The proposals adopted in February 1978 included

DO YOU NEED A LAWYER?

LEGAL SERVICES AT VERY REASONABLE FEES

- Divorce or legal separation – uncontested (both spouses sign papers)

  $175.00 plus $20.00 court filing fee

- Preparation of all court papers and instructions on how to do your own simple uncontested divorce

  $100.00

- Adoption – uncontested severance proceeding

  $225.00 plus approximately $10.00 publication cost

- Bankruptcy – non-business, no contested proceedings

  Individual
  $250.00 plus $55.00 court filing fee

  Wife and husband
  $300.00 plus $110.00 court filing fee

- Change of Name

  $95.00 plus $20.00 court filing fee

Information regarding other types of cases furnished upon request.

Legal Clinic of Bates & O'Steen
817 North 3rd Street
Phoenix, Arizona 85004
Telephone: (602) 555-5555

EXHIBIT 4–3 Bates & O'Steen Ad

a list of 25 types of information lawyers were permitted to communicate in an advertisement. Included in the list were provisions allowing the announcement of fields of practice, professional memberships, foreign-language ability, and six provisions governing fees. The list was preceded by a requirement that any such information be presented in a "dignified manner." The term *dignified manner* was further defined in later case law.

Lawyers' advertisements began to test the regulations. A California lawyer ran a score card of his murder trials and their dispositions in a newspaper. Another attorney, Ken

Hur, ran a television ad in Madison, Wisconsin, in which he played a convict whose final words from the electric chair were that he wished he would have called Hur's legal clinic. A Connecticut firm ran an ad of an actor taking a chain saw to furniture while a voice-over talked about better ways to divide community property. Each of these ads was subject to scrutiny by the state bars, which tried to ban them. In 1980, the U.S. Supreme Court heard the case of *Central Hudson Gas & Electric Corporation v. Public Service Commission of New York*, 447 U.S. 557 (1980). In that case, the Supreme Court developed a four-part test to determine whether a state's restriction of lawyer advertising was unconstitutional. It ruled that in order to enjoy First Amendment protection

- the advertisement must not concern unlawful activity or be misleading.
- there must be a substantial state interest in the regulation.
- the regulation must directly advance the asserted interest.
- the court will ask whether the regulation is more extensive than necessary.

ABA Model Rule 7.2 regulates lawyers' advertising activities by imposing the following guidelines:

> (a) . . . [A] lawyer may advertise services through written, recorded or electronic communication, including public media.
>
> (b) A lawyer shall not give anything of value to a person for recommending the lawyer's services except that a lawyer may
>
> > (1) pay the reasonable costs of advertisements or communications permitted by this Rule;
> >
> > (2) pay the usual charges of a legal service plan or not-for-profit or qualified lawyer referral service. A qualified lawyer referral service is a lawyer referral service that has been approved by an appropriate regulatory authority;
> >
> > (3) pay for a law practice in accordance with Rule 1.17, and
> >
> > (4) refer clients to another lawyer or a nonlawyer professional pursuant to an agreement not otherwise prohibited under these Rules that provides for the other person to refer clients or customers to the lawyer, if the reciprocal referral agreement is not exclusive, and the client is informed of the existence and nature of the agreement.
>
> (c) Any communication made pursuant to this rule shall include the name and office address of at least one lawyer or law firm responsible for its content.

In addition to the ABA's Model Rules, states have devised their own rules concerning attorney advertisements. Every state now has incorporated advertising regulations in their ethics rules. In fact, in the 15-month period from April 1991 to June 1992, more advertising regulatory activity took place than in the 15 years since the *Bates* decision. Since 1992, there has been little change in lawyer advertising regulations. The Supreme Court's expansion of commercial free speech, coupled with aggressive regulatory efforts, ensures that the advertising debate will continue into the foreseeable future.

A typical law firm spends between 2 and 4 percent of its gross revenue on advertising. A law firm that does television advertising will spend more. One firm that advertises on television reported that it spent 14 percent of its gross revenues on advertising.

Attorneys have used the following advertising techniques: print media, radio, television, and the Internet.

PRINT MEDIA Advertising in print media includes letterheads, newspapers, periodicals, and telephone directories. In regulating print media advertisements, the ABA adopted Model Rule 7.1:

> A lawyer shall not make a false or misleading communication about the lawyer or the lawyer's services. A communication is false or misleading if it contains a material

misrepresentation of fact or law, or omits a fact necessary to make the statement considered as a whole not materially misleading.

Letterhead   Although not circulated among the public like other, more conventional print advertising, an attorney's letterhead has been determined to be an advertising medium and, therefore, is subject to Model Rule 7.5:

> (a) A lawyer shall not use a firm name, letterhead or other professional designation that violates Rule 7.1. A trade name may be used by a lawyer in private practice if it does not imply a connection with a government agency or with a public or charitable legal services organization and is not otherwise in violation of Rule 7.1.
>
> (b) A law firm with offices in more than one jurisdiction may use the same name or other professional designation in each jurisdiction, but identification of the lawyers in an office of the firm shall indicate the jurisdictional limitations on those not licensed to practice in the jurisdiction where the office is located.
>
> (c) The name of a lawyer holding a public office shall not be used in the name of a law firm, or in communications on its behalf, during any substantial period in which the lawyer is not actively and regularly practicing with the firm.
>
> (d) Lawyers may state or imply that they practice in a partnership or other organization only when that is the fact.

It is acceptable to have the firm's website address on its letterhead, but trade names must be used so it is not misleading. For example, the name "Jefferson County Legal Clinic" might be confused with a governmental legal aid agency, so it would be misleading if it is used by a private law firm.

Rules regarding specialty advertising vary by state. In those states that have certified specialist programs, only attorneys who have passed an exam in that area may advertise themselves as a certified specialist in that area of law (see Chapter 2). Some states, especially those with no specialist program, prohibit the use of the term *specialist* on letterheads and promotional material. ABA Model Rule 7.4 states in pertinent part:

> (a) A lawyer may communicate the fact that the lawyer does or does not practice in particular fields of law.
>
> . . .
>
> (d) A lawyer shall not state or imply that a lawyer is certified as a specialist in particular field of law, unless:
>
> > (1) the lawyer has been certified as a specialist by an organization that has been approved by an appropriate state authority or that has been accredited by the American Bar Association; and
> >
> > (2) the name of the certifying organization is clearly identified in the communication.

Illinois attorney Gary E. Peel indicated on his letterhead that he was "certified as a civil trial specialist by the National Board of Trial Advocacy." The Illinois Attorney Registration and Disciplinary Commission accused Peel of violating its ethical rules pertaining to the specialist prohibition. The Illinois Supreme Court agreed and said that the title was misleading (*In re Peel*, 126 Ill. 2d 397 [1989]). The U.S. Supreme Court heard the case and disagreed with the Illinois ruling (*Peel v. Illinois*, 110 S.Ct. 2281 [1990]). The Court ruled that a state cannot completely ban statements that are not misleading, such as certification as a specialist by bona fide organizations such as the National Board of Trial Advocacy. Illinois and other states were forced to amend their rules to accommodate the U.S. Supreme Court's ruling.

Newspapers   Advertising in the newspaper was the original method lawyers used to reach the public. The ads originally appeared in the classifieds section of a newspaper, but in the 1980s, lawyers have found that a much more lucrative location is the business page. Now, attorney ads are found in all areas of the newspaper.

TRENDS

ATTORNEYS' LETTERHEADS
LESS TRADITIONAL

Traditionally, law firm letterheads had the same style: firm name centered at the top of the page in black with partners' and associates' names listed. In 1992, Baker & McKenzie became the first major firm to have its name in a brilliant red color across the top of the stationery. Now, law firms are having stationery printed in two colors and are creating firm logos and letterheads with a less traditional look. Partners' and associates' names are being left off the letterhead. Producing new letterheads every time there was a change in the firm proved to be too expensive. Another money-saving trend is to print the letterhead on laser printers at the same time a letter is printed. However, a survey conducted by Altman Weil Pensa titled "Comparative Study of Law Firm Identity Systems" indicated that such practices make a poor impression on clients.

Saddleback Financial Center   Telephone (949) 465-0011
24012 Calle de la Plata, Suite 120   Facsimile   (949) 465-9910
Laguna Hills, California 92653   E-Mail ssgapc@ix.netcom.com
                                      Practice Established 1970

SHELDON S. GOODMAN
ATTORNEY AT LAW
A PROFESSIONAL CORPORATION

Periodicals   Law firms also advertise in various periodicals, including magazines and news-letters. Once a firm's target market is identified, ads are placed in periodicals directed to that market. For example, an attorney specializing in defending attorneys in discipline proceedings would place an ad, such as the ad shown in Exhibit 4–4, in bar association periodicals.

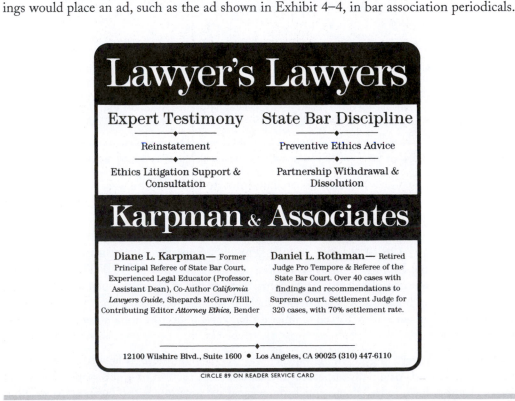

EXHIBIT 4–4   Ad from a Bar Association Periodical *(California Lawyer)* *(Reprinted with Permission of Karpman & Associates.)*

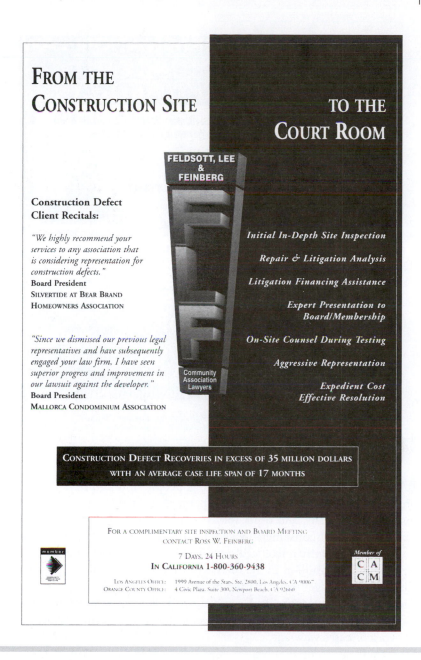

EXHIBIT 4–5   Ad from a Homeowners' Association Newsletter *(Reprinted with Permission of Feldsott, Lee & Feinberg.)*

A firm specializing in construction defect litigation would place an ad, such as the ad shown in Exhibit 4–5, in a homeowners' association newsletter.

The type of periodical or directory in which attorneys advertise has been the subject of a state's ethics rules. In 2007, the New Jersey Supreme Court Committee on Attorney Advertising issued an opinion banning attorneys from advertising in "Super Lawyer" or "Best Lawyers" publications. In their opinion, the name of the directory compared their lawyers with other lawyers, which is a violation of the state's ethical rules. The ban was stayed pending review by the New Jersey Supreme Court.

Yellow Pages   The most common method of attorney advertising is a listing in the Yellow Pages of the telephone book (see Exhibit 4–6). More lawyers advertise in the Yellow Pages than any other method by an overwhelming percentage. In some communities, more space in the Yellow Pages is dedicated to lawyer ads than to any other product or service. According

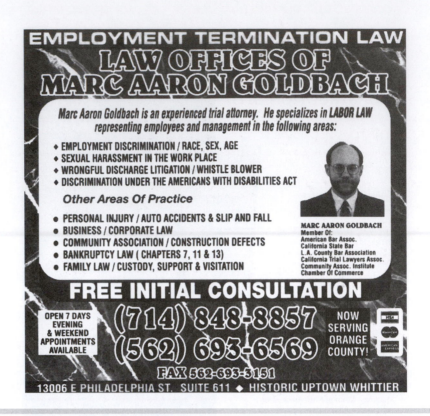

EXHIBIT 4–6   Ad from the Yellow Pages

to the ABA Commission on Lawyer Advertising, people find attorneys through the Yellow Pages more than any other method of selection, more so than bar-sponsored lawyer referral services, prepaid legal plans, and other forms of advertising. The Yellow Pages Publishers Association reported that consumers looked up attorneys about 350 million times, making it the eighth most frequently referenced classification in the Yellow Pages.

Lawyers spent $800 million in Yellow Pages advertising in 2000. Most attorneys who advertise in the Yellow Pages feel that their money is well spent. Pennsylvania attorney Mark David Frankel reserved the entire back cover of two Yellow Page directories. He said, "Since we began using the back cover in April 1994, we've seen a 75 percent increase in clients. And they're the types of cases we want."

However, there are some disadvantages to Yellow Pages advertising. According to Los Angeles sole practitioner Susan Lavian, a full-page Yellow Pages ad is expensive. A full-page display ad with a photo in the Yellow Pages costs about $60,000. In addition, there are added overhead costs in hiring additional staff to screen calls and follow up on the calls. Ms. Lavian indicated that out of every 100 calls, 25 percent are cases she would take, 10 percent bring in referral income, and the remainder are put on her mailing list.

Yellow Pages advertising popularity is decreasing because of its expense. Lawyers are spending less on Yellow Pages advertising today than they did three years ago. They are putting those dollars in netvertising.

RADIO   Advertising on the radio is becoming more common. Often, law firms will sponsor segments of a radio program, such as news or special announcements. Producing a radio talk show about the law, with an attorney moderator, is a popular method of exposing a firm to the public. The Los Angeles firm of Sheppard, Mullin, Richter & Hampton sponsors *The NewsHour with Jim Lehrer* for about $200,000 a year. The firm reported that the sponsorship has surpassed print advertising in terms of name recognition.

TELEVISON   Lawyers take advantage of the public exposure afforded them by television advertisements. Television advertising was largely responsible for the legal clinics' success.

Jacoby & Meyers Legal Clinic started advertising on television in the early 1970s and quickly expanded to 150 offices nationwide by 1977. It sparked their competitors to follow suit, resulting in many television ads in the 1980s.

Television advertising has come under the scrutiny of state bar associations, and many attorneys have been disciplined for advertising messages that mislead the public. For example, an attorney advertised, "If you are injured in an automobile accident, or at work, call me. No fee until I win for you." The California State Bar found this advertising to be misleading because, even though the case was a **contingency** case, the client incurred fees for costs, such as filing fees, investigation fees, deposition costs, and so on. The attorney was required to stop this advertisement and develop a new one. The new advertisement said the same thing, except it had a disclaimer stating, "Does not include fees for costs."

contingency
A case in which a lawyer receives a percentage of the recovery rather than a flat amount of money.

Of Interest . . .

THE PIT BULL LAWYERS

Two Florida lawyers have received a public reprimand from the state's Supreme Court for branding themselves as the Pit Bull lawyers. They used the image of a pit bull as a logo and advertised the telephone number 1-800-Pit-Bull in their TV ads. Stressing the issue of the legal profession's image, the court stated that the logo and phone number "demean all lawyers and thereby harm both the legal profession and the public's trust and confidence in our system of justice."

The court overturned a referee's finding that the ethics rules where unconstitutional as applied to this matter. At the time of the referee's decision, it was reported that the only nonlawyer who complained was a pit bull breeder who claimed that the association with lawyers was pulling down the image of the breed.

Concerns about television advertising have prompted state legislation. The Iowa and New Jersey Supreme Courts require that television advertisements be "predominantly informational." Some states do not allow dramatizations. Others specifically exclude scenes of wrecked vehicles or planes. Many states have determined that testimonials create unrealistic expectations. In Florida, the attorney must be in the commercial—no actors are allowed. The key consideration in evaluating the content of lawyer advertising is that it not be false, misleading, or deceptive. Many state bar associations have special task forces to regulate lawyers' television ads, and some have considered banning television ads altogether.

Television ads have been used to attract a specific class of people. For example, when phen-fen was discovered to be harmful to people's health, law firms representing former phen-fen users produced television ads that informed the public that they may be entitled to compensation if they had previously taken the drug. The phen-fen settlement fund increased from $1 billion to $13 billion. Wyeth, the drug's manufacturer, asserts that it traced the increase to the mass recruitment of new claimants through television and newspaper advertising.

Television is used for other issues as well. Known as "issues advertising," television segments directly target those with a specific problem. In Texas, the issue is house mold. In Illinois, it is nursing home care. Television is also used for political issues. Critics claim that issues advertising sways potential jurors and damages the jury pool.

Television advertising is expensive. An average commercial in a midsized market can cost as much as $500,000. Two or three customized ads cost about $20,000 to produce, and a modest run of the ad will cost about $25,000 a month. Attorneys who advertise on television have reported a return of $6 to $10 on every dollar spent on television advertising. One firm that advertises its personal injury services reported a 300 percent return on each dollar spent on television advertising.

Another method of promoting a firm through television is to host a television show. Frederic G. Levin of Levin, Middlebrooks, Mabie, Thomas, Mayes & Mitchell in Pensacola, Florida, is the creator of Blab Television, which produces *Law Line*. On this show, Levin interviews prominent lawyers on various legal subjects of interest to the public. Levin indicates that in the approximately 5 years following the show's first airing, the firm's gross fees tripled.

THE INTERNET The Internet has become an essential tool for law firms. Lawyers use the Internet to locate experts, research opinions, retrieve court rules and information, and obtain continuing education credits. Lawyers also use the Internet to advertise their services and promote their firms. This form of electronic advertising is called netvertising. Among the benefits of advertising on the Internet are the following:

- It can reach untapped client bases.
- It is cost effective.
- It delivers information effectively.
- It provides an excellent marketing complement.
- It can enhance the firm's image.
- It reduces geographic barriers.
- It can be used as a recruitment tool.

In November, 1994, five law firms had websites on the Internet. Seven months later, that figure grew to 500. In 2007, 80 percent of all law firms have a website. The firm website is considered the firm's most valuable marketing tool.

The ABA has not issued a specific rule for Internet advertising, but it applies Model Rule 7.1 to websites. Most states have concluded that advertising on the Internet is acceptable if it complies with its other advertising guidelines.

Of Interest . . .

ARE WEBSITES CONSIDERED NETVERTISING?

This controversial subject has drawn the attention of state regulatory agencies for the past decade. Adding things to websites such as blogs, hyperlinks to legal information, and inducements to the reader, the sites begin to look more and more like legal advertising. According to *Zauderer v. Office of Disciplinary Counsel,* 471 U.S. 626,639, 105 S.Ct. 2265, 2274-75 (1985), websites that include free legal information are advertising. Under the *Zauderer* reasoning, informative websites that contain any kind of solicitation are advertising and subject to regulation.

In *Texans Against Censorship, Inc. v. State Bar of Texas,* 888 F.Supp. 1328 (E.D. Tx 1995), the court found that it is only when the message conveyed by the communication suggests to the public, or a specific individual, that the lawyer's professional services are available for hire that the communication must meet the ethical rules of the state. It would seem that this statement suggests that any time an attorney includes the firm name or address, that he may be suggesting that he is available for hire. Firms have put disclaimers on their websites indicating that the information in the website is for general information only, but disclaimers may not stop the website from being subject to state regulation.

To summarize a complicated subject matter, it appears that a home page that only provides accurate general information about the law and law firm is not advertising and not subject to regulation. However, if the general information is followed by an invitation to employ or contact the attorney, the entire page will be considered an advertisement and will be subject to regulation. An attorney may also be subject to discipline for fraudulent behavior if he hides his identity as the author of the website and then uses it to gain new clients.

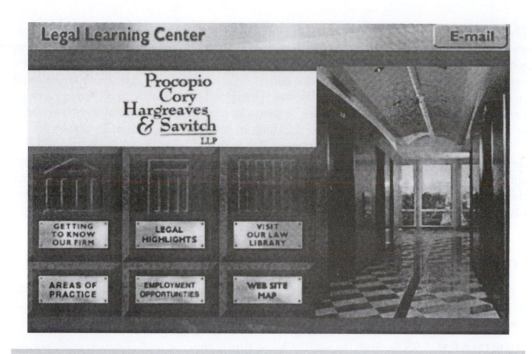

EXHIBIT 4–7   Example of Law Firm Website *(Reprinted with Permission of Procopio, Cory, Hargreaves & Savitch, LLP and SiteLab International.)*

Since the Internet has no state boundaries, it is difficult to determine which state's rules apply. To determine what rules apply to a website, the following factors are considered:

- The state in which members of the firm are authorized to practice
- The state in which the firm is seeking clients
- The state in which the firm practices
- The website's content

If the website's content is for information purposes only (newsletters, articles, public information), chances are that it would not fall under the jurisdiction of advertising rules. If the website's content is for the purpose of attracting clients (attorney biographies, areas of specialties), it would fall under the jurisdiction of the state's ethics rules. Many lawyers view their websites to be an electronic firm brochure. While some aspects of a website are analogous to print advertising, other elements are unique to cyberspace. An example of a law firm website is shown in Exhibit 4–7.

Virtually every state has incorporated Rule 7.1 into its ethics rules prohibiting false and misleading information and lawyer comparisons in netvertisements. As such, phrases used in websites, such as "best lawyers," "highly qualified," and "expert" have been determined to violate Model Rule 7.1 since they make a comparison to other attorneys.

Netvertising may pose other ethical problems, such as the unauthorized practice of law. Other advertising mediums such as newspaper, radio, and television have a limited jurisdiction of the advertisement. In comparison, the Internet has no such boundaries. Once a lawyer posts an advertisement on the Internet in the form of a website, the netvertisement solicits clients from all over the world. The Internet has no station range or circulation limitation, and this poses one of the biggest ethical problems with netvertising. For example, a Georgia lawyer might place an advertisement on a local television station where the broadcast range of that advertisement will not go outside of Georgia and thus not outside the area in which the lawyer is licensed to practice law. However, a Georgia lawyer's netvertisement may be read around the world or at the very least, outside the jurisdiction in which the lawyer is licensed to practice law. Not only is this misleading, but it is also potentially the unauthorized practice of law.

blog
The term blog is short for web log. A web log is a journal (or newsletter) that contains Internet links and is intended for public consumption and participation.

Blogs   For many lawyers, **blogs** have become a popular marketing tool. The term blog is short for weblog. A weblog is a journal (or newsletter) that contains Internet links and is intended for public consumption and participation. Most weblogs allow readers to follow conversations by following links between entries on related topics. Legal blogs are devoted to one or two subjects that pertain to the law. Developed primarily by small-firm practitioners and legal scholars, some large firms' websites link to blogs authored by their attorneys, and the trend is catching on. There are hundreds of blogs on hundreds of legal subjects.

State bars are looking at blogs to determine if they should be regulated as advertising. If so, the requirement that law firms file their advertisements with their state's ethics committee could stifle blogs. Some blog owners are putting lengthy disclaimers on their websites to clarify that the blog is not intended as an advertisement. But some legal scholars think that the disclaimer makes no difference in determining whether states can regulate blogs as commercial speech.

Promotional Activities

Law firms have undertaken other activities to promote their business, including sponsoring seminars, joining community organizations, writing articles for trade publications, speaking at conferences or continuing education classes, and publishing brochures, newsletters, and articles.

SEMINARS   Some firms, especially large firms, sponsor and conduct seminars for their clients, as shown in Exhibit 4–8. A firm with a large corporate client may give an educational seminar to that client, free of charge, in areas that are of interest to that client. This helps keep the corporate client informed and creates a personal rapport with the client. Firms may also cosponsor seminars with other organizations, such as banks, real estate companies, and accounting firms.

COMMUNITY ORGANIZATIONS   A potential client base exists in various community organizations. Such groups as the Rotary Club, Lions Club, Elks Club, and Moose Lodge are known for providing networking opportunities for various professionals. Some community organizations allow only one representative from each profession.

ARTICLES   Writing articles for legal or nonlegal publications gives an attorney and a firm exposure. In addition, writing on a particular area of law that other attorneys rely on gives an author a reputation of "expert" in the field. Often, the author is invited to speak publicly on the subject. Attorneys also post the articles they write on a website.

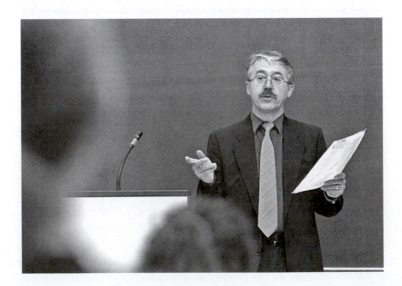

EXHIBIT 4–8   Law Firms Sponsor Seminars for Clients

welcome to the

B&B

LAW OFFICES of

Boyd & Boyd, P.C.

403 Masonic Street
Dyersburg, Tennessee 38024
901-285-8900

we thank you
for choosing
our law firm

* * * *

We appreciate your confidence in us. We will do all we can to earn your continued faith.

If you are a new client, you will benefit from knowing some things about your new law firm, and this booklet will help explain our office procedures so you can best follow the progress of your legal matter. If you are an "old" valued client, perhaps this will refresh your recollection. We will try to answer each of your questions as best we can. And we truly welcome your friendship and comments.

Why Choose a Firm of Lawyers?

In this age of specialization, we have divided our staff into various categories based on each lawyer's training, knowledge, and experience. By choosing our firm, you are getting more than one lawyer who will be interested in your case and who will use his or her knowledge in seeing that your case is properly handled.

How Will I Know Which Lawyer In the Firm Is Best for Me?

Choosing the lawyer on our staff who can best represent you will be carefully done so

that you can take full advantage of our skills. Accordingly, it may not be possible, or even advantageous, to have one attorney handle all of your legal matters. However, our weekly staff meetings are designed to keep each of us informed of all developments. One lawyer will be responsible for the overall progress of your case, but from time to time another lawyer may perform certain duties within the case itself. Please do not be disturbed if your case is handled by a different attorney within our firm. "Your lawyer" will still be your lawyer. This is merely another sign to you that we are doing our best to handle your case as professionally as possible.

How Will I Be Kept Informed of My Case?

We intend to keep you informed whenever there is something important happening concerning your case. Therefore, we normally send you copies of all incoming and outgoing correspondence and other documents which relate to your case. These materials are stamped "For Your Information," and you should look them over carefully to see if any mistakes or misunderstandings have occurred or if we have missed any point which you think might be important.

In addition, you should receive a letter from us about every 60 days concerning the status of your case, if it takes several months to resolve.

Although we would like to talk to you every week, this is not very practical, so we ask you to call us only if you have important new information. If you change your address or job, or if there is a mistake or misunderstanding in any of the materials we have sent you. Much of this information can be given to the secretary or to the legal assistant without the necessity of talking to your lawyer, and your lawyer will

then call you back if it is necessary to discuss the information with you.

What Do I Do When I Have a Question?

We are interested in your questions. We want you to ask them. Unfortunately, much of a lawyer's time and duties take him or her out of the office for trials and other work, even for days at a time. Also, like all professional people, we frequently have clients in our office, and cannot manage to answer all our calls. In that case, ask the secretary; you will be pleased at how informed and helpful she can be. If she cannot answer your question, she will get the answer for you, or arrange to have your legal assistant or attorney contact you. Oftentimes she will refer you to the legal assistant handling your case, who will be familiar with the details of your matter and will be in a position to discuss it with you. Above all, leave a message so we know your concern in advance. If you do that, we will always try to get an answer back to you even if your attorney is out of the office when you call.

Who Is the Legal Assistant?

As an essential part of our team, our office employs legal assistants to handle various aspects of your matters. These are highly trained and very competent persons who have taken special college courses to be able to assist the lawyers in rendering legal services. If a legal assistant is assigned to your case, you will normally be introduced to that person during your initial visit to our office. If you have any questions about your case or matter or need to furnish additional information, call the legal assistant first. If the legal assistant feels that you need to talk to the lawyer handling the case, you will be put in touch with that lawyer as soon as possible.

EXHIBIT 4–9 Sample Law Firm Brochure

PUBLIC SPEAKING Speaking at lawyers' conventions, continuing education courses, and organizational meetings gives an attorney and a firm exposure. Although not directed at the public for cultivating clients, being known as an expert in a particular field gives a firm an opportunity for referrals from other attorneys. When an attorney refers a client to a firm, that client has the potential of referring other clients to the firm.

BROCHURES Most law firms have brochures, such as the one shown in Exhibit 4–9. Typically, a law firm brochure is 8 to 20 pages in length, is professionally designed, and includes inserts showing a firm's practice areas and lawyer biographies. Midsize firms are more likely than large firms to include biographical information about their owner or owners. Many brochures are illustrated with photos or drawings, and some include photos of a firm's lawyers. Firm brochures are considered an effective marketing tool by most attorneys.

NEWSLETTERS Almost three-fourths of all large firms publish a newsletter. A newsletter can help a firm attain a variety of goals, including the following:

- Reminding clients of their obligation to file reports with government agencies
- Informing clients about new developments in the law
- Informing clients about services available from the firm

Jones Day, a 2,200-lawyer firm with offices in 30 cities around the world, distributes a number of newsletters from its information systems services group. Its first newsletter came out in 1988. A list of its newsletters is found on its website at <http://www.jonesday.com>.

A combination of four different trends has contributed to the success of the law firm newsletter.

1. Desktop publishing and laser printers
2. Increased usage of personal computers in law firms
3. Awareness of increasing demands for technical support
4. Spread of multiple offices that are connected to a computer network

Newsletters are used to get referrals, obtain clients, keep existing clients, and create visibility, as shown in Exhibit 4–10. Newsletters are also tied to promotional strategies. For example, articles published in newsletters can be sent to prospective clients and distributed at trade conferences. Newsletters can also be posted on a firm's website. To save postage and expedite delivery, firms are posting their newsletters on their websites and sending e-mails to clients with a link to the newsletter.

On the whole, newsletters are read and are useful. They generate goodwill and enhance client relations. General counsels state that they appreciate a little free legal advice and that a firm increases its recognition through newsletters.

The various marketing activities discussed here are important to build a law practice. In 2005, LexisNexis Martindale-Hubbell commissioned a study on how small law firms market their firms to clients. The *Martindale-Hubbell Small Firm Marketing Index*, conducted by Harris Interactive, surveyed 1,000 small firms throughout the country. The results of the study revealed that networking and word-of-mouth are still essential to building a law practice. As to marketing activities, it revealed that 89 percent of law firms view their

EXHIBIT 4–10 How Managing Partners and Marketing Directors Rate Newsletters *(National Law Firm Marketing Association survey on newsletters to clients.)*

websites as advertising and that most of a firm's advertising budget is spent on print advertising (Yellow Pages).

Public Relations

Most professionals do not know the difference between advertising and public relations. These are different methods of communicating a firm's services to the public. Advertising involves purchasing media space to promote a firm's practice and build a firm's image. Public relations is developing and maintaining a favorable public image between a law firm and a community.

Public relations consists of participation in community and social activities as well as the publicity a firm receives on high-exposure cases. Once a firm gets its name in a newspaper, the chances of the paper repeating its name are very slim—unless the firm has another story that is newsworthy. A firm cannot dictate when the agencies of mass communication will run a story or where the story will be located in a newspaper. A journalist creates a story's content and may leave out important information, such as the firm's location and phone number.

Law firms hire public relations firms to increase the firm's visibility and create a positive public image. The public relations firm teams up with the law firm in its marketing strategies to create press releases and advertisements for the firm, such as the one shown in Exhibit 4–11.

Advertising allows a firm to repeat publicity as often as it would like. Repetition is very important in building awareness of a firm and its specialties. Most important, a firm has total control over a message conveyed to the public and may include information it feels is important to attract new clients. In addition, an advertisement can be scheduled to appear at specific times when potential clients would most likely see it.

Public relations has more credibility than advertising since its source is presumably objective and nonbiased. Making reprints of public relations news stories and sending them to clients is a clever marketing tool.

Solicitation

Solicitation of clients is one of the most complicated—and ethically dangerous—areas in which attorneys and paralegals work. The rules vary from jurisdiction to jurisdiction and include such areas as in-person contact, direct-mail solicitation, conduct of agents, and the Internet. However, the various rules do not define exactly what solicitation is, so it must be determined by case law that defines the term. One of the most difficult questions in lawyer solicitation involves multistate compliance with rules. *What is proper in one state may be improper in another.*

The ABA has strict rules prohibiting lawyers' direct solicitation of potential clients. Its Model Rule 7.3 has four parts dealing with solicitation, as follows:

(a) A lawyer shall not by in-person, live telephone, or real-time electronic contact solicit professional employment from a prospective client when a significant motive for the lawyer's doing so is the lawyer's pecuniary gain, unless the person contacted:

(1) is a lawyer; or

(2) has a family, close personal, or prior professional relationship with the lawyer.

(b) A lawyer shall not solicit professional employment from a prospective client by written, recorded or electronic communication or by in-person, telephone or real-time electronic communication or by in-person, telephone or real-time electronic contact even when not otherwise prohibited by paragraph (a) if:

(1) the prospective client has made known to the lawyer a desire not to be solicited by the lawyer; or

(2) the solicitation involves coercion, duress or harassment.

NEWS RELEASE

FROM: Law offices of Black, White & Greene LLC

FOR IMMEDIATE RELEASE
REAL ESTATE ATTORNEY AYERS CALLS ON LAWYERS TO
DEMONSTRATE RELIABILITY OF TIME-SHARE INDUSTRY

LOS ANGELES, CA, June 6, 2003—"As an industry that has come into its own and has already passed the billion dollar mark, time-sharing doesn't need to prove its viability any longer. What it does need to prove is its *reliability.* And real estate attorneys must aid in that process, by ensuring that the time-share projects they structure or represent are well planned and honestly presented to the public."

That statement reflected the tone of remarks presented today by Robert Black, partner in charge of the Real Estate Department of the Law Offices of Black, White & Greene, to the Real Estate Section of the California State Bar Association.

A leader in the area of time-share law, Black explained the basic concept of real estate time-sharing and discussed existing and proposed state and federal regulations for the industry. "In addition to the many proposed state regulations, which are often needed to ensure consumer protection in this relatively new industry, I think we will see greater self-regulation by the industry. That will occur simply because reputable developers will insist on it to guarantee their credibility," he said.

"Image is the key today in time-share projects," Black added. "Not only must the projects we represent be structured honestly, employ ethical marketing techniques, and obtain sufficient capitalization, but they must also be seen to possess those attributes. And we must work with regulators, not against them, to see that the industry is established on a strong regulatory foundation."

A member of the National Timesharing Council of the American Land Development Association, Black serves on the NTC's State and Federal Regulations and Standards and Ethics Committee. He was co-chairman of the NTC—National Association of Real Estate Licensed Law Officials committee that drafted the model time-share law now being considered for state-by-state implementation.

As an attorney, Black has represented numerous developers of both domestic and foreign time-share projects over the past 8 years. His articles on time-share law have appeared in such publications as *Real Estate Update, Resort Timesharing,* and the *National Law Journal.*

In addition to his law and real estate industry activities, Black is Chairman of the Board of Commissioners of the Los Angeles Housing Authority, a member of the California Real Estate Commission, and advisor to the American Resort Commission.

A graduate of the University of Southern California and UCLA School of Law, Black lives in Santa Monica, California.

EXHIBIT 4–11   Sample Press Release

(c) Every written, recorded or electronic communication from a lawyer soliciting professional employment from a prospective client known to be in need of legal services in a particular matter shall include the words "Advertising Material" on the outside envelope, if any, and at the beginning and ending of any recorded or electronic communication, unless the recipient of the communication is a person specified in paragraphs (a)(1) or (a)(2).

(d) Notwithstanding the prohibitions in paragraph (a), a lawyer may participate with a prepaid or group legal service plan operated by an organization not owned or directed by the lawyer that uses in-person or telephone contact to solicit memberships or subscriptions for the plan from persons who are not known to need legal services in a particular matter covered by the plan.

Generally, a lawyer may not personally contact a person, unrelated or unassociated with the lawyer, and inform that person of the legal services the lawyer has to offer if the lawyer's objective is monetary gain. The justification for the prohibition is that lawyers are trained in the art of persuasion and that people in need of legal services may be emotionally vulnerable and subject to overreaching. The U.S. Supreme Court stated in *Ohralik v. Ohio State Bar Association*, 426 U.S. 447 (1978), "In-person solicitation is a practice rife with possibilities for overreaching, invasion of privacy, the exercise of undue influence fraud."

For example, if a lawyer is attending a cocktail party one evening and is speaking to an acquaintance who informs the lawyer that she is deeply in debt and is considering bankruptcy, the lawyer may not inform the acquaintance of his ability to represent her in the bankruptcy proceeding. However, if the acquaintance mentions her desire to file bankruptcy and requests the lawyers' services, the lawyer may accept the case without being accused of soliciting.

DIRECT MAIL Through time, the ABA's rules regarding direct mail have changed with case law rulings. For example, in 1988, Model Rule 7.3 prohibited direct-mail solicitation. The Supreme Court ruled in *Shapero v. Kentucky Bar Association*, 108 S.Ct. 64 (1988), that direct-mail solicitation was constitutionally protected free speech. The Court said that lawyers could send mail specifically to those known to be in need of services, such as accident victims, judgment debtors, and foreclosure defendants. In 1989, the ABA modified Rule 7.3 to comply with the court's ruling, but added a provision that all such direct-mail advertisements be clearly labeled as such.

Direct-mail advertising has never been a popular form of advertising with bar associations. In 1989, Florida attorneys were mailing 700,000 direct-mail solicitations per year, 40 percent of which were aimed at accident victims or their survivors. The Florida Bar Association conducted a random sampling of recipients of the direct-mail campaign that revealed that 45 percent believed that the solicitation was designed to take advantage of gullible people, and 27 percent reported having a lower regard for the legal profession because of the mailings. The Florida Bar Association sought to ban direct-mail solicitation to accident victims and their families, and the lawyers challenged the ban.

The case of *Florida Bar v. Went For It, Inc.,* was heard by the Florida Supreme Court, which rejected the ban but imposed a 30-day waiting period for direct-mail solicitation to accident and wrongful death victims and their families. The waiting period was challenged in federal court and the U.S. Court of Appeals for the Eleventh Circuit, which found the 30-day waiting period unconstitutional and a violation of free speech. The U.S. Supreme Court heard the case (115 S.Ct. 897 [1995]) and overruled the federal court's decisions. It ruled that the 30-day waiting period was proper.

At the time the Supreme Court heard the case, state bar associations and eight local bar associations joined in an **amicus curiae** brief, urging the court to implement the waiting period. The case has sparked state bar associations to consider restrictions on solicitation and television advertising. Maryland adopted a similar rule and extended the 30-day ban to solicitation of criminal and traffic defendants. The U.S. Court of Appeals for the Fourth Circuit rejected the ban for criminal and traffic defendants (*Ficker v. Curran*, 96-2724), stating that criminal defendants are in immediate need of legal assistance and would not benefit from the 30-day waiting period.

Wisconsin also considered implementing the 30-day ban, but, before doing so, conducted a survey of more than 500 accident victims to determine whether such restriction was necessary. The survey resulted in the findings shown in Exhibit 4–12. Wisconsin's State Bar President, David Saincheck, was quoted as saying, "It is pretty clear . . . that the public is nowhere near as negative about [direct mail] as attorneys might think."

amicus curiae
Friend-of-the-court brief that states the position of the author relating to a case pending before the court.

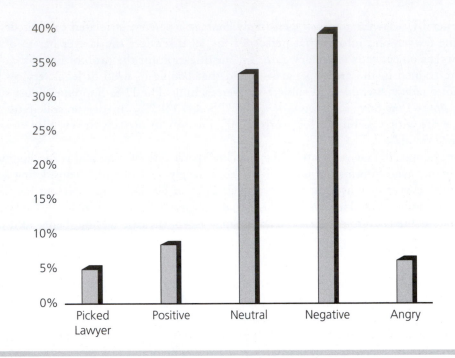

EXHIBIT 4–12   Results of Wisconsin State Bar Regarding Direct-Mail Advertising

An example of a direct-mail piece targeted to a specific audience (homeowners) is shown in Exhibit 4–13. An example of a direct-mail piece that violates the ABA Model Rules is shown in Exhibit 4–14.

spam
To send unsolicited commercial e-mail messages to large numbers of persons on the Internet in an indiscriminate manner.

E-MAIL   Indiscriminate posting of e-mail messages to consumers promoting services or products is defined as **spam.** In April, 1994, Phoenix lawyer Lawrence Canter of the firm Canter & Siegal posted an advertisement for immigration services to thousands of Internet newsgroups without regard for the subject matter of the newsgroup. The firm received thousands of angry e-mails, including death threats. Cantor's endeavor resulted in hundreds of complaints that led to his suspension for 1 year for violating several ethics rules, including the following:

- Failure to label his e-mail as advertising material
- Failure to submit a copy of the e-mail to the state bar disciplinary authorities
- Making reference to himself as an "immigration lawyer" in violation of a rule on government specialization
- Engaging in conduct prejudicial to the administration of justice

Another question regarding electronic advertising is whether a lawyer's participation in chat rooms and list servers constitutes solicitation. Some attorneys have admitted that their participation in such activities is solely for the purpose of generating business. If so, is that wrong? If it is, would every chat room session have to include a header with the phrase "Advertising Material?" Answers to these and other questions are currently being addressed by the ABA and individual states. In the next few years, new regulations of lawyers' solicitation activities over the Internet will be implemented.

capper
A person who is paid to obtain cases for a lawyer.

CAPPERS   A **capper** is a person paid to get business for an attorney. Potential cappers include insurance adjusters, medical personnel, and police officers. An insurance adjuster or police officer investigating an accident is able to recommend an attorney to an accident victim. If the victim retains the lawyer, the capper is paid a fee. *This type of activity is highly illegal* and, unfortunately, occurs often.

JAMES F. ROBERTS

IRVINE OFFICE	*Attorney at Law*	BREA OFFICE
18300 VON KARMAN	1-800-244-4882	770 S. BREA
SUITE 820		SUITE 207
IRVINE, CALIFORNIA 92715		BREA, CALIFORNIA 92621
FAX: (714) 863-9002		FAX: (714) 256-1070
TELEPHONE: (714) 863-1313		TELEPHONE: (714) 256-1065
		October 27, 2003

Dear Homeowner:

This is not a summons to appear in court and I am not a bill collector. I help people avoid probate and I save them money; I am an estate planning attorney.

Doing nothing or doing the wrong things can actually cost you money. To prevent this from happening to you, I am inviting you to a FREE seminar meeting on family estate planning. We'll discuss living trusts, wills, health power, conservatorship, and a number of other topics of vital importance and ... I'll answer your questions.

If all of your assets equal $60,000 or more, your estate will have to go through probate in California, and, if you own real property in other states you may have to hire an attorney and go through probate in those states as well.

If you're like me, you don't want any part of a process that takes 6% to 10% of everything you own, requires mounds of paperwork, and often takes 2 years or longer before the people you care about can claim their rightful inheritance.

There are many reasons why you don't want to go through probate. We'll be discussing those as well as discussing other important legal documents you should have to protect yourself now and in the future. I could not begin to cover these in a letter; that's why I'm inviting you and your family and friends to a FREE educational meeting.

I've been in business for over 11 years; I have set up more than 2,500 Living Trusts. The key is quality, customized legal documents that do a good job for you, follow your wishes, and keep you in control.

For your convenience, I'm presenting two seminars:

Tues., Nov. 10, 9:00 a.m.	Tues., Nov. 17, 7:30 p.m.
Velvet Turtle Restaurant	Holiday Inn (Off Harbor)
1450 N. Harbor, Fullerton	222 W. Houston, Fullerton
(Free Breakfast Meeting)	(Refreshments)

Seating is limited, so please call 1-800-244-4882 for reservations. Don't wait until it's too late to plan. You need this information to PROTECT yourself and your loved ones.
Sincerely,

James F. Roberts
Estate Planning Attorney

EXHIBIT 4–13 Sample of an Unsolicited Direct-Mail Advertisement

Cappers are very creative in their solicitation efforts. They hang out in emergency room lobbies waiting for automobile accident victims. They come equipped with retainer agreements already completed so that all they have to do is fill in a victim's name and have the victim sign the agreement.

EXCEPTIONS TO SOLICITATION AND PROHIBITIONS An attorney may inform a potential client of services if no financial benefits will be gained by doing so. For example, a lawyer employed by a public defender's office may inform a potential indigent client of his services without being accused of solicitation. A public defender and a

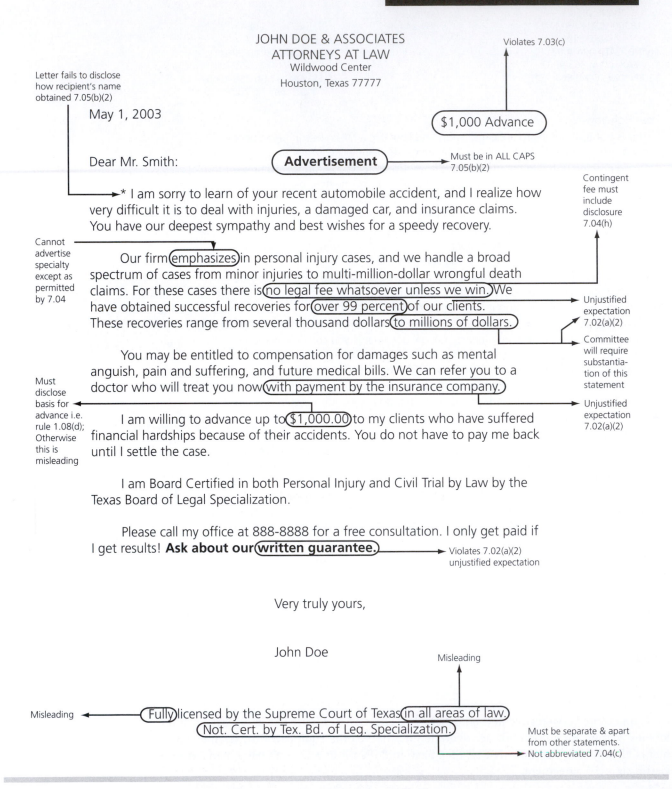

Not In Compliance

Violates 7.03(c)

JOHN DOE & ASSOCIATES
ATTORNEYS AT LAW
Wildwood Center
Houston, Texas 77777

Letter fails to disclose
how recipient's name
obtained 7.05(b)(2)

$1,000 Advance

May 1, 2003

Dear Mr. Smith: **Advertisement**   Must be in ALL CAPS
7.05(b)(2)

Contingent
fee must
include
disclosure
7.04(h)

* I am sorry to learn of your recent automobile accident, and I realize how
very difficult it is to deal with injuries, a damaged car, and insurance claims.
You have our deepest sympathy and best wishes for a speedy recovery.

Cannot
advertise
specialty
except as
permitted
by 7.04

Our firm emphasizes in personal injury cases, and we handle a broad
spectrum of cases from minor injuries to multi-million-dollar wrongful death
claims. For these cases there is no legal fee whatsoever unless we win. We
have obtained successful recoveries for over 99 percent of our clients.
These recoveries range from several thousand dollars to millions of dollars.

Unjustified
expectation
7.02(a)(2)

Committee
will require
substantia-
tion of this
statement

You may be entitled to compensation for damages such as mental
anguish, pain and suffering, and future medical bills. We can refer you to a
doctor who will treat you now with payment by the insurance company.

Must
disclose
basis for
advance i.e.
rule 1.08(d);
Otherwise
this is
misleading

I am willing to advance up to $1,000.00 to my clients who have suffered
financial hardships because of their accidents. You do not have to pay me back
until I settle the case.

Unjustified
expectation
7.02(a)(2)

I am Board Certified in both Personal Injury and Civil Trial by Law by the
Texas Board of Legal Specialization.

Please call my office at 888-8888 for a free consultation. I only get paid if
I get results! **Ask about our written guarantee.**

Violates 7.02(a)(2)
unjustified expectation

Very truly yours,

John Doe

Misleading

Misleading   Fully licensed by the Supreme Court of Texas in all areas of law.
Not. Cert. by Tex. Bd. of Leg. Specialization.

Must be separate & apart
from other statements.
Not abbreviated 7.04(c)

EXHIBIT 4–14   Sample of a Direct-Mail Piece That Violates the ABA Model Rules *(Reprinted with Permission of The State Bar of Texas. Texas State Bar Journal, 58(7), p. 663. July, 1995.)*

district attorney are employed by a county or state and receive a salary from taxpayer dollars. Therefore, they will not increase their income by representing a client.

In addition, sponsored attorney referral services are exempt from capping allegations. These services charge a small fee to put an attorney on a list. When clients call a referral service for a recommendation, the service will give them an attorney's name and telephone number. The attorney agrees to charge the referred client a reduced fee for a consultation. After the consultation, the attorney sends the referral service a fee for the referral. An employee of an attorney referral service cannot be accused of soliciting for referring a client to an attorney, even though the attorney compensates the service.

Also exempt from solicitation allegations are attorneys employed by prepaid legal service plans. An attorney employed by an insurance plan may inform a member of the plan of the availability of legal services. Since the attorney is employed by the insurance company, the attorney's income will not increase by representing the member. The client will receive legal services at a reduced rate, and the fees will be paid by the insurance company.

There are other circumstances that are not considered overreaching and in which the prohibition against direct solicitation is not necessary. These circumstances are direct communications with a family member or current or former client, a person who requests the information, and a pro bono client. However, in some cases, states have ruled that a pro bono client may be subject to the solicitation ban. Although the attorney may receive no monetary gain from representing the client, if the case is a high-profile case, the attorney would receive name recognition from media attention and would realize future profits.

STAFF REFERRALS   A firm's employees can refer their friends to the attorneys in their firm. *A problem occurs, however, if an employee is compensated for a referral.* Even a small gratuity or thank-you gift is considered payment for a referral in some states. Therefore, if a paralegal refers a friend to a firm, the paralegal may not receive any compensation for the referral.

DEPARTING ATTORNEYS   An attorney terminating employment with a firm may contact clients and inform them of the departure. However, case law rulings state that clients are a firm's property and not an individual attorney's property. It is considered improper for an attorney to try to persuade clients to leave a firm with the attorney. It is the client's decision to choose the attorney or the firm.

THE ATTORNEY-CLIENT RELATIONSHIP

An attorney-client relationship consists of many elements, including trust, loyalty, honesty, openness, and understanding. When any of these elements is missing from the relationship, the relationship suffers. When an attorney-client relationship suffers, it affects the entire firm.

When Does the Attorney-Client Relationship Begin?

Traditionally, determining when an attorney-client relationship began was based on contract law and principles of agency. Prior case law stated that the relationship began with the client's request that the lawyer act on the client's behalf and the lawyer's agreement to represent the client. Some courts have ruled that no attorney-client relationship exists unless a written contract exists.

Recent case law indicates that determining when an attorney-client relationship begins is based on other factors that do not involve a written agreement. The Iowa Supreme Court used the following three conditions to test when an attorney-client relationship exists:

1. The client sought legal advice.
2. The advice sought was within the areas of the lawyer's competence.
3. The lawyer gave, or agreed to give, the advice sought.

A Michigan ethics opinion states that an attorney-client relationship can begin from a brief, informal conversation in person or by telephone where legal advice was given although no fee was charged and no contract of employment was signed. If a lawyer gives gratuitous advice, he or she is held to the same standard of care as if formerly retained. Therefore, an attorney-client relationship may exist without a formal agreement and may be implied by a lawyer's conduct. If a lawyer's conduct would make a person believe that the lawyer is acting on the person's behalf, an attorney-client relationship is established. For example, in a Minnesota case, *Togstad v. Vesely, Otto, Miller & Keefe,* 291 N.W. 2d 686 (1980), the court found that although the attorney did not agree to take the client's case, his action in telling the client that he did not think she had a case established a lawyer-client relationship. The client was awarded $650,000 because the lawyer did not warn her about a statute of limitations. However, the existence of an attorney-client relationship and the circumstances surrounding a case must be determined on a case-by-case basis.

Most frequently, an attorney-client relationship is created by an expressed agreement to represent a client. Paying a fee is only one element of the existence of a lawyer-client relationship. When a lawyer is consulted, is advised of facts, and agrees to take a case on the request of a client, a relationship is established.

The Five Cs of Client Relations

The attorney-client relationship consists of five major areas known as the five Cs of client relations: competence, commitment, communication, conflict of interest, and confidentiality. The attorney is ultimately responsible for ensuring that the five Cs are performed. A lawyer's staff, especially paralegals, must also be attentive to the five Cs.

COMPETENCE The law has always recognized the importance of competent legal representation. However, the profession did not especially require lawyer competence until after 1970 when the ABA Model Code was amended to include lawyer competence.

Rule 1.1 of the Model Rules states:

> A lawyer shall provide competent representation to a client. Competent representation requires the legal knowledge, skill, thoroughness and preparation reasonably necessary for the representation.

A lawyer is expected to have knowledge of the principles of law applicable to the client's problem. In addition, a lawyer is expected to know procedural rules and court rules for all the courts in which the lawyer practices. Paralegals are helpful in this area. A new attorney often relies on paralegals for this information.

Legal skills include technical skills such as the ability to draft documents, review documents, conduct research, and perform such administrative tasks as record keeping. Some important legal skills—such as analysis of **precedent**, evaluation of evidence, and legal drafting—are required in all legal problems. Perhaps the most basic legal skill is determining what kind of legal problems a situation may involve.

The standard of thoroughness required by the ABA Model Rules is the degree of thoroughness ordinarily employed by lawyers undertaking similar matters.

Adequate preparation requires necessary legal research and investigation of the facts of a case. Attorneys have been disciplined for neglect and inadequate preparation, specifically for failure to ascertain basic statutory points of law readily ascertainable by any member of the bar. This rule does not, however, require that an attorney investigate remote theories of law or every fact of a case, unless the circumstances reasonably indicate the need for such investigation.

An attorney need not be experienced in an area of law before accepting a case. It is not possible for a lawyer to be an expert in all fields of law. If an attorney is inexperienced in an area of law before accepting a case in that area, the attorney must make an effort to become knowledgeable in that area without jeopardizing the client's case. For example, an attorney who has had no experience in probate may accept a probate case if, through diligent research

precedent
A court decision on a question of law that gives authority or direction on how to decide a similar question of law in a later case with similar facts.

and study, the attorney can become knowledgeable about probate without exposing the client's case to risk.

A lawyer who knows that he or she does not have the necessary skills to undertake a complex matter is bound by the Rules of Professional Responsibility of many states either to decline the case or to associate another attorney on the case who is competent in the subject matter. Lawyers have been suspended from the practice of law for failure to gain the necessary knowledge or to associate another lawyer on a complex case. If a lawyer chooses to associate another lawyer, that lawyer must have the client's consent. Furthermore, the fees charged the client cannot be increased because of the involvement of the additional lawyer.

COMMITMENT   Commitment to a client's case forbids a lawyer to neglect the case. Prejudicial delay is clearly a violation of an attorney's commitment to a client. In addition, failure to act promptly may cause a client needless anxiety, worry, and frustration.

Rule 1.3 of the Model Rules states:

> A lawyer shall act with reasonable diligence and promptness in representing a client.

This rule imposes a duty on a lawyer to be committed to a client's matter with reasonable speed and readiness. The case of *Mendicino v. Magagma*, 572 P. 2d 21, 23–24, states, "Lawyers . . . everywhere are, themselves, on public trial. . . . The procrastination of one of us results in the condescension of all and, in this context, we must stand responsible for each other as we discharge our obligation to our clients, the courts, and the public at large."

In addition to possibly damaging a client, a lawyer's procrastination and delay interfere with the administration of justice. Some examples of a lack of commitment to a client's case follow:

- Failure to begin an action
- Failure to appear at a hearing
- Failure to file pleadings
- Filing carelessly drafted pleadings
- Failure to respond to interrogatories
- Failure to respond to correspondence from opposing counsel
- Failure to correct a known defect in a case
- Failure to notify clients of a lawyer's new office address or telephone number

Commitment to a client's case also includes loyalty to the client. Under the ABA Model Code, this duty is expressed as zealousness. The term **zeal** first appeared in formal standards of conduct in ABA Canon of Professional Ethics 15, which states, in part,

> [T]he lawyer owes entire devotion to the interest of the client, [and should] apply zeal in the maintenance and defense of his rights and the exertion of his utmost learning and ability, to the end that nothing be taken or withheld from him, [save] by the rules of law, legally applied.

The term *zeal* suggests the frame of mind appropriate in advocacy but not appropriate in a lawyer's role as advisor. Although a lawyer must represent a client with zeal, the lawyer's zeal must always respect the decisions made by the client.

zeal
Enthusiastic and diligent devotion.

COMMUNICATION   The obligation to communicate with a client has been recognized throughout the history of the legal system and the legal profession as one of a lawyer's primary duties. Breach of that duty is a very serious failure. However, attorneys' failure to communicate with clients is the most common complaint clients have about attorneys.

Rule 1.4 of the Model Rules states:

(a) A lawyer shall:

(1) Promptly inform the client of any decision or circumstance with respect to which the client's informed consent, as defined in Rule 1.0(e), is required by these Rules;

(2) reasonably consult with the client about the means by which the client's objectives are to be accomplished;

(3) keep the client reasonably informed about the status of the matter;

(4) promptly comply with reasonable requests for information; and

(5) consult with the client about any relevant limitation on the lawyer's conduct when the lawyer knows that the client expects assistance not permitted by the Rules of Professional Conduct or other law.

(b) A lawyer shall explain a matter to the extent reasonably necessary to permit the client to make informed decisions regarding the representation.

A lawyer can keep clients informed by doing the following:

- Advising them of the status of their affairs in a timely manner
- Responding to their requests for information
- Responding to clients' letters and telephone calls
- Notifying them of changes in the lawyer's address and telephone number
- Apprising them of any reason why the lawyer cannot provide them with diligent representation
- Advising them of the proper course of action and the risks involved and possible alternative action
- Informing them of their rights, especially in criminal cases
- Advising them on both the legal and the practical aspects of a matter
- Providing them with copies of all documents received or prepared in their case

The duty to communicate effectively is also necessary to maintain public confidence in the legal profession. Warren Burger states in *The Role of the Law School in Teaching Legal Ethics and Professional Responsibility,* "The findings of . . . polls . . . [suggest] that the public's perception of lawyers is that . . . lawyers do not care whether their clients fully understand what needs to be done and why."

Providing a client with information relates to two areas of the client's case: informing the client of the status of the case and advising the client of the law to allow the client to make informed decisions concerning the case. Therefore, a lawyer must communicate information sufficient to permit a client to appreciate the significance of a case.

Communication reassures a client that matters of importance are not being left unresolved, prevents prejudice to a client's rights, and preserves the trust and confidence that clients normally expect of their lawyers.

CONFLICT OF INTEREST   A lawyer may not represent one client whose interests are adverse to another client, even if the two representations are unrelated, unless the client consents and the lawyer believes the representation will not adversely affect a client. This rule has its roots in a lawyer's duty of loyalty to a client. It is generally agreed that a greater obligation is owed to a former client than to a potential client.

Rule 1.7 of the ABA Model Rules states:

(a) Except as provided in paragraph (b), a lawyer shall not represent a client if the representation involves a concurrent conflict of interest. A concurrent conflict of interest exists if:

(1) the representation of one client will be directly adverse to another client; or

(2) there is a significant risk that the representation of one or more clients will be materially limited by the lawyer's responsibilities to another client, a former client or a third person or by a personal interest of the lawyer.

(b) Notwithstanding the existence of a concurrent conflict of interest under paragraph (a) a lawyer may represent a client if:

(1) the lawyer reasonably believes that the lawyer will be able to provide competent and diligent representation to each affected client;

(2) the representation is not prohibited by law;

(3) the representation does not involve the assertion of a claim by one client against another client represented by the lawyer in the same litigation or other proceeding before a tribunal; and

(4) each affected client gives informed consent, confirmed in writing.

The first part of the rule states that a lawyer may not act as an advocate against a person whom the lawyer represents in another matter, even if it is totally unrelated. Doing so would cause the attorney's loyalty and commitment to the client to be compromised. The client is likely to doubt the loyalty of a lawyer who opposes him or her in an unrelated matter.

The second part of the rule refers to an attorney representing multiple clients in the same matter. For example, a husband and wife who seek a divorce and agree on the division of property may ask a lawyer to prepare the appropriate documents for the action. In some cases, this may limit the attorney in representing either the husband or the wife. If the division of the community property is unequal, the attorney will be limited in asserting the rights of the damaged party because the attorney represents both parties.

Representing both parties may subject an attorney to a malpractice claim. In *Ishmael v. Millington*, 241 Cal. 2d 520 (1966), the court upheld a judgment for malpractice when the attorney represented both sides in a dissolution of marriage. Courts have expressed concern that a lawyer's representation of one client may be diminished to avoid antagonizing a second client. However, according to ABA Model Rule 1.7, an attorney may represent both parties in a matter if the lawyer believes that the representation would not be limited and each client gives his or her consent in writing.

Rule 1.9 of the ABA Model Rules states:

(a) A lawyer who has formerly represented a client in a matter shall not thereafter represent another person in the same or a substantially related matter in which that person's interests are materially adverse to the interests of the former client unless the former client gives informed consent, confirmed in writing.

(b) A lawyer shall not knowingly represent a person in the same or substantially related matter which a firm with which the lawyer formerly was associated had previously represented a client (1) whose interests are materially adverse to that person and (2) about whom the lawyer has acquired information protected by Rule 1.6 and 1.9(c) that is material to the matter; unless the former client gives informed consent, confirmed in writing.

(c) A lawyer who has formerly represented a client in a matter or whose present or former firm has formerly represented a client in a matter shall not thereafter

(1) use information relating to the representation to the disadvantage of the former client except as these Rules would permit or require with respect to a client, or when the information has become generally known, or

(2) reveal information relating to the representation except as these Rules would permit or require with respect to a client.

The reason for this rule is the potential for the violation of a lawyer's duty of loyalty to a former client as well as the risk that confidential information gained in a prior representation will be used to the disadvantage of the former client.

When a client retains an attorney in a law firm, the client retains every attorney in the firm. Therefore, *two attorneys in the same firm cannot represent two sides of a dispute because to do so would be a conflict of interest.* An attorney in an office-sharing arrangement may refer the opposing party to an attorney in the same suite if the two attorneys do not hold themselves out to be members of the same firm, the files are kept separate, and the clients' confidences are guarded.

ETHICS ALERT

direct conflict
When an attorney or firm has a relationship with a person who may be involved in the conflict or when the attorney or firm has a financial interest in an entity involved in the conflict.

potential conflict
Arises when an attorney has an indirect relationship with a person who may be involved in the conflict.

positional conflict
An attorney's or firm's representation of the competition of a client.

There are three types of conflicts: direct conflict (also known as concurrent), potential conflict, and positional conflict. With a **direct conflict,** an attorney or firm has a direct relationship with, or financial interest in, an entity or person who is likely to be involved in the case. For example, one of the firm's attorneys may own stock in the opposing party or be related to the opposing party. With a **potential conflict,** a member of the firm may not be directly related to the opposing party but may have ties to the opposing party from a past or current relationship. For example, an attorney's daughter may be engaged to the opposing party's son. Another type of potential conflict is when a firm's employees have worked for the opposing party and may have knowledge of confidential information. This type of conflict must be determined on a case-by-case basis. A **positional conflict** arises when a firm agrees to represent a client's competitor. Clients, especially large corporate clients, are insisting that their attorneys demonstrate their loyalty by not representing their competition.

Most law firms today, especially large ones, build extensive databases to track their clients and potential conflicts of interest. Some firms create their own conflict-checking software, but most firms use commercial software.

When lawyers leave one firm to join another, the question of whether a lawyer has a conflict of interest is more complicated. Rule 1.9 operates to disqualify a lawyer only when the lawyer involved has actual knowledge of information about the client or the client's case. If a lawyer acquired no knowledge or information relating to a particular client while with one firm, neither the lawyer nor the second firm has a conflict representing another client in the same or a related matter even though the interests of the two clients conflict.

Model Rule 1.10(b) states:

> (b) When a lawyer has terminated an association with a firm, the firm is not prohibited from thereafter representing a person with interests materially adverse to those of a client represented by the formerly associated lawyer and not currently represented by the firm, unless:
>
> > (1) the matter is the same or substantially related to that in which the formerly associated lawyer represented the client; and
> >
> > (2) any lawyer remaining in the firm has information protected by Rules 1.6 and 1.9(c) that is material to the matter.

Independent of the question of disqualification of a firm for conflict of interest, a lawyer changing employment has a continuing duty to preserve confidentiality of information about a former client.

CONFIDENTIATILTY   One major characteristic that differentiates a law firm from business in other industries is the requirement that all matters within the office be kept confidential. *Information a legal team learns from or about a client during representation of that client is confidential.*

Rule 1.6 of the ABA Model Rules states:

> (a) A lawyer shall not reveal information relating to the representation of a client unless the client gives informed consent, the disclosure is impliedly authorized in order to carry out the representation, or the disclosure is permitted by paragraph (b).
>
> (b) A lawyer may reveal information relating to the representation of a client to the extent the lawyer reasonably believes necessary:
>
> > (1) to prevent reasonably certain death or substantial bodily harm;
> >
> > (2) to prevent the client from committing a crime or fraud that is reasonably certain to result in substantial injury to the financial interests or property of another and in furtherance of which the client has used or is using the lawyer's services;
> >
> > (3) to prevent, mitigate or rectify substantial injury to the financial interests or property of another that is reasonably certain to result or has resulted from the

client's commission of a crime or fraud in furtherance of which the client has used the lawyer's services;

(4) to secure legal advice about the lawyer's compliance with these Rules;

(5) to establish a claim or defense on behalf of the lawyer in a controversy between the lawyer and the client, to establish a defense to a criminal charge or civil claim against the lawyer based upon conduct in which the client was involved, or to respond to allegations in any proceeding concerning the lawyer's representation of the client; or

(6) to comply with other law or a court order.

The primary justification for the strict rules on confidentiality is the desirability of complete candor between client and lawyer. Confidentiality not only facilitates the full development of facts essential to proper representation but also encourages people to seek legal assistance at an early stage.

Whenever attorneys get together, the primary topic of conversation is the cases they are working on. "I had a case where the plaintiff . . ." "While working on a bankruptcy case, I discovered that . . ." "I've been in trial all day on a drunk driving case where the defendant . . ." Are these attorneys breaking the confidentiality rule? The answer is, maybe. If the attorney reveals facts of the case that would reveal the client's identity, the confidentiality rule has been violated. Otherwise, the confidentiality rule has not been violated. If the statements were made to other attorneys within the same firm, the attorney may reveal the client's identity since the entire firm represents the client.

Technology is adding to the burden of keeping a client's case confidential. Lawyers and staff members who work on cases away from the office are taking advantage of remote access technology and can access the firm's computers from home, hotel rooms, and other remote areas. This remote access leaves the firm's computer vulnerable to others who are not authorized access to the information. For example, temporary help and contract attorneys who have no long-term commitment to the firm learn passwords and log-in codes to the firm's computer. On occasions, disgruntled employees and contract workers have gained access to a computer by remote access and done great harm to the firm's computer system. Every employee should guard computer information by performing backups regularly. Passwords should be changed often and laptops guarded against theft.

Another concern lawyers have regarding confidentiality is e-mail. This area is an especially hot topic for attorneys who receive inquiries from the general public through websites. Many attorneys who have established websites on the Internet provide their e-mail address and invite communication from their readers. If a person sends an attorney a question regarding a particular area of the law and the attorney responds, has the attorney-client relationship been created? If so, have the client and the attorney impliedly waived their right to confidentiality by communication over the Internet where access to such information by others is relatively easy? Does the attorney have the duty to warn the person at the outset that they may give up their right to confidentiality by sending any information to the attorney via e-mail?

In *City of Reno v. Reno Police Protective Association*, 59 P.3d 1212 (Nev. 2002), the Nevada Supreme Court held that a privileged attorney-client communication retained its privileged status despite claims by the opposing side that the privilege had been waived by the fact that the message had been e-mailed. The court relied on ABA Formal Opinion 99-413 (1999), which held that sending unencrypted Internet e-mail does not violate a lawyer's duty of confidentiality. The court also noted that both federal and California statutes say that unlawfully intercepted electronic communications do not lose their confidential status.

Exceptions to Confidentiality Rule   Exceptions to the confidentiality rule include the following:

- A client may consent to a lawyer's divulging confidential information, but only after full disclosure and consultation.

- A lawyer may reveal a client's intentions to commit a crime and the information necessary to prevent a crime.
- If a client commits perjury, an attorney has an obligation to reveal the perjury. Perjury is a fraud on the court, and the Model Rules require total candor with the court. The Model Rules further forbid lawyers to "knowingly use perjured testimony or false evidence" or to "knowingly make a false statement of law or fact." The lawyer is obligated to encourage the client to rectify the fraud and reveal the fraud to the court.
- If a law or a court order requires a lawyer to disclose otherwise confidential information, the lawyer may do so.
- A lawyer may reveal a client's confidences to collect fees and defend him- or herself against claims of criminal or unethical conduct arising out of her representation of the client.

The principle of confidentiality is based on two bodies of law: the rule of confidentiality established in professional ethics and the attorney-client privilege (which includes the work-product doctrine). The scope of the attorney-client privilege is much more limited than the confidentiality rule.

ATTORNEY-CLIENT PRIVILEGE   The purpose of the attorney-client privilege is to encourage full and frank communication between attorneys and their clients and to promote broader public interests in the observance of law and administration of justice. Attorney-client privilege permits a client to refuse to testify and to keep an attorney from testifying in a legal proceeding about communications made between the two in strict confidence. The privilege applies only to communications between lawyer and client and does not apply to information that the firm learns on its own during the representation.

In order for a communication between an attorney and client to be privileged, it must be made in confidence, must be made to obtain legal advice, and must be with an attorney. The client runs the risk of losing the privilege if third persons (i.e., other than the lawyer's agents and employees) are present during the consultation. However, the courts have ruled that, in some circumstances, a third party may be present during the consultation without voiding the attorney-client privilege. For example, a prisoner in conference with his or her attorney does not waive the attorney-client privilege by the presence of a guard.

EXHIBIT 4–15 The Attorney-Client Privilege Protects Communications Between a Client and Lawyer

A comparison of the attorney-client privilege and confidentiality follows:

- Attorney-client privilege protects only information covered by attorney-client communication. It does not protect the facts generating the confidences or the knowledge of the client.
- Information that is open to the public is not covered by the attorney-client privilege. However, the lawyer's obligation to keep information confidential includes information that is public.
- Attorney-client privilege includes information that the lawyer obtains from the client only. Confidentiality includes all information "relating to the representation of a client" regardless of its source.
- Attorney-client privilege prevents disclosure in the litigation process.
- Confidentiality prevents disclosure anywhere at any time, even after the death of the client.

Paralegals often witness the development of attorney-client privilege. If a paralegal attends a conference, such as the initial client interview, wherein the client reveals the facts of his or her case to the attorney and requests legal advice, the paralegal has witnessed the development of attorney-client privilege. As an agent of the attorney, the paralegal is protected and may be present without damaging the attorney-client privilege. However, if the client brings a friend to the meeting, the confidential nature of the communication that creates attorney-client privilege is breached. Paralegals must be cautious to guard attorney-client communications and alert the attorney where a potential breach of attorney-client privilege is possible.

Attorney-client privilege is a bit more complicated with corporate clients. Since many people comprise a corporation, it must be clear that it is the corporation and not an employee that holds the privilege and thus, only the corporation may waive the privilege.

Certain exceptions to the privilege do exist. One such exception is when a client questions the attorney's professional competence through criminal charges or a malpractice suit, for example. Also, when an attorney represents two clients who later become adversaries, privileged matters relating to the joint matter are waived as well. Confidential disclosure about a future crime is not protected because lawyers are required to reveal such information to enforcement officials.

Other information the lawyer learns about the client that could hurt or embarrass a client is protected under confidentiality rules or the attorney work-product doctrine.

ATTORNEY WORK-PRODUCT DOCTRINE   The attorney work-product doctrine requires that information an attorney learns in representation of a client be kept confidential and not be revealed to third parties. For information to be protected under this doctrine, it must be obtained by an attorney through the attorney's investigation and analysis of a case. Opposing counsel may not require disclosure of this information.

The cases of *Dabny v. Investment Corporation of America*, 82 F.R.D. 464 (1979), and *United States v. Cabra*, 622 F. 2d 182 (5th Cir. 1980), extend the work-product privilege to paralegals. Paralegals are most often the first members of a legal team to become aware of sensitive issues and confidential documents. Some examples of paralegals' work products that are subject to the work-product doctrine include the following:

- Interoffice memorandums discussing case status or case strategy
- Telephone memos of conversations with clients, witnesses, and others related to the investigation
- Notes of meetings with clients
- Document-screening and site inspection notes
- Investigation memos and interview notes
- Document production notes
- Case memorandums and task assignment documents
- E-mails

When Does the Attorney-Client Relationship End?

When a client retains an attorney, he or she may end the relationship at any time without justifying the termination. When an attorney agrees to take a client's case, the commitment creates an obligation that the lawyer will continue the case until judgment, settlement, or resolution. If a lawyer wants to end a relationship with a client and the client will not release the lawyer from the obligation, in most cases the lawyer must have the court's permission. To get the court's permission, the lawyer must show that good cause exists for terminating the attorney-client relationship. Permission may be denied if withdrawal would adversely affect the opposing party or the client or interfere with the administration of justice, as would withdrawal on the eve of trial.

Model Rule 1.16, directed toward declining or terminating representation, states when withdrawal is mandatory and when it is discretionary, as follows:

(a) (Mandatory withdrawal) Except as stated in paragraph (c), a lawyer shall not represent a client or, where representation has commenced, shall withdraw from representation of a client if:

(1) the representation will result in violation of the rules of professional conduct or other law;

(2) the lawyer's physical or mental condition materially impairs the lawyer's ability to represent the client; or

(3) the lawyer is discharged.

(b) (Discretionary withdrawal) Except as stated in paragraph (c), a lawyer may withdraw from representing a client if:

(1) withdrawal can be accomplished without material adverse effect on the interests of the client;

(2) the client persists in a course of action involving the lawyer's services that the lawyer reasonably believes is criminal or fraudulent;

(3) the client has used the lawyer's services to perpetrate a crime or fraud;

(4) the client insists upon taking action that the lawyer considers repugnant or with which the lawyer has a fundamental disagreement;

(5) the client fails substantially to fulfill an obligation to the lawyer regarding the lawyer's services and has been given reasonable warning that the lawyer will withdraw unless the obligation is fulfilled;

(6) the representation will result in an unreasonable financial burden on the lawyer or has been rendered unreasonably difficult by the client; or

(7) other good cause for withdrawal exists.

(c) A lawyer must comply with applicable law requiring notice to or permission of a tribunal when terminating a representation. When ordered to do so by a tribunal, a lawyer shall continue representation notwithstanding good cause for terminating the representation.

(d) Upon termination of representation, a lawyer shall take steps to the extent reasonably practicable to protect a client's interests, such as giving reasonable notice to the client, allowing time for employment of other counsel, surrendering papers and property to which the client is entitled and refunding any advance payment of fee or expense that has not been earned or incurred. The lawyer may retain papers relating to the client to the extent required by other law.

Under the ABA Model Rules, a lawyer may terminate an attorney-client relationship at his or discretion if any of 10 conditions exist:

1. The client insists on a claim or defense that cannot be supported by a good-faith argument on existing law.

2. The client acts unlawfully or insists that the lawyer do so.

3. The client makes it unreasonably difficult for the lawyer to be effective.

4. Before the case goes to court, the client insists that the lawyer act contrary to the lawyer's judgment and advice.

5. The client deliberately disregards an agreement with the lawyer as to fees or expenses.

6. The lawyer's continued employment is likely to result in a violation of an ethics rule.

7. The lawyer is unable to work with co-counsel, to the detriment of the client's interest.

8. The lawyer has physical or mental problems that make it difficult to provide the client with an effective representation.

9. The client consents to the withdrawal.

10. Any other reason is found by the court to be good cause for withdrawal.

A lawyer must still protect a client's interest even after the lawyer has either withdrawn or been terminated from a case. If, for example, a lawyer is terminated or withdraws from employment 4 days before a court hearing and the client has not retained other counsel, the attorney must take all steps necessary to protect the client's rights, including appearing at the hearing and requesting a continuance for the client.

In some cases, the permission of the court is required before an attorney may withdraw from representation. Each state varies as to this requirement and the circumstances surrounding attorney withdrawal.

ATTORNEY DISCIPLINE

Attorneys who fail to abide by the ethical rules of their state are subject to discipline by their state bar association or other attorney disciplinary agency. Most state bar associations have rules governing discipline. In 1993, the ABA adopted the Model Rules for Lawyer Disciplinary Enforcement, the last amendment of which was 2002. These rules were developed as a guide for state bar associations' disciplinary systems. Some states have incorporated the ABA's Model Rules, and others have developed their own disciplinary system.

If a client complains to a state bar about an attorney, the state bar or other attorney disciplinary agency will investigate the matter, and a hearing will be held to determine whether the attorney has violated a rule. The attorney is entitled to be represented by an attorney. If the attorney is found guilty, the state bar or other agency imposes discipline on the lawyer in any one of five ways: admonition, reprimand, probation, suspension, or disbarment. Other forms of discipline may be used in conjunction with any of these five in some circumstances.

Admonition

Admonition, also known as a private reprimand or private reproval, is the least severe form of discipline. When it is imposed, a state bar or other attorney disciplinary agency declares an attorney's conduct improper but keeps the information private. The charge, facts of the case, proceedings, and outcome go into the attorney's file, and no further action is taken on the matter. However, if the attorney faces similar charges in the future, the state bar or other attorney disciplinary agency will consider past offenses when imposing discipline.

For example, a client complained that his attorney consistently failed to return telephone calls. The attorney was contacted and asked why she had not communicated with the client.

admonition
A reprimand given to a lawyer.

If the attorney's failure was by oversight or inadvertence, the attorney would be admonished to be more responsive to the client. The matter would be closed, and the attorney's file would be documented that the admonishment occurred.

Reprimand

reprimand
A formal rebuke; to strongly criticize.

Reprimand, also known as public censure or public reproval, is a form of discipline that publicly declares an attorney's conduct improper. A state bar or other attorney disciplinary agency publishes the name of the attorney, facts surrounding the discipline, and the form of reprimand in newspapers, magazines, journals, and other publications. The attorney's reputation and the firm's reputation suffer when a reprimand is published. An attorney who is reprimanded loses client confidence.

For example, an attorney was reprimanded for failing to maintain accurate records of his client funds trust account. The attorney was responsible for managing funds from the sale of his client's business, and received and deposited into the client funds trust account funds from the sale of the client's business. He wrote checks on behalf of the client resulting from the sale of the business. Two of the checks were returned for insufficient funds, and the attorney quickly deposited the requisite funds into the client funds trust account to satisfy the checks. On investigation by the disciplinary agency, it was found that the attorney had mismanaged his client funds trust account and was publicly reproved. In addition, the attorney had to complete 4 hours of training in client funds trust account management. The matter was published in a state bar association magazine.

Probation

probation
A form of discipline that allows a person convicted of an offense to forgo more drastic punishment under supervised conditions.

When an attorney is on **probation,** a state bar or other disciplinary agency imposes certain conditions that must be met for the lawyer to continue to practice law. Probation may be ordered alone or with an admonition or reprimand. Probation also may be imposed as a condition on reinstatement of a suspended or disbarred attorney. The conditions of probation may include the following:

- Quarterly or semiannual reports on caseload status
- Supervision by a local disciplinary committee member
- Periodic audits of trust accounts
- Participation in local drug or alcohol abuse programs
- Passing the Professional Responsibility section of the state bar exam
- Other limitations on the attorney's practice.

For example, an attorney represented a client in a personal injury case. The attorney filed a complaint and shortly thereafter gave the case to another attorney without the client's knowledge and consent. Although she was the attorney of record, she failed to monitor the other attorney's work and failed to perform further work for the client. The court dismissed the complaint for failure to prosecute.

The client complained to the state bar, and on investigation, the state bar found that the attorney had a prior record of discipline. The state bar ruled that the attorney was guilty of failure to competently perform legal services, improper withdrawal, and failure to return unearned fees. She was ordered to pay restitution to the client and was placed on 3 years' probation.

Suspension

suspension
The temporary cessation of the right to practice law as punishment for wrongdoing.

A more severe form of discipline, **suspension** means that an attorney may not practice law for a specific period of time, usually from 6 months to 3 years. After the period of suspension has ended, the attorney may apply for **reinstatement,** or restoration of the right to practice law. The attorney must be able to prove **rehabilitation,** or restoration to a useful life, and may be put on probation as a condition of reinstatement.

A suspended attorney must notify all clients, usually in writing, that he or she has been suspended. The attorney also must find these clients another attorney if they so request. If the suspension jeopardizes a client's case, the suspended attorney must be diligent to minimize the client's inconvenience or damage caused by the suspension.

A suspension is open to public scrutiny. The name of the attorney, facts of the case, and findings of the state bar or other attorney disciplinary agency are published in newspapers, magazines, or other periodicals. Suspension not only interrupts an attorney's career and ability to earn a living but is also damaging to the attorney's and the firm's reputation.

For example, an attorney worked for a distribution company owned by his father. The company contracted with a packing company that packed, stored, and sold the product. The attorney began to defraud the packing company by underpaying them and using false invoices. The case was litigated, and the jury found the attorney guilty of five counts of aiding and abetting mail fraud and conspiracy to commit mail fraud. The state bar investigated and found that the attorney's conduct involved multiple acts of wrongdoing based on his convictions. His license to practice law was suspended for 3 years.

Disbarment

Disbarment, the most drastic attorney discipline, terminates a lawyer's status as a lawyer and cancels the attorney's license to practice law. Disbarments are subject to public scrutiny. The name of the attorney, facts of the case, and findings of the state bar are published in newspapers, magazines, or other periodicals.

Some state bar associations do not have the ultimate authority to disbar an attorney. Since disbarment directly affects an attorney's ability to make a living, some states require that all disbarment proceedings be appealed or reviewed by the state's high court. The state court will review the allegations and the facts of the case and will either **confirm** (verify) or **overrule** (reject) the disbarment and order a suspension, reprimand, or other form of discipline.

A disbarred attorney may not practice law in any other state. When an attorney applies for membership in a state bar of another state, the application asks whether the attorney is disbarred in another state. If a disbarred attorney lies on the application and the lie is discovered, the attorney will be immediately disbarred again and prosecuted for fraud.

Disbarment is not always permanent. An attorney may apply for reinstatement after a sufficient amount of time has elapsed, usually about 5 years. The attorney must show proof of rehabilitation. Reinstatement may have conditions imposed, such as probation.

For example, an attorney was paid $20,000 to represent two clients in a civil case. She failed to perform the work, and the case was set for a hearing to determine whether the case should be dismissed. The attorney did not show up at the hearing, and the case was dismissed. The attorney failed to refund unearned fees to the client.

In a second matter, the same attorney represented a different client in a personal injury case. The client made numerous attempts to reach the attorney, but without success. Subsequently, the attorney settled the case without the client's knowledge or consent. She signed the client's name to the settlement draft and deposited the money into the client funds trust account. The attorney failed to notify the client that settlement funds were received and did not disburse the funds to the client. On investigation, the disciplinary agency found that the attorney had a prior record of similar acts of misconduct and that she had caused great harm to her clients. The attorney was disbarred for misappropriation of funds, failure to competently perform legal services, failure to refund unearned fees, failure to communicate, failure to notify clients of receipt of settlement funds, failure to disburse settlement funds, failure to maintain client funds in trust, and failure to cooperate in disciplinary proceedings.

reinstatement
The restoration of a right that had ceased.

rehabilitation
Restoration to a useful life through education and therapy.

disbarment
The taking away of a lawyer's right to practice law.

confirm
To corroborate or verify (ratify) the ruling of a lower court.

overrule
To reject or supersede an existing judicial opinion; to invalidate.

Other Forms of Discipline

Other forms of discipline frequently imposed with the five standard forms of discipline include the following:

- Restitution, if a lawyer has stolen a client's funds
- Payment of costs
- Limitation on practice
- Requirement that a lawyer take the Professional Responsibility exam
- Resignation

Occasionally an attorney will resign his or her license to practice law instead of going through disciplinary proceedings. If the grievance is serious enough to warrant disbarment, an attorney will resign to avoid publication of his or her conduct. When an attorney resigns, the resignation is published, but the actions of the attorney and the facts of the case are not published since resignation halts disciplinary and investigative proceedings.

Clients who have been damaged by the ethical violations of their attorneys may sue them for damages in addition to reporting them to disciplinary authorities.

CIVIL AND CRIMINAL LIABILITY   To be licensed as an attorney, a person must be of high moral character. If an attorney is convicted of a crime or commits an illegal act, regardless of client involvement, a state bar association or other attorney disciplinary agency will consider the crime a moral offense and therefore subject the attorney to discipline. In addition, an attorney will be subject to any sentence or fines imposed by a judge in a criminal matter.

If an attorney's breach of an ethical rule involves fraud or any other civil offense, the client also may sue the attorney in civil court and may recover damages. If an attorney fails to act competently or represent a client diligently, the client may sue the attorney for malpractice.

ATTORNEY MALPRACTICE   A negligent attorney may be sued for malpractice. The case may be tried through the state court system or without court involvement through **arbitration.**

arbitration
The resolution of a dispute without court involvement.

Most attorneys carry malpractice insurance to cover the costs of malpractice suits and arbitration. The price of this insurance has risen tremendously since the early 1970s because of the high cost of claims paid successful litigants. No matter how diligent a firm represents its clients, mistakes are made. In the practice of law, mistakes are costly not only for the firm but also for the client. Most legal malpractice claims have their origin in the breakdown of the attorney-client relationship. A client who has been treated professionally, courteously, and respectfully will rarely file a formal malpractice claim against an attorney. A disgruntled client, one who has been treated unprofessionally and without respect, is more likely to file a malpractice claim to make the attorney's life just as miserable.

In a conventional malpractice case, the plaintiff must prove the following four elements:

1. The existence of an attorney-client relationship
2. That the attorney's action (or inaction) was negligent
3. That the attorney's action (or inaction) caused injury to the client
4. The nature and amount of damages to the client

Stephen M. Blumberg and Willis S. Boughman researched legal malpractice claims and published their findings in their book *Preventing Legal Malpractice: California Case Studies.* They found the 10 most common legal practice claims, which are shown in Exhibit 4–16. They also found that certain types of cases experienced more malpractice claims than others, as shown in Exhibit 4–17.

An attorney breaching a provision of the code of ethics damages his or her reputation and the reputation of the firm in addition to costing the firm high malpractice insurance rates. Clients are the victims of unethical behavior. The importance of good client relations cannot be overemphasized.

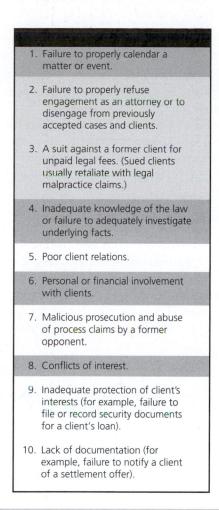

1. Failure to properly calendar a matter or event.

2. Failure to properly refuse engagement as an attorney or to disengage from previously accepted cases and clients.

3. A suit against a former client for unpaid legal fees. (Sued clients usually retaliate with legal malpractice claims.)

4. Inadequate knowledge of the law or failure to adequately investigate underlying facts.

5. Poor client relations.

6. Personal or financial involvement with clients.

7. Malicious prosecution and abuse of process claims by a former opponent.

8. Conflicts of interest.

9. Inadequate protection of client's interests (for example, failure to file or record security documents for a client's loan).

10. Lack of documentation (for example, failure to notify a client of a settlement offer).

EXHIBIT 4–16   The 10 Most Common Malpractice Claims, by Frequency *(Reprinted with Permission of Legal Assistant Today. Copyright by James Publishing, Inc.)*

By Percentages:

Plantiff personal injury practices see the highest number of legal malpractice suits.

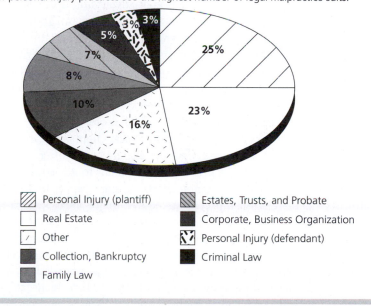

Personal Injury (plantiff)   Estates, Trusts, and Probate
Real Estate   Corporate, Business Organization
Other   Personal Injury (defendant)
Collection, Bankruptcy   Criminal Law
Family Law

EXHIBIT 4–17   Frequency of Malpractice Claims, by Type

CONCLUSION

Lawyers are paid for satisfying clients. Therefore, client satisfaction should be the basis for measuring law firm performance. Studies have shown that clients, in general, are not satisfied with how lawyers communicate with them or handle their legal matters. According to a 2007 survey conducted by BTI Consulting in Boston, almost 70 percent of clients are dissatisfied with their attorneys. Client satisfaction rates among the Fortune 1000 companies declined 15 percentage points in one year. The survey identified three areas that contributed to client dissatisfaction:

1. Not keeping up with changing client needs
2. Doing a poor job of articulating and delivering value
3. Poor communication

If all members of a legal team devoted their efforts to strengthening the attorney-client relationship, a firm would be rewarded by satisfied clients telling their friends about the firm. The future of every law firm rests on its ability to attract and hold satisfied clients. Lawyers do not build law firms—clients do.

SUMMARY

Before the 1970s, lawyers enjoyed fairly stable relationships with their clients. Since the 1970s, however, certain variables have affected the traditional attorney-client relationship. The economic flux of the United States and rules governing the attorney-client relationship have caused changes in the traditional relationship.

Lawyers are clients' representatives, officers of the legal system, and public citizens having special responsibility for the quality of justice. As a client's representative, a lawyer performs three functions: advisor, advocate, and agent.

A firm's marketing activities are set forth in a marketing plan. This plan is an essential element of successful client cultivation.

Law firms use various methods to attract clients, including advertisements, promotional activities, public relations, and solicitation. Each state has devised its own rules concerning attorney advertisements. Advertising in a newspaper was the original method lawyers used to reach the public. The most common method of advertising is listing in the Yellow Pages of a telephone book. Most recently, lawyers have taken advantage of the public exposure afforded them by Internet advertising, known as netvertising.

Some firms promote their business by sponsoring and conducting seminars for their clients. Writing articles for legal or nonlegal publications gives an attorney and a firm great exposure. Speaking at lawyers' conventions, continuing education courses, and organizational meetings also gives an attorney and a firm exposure.

The ABA Model Rules and the states' codes of professional responsibility have strict rules prohibiting lawyers' direct solicitation of potential clients. A lawyer may not approach a person and inform that person of the legal services he has to offer.

A capper is an agent of an attorney paid to obtain business for the attorney. Cappers have been known to be very creative in their solicitation efforts. Paying a capper for business is illegal.

The attorney-client relationship consists of five major areas known as the five Cs of client relations. They are competence, commitment, communication, conflict of interest, and confidentiality.

The law has always recognized the importance of competent legal representation. Four things are required to represent a client competently: legal knowledge, skill, thoroughness, and preparation. The legal skills required of a lawyer include technical skills such as the ability to draft documents, review documents, conduct research, and perform administrative tasks, such as record keeping.

Commitment to a client's case forbids a lawyer to neglect the case. ABA Model Rule 1.3 imposes a duty on a lawyer to be committed to a client's matter with reasonable promptness. Commitment to a client's case also includes loyalty to the client.

The obligation to communicate with a client has been recognized throughout the history of the legal system and profession as one of a lawyer's primary duties. Lack of communication is a client's biggest complaint against an attorney.

A lawyer may not represent one client whose interests are adverse to another client, even if the two representations are unrelated, unless each client consents and the lawyer believes he or she is able to represent the one client without adversely affecting the other. The reason for this rule is that without it, a lawyer's duty of loyalty to a former client may be violated, and confidential information gained in a prior representation may be used to the disadvantage of the former client.

One major characteristic that differentiates a law firm from businesses in other industries is the requirement that all matters within that office be kept confidential. Even though court actions are public record, a client's case cannot be discussed outside the office.

Attorneys who fail to abide by the ethical rules of their state are subject to discipline. Admonition is the least severe form of discipline. Reprimand is a form of discipline that publicly declares an attorney's conduct improper. When an attorney is on probation, a state bar or other attorney disciplinary agency imposes certain conditions that must be met for the lawyer to continue to practice law. Suspension, a more severe form of discipline, means that an attorney may not practice law for a specific period. Disbarment, the most drastic attorney discipline, terminates a lawyer's status as a lawyer and cancels the attorney's license to practice law.

An attorney breaching a provision of the code of ethics damages that attorney's reputation and the reputation of the firm in addition to costing the firm high malpractice insurance rates.

CHAPTER ILLUSTRATION

The law firm of Black, White & Greene continued to grow. Robert felt that it was time that the firm prepared a formal marketing plan to position the firm in the legal community. He and Tricia decided that the first step was to develop and circulate a client survey to determine the firm's strengths and weaknesses.

The survey was completed and distributed to current and past clients. Approximately 40 percent of the questionnaires were returned. The majority of the clients were satisfied with the service they received from the firm, and others gave the firm helpful suggestions on improving its service. Among the areas that needed improvement were keeping the client adequately informed and communicating with clients in a prompt manner. Some clients indicated that their telephone calls were not promptly returned. Tricia quickly prepared a new policy that allowed an attorney to delegate returning telephone calls to the paralegals. She circulated a memorandum that set forth the guidelines for the returned calls, including cautioning the paralegals against giving legal advice, accepting a case, and communicating legal fees to a client.

The next step was to identify the firm's target market. Because of Dennis White's successful outcome in a business litigation case that received favorable publicity, the firm was attracting small- and medium-size business clients. Robert and Tricia agreed to target their marketing efforts to the business community, offering intellectual property and litigation services to them. The marketing plan was developed to reach the target market, and the firm committed $100,000 to the advertising budget.

Tricia and Robert determined that print advertising and netvertising were the best vehicles to market its services. They placed an ad in the business-to-business Yellow Pages. They also researched what magazines and periodicals were used by the local business community. They determined that the *County Business Journal* was the most popular periodical for businesses, so they placed a full-page ad in the *Journal*. Although expensive, they determined that the ad would receive the best exposure there.

To increase the firm's exposure on the Internet, the firm hired Internet Innovations, Inc., a company specializing in web-page development and internet placement. The company reconstructed the firm's website and created a business blog for the firm's clients. The company also placed the firm's website in search engines to receive the most exposure.

Robert and Tricia also determined that the firm should join the local Chamber of Commerce, an organization of business owners in the community. The Chamber has breakfast meetings once a week and offers many benefits to its members. Robert joined and attends regularly. With his participation, the firm became known to many local businesses.

Robert and Tricia wanted to involve the entire firm in the firm's marketing plan. Robert expects the attorneys to participate in marketing activities with the assistance of the paralegals and secretaries. Dennis agreed to write articles on business litigation for the blog and to contribute to it weekly. Grant agreed to participate in the next educational seminar being offered by the local bar association. Milton was assigned to watch the newspaper for announcements of new businesses in the county to mail them the firm's brochure. Sandra volunteered to prepare a firm newsletter containing Dennis's articles and general information about the firm.

The marketing plan was completed and implemented. Although it took time, effort, and money, the firm's marketing strategy was successful, and the firm eventually received the exposure it desired. The firm's client list was getting longer.

One of the firm's new clients was Tinker Town Toy Company, a toy manufacturer. Tinker has a dispute with County Construction Company, which was contracted to build a new manufacturing facility for Tinker. According to Tinker, the facilities were built contrary to the contract and are totally inadequate. County refuses to remedy the situation and fix the problems. Tinker wants to sue. Grant accepted the case and filed a complaint on behalf of Tinker.

The case went into the discovery stage, and Grant scheduled the deposition of Henry Gonzales, County's president. At the deposition, Grant learned that County is a wholly owned subsidiary of Statewide Construction, Inc. Grant thought for a moment and immediately terminated the deposition. "What's going on?" County's attorney asked. "I'll talk to you later," said Grant.

Grant went into the file room and looked in the firm's closed files. There it was: *Statewide Construction, Inc. v. Carpenters Local 101*. The firm represented Statewide 2 years ago. Statewide Construction is the firm's client. Now the firm is suing a subsidiary of its client, a direct conflict of interest. "Oops," said Grant.

Grant went directly to Tricia and asked her about the firm's policy for checking conflicts. Tricia said, "I'm right now in the process of reviewing conflict-checking software to determine which one is best for the firm. But I haven't chosen one yet. As soon as I do, we'll have to go back into all the files since the beginning and input all the clients in the database. Then the database will be searched whenever a case is opened."

"That's great, but it won't help us now! I need to talk to Robert."

Grant conveyed to Robert his problem with the Tinker case. They knew they were in trouble. Grant immediately contacted Tinker and talked to the president about the problem. "The firm must immediately withdraw as your attorney," said Grant. Tinker's president was furious and said, "But then we'll have to start the case over with new attorneys. That will delay this problem even longer! We've already paid you thousands of dollars. This problem has hurt this case, and we are going to take this matter to the State Bar Disciplinary Committee!" He then hung up the phone.

Two weeks later, Grant received a telephone call from Alice Verstegan, investigator for the state bar. She informed him that the Tinker matter is under investigation. Grant cooperated with Alice during the investigation. In 5 months, the investigation was finished. Alice informed Grant that the state bar had made the following findings:

- The firm was negligent in not checking into the ownership of County Construction and failing to check for conflicts when it accepted the case.
- The negligence delayed the client's case and resulted in financial damage to the client.
- The firm must reimburse Tinker the amount of its attorney's fees, or $34,500.
- The firm must implement a conflict-checking program immediately. A legal management consultant would visit the firm in 30 days to check on the program and will submit a report to the state bar reporting the status of the program.
- Since there were no prior discipline proceedings and the firm cooperated with the investigation, the state bar would give the firm an admonishment and put the firm on probation for 2 years. During the 2-year period, the firm must submit quarterly reports informing the state bar of the firm's conflict-checking policies and have no further client complaints.

Everyone in the firm felt the effects of the discipline. Robert and Tricia made sure that every employee received comprehensive ethics training. Now, more than ever, the firm's relationship with its clients is the primary focus of the firm, and it has a state-of-the-art conflict-checking program.

CHAPTER REVIEW

1. What factors have affected the traditional attorney-client relationship?
2. What are the functions of a lawyer when representing a client (the three As)?
3. What four things do clients want from their attorneys? Which one do they consider the most important?
4. What types of marketing activities do firms employ?
5. What is the name of the case that permits lawyers to advertise?
6. What is the most common type of attorney advertising?
7. What are the exceptions to "solicitation" allegations?
8. What are the five Cs of client relations?
9. What is attorney-client privilege?
10. What are the differences between confidentiality and attorney-client privilege?
11. How does the attorney work-product doctrine affect paralegal?
12. What are the five types of attorney discipline?

EXAMPLES FOR DISCUSSION

1. NEW CLIENT

Tim Hemstreet is a sole practitioner. He advises you, his paralegal, that he is planning to visit a potential client in the hospital who, he read in the newspaper, had been involved in a serious accident. He plans to inform her of his services to retain her as a new client.

1. Is his conduct ethical? Yes, page 131
2. Tim informs you that the potential client is his sister. Is his conduct ethical? no, page 137
3. Tim informs you that he plans to offer his services to the potential client for free because she has six children under the age of 7 years. Is his conduct ethical?
4. Tim informs you that he plans to offer his services to the potential client for free because the accident is suspected to be an attempted murder plot by her husband,

the governor of the state. He expects the case to draw nationwide media attention that would give him fame and fortune. Is his conduct ethical?

5. Tim asks you to visit the potential client in the hospital to retain her as a client. He offered to give you a "substantial bonus" if you get a signed retainer agreement. Is his conduct ethical? Is your conduct ethical?

6. Which ABA Model Rule(s) applies to this situation?

2. THE BATTLES' BATTLE

Brenda Battle made an appointment with Gary Athman, a well-known divorce attorney. During the client interview, Brenda told Gary that she wanted a divorce and requested legal advice as to her rights. Gary informed her of her legal rights and counseled her on separate and community property. He also made recommendations on the steps she should take before beginning proceedings. Brenda did not retain Gary to handle her divorce proceedings but paid him for his time and his legal advice.

Two weeks later, Sam Battle, Brenda's estranged husband, made an appointment with Gary. He asked Gary to begin divorce proceedings against Brenda.

1. Should Gary represent Sam against Brenda? If so, why? If not, why not?

2. What ethical rule or rules apply to this case?

3. WHERE IS THE CLIENT?

Client Steven Bristol was scheduled to have his deposition taken regarding his lawsuit against the city. He had forgotten when the deposition was scheduled but was certain it was coming up soon. He contacted his lawyer to ask for the date of the deposition. The secretary told him the attorney was in court but took his name and number and said he would ask the attorney to return Steven's call. The attorney did not return Steven's call, so 2 days later, Steven phoned the attorney again.

Again, the attorney did not return Steven's call. Steven made two more attempts to contact the attorney for the deposition date and each time received the same reply from the secretary. Two weeks later, Steven was at work when he received a telephone call from his attorney's secretary:

"Mr. Bristol! Where are you? We are all here in the office ready to take your deposition! We're waiting for you. When will you be here?"

"What!" said Steven. "I had no idea my deposition was today. I've called you four times over the last two weeks to determine the date and could get no information at all! I have made no arrangements with my work to be gone this afternoon, and I have an important meeting to attend. What type of law firm do you run down there, anyway?! Tell the attorney that I want to speak to him immediately!"

Steven's deposition had to be canceled, the court reporter was sent home, and Steven's attorney and the city's attorney wasted an afternoon because of lack of communication.

1. What do you suppose Steven's response was when he received a bill for legal fees and court reporter costs for that afternoon?

2. How did this incident affect the attorney-client relationship?

3. How should the situation have been handled?

4. Which one of the five Cs of client relations does this situation illustrate?

5. What ethical obligation did the attorney violate?

6. How could a paralegal have helped in this situation?

4. THE INITIAL CLIENT INTERVIEW

Norma Hunter, a paralegal, works for the law firm of Everett & Mullins, a respected medium-size law firm. Her supervising attorney is Rick Everett, who specializes in criminal defense work. Norma assists Rick in the initial client interview by taking notes to be sure that they do not miss any facts. She often accompanies Rick to the jail to interview incarcerated clients. Rick was called to represent Charles Nix, a man accused of raping and murdering several women in the area. Rick and Norma went to the jail to interview Charles. The arraignment was scheduled for the next week.

As they entered the interview room, Charles was present, as was a guard who would not let Charles out of his sight. Halfway through the interview, Rick was called out of the room to answer a telephone call. While he was gone, Charles continued his story and asked Norma many questions that affected his rights. He also asked Norma for some legal advice concerning his case.

1. What should Norma's response be?
2. Does attorney-client privilege apply to this situation?
3. Does attorney-client privilege apply to the time Rick was out of the room?
4. If you were Norma, what would you do?
5. If you were Norma, how would you protect attorney-client privilege?

5. THE WEB PAGE

You are a paralegal for sole practitioner, Irene Bunnell. Irene asks you to be in charge of developing a website for the firm. She gives you the following directions:

a. The title of the website is "The Best Lawyer in Town."
b. It must contain her biography.
c. It must contain the following phrase: "a specialist in family law, criminal law, and probate." (Your state has no recognized specialist program.)
d. It must include a list of her recent clients, including some comments they made about what great service they received from her.
e. It must include a list of articles she wrote for the local bar association and include links to the articles.
f. It must include her picture and a picture of her law office shingle.

   1. What ABA Model Rule(s) applies to Irene's website?
   2. What elements are ethical?
   3. What elements are unethical?

ASSIGNMENTS

1. For each situation, answer the questions given with the situation as well as the following questions:

   a. What is the attorney's ethical responsibility to the client?
   b. Under what section in the ABA's Model Code does the situation fall, if any?

SITUATION 1: Attorney Pascal Chastain has received a notice of trial in the case of *Jensch v. Quenzer.* The trial will be held in 90 days. Numerous depositions have been taken in the case, but one more is necessary for the trial. It is the deposition of the eyewitness in the matter and is the most important deposition. The bill for the previous depositions exceeds $1,000 and has not been paid. Pascal's client originally agreed to pay the bill but now says he is unable to do so. In addition, the client has not paid his legal fees to Pascal's firm in 3 months and says he cannot do so. The court reporting service will not provide any more services to the firm until its bill is paid. All discovery must be completed 30 days before trial. What should Pascal do?

SITUATION 2: John Korengold asks Rose Riley to represent him in an action against the county. After hearing John's story, making an independent investigation of the facts, and researching the applicable law, Rose concludes that present law does not support John's position but that an argument exists for a change in the law. Should Rose take the case?

SITUATION 3: A disastrous airplane crash occurred at Los Angeles airport, and many people were killed. Lee Erickson specializes in airplane accident litigation and was interviewed on a local television show after the crash. During the interview, Lee remarked that the families of the victims should seek representation from attorneys experienced in air crash matters and that his firm is one of the few with such experience. If Lee's primary reason for granting the interview was to solicit clients, was the interview proper?

After the air crash, Lee placed an ad in the newspaper that gave the name, address, and telephone number of the firm and stated, "We specialize in air crash matters. No charge for initial consultation." Was the ad proper?

Lee paid a personal visit to each of the victims' families. After expressing condolences, he advised them of their rights against the airline and informed them that his firm would represent them against the airline. Was Lee's conduct proper?

SITUATION 4: Zoua Xiong represented Darla Schlattman and Janet Jeffrey by preparing a partnership agreement for their business venture. Darla and Janet revealed to Zoua certain confidential information about their personal financial situations. A year later, the partnership broke up, and Darla has asked Zoua to represent her in litigation against Janet. Should Zoua accept the case?

SITUATION 5: Eric Anderson's firm is representing Ernest Walker in a wrongful death action resulting from an automobile accident. Eric has worked extensively on the case, which has received substantial publicity in the local news media, including allegations that Ernest was under the influence of drugs at the time of the accident. A friend asks Eric whether the news reports are true concerning the condition of his client. What should Eric say?

SITUATION 6: Angela Pavek is representing Paula Erdmann in a matter involving a claim by the Internal Revenue Service (IRS) for unpaid income taxes for the years 2003–2005. Paula has informed Angela that, before consulting Angela, she gave the IRS false financial statements for the years in question. What should Angela do?

SITUATION 7: Theresa Enrica is on an annual retainer for Bendix Corporation to handle all its litigation. Bendix consults Theresa on a complex workers' compensation matter. Theresa has had minimal training and no experience in such matters. Should she accept the case?

SITUATION 8: At the trial of a civil case, *McCauley v. Jeffers,* judgment was for client Molly McCauley, but she was not satisfied with the amount of damages awarded. She felt that she should have received more money. Client Molly demanded that her attorney, Patrizia Boen, appeal the matter on the basis of jury prejudice as evidenced by the small amount of the judgment. Ms. Boen polled the jury and does not believe that a good-faith argument can be made in support of Molly's position. She informed Molly that she did not believe that an appealable issue exists, but Molly insisted that the matter be appealed. What should Patrizia do?

SITUATION 9: Rochelle Betterly is a new paralegal in a small law firm. She has a conversation with her attorney, at which time the attorney informs her that she will give Rochelle 10 percent of the fees on all legal cases Rochelle refers to the firm. What should Rochelle do?

SITUATION 10: Renee Farber has interviewed Brett Atkinson regarding a civil lawsuit for damages sustained by Brett as a result of a fight he was involved in at a downtown bar. Brett wants to sue a man for assault and battery. Renee reviews the documents and investigates the matter. She finds that Brett started the fight and that his opponent has filed many complaints against Brett for harassment. She also learns that Brett filed three previous lawsuits against this person for separate incidents of assault and battery. All three lawsuits were dropped when it was learned that Brett instigated each confrontation. Should Renee take the case?

2. Look in the Yellow Pages of your phone book, under "Attorneys." Do you see any "improper" ads? If so, why are they improper?

3. Interview friends who recently retained the services of a lawyer. Do they feel that the lawyer provided them with good legal services? Why or why not? What impressed your friends about the services? What upset your friends about the services? Where do their comments fall in the five Cs of client relations?

4. Obtain a copy of your state bar association's magazine, journal, or newsletter. Notice the section dealing with disciplined attorneys. What were the ethical violations that caused the attorneys' discipline? Report your findings to the class.

5. You are the office manager for a medium-sized law firm in a large metropolitan area. Business is slow, and no new clients have retained your firm in a long time. The owners of the law firm want to promote the firm and have put you in charge of developing a marketing plan to attract clients. Your target market is small- and medium-sized businesses since your firm specializes in real estate and business litigation. You have a budget of $100,000. Describe your plan in a written report. For each item, include a breakdown of cost and describe the members of the legal team who will be involved.

6. Obtain a copy of your state's code of professional responsibility. Compare it with the provisions of the ABA Model Code in the text. Do the two differ? If so, in what ways?

7. For Black, White & Greene, write the client-relations policies you would establish for the firm. Include the following:
   a. Marketing strategies
   b. Marketing assignments for various personnel
   c. Firm policy regarding client referrals
   d. Confidentiality requirements
   e. Conflict of interest policy
   f. Client communications and legal advice
   g. Procedures for reporting unethical behavior
   h. Advertising guidelines and ethics
   i. Newsletter
   j. Seminars
   k. Press releases
   l. Community programs
   m. Client surveys

SELF TEST

How well did you grasp the material in the chapter? Test yourself by answering the following questions, and check your answers against the answers found in Appendix A.

1. What are the four things that have affected the traditional attorney-client relationship?
2. What type of approach does a state bar's code of ethics provide?
3. What is the current name of the rules of ethics adopted by the ABA?
4. As a client's representative, a lawyer performs what three functions (the three As)?
5. As an advisor, the lawyer performs what five functions?
6. As a client's advocate, what are a lawyer's three obligations?
7. What are the eight duties the ABA's Model Rules impose on the attorney as an advocate?
8. As a client's agent, what four functions will the lawyer perform?
9. Who is ultimately responsible for the attorney-client relationship?
10. Who is responsible for a paralegal's actions?
11. Are paralegals bound by the Rules of Professional Responsibility of state bar associations?
12. Paralegals are considered lawyers' _____.
13. What are the four factors clients want from their attorneys? Which is the most important?
14. What is the best source of new clients for a firm?
15. What kind of plan is a firm's marketing strategy stated in?
16. What is "positioning" a law firm?
17. What is a target market?
18. Why was attorney advertising banned by the ABA?
19. In the case of *Bates v. State Bar of Arizona*, what was the U.S. Supreme Court's ruling?
20. What is the most common method of advertising?
21. What are the key considerations in evaluating the content of lawyer television advertising?
22. What is "issues advertising"?
23. What is netvertising?
24. What is considered a law firm's most valuable marketing tool?
25. What Model Rule is applied to Internet advertising?
26. What are some of the problems associated with advertising on the Internet?
27. What information about a lawyer's services is prohibited in Internet advertising?
28. What is a blog?
29. What type of firm is most likely to sponsor seminars for their clients?
30. Why do firms conduct seminars for clients?
31. What goals can a firm's newsletter help a firm attain?
32. What were the four trends that contributed to the demand for newsletters?
33. What is public relations?
34. Why does public relations have more credibility than advertising?
35. What is the general rule against soliciting?
36. Why can't lawyers make the first contact with a potential client?
37. What was the U.S. Supreme Court's ruling in *Shapero v. Kentucky Bar Association*?
38. What is spam, and what happened to an attorney who spammed?
39. What is a capper?

40. Who is exempt from solicitation accusations?
41. What types of people are potential cappers?
42. When may an attorney inform a potential client of his or her legal services?
43. When does a problem occur if an employee refers a friend to an attorney?
44. If an attorney terminates his or her employment with the law firm, is the attorney entitled to take all his or her clients with him or her? Why?
45. What are the five Cs of the attorney-client relationship?
46. What determines when the attorney-client relationship begins?
47. What are the three factors the Iowa Supreme Court uses to test when an attorney-client relationship exists?
48. Is payment of a fee essential for an attorney-client relationship to exist?
49. What four things are required to represent the client competently?
50. What are the legal skills required of a lawyer?
51. What is "thoroughness" as required by the ABA Model Rules?
52. What does adequate preparation consist of?
53. Must an attorney decline a case if he or she has no experience in the applicable area of law?
54. If the case is complex and the lawyer knows that he or she does not have the skill or experience to take the case, the attorney may do one of two things. What are they?
55. If the lawyer chooses to associate another lawyer on the case, what must the attorney obtain?
56. Can the attorney charge the client increased fees if he or she associates another lawyer on the case?
57. What does commitment to a client's case forbid the lawyer to do?
58. What are some examples of a lack of commitment to a client's case?
59. What does *zeal* mean?
60. What is clients' most common complaint of their lawyers?
61. What are some of the things a lawyer can do to keep clients informed?
62. Providing the client with information relates to two areas of the client's case. What are they?
63. When may a lawyer represent a client whose interests are adverse to another client?
64. What client is owed a greater obligation by the lawyer? Former or potential?
65. Can two attorneys in the same firm represent two sides of a dispute? Why?
66. What is a direct conflict of interest?
67. What is a potential conflict of interest?
68. What is a positional conflict of interest?
69. What is one of the major factors that differentiates a law firm from other industries?
70. What are the reasons for confidentiality?
71. What are the exceptions to the confidentiality rule?
72. What is attorney-client privilege?
73. What three factors must be present for a communication between an attorney and a client to be privileged?
74. What are the differences between confidentiality and attorney-client privilege?
75. What are some exceptions to the attorney-client privilege?
76. What is the attorney work-product doctrine?
77. What are some examples of a paralegal's work product that are subject to the work-product doctrine?

78. When may a client terminate the attorney-client relationship?

79. When must an attorney obtain the court's permission to withdraw from a case?

80. According to the ABA Model Rule 1.16, under what circumstances may an attorney terminate the attorney-client relationship?

81. If a lawyer has withdrawn or been terminated, what must the lawyer do?

82. What are the five ways an attorney can be disciplined by the state bar?

83. What is an admonition?

84. What is a reprimand?

85. What is probation?

86. What is suspension?

87. What is disbarment?

88. Who has the ultimate authority to disbar an attorney in most states?

89. Is disbarment permanent?

90. What are some other forms of discipline for an attorney?

91. If an attorney fails to act competently, what is the client's recourse?

92. If an attorney is negligent, what may the attorney be sued for?

93. What type of firm is sued for malpractice the most often?

94. What is the basis for measuring a law firm's performance?

95. According to a 2007 survey of client satisfaction, what are the three reasons respondents were dissatisfied with their attorneys?

Key Words

admonition	disbarment	probation
amicus curiae	joint venture	rehabilitation
arbitration	netvertising	reinstatement
blog	overrule	reprimand
capper	positioning	spam
compulsory organization	positional conflict	suspension
confirm	potential conflict	target market
contingency	precedent	zeal
direct conflict		

Cybersites

LAW FIRM MARKETING

Law Marketing Portal—<*http://www.lfmi.com*>

Website for the Legal Marketing Association—<*http://www.legalmarketing.org*>

Law firm marketing portal—<*http://www.lawmarketing.com*>

Website of Integrity Marketing Solutions (newsletters)—
    <*http://www.imslegalmarketing.com*>

Lawyer advertising —<*http://www.smartmarketingnow.com*>

Lawyer advertising commercials and videos—<*http://www.stuff4lawyers.com*>

A.L.T. Legal Professionals Marketing Group—
    <*http://www.legalprofessionalsmarketing.com*>

NETVERTISING

Web Counsel LLC—*<http://www.Webcounsel.com>*

Attorney portal. Good website to view various netvertising techniques.
<http://www.attorneys-online.net>

Legal website design—*<http://www.poweradvocates.com>*

Consultwebs.com website—*<http://www.lawwebmarketing>*

Legal website design—*<http://www.ScorpionDesign.com>*

Internet Advertising Company—*<http://www.360netvertising.com>*

LEGAL ETHICS

Articles regarding lawyers' ethics. Hiros Gamos—
<http://www.hg.org/practic.html>

ABA center for Professional Responsibility—*<http://www.abanet.org/cpr.html>*

Ethics and technology—*<http://www.legalethics.com>*

Association of Professional Responsibility Lawyers—*<http://www.aprl.net>*

BLOGS

Legal marketing. Will Hornsby—*<http://www.willhornsby.com>*

Legal marketing. Larry Bodine—*<http://www.legalmarketing.typepad.com>*

Environmental legal blog—*<http://www.environmentallegal.blogs.com>*

How blogs affect public relations—*<http://www.micropersuasion.com>*

Public relations by Tom Murphy—*<http://www.natterjackpr.com>*

Portal for legal blogs by blawg—*<http://www.blawg.com>*

Inside opinion – legal blogs—*<http://www.legalblogwatch.typepad.com>*

Wall Street Journal law blog—*<http://blogs.wsj.com>*

TOP LAW FIRM SITES

Arent Fox —*<http://www.arentfox.com>*

Bricker & Eckler—*<http://www.bricker.com>*

Buchalter Nemer—*<http://www.buchalter.com>*

Buck & Gordon—*<http://www.buckgordon.com>*

Carrington Coleman—*<http://www.ccsb.com>*

Divorce attorney listings—*<http://www.divorcenet.com>*

Faegre & Benson—*<http://www.faegre.com>*

Frederikson & Byron—*<http://www.fredlaw.com>*

Goodwin Procter—*<http://www.goodwinprocter.com>*

Gordon & Glickson, PC—*<http://www.ggtech.com>*

Jeffery Kuester. Top 5 percent of best legal websites—
<http://www.Kuesterlaw.com>

Joseph C. Grasmick, Esq.—*<http://www.grasmick.com>*

Larry King—*<http://www.larrykinglaw.com>*

Lipcon, Margulies & Alsina—*<http://www.lipcon.com>*

Miller Nash—*<http://www.millernash.com>*

Moye White—*<http://www.mgovg.com>*

Parker Waichman Alonso—*<http://www.yourlawyer.com>*

Robert L. Sommers, Esq.—<*http://www.taxprophet.com*>
Venable LLP—<*http://www.venable.com*>

ATTORNEY DISCIPLINE

Louisiana Attorney Disciplinary Board—<*http://www.ladb.org*>
Arizona Attorney Discipline Unit—<*http://www.supreme.state.az.us/dc*>
Attorney discipline defense—<*http://www.fishkinlaw.com*>

 Student CD-ROM
For additional materials, please go to the CD in this book.

 Online Companion™
For additional resources, please go to http://www.paralegal.delmar.cengage.com

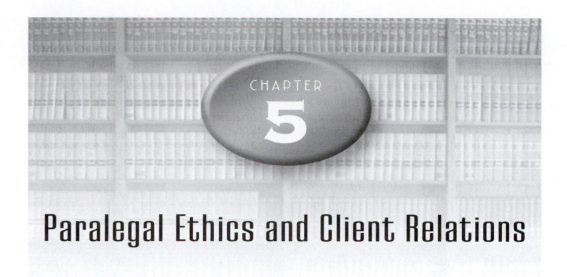

Paralegal Ethics and Client Relations

OBJECTIVES

After completion of this chapter, the student should be able to do the following:

- Understand how paralegal ethics have evolved.
- Describe the disciplinary authority of paralegal associations.
- Develop competency.
- Prepare a goodwill letter.
- Define legal advice and know what activities constitute legal advice.
- Guard against conflict-of-interest violations.
- Erect a Chinese wall around a person with a conflict of interest on a case.
- Understand the importance of keeping clients' matters confidential.
- Identify the three main areas of the unauthorized practice of law.
- Identify an independent paralegal and discuss the issues surrounding them.
- Understand what activities constitute the unauthorized practice of law.

INTRODUCTION

A number of factors contribute to our ethical values: family, friends, religious upbringing, education, environment, and past experiences. The *Living Webster Encyclopedic Dictionary* defines ethics as "the principles of morality, or the field of study of morals or right conduct." Morality and ethics are intangible. They cannot be defined as honest versus dishonest, right versus wrong, or good versus bad. There are many gray areas in between. Sometimes it is difficult to determine what is ethical because of the many gray areas involved in ethical issues.

Our personal characteristics influence the degree to which we can recognize ethical issues. People with good intentions sometimes violate ethical standards because they are unaware of ethical boundaries or do not give their actions serious thought. It is important to establish a foundation of ethical standards before you are faced with an issue. This foundation is established through education and knowledge of ethics and professional responsibility.

Many organizations—such as national and state bar associations; national, state, and local paralegal associations; and the courts—have developed ethical guidelines for paralegals to follow. Paralegals are not lawyers and, therefore, are not legally bound by the attorney's state bar code of ethics. However, paralegals are lawyers' agents, and as such, they are morally bound to adhere to the lawyers' code of professional conduct and be familiar with the attorney's ethical responsibility to the client. Paralegals comply with ethical codes to protect their employers from liability. Law firms expect a high standard of conduct from their employees. Therefore, paralegals must adhere to strict ethical guidelines and be knowledgeable about what ethical behavior is expected from them.

EVOLVEMENT OF PARALEGAL ETHICS

Role of Bar Associations

The paralegal profession was born in the 1960s out of concern for the legal profession as it was structured. The rising cost of legal services was preventing low- and middle-income people from access to the legal system. This caused the organized bar and the lawyers themselves to examine their profession. A study conducted by the American Bar Association (ABA) in the early 1960s revealed that lawyers' businesses were not as profitable as other professionals, such as doctors, dentists, and architects. To discover the reason, the ABA took a hard look at the other professions. They found some distinct differences. Doctors and dentists were professionally managed and used assistants. The ABA considered the use of assistants and determined that it would (1) increase lawyers' efficiency, (2) decrease costs to the client, and (3) increase the attorney's profitability. Thus the paralegal profession was born.

In 1967, the ABA promoted the concept of paralegals and established a committee on paralegals in 1968. The committee, now called the ABA Standing Committee on Paralegals, promotes the paralegal concept and conducts surveys of attorneys regarding their use. Although attorneys were slow to accept paralegals, today they are a common and essential member of the legal team.

The first formal paralegal educational programs were established in the early 1970s. In 1971, there were 11 paralegal educational programs in the entire country. Today, there are more than 800. In 1974, the ABA adopted guidelines for paralegal education and curriculum, and began its approval process of paralegal programs in 1975. The ABA has attempted to further define the role of the paralegal and to educate attorneys in the effective use of paralegals by adopting the ABA Model Guidelines for the Utilization of Paralegal Services in 1991. In 2003, the Guidelines were revised and updated.

The ABA Model Guidelines contain 10 guidelines, directed to attorneys, as follows:

Guideline 1: A lawyer is responsible for all of the professional actions of a paralegal performing services at the lawyer's direction and should take reasonable measures to ensure that the paralegal's conduct is consistent with the lawyer's obligations under the rules of professional conduct of the jurisdiction in which the lawyer practices.

Guideline 2: Provided the lawyer maintains responsibility for the work product, a lawyer may delegate to a paralegal any task normally performed by the lawyer except those tasks proscribed to a nonlawyer by statute, court rule, administrative rule or regulation, controlling authority, the applicable rule of professional conduct of the jurisdiction in which the lawyer practices, or these Guidelines.

Guideline 3: A lawyer may not delegate to a paralegal:

A. Responsibility for establishing an attorney-client relationship.

B. Responsibility for establishing the amount of a fee to be charged for a legal service.

C. Responsibility for a legal opinion rendered to a client.

Guideline 4: A lawyer is responsible for taking reasonable measures to ensure that clients, courts, and other lawyers are aware that a paralegal, whose services are utilized by the lawyer in performing legal services, is not licensed to practice law.

Guideline 5: A lawyer may identify paralegals by name and title on the lawyer's letterhead and on business cards identifying the lawyer's firm.

Guideline 6: A lawyer is responsible for taking reasonable measures to ensure that all client confidences are preserved by a paralegal.

Guideline 7: A lawyer should take reasonable measures to prevent conflicts of interest resulting from a paralegal's other employment or interests.

Guideline 8: A lawyer may include a charge for the work performed by a paralegal in setting a charge and/or billing for legal services.

Guideline 9: A lawyer may not split fees with a paralegal nor pay a paralegal for the referral of legal business. A lawyer may compensate a paralegal based on the quantity and quality of the paralegal's work and the value of that work to a law practice, but the paralegal's compensation may not be contingent, by advance agreement, upon the outcome of a particular case or class of cases.

Guideline 10: A lawyer who employs a paralegal should facilitate the paralegal's participation in appropriate continuing education and **pro bono publico** activities.

In addition to these 10 guidelines, the ABA adopted Model Rule 5.3, which states the following:

With respect to a nonlawyer employed or retained by or associated with a lawyer:

a. a partner, and a lawyer who individually or together with other lawyers possess comparable managerial authority in a law firm shall make reasonable efforts to ensure that the firm has in effect measures giving reasonable assurance that the person's conduct is compatible with the professional obligations of the lawyer;

b. A lawyer having direct supervisory authority over the nonlawyer shall make reasonable efforts to insure that the person's conduct is compatible with the professional obligations of the lawyer; and

c. A lawyer shall be responsible for the conduct of such a person that would be a violation of the Rules of Professional Conduct if engaged in by a lawyer if:

1. The lawyer orders or, with the knowledge of the specific conduct, ratifies the conduct involved; or

2. The lawyer is a partner or has comparable managerial authority in the law firm in which the person is employed, or has direct supervisory authority over the person, and knows of the conduct at a time when its consequences can be avoided or **mitigated** but fails to take reasonable **remedial** action.

Further, ABA Ethical Consideration 3-6 states: "A lawyer often delegates tasks to clerks, secretaries and other laypersons. Such delegation is proper if the lawyer maintains a direct relationship with his client, supervises the delegated work, and has complete professional responsibility for the work product."

In addition to the ABA, some local and state bar associations have also adopted guidelines for the use of paralegals. Limitations of delegable tasks differ widely. Some states prohibit paralegals from attending real estate closings, while other states allow it. Some states prohibit paralegals from supervising will executions, while other states allow it. Paralegals must be familiar with their state's ethical boundaries.

Role of Paralegal Associations

During the 1970s, two national paralegal associations were established: the National Federation of Paralegal Associations (NFPA) and the National Association of Legal Assistants (NALA). In 2003, a third national association was formed: the American Alliance of Paralegals, Inc. (AAPI). The NFPA is an association of local paralegal associations and individual members.

pro bono publico
Latin for "for the good"; used to describe work or services performed free of charge for indigent people. Most commonly known as pro bono.

mitigated
To make less severe; alleviation, reduction, abatement, or diminution of a penalty or punishment imposed by law.

remedial
Affording a remedy; giving means of obtaining redress.

The NALA is an association of individual members and has local paralegal groups affiliated with it. The AAPI is an association of individual members. Numerous local and state paralegal associations were also established.

Each national paralegal association has established a code of ethics for which their members are responsible. These codes are set forth in Appendix C. Some state and local paralegal associations have developed their own ethical code, while others have adopted the ethical code of a national paralegal association. Some national, state, and local paralegal associations have an enforcement committee that investigates an alleged violation of its ethical code. If the committee finds that misconduct occurred, it may impose any of the following sanctions:

- Letter of reprimand
- Counseling
- Attendance at an ethics course approved by the committee
- Probation
- Suspension of authority to practice
- Revocation of authority to practice
- Imposition of a fine
- Assessment of costs
- Referral to the appropriate authority if criminal activity is found

Although the Committee may impose any of the above sanctions, it is not a governmental agency, and therefore, it has no authority to legally bind a member to pay a fine or suspend practice. It may impose probation as to the violator's membership status in the organization, but not as a practicing paralegal. Paralegal ethical standards committees have no authority to impose stricter discipline. It has been a problem to monitor adherence to the organization's ethics code. Unless the violation is reported to the association, the association is unaware of the violation.

PARALEGAL ETHICS AND CLIENT RELATIONS

We discussed the five Cs of client relations in Chapter 4 as they relate to the attorney. The same elements apply to paralegals. The five Cs of client relations are competence, commitment, communication, conflict of interest, and confidentiality.

Competence

It is important to the effective representation of a client that all members of the legal team be competent. A paralegal has an obligation to strive for increased competency. The four aspects of a lawyer's competency also apply to paralegals: legal knowledge, skill, thoroughness, and preparation.

You acquire legal knowledge in school and continuing legal education. Applying that knowledge to clients' cases creates skill. Your knowledge and skill are continuously growing. You will increase your knowledge and skill by experience and continuing your legal education. The NALA expects its members to complete a certain number of continuing education units in order to maintain active status in their association, and the NFPA requires continuing education for registered paralegals to maintain their Paralegal Advanced Competency Exam (PACE) credential. The AAPI also requires continuing education to maintain its certification.

Of Interest . . .

COMMON TIME WASTERS

The following are things that waste time and affect the efficiency of paralegals:

- Accepting too many jobs at one time
- Attempting to blame people for mistakes
- Changing priorities unnecessarily
- Commuting
- Daydreaming
- Delayed decisions
- Excessive clutter
- Excessive neatness
- Failure to delegate
- Failure to let subordinates work on their own
- Failure to set priorities
- Failure to set standards
- Fatigue
- Inability to say no
- Inadequate planning
- Inadequate staffing
- Incompetent staff
- Interruptions
- Lack of authority to carry out responsibilities
- Lack of clear objectives
- Lack of concentration
- Lack of information
- Lack of methods for handling recurring problems

Thoroughness is accomplished by adequate preparation. A law office relies heavily on its staff for various aspects of a case. A busy lawyer with little time to research a case relies on the paralegal (or law clerk) for the research. If the research is not thorough, the lawyer has no way of knowing it unless he or she did the research him- or herself or was "surprised" at a court hearing.

Even minor errors can cause irreparable harm in a legal case. Typographical errors, wrong dates, wrong names, or a comma in the wrong place can have dire consequences to a client's case. Failing to prepare a document correctly or being sloppy in work habits affects thoroughness. It is vital to be meticulous about every detail in a task.

Surprisingly, technology has been responsible for a lack of thoroughness. A task can be accomplished faster, and it is easy to rely on technology to be thorough for us. We tend to be lazy in the details. A paralegal cannot afford to be lazy with details. Many legal malpractice lawsuits have their origin in minor, inadvertent errors that caused a client great harm. Thoroughness is one of the most important aspects of paralegal work.

Canon 9 of the NALA's Code of Ethics and Professional Responsibility provides the paralegal with the following ethical guideline in this area:

A legal assistant shall work continually to maintain integrity and a high degree of competency throughout the legal profession.

Section 1 of the NFPA Model Disciplinary Rules states:

> A paralegal shall achieve and maintain a high level of competence. A paralegal shall achieve competency through education, training and work experience. A paralegal shall participate in continuing education in order to keep informed of current legal, technical and general developments. A paralegal shall perform all assignments promptly and efficiently.

How do you know when you are competent? It is like being in love; you will know it when it happens. The more you perform certain tasks, the more competent you become. As you are exposed to various aspects of a task, you gain knowledge about that task. This exposure comes from experience. The more knowledgeable you become, the more skillful you are. The more skillful you are, the more thorough you are. The more thorough you are, the more competent you are.

Of Interest . . .

PARALEGAL'S SLOPPY WORK HABITS COST FIRM HALF MILLION DOLLARS

A complaint was delivered to a California firm when the responsible paralegal was away from her desk. The paralegal found the complaint 38 days later, long after the 20-day response period had expired. The court awarded the plaintiff a default judgment for $562,489.

The firm attempted to reverse the judgment on the grounds that the complaint got lost on the paralegal's desk, but the court refused to vacate the default judgment. On appeal, the appellate court refused to reverse the decision and the U.S. Supreme Court declined to hear the case.

The firm investigated the incident and informed the court that an effective system is in place so that the incident does not happen again. The problem could have been avoided if the paralegal had neater work habits.

For example, say that an attorney represented a client to incorporate the client's business. The paralegal was responsible for many of the tasks associated with forming a corporation. The attorney, with the assistance of the paralegal, prepared and filed the articles of incorporation. The client called the attorney to inquire about when the remainder of the corporate documents would be ready so that he could set and plan the first meeting of the board of directors of the corporation. The attorney asked the paralegal how long it would take to get the remainder of the documentation ready for the first meeting, and the paralegal said that they would be completed in 10 days. The attorney told the client, and they set the first meeting of the board of directors for 10 days hence.

Two days before the first meeting, the paralegal realized that she had not ordered the corporate seal, stock certificates, and other corporate supplies. She called the company that prepares the corporate supplies, and they informed her that the earliest the corporate materials could be ready was in 5 business days.

The paralegal told the attorney of the problem. The board of directors' meeting had to be postponed. The attorney was furious and knew that the client had spent a lot of time setting the meeting date because it was difficult to get the entire board of directors together. Some board members lived in adjacent counties and had to rearrange their schedules to attend the meeting. The attorney called the client, saying that they had to postpone the meeting. The client was furious. The consequences of the paralegal's mistake are as follows:

- The client and other board members were inconvenienced.
- The formation of the corporation was delayed.
- The attorney's trust in the paralegal suffered.
- The client's trust in the attorney suffered.
- The attorney-client relationship suffered.

Commitment

Paralegals must be committed to the client's case. Since paralegals are actively involved in cases, a paralegal can easily identify potential problems and be assertive to bring potential problems to the attorney's attention. Paralegals may then assist the attorney in preventing a problem before it interferes with the attorney-client relationship. Eight areas that indicate a lack of commitment and that will alert paralegals to possible problem areas follow:

1. Failure to begin an action
2. Failure to appear at a hearing
3. Failure to file pleadings
4. Filing carelessly drafted pleadings
5. Failure to respond to interrogatories
6. Failure to respond to correspondence from opposing counsel
7. Failure to correct a known defect in a case
8. Failure to notify clients of a lawyer's new office address or telephone number

For example, an attorney represented a client in a case involving the client's apartment unit. The client's tenants were suing her for construction code violations. The client was very upset about the lawsuit and called the attorney every day to learn of new developments. The attorney refered the calls to a paralegal. Every time the client called, she complained about the lawsuit and the problems she had with her tenants. Each telephone call took at least 15 to 20 minutes of the paralegal's time. The case was moving slowly, and there were few if any new developments to report.

The client called to talk to the paralegal. When the paralegal heard that the call was from the client, he had no new information to give to her and did not take her call. The client called the next day and then the next. The paralegal, being busy with other projects, did not return her calls. The paralegal's lack of responsiveness to the client not only is unprofessional but also indicates a lack of commitment to the client's case.

Communication

Paralegals can greatly assist an attorney in communicating with clients. Most often, when a client requests information about a case, a response from anyone in the firm will be sufficient. Paralegals, being responsible for the day-to-day maintenance of a case, usually have information about the case readily available. In addition, a paralegal is usually in the office. If a client gets into the habit of requesting information from a paralegal, who is almost always available, it will relieve the attorney from returning numerous telephone calls after a day in court. Paralegals are often the bridge between a distraught client and a busy attorney and can contribute to easing the concerns of clients.

Responding to a client's correspondence or request for a status report consists of writing a letter to the client or telephoning the client with the information. Often, attorneys will not respond to a client's request because they have nothing new to tell the client. If this is the case, a paralegal can respond to the client's concerns, and this will enhance the attorney-client relationship. A paralegal may draft a letter for the attorney's review without being specifically directed to do so. **Goodwill letters** are easily written, and if nothing has happened on the client's case in a month, a short letter to that effect should keep the client satisfied. The time it takes to write a simple letter comes back to the firm a hundredfold by way of satisfied clients. When the only correspondence a client receives from an attorney is a bill, the client begins to lose confidence in the attorney, and the attorney-client relationship suffers. Examples of goodwill letters are shown in Exhibits 5–1 and 5–2.

For example, a client called an attorney for updated information about his case. The attorney, being involved in trial, did not come into the office and did not return the client's call. The client called the next day. The paralegal received the attorney's phone messages and noticed that the client had called again. The paralegal called the client and told him that the attorney was in trial and asked whether she could help him. The client wanted to know whether they had received a deposition transcript that was taken of the adverse party. The paralegal told the client that she would check and get back to him. The paralegal documented the file that the conversation took place and called the court reporter to find out the status of the deposition. She learned that the transcript would be ready in a week and called the client to inform him. In addition, she wrote the client a goodwill letter and repeated the information. The goodwill letter served two purposes: It gave the client the requested

goodwill letter
Letter written to create rapport and good relations.

Black, White & Greene, LLP
Attorneys at Law
1212 Main St.
Anytown, IL
999-555-9876

Date

Clarence Client
345 Broadway St.
Anytown, Pa 00000

Dear Mr. Client:

This letter is written to inform you of the status of your case for the thirty-day period from January 1 through January 30.

There has been no activity on your case within this thirty-day period. However, we will keep you informed of future events as they occur.

If you should have any questions or comments, please do not hesitate to contact us at any time.

Sincerely,
Black, White & Greene

Milton Nollkamper, Paralegal to Dennis White

MN:pe

EXHIBIT 5–1   Sample Goodwill Letter, No Activity

Black, White & Greene, LLP
Attorneys at Law
1212 Main St.
Anytown, IL
999-555-9876

Date

Clarence Client
345 Broadway St.
Anytown, Pa

Dear Mr. Client:

This letter is written to inform you of the status of your case for the period January 1 through January 30.

The opposing attorney contacted us on January 15 and expressed a desire to take your deposition. However, no deposition date has been scheduled. We will inform you in the event your deposition is requested by the opposing attorney.

If you should have any questions or comments, please do not hesitate to contact us at any time.

Sincerely,
Black, White & Greene

Milton Nollkamper, Paralegal to Dennis White

MN:pe

EXHIBIT 5–2 Sample Goodwill Letter, Activity

information in writing so that the client's records are complete, and it served to document the file that the conversation took place.

LEGAL ADVICE Paralegals and other nonattorney staff are constantly communicating with clients. Unlike other industries, the legal profession places strict boundaries on paralegal-client communication. The paralegal must have a firm understanding of what is legal advice and what is not. *If the paralegal suspects that the information the client seeks requires legal advice, the attorney must respond to the client.* Further, a client must be informed that the paralegal is not an attorney and cannot give legal advice. What is legal advice?

ETHICS ALERT

There is no definitive definition of legal advice. An article written by Barbara Rosen for *Legal Assistant Today* describes the problem Susan Kaiser, policy vice president for the NFPA, had when she tried to determine the definition. She was helping the NFPA draft its ethical code and asked attorneys for the definition of legal advice. She was directed to the ABA for a definition. She said, "But when I asked the ABA myself, I was passed from department to department. I was finally told, 'We have no definition. Check the court cases in each state to see what they say.'"

Without researching each state's case laws concerning legal advice, a general guideline for legal advice is this: *If a paralegal applies knowledge of the law to the facts of a case and renders an opinion, it is legal advice.* This would include the following activities:

ETHICS ALERT

- Recommending a course of conduct or action to a client
- Evaluating a case and predicting the possible outcome
- Evaluating a case and suggesting a course of action
- Explaining the client's rights or obligations to a client
- Independently interpreting statutes, decisions, or legal documents to a client

Court cases have ruled that legal advice requires knowledge that can be obtained only through a law school education and is, therefore, the exclusive domain of lawyers. This area is especially difficult for experienced paralegals who have worked in a specialized area of law for many years. They know the law and the answers to questions. The line between giving information and giving legal advice is confusing. Although a paralegal is very knowledgeable in his field, he cannot answer a client's questions if it requires applying the facts of the case to his knowledge. Paralegals need to be careful of "hot" questions, such as "What are my options?" "How do you interpret this?" and "What does this mean?" Prefacing an opinion with "If I were you" or "If it were my problem, I would . . ." does not negate the legal advice. The impact on the client is the same as if the advice was not prefaced with a personal opinion.

If a paralegal is asked a question that requires legal advice, she must ask the attorney for the answer even though she may know the answer. She may then relay the information to the client. However, it must be the exact legal opinion of the attorney without any expansion or interpretation by the paralegal. The paralegal must add that it is not the paralegal's opinion since, as a paralegal, she cannot give legal advice.

ETHICS ALERT

In addition to verbal legal advice, *a paralegal assistant must be careful not to sign a letter to a client containing legal advice.* A paralegal may draft the letter for the attorney's approval and signature, but the paralegal may not sign the letter. An example of a letter containing legal advice is shown in Exhibit 5–3.

There are a couple of exceptions to the prohibition of paralegals giving legal advice. The case of *Johnson v. Avery,* 393 U.S. 484 (1969), lifting the legal advice prohibition from inmates to encourage them to help each other prepare **postconviction writs,** created the "jailhouse lawyer."

Another exception is that you may give legal advice to a client you are representing at an administrative hearing if the administrative agency allows nonattorney representation. In addition, some states allow nonattorney legal advice in their pro bono program. As a general

postconviction writs
A written judicial order to perform a specified act or giving authority to have it done after a criminal conviction.

Black, White & Greene, LLP
1212 Main St.
Anytown,
IL-999-555-9876

Clarence Client
234 Fourth St.
Anytown, State 000000

Re: Marriage of Client

Dear Mr. Client:

Enclosed is a copy of the documents that were filed with the court this date.

As you will note, the bank account with Gimme Money Bank has been listed as separate property. According to the information you provided us, the bank account was a gift from your deceased father so would be considered your separate property and not subject to division by the court.

The opposing party has scheduled your deposition for June 4 at 10:00 in our offices. I will contact you prior to that time to discuss your testimony.

Sincerely,

Milton Nollkamper, Paralegal

EXHIBIT 5–3 Sample Letter Containing Legal Advice

rule: if you are not sure whether it is legal advice, it probably is. It is better to err on the side of caution and not give the advice.

Consider the following five examples:

1. Your friend has a dispute with his landlord. Under the terms of the lease, the landlord agrees to replace the roof of your friend's house. The landlord does not replace the roof, and the roof leaks and damages your friend's stereo system. Your friend asks you for advice. You review the lease and tell your friend that the landlord breached the lease by not replacing the roof and that he does not have to pay the rent. You are giving legal advice. You are applying your knowledge of landlord-tenant law to the facts of your friend's case and giving him an opinion.

2. At a party, a woman finds out that you are a paralegal. "I had an auto accident about a year ago," she groans. "My attorney still hasn't filed the complaint with the court. If he was your attorney, would you fire him?" You answer, "You bet I would." Your reply is legal advice. You are applying your knowledge of personal injury cases to the facts of the woman's case.

3. A patent attorney from the law firm across the hall does not know family law as well as you do. "My divorce client asked me what chance she has of getting custody of the children," he says. "What do you think I should tell her?" You say, "Tell her it's about 80/20 in her favor." Your response is not legal advice because the comment is made to an attorney. If you made the same comment to a nonattorney, it would be legal advice. Since the attorney is responsible for giving legal advice to clients, he is responsible for verifying the paralegal's information before he relays it to his client.

4. You and your supervising attorney are interviewing a new client. The attorney has to leave the room. While the attorney is gone, you made the following comments to the client: "A plaintiff is a person who starts a lawsuit. A defendant is a person being sued. If the attorney decides to proceed with your case, you will be the plaintiff. From what you've told us so far, it sounds like your complaint would be based on a claim of negligence and intentional infliction of emotional distress." The first two sentences would not be legal advice because you are not applying the facts of the client's case to the definitions. The next two sentences are legal advice.

5. A client calls to speak to your supervising attorney, who is not available. The client asks you whether you think she could win her case. You say, "You have to remember that I am a paralegal and cannot give you a legal opinion, but in my personal opinion, I think you have a very good case." The statement is inappropriate. Your personal opinion is based on your legal knowledge as it applies to the client's case and is, therefore, legal advice.

IDENTIFYING THE PARALEGAL   When communicating with clients, paralegals must always identify themselves as a paralegal so that the client understands that the paralegal is not an attorney. *All business cards and law firm stationery must clearly identify the paralegal's status.* If the paralegal writes a letter to clients or others on law firm stationery, the term paralegal, or other appropriate title, must follow the paralegal's name. This will ensure that no one is confused as to the paralegal's status.

An ethics opinion issued by the NFPA urged paralegals to always disclose their title and jurisdiction on all professional electronic communication to avoid any misunderstanding about their status. All e-mails, whether over the Internet or an **intranet**, should include the paralegal's title and jurisdiction. They should also include a disclaimer, such as "Nothing in this e-mail message should be construed as a legal opinion or legal advice."

ACCEPTING THE CASE   Another area of a paralegal's communication with clients that is forbidden is accepting a case. *It is the attorney's responsibility to accept or reject a case.*

intranet
A private collection of information that is viewed by Internet Web browser software and is accessible only to authorized members of a private network; a private Internet site.

Accepting a case creates the attorney-client relationship, for which the attorney is responsible. A comment that can be construed as accepting a case is forbidden to nonlawyers.

For example, a paralegal received a telephone call from a potential client who said, "I was involved in an automobile accident about 10 months ago, and I want to sue. Does your firm handle such cases?" The paralegal replied, "Yes, we do. We'd have to get started on your case right away because the **statute of limitations** expires in 2 months. When was the exact date of the accident?" The potential client said, "June 23." "Okay," said the paralegal. "I'm going to send you a questionnaire for you to complete and return." "Okay," said the client.

The paralegal sent the potential client the questionnaire, but he did not return it. The paralegal did not hear from him until 4 months later. "How's my case going?" asked the potential client. The paralegal forgot about the previous call and searched the client list for the potential client but could not find him. "I think you have the wrong law firm," responded the paralegal. "No," said the potential client. "This is the right firm." The paralegal gave the call to the attorney. The next time the firm heard from the potential client, it was in the form of a legal malpractice suit for abandoning a client and missing the statute of limitations.

Even though the paralegal did not intend to accept the case, the potential client perceived her comments as such. If he would have returned the questionnaire, the paralegal would have given it to an attorney and set an appointment for the potential client to consult with the attorney. However, that process was not made clear to the potential client. The paralegal's mistake was in not following up on return of the questionnaire.

The following are the results of the paralegal's mistake:

- The statute of limitations expired that prevented the potential client from pursuing his case.
- The paralegal was admonished by the firm, resulting in damage to her reputation.
- The firm had to defend the lawsuit and ethics complaint, costing it money and damaging its reputation.

Conflict of Interest

Canon 8 of the NFPA's Model Code of Ethics and Professional Responsibility states:

> A paralegal shall avoid conflicts of interest and shall disclose any possible conflict to the employer or client, as well as to prospective employers or clients.

Although paralegals do not represent clients, case law from 1985 to the present has opened a new area of concern for paralegals: nonlawyer conflict of interest. Paralegals have access to confidential information about a case. Furthermore, they are included in strategic planning meetings for a case and obtain knowledge about how a firm manages its cases. If the paralegal terminates employment with one firm to become employed by another firm, she may work for a firm that represents the opposing party on a case she handled for the previous firm. *This presents a conflict of interest for the paralegal.*

ETHICS ALERT

In the case of *Quinn v. Lum* (Haw. Ct. App.), attorney Richard Quinn filed suit against his former legal secretary, Rogerlene Lum, for accepting employment with Cronin, Fried, Sekiya & Kekina. Quinn's firm was known for specializing in representing doctors and hospitals in medical malpractice cases. The Cronin firm was known for representing plaintiffs in medical malpractice cases. Quinn held that Lum was exposed to confidential information in case review meetings about a case in which the Cronin firm represented the plaintiffs. He requested a **temporary restraining order** to stop Cronin's hiring of Lum.

The court denied Quinn's temporary restraining order, but the Cronin firm agreed that Ms. Lum would not work on the case the firm had with Quinn.

In a California case, *In re Complex Asbestos Litigation*, an attorney who represented many plaintiffs in asbestos cases hired a paralegal, Michael Vogel, who had previously worked for one of the defendant's attorneys. The defendant's attorney filed a motion to disqualify the plaintiffs' attorney on the basis of Mr. Vogel's conflict of interest. The court granted the defendant's attorney's motion and disqualified the plaintiffs' attorney from representing plaintiffs in all the cases on which Vogel worked. In addition, the plaintiffs' attorney was fined $10,000 for failing to ensure confidentiality. The plaintiffs' attorney was also ordered to review all the files on which Mr. Vogel worked and to delete any information that Vogel contributed to the case. On appeal, the appellate court upheld the lower court's ruling and set forth two options for a firm hiring a paralegal from opposing counsel's firm: The hiring firm must (1) obtain a written waiver from the former employer or (2) construct a **Chinese wall,** also known as a cone of silence or a screen, around the new paralegal and prohibit the paralegal from working on any case with the paralegal's former employer. If the new firm does not do so, it is subject to disqualification and sanctions.

A Chinese wall imposes the following restrictions:

- The firm must educate all employees about the importance of the Chinese wall.
- The isolated person may not discuss the case with others or be near others who are working on the case. All firm employees must be aware of the wall that is constructed around the employee.

Chinese wall
Prohibits a person from working on or discussing a case if that person has a conflict of interest.

Of Interest . . .

CONFLICT OF INTEREST SITUATIONS

If a paralegal suspects that there may be a conflict of interest, the paralegal must bring the situation before the supervising attorney. It is the supervising attorney's responsibility to make the ultimate decision of whether there is, or is not, a conflict of interest. Conflict-of-interest situations include the following:

Changing Jobs: If a paralegal works at a law firm that is handling a legal matter on behalf of a client and then goes to work for another law firm that is handling the same legal matter on behalf of the adversary, there is a conflict of interest.

Family and Personal Relationships: If a paralegal is related to, or close friends with, a party in a matter, a client, or someone involved in the matter, there may be a conflict of interest.

Other Interests Outside Employment: If the paralegal is involved in an organization or is affiliated with an organization that is a party to a matter, there may be a conflict of interest.

TIPS AND SUGGESTIONS

- If you suspect that you may have a conflict of interest in a matter, bring it to the supervising attorney's attention immediately. Provide only the information necessary to determine whether there is a conflict of interest.
- When you start a new job, ask for a list of legal cases that your new employer is handling. Review the list for possible conflicts. Identify possible conflicts of interest, and have a Chinese wall erected around those cases.

- The isolated person may not have access to files and documents of the case. The subject case files must be "flagged" in a manner that is identifiable from a distance and is obvious to all who see the file that it is subject to a Chinese wall.
- The client must be notified of the potential conflict and of the firm's efforts to isolate the person from those working on the case.

Freelance paralegals, working for various firms on a per case basis, have a particular duty to guard against conflict of interest. If a freelance paralegal worked on a case for one firm, he may not work on the same case for another firm. To do so would damage the paralegal's credibility and reputation and expose the second firm to conflict-of-interest allegations. It is important that all freelance paralegals keep a list of cases on which they have worked and a current client list.

For example, a freelance paralegal worked on a very large, complex litigation case for one of her clients. The project took many months of the paralegal's time. When she was finished, she received a call from a new law firm that was one of the defendants in the complex case she was working on for the previous law firm. They requested that the freelance paralegal work on the same complex case for them. The freelance paralegal had to decline the assignment; accepting it would have been a conflict of interest.

Confidentiality

Paralegals have a lot of direct client contact. A lawyer's duty to maintain clients' confidences extends to paralegals. The lawyer has an ethical responsibility to ensure that all employees understand the obligation of confidentiality.

Although court actions are public record, a client's case cannot be discussed outside the office. In addition, caution should be taken when discussing a client's case while in the office. *Never discuss a client's case near the waiting area where other clients may be sitting.* Conferring about a case in an elevator is also dangerous. Confidentiality also extends to the maintenance of a client's files. To ensure confidentiality, some firms number files so that a client's name is not on the outside of a file folder. Also, locked filing cabinets protect a client's confidentiality. Client files must be out of the view of other clients or other people not affiliated with the law firm. Some pointers to remember when meeting with clients are shown in Exhibit 5–4.

CONFIDENTIALITY TIPS FOR CLIENT MEETINGS

1. Do not have case files on your desk that may reveal the identity of another client.

2. Do not accept telephone calls from other clients while meeting with a client. This not only jeopardizes the confidentiality of a client's matter, it conveys a message to the client you are meeting with that his or her matter is not as important as the other client's matter.

3. When in a meeting with a client, do not answer your phone with the speaker turned on. Mute the speaker, or do not take telephone calls.

4. Always close your door while meeting with a client.

5. Never mention that a certain client visited your office.

6. Do not have a document relating to a client's case on your computer while meeting with a client. Close the file or use a screen saver.

7. Do not discuss other cases in the office with a client. The client may assume that you also discuss his or her case with others.

8. Do not discuss client matters with coworkers in an area where clients may overhear the conversation. Make sure your surroundings are private.

EXHIBIT 5–4   Tips for Client Meetings

Caution should be taken when communicating with clients by e-mail. If you transmit confidential information to a client by e-mail, the client must receive the communication on a secure server. If the communication is sent to the client, and others have access to the client's e-mail, the attorney-client privilege may be lost. *Before electronically communicating with a client, be sure to ascertain whether the client is the only person with access to the e-mail.*

The same caution should be used when faxing information to a client. Be sure that the client is the only person on the other end of the fax when faxing to a client. A confidentiality notice should be at the bottom of the fax cover sheet and "confidential" in large letters should also be on the fax cover sheet.

No client information, even conveyed without identifying names, should be discussed with family or friends. An example of how a casual conversation can expose a client's confidence is as follows: A paralegal and a friend were having dinner in a restaurant and were discussing how easy it is to get a credit card. The paralegal told her friend that abusing credit cards has caused many people to file bankruptcy. She said, "We filed bankruptcy for a couple a month ago. She is a housekeeper, and he is a painter. There is no way they could qualify for a personal loan, but they received three credit cards in the mail. After a while, they had $75,000 in credit card debt that will be discharged in their bankruptcy." Her friend said, "You mean Jose and Ann Hernandez?" "Uhhhhh . . . how did you know?" asked the paralegal. "Remember? She is my housekeeper, and I referred them to your firm. I didn't know they had to file bankruptcy. They told me they wanted a will. Did they really have $75,000 in credit card debt? Wow!"

Even though the paralegal did not mention any names, she did reveal information that identified the clients. Her mistake revealed confidential information about her friend's housekeeper.

THE UNAUTHORIZED PRACTICE OF LAW

Before we can understand what activities constitute the *unauthorized* practice of law, we must first understand the activities that constitute the *authorized* practice of law. There is no precise definition of the practice of law that is accepted throughout the country. Each state has developed its own definitions of the practice of law. A synopsis of each state's definition of the practice of law is found on the accompanying CD.

Concerning the practice of law, ABA Ethics Code 3-5 states:

It is neither necessary nor desirable to attempt the formulation of a single, specific definition of what constitutes the practice of law. Functionally, the practice of law relates to the rendition of services for others that call for the professional judgment of a lawyer. The essence of the professional judgment of the lawyer is his ability to relate the general body and philosophy of law to a specific legal problem of a client; and thus, the public interest will be better served if only lawyers are permitted to act in matters involving professional judgment.

Since there is no generally accepted standard or definition of the authorized practice of law, there is no generally accepted definition of the unauthorized practice of law. However, each state has created its own definition of the unauthorized practice of law and the activities that constitute the unauthorized practice of law by statute, regulation, or case law. In most states, the unauthorized practice of law is a crime.

To ensure competent representation, states issue a license to those it feels are competent to represent others. Since legal problems often involve complex issues, only those with an adequate legal education are authorized to resolve legal problems for others. Therefore, all states have statutes that limit the practice of law to licensed attorneys. The public is jeopardized if incompetent persons attempt to represent others.

Court decisions throughout the country have identified various elements of the practice of law. The unauthorized practice of law is performing any of those elements without authorization. The main elements of the practice of law are summarized by the following three tasks:

1. Representing clients in court or government agency proceedings
2. Preparing legal documents
3. Giving legal advice

The unauthorized practice of law would therefore be performing any of the above tasks without authorization:

1. Representing clients in court or government agency proceedings
2. Preparing legal documents without the supervision of an attorney
3. Giving legal advice

Representing Clients in Court or Government Agency Proceedings

Paralegals may not represent a client in court. However, many states allow law students to represent clients in court under a lawyer's supervision in certain types of cases. The law student must meet certain qualifications and be registered with the court. In some states' lower courts, paralegals are allowed to make court appearances in certain uncontested matters if they meet certain qualifications. For the most part, however, paralegals may not appear in court on behalf of a client.

In the case of *People v. Alexander*, 53 Ill. App. 2d 299, 202 N.E. 2d 841 (1964), a law clerk appeared in court to advise the court that his employing attorney was involved in a trial and was unable to attend. The clerk informed the court that the case had not yet been settled. The clerk was prosecuted for the unauthorized practice of law even though he just relayed factual information to the court. At the clerk's trial, the court ruled that the clerk's appearance was an unauthorized practice of law, but the appellate court overruled the decision, stating, "[I]f apprising the court of an employer's engagement or inability to be present constitutes the making of a motion, we must hold that clerks may make such motions for continuances without being guilty of the unauthorized practice of law."

Paralegals may represent clients before many federal or state administrative agencies. The Administrative Procedure Act states, "A person compelled to appear in person before an agency or representative thereof is entitled to be accompanied, represented and advised by counsel or, if permitted by the agency, by other qualified representative." Some agencies have no requirement for the representation. Others have certain requirements that an individual must meet in order to represent a person. For example, immigration regulations provide that nonattorneys become certified representatives before the Board of Immigration Appeals. Some federal agencies that allow nonlawyer representation include the following:

- Department of Treasury, Internal Revenue Service, and Tax Court
- Immigration and Naturalization Service
- Department of Energy
- Social Security Administration
- Drug Enforcement Agency
- National Labor Relations Board
- Equal Employment Opportunity Commission
- Health and Human Services

ETHICS ALERT

deponent
A person whose deposition is taken.

Paralegals are also prohibited from representing a client at a deposition. While paralegals may attend depositions with their supervising attorney, they may not ask the **deponent** questions. In the California Municipal Court case of *People v. Miller*, a paralegal was prosecuted for the unauthorized practice of law for representing a client in a deposition because the employing attorney had a schedule conflict. Although the paralegal originally intended to simply accompany the deponent to the deposition, the opposing counsel badgered the deponent to tears. The paralegal tried to calm the client by asking her a couple of yes-or-no questions to clarify some statements that could be misconstrued. The paralegal was prosecuted for the unauthorized practice of law. At the hearing, he was convicted of a misdemeanor and fined.

Preparing Legal Documents

Preparing legal documents is a task that paralegals perform often. A problem arises when legal documents are prepared *without the attorney's direct supervision*. Legal documents include preprinted legal forms. Some may argue that completing a form is not a complicated task, but courts have ruled that completing a court form for a client requires knowledge obtained by a law school education and constitutes giving legal advice. Paralegals may prepare the forms under the supervision of an attorney or for their own case if they represent themselves, but they may not complete forms for another person. Typing and legal secretarial services that choose a legal form for a customer or that tell the customer what information to put on the form have been found guilty of the unauthorized practice of law. There have been other court rulings that said that even informing a person what form to use constitutes the unauthorized practice of law.

There are exceptions to this rule. In the 1930s, state and local bar associations entered into a series of "turf agreements" with other professions, such as accountants, real estate agents, and bankers, that set forth what those professionals could and could not do in the legal area. Nonattorneys who are real estate salespersons often complete sales offer forms for their clients; such forms are binding legal documents. However, they are not prosecuted for the unauthorized practice of law pursuant to the turf agreements.

In a class-action lawsuit filed on behalf of more than 8,000 real estate borrowers in 2001, titled *Dressel v. AmeriBank*, 635 N.W.2d 328, the Michigan Court of Appeals ruled that AmeriBank had engaged in the unauthorized practice of law by charging borrowers $400 for the preparation of standard loan documents the bank completed without an attorney's supervision. The bank contended that it was preparing the papers for its own benefit and, therefore, was covered by a **pro se** exception. The court rejected the bank's claim because the bank charged a fee for the service. The Michigan Supreme Court reversed the judgment (*Dressel v. AmeriBank*, 468 Mich. 557, 664 N.W.2d 151) in 2003.

pro se
For one's own behalf; appearing for oneself in court.

Experts disagree on where to draw the line in this area. Some states forbid their court clerks to tell a person who wants to process his or her own divorce what forms to use. Other states' courts employ paralegals and other nonattorney staff solely for that purpose. They help pro se parties complete their paperwork consisting of legal forms for dissolutions of marriage, restraining orders, and small-claims cases. Without this assistance, wrong and incomplete forms are filed, causing delays in the court system. Helping pro se litigants complete their paperwork ensures that their rights are protected and their case is heard in a timely manner. These nonattorneys are giving legal advice as defined by case law in some jurisdictions, but they are contributing a service to the public and the court system. No one is complaining about their potential unauthorized practice of law activities.

Some states are establishing laws and guidelines for nonattorneys to be able to complete forms for the public. In 2001, the Washington State Bar requested that its Supreme Court approve a rule that would authorize highly skilled paralegals to do tasks routinely done by attorneys in an effort to provide affordable legal services to the public. In 2002, North Carolina followed by requesting approval for paralegals to compete with lawyers to perform real estate closings. It is the opinion of the FTC and Justice Department that consumers can save money by having the option to hire less expensive lay closers. Other states are considering similar rules.

After learning of the increase in pro se cases, the ABA Standing Committee on the Delivery of Legal Services investigated the growing trend of do-it-yourself legal services. They found that 80 percent of the legal needs of the poor are left unmet. They conducted a survey in Maricopa County, Arizona, and found that there was a pro se litigant in 88 percent of all divorce cases. Two-party pro se divorces were recorded in 52 percent of the proceedings.

In response to the public's growing need for affordable legal services, the ABA and individual state courts developed self-service centers. In these centers, litigants can obtain nonattorney services as well as attorney services. Known as **unbundled legal services** or discrete task representation, the legal representation is separated into tasks, such as giving advice, preparing documents, and appearing in court. A pro se litigant who cannot afford full attorney representation can use the lawyer for just one part of the case and a nonattorney for others. Proponents of unbundled legal services believe that clients are more satisfied with the handling of their legal matters because they are empowered to make their own informed decisions. Opponents state that there are ethical risks involved with unbundling legal services.

The Bankruptcy Code allows nonattorneys (bankruptcy petition preparers) to prepare bankruptcy forms for others under its guidelines, which are found on the accompanying CD. It is estimated that as many as 2 million people a year represent themselves in California courts. To accommodate these people, California allows nonattorneys to prepare forms in certain areas of law without prosecution for the unauthorized practice of law if they register in the county in which they do business. These nonattorneys are known as **legal document assistants,** discussed in more detail below.

Paralegals may draft and prepare pleadings, *but they may not sign the pleadings.* Every pleading or other document filed with the court (except **certificates of service**) must be signed by the attorney of record. The attorney's signature is verification that the attorney read and knows the contents of the document.

In 2006, The North Carolina State Bar Ethics Council passed Formal Ethics Opinion 13, which states that paralegals can sign pleadings and court documents on behalf of their supervising attorneys in the attorney's absence if exigent circumstances exist. Before authorizing a paralegal to sign a document on the lawyer's behalf, the attorney must carefully and thoroughly review both the substance and form of the pleading and supervise the paralegal while preparing the document. To clarify that the paralegal is signing on behalf of, and not in place of, the attorney, the paralegal must put his or her initials after the lawyer's signature. Some states consider it a UPL violation when paralegals sign on behalf of their attorneys, even with the attorney's permission.

Giving Legal Advice

There have been many court rulings that have dealt with the area of legal advice and the unauthorized practice of law. In the 1970s, Dacey, a nonlawyer, wrote a book entitled *How to Avoid Probate.* The book provided forms and instructions on how to complete the forms for probating a decedent's estate through **probate.** He was prosecuted for giving legal advice and the unauthorized practice of law (*New York County Lawyer's Association v. Dacey,* 234 N.E. 2d 459 [1967]. The court ruled that publication of forms and instructions on how to complete the forms did not constitute legal advice if the instructions were directed toward the public and not individual clients.

Since that time, many self-help legal books directed to the public have been published. Nolo Press, a legal book publisher, has a number of books written for this purpose and has been involved in a number of UPL proceedings with varying degrees of success.

Legal "kits" followed self-help books. Legal kits contain the requisite forms for a particular area, such as wills, trusts, and dissolutions of marriage, along with instructions on how to complete the forms. The publishers were prosecuted for the unauthorized practice of law. Consistent with the *Dacey* ruling, the courts ruled that the legal kits do not constitute the unauthorized practice of law because they are directed to the public rather than to an individual client. Today, legal kits for dissolution of marriage, bankruptcy, and will preparation are available in most stationery stores and are also available in software products.

There are a number of legal software products available by various software companies. Some products are marketed to the general public to help them with their legal needs. These

unbundled legal services
Breaking a legal representation into tasks that are performed by a lawyer and nonlawyer.

legal document assistant
An independent paralegal in California who has registered with his or her county and does legal work for the public.

certificate of service
A document appended to the end of a legal document that contains the date and place of mailing.

probate
A court procedure by which a will is proved to be valid or invalid; refers to the legal process wherein the estate of a decedent is administered.

products have been attacked for the unauthorized practice of law. In 1999, a Texas federal judge ruled that Parsons Technology, Inc.'s *Quicken Family Lawyer '99* software constituted the unauthorized practice of law and was therefore banned from the state of Texas. Parsons' lawyers argued that the computer program did not constitute the unauthorized practice of law because there is no direct personal contact that creates an attorney-client relationship. The court ruled that the software illegally functioned as a lawyer and placed the software in a new category—**cyberlawyer.** According to the judge, the software went beyond providing instructions on how to fill out a legal document *(Unauthorized Practice of Law Committee v. Parsons Technology, Inc., 1999 WL 47235 [N.D. Tex., Jan. 22, 1999] [Civ.A. 3:97CV-2859H].* The *Quicken Family Lawyer* software is the first self-help legal product to be banned anywhere in the United States since the *Dacey* case in 1967. Before Parsons could appeal the decision, the Texas Legislature enacted an amendment to Texas Government Code § 81.101 providing that "the 'practice of law' does not include the design, creation, publication, distribution, display, or sale . . . [of] computer software, or similar products if the products clearly and conspicuously state that the products are not a substitute for the advice of an attorney.

In a more recent ruling in 2007, the U.S. Court of Appeals for the Ninth Circuit agreed with the Ninth Circuit Bankruptcy Appellate Panel that computers can engage in the unauthorized practice of law in its ruling of *Reynoso v. Frankfort Digital Services, Ltd [In re Reynoso,* 315 B.R. 544. See also 477 F.3d 1117]. Frankfort Digital Services created the Ziinet Bankruptcy Engine, which prepared bankruptcy filings for its customers via the Internet. It advertised itself as an expert system that "knows the law." For $219, the customer gained access to the system and gained entry to the website's vault of information. The customer entered his information into the system as prompted. The software prepared the forms, chose the customer's exemptions and supplied the relevant legal citations. The customer then printed out the completed forms and filed them with the court. The court found that the owners of the program were "bankruptcy petition preparers" and violated the rules that apply to bankruptcy petition preparers. The non-lawyers who operate the software's company were found guilty of UPL. A copy of this ruling is on the accompanying CD.

The majority of court rulings, however, indicate that the software, kits, and books themselves do not constitute legal advice as long as they are not sold in conjunction with personalized assistance in completing the process. A problem arises when you apply the information directly to a client's matter. For example, you can write a book about completing a petition for dissolution of marriage but cannot complete a petition for a client without the supervision of an attorney. You can direct a person to read a self-help legal book but cannot tell the person what the book says or, some experts would say, direct the person to a particular chapter or page. You can use legal software to prepare your own will, but may not use it to prepare a will for others for compensation.

The parameters of legal advice are constantly being revised. In the case of *Doe v. Condon,* 532 S.E.2d 879 (4th Cir. 2000), the question of legal advice arose when a paralegal taught an estate planning seminar without an attorney being present. The court held that a paralegal cannot make unsupervised public presentations or conduct initial client interviews in which the paralegal answers general legal questions. However, the court made no distinction between general and specific legal questions, ruling that a paralegal may not give legal advice, period.

Independent Paralegals

There are two types of self-employed paralegals: freelance paralegals, who work only for attorneys on a contract basis, and independent paralegals, who work directly for the public.

According to *Legal Assistant Today's* Freelance Survey conducted in 2006, 80.6 percent of freelance paralegals have a home office and 19.4 percent rent office space. The three practice areas most commonly practiced by freelance paralegals are litigation (42.1 percent), personal injury (39.5 percent), and real estate (39.5 percent). Their most common duties include document management (73.7 percent), drafting documents (86.8 percent), factual research (71.1 percent), and legal research (84.2 percent). Most freelance paralegals work

cyberlawyer
Software that assists the public with legal issues.

alone, but some (29.7 percent) have employees or outside contractors working for them. Their clientele are mostly small firms and sole practitioners (68.4 percent). Most freelance paralegals (59.5 percent) have a paralegal certificate, the majority of which are from ABA-approved paralegal programs (58.3 percent). Most freelancers (73.7 percent) have not completed certifications from a national or state paralegal association.

Independent paralegal services emerged in the early 1970s. In 1972, Ralph Warner, co-founder of Nolo Press and author of *The Independent Paralegal's Handbook: How to Provide Legal Services without Going to Jail,* helped launch the Wave Project, a chain of do-it-yourself divorce centers. Wave centers were independent paralegal services that provided typing and information services to the public for $50 to $75.

Since the early 1970s, many independent paralegals have been prosecuted for the unauthorized practice of law. In a well-publicized case, *Florida Bar v. Furman,* 376 So. 2d 378 (1979), Rosemary Furman operated Northside Secretarial Service and helped customers prepare legal forms for their own cases. She was convicted of the unauthorized practice of law for giving them advice on the correct information to insert on the forms. The court prohibited her from helping customers complete the forms. She could prepare the forms, but only with information given by her customers. Furman protested that her customers did not know legal terminology or the correct form to use and that such a restriction would result in forms being completed incorrectly, and this would be a disservice to her clients. The court eventually imposed a jail sentence on her for failing to abide by its order. Her sentence was canceled in 1984 after she agreed to close her business.

In the late 1980s, the State Bar of California found that there was "an overwhelming unmet need" for better access to legal services for low- and moderate-income people. The bar created a commission to study whether independent paralegal services could meet this need. The committee, called the Public Protection Committee, held hearings of laypersons and members of the legal community and found that independent paralegals could help meet this need. The committee issued a report that recommended that the California Supreme Court adopt a rule authorizing independent paralegals to engage in the practice of law in bankruptcy, family law, and landlord-tenant law in uncomplicated, routine cases. The report caused an uproar in the state bar, and its president at the time vowed that it would "never see the light of day."

In late 1998, California enacted California Business and Professions Code Sections 6400–6415, which allows paralegals to do "**scrivener**-type" services for the public if they register with the county and post a bond. They may help clients who are representing themselves by completing, filing, and serving legal documents. They may make legal information available to customers but may not offer legal advice. They are identified as "Legal Document Assistants." See the accompanying CD for the complete law for California Legal Document Assistants. Other states are enacting similar legislation or are considering similar legislation. See the Regulation Chart on the accompanying CD, which indicates the states who have enacted legislation of this nature.

An organization with its roots in California, Help Abolish Legal Tyranny (HALT) estimates that as many as 128 million Americans—more than half the U.S. population—have no access to legal services. It also estimates that U.S. consumers could save $1.3 billion per year on matters such as divorces, wills, bankruptcy, and incorporations by using independent paralegals instead of lawyers. Recent statistics in California indicate that 75 percent of dissolution of marriage cases have at least one party who is not represented by an attorney.

Are independent paralegals fulfilling an unmet need for lower cost legal services? The question can be answered by the public's response to independent paralegals. The Central District of California is the largest bankruptcy court in the nation. More than 50 percent of its bankruptcy filings are prepared by independent paralegals called bankruptcy petition preparers. Some are qualified and some are not, causing havoc in the court system. To eliminate the havoc and control the situation, the Congress passed legislation to regulate bankruptcy petition preparers at 11 U.S.C. § 110. The rules for bankruptcy petition preparers are found on the accompanying CD.

Bankruptcy petition preparers are not favored by trustees or the courts. The Justice Department officials have filed almost 4,000 motions seeking to stop bankruptcy petition preparers in the 7-year period from 1995 to 2002. Since there are no educational requirements

scrivener
A clerk or scribe; a notary.

to be a bankruptcy petition preparer, some are making grievous mistakes that have thrown the bankruptcy system into chaos. During the procedural 341(a) creditors meeting held in a bankruptcy proceeding, the debtor must disclose to the trustee whom, if anyone other than an attorney, helped prepare the bankruptcy petition. One bankruptcy petition preparer said, "I've heard from a number of customers that they feel they've been harassed by the trustee's office at their 341(a) creditors meeting for having used a bankruptcy petition preparer. The trustee was actually turning the 341(a) meeting into inquisitions about what the bankruptcy petition preparer did."

The battle against independent paralegal services continues today. It has created a need to separate independent paralegals from paralegals who work under the supervision of attorneys, called traditional paralegals. Traditional paralegals object to independent paralegals using the term *paralegal* or *legal assistant* in their title because they see the two as distinct professions. Attempts have been made to codify and define the term *paralegal* as one who works under the direct supervision of an attorney.

In California Business and Professions Code Sections 6400–6415 mentioned previously, persons who provide independent paralegal services to the public are titled "legal document assistants" and "unlawful detainer assistants." Traditional paralegals object to this term because it is too close to the title "legal assistant." In California, the opposition campaign was spearheaded by the California Alliance of Paralegal Associations (CAPA), which states that independent paralegal activities are scrivener-type work, and CAPA sees the role of paralegals as much more substantive. Other terms for independent paralegals are "legal technician," "legal document assistant," "public paralegal," and "limited law advisers."

A landmark case further identifying the unauthorized practice of law in California is the case of *People v. Landlords Professional Services*, 215 Cal. App. 3d 1599; 264 Cal. Rptr. 548 (1989), which stated that the following actions, when clerical, do not constitute the unauthorized practice of law:

- Giving customers written instructions and legal information needed to handle their own cases, even detailed instructions containing specific advice
- Providing the appropriate court forms for the customer's use
- Typing the forms at the direction of the customer
- Filing the papers so that they will be accepted by the court
- Having the forms served as directed by the customer

Abuses

The lack of regulation of the paralegal profession, especially independent paralegal services, has created problems for the paralegal profession as a whole. Laypersons with little or no paralegal education or experience are starting independent paralegal services and processing legal cases for the public. The documents filed on their customers' behalf are often wrong or incomplete, causing great harm to the client and damage to the court system. Since there are few laws governing these services, damaged clients often have no recourse against the paralegal service. If clients were damaged by an attorney, they could sue the attorney for malpractice or complain to the state bar about the attorney's conduct.

We The People USA is a document preparation service company that sells franchises throughout the United States. They have been in business for over 20 years and have served over 600,000 customers. They have 128 centers in 28 states. They advertise that no legal background or experience is necessary to operate a center, and state they will train their franchisees. Numerous UPL complaints have been filed against them. In response to the complaints, We The People state that they are providing a necessary service to those who cannot afford an attorney.

"Fly-by-night" independent paralegal programs are programs or independent paralegal services that are unqualified and damage their customers and the paralegal profession, such as the one shown in the advertisement in Exhibit 5–5. The advertisement contains numerous inaccuracies and false statements and misleads the public. With the limited knowledge

---

Make Over $200,000 a Year Working at Home Part Time

"I work only two evenings a week. I only have a high school education, and it took only ten days (one Saturday a week for ten weeks) to learn how to be a Board Certified Independent Paralegal. I made $245,000 last year doing legal work in my spare time."

Two years ago, James Jones was a construction worker working for $12.50 an hour. Today, he is a wealthy entrepreneur with his own paralegal business.

Owns a Ranch in Flower Falls and a $750,000 home in Roland Heights

After attending our prestigious paralegal school, James now enjoys frequent vacations to Europe and has been around the world twice!

At our school, James learned how to help others with their divorces, bankruptcies, wills, name changes, incorporations, and landlord-tenant matters. At first he started out by charging his clients a nominal fee but then learned that the demand was so great he tripled his fees and reduced his hours.

Hottest Profession in the Country

The Department of Labor said that the paralegal profession was one of the hottest professions in the country. Start NOW to become part of the fastest-growing profession in the United States. In just ten tutorial visits, you can become a Board Certified Independent Paralegal, certified by the prestigious Professional Paralegal Bar Association of the United States of America, of which Jones is the president. For the low price of $1,200 per lesson, you can learn the secrets of successful independent paralegals. The fee includes software and manuals.

NO legal education required!
NO legal experience required!
We'll teach you all you need to know!

Cruises the Bahamas Six Months a Year in His Own Private Yacht

A FREE seminar is offered at the Holiday Inn, 346 Main St., Anytown, on Saturday, June 30, at 10 A.M. The seminar is sponsored by the prestigious Professional Paralegal Bar Association. At this seminar, you will find out how becoming an independent paralegal is the easiest and most lucrative home business in the country. CALL NOW (999) 555-5555 for your reservation in this seminar. The first ten calls will receive a FREE $50 manual entitled "How to Sue Any SOB for Millions without a Lawyer."

James Jones Is Booked to Make Over $400,000 Next Year

The time is NOW to get started. Riches await you. Because of the demand for this program, all the Monday and Wednesday evening tutorial classes are filled, and there is a waiting period of over ten months. There are still a few seats left in our Tuesday/Thursday evening tutorial sessions and two seats left for the Saturday session. HURRY! Call (999) 555-5555 for a schedule of classes at a location near you.

EXHIBIT 5–5   Sample Advertisement Promoting an Independent Paralegal Service Franchise

unlawful detainer
A statutory procedure whereby a landlord can legally evict a tenant in default on the rent.

that the public has about the paralegal profession, they are not aware of these inaccuracies. The program offered in the advertisement is actually a promotion for a paralegal school that teaches its students how to operate an independent paralegal service by purchasing its software and program at a very high price. No legal education or experience is required. Graduates of the program are calling themselves paralegals and doing legal work for the public. The public has no way of knowing whether the independent paralegal service is operated by a knowledgeable, experienced paralegal or by one with no paralegal training.

Exhibits 5–6, 5–7, and 5–8 are examples of notices sent to people who were being evicted from their home or apartment. The independent paralegal service searches court records for new **unlawful detainer** actions and mails the notice to the evictees. One of the methods used by the independent paralegal service to delay a customer's eviction proceedings is filing bankruptcy for the customer. Unsophisticated people subject to eviction proceedings often are not aware of the ramifications of a bankruptcy proceeding and suffer its consequences for years in the future. To curb this illegal activity, the California legislature passed a law making access to unlawful detainer court records restricted to authorized personnel only. However, this type of activity still exists today. See the accompanying CD for the complete law of Legal Document Assistants *in California.*

Without some type of regulation, these illegitimate programs and services will continue to proliferate. Regulating independent paralegals is currently being considered by many

Brown Legal Offices
555-555-1000

YOUR ACTION IS REQUIRED

Dear Tenant:

Your landlord has filed an EVICTION LAWSUIT against you. This is the first step in an action to EVICT you from your residence.

Please take note. You have only five (5) CALENDAR DAYS to file a response in person with the court. If you do not answer within these five days, you could lose the case by default. A Marshal will post a "FIVE-DAY NOTICE TO VACATE" within a few days.

Our office can help you STOP THIS ACTION. By calling NOW, we can help you get the time required to find a new residence or even stay in the premises you now occupy. Don't be forced out of your home with only a few days to relocate. We will extend the time or prevent the action. Don't be misled by other companies claiming to get you more than two months or that others only give you the forms to complete.

WE COMPLETE ALL FORMS FOR YOU. YOU ONLY NEED TO SIGN THEM.

DO NOT DELAY - CALL NOW

YOUR QUICK ACTION IS A MUST. Call us today for an appointment. You will need to bring this letter and any other documents you have received.

EVENING/WEEKEND APPOINTMENTS ARE AVAILABLE
OUR COMPLETE FEE IS ONLY $50.00
WE FILE ALL COURT DOCUMENTS
WE CAN COME TO YOU

EXHIBIT 5–6   Sample Independent Paralegal Service Letter to a Tenant Facing Eviction #1

OFFICIAL NOTICE

OUR RECORDS INDICATE THERE IS A NOTICE OF TRIAL/HEARING

TO ALL PARTIES:

PLEASE TAKE NOTICE that your Answer–Unlawful Detainer case has been set for COURT TRIAL on _____ at _____ [time] _____ in Division _____ of the _____ [name of court and address]_____.

**RESPONDING TO THIS NOTICE WILL GIVE YOU
ADDITIONAL TIME TO RESOLVE YOUR SITUATION.**

REMAIN IN YOUR PREMISES UP TO SIX (6) MONTHS

CALL TODAY FOR MORE INFORMATION

International Paralegal Services
Bankruptcy * Eviction Defense
24-Hour Service

EXHIBIT 5–7   Sample Independent Paralegal Service Letter to a Tenant Facing Eviction #3

SPEEDY PARALEGAL SERVICES
555-555-2000

DEAR TENANT:

An EVICTION LAWSUIT has been filed against you by your landlord. The purpose of the lawsuit is to evict you from your premises. **REMEMBER This OFFICE IS HERE TO HELP YOU!!!!!**

If you have been served with a Court summons, you only have five (5) days "including weekends" in which to file a proper legal response. If you fail to answer within this time period, your landlord may win a JUDGMENT BY DEFAULT AND WILL THEN HAVE THE MARSHAL POST A "FIVE-DAY NOTICE TO VACATE" AND HAVE YOUR DOORS LOCKED AT YOUR RESIDENCE WITHIN A FEW DAYS.

If you have received your notice **CALL ME IMMEDIATELY!!!! "YOU MUST ACT IMMEDIATELY." TIME IS OF THE ESSENCE!!!!!!**

All County Paralegal Services will help you prepare your legal documents, including any legal defenses and follow-up consultation.

WE CAN HELP YOU TO REMAIN IN YOUR PREMISES FOR UP
TO FOUR MONTHS. RESPONDING TO THIS LETTER WILL GET
YOU ADDITIONAL TIME TO RESOLVE YOUR SITUATION.

Call our office as soon as you receive this letter and have a Counselor come out to your home with no trouble to you, or come in to one of our offices. Office hours are 8:00 A.M. to 8:00 P.M. seven days a week. **"REMEMBER YOU MUST ACT NOW"**

WE MAKE HOME CALLS
24-HOUR SERVICE
BANKRUPTCY CONSOLATION

EXHIBIT 5–8   Sample Independent Paralegal Service Letter to a Tenant Facing Eviction #2

states and will be developed in the next decade. One thing is for sure: The debate over the unauthorized practice of law will continue into the future.

CONCLUSION

According to Therese Cannon in her book *Ethics and Professional Responsibility for Legal Assistants*, paralegals can advance professionalism through commitment to the following eight areas:

1. Public service
2. Education
3. High standards of ethical conduct
4. Excellence
5. Strong work ethic
6. Integrity and honor
7. Development of the whole person
8. Exercising good judgment, common sense, and communication skills

   It is important that all paralegals exhibit the professionalism that comes from a commitment to these elements to ensure that the paralegal profession will be strong and continue to grow in future decades.

SUMMARY

Many organizations such as national and state bar associations; national, state, and local paralegal associations; and the courts have developed ethical guidelines for paralegals to follow. Paralegals are not bound by the attorney's state bar code of ethics but comply with them to protect their employers from liability.

In 1967, the ABA promoted the concept of paralegals and developed guidelines for lawyers' use of them. In addition to the ABA's guidelines, some local and state bar associations have adopted guidelines for the use of paralegals as well as the three national paralegal associations. Some state and local paralegal associations developed their own ethical code or adopted the ethical code of a national paralegal association.

The same elements of the five Cs of client relations discussed in Chapter 4 apply to paralegals. They are competence, commitment, communication, conflict of interest, and confidentiality.

The four aspects of a lawyer's competency apply to paralegals: legal knowledge, skill, thoroughness, and preparation. You acquire legal knowledge in school and continuing legal education, and applying that knowledge to clients' cases creates skill. Thoroughness is accomplished by adequate preparation. The more knowledgeable you become, the more skillful you are. The more skillful you are, the more thorough you are. The more thorough you are, the more competent you are.

Knowledge of the eight areas that indicate a lack of commitment will alert paralegals to possible commitment problem areas.

Paralegals can greatly assist an attorney in communicating with clients. Responding to a client's correspondence or request for a status report consists of writing a letter to the client or telephoning the client with the information. A paralegal may draft a letter for the attorney's review without being specifically directed to do so. When communicating with clients, a paralegal must have a firm understanding of what is legal advice and what is not. If a paralegal applies knowledge of the law to the facts of a case and renders an opinion, it is legal advice. If a paralegal is asked a question that requires legal advice, she or he must ask the attorney for the answer even though she or he may know the answer. A paralegal must also be careful not to sign a letter to a client containing legal advice and must always identify her- or himself as a paralegal so that the client understands that the paralegal is not an attorney. Another area of a paralegal's communication with clients that is forbidden is accepting a case. It is the attorney's responsibility to accept or reject a case.

A lawyer's duty to maintain clients' confidences extends to paralegals. Confidentiality also extends to the maintenance of clients' files. Be careful when communicating with clients by e-mail. Transmitting information to an unsecured e-mail address may interfere with attorney-client privilege.

The activities that constitute the unauthorized practice of law are subject to statute, regulation, or case law interpretation of each state. Court decisions throughout the country have identified various elements of the practice of law. Paralegals may not represent a client in court. However, paralegals may represent clients before many federal or state administrative agencies. Paralegals are also prohibited from representing a client at a deposition.

When paralegals prepare legal documents, a problem arises when the documents are prepared without the attorney's direct supervision. Experts disagree on where to draw the line in this area. Some states forbid their court clerks to tell a person who wants to process his or her own divorce what form to use. Other states' courts employ paralegals and other nonattorney staff solely for that purpose. Some states are establishing laws and guidelines for nonattorneys to be able to complete forms for the public. Paralegals may draft and prepare pleadings, but they may not sign the pleadings.

There been many court rulings that have dealt with the area of legal advice and the unauthorized practice of law. The majority of court rulings indicate that legal kits and books themselves do not constitute legal advice as long as they are not sold in conjunction with personalized assistance in completing the process. The parameters of legal advice are constantly being revised.

Independent paralegals provide legal services directly to the public in areas such as divorce, bankruptcy, immigration, and landlord-tenant matters. They direct their services to low- and moderate-income people who cannot afford an attorney. When independent paralegal services emerged in the 1970s, their owners were prosecuted for the unauthorized practice of law.

In the late 1980s, the State Bar of California found that there was "an overwhelming unmet need" for better access to legal services for low- and moderate-income people and that independent paralegals can help meet that need. In late 1998, California enacted sections 6400–6415 of the California Business and Professions Code, which allows paralegals, known as legal document assistants, to do "scrivener-type" services for the public if they register with the county and post a bond. Other states are enacting similar legislation or are considering similar legislation. The lack of regulation of the paralegal profession, especially independent paralegal services, has created problems for the paralegal profession as a whole. "Fly-by-night" independent paralegal programs and services are unqualified and damaging to their customers and the paralegal profession.

It is important that all paralegals exhibit the professionalism that comes from a commitment to ethical behavior to ensure that the paralegal profession will be strong and continue to grow in future decades.

CHAPTER ILLUSTRATION

The law firm of Black, White & Greene was still reeling from the Tinker Town Toy conflict-of-interest problem that plagued them in Chapter 4. Tricia worked hard to get their conflict-checking system up and running. They hired outside data processing people to go through every case the firm has handled and input all parties and other pertinent information into the system. Now, before the firm accepts a case, they will check their conflicts system to determine whether the firm has a potential or direct conflict of interest.

Tricia arranged for all the employees to be trained on the system, including each attorney. As Milton was being trained, he noticed that he may have a conflict of interest in a case the firm was handling against MidTown Manufacturing Company. He noticed that MidTown was represented by the law firm for which he used to work. He remembered working on the case, but he could not remember much about it. He thought that he had better bring it to Robert's and Tricia's attention.

He consulted with Robert and Tricia about the potential conflict problem. The case is Patrizia Boen's case, so Milton has not worked on it. Melvin, Patrizia's paralegal, has worked on it. However, to avoid any more conflict-of-interest problems, Robert and Tricia decided to erect a Chinese wall around Milton as it pertained to the MidTown Manufacturing case.

Tricia immediately prepared a memorandum to all employees explaining that Milton must be isolated from the MidTown Manufacturing case. All employees were forbidden to discuss the case around Milton, and he could not be near anyone when they were working on the case. They gathered the documents concerning the MidTown case and transferred them to bright-red file folders. The folders had large letters on the front: "SUBJECT TO CHINESE WALL ERECTED AROUND PARALEGAL MILTON NOLLKAMPER." Patrizia Boen, the responsible attorney, was instructed to keep the files in her office in a locked filing cabinet. The files were not to be filed in the general filing area with the other clients' files, where Milton could see them. She was to work on the case in her office with the door closed. Melvin was also instructed to work on the case in his office with the door closed. In addition, Patrizia was instructed to inform her client, JB Asphalt Service, of the potential conflict and the efforts of the firm to isolate Milton from the case. Patrizia was also directed to obtain a release from JB indicating that they are aware of the potential conflict of interest and that they have been informed about the efforts of the firm to isolate the employee with the conflict.

With the Chinese wall firmly erected around Milton, the firm was comfortable with their efforts to eliminate the MidTown conflict. A conflict of interest, however, was not the only problem they would have with the MidTown case.

Melvin was working on JB Asphalt's response to MidTown's request for the production of documents. Patrizia wrote Melvin a memo with instructions on how to prepare the response. The memo told him to object to requested documents 10 through 15 as being protected under attorney-client privilege and documents 18 through 21 as subject to the attorney work-product doctrine. He was instructed to submit the other requested documents. Melvin was instructed to obtain all the requested documents from the client. The response was due in 30 days. Melvin obtained all the documents from JB and started to draft the response. He got sick with the flu and did not come to work for a week. Patrizia was getting ready to go on vacation to Europe and was starting to panic because her work was not getting done because Melvin was out sick. The other paralegal, Milton, was isolated from the MidTown case, so he could not step in to help Melvin with the response. Melvin returned to work the day Patrizia was leaving for Europe.

The MidTown response was not the only deadline that faced Melvin when he returned. His desk was piled high with files that needed to be processed before Patrizia left for Europe. He was overwhelmed. Patrizia instructed him, "We have to get the complaints done on the two eminent domain cases today. They have to be filed tomorrow. Call MidTown's attorney and get a continuance on the responses until I return." "OK," said Melvin. Melvin called MidTown's attorney, who was not available. His secretary told him that he would return his call. He worked on the two eminent domain complaints and completed them. Patrizia reviewed them, signed them, and left for Europe.

The next day, MidTown's attorney returned Melvin's call. Melvin informed him that Ms. Boen was out of town and would return in 2 weeks. He requested a continuance on the responses until after she returned. MidTown's attorney blew up. "What! You want a continuance? This case is set to go to trial in 2 months! No, you may not have a continuance. Get that response to me today!" Melvin tried to explain the situation. He told him that he had been ill for a week, putting the project behind schedule. "I don't want to hear your excuses," said MidTown's attorney. "I'd better have that response today, or I'll ask the court for sanctions against you!"

Melvin went right to work on the response. He was under pressure to get them done before 4 p.m., the time when the messenger was coming to pick it up to deliver it to MidTown's attorney. He quickly prepared it, included all the documents, signed Patrizia's name to it without adding his initials, and sent it off with the messenger.

At 7 p.m. that evening, as Melvin relaxed in front of the television set, he remembered Patrizia's memo about the response. "Ohhhh shi———!" Melvin jumped into his car and went directly to the office. He found the memo in the file. "Object to requested documents 10 through 15 as being protected under attorney-client privilege and documents 18 through 21 as subject to the attorney work-product doctrine." Melvin's response did not object to anything. He had included those protected documents. He knew he was in trouble. The documents he attached that were subject to privilege were very important. They showed their client in a negative light, and if the opposition saw them, they might lose the case. He had to get the response back.

Melvin called MidTown's attorney the first thing in the morning. "I have to have the response back," Melvin said. "It is incorrect." "What do you mean it's incorrect?" asked MidTown's attorney. "It contains all the documents I requested, and it is signed by Ms. Boen." "But," said Melvin, "she did not sign it. I was in a hurry to get it to you, and I signed it." "I don't believe you," MidTown's attorney responded. "You know that a paralegal can't sign pleadings. No, I won't return it to you. Have Ms. Boen call me as soon as she returns."

When Patrizia returned, Melvin told her what happened. She turned pale. She consulted with Robert and Tricia about the problem. They all agreed that Melvin should be fired, and he was.

The attorneys in the firm expect their staff to know the ethics involved in legal practice, but this problem alerted them to the possibility that their employees' ethics training needed improvement. Tricia consulted with an attorney who specialized in ethics and hired him to develop and conduct ethics workshops for the firm. The workshops were conducted every Wednesday evening for 2 months, and attendance was mandatory for all employees, including the attorneys.

CHAPTER REVIEW

1. Who conceived of the concept of paralegals, and why was the profession created?
2. How is a paralegal's competence increased?
3. What are the eight things that indicate a lack of commitment to a client's case?

4. What is legal advice?
5. What five activities constitute giving legal advice?
6. What are the exceptions to paralegals giving legal advice?
7. A paralegal may not accept a case. Why?
8. When does a paralegal have a conflict of interest?
9. What are some things a paralegal can do to keep a client's matter confidential?
10. What three activities are the main elements of practicing law?
11. What is the unauthorized practice of law?
12. What determines the unauthorized practice of law for each state?
13. What is an independent paralegal?
14. According to *People v. Landlords Professional Services,* what clerical activities are not included in the unauthorized practice of law?
15. What are some abuses of the lack of regulation of the paralegal profession?

EXAMPLES FOR DISCUSSION

1. *ADAPTED FROM* LOUISIANA STATE BAR ASSOCIATION V. EDWINS, *540 SO. 2D 294 LA. (1989)*

Stacy Williams is a freelance paralegal doing business in New York City under the name Prompt Paralegal Service. She employs her daughter as a secretary. Stacy works mainly for attorneys who need extra help in the area of litigation support.

One afternoon, Stacy was contacted by Tim Hemstreet, an attorney with an office in Washington, DC. He asked Stacy for some help on a case he had in New York. He asked Stacy to serve a defendant and prepare some interrogatories for him. He was impressed with Stacy's abilities and soon gave her more work. One morning, Hemstreet telephoned Stacy with a proposal. Tim wanted to develop a New York clientele and needed a branch office. He proposed to use Stacy's office as a New York branch office. He would list Stacy's office address as a branch office and would split office expenses with her. Stacy could still be a freelance paralegal, but Tim wants her to make his cases her first priority. Stacy agreed. The first thing Stacy did was take down the sign in front of her office that read "Prompt Paralegal Service" and exchanged it for a sign that said "Law Offices." If someone should walk in looking for an attorney, the secretary would direct the client to Stacy, who would interview the client, prepare a fee agreement, and get the case started.

Tim was busy with his Washington, DC, cases and was never in the New York office. Stacy handled all his New York cases. She prepared complaints, answers, motions, and discovery. She faxed drafts of the documents she prepared to Tim for his approval and review. Tim would okay the documents and instructed Stacy to sign the pleadings for him. When Stacy complained about signing his name, he sent her a signature stamp of his signature so that all she had to do was stamp the document with the signature stamp. Soon, he became so confident in Stacy's abilities that he told her not to bother faxing the documents to him for his review. He was too busy to look them over. He told her to just sign the pleadings and file them with the court. Tim made all the court appearances, but Stacy did all the rest of the work for his New York clients.

1. Did Stacy violate any ethical guidelines? If so, what are they?
2. Did Tim violate any ethical guidelines? If so, what are they?
3. If you were Stacy, how would you handle the situation?
4. If you were Tim, what would you do differently?
5. If the State Bar of New York learned of Stacy's and Tim's arrangement, what would they do to Stacy? To Tim?

2. *ADAPTED FROM* IN RE ANDERSON, *79 B.R. 482; BANKR. S.D. CAL. (1987)*

Janis is a factory worker employed by a paper manufacturing company. She is having financial difficulties and wants to know more about bankruptcy. She noticed an ad in the newspaper placed by J. R. Elms & Associates, a local independent paralegal service that advertised that they specialized in bankruptcy. Janis called for more information, and Joe Elms came to her house for an interview.

Joe told Janis that J. R. Elms was a legal typing service. He explained that he was not an attorney and could not give her legal advice. He gave her a questionnaire to complete to list her assets and liabilities and creditors' names and addresses. Janis had only a few creditors. She owed her home mortgage and a couple of credit card companies. Her credit card debt totaled $5,000. Janis asked Joe a number of questions pertaining to the consequences of bankruptcy. He said, "Bankruptcy no longer has a stigma attached to it. Everyone is filing bankruptcy now." She asked him what the difference was between a Chapter 7 bankruptcy and a Chapter 13 bankruptcy. Joe told her that she was ineligible to file a Chapter 13 bankruptcy (although she was eligible) and that a Chapter 13 would cost her more money. She asked Joe whether she would lose her house if she filed for Chapter 7. He said yes. She also asked him whether she would be able to keep her income tax refund that she expected to get. He said yes. She told Joe that she was expecting to receive some money from her grandmother as an inheritance and asked whether she would have to report it. Joe responded, "No, don't worry about it. I'll handle everything for you." She paid Joe the total fee for the bankruptcy. He assured her that he would handle everything and asked her to sign an agreement and guarantee that read:

> I, the undersigned, hereby authorize J. R. Elms & Associates, a legal scrivener service, to transcribe the information submitted herewith, in order for them to complete the proper legal forms for me to file bankruptcy. I consider myself competent to represent myself in court and do not expect J. R. Elms & Associates to give me any legal advice or represent me in court or in any manner whatsoever.

1. Did Joe engage in the unauthorized practice of law? How?
2. Did Joe give Janis legal advice? When?
3. How would Joe's activities not be construed as unauthorized practice of law?

3. DO INDEPENDENT PARALEGALS CONTRIBUTE A SERVICE OR BREAK THE LAW?

There is a controversy surrounding independent paralegal services and the unauthorized practice of law. Proponents of independent paralegals doing work directly for the public list the following in support of their position:

- Low-income people cannot afford the services of a licensed attorney and have no background or training to process legal cases for themselves. Without low-cost assistance, they would have no access to the legal system.
- Independent paralegals contribute a service to the community by making the legal system more accessible to people.
- Independent paralegals contribute a service to the legal system by helping pro se parties process cases for themselves correctly, thereby reducing misfilings with the court.
- The cases processed by independent paralegals are normally routine and uncomplicated and do not involve complex issues. They are the types of cases that attorneys normally delegate to paralegals under their supervision.

Opponents to independent paralegals list the following in support of their position:

- Most states do not regulate independent paralegals. Therefore, unqualified persons can become independent paralegals, and this does great harm to the reputations of qualified independent paralegals and harm to the customers they serve.
- Completing forms and documents for others has been determined in various jurisdictions as giving legal advice, an activity forbidden to paralegals.

- Independent paralegals have no law school education, so are unable to spot complicated issues that require more sophisticated legal services, to the detriment of their customers.
- Paralegals should abide by the law and not step outside the boundaries of the law.

1. Should independent paralegals be allowed to prepare documents for the public without an attorney's supervision? Why or why not?
2. When should independent paralegals be authorized to do work for the public?
3. When should independent paralegals not be authorized to do work for the public?
4. Should independent paralegals be licensed?
5. If independent paralegals should be licensed, should traditional paralegals be licensed also?
6. If independent paralegals should be licensed, who should the licensing agency be?
7. What qualifications should an independent paralegal have?

4. Conflicts of Interest

As seen in this chapter, a firm can be disqualified from a case if its paralegal worked on the case when employed by the opposing law firm. Do you think that paralegals should be subject to the same rules on conflicts of interest as those governing lawyers? Do you think that different conflict rules should be applied to government lawyers and paralegals? Why or why not?

5. *Adapted from* De Vaux v. American Home Assurance Co., *387 Mass. 814, 444 N.E. 2d 355 (1983)*

A client called an attorney's office seeking legal advice for injuries she received in a fall in a department store. The secretary told the client to write a letter to the store informing them of her fall and injuries, and she arranged for the client to receive a medical examination with the store's doctor. She also told the client to write a letter to the attorney requesting legal services. The client wrote the letters and personally delivered the attorney's letter to the attorney's office, but it was misfiled and not seen by the attorney.

The client called the attorney a number of times, but the attorney did not return her calls. After 3 years, the statute of limitations expired, and the client sued the attorney for malpractice. In his answer, the attorney stated that he was never retained to represent the client and that no attorney-client relationship was established. The client stated that the secretary was the attorney's agent and therefore had *apparent authority* to establish the attorney-client relationship and that the client reasonably relied on the attorney's secretary. Her reliance established the attorney-client relationship. *Apparent authority* was defined as "authority that results from conduct by the principal which causes a third person reasonably to believe that a particular person has authority to enter into negotiations or make representations as his agent." The attorney asserted that the secretary had no authority to establish the attorney-client relationship. Where there is no attorney-client relationship, there can be no breach of duty and therefore no liability. The client claimed that the attorney placed the secretary in a position in which prospective clients might reasonably believe that she had the authority to establish the attorney-client relationship.

1. How do you think the court ruled in this case?
2. Did the secretary create the appearance of having the authority to establish the attorney-client relationship?
3. What aspects of the five Cs of client relations apply to this case?
4. What were the secretary's ethical violations, if any?
5. What were the attorney's ethical violations, if any?
6. If you were the secretary, what would you have done?
7. If you were the attorney, what would you have done?
8. What ABA ethical rule(s) was violated?

6. Are the Restrictions on the Unauthorized Practice of Law too Stringent?

Do you think some activities that currently constitute the unauthorized practice of law should be allowed? If so, what activities? When should the activity be allowed? When should they not be allowed? How would relaxing the restrictions on the unauthorized practice of law affect the legal profession? The paralegal profession? The public? The court system?

7. Clerical versus Substantive Legal Work

The case of *People v. Landlords Professional Services* found on page 191 lists the clerical activities that do not constitute the unauthorized practice of law. When would those activities be considered the unauthorized practice of law? What is the difference between clerical and substantive activities? What activities would not be considered clerical? Discuss.

ASSIGNMENTS

1. Look in the telephone book for ads from independent paralegals. Clip them out and insert each one on a separate sheet of paper. Also, find ads for freelance paralegal services. What are the differences in the ads? Do you see any ads for bankruptcy petition preparers that violate Rule 6 of Section 110 of Title 11 of the United States Code, which is on the accompanying CD (Bankruptcy Petition Preparers) prohibiting the word *legal* in the company's name or advertisements? Do you see any statements in advertisements for independent paralegal services that may mislead the public into believing that the independent paralegal is an attorney?

2. Describe what a paralegal must do when changing employment to avoid potential conflicts of interest.

3. Describe some things a paralegal can do to increase competence. What are some things a paralegal can do if her or his workload is too heavy to ensure thoroughness?

4. Refer to the Paralegal Regulation Chart on the accompanying CD and find your state. Obtain a copy of the state's regulation concerning paralegals. If your state has no regulation of paralegals, contact your state or local paralegal association and obtain a copy of its code of ethics. Prepare an outline of a paralegal's ethical responsibilities in your jurisdiction.

5. Role play the situations described in the examples to legal advice found on page 181. What would be the correct response in each situation?

6. Review the advertisement in Exhibit 5–5 and list all the inaccuracies and false or misleading statements made. If you cannot prove that some statements are false, how can you assume that some statements are false?

7. Research the websites listed in the Cybersites section at the end of the chapter relating to freelance paralegals and independent paralegals. What are the differences between the services offered by freelance paralegals and independent paralegals? What are the rates for independent paralegal services? What type of activities do they advertise?

SELF TEST

How well did you grasp the material in the chapter? Test yourself by answering the following questions and check your answers against the answers found in Appendix A.

1. What factors contribute to a person's ethical values?
2. How does the *Living Webster Encyclopedia Dictionary* define ethics?
3. Ethics cannot be defined as honest versus dishonest, right versus wrong, or good versus bad. Why?

4. What factors contribute to how we can recognize ethical issues?
5. Why do people with good intentions sometimes violate ethical standards?
6. How is the foundation of ethical standards established?
7. What organizations have developed ethical guidelines for paralegals to follow?
8. Are paralegals bound to an attorney's state bar code of ethics? Why?
9. Paralegals are lawyers'---------.
10. Can a paralegal be prosecuted by a state bar or governing agency for unethical behavior?
11. Who suffers from a paralegal's unethical conduct?
12. Why must paralegals abide by ethical codes?
13. Why was the paralegal profession established?
14. What did the ABA study conducted in the early 1960s reveal?
15. What differences did the ABA find between the legal profession and other professions?
16. The ABA determined that paralegals could enhance the legal profession by what three things?
17. What is the ABA's paralegal committee called?
18. When were the first formal paralegal education programs established?
19. When did the ABA begin its approval process of paralegal programs?
20. What are the names of the three national paralegal associations?
21. What are the sanctions that a paralegal association can impose on paralegals who violate its code of ethics?
22. Why has it been a problem to monitor adherence to an organization's ethical code?
23. What are the five Cs of client relations for paralegals?
24. What are the four aspects of a lawyer's competency that apply to paralegals?
25. How do you acquire legal knowledge?
26. How do you create skill?
27. How do you increase your knowledge and skill?
28. How do you develop thoroughness?
29. What factors affect thoroughness?
30. Why has technology been responsible for a lack of thoroughness?
31. What are the eight areas that indicate a lack of commitment to a client's case?
32. How can paralegals assist an attorney in communicating with clients?
33. What is a goodwill letter?
34. Who may give legal advice to a client?
35. What is a general guideline for legal advice?
36. What five activities constitute legal advice?
37. Why is the prohibition against giving legal advice difficult for experienced paralegals?
38. If a paralegal is asked a question that requires legal advice, what must she or he do?
39. May a paralegal sign a letter that contains legal advice?
40. What are the exceptions to the prohibition of paralegals giving legal advice?
41. What is the name of the case that created the "jailhouse lawyer"?
42. Why must paralegals always identify themselves as a paralegal?
43. Why is a paralegal prohibited from accepting a case?
44. What is nonlawyer conflict of interest?
45. What is a Chinese wall?
46. What restrictions does a Chinese wall impose?
47. Why must freelance paralegals keep a list of cases on which they have worked?
48. How can a paralegal ensure that a client's matter is kept confidential?
49. Why must an e-mail sent to a client be sent on a secure server?

50. How are the activities that constitute the unauthorized practice of law determined?
51. What three activities are determined to be the unauthorized practice of law?
52. When may paralegals represent clients?
53. May a paralegal ask a client questions at a deposition?
54. When does a paralegal's preparation of documents constitute the unauthorized practice of law?
55. What are unbundled legal services?
56. How have courts ruled concerning completion of a legal form?
57. Many courts employ nonattorneys to assist people with what function?
58. Why do courts employ nonattorneys to assist people in pro se cases?
59. May a paralegal sign a pleading?
60. Why must an attorney sign a pleading?
61. How did the court rule on the *Dacey* case?
62. What is a legal kit?
63. How did the courts rule concerning legal kits?
64. Where can you find a legal kit?
65. What is an independent paralegal?
66. What is a freelance paralegal?
67. What is the difference between an independent paralegal and a freelance paralegal?
68. What was the Wave Project?
69. What did Wave centers do?
70. What was the court's ruling in *Florida Bar v. Furman*?
71. Why was Furman's jail sentence commuted?
72. What type of services will California's SB 1418 allow?
73. According to California's SB 1418, what may independent paralegals not do?
74. What are independent paralegals called pursuant to SB 1418?
75. Why are bankruptcy petition preparers disfavored by trustees and bankruptcy courts?
76. What does HALT stand for?
77. What is a traditional paralegal?
78. Why do traditional paralegals and CAPA object to the title "legal document assistants"?
79. What are some other terms for independent paralegals?
80. What is the name of the case that lists the clerical activities that are not considered to constitute the unauthorized practice of law?
81. What has created problems for the paralegal profession and independent paralegals?
82. What are "fly-by-night" paralegal programs and services?
83. Why are "fly-by-night" paralegal programs dangerous?
84. How are unqualified paralegals allowed to proliferate?
85. What are the eight things to which a paralegal must be committed to ensure professionalism?

Key Words

certificate of service	legal document assistant	remedial
Chinese wall	mitigated	scrivener
cyberlawyer	postconviction writs	statute of limitations
deponent	probate	temporary restraining order
goodwill letter	pro bono publico	unbundled legal services
intranet	pro se	unlawful detainer

 **Cybersites**

UNAUTHORIZED PRACTICE OF LAW

Texas State Bar UPL Committee—<*http://www.txuplc.org*>

Mediation and UPL—<*http://www.mediate.ca/avoidingunauth.htm*>

Legal Ethics—<*http://www.legalethics.com/*>

Legal Ethics Forum—<*http://www.legalethicsforum.com*>

The Cato Institute—<*http://www.cato.org/pubs/regulation/*>

San Diego County Bar Association—<*http://www.sdcba.org/ethics/*>

American Bar Association—<*http://www.abanet.org/rppt/*>

HALT—<*http://www.halt.org*>

FREELANCE PARALEGALS

Paralegal Consultant Associates—<*http://www.paraconn.com*>

Paralegal Gateway—<*http://www.paralegalgateway.com/*>

Paralegal Press—<*http://www.njparalegal.com/*>

Midwest Paralegal Services, Inc. —<*http://www.midwestparalegal.com/*>

Chester County Freelance Paralegal Services—
     <*http://www.chescofreelanceparalegal.com*>

Colorado Freelance Paralegal Network—<*http://www.paralegalsfreelance.com/*>

Full Service Legal Support, LLC—<*http://www.fullservicesupport.com*>

Paralegal Services USA—<*http://www.paralegalservicesusa.com/*>

INDEPENDENT PARALEGALS

Divorce Services (Arizona)—<*http://www.paralegal-plus.com*>

California Association of Legal Document Assistants—<*http://www.calda.org*>

Robin Schumacher, LDA—<*http://www.robinschumacher.com/*>

Laguna Preparers Service—<*http://www.lagunaparalegal.com/*>

Document Assistant—<*http://www.documentassistant.com/*>

Cox & Associates A La Carte Real Estate Services—<*http://www.bayliving.com/*>

Alliance of Legal Document Professionals—<*http://www.aldap.com/*>

Tamara Parker, Legal Document Services—<*http://www.legaldocumentassistant.net*>

Legal Document Assistants Online—<*http://www.ldasource.com*>

BANKRUPTCY PETITION PREPARERS

Bridgeport Bankruptcy—<*http://bridgeportbankruptcy.com/*>

National Association of Bankruptcy Petition Preparers—<*http://www.nabpp.org/*>

Do It Yourself Documents—<*http://www.doityourselfdocuments.com/*>

 Student CD-ROM
For additional materials, please go to the CD in this book.

 Online Companion™
For additional resources, please go to http://www.paralegal.delmar.cengage.com

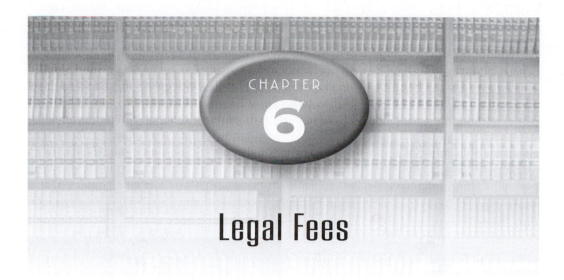

CHAPTER 6

Legal Fees

OBJECTIVES

After completion of this chapter, the student should be able to do the following:

- Describe the various types of fees charged in a law office.
- Explain the rules and ethics that apply to lawyers and paralegals regarding fees.
- Describe other methods of producing profits besides fees.
- Explain the factors considered when determining a reasonable fee.
- Calculate a lodestar fee.
- Explain liens for fees.
- Describe a paralegal's ethical responsibility concerning fees.
- Identify requirements for fee agreements.

INTRODUCTION

How law firms charge for their services makes the practice of law different from other businesses. A retail store prices its product according to the product's cost; a merchant **marks up** the product to ensure a profit. Law firms use different methods to price their product. They charge for lawyers' and paralegals' services. A thorough knowledge of legal fees will prepare a paralegal student to participate in firm profitability and management.

One of the goals of a law firm is to make a profit, and legal fees are a major part of law firm profitability. Other goals—to provide quality legal services at reasonable prices and to ensure employee growth—cannot be compromised to achieve profitability. Keeping a law firm profitable, while satisfying clients and employees, is a constant challenge for legal management.

A law firm goes to great lengths to establish a fee structure that is reasonable and maximizes profitability. In the competitive legal marketplace, it is a challenging task to keep fees affordable for a client and profitable for a firm. To do this, firms use various types of fees and charge different fees for different services. Developing a fee structure is not an arbitrary process; many issues are considered before a fee structure is established.

This chapter will discuss the history of legal fees, the various types of fees, the ethics involved in charging for legal services, the issues involved in setting fees, and fee agreements. Even though paralegals may not set fees, knowledge of the methods used to do so will give

mark up
To add a percentage on the cost of an item for profit.

them an understanding of law firm management. The chapter will explain when the different fees are used and will discuss the division of fees and other forms of law firm income.

Federal and state laws, and national and state bar associations, produce guidelines concerning legal fees. This chapter will review these guidelines and examples of fee agreements. Since paralegals often draft fee agreements, these examples will enable paralegal students to become familiar with fee agreement provisions. The chapter will review paralegals' ethical responsibilities concerning legal fees. Finally, the chapter will discuss legal fee agreements.

HISTORICAL PERSPECTIVE

Throughout history, lawyers' fees have been the subject of debate and controversy. At the time of the Roman republic, legal services were free of charge—rendered for the honor and personal satisfaction the advocate received by providing them. As Roman law became more complex, providing legal services became more complicated, and the advocates requested money or some other form of compensation for doing so. This practice was highly scandalous, and a law was passed prohibiting advocates from charging for their services.

With the fall of the Roman republic, lawyers again sought monetary compensation for their services. Emperor Augustus decreed this practice unlawful and assessed lawyers who charged for their services a fine of four times the amount charged. However, this decree did not eliminate lawyers' attempts to charge for their services.

After hearing arguments on the advantages and disadvantages of lawyers' fees, Emperor Claudius passed a law permitting lawyers to accept a fee as long as the fee did not exceed a certain amount. Under this law, however, a client was under no legal obligation to pay a lawyer a fee.

The ancient practice of providing gratuitous legal services certainly has not prevailed into modern times, but accountability for a fee has remained. Society's reluctance to pay lawyers has created the requirement that a lawyer's fee be reasonable and proper. To ensure that a lawyer's fee is reasonable and proper, bar associations have established rules and guidelines that govern legal fees. Various types of fees have evolved to ensure client satisfaction, reasonableness, and profit for a firm.

TYPES OF FEES

To gain a complete understanding of law firm profitability, one must have an understanding of the types of fees charged to clients. The different types of fees are retainer, hourly, flat (or fixed), task-based, contingency, statutory, referral, premium, value-based, and combination, or hybrid, fees.

Retainer Fees

A considerable amount of confusion arises over the meaning of the term *retainer*. The legal profession has used the term for decades—but with different meanings. It is common to hear the statement "The client has retained the firm." This means that the client has secured the services of the law firm. It also may mean that the client has paid the firm a retainer fee. But what type of retainer fee? Four types of retainer fees are used: true, nonrefundable chargeable, nonrefundable nonchargeable, and refundable chargeable.

TRUE RETAINER   A true retainer fee is paid to a law firm to ensure the firm's availability to a client. No services are provided in return for the fee. This type of fee was prevalent before the 1960s, when few law firms existed. A client paid a true retainer fee to secure a firm's loyalty and availability to the client and to ensure that the firm would not accept a case against the client.

No standard amount was used for a true retainer fee; the fee was agreed on between the client and the firm. The payment schedule was also subject to agreement—the fee could be paid annually, biannually, quarterly, or monthly.

Since the 1960s, it is rare for a law firm to receive a true retainer fee. Increased competition in the legal arena and the advent of ethical rules that mandate a lawyer's loyalty to clients and former clients have made a true retainer fee unnecessary.

NONREFUNDABLE CHARGEABLE RETAINER   A nonrefundable chargeable retainer fee is paid in advance of representation, is not refundable to a client in most circumstances, and is applied toward the total fee. If a client's case should end before the retainer fee is used or if the client should discharge the firm, the remaining retainer fee is not returned to the client. For example, if the fee for a divorce is $2,000 and a lawyer requires a $1,000 nonrefundable chargeable retainer, the $1,000 is applied as advance payment for the $2,000 fee but is not returned to the client if the client has second thoughts about filing for divorce or terminates the attorney-client relationship.

Nonrefundable chargeable retainers are also used to make an attorney available to a client. For example, when a client needs to have access to an attorney by telephone, the client will pay a firm a nonrefundable chargeable retainer for anticipated services for the coming month. Any time spent by the attorney is deducted from the retainer. The remaining retainer at the end of the month is not returned to the client. If the client should not use the attorney's services during the month, the client is not entitled to reimbursement of the fee. This type of fee encourages a lawyer's availability and gives the client a priority on the lawyer's time.

NONREFUNDABLE NONCHARGEABLE RETAINER   A nonrefundable nonchargeable retainer is paid to a firm at the beginning of a case and is not applied to a client's bill. It is not returned to a client should the client decide not to retain the firm or elect to discharge the firm for any reason. This type of retainer is often called a sign-up bonus.

Many firms use nonrefundable nonchargeable retainers to ensure client loyalty to a firm. It also discourages a client from **lawyer hopping,** or seeking advice and representation from a series of lawyers, which is very time consuming for lawyers. This type of retainer also tests a client's commitment to a case. Some clients are willing to pay this type of fee for the services of a prominent lawyer.

Each state has its own rules governing nonrefundable retainer fees. In some states, conditions are imposed on nonrefundable retainers, and in others nonrefundable retainers are not allowed. A New York lawyer charged his criminal client a nonrefundable fee of $15,000, and a fee agreement was signed indicating the nonrefundable nature of the fee. A month later, the client discharged the attorney and demanded a refund of the fee. The request was denied, and the client filed a grievance against the lawyer. At the grievance hearing, the court found that the nonrefundable nature of the fee was attorney misconduct, and the attorney was suspended from practicing law for 2 years. On appeal, the New York Court of Appeals upheld the 2-year suspension and stated that the nonrefundable fee agreement interfered with the client's right to discharge the lawyer and was a form of economic coercion against that right (*In the Matter of Cooperman,* March 17, 1994, New York Court of Appeals).

REFUNDABLE CHARGEABLE RETAINER   A refundable chargeable retainer fee is applied to a total fee and is returned if a client terminates an attorney-client relationship. This type of retainer is used in cases in which a client will likely not pay the bill.

For example, Melissa Edwards secured the services of Consuelo Lagos to defend her in a lawsuit filed by her landlord. Consuelo told Melissa that the firm would charge $200 an hour for each hour spent on the case and requested a $2,000 refundable retainer fee that would be applied toward her bill. In essence, the retainer fee was prepayment for 10 hours of Consuelo's time. The $2,000 was collected from Melissa and deposited in the firm's client funds account, and Consuelo would withdraw the money as the fee was earned.

Consuelo answered the complaint and began negotiations with the landlord's attorney. After about 5 hours' work, they reached a settlement, and the landlord dismissed his case against Melissa. Consuelo withdrew $1,000 from the funds account as payment of the fee and returned the remaining $1,000 to Melissa. Had the $2,000 retainer fee been nonrefundable and chargeable, the services fee would have been deducted from it, but Melissa would have received no

lawyer hopping
Going from lawyer to lawyer for advice and representation.

money back. If the $2,000 had been a nonrefundable nonchargeable retainer fee, Melissa would have received no money back and also been sent a bill for $1,000 for Consuelo's time.

★ Hourly Fees

Hourly fees are the most common fees charged. In some areas, they are the only acceptable method of charging clients. With hourly fees, a client is charged by the hour for each hour or portion of an hour spent on a case.

Clients are billed according to the hourly rate of a person working on a case. Different hourly rates are set for partners, associates, paralegals, and law clerks. In addition, different hourly rates are established within those categories to compensate a person for education, experience, specialty, and seniority.

Hourly rates vary according to specialty, geographic area, and years of experience. An experienced antitrust attorney may charge $500 an hour in the Midwest and as much as $800 an hour in major metropolitan areas, such as New York. Some firms vary their hourly rates according to the type of client served; they charge higher hourly rates for corporate clients and lower hourly rates for individual clients. The reasoning is that corporate clients have more complex issues than individual clients.

A typical case will involve a senior attorney, a junior attorney, and a paralegal. A senior attorney may bill $500 an hour, a junior attorney $300 an hour, and a paralegal $100 an hour. It is not uncommon to have five or six different people working on a case, each with a different hourly rate.

Exhibit 6–1 shows paralegal billing rates as reported by the *Legal Assistant Today* 2007 Annual Salary Survey. Large, metropolitan areas have higher billing rates than rural areas, and some areas of the country have lower billing rates.

BLENDED HOURLY RATES Instead of charging a client different hourly rates for different employees working on a case, a firm may offer the client a blended hourly rate, which is an average hourly rate of the people working on the case. For example, the average of a senior partner billing at $400 an hour, a junior partner billing at $300 an hour, an associate billing at $200 an hour, a junior associate billing at $150 an hour, and a paralegal at $100 an hour is $230 per hour. A client is billed $230 an hour for the time spent by each timekeeper. This eliminates complicated billing statements setting forth the billing rates of each person.

For example, Sam Aparacio is the owner of a real estate development firm. Sam had an hourly fee agreement with Black, White & Greene. Sam consulted Grant Greene on a case

HOURLY RATE	PERCENTAGE
$156 or more	9
$136–$155	9
$116–$135	12.4
$96–$115	13.5
$86–$95	21.3
$76–$85	9
$66–$75	12.4
$56–$65	6.7
$46–$55	1.1
$36–$45	1.1
$26–$35	2.2
$15–$25	2.2

EXHIBIT 6–1 Paralegal Billing Rate (*As seen in the March/April 2007 issue of* Legal Assistant Today. *Copyright 2007 James Publishing, Inc. Reprinted courtesy of* Legal Assistant Today. *For subscription information call 800-394-2626, or visit <http://www.legalassistanttoday.com>.)*

Black, White & Greene, LLC

For services rendered for initial conferences regarding real estate case:

SERVICES	HOURS	AMOUNT
Partner Grant Greene	4.0	$1,600.00
Senior partner Dennis White	2.0	900.00
Associate Patrizia Boen	2.0	600.00
Associate George Templeton	4.0	1,200.00
Paralegal Milton Nollkamper	2.0	200.00
Paralegal Julie Stockstill	2.0	200.00
Total		**$4,700.00**

Hourly rates

Partner Grant Greene	400.00	
Senior partner Dennis White	450.00	
Associate Patrizia Boen	300.00	
Associate George Templeton	300.00	
Paralegal Milton Nollkamper	100.00	
Paralegal Julie Stockstill	100.00	

EXHIBIT 6–2 Invoice for Straight Hourly Rate

for which he wished to retain the firm. They had agreed on the usual fee agreement of $450 an hour for senior partners, $400 for partner Grant, $300 an hour for associates, and $100 an hour for paralegals.

Sam had a 2-hour conference with Grant, explaining the case to him. Since the case was sizable, Grant included a senior partner and an associate in the conference. A week later, the Grant spent 2 hours going over the case with George, another associate. The next day, George had a 2-hour conference with the firm's two paralegals to inform them about the case.

To apprise the law firm of the case, and before any work was done, Sam received a bill, as shown in Exhibit 6–2, that set forth the various hourly rates for each timekeeper. Exhibit 6–3 is an example of a bill for the same services using blended hourly rates.

Black, White & Greene, LLC

For services rendered for initial conferences regarding real estate case:

SERVICES	HOURS	AMOUNT
Partner Grant Greene	4.0	$1,100.00
Senior partner Dennis White	2.0	550.00
Associate Patrizia Boen	2.0	550.00
Associate George Templeton	4.0	1,100.00
Paralegal Milton Nollkamper	2.0	550.00
Paralegal Julie Stockstill	2.0	550.00
Total		**$4,400.00**

Hourly rate is blended hourly rate at $275 per hour.

EXHIBIT 6–3 Invoice for Blended Hourly Rate

Note that the bill for the blended hourly rate is less than the one for the straight hourly rate. This is because more time was spent by senior attorneys than by paralegals. If paralegals spent most of the time on the case, the blended rate would result in higher fees than the straight hourly rate. In our example, $275 per hour is the average timekeepers' billing rate. This average is the blended hourly rate.

METHOD FOR DETERMINING HOURLY RATES   Putting a monetary value on legal services requires a great deal of skill, knowledge, and management expertise. Too often, hourly rates are determined by what the market will bear or what the competition is charging rather than on sound management principles. To determine what rates need to be charged in order to obtain a desired level of income and profit for a firm, a number of variables must be considered. Among them are the following:

- Planned or budgeted expenses, excluding partner or shareholder compensation and benefits
- Anticipated billable time by partner, associate, or paralegal
- Desired profit percentage
- Reasonable allocation of expenses by partner, associate, and paralegal
- Firm collection rate—billings divided by cash receipts
- Billing rate—work-in-progress billable time versus past billed hours

Other variables are also considered. The following is a list of examples of variables:

- Local living standards
- Experience of attorney
- Attorney's seniority
- Client's ability to pay
- Rates of competitors
- Attorney's specialty
- Attorney's ability
- Firm's prestige

The more experienced and reputable an attorney, the higher the hourly rate. A new associate attorney will have a lower hourly rate than an experienced senior partner. The reasoning is that an experienced attorney can produce work faster and with greater efficiency than an inexperienced attorney. Therefore, a higher rate is warranted for a more experienced legal professional. As of this writing, the highest hourly rate for a U.S. attorney is $1,000 per hour. Benjamin Civiletti, senior partner of Venable, LLC, was the U.S. Attorney General under President Jimmy Carter and specializes in internal investigations and corporate defense. He charges $1,000 per hour.

To calculate an hourly rate, one must consider overhead, profit, salary, and billable hours. For example, a junior attorney right out of law school desires a salary of $80,000 per year. He is expected to bill 1,500 hours a year (6.25 hours a day) for the salary. Overhead is 50 percent of his salary, and profit for the firm is 25 percent of overhead plus salary. How much money per hour must the junior attorney charge?

$$\$80,000 + \$40,000 \text{ overhead} + \$30,000 \text{ profit} = \$150,000 \text{ total receipts}$$

$$\$150,000 \div 1,500 = \$100.00 \text{ per hour}$$

Flat Fees

flat fee
One fee that is charged for an entire case; also known as a fixed fee.

A **flat-fee,** or fixed fee, is a set fee for a service rendered. For example, a simple will, uncontested dissolution of marriage proceedings, or drunk driving defense is usually charged one fee for the entire case.

PER DIEM FLAT FEES A **per diem** flat-fee is a fee charged by an attorney for a day's work. It is based on an attorney's hourly rate for 8 hours of the attorney's time. For example, if an attorney charges $200 an hour, the per diem charge would be $1,600 a day ($200 × 8 = $1,600). Attorneys charge per diem fees when they are in trial and cannot anticipate the length of the trial.

per diem
Latin term meaning "by the day".

MINIMUM AND MAXIMUM FLAT FEES In some cases, a firm may quote a client two flat fees: a minimum and a maximum. These types of flat fees are based on the outcome of a matter. If the outcome is extremely satisfying for the client, the maximum fee is charged. If the outcome is not as the client had hoped, the minimum fee is charged.

METHOD FOR ESTABLISHING FLAT FEES A law firm knows from experience approximately how long it takes to complete a certain type of case. If time records have been routinely kept, it is not difficult to compute an average of the time it takes to complete a case that falls in a particular category. An attorney's and paralegal's times are estimated, and a flat-fee is established based on their hourly rates for completion of the case. For example, for a simple will, a flat-fee might be determined as follows:

$$\text{Attorney 1 hour at \$300 an hour} = \$300$$
$$\text{Paralegal 2 hours at \$100 an hour} = \underline{200}$$
$$\text{Total cost} = \$500$$

Task-Based Fees

The trend toward task-based billing was created in the late 1990s by corporate legal departments who wanted to manage their legal costs more effectively and economically. It was developed as an alternative to hourly fees. For decades, various entities, especially corporate legal departments, have objected to hourly fees. They felt that charging by the hour encourages inefficiency and overstaffing projects. They also felt that hourly rates discourage delegating a task downward to a qualified member of the legal team with a lower hourly rate.

To eliminate some of these problems, representatives from the Litigation Section of the American Bar Association (ABA), the American Corporate Counsel Association, and corporate legal departments coordinated by Price Waterhouse LLP developed a task-based management system, which is shown in Exhibit 6–4. In a task-based system, legal work is categorized by phase. Each phase contains a list of tasks, and each task contains activities. Each task is given a specific fee or hourly rate that is appropriate to the level of complexity of the task. For example, in the pretrial pleadings and motions phase (code L200), there are six tasks: pleadings, preliminary injunctions, court-mandated conferences, dispositive motions, other written motions, and class-action certification and notice. The pleadings task includes such activities as researching, drafting, editing, filing and reviewing complaints, answers, and cross-complaints. For the pleadings task, the firm charges X dollars or X dollars per hour. For the preliminary injunctions task, the firm charges X dollars or X dollars per hour.

Categorizing legal services by task offers corporate clients many advantages over hourly billing. They can budget for legal costs and can estimate how much a case should cost. In addition, if all of the corporation's outside counsel use the same codes, such as the uniform coding system shown in Exhibit 6–4, corporations can compare their attorney's invoices and see which firm's services are the most reasonable.

Most firms find task-based timekeeping difficult to implement. Timekeepers must consult a long and detailed code list every time they make an entry on their time sheets. This process has been estimated at 5 to 10 percent of the total time devoted to the case. As a solution to this problem, firms are finding it necessary to acquire software that will calculate the fees and track the profitability of each phase or task. As more software is developed,

L100—Case assessment, development, and administration
    L110—Fact investigation/development
    L120—Analysis/strategy
    L130—Experts/consultants
    L140—Document/file management
    L150—Budgeting
    L160—Settlement/nonbinding ADR
    L190—Other case assessment, development, and administration
L200—Pretrial pleadings and motions
    L210—Pleadings
    L220—Preliminary injunctions/provisional remedies
    L230—Court-mandated conferences
    L240—Dispositive motions
    L250—Other written motions/submissions
    L260—Class-action certification and notice
L300—Discovery
    L310—Written discovery
    L320—Document production
    L330—Depositions
    L340—Expert discovery
    L350—Discovery motions
    L390—Other discovery
L400—Trial preparation and trial
    L410—Fact witnesses
    L420—Expert witnesses
    L430—Written motions/submissions
    L440—Other pretrial preparation and support
    L450—Trial and hearing attendance
    L460—Posttrial motions and submissions
    L470—Enforcement
L500—Appeal
    L510—Appellate motions and submissions
    L520—Appellate briefs
    L530—Oral argument

EXHIBIT 6–4   Uniform Task-Based Management System—Litigation Code Set

more firms will be able to offer their clients this type of fee. Software will allow a firm to use the task-based system (Exhibit 6–4) or develop individualized systems for each corporate client.

Paralegals who work for firms that charge task-based fees must be conscious of the budget and be careful not to exceed preset fee guidelines. For example, if a firm has projected that it would take 25 hours to summarize eight depositions, it has calculated its fee on the basis of that time prediction. If the paralegal should exceed the 25 hours, the firm's profit margin is affected. This kind of fee structure calls for strict discipline in work habits.

Contingency Fees

contingency fee
A fee consisting of a percentage of the possible recovery from a lawsuit.

A **contingency fee** is a fee based on a percentage of a client's recovery in a case. The average rate charged is normally 33.33 to 40 percent of the recovery. For example, if a client is awarded a judgment for $15,000, a lawyer might receive one-third of the recovery, or $5,000, for the fee, and the plaintiff would receive the remaining $10,000.

Contract required (handwritten margin note)

Judgment	$15,000
Attorney's Fee (one-third)	−5,000
Subtotal	10,000
Costs	−1,000
Total to client	$ 9,000

EXHIBIT 6–5   Gross Fee Method

Judgment	$15,000.00
Costs	−1,000.00
Subtotal	14,000.00
Attorney's fee (one-third)	−4,666.67
Total to client	$9,333.33

EXHIBIT 6–6   Net Fee Method

A typical contingency fee arrangement follows:

- 25 percent of sums recovered by way of settlement prior to filing a lawsuit
- 33.33 percent of sums recovered after filing a lawsuit but before trial
- 40 percent of sums recovered within 30 days of commencing trial or after trial
- 45 percent of sums recovered if any judgment is appealed or if garnishment or any proceeding after judgment has to be brought to collect the judgment or any portion thereof
- 50 percent of sums recovered if a matter is subject to retrial as ordered by a trial or appellate court

In addition to a contingency fee, a client must pay all **costs** of a litigation that may be advanced by a law firm. In complex litigation cases, costs can be substantial. The manner in which costs are deducted from the total amount of a judgment determines the amount of a client's recovery and an attorney's fee.

Two methods are used to calculate a contingency fee: the gross fee method and the net fee method. Some states require that attorneys use the net fee method. Exhibits 6–5 and 6–6 show these methods for a case in which a client was awarded a judgment for $15,000, had a costs bill of $1,000, and had a one-third contingency fee agreement with an attorney.

Contingency cases are mainly plaintiff matters, but defense cases also may be taken on contingency. A contingency fee for a defense contingency case is called a modified contingency fee.

MODIFIED CONTINGENCY FEE   In a modified contingency fee case, a lawyer's percentage is not based on the amount of the recovery; rather, the lawyer is paid a percentage of the difference between the amount at issue and the amount of the final judgment. For example, a lawyer represents an insurance company in a case with a potential liability of $1,000,000. The lawyer's fee is based on the difference between $1,000,000, which is the client's exposure, and the actual judgment. Therefore, if the judgment is for $250,000, the lawyer's fee is a percentage of $750,000, which is the difference between the amount of exposure ($1,000,000) and the total judgment ($250,000). This fee arrangement encourages the lawyer to obtain the best possible judgment for the insurance company. If the judgment

costs
Expenses of one side of a lawsuit that a judge orders the other side to reimburse; includes filing fees, service fees, and recording fees.

is for $1,000,000, the lawyer essentially loses the case and gets a reduced hourly rate or a retainer fee as compensation.

CONTINGENCY FEE CONSIDERATIONS   Four considerations are involved in taking a case on a contingency basis. They can be described by the acronym RISC: *r*isk, *i*nflation, *s*ignificant expense, and *c*ash flow.

Risk   An element of risk is involved in taking a case on a contingency basis. If a client should lose the case, the attorney is entitled to no fee: One-third of zero is still zero. In addition, the case may not adequately compensate the attorney for the amount of time expended on it. On the other hand, in large cases a firm may make more than it would if it charged a client by the hour. Another risk is that a judgment debtor will be unable to pay a judgment, which would render the judgment uncollectible.

Inflation   In large areas, courts are extremely crowded, and it is not uncommon to wait as long as 5 years for a trial date. A firm will work on a case for the entire 5-year period until trial. In the event of appeal, the case may be active for a longer period. Furthermore, the losing party does not necessarily put a check in the mail the day of the judgment. The firm may have to collect the judgment, which takes more time and effort.

If it takes a firm 5 or more years to complete a case, the value of the dollar will most likely decrease during that period. In addition, the firm's expenses and the attorney's hourly rate will increase. Therefore, the dollars received at the end of the case are worth less than the dollars that could have been earned at the beginning of the case.

Significant Expense   Some cases require expert witnesses, investigation, and other expenses. Most often, the client cannot afford the services of an expert witness, so a firm will **advance**, or loan, these costs to the client, to be reimbursed at the end of the trial. In complex cases, the services of expert witnesses can cost tens of thousands of dollars. In short, litigating cases is very expensive and requires a large amount of cash resources.

Cash Flow   If a firm works on a case for 5 years on a contingency basis, it is expending time that is not paid by the client when the service is rendered. Had the attorney or paralegal spent time on a case that billed the client by the hour, the firm would have received compensation for that time fairly soon after the client was billed. In a contingency case, the firm may wait for 5 or more years to be paid for its efforts. In the meantime, employees must be paid, overhead expenses must be paid, and the attorney must receive a salary. Spending a lot of time on contingency cases affects a firm's cash flow.

The ABA, state law, and state bar association Codes of Ethics have restricted the types of cases that can be taken on a contingency basis. Cases that are taken on contingency basis include personal injury, medical malpractice, wrongful death, and other **tort** cases, or cases involving a legal wrong done to a person or a civil wrong that is not based on a contract.

ABA Model Rule 1.5(d) expressly prohibits contingency fee agreements in domestic relations cases. A lawyer cannot agree to represent a family law client for a percentage of the client's property settlement. Contingency fees are also prohibited in criminal and other types of cases that vary by state:

> (d) A lawyer shall not enter into an arrangement for, charge, or collect:
>
> 1. Any fee in a domestic relations matter, the payment or amount of which is contingent upon the securing of a divorce or upon the amount of alimony or support, or property settlement in lieu thereof; or
>
> 2. A contingent fee for representing a defendant in a criminal case.

CONTINGENCY FEE LIMITS   Several states have put limits on contingency fees, particularly in medical malpractice cases. It was felt that doing so would discourage lawsuits. High plaintiffs' recoveries in personal injury and medical malpractice cases have affected automobile and medical malpractice insurance rates. It has been argued that a ceiling on

advance
To pay money before it is due; to loan money.

tort
A legal wrong done to a person; a civil wrong that is not based on a contract.

contingency fees would reduce awards and judgments and therefore keep insurance rates down. A list of states that have limits on contingency fees for medical malpractice cases is on the accompanying CD.

In California, for example, medical malpractice insurance premiums increased to the point that doctors were having difficulty paying them. They lobbied for a ceiling on contingency fees in medical malpractice cases, which resulted in legislation adopting a sliding scale limitation on the amount of contingency fees that could be recovered in medical malpractice cases. Attorneys' contingency fees are structured in California medical malpractice cases as follows (Business and Professions Code § 6146):

- 40 percent of the first $50,000 of recovery
- 33.33 percent of the next $50,000 of recovery
- 25 percent of the next $500,000 of recovery
- 15 percent of any amount of recovery over $600,000

Recovery means the net sum after costs are deducted.

Statutory Fees

Statutory fees are set by statute and vary with each state. These fees are usually a structured percentage of a case. For example, attorneys may be paid statutory fees in probate or workers' compensation matters, in which case the amount of a fee is based on the value of an entire estate and may be calculated as follows:

- 7 percent of an estate up to $200,000
- 5 percent of the next $500,000
- 3 percent of the next $1,000,000
- 2 percent of the estate in excess of $1,000,000

According to this schedule, an attorney representing an estate worth $1,000,000 would receive the following fee:

7 percent of $200,000	$14,000
5 percent of $500,000	25,000
3 percent of $300,000	9,000
Total fee	$48,000

If an attorney spends more time on a case than usual, or a case is more complex than the average case, the attorney may request that a court grant **extraordinary fees,** which are added to the statutory fees.

extraordinary fee
A fee that is awarded in addition to statutory fees and that compensates an attorney for extra work required by the circumstances of a case.

Referral Fees

A referral fee is a payment for referring a client to a firm. Courts and bar associations have discouraged gratuitous referral fees, or fees for which no other service is rendered, and most states prohibit them. Model Rule 7.2(b)(4) states:

A lawyer shall not give anything of value to a person for recommending the lawyer's services except that a lawyer may: . . .

(4) refer clients to another lawyer or nonlawyer professional pursuant to an agreement not otherwise prohibited under these Rules that provides for the other person to refer clients or customers to the lawyer if:

(i) the reciprocal referral agreement is not exclusive, and

(ii) the client is informed of the existence and nature of the agreement.

Those against referral fees feel that such a fee may unfairly increase a client's bill. They feel that referral fees damage the image of lawyers who receive payment for doing little or no work and that most clients are offended by referral fees. They also feel that referral fees are beneath the dignity of the legal profession.

Those in favor of referral fees feel that clients, being unfamiliar with lawyers' reputations, benefit by being referred to the most competent attorney who will give them excellent legal services. They feel that a client is protected against increased fees by other rules of professional conduct that prohibit increasing a client's fee to pay a referral fee.

Rules against referral fees are difficult to enforce. Often, a client is not aware that a referral fee is paid. A few states allow referral fees if a client consents and the fee is reasonable. An example of a letter informing a client of a referral fee is on the accompanying CD.

Of Interest . . .

THE LARGEST LEGAL FEE EVER!

The $206 billion settlement of state lawsuits against the tobacco industry generated the largest attorneys' fees award in history—$10 billion—and some experts predict that legal fees could be even higher. The attorneys' fees provision is a small part of a complex settlement agreement with the tobacco industry and represents about 5 percent of the total settlement package. Some lawyers involved in the case had contingency fee agreements from 20 to 40 percent of the recovery and are expected to enforce their fee agreements through litigation or arbitration. The outcome of the arbitration and litigation could increase the total attorneys' fees award substantially. A legal expert hired by the state of Texas to fight the litigation brought about by its attorneys to enforce the contingency fee agreements calculated that the Texas lawyers were asking for fees that amounted to $92,000 an hour.

Premiums

Premiums can be best described as tips. In some situations, if an attorney obtains an especially favorable result for a client, the client will give a firm a premium fee in addition to the usual attorney's fee, whether it is a contingency fee, flat-fee, or hourly rate. Some firms negotiate a premium at the beginning of a case. If, for example, a client requires a case to be handled immediately, an attorney and staff are required to put aside other cases. The firm will be entitled to a higher fee. However, until it is known that the case was handled in such a manner, the client does not want to commit to paying the higher fee. To encourage the firm to handle the case in an expeditious manner, a client will offer the firm a premium fee if the outcome is satisfactory to the client. A premium fee may be payment of an increased hourly rate, a flat-fee, or a contingency fee.

A premium gives a law firm an incentive to obtain the best possible result for a client. For example, a bank gives a law firm a case to collect $50 million in loans from a real estate developer. The bank agreed to an hourly rate of $X. However, if the firm can collect 80 percent of the loans within a certain amount of time, it would be entitled to a premium. If collecting the money took longer or resulted in a lesser amount, a premium would not be due.

A well-known example of a premium fee is when New York's Cravath, Swaine & Moore told the Federal Deposit Insurance Corporation (FDIC) that it would bill it $300 per hour. If, however, Cravath could recover more than $22 million from Michael Milliken, a junk bond trader, the firm was entitled to a premium that brought its hourly rate up to $600 an hour.

Value-Based Fees

A **value-based fee** is determined after the work is completed and is based upon the value of the work to the client as defined by the client. The agreement between lawyer and client sets forth the factors to be considered in setting the final fee and is set at the beginning of the case. A maximum fee and minimum fee may also be established. This type of agreement requires a great deal of trust between the lawyer and the client. In addition, the type of case must be one where the value to the client can be calculated.

This type of fee is most often used with straight or discounted hourly billing up to an agreed upon minimum fee with a bonus due based on achieving shared objectives. These shared objectives include reducing overall costs, meeting deadlines, or an early resolution to a dispute.

For example, Black, White & Greene was retained to defend XYZ corporation in a lawsuit that was filed against them. They agreed on a value-based legal fee as follows:

The client would pay the firm a discounted hourly fee (30 percent) for time spent preparing the case for trial. If the case was settled prior to trial for $1,500,000 or above, the firm would be entitled to a small bonus of $50,000. If the case settled for $1,000,000 to $1,499,000, the firm would be entitled to a bonus of $75,000. If the case settled for under $1,000,000, the firm would receive an additional fee of $100,000. If the case went to trial and the judgment was $1,500,000 or above, the firm would receive a 20 percent contingency fee. If the judgment was for $1,000,000 to $1,499,000, the firm would receive a 25 percent contingency fee. If the judgment was under $1,000,000, the firm would receive 33.33 percent of the recovery.

> **value-based fee**
> A fee that is based on the amount of value the case had for the client.

Of Interest . . .

THE ENRON BANKRUPTCY—DO LEGAL FEES EXCEED THE COMPANY'S VALUE?

Legal fees for law firms representing Enron in its bankruptcy proceedings are expected to exceed $250 million. In the first four months of the bankruptcy case, 12 law firms charged nearly $64 million in fees and expenses. Senior attorneys charged as high as $725 per hour and associates charged as high as $460 hour. Paralegal billing rates ranged from $50 to $175 per hour. One attorney, Steve Susman of Susman Godfrey, charged $900 an hour to handle Enron's securities litigation. Experts have calculated that legal fees can be as much as 3 to 4 percent of the total value of the company. Enron, however, estimates its total assets at $50 million.

Combination Fees

Combination fees, also known as hybrid fees, are a combination of retainer, hourly, flat, contingency, statutory, referral, and premium fees. Possible combinations follow:

- Nonrefundable nonchargeable retainer and hourly fee (no portion of the retainer is returned to a client or applied to the hourly fee)
- Nonrefundable nonchargeable retainer and flat-fee (no portion of the retainer is returned to a client or applied to the flat-fee)
- Nonrefundable nonchargeable retainer and contingency fee (no portion of the retainer is returned to a client or applied to the contingency fee; if the retainer is substantial, a lower contingency fee—20 to 25 percent—may be charged)

- Nonrefundable nonchargeable retainer and statutory fee (no portion of the retainer is returned to a client or applied to the statutory fee)
- Refundable chargeable retainer and hourly fee (the retainer is applied to prepay the hourly fee)
- Refundable chargeable retainer and flat-fee (the retainer is applied to prepay a portion of the flat-fee)
- Refundable chargeable retainer and contingency fee (the retainer is deducted from the contingency fee at the conclusion of a matter)
- Refundable chargeable retainer and statutory fee (the retainer is deducted from the statutory fee at the conclusion of a matter)
- Hourly fee and flat-fee (the flat-fee is charged up to a certain point in the case, and then the firm begins charging by the hour)
- Hourly fee and contingency fee (a reduced hourly rate and a reduced contingency rate are charged)
- Flat-fee and contingency fee (the flat-fee may apply to anticipated costs or be considered a nonrefundable chargeable retainer and be deducted from the contingency fee)
- Hourly rate and premium (the hourly rate increases, depending on the outcome)
- Flat-fee and premium (the flat-fee increases, depending on outcome)
- Contingency fee and premium (either the contingency fee percentage is increased or an additional flat-fee is charged, depending on the outcome)

TRENDS

ALTERNATIVE FEES

As clients become dissatisfied with current billing techniques, creative fee structures will be developed to satisfy the demand. Legal fee structures are predicted to change more in the first 10 years of the new millennium than they have in the previous 50 years.

Most law firms charge an hourly fee. Firms have been reluctant to accept alternative fee structures because there are unknown variables in legal cases. These unknown variables were not known when the fee was set, causing the firm's profitability to decrease. With an hourly fee, these variables are tackled with no financial consequences to the firm. However, the pressure of economics has caused corporate clients to demand alternative billing methods. According to a survey sponsored by Chicago law firm Butler Rubin Saltarelli & Boyd, 85 percent of the 162 in-house counsel surveyed are testing alternative billing methods, and 60 percent reported success with alternative billing methods. The trend away from the billable hour will gain momentum in the next decade. Exhibit 6–7 shows the results of a 2006 survey conducted by the *National Law Journal* that describes a firm's billing methods other than the hourly rate. Note than some firms are moving away from the standard hourly rate charge.

DIVISION OF FEES

The ABA and state bar associations have set guidelines for the division of fees among lawyers and with nonlawyers.

NAME OF FIRM	# OF ATTORNEYS	VARIATIONS OF HOURLY RATE	ALTERNATIVES TO HOURLY RATE
Armstrong Teasdale	266	17%	17%
Burr & Forman	188	35%	6%
Butzel Long	217	10%	10%
Curtis, Mallet, Colt	196	33%	10%
Day, Berry & Howard	251	77%	23%
Dorsey & Whitney	600	15%	10%
Dykema Gossett	341	82%	18%
Fowler White Boggs Banker	227	25%	10%
Holme Roberts & Owen	206	5%	10%
Jenner & Block	467	50%	5%
Loeb & Loeb	240	15%	15%
McKenna Long & Aldridge	400	20%	20%
Powell Goldstein	282	2%	13%
Snell & Wilmer	448	20%	15%
Ulmer & Berne	179	40%	5%
Whiteford, Taylor & Preston	155	1%	1%
Womble Carlyle Sandridge	520	25%	5%

Variations: Discounted rate, blended rate

Alternatives: Flat fee, contingency, hybrid, and value-based

EXHIBIT 6–7 Firms That Charge Legal Fees Other Than the Standard Hourly Rate *(Adapted from the National Law Journal's research on alternative billing practices.)*

Division of Fees among Lawyers

Most states prohibit attorneys dividing, or splitting, fees with other attorneys who are not members of their firm unless the division is in proportion to services rendered and the client consents.

Model Rule 1.5(e) states:

A division of a fee between lawyers who are not in the same firm may be made only if:

(1) the division is in proportion to the services performed by each lawyer or, each lawyer assumes joint responsibility for the representation;

(2) the client agrees to the arrangement, including the share each lawyer will receive, and the agreement is confirmed in writing; and

(3) the total fee is reasonable.

According to this rule, a lawyer must perform some work or share responsibility for a case in order to deserve a fee from another lawyer, unless the client consents to the contrary.

Fee splitting among lawyers is appropriate when an attorney is discharged in a contingency case. A new attorney will make arrangements with a former attorney to pay the former attorney a percentage of the fee based on the amount of his or her services rendered on the case. The extent of a fee division, responsibility, and services rendered varies from case to case and is subject to agreement between the attorneys. Although Model Rule 1.5(e) does not state that the amount of the fee must be disclosed to a client, various states have rules requiring such disclosure. An example of a letter informing a client of the referral fee arrangement is located on the accompanying CD.

Division of Fees with Nonlawyers

A lawyer is prohibited from sharing fees with a nonlawyer except in certain circumstances. Those circumstances are found in Model Rule 5.4(a), which states:

> (a) A lawyer or law firm shall not share legal fees with a nonlawyer, except that:
>
> (1) an agreement by a lawyer with the lawyer's firm, partner, or associate may provide for the payment of money, over a reasonable period of time after the lawyer's death, to the lawyer's estate or to one or more specific persons;
>
> (2) a lawyer who purchases the practice of a deceased, disabled, or disappeared lawyer may, pursuant to the provisions of Rule 1.17, pay to the estate or other representative of that lawyer the agreed-upon purchase price;
>
> (3) a lawyer or law firm may include nonlawyer employees in a compensation or retirement plan, even though the plan is based in whole or in part on a profit-sharing arrangement; and
>
> (4) a lawyer may share court-awarded legal fees with a nonprofit organization that retained or recommended employment of the lawyer in the matter.

A lawyer may be in violation of this rule if the lawyer does any of the following:

- Provides services in association with a member of another profession, such as a tax consultant, real estate developer, or financial analyst
- Works as a salaried employee of a nonlawyer who charges clients more for legal services than the attorney's salary costs the employer
- Owns an interest in a corporation in which nonlawyers provide services traditionally provided by lawyers
- Pays nonlawyer personnel according to a percentage of the fees earned by a firm
- Pays nonlawyer consultants a percentage of the proceeds of contingent fee litigation

Most states have adopted this prohibition of dividing fees with nonlawyers. However, in 1990, the District of Columbia stunned the legal community by adopting a rule that nonlawyers may own a portion of a law firm and receive a portion of the law firm's profits in certain circumstances.

An argument supporting the prohibition of fee splitting with a nonlawyer is that a fee division may allow a lawyer's independent judgment to be controlled by a nonlawyer who is interested in his or her own profit rather than the legal needs of a client. *Prohibiting fee splitting also discourages nonlawyers from engaging in the unauthorized practice of law and referring clients to a lawyer for a percentage of a fee, known as capping.* (See Chapter 4.)

An argument against this prohibition is that it prevents the development of "full-service" law firms, in which members of different professions work together to meet the needs of clients, such as tax counseling and financial planning.

Law firms may, however, offer their employees compensation through a profit-sharing plan if the compensation relates to the net profits of the firm and not to fees received in a particular case. Law firms may also give a small percentage of a fee received to a nonprofit attorney referral service. Some states, however, have ruled that a referral service may charge only flat fees and may not charge a fee based on a percentage of the fee received from a client referred by the service.

OTHER FEES AND CHARGES

Traditionally, a lawyer's hourly rate was intended to pay the attorney's salary and overhead expenses (salaries of support staff, rent, taxes, supplies, equipment, and related expenses) and to provide profit for a firm. However, law firm expenses, overhead, and staff compensation have increased more than revenues. Lawyers have not been able to raise their hourly rates fast enough to accommodate the increased expenses. This has resulted in a "profit crunch," which requires law firm management to devise ways to recoup overhead and expenses to retain profit earnings for a firm.

Emerging since the early 1980s are law firms charging clients additional fees. To reduce overhead, these firms are charging clients for services that were traditionally considered overhead and included in a lawyer's fee. In addition to professional and paraprofessional fees, law firms are charging for the services of other law firm personnel, hard costs, and soft costs.

Other Law Firm Personnel

Some law firms bill clients for the time of secretaries, litigation support personnel, messengers, and temporary personnel.

SECRETARIES   As we saw in Chapter 2, the traditional role of secretary is eroding with advances in technology. The functions and responsibilities of secretaries are changing into an administrative position. With computers sitting on most attorneys' desks, attorneys are performing some of their own clerical functions. E-mail and automated phone answering programs are changing a secretary's phone responsibilities. Firms are e-mailing rather than mailing documents. Secretaries are given more responsibility.

With the changes in a secretary's function comes the necessity that secretaries be trained in new technology. Since new technology and computer capabilities are being introduced often, secretarial training costs for computer programs have also increased. In addition, since legal secretaries are scarce, they are demanding higher salaries than ever before. Therefore, firms have a substantial investment in their secretarial staff.

For some firms, secretaries are moving out of the overhead category into the income producer category as the firms bill a client for a secretary's time, especially if the secretary performs paralegal duties.

LITIGATION SUPPORT   Only firms that handle a lot of complex litigation hire litigation support personnel. Some use outside litigation support services for this function. In either case, firms pass this cost on to a client. If a firm utilizes the services of its own personnel, it will charge a client more than the **actual cost,** or true cost, of the service. If a firm uses an outside litigation support service, the firm may or may not charge more than the actual cost.

actual cost
The true cost without consideration of a markup for profit.

MESSENGERS   Special messenger services have traditionally been billed to a client but were not considered a profit center for a firm. In the past, a firm would bill a client the actual cost of messenger services or include the services in the overhead of the firm. Now, however, whether an outside messenger service or in-house messenger is used, most firms charge a client more than the actual cost to increase a firm's profit. In large cities, firms that have their own messengers have a flat charge to each client for each delivery, plus out-of-pocket expenses. Some messengers charge for their time and have a flat rate for each run for each client to cover the costs of transportation.

TEMPORARY EMPLOYEES   If additional staff is required because of an absent employee or an abundance of work, the expense of hiring them is passed on to the client. Temporary employees can be an attorney or a file clerk.

In the past, the services of law firm personnel were incorporated into an attorney's fee. It has been argued that this was unfair to clients who did not use those services. One client may require heavy secretarial time, and another may require none. Therefore, separate charges for these services were justified out of fairness to a client. However, if these services are taken out of the overhead of a firm and are no longer included in an attorney's hourly rate, the attorney's hourly rate should be reduced.

Hard Costs

hard cost
A cost incurred for filing fees, service fees, deposition expenses, and so on.

Hard costs, also called direct costs, are directly attributable to a client's case—such as filing fees, service fees, deposition expenses, online legal research, and so on.

The term *costs of litigation* should not be confused with the term *expenses of litigation.* Although the terms are almost synonymous, they have different legal definitions. Costs are recoverable by the prevailing party in some cases, and expenses are not recoverable. Costs are defined in state statutes and include filing fees, service fees, recording fees, and other fees as provided by statute. Expenses of litigation include investigator's fees, deposition fees, expert witness fees, and expenses of obtaining and presenting evidence.

A client usually must pay for all the costs and expenses of a case. Model Rule 1.8(e) states:

> A lawyer shall not provide financial assistance to a client in connection with pending or contemplated litigation, except that:
>
> (1) a lawyer may advance court costs and expenses of litigation, the repayment of which may be contingent on the outcome of the matter; and
>
> (2) a lawyer representing an indigent client may pay court costs and expenses of litigation on behalf of a client.

If a lawyer loses a contingency case and the client cannot afford to pay the costs and expenses, a court may not require the client to pay the costs and expenses. However, some states require a client to reimburse a lawyer for all expenses of litigation regardless of financial status or outcome of the case.

If a client is severely injured and cannot work, some states allow a firm to pay a client a reasonable sum for the client's living expenses when involved in lengthy litigation. The client must sign a promissory note to repay the firm out of the proceeds of the judgment. Some states do not allow lawyers to do this. In 1979, an Arizona lawyer was suspended for advancing an unemployed client $215 for living expenses pending the outcome of his case.

The prohibition against payment of costs and expenses originates from an early common law that prohibited an attorney from financing litigation for a portion of a recovery. Modern-day reasoning for not allowing attorneys to pay for the expenses of litigation is to discourage lawyers from putting their own recovery before that of a client and therefore creating a conflict of interest.

Soft Costs

soft cost
A cost incurred for photocopying, long-distance telephone calls, faxes, and so on.

Soft costs, also known as indirect costs, cannot be directly attributable to a client's case until applied to the client's case. These costs include overhead expenses for items such as the following:

- Photocopies
- Attorney's time in preparing forms or other multiple-use documents
- Use of conference rooms
- Housekeeping services for meetings and depositions
- Use of substantive systems (substantive systems developed by law firm personnel to increase efficiency and decrease the amount of time spent on a project)
- Local and long-distance telephone charges
- Transportation and meals on occasions of overtime
- Telex and fax communications

- Supplies
- Storage of documents
- Destruction of documents
- Online legal research
- Interest on accounts receivable
- Outside services (refer to Chapter 2)
- Postage
- Use of a firm's extranet (see Chapter 10)

PHOTOCOPIES Photocopies were the first and are the most frequent soft cost charged. Firms charge for photocopies on a per copy basis, and their charges vary. When considering the cost of the equipment, paper, supplies, and maintenance contracts, the actual cost of each copy may be about 8¢. However, when you add the time and expense of an employee's time to make the copy, the actual cost increases. Firms have made their photocopy service a profit center, with some firms charging from 30¢ to $1 a copy. A firm rarely charges clients the actual cost for photocopies.

In high-volume litigation cases, some firms reduce charges after a set number of pages. Costs for outside duplication work are passed on, usually without a surcharge. Firms with their own binding equipment often charge for each item bound to cover the cost of supplies and machinery.

MULTIPLE-USE DOCUMENTS Standard documents, such as complaints, that are programmed into the computer take very little time to complete. For example, an attorney's time consists of changing a standard document to insert information particular to a client's case. This may take as little as 5 minutes of an attorney's time. If an attorney billed a client by the hour for preparation of a complaint that took 5 minutes, the firm would not be compensated for the value of the product to the client. Therefore, the attorney imposes an extra charge for multiple-use documents.

If a complex document is used in another case, can the attorney charge a new client for the actual time spent altering the document for the new client or for the original time spent creating the document? This is a difficult question since the expense of the new document is negligible compared to what a client paid for the original document. Experts differ in their opinions. Opponents say that the original client should not pay to benefit another client. Proponents say that the value of the document to the new client is the same as the value to the original client and that they should pay the same amount. The ABA addressed this question and stated that lawyers who charge a previous client by the hour cannot charge the new client the same amount for recycled work product. Some state bar associations have adopted the same prohibition.

USE OF CONFERENCE ROOMS Some firms charge an hourly rate or flat-fee for the use of conference rooms for meetings or depositions.

HOUSEKEEPING SERVICES In addition to charging for the use of conference rooms, firms may charge for housekeeping services to come in and clean a conference room after its use. This charge also might be assessed if a meal is served at an office. However, most firms bill a client for food costs without passing on housekeeping service costs.

USE OF SUBSTANTIVE SYSTEMS When a firm develops systems that streamline services rendered to a client being charged by the hour, the law firm is being penalized for its efficiency. Therefore, clients who benefit from the systems pay for the systems and are billed an extra charge similar to the multiple-use document charge. For example, a firm with a custom database system for discovery documents will save a client money by organizing discovery documents. The cost of the database's development is paid for by the clients who use it.

T R E N D S

TECHNOLOGY CREATING SOFT COST DILEMMA

Technology is reducing overhead costs for law firms, including soft costs that are billed to the client. Many law firms bill clients for faxing documents, as much as $1 to $2 per page to cover telephone costs associated with the fax. Now that documents can be e-mailed directly from a computer workstation, questions of whether and how to charge for those e-mails arise. The ABA issued an opinion regarding soft costs, stating that lawyers should charge "no more than the direct cost associated with the service plus a reasonable charge for the overhead associated with the expense." Calculating the direct cost and overhead allocation creates problems for many firms. Some firms disagree with the ABA's opinion and charge "whatever the client is willing to pay" for soft costs. However, clients are becoming increasingly intolerant of soft costs, which is causing some law firms to eliminate charging for them.

LOCAL AND LONG-DISTANCE TELEPHONE CHARGES   In addition to the time a lawyer spends on a telephone call, a client is billed for telephone charges. Some firms assess actual charges; others add a substantial percentage for profit and to cover the cost of equipment and line charges. Most firms charge clients for long-distance calls, and some charge clients message units for local calls. Expenses for the attorney's cell phone are also charged.

portal-to-portal
Of or relating to the time spent traveling from one place to another.

ETHICS ALERT

TRANSPORTATION AND MEALS   Travel is the expense most often billed by attorneys. Some firms add on a percentage of the cost to cover a travel-accident insurance policy in force at a firm. Some attorneys charge a client for the amount of time spent traveling. **Portal-to-portal** charges means that an attorney's clock starts to run when he gets into his car to travel to the courthouse for a hearing and does not stop until he gets out of his car at the office after the hearing. In addition, when traveling by air, attorneys often bill clients for the time spent on the airplane. Some attorneys double-bill by working on another client's case while traveling on behalf of a client who is being charged for that time. Working while traveling is double billing only if the same client is billed for both. *Double billing is considered unethical in most states.*

Travel time may be charged at an attorney's regular hourly rate or at a reduced rate. The argument in support of charging for travel time is that it is time taken away from other billable work. In addition to travel time, a client is charged for other travel expenses, such as hotels and meals.

If a firm is required to work overtime on a case, the firm will charge a client for meals for the staff as well as additional overtime charges.

FAX COMMUNICATIONS   Most firms charge for sending faxes. Many firms have a flat rate for most faxes, with an additional charge for phone-line charges. These charges are usually in two parts: an amount associated with the telephone charge and a charge for each page. The amount for each page may decrease with the volume of a particular transmittal. Some firms also charge for incoming faxes—either a flat-fee for each document or a fee for each page. Some firms charge as much as $1.75 per page for faxes.

SUPPLIES   The costs of supplies are often billed to clients in complex litigation cases when a large quantity of supplies is used.

DOCUMENT STORAGE In cases that have a large volume of documents, storing the documents becomes a problem. Firms must increase their office space to provide for storage space, which costs a firm additional money for rent. Therefore, a firm will charge a client a storage fee if a case generates many documents. Firms that put documents on microfilm also will charge a client for this service, as well as for storing the microfilm.

DESTRUCTION OF DOCUMENTS If a client does not want documents returned at the end of a case, a firm will charge the client to destroy those documents, including the time for an employee to shred the documents.

USE OF COMPUTER AND COMPUTER DATABASE In a complex litigation case for which documents or other information is input into a firm's computer **database,** a client is charged for use of the database as well as for the space used on the firm's computer. The more computer space a client uses, the higher the charge. The charge continues while the information is retained in the firm's computer.

> **database**
> A collection of information for computer retrieval.

Most firms also charge a client for use of online legal research databases in addition to the time spent by the person doing the research. Since a firm is charged for each minute of use, it recovers this cost by billing a client. The amount charged to a client can be the actual amount, a fixed rate for each minute online, or a "type-of-job" charge. Legal databases include WESTLAW and Lexis-Nexis.

INTEREST ON ACCOUNTS RECEIVABLE Charging interest on a client's past-due account was previously taboo for the legal profession. However, with the increasingly high costs of overhead and interest rates, attorneys have followed other professionals in doing so. Some state bar associations have rules that state that an attorney must inform a client in writing of interest charges. A few states require a client's consent to charge interest on an account.

POSTAGE Many firms charge a client for regular postage as well as overnight mail and private document delivery.

USE OF THE FIRM'S EXTRANET An **extranet** is a web-based interface to a firm's private network. It is used to communicate privately with clients and post documents and other communications for the client's use. Extranets can be established for individual cases, as well as for individual parties.

> **extranet**
> A Web-based interface to a private network; used to communicate directly with clients.

No uniformity exists in recovering costs. A firm may impose all, some, or no soft charges. Soft costs charged to clients vary by area of the United States. In the Midwest, firms are less likely to charge clients soft charges. Some firms just add on 5 to 10 percent of the bill as a general overhead charge instead of listing every category separately. Photocopies, postage, and telephone charges are most likely included in this general overhead charge, but other costs, such as messenger and computer charges, are listed separately.

As technology continues to introduce new automation, we will see new soft costs emerge. If the market will bear such charges, attorneys will continue to assess them until clients scream. Soft costs that clients most often resent are photocopies over $1 per page, fax charges, and postage. A large corporate client that receives a bill from its attorneys for thousands of dollars resents being charged the postage used to send them the bill. They also object to high fax charges that are imposed at the law firm's discretion when many faxes are not absolutely necessary. In 1993, the U.S. Department of Energy paid one firm $175,000 for photocopies and $49,000 for faxes in one case.

In December 1993, the ABA addressed soft costs in its Formal Opinion 93-379, which states:

> A lawyer may not charge a client for overhead expenses generally associated with properly maintaining, staffing and equipping an office; however, the lawyer may recoup expenses reasonably incurred in connection with the client's matter for services performed in-house, such as photocopying, long distance telephone calls, computer research, special deliveries, secretarial overtime and similar services, so long as the charge reasonably reflects the lawyer's actual cost for the services rendered.

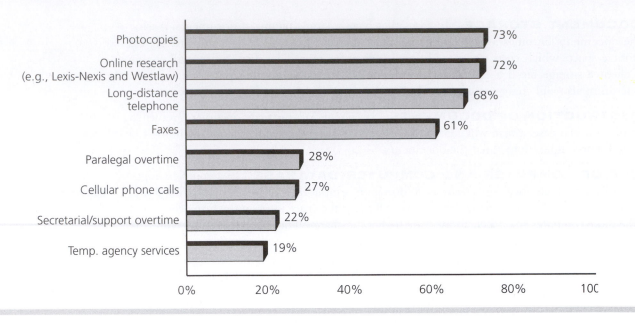

EXHIBIT 6–8   Percentage of Firms that Charge Soft Costs

The ABA states that it is improper for the lawyer to impose a surcharge on disbursements over and above the actual cost, unless the client agrees in advance to the amount of soft costs charged. When no specific cost is agreed on, the ABA states that the lawyer is obligated to charge the client no more than the direct cost associated with the service (i.e., the actual cost of making a photocopy) plus a reasonable allocation of overhead expenses directly associated with the service (i.e., the cost of the photocopy machine operator's time to make the copy). Exhibit 6-8 shows the percentage of firms that charge for soft costs as reported by the Law Firm Services Association.

STATUTORY AND JUDICIAL GUIDELINES

Statutes, case law, and state and national bar associations have set forth the elements to consider when determining whether a legal fee is reasonable. For bankruptcy cases, reasonableness factors are set forth in 11 U.S.C. § 330(3) as follows:

> In determining the amount of reasonable compensation to be awarded, the court shall consider the nature, the extent, and the value of such services, taking into account all relevant factors, including
>
> (A) the time spent on such services;
>
> (B) the rates charged for such services;
>
> (C) whether the services were necessary to the administration of, or beneficial at the time at which the service was rendered toward the completion of, a case under this title;
>
> (D) whether the services were performed within a reasonable amount of time commensurate with the complexity, importance, and nature of the problem, issue, or task addressed; and
>
> (E) whether the compensation is reasonable based on the customary compensation charged by comparably skilled practitioners in cases other than cases under this title.

The ABA has set forth guidelines to help lawyers keep their fees reasonable. These guidelines concerning legal fees were established for two reasons:

1. to preserve the effectiveness, integrity, and independence of the profession and
2. to give society reasonable access to the legal system.

What constitutes a reasonable fee varies from case to case. Furthermore, federal and state laws, as well as case law, continue to define the elements that constitute reasonableness.

Calculating a Reasonable Fee

To set standards that will satisfy reasonableness without compromising a lawyer's compensation, the ABA set forth eight elements of a reasonable fee in Model Rule 1.5(a), which states:

> (a) A lawyer shall not make an agreement for, charge, or collect an unreasonable fee or an unreasonable amount for expenses. The factors to be considered in determining the reasonableness of a fee include the following:
>
> > 1. The time and labor required, the novelty and difficulty of the questions involved, and the skill requisite to perform the legal service properly;
> >
> > 2. The likelihood, if apparent to the client, that the acceptance of the particular employment will preclude other employment by the lawyer;
> >
> > 3. The fee customarily charged in the locality for similar legal services;
> >
> > 4. The amount involved and the results obtained;
> >
> > 5. The time limitations imposed by the client or by the circumstances;
> >
> > 6. The nature and length of the professional relationship with the client;
> >
> > 7. The experience, reputation and ability of the lawyer or lawyers performing the services;
> >
> > 8. Whether the fee is fixed or contingent.

The above eight factors are not exclusive, nor will all eight factors be relevant in each instance. Most state bars' codes of professional responsibility list the factors that constitute reasonableness in their states. Some guidelines include more than the eight factors identified by the ABA, and some guidelines have fewer factors.

The eight factors that are considered by the ABA in determining a reasonable fee can be remembered by the acronym TOCATPET (think of petting your two cats):

1. **T**ime and labor required
2. **O**ther employment opportunities
3. **C**ustomary fees in a community
4. **A**mount involved and results obtained
5. **T**ime limitations
6. **P**rofessional relationship with a client
7. **E**xperience, reputation, and ability of a lawyer
8. **T**ype of fee (fixed or contingent)

TIME AND LABOR REQUIRED The amount of time and labor required on a case is the basis of fee determinations. Each member of the legal team must keep an accurate accounting of the time spent on a matter, even though the case may be a contingency fee case or fixed-fee case. This accounting need not be extremely detailed but must give some idea of the legal service performed during the time period. It also should reflect which lawyer or paralegal performed the work. If the client should contest the fee, the firm can show the accounting of time expended on the matter. A judge will rule on the reasonableness of the amount of time spent and may adjust the time to eliminate excessive or unproductive time.

In addition to the time and labor required on a case, the novelty and difficulty of the questions involved and the skill necessary to represent a client are considered. A case with many complex issues not only requires more time but also calls on the skill and the experience of a lawyer to manage the issues effectively.

For example, a client retained a lawyer in a case involving a patent infringement of the client's new technological invention. The case was very complicated. Since the case involved a new area of law, few other cases involved the client's issue. This made research difficult.

The case required the skill of a senior attorney because it was too complex for an inexperienced associate to handle. It also required more time than usual to be spent on research and discovery. The lawyer was entitled to a higher fee than usual because of these issues.

OTHER EMPLOYMENT OPPORTUNITIES On occasion, the magnitude of a case will not allow a firm to accept other cases without significantly increasing its workforce and overhead. One case can consume the time of a law firm staff, which will not allow a firm to accept other cases. This severely affects the financial base for a firm.

Other employment opportunities also may be affected when a firm represents a party in a highly publicized, highly controversial case. If, for example, a firm represents a criminal defendant who has been accused of heinous crimes against people, defending that person is not going to win the firm any popularity contests.

To illustrate, suppose the owners of ABC Nursery School were accused of abusing the children in their care. The case received extensive media attention and included a very long criminal trial. The proceedings lasted almost 5 years. The attorney who defended the owners could accept no other employment during the proceedings because the *ABC* case consumed all her time. Luckily, the lawyer had the support of her partners, who agreed to the representation and even agreed to contribute some of the firm's resources to the case. The lawyer commented that if the trial had lasted much longer, her firm would not have been able to continue and would have had to dissolve. In addition, because of the negative impression the case had on the public, the attorney's firm suffered a loss of other clients. The firm was entitled to larger fees for the effect the case had on it.

CUSTOMARY FEES IN A COMMUNITY The amount charged by other law firms in a community for a similar service is a consideration in calculating a reasonable fee. If a fee charged to a client is not wholly disproportionate to the fees charged by other firms in the area, it may be considered a reasonable fee.

AMOUNT INVOLVED AND RESULTS OBTAINED A lawyer's fee must be reasonably comparable to the results a client obtains. A bill of $300 an hour for 4 hours spent negotiating a contract that saves a client $1,000,000 is disproportionate to the results of an attorney's efforts. On the other hand, a charge of $20,000 for litigating a case worth $15,000 is also disproportionate to the results obtained for a client.

In certain circumstances, a lawyer's fee may be more than the amount a client recovers in a case. A case that has a high value because it establishes precedent is an example of this type of circumstance. A case that challenges existing law requires more time and effort from an attorney. In some cases, however, the low value of a case will not justify the attorney's spending the extra amount of time or effort it takes to appeal the case. Few clients can finance an attorney to take a case to the U.S. Supreme Court. In the 1950s, when civil rights laws were being litigated, attorneys found that they were not compensated for establishing precedent in this area. To remedy this problem, the Legislature passed the Civil Rights Attorneys' Fees Act. This act stated that a successful plaintiff in a civil rights lawsuit would be awarded reasonable attorneys' fees, recognizing the low amounts of awards in comparison with the high cost of bringing an action. Other types of litigation award the cost of reasonable attorneys' fees to successful litigants.

TIME LIMITATIONS When the circumstances of a case are such that unreasonable time demands are imposed on a firm, the firm should be paid for this effort. Time limitations may require that a legal team suspend its work on other clients' cases to attend to the needs of one case. They also may require that attorneys, paralegals, and other office staff work overtime to ensure the timeliness of a case. Therefore, a firm incurs additional expenses that should be paid by the client.

For example, a client who retains an attorney a week before the statute of limitations expires—the time period within which a lawsuit must be filed—is putting time constraints on the attorney, the paralegal, the secretary, and other law firm personnel. The legal team must attend to this new client's case immediately, causing them to stop working on other clients' matters. The firm should be compensated for the inconvenience.

PROFESSIONAL RELATIONSHIP WITH A CLIENT   When a client provides a firm with many cases during a year, that client may be entitled to fee consideration from the firm. The concept of volume discounts is appropriate for law firms.

EXPERIENCE, REPUTATION, AND ABILITY OF A LAWYER   The more experienced and reputable an attorney, the more that attorney should be compensated. The more experienced an attorney, the higher the attorney's hourly rate. The rationale for this is that an experienced lawyer will take less time to complete a project than an inexperienced lawyer.

Attorneys with a high profile who have received publicity for their performance in high-visibility cases will demand a higher fee for their work. An attorney's reputation affects a case. For example, a product liability attorney who has earned very high judgments for clients and has received publicity for this influences the manner in which an opposing party will litigate a case. If an attorney has a reputation for winning cases, an opposing defendant or insurance company will likely settle a case rather than go to trial.

TYPE OF FEE   A contingency fee contains elements of risk for a law firm, and the firm should be compensated for all elements involved in taking a contingency case (RISC factors are discussed earlier). Courts have generally awarded a higher fee for RISC factors in a contingency fee case. However, some courts have ruled that RISC factors are contained in an attorney's hourly rate. Some courts have felt that to increase a fee to include the RISC factors would encourage frivolous lawsuits.

Average cases involving a higher-than-average contingency fee have been held to be unreasonable. For example, in a personal injury case of average complexity and average recovery, a contingency fee of 50 percent has been determined to be unreasonable (*In re Kennedy*, 472 A. 2d 1317 [1984]). Such a standard has received various interpretations by different courts. If a client agreed to pay an attorney 50 percent of a recovery, some courts are reluctant to interfere with a valid fee contract between the client and the attorney. Other courts feel an obligation to supervise fee agreements. However, in general, contingency fees providing for an exorbitant percentage of a recovery have been held to be unreasonable (see *United States v. 115.128 Acres of Land*, 101 F. Supp. 796 D. N. J. [1951]).

Contingency fees can be set aside by a court and an hourly rate applied to a case. Events occurring after a fee agreement is signed may affect the reasonableness of a fee. For example, an attorney represented a client in a personal injury case for a one-third contingency fee. Doctors who treated the client filed liens, or charges, on the outcome of the suit for payment of medical services rendered the client, and an insurance company put a lien against the net recovery for the amount of past benefits paid the client. At the end of the case, after the attorney, doctors, and insurance company were paid, the client received nothing. The attorney's time records indicated that if billed by the hour, the attorney would have received about 10 percent of the contingency fee. Considering the events, the contingency fee was unreasonable, and the attorney's fee was reduced to reflect hourly compensation (see *MacKenzie Construction v. Maynard*, 758 F. 2d 97).

Lodestar and Multipliers

A number of federal circuit courts adopted a two-step approach to calculating reasonable attorneys' fees: lodestar and multipliers. The term **lodestar** originated in the U.S. Court of Appeals for the Third Circuit in the case *Lindy Bros. Builders v. American Radiator & Standard Sanitary Corp.*, 487 F. 2d 161, and has been the basis of most fee awards in the court system since 1973. Calculation of a lodestar figure is accomplished by determining the number of hours reasonably spent in a case and applying the attorney's hourly rate thereto to arrive at a reasonable fee. A court will limit lodestar hours to hours reasonably expended and may discount hours spent unproductively. In addition, a court may rule that an attorney's hourly rate is not reasonable and make adjustments. In most cases, however, an attorney's established hourly rate is presumed to be reasonable.

lodestar
A method of calculating an attorney's fee using the attorney's hourly rate multiplied by the number of hours worked on a case.

Courts have determined that the factors listed in ABA Model Rule 1.5(a) (TOCATPET) are inherent in the lodestar calculation. For example, the complexity and difficulty of a case would be reflected in the number of hours expended. The experience, reputation, and skill level of an attorney would be reflected in the hourly rate.

Some courts have ruled that factors such as time limitations and contingency fees are not considered in lodestar calculations. If a court determines that lodestar does not adequately compensate for all factors of a case, the court may apply a **multiplier** to the lodestar figure, thereby increasing the fee. A court may award an additional flat-fee or percentage to a lodestar figure to compensate an attorney for time limitations imposed by a client. As an example, if an attorney's lodestar is calculated to be $200 an hour and the attorney's time records indicate that he or she spent 100 hours on a case, a judge will calculate the lodestar fee at $20,000. To compensate the attorney for the RISC factors of a contingency case, the judge may increase the figure by 20 percent, or $4,000, for a total fee award of $24,000. Lodestar multipliers occur only in rare circumstances.

multiplier
An amount that is added to an attorney's lodestar fee to compensate for time limitations and risks.

Of Interest . . .

UNREASONABLE MULTIPLIER?

The state of Minnesota hired the law firm of Kaplan, Miller & Ciresi LLP to represent it in its lawsuit against the tobacco industry. Under the settlement, the tobacco industry agreed to pay the firm $444 million for fees. A controversy arose about how the fee was calculated. The fee agreement contained a complex formula that totaled the $444 million. The agreement indicated $27.5 million was for the firm's billable fees. To that sum, a multiplier of 14 was added for a total of $385 million. A "contingency component" of $58.8 million was then added for a total of $444 million.

There is no question that the firm worked hard on the case. More than 100 firm employees worked on the case. They conducted 300 depositions, 190 motions, 18 appeals, and a 74-day trial.

A multiplier is applied to compensate the firm for the risk the firm took in the case. Since the firm took the case on a contingency, the firm had compensable risk factors. A multiplier of two or three is normal and a multiplier of five is considered very high. Professor Brickman, Professor of Law at Benjamin N. Cardozo School of Law, who testified before Congress on the matter, said, "This multiplier is not from this planet—it's hocus pocus." A lawsuit was filed to block payment of the fee.

While calculating a lodestar fee is simple (hours times hourly rate), determining the reasonablness of these two factors requires a detailed analysis of the facts of each case. In the case of *In re Atwell*, 148 B.R. 483 (Bankr. W.D. Ky. 1993), the court listed the factors to consider when applying the lodestar method to determine a reasonable fee. It also set guidelines to follow to determine whether to decrease the fee or apply a multiplier. These factors are illustrated in Exhibit 6–9.

Liens

Courts have ruled that an attorney's payment of expenses of litigation without reimbursement creates a proprietary interest in a case. ABA Model Rule 1.8(i) prohibits a lawyer from

LODESTAR CALCULATION

IS THE HOURLY RATE REASONABLE?	IS THE NUMBER OF HOURS REASONABLE?
1. What is the attorney's customary hourly rate?	1. Are the issues of the case difficult and complicated?
2. Is the attorney's customary hourly rate commensurate with rates charged by other attorneys in the area?	2. What is the amount of time spent on comparable matters with similar issues by comparable counsel?
3. What is the skill of the attorney and the quality of legal services provided?	3. What are the nature and characteristics of the case.
4. What is the difficulty level of the issues involved with the case?	4. How many issues in the case are litigated, and to what degree?
5. Can some tasks be regarded as "clerical" and be considered overhead or compensated at a lower rate?	5. How much time was spent in preparing attorney's fees applications?
6. What is the billing agreement between lawyer and client?	6. Did the attorney use good billing judgment when billing the client? Were bills reviewed properly?

Should the Lodestar Be Increased?

YES	NO
1. The attorney complied with the requirements of his or her employment.	1. The attorney did not comply with the requirements of his or her employment.
2. Working on the case has interfered with the attorney's ability to work on other cases.	2. Working on the case has not interfered with the attorney's ability to work on other cases.
3. The case is an undesirable case.	3. The case is not an undesirable case.
4. The case is a contingency case and involves RISC factors.	4. The case is not a contingency case and does not involve RISC factors.
5. The results obtained for the client were extraordinary.	5. The results obtained for the client were average or not extraordinary.

EXHIBIT 6–9   Lodestar Calculation Considerations

acquiring an ownership or proprietary interest in a client's case, except under two conditions. The rule states:

> A lawyer shall not acquire a proprietary interest in the cause of action or subject matter of litigation the lawyer is conducting for a client, except that the lawyer may:
>
> (1) acquire a lien granted by law to secure the lawyer's fee or expenses; and
>
> (2) contract with a client for a reasonable contingent fee in a civil case.

Examples of an attorney acquiring a proprietary interest in a case include giving a client advice on various courses of action if the attorney stands to profit by one of the courses of action (allowing the outcome of a case to affect an asset of the attorney) and obtaining literary rights to a book about the case.

It is unethical for an attorney to profit by writing a book or making a movie about his or her representation in a high-profile case. However, an attorney may charge a client in a literary property case a share in the ownership of the property as a fee if the arrangement is not adverse to the client. Model Rule 1.8(d) states:

> Prior to the consultation of representation of a client, a lawyer shall not make or negotiate an agreement giving the lawyer literary or media rights to a portrayal or account based in substantial part on information relating to the representation.

A lawyer may place two types of liens on a case: a charging lien and a retaining lien.

CHARGING LIEN   A **charging lien** is placed on a judgment that a lawyer obtained for a client. The lien may be created by a specific contract or by a provision in a retainer agreement. When the client is paid the judgment, the lawyer is paid from the proceeds of

charging lien
A lien placed on a client's proceeds or judgment for payment of an attorney's fees.

the judgment. A charging lien will have priority over other liens, except tax liens. *In many states, a lawyer cannot place a charging lien on the judgment of an unrelated case or on alimony or child support.* Most states allow charging liens, but some have specific requirements, such as the client's consent, to perfect a charging lien.

RETAINING LEIN   A **retaining lien** allows a lawyer to retain papers, money, or other property received from a client until the lawyer is paid a fee. If the lawyer relinquishes the property on which the lien is placed, the lawyer may lose the lien. *In many states, a lawyer cannot place a lien on any property received for a specific purpose or on property received in an unrelated case.*

Controversy has arisen regarding retaining liens. Courts have questioned a lawyer's right to retain property that was entrusted to the lawyer for safekeeping. It is a lawyer's ethical responsibility to take reasonable steps to avoid prejudice to a client, and retention of a client's property may prejudice the client. Some states have ethical rules prohibiting a retaining lien, but several states allow retaining liens.

retaining lien
A lien placed on property that belongs to a client and is in an attorney's possession.

OTHER LIENS   An attorney may secure payment of fees by having a client sign a promissory note secured by a deed on the client's property. Lawyers also may obtain a security interest in a client's property, such as a client's car, to secure payment of fees.

Paralegal Guidelines

A lawyer has full responsibility for a client's fee. However, paralegals are agents of an attorney and are responsible for complying with guidelines concerning fees. Paralegals must be careful in two areas of legal fees: quoting and setting.

QUOTING FEES   There has been much debate over whether paralegals should quote fees to a client. Paralegals will often be asked how much a firm charges for its services. In cases that have a flat-fee established—such as for simple wills, uncontested divorces, bankruptcies, and some criminal cases—paralegals are often permitted to quote fees to a client.

Paralegals should be cautioned against quoting fees regardless of an attorney's authorization to do so. Cases have ruled that it takes the independent judgment of a person with a law school education to quote fees. Clients frequently do not know the law in their case and cannot determine their legal needs. A client who contacts an office for a simple will may in fact require complex estate planning to protect an estate. Only an attorney can identify potential issues in a case and anticipate potential problems that affect the fee. Since an attorney is ultimately responsible to a client for fees, the attorney should quote all fees.

An attorney is ultimately responsible for the acts of a paralegal. A paralegal who quotes a standard fee to a client may damage a potential attorney-client relationship if the client needs more than standard services. Firms have been accused of **bait-and-switch tactics** by clients who were quoted low fees on a case that required more complex work. A paralegal is not to blame in this circumstance. However, to avoid potential problems, paralegals should not quote fees.

bait-and-switch tactics
A tactic used in advertising to attract customers to a sale item and switch that item with one that is not on sale.

SETTING FEES   *A paralegal may not set a fee.* A paralegal does not have the requisite training to anticipate the facts and issues of a case and is not qualified to set a fee. This is an attorney's responsibility. Paralegals who manage a law firm may be involved in fee setting from a management perspective, but all standard fees set by management must be reviewed and accepted by the attorneys in authority.

RECOVERABILITY OF PARALEGAL FEES   In certain types of cases, the prevailing party in a lawsuit may be awarded attorneys' fees. This means that the losing party must pay the prevailing party's **reasonable attorneys' fees.** In the past, paralegals' fees were not recoverable by a prevailing party. However, the U.S. Supreme Court considered this issue in the case of *Missouri v. Jenkins*, 109 S. Ct. 2463 (1989), and ruled that paralegals' fees are recoverable. The Supreme Court stated, "By encouraging the use of lower cost paralegals rather than attorneys wherever possible, permitting market rate billing of paralegal hours encourages cost-effective delivery of legal services."

reasonable attorneys' fees
The amount of attorneys' fees determined by a governing entity to be reasonable.

However, what constitutes paraprofessional duties is an issue. A U.S. bankruptcy judge denied claims for paralegals' fees when the duties were considered clerical in nature, such as photocopying, preparing envelopes, and mailing pleadings and orders. The judge stated that the costs for clerical duties are considered overhead expenses and are covered in professional hourly rates.

Courts have ruled that the following criteria apply when an attorney's fee award may include expenses for paralegals:

- The service performed must be legal in nature.
- The performance of services must be supervised by an attorney.
- The qualifications of the person performing the services must be specified in the request to determine such qualifications.
- The nature of the service must be specified to allow the court to determine whether the service is legal or clerical.
- The amount of time must be reasonable.
- The amount charged must reflect reasonable community standards.

Fees awarded for paralegals vary from $25 an hour (*Mason v. Oklahoma Turnpike Authority* 1997, W.L. 311880, U.S.C.A., 10th Cir. Okla. [1997]) to $250 an hour for a class-action suit (*Berchin v. General Dynamics Corp.* W.L. 465752, S.D.N.Y. [1996]). The case of *Spegon v. The Catholic Bishop of Chicago*, 989 F. Supp. 984 (1998), ruled that $90 an hour was an appropriate award for paralegal services. A list of cases that have considered the recovery of paralegal fees is on the accompanying CD.

Of Interest . . .

NINE WAYS PARALEGALS CAN HELP REDUCE LEGAL FEES

1. *Promote Partnering:* Share responsibility for legal work with the client. In-house legal staff can perform some of the tasks performed by outside counsel.
2. *Scrutinize Discovery Procedures:* Establish clear procedures that streamline the discovery process.
3. *Act as Liaison:* Outline requirements of a case to avoid costly and unnecessary delays.
4. *Draft Detailed Retention Letters:* A retention letter summarizes the terms of the representation and prevents misunderstandings at the case's conclusion. The letter sets forth the limits of the representations and helps staff keep within those limits during the course of the representation.
5. *Use Task-Based Billing:* Task-based billing sets limits on each task and helps paralegals stay within those limits.
6. *Employ Information Technology:* Use technology whenever possible to save time and reduce costs.
7. *Consolidate Vendor Contracts:* If the firm does a lot of business with an outside vendor, volume discounts can be negotiated and passed on to the client.
8. *Preapprove Disbursements:* Obtain approval from the client before incurring costs for such expenses as temporary staff and online legal research.
9. *Control Case Staffing:* Some firms overstaff a case, resulting in duplication of effort and wasted time bringing additional personnel up to speed. Set the staffing needs at the beginning of the case to avoid these costs.

SOURCE: *Reprinted with permission of* Legal Assistant Today, *September 1997.*

FEE AGREEMENTS

A misunderstanding about fees is frequently a source of dispute between a client and a lawyer and erodes an attorney-client relationship. Fee agreements that result in disputes often are informal, oral agreements that are miscommunicated.

Model Rule 1.5(b) and (c) states:

> (b) The scope of the representation and the basis or rate of the fee and expenses for which the client will be responsible shall be communicated to the client, preferably in writing, before or within a reasonable time after commencing the representation, except when the lawyer will charge a regularly represented client on the same basis or rate. Any changes in the basis or rate of the fee or expenses shall also be communicated to the client.

> (c) A fee may be contingent on the outcome of the matter for which the service is rendered, except in a matter in which a contingent fee is prohibited by paragraph (d) or other law. A contingent fee agreement shall be in a writing signed by the client and shall state the method by which the fee is to be determined, including the percentage of percentages that shall accrue to the lawyer in the event of settlement, trial or appeal; litigation and other expenses to be deducted from the recovery; and whether such expenses are to be deducted before or after the contingent fee is calculated. The agreement must clearly notify the client of any expenses for which the client will be liable whether or not the client is the prevailing party. Upon conclusion of a contingent fee matter, the lawyer shall provide the client with a written statement stating the outcome of the matter and, if there is a recovery, showing the remittance to the client and the method of its determination.

The requirement that fee agreements be in writing is to prevent misunderstandings, enhance an attorney-client relationship, and provide protection for a lawyer in case of a fee dispute. Any ambiguity in a fee agreement is determined against the lawyer.

Some states require that all fee agreements be in writing. California, for example, requires a written fee agreement when fees in a case are expected to exceed $1,000. The agreement must contain an explanation of the fee, the nature of the services to be provided to the client, the responsibility of the lawyer, and the responsibility of the client.

Retainer Fee Agreements

Many states require that nonrefundable retainers, if allowed, be clearly explained to clients. A fee agreement must clearly state that the entire retainer will be nonrefundable on discharge and the circumstances surrounding the retainer (chargeable or nonchargeable). An example of a nonrefundable chargeable fee agreement is on the accompanying CD.

Hourly Fee Agreements

Hourly agreements must set forth a schedule with the hourly rate of each employee clearly stated. All hard and soft costs must be indicated to avoid disputes about the entire fee. An example of an hourly fee agreement is on the accompanying CD.

Flat-Fee Agreements (Fixed Fee)

Some states require that flat fees be in writing. If any additional charges are assessed, those charges must be clearly stated. An example of a flat-fee agreement is on the accompanying CD.

Contingency-Fee Agreements

Most states require that a contingency-fee agreement be in writing. ABA Model Rule 1.5(c) requires that a contingency-fee agreement state whether the fee is calculated by a gross-fee or by a net-fee method. At the conclusion of a case, a client must receive a full accounting of the fee, including an itemization of the costs. An example of a contingency-fee agreement is on the accompanying CD.

CONCLUSION

The high cost of attorneys is the subject of many conversations. Attorneys' fees are expensive—so expensive that many people cannot afford them. In 2007, a well-known attorney stated that she could not afford her own fees.

When considering fees, one must consider the value of the service one receives. A lawyer's work involves people's lives, and the outcome of a case can dramatically affect the quality of a person's life. Consumers pay a price for a product based on its value. They place a high value on an attorney's service to society.

SUMMARY

The various types of fees are retainer, hourly, flat, task-based, contingency, statutory, referral, premium, value-based, and combination, or hybrid, fees. A true retainer fee is paid to a law firm to ensure the firm's availability to a client. Hourly fees are the most common type of legal fees and in some jurisdictions the only acceptable method of charging clients. A flat-fee is a set fee for a service rendered. A task-based fee is a flat rate for specific tasks in a matter. A contingency fee is a fee based on a percentage of a client's recovery in a case. A statutory fee is set by statute and varies with the state. A referral fee is a fee for referring a client to a firm. Premium fees can be best described as tips. Value-based fees are based upon the value of the service to the client. Combination fees are a combination of any of the various types of fees.

Changes are occurring in the traditional delivery of legal services. Emerging since the early 1980s are law firms charging clients additional fees. Some law firms are now billing clients for the time of staff members and for costs, such as hard and soft costs.

Statutes, case law, and state and national bar associations have set forth the elements to consider when determining whether a legal fee is reasonable. The ABA established rules and guidelines concerning legal fees for two reasons: (1) to preserve the effectiveness, integrity, and independence of the profession and (2) to give society reasonable access to the legal system. To set standards that will satisfy reasonableness without compromising a lawyer's compensation, the ABA set forth the ingredients of a reasonable fee in Model Rule 1.5(a).

What constitutes a reasonable fee varies from case to case. The eight factors that are considered in determining a reasonable fee can be remembered by the mnenonic TOCATPET.

A number of federal circuit courts adopted a two-step approach to calculating reasonable attorneys' fees: lodestar and multipliers. Courts have determined that the factors listed in ABA Model Rule 1.5 (TOCATPET) are inherent in the lodestar calculation.

A lawyer may place two types of liens on a case: a charging lien and a retaining lien. A charging lien is placed on a client's judgment. A retaining lien allows a lawyer to retain papers, money, or other property received from a client until the lawyer is paid a fee. An attorney may also secure payment of fees by having a client sign a promissory note secured by a deed on the client's property and a security lien on the client's property, such as a car.

A lawyer has full responsibility for a client's fee. Much debate has taken place over whether paralegals should quote fees to a client. Paralegals should be cautioned against quoting fees regardless of an attorney's authorization to do so. In addition, a paralegal may not set a fee.

Many states require that nonrefundable retainers be clearly explained to clients. Hourly agreements must set forth a schedule with the hourly rate of each employee clearly stated. Some states require that flat-fees be in writing. Most states require that a contingency fee agreement be in writing.

CHAPTER ILLUSTRATION

The law firm of Black, White & Greene charges its clients four types of fees: hourly, fixed, statutory, and contingency. Certain criminal cases that Dennis White handles, such as drunk driving defenses, are charged a fixed fee. To arrive at the fee, the firm averaged the amount of time Dennis and his paralegal, Milton, spent on drunk driving cases and applied their hourly rates to the total number of hours to arrive at a fixed fee of $2,000 for each representation. Robert and Tricia monitor the cases closely to determine whether the fixed fee is providing the firm with a profit. They found that some cases warranted additional time that was not originally anticipated but that others required less time than originally anticipated. Therefore, it averages out, and they are satisfied with the charge. If the firm's expenses increase, such as an increase in Dennis's or Milton's hourly rate, they will adjust the fee accordingly.

Associate Patrizia Boen handles personal injury cases for the firm and charges those clients a contingency fee. She charges 33.33 percent of the recovery before trial, 40 percent 30 days before trial, and 50 percent if the case is appealed. Her clients are required to deposit $1,000 in the firm's client funds trust account for costs such as filing fees, service fees, and depositions. If the case exceeds those costs, the client must reimburse the firm out of the proceeds of the case. The firm uses the net fee method to calculate the contingency fee. Ms. Boen also handles the firm's workers' compensation cases. The fee for these cases is a 10 percent contingency fee and is set by statute. Additionally, Ms. Boen handles domestic cases on an hourly fee basis.

Tricia and Robert monitor the contingency cases closely. The firm's computer keeps track of the employees' time spent on contingency matters. When discussing settlement, Patrizia can ask for a management report of the time spent on the case to determine the case's settlement value. She can also determine whether the case was profitable by looking at time reports. The firm has a policy that no more than 50 percent of Patrizia's caseload can be contingency cases because of the amount of time it takes to get paid on the case. It affects the firm's cash flow to have too many contingency cases.

George Templeton, now an associate, handles probate and estate planning for the firm. The fee for probate cases is set by statute and is a percentage of the total amount of the estate. Most of the time, the probate cases involve issues that are not anticipated at the beginning of the case. To be compensated for these problems, George requests extraordinary fees from the probate court. Estate planning cases are charged by the hour or a flat-fee.

Most of the firm's clients are charged an hourly rate for legal services. To establish their hourly rates, Tricia researched what the standard hourly rates were in the community. She calculated the rate after applying the firm's overhead expenses and profit margin to the rate schedule to arrive at the final schedule of hourly rates. She came up with the following rate schedule:

Robert Black, senior attorney:	$450/hour
Dennis White, senior attorney:	$450/hour
Grant Greene, partner:	$400/hour
Patrizia Boen, associate	$300/hour
George Templeton, associate:	$300/hour
Milton Nollkamper, paralegal:	$100/hour
Julie Stockstill, paralegal:	$100/hour

In addition to direct costs, the firm also charges its clients for indirect, or soft, costs. It developed the following soft-cost schedule:

Photocopies: 30¢/page

Faxes: 75¢/page

Long-distance telephone calls: Actual cost plus 10 percent

Postage: Actual cost

Employee overtime: Time-and-a-half of hourly rate

Messenger service: Actual cost plus 20 percent

A potential new client, Technology Enterprises, Inc., called and made an appointment with Robert to discuss the possibility of the firm handling all its business litigation. Technology Enterprises is a very large corporation with a corporate legal department of 24 attorneys. The company's general counsel met with Robert and told him that they are dissatisfied with their current outside law firm and wanted to replace it with a new firm. He said that they were interviewing three firms in the area and would choose one to handle all their litigation. Since Black, White & Greene had such a good reputation in the business community, he requested that they submit a proposal describing their fees for litigation work. Robert was very excited about the possibility of working for this new client because they could provide the firm with a lot of work.

Robert went right to work on the proposal. He asked for the assistance of Tricia and of Sandra, who is the desktop publishing expert in the firm. Robert wanted the proposal to stand out among their competition, so the firm hired a temporary secretary to fill in for Sandra as she worked on this proposal.

The proposal included a complete history of the firm, a biography of its attorneys, and a list of major clients the firm represented. It included a history of the firm's successful cases. It also included a schedule of the firm's hourly rates and a list of costs billed to the client. The firm hired a professional photographer to take pictures of the firm and employees to put in the proposal.

Sandra worked hard on the proposal, which, when she finished it, was beautiful. She had it professionally bound with a beautiful cover. It was quite impressive. Robert had the proposal personally delivered to Technology and was confident that they would get the account.

A week passed, and Robert heard nothing from Technology. He called the general counsel, who told him that they were reviewing all the proposals and had not made a decision yet. He commented on Robert's proposal as one of the most beautiful he had ever seen. Robert was sure that they would get the account and started thinking about hiring additional employees to handle all the work they would get.

A week later, Technology's general counsel called Robert, but Robert was not in. Robert returned the call the next day, but the general counsel was not in. Robert was very anxious and told Tricia to cancel all his appointments for the next 2 days so that he would be available when Technology called. They called the next day.

"Hello, Robert," said Greg Meyers, the general counsel of Technology Enterprises. "Hello, Greg," said Robert, "it's good to hear from you. Have you made your decision yet?"

"Yes we have, and I'm sorry to tell you that your firm was not chosen," said Greg. "We chose the Smith & Jones firm."

Robert was stunned. He was sure he did not hear him correctly. "What?" asked Robert.

Greg continued, "We chose the Smith & Jones law firm. It was a tough decision. Your proposal was by far the nicest, but the Smith firm charges its corporate clients task-based fees. We prefer task-based fees because it is easier to monitor cases and track our litigation expenses. We are moving away from hourly fees. Another problem with your proposal was the soft costs you charge. We have a problem paying for postage, faxes, and telephone charges. The Smith firm just adds a low monthly administrative fee to cover those things. I want to thank you for submitting your proposal and wish you much success."

Robert thanked him and hung up the phone. He was shocked and very disappointed. "Task-based fees?" he thought. "I've heard of them but don't quite understand how it works." He called Tricia into his office and told her the bad news. He instructed her to research task-based billing and to do whatever was required to implement it into the firm's fee structure. The next time a large client requests a proposal, they will be prepared.

CHAPTER REVIEW

1. Describe the four types of retainer fees. How is each used?
2. Explain the difference between straight hourly rates and blended hourly rates.
3. What variables are considered when determining a lawyer's hourly rate?
4. What variables are considered when determining a set fee?
5. What is task-based billing?
6. What is the difference between a contingency fee and a modified contingency fee?
7. What is the difference between the gross-fee and net-fee methods for calculating a contingency fee?
8. What four considerations are involved in taking a case on a contingency basis?
9. What are premium fees?
10. What are value-based fees?
11. What are hard costs?
12. What are soft costs?
13. What eight factors are considered when determining a reasonable fee?
14. What is the lodestar approach to calculating a reasonable fee?
15. What is the difference between a charging lien and a retaining lien? In what circumstance is each used?
16. Why should paralegals not quote fees?

EXAMPLES FOR DISCUSSION

1. THE FEE FEUD

Research Data, a large corporation, retained Attorney Cecilia Patino to represent it in a breach-of-contract action. Research Data agreed to pay Cecilia a one-third contingency fee. After filing suit and initiating discovery, Cecilia found the case to be more complex than she had originally anticipated, so she associated Melvin Goldberg, a successful civil fraud specialist who agreed to handle the litigation. The attorneys agreed to share equally in the work and the fee. Research Data signed a new contingency agreement, incorporating Melvin into the agreement.

Research Data received a favorable outcome and paid the attorneys the contingency fee. When it came to splitting the fee, however, a dispute arose between the attorneys. Melvin alleged that Cecilia was not entitled to one-half of the fee because she did not do one-half of the work on the case.

1. If you were the judge in this matter, how would you resolve the conflict?
2. Should Cecilia be given consideration because it was her case to begin with? If so, how much? If not, why not?
3. What Model Rule applies to this case?

2. HIGH-OVERHEAD SOLUTION

Reingold & Feinstein found that its overhead and expenses were too high. It decided to hire an experienced law firm administrator to keep costs down and bring the profits of the firm up. As compensation, the firm offered the administrator a salary and a percentage of the profits. If the administrator did a good job, the percentage of the profits could be as much as one-fourth to one-third the administrator's total compensation. It was believed that such compensation would be an incentive for the administrator to produce greater efficiency and productivity, which would increase profits for the firm.

1. Was the administrator's compensation proper?
2. What area of the United States would condone such a financial arrangement?
3. What Model Rule applies to this case?
4. What are some possible repercussions of this arrangement?
5. Do any advantages accompany this arrangement? If so, what are they?

3. THE FEE IS MINE!

Rachel Anderson is a bankruptcy lawyer who represented Phyllis Swiftarrow in a bankruptcy case. During the bankruptcy, Phyllis was injured on the job and asked Rachel whether she would handle her new workers' compensation and personal injury case. Since Rachel is a bankruptcy lawyer, she referred the case to Ming Liao, a workers' compensation specialist. Ming, specializing in only workers' compensation cases, would not take the personal injury part of the case.

Rachel told Phyllis that she would continue to look for a personal injury lawyer and called many of her colleagues to ask them whether they were interested in the case. Because the case involved complex issues for little recovery, the lawyers declined it. The statute of limitations had almost expired, so Rachel prepared and filed a complaint for Phyllis, listing Phyllis as in propria personna, or representing herself. Rachel continued to search for a personal injury attorney for Phyllis and mentioned to Ming that she was unable to find one. Ming recommended that Rachel call Albert Franzmeir, who agreed to take the case.

Phyllis indicated that she would agree to a referral fee for finding Albert. Rachel feels that she is entitled to the fee, but Ming insists that he is entitled to it. Albert says he does not want the case if it will involve a referral fee war between Rachel and Ming.

1. How would you resolve this problem?
2. In your opinion, who is entitled to the referral fee? Why?
3. What Model Rule applies in this case?
4. What are the advantages of paying a referral fee in this case?
5. What are the disadvantages of paying a referral fee in this case?

4. ATTORNEY REFERRAL FEES

Discuss attorney referral fees. Do you think they are proper? If so, why? If not, why not? Do you think there is a problem monitoring referral fees? How could they be monitored?

5. CREATIVE FEE STRUCTURING

Shannon Freer contacted Joel Olson to represent her in her personal injury case. She asked Joel to take the case on a contingency since most firms take personal injury cases on a contingency basis and she had no funds for a lawyer. Joel is a new sole practitioner, right out of law school, and is struggling to meet the overhead expenses of the office. He told Shannon that he could not afford to take the case on a contingency fee basis. Shannon was very impressed with Joel, however, and asked him to reconsider his decision.

1. What are some possible fee structures that could meet both Joel's and Shannon's needs?

6. DRILL AND FILL DENTAL SERVICES

You go to the dentist twice a year to get your teeth cleaned. You heard that your dentist had devised a new method of charging for the service, but you were surprised to receive the following bill:

DRILL & FILL DENTAL SERVICES

For dental services rendered on July 10.

Call for appointment

Receptionist time	.2 hr.	$ 7.00
Use of 800 number		2.00

Appointment Setup

Secretarial services	.3 hr	12.00
One page in appointment book		.25
Computer charges		10.00
Reminder card		5.00
Postage for reminder card		.50
Copy of reminder card for file		.50

Appointment

Receptionist services	.2 hr.	7.00
Use of reception area	.8 hr	20.00
Magazine rental		5.00
Professional services		50.00
One set of rubber gloves		10.00
Dental floss		.05
Dental tools rental		10.00
Dental equipment rental		45.00
Parking space rental, 1.5 hrs		15.00
Free toothbrush		3.00

Billing

Bill preparation, secretarial	.3 hr	12.00
Dentist review	.2 hr	25.00
3 photocopies		1.50
Postage		.50
TOTAL		$241.30

All accounts charged 18% annual interest if not paid within 15 days

---

1. How do you react to the bill?
2. Are the charges proper?
3. Why do doctors and dentists not bill their patients as shown in the example?
4. Why do attorneys charge for soft costs?
5. Why are attorneys' charges and soft costs tolerated?

7. WHO PAYS TO EDUCATE THE LAWYER?

Adam Hunt retained the services of Anne Sheridan in his case involving a title dispute on his property. Anne charged Adam $150 an hour for each hour she spent on the case. At the conclusion of the case, Anne gave Adam a bill as follows:

Client interview	1.0 hour	$150
Research	3.0 hours	450
Document preparation	1.0 hour	150
Conversation with title officer	0.5 hour	75
Total		$825

Adam paid the bill, thanked Anne, and left.

A week later, Mark Edwards retained the services of Anne with the same title problem on his property. He asked Anne how much the service would cost. Since knowledge of the transaction was fresh in Anne's mind from Adam's case, Anne would not have to do research on the case. In addition, the necessary documents were in Anne's computer, so she would not need a full hour to prepare them. Altogether, it would only take Anne about 2 hours to handle Mark's case.

1. If Anne charged Mark $150 an hour based on her actual time, would it be fair that Adam paid for Anne's education to benefit Mark?
2. Could Anne qualify herself as an expert in this area to justify charging Mark a higher hourly rate than she charged Adam?
3. If Anne charged Mark an $825 flat-fee, would this be fair to Mark?
4. If Anne charged Mark a lower flat-fee, would this be fair to Adam?
5. What Model Rule applies to this case?

8. BOND OR BUST

Brenda Camp gave Attorney Doug Lillehei $100,000 to pay for a bond in a foreclosure proceeding on her casino. When Brenda later failed to pay Doug's fees, Doug argued that the $100,000 was given as partial payment of those fees and that he had advanced the remainder of the money for posting the bond. When the money from the bond was released, Doug indicated that he had a right to retain it because he had placed a retaining lien on it for attorneys' fees owed.

1. Who is entitled to the bond money?
2. What Model Rule applies to this case?
3. Was a retaining lien proper in this case?
4. If you were Doug, what would you have done in this case?

9. THE OLD BAIT-AND-SWITCH TACTIC

Gail Dahl contacted Lawyer Susan Crowe to file bankruptcy. When Gail called the office, she talked with Jan Odegard, the paralegal, and inquired how much a Chapter 7 bankruptcy would cost. Jan told her the fee was $650 and mailed her a questionnaire to complete for her appointment, which was set for a week later. The procedure for the firm is to have the paralegal interview a client and then refer the client to a lawyer.

When Gail came in for her appointment, Jan interviewed her and told her again that the fee for the bankruptcy would be $650, payable in advance. Gail paid the fee to Jan. Gail was then interviewed by Susan. During the course of the interview, Susan discovered that Gail was the owner of a small business that was also heavily in debt. Further questioning revealed that Gail's business debts consisted of more than $350,000, with over 150 creditors. Since the business was a sole proprietorship, it would have to be included in the Chapter 7 bankruptcy.

Susan told Gail that because of the magnitude of the bankruptcy, the case would cost $1,500. Gail protested vehemently, stating that Jan told her it would cost $650 and she refused to pay more. Gail accused Susan of bait-and-switch tactics and threatened to file a complaint with the state bar.

1. What did this incident do to the reputation of Susan?
2. How did this incident affect the reputation of lawyers in general?
3. What did Jan do wrong?
4. What did Susan do wrong?
5. What did Gail do wrong?
6. How could this type of incident be avoided?

ASSIGNMENTS

1. You are a judge for fee disputes for lawyers and clients. To determine whether a fee is reasonable, consider the concepts discussed in this chapter, including the eight factors (TOCATPET) that contribute to the reasonableness of a fee. For each situation, list the issues involved and the factors that apply and make your ruling.

SITUATION 1: Anthony Vegas retained Howard O'Brien to represent him in his divorce proceedings. Anthony executed a fee agreement that provided for a nonrefundable retainer of $2,500. The agreement stated:

> A client will pay a lawyer a nonrefundable retainer of $2,500, which is not to be affected by any possible reconciliation between the client and a spouse. Said retainer is to be credited against charges of $200 an hour.

After Howard had spent 10 hours on Anthony's case, Anthony discharged Howard and gave no reason for doing so. Howard refused to refund the remainder of the retainer fee to Anthony. Anthony contested. Is Anthony entitled to a refund of the retainer?

SITUATION 2: A court determined a lodestar fee for a contingency case and doubled that fee to account for a "risk premium." The court determined that since the client's chance of success was 50 percent, a doubling of the lodestar was necessary to account for the lawyer's risk in taking the case. The client appealed the ruling to an appellate court, stating that the multiplier was excessive. Was it?

SITUATION 3: Paula O'Connor agreed to defend Glen Hageman in a criminal proceeding. Paula prepared a fee agreement calling for a flat-fee of $15,000 to cover all services, including the trial. The fee was payable up front. Glen signed the agreement but paid no money. Three months later, after Paula had worked on the case, she refused to represent Glen further until she received the money. Glen had no money, so Paula demanded a $25,000 note secured by a second mortgage on Glen's vacation home. When Glen did not pay the fee, Paula started foreclosure proceedings on the home. Glen objected. May Paula foreclose on Glen's vacation home to satisfy the note?

SITUATION 4: Ray Addington, a businessman, employed Ellen Henley regarding a contract action. Ellen stated that her hourly rate would be $200. When Ray indicated he had no money to pay on an hourly basis, Ellen presented a one-third contingency fee agreement, which Ray signed. Ellen participated in settlement negotiations for a year and obtained a settlement figure of $195,000 for her client. Under the contingency fee agreement, the lawyer's fee was $65,000. When payments were made to the lawyer, creditors, and subcontractors out of the settlement proceeds, nothing was left for Ray. Time sheets indicated that if Ellen had charged $200 an hour, her services would have been worth $20,000. Is a contingency fee appropriate in this case?

SITUATION 5: Donna DeMaster, owner of a piece of property worth $70,000, hired Bill Schuster to represent her in a quiet title lawsuit brought by Donna's brother. Bill took the case on a one-third contingency. The case never went to trial but was settled because of the efforts of the parties' mother. No novel or difficult legal questions were involved, and the pleadings filed in the matter were not complicated. Bill charged Donna $23,000 for the representation. He kept no time records since he had the case on a one-third contingency basis. Is the fee excessive?

SITUATION 6: Al Houser paid Walter Krogen $45,000 to represent him in a felony case. Al pleaded guilty, did not go to trial, and was sentenced to 1 year in prison. He felt that the fee was excessive. Al's co-defendant, who went to trial, paid his attorney $12,000. However, Walter stated that he spent more than 800 hours representing Al on the case. Was the fee appropriate?

SITUATION 7: Laura Albertson retained Leslie Olson regarding the final distribution of property from her divorce. A detailed retainer agreement set forth a minimum number of hours required for the representation and specified Leslie's hourly rate under two alternative time schedules. It also provided for the payment of additional attorneys' fees of a percentage of the net property distribution obtained for Laura. Was the fee agreement proper?

SITUATION 8: Meghan Schuh represented Joshua Anderson in a product liability case that was taken on a contingency and that included an appeal. The trial court ruled against Joshua, and Meghan sought an appeal of the ruling. However, Meghan had no experience with appellate work, so she hired an experienced appellate attorney to prepare the appeal and argue the case before the appellate court. In return for the appellate attorney's services, Meghan agreed to pay him 25 percent of the total fee. Meghan did not inform Joshua of her association of the appellate attorney. Did Meghan act properly?

SITUATION 9: Erin Brown's fee agreement with Nathan Bunnell entitled her to one-third of a gross recovery received by compromise or settlement prior to filing an insurance suit and 40 percent thereafter. The fee agreement also gave Erin a charging lien on any recovery. Erin opened the file, collected certain information, and notified the insurance carrier of the case. The carrier declined Nathan's claim. A suit was filed in the hope of receiving a favorable disposition from the insurance company, but no offer was forthcoming. Erin wrote Nathan a letter that stated that no further work would be done on the case and advised Nathan that he could seek other counsel, pursue the case himself, or have the matter dismissed. Nathan retained another law firm to represent his interests. When the second firm received his file from Erin, it was accompanied by a statement of Erin's charging lien on the proceeds of the case. Was Erin entitled to collect on the charging lien?

SITUATION 10: Sonia Feldbrugge represented Erica Lukk in a criminal case. During the course of representation, Erica was injured in an automobile accident and requested that Sonia represent her in the personal injury case. Sonia agreed to represent Erica for a one-third contingency fee. Erica's criminal matter ended, but she did not pay Sonia for that case. Erica owed Sonia $5,000 for the criminal case. Therefore, Sonia put a charging lien on the proceeds of the personal injury case for the $5,000 fee not paid in the criminal case. Was the lien proper?

2. Draft a contingency fee agreement for a one-third fee before trial, 40 percent if the case goes to trial, and 45 percent if an appeal is made. Use the examples on the accompanying CD as a guide.

3. Draft a fee agreement that includes a nonrefundable chargeable retainer and hourly rates for the following:

Senior attorney at $400 an hour

Associate attorney at $300 an hour

Paralegals at $110 an hour

4. Draft a fee agreement that includes a $5,000 refundable chargeable retainer and a flat-fee of $10,000, using the examples on the accompanying CD as a guide.

5. In your ficticious law firm, the owner's hourly rate is $400 an hour, senior attorneys $350 an hour, junior attorneys $275 an hour, paralegals $125 an hour, and law clerks $100 an hour. Assuming that the owner and one senior attorney, one junior attorney, one paralegal, and one law clerk work on a case, what would be the blended hourly rate?

6. For Black, White & Greene, write about their fee structure. For this exercise, it is okay to set fees.

   a. Include hourly rates for all attorneys, paralegals, and law clerks.
   b. Describe what types of cases are flat-fee cases and the amount of each.
   c. Describe what types of cases are contingency cases and the percentage factors.
   d. Describe whether the firm calculates its fees by the gross fee or net fee method.
   e. Describe the firm's policy of retainer fees, and describe the type of retainer fee charged.
   f. Describe the firm's policy concerning referral fees.
   g. Describe the firm's policy on premium fees and combination fees.
   h. Describe the firm's policy concerning hard costs.
   i. Describe the firm's policy concerning soft costs, and list all soft costs and the charges.
   j. Describe the firm's policy concerning liens.
   k. Describe the firm's policy regarding paralegals quoting fees and describe what a paralegal should do if a client asks the paralegal for fee information.

SELF TEST

How well did you grasp the material in the chapter? Test yourself by answering the following questions, and check your answers against the answers found in Appendix A.

1. At the time of the Roman republic, how much did legal services cost?
2. Name the 10 different types of fees.
3. Name the four types of retainer fees.
4. What is a true retainer fee?
5. Why is a true retainer fee used?
6. What is a nonrefundable chargeable retainer fee?
7. What is a nonrefundable nonchargeable retainer fee?
8. Why do many firms use nonrefundable retainers?
9. What is a refundable retainer?
10. What are hourly fees?
11. Hourly rates vary according to what three things?
12. What is a blended hourly rate?
13. What are the six factors used to determine hourly rates?
14. What is the most common fee found in law offices?
15. What is a flat (fixed) fee?
16. What is a per diem flat-fee?
17. What are minimum/maximum flat-fees?
18. How are flat-fees established?
19. What is task-based billing?

20. What is a contingency fee?
21. What are the two methods of calculating the attorney's contingency fee?
22. What is the difference between the gross-fee method and the net-fee method of calculation?
23. What type of fee calculation gives the client the most money?
24. What is a modified contingency fee?
25. What are the four considerations in taking a case on a contingency fee basis?
26. Why have a number of states put limits on contingency fees?
27. What are statutory fees?
28. According to Model Rule 1.5(e), what are the three occasions when an attorney may divide a fee with another attorney?
29. According to Model Rule 5.4, what are the three occasions when a lawyer may share legal fees with a nonlawyer?
30. Why are lawyers prohibited from fee splitting with nonlawyers?
31. According to Model Rule 7.2(b)(4), what are the three occasions when an attorney may pay a referral fee?
32. What are the four arguments against referral fees?
33. What are the two arguments for referral fees?
34. What are premium payments?
35. What are value-based fees?
36. What are combination fees?
37. What are hard costs?
38. What is the difference between costs of litigation and expenses of litigation?
39. Why are attorneys not allowed to pay for the expenses of litigation?
40. What are soft costs?
41. What are some examples of soft costs?
42. What are the two reasons that the ABA established rules and guidelines concerning legal fees?
43. What are the eight considerations in determining a reasonable fee (TOCATPET)?
44. What is the lodestar calculation?
45. What are multipliers?
46. What are the two types of liens that an attorney may place to secure payment of fees?
47. What is a charging lien?
48. What is a retaining lien?
49. In addition to a charging lien and a retaining lien, what else may a lawyer do to secure payment of fees?
50. Who has full responsibility for a client's fee?
51. Why must paralegals comply with attorney guidelines concerning fees?
52. What has case law ruled that a person must have to quote fees?
53. Whose responsibility is it to set fees?
54. What is the name of the case that ruled that paralegal fees are recoverable?
55. What is most often the source of dispute between a client and a lawyer?
56. What is an essential ingredient for any fee agreement?
57. What type of fee must be in writing according to Model Rule 1.5(c)?
58. Why are written fee agreements desirable?

Key Words

actual cost	extraordinary fee	portal-to-portal
advance	flat-fee	reasonable attorneys' fees
bait-and-switch	hard cost	retaining lien
charging lien	lawyer hopping	soft cost
contingency fee	lodestar	tort
costs	mark up	value-based fee
database	multiplier	
extranet	per diem	

Cybersites

LEGAL FEES

Devil's Advocate: Legal fee management and consulting—
    <*http://www.devilsadvocate.com*>

Understanding Fee Agreements—<*http://www.consumerlawpage.com*>

How do Attorneys Charge?—<*http://www.tba.org/*>

Washington State Bar Association – Legal Fees—
    <*http://www.wsba.org/media/publications/*>

Accountability Services—<*http://www.legalbills.com*>

Student CD-ROM
For additional materials, please go to the CD in this book.

Online Companion™
For additional resources, please go to
http://www.paralegal.delmar.cengage.com

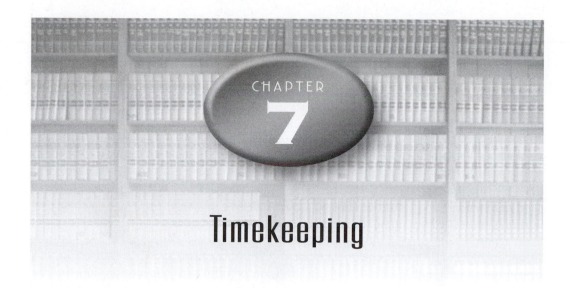

Timekeeping

OBJECTIVES

After completion of this chapter, the student should be able to do the following:

- Define annual billable hours requirements.
- Explain what constitutes nonbillable time.
- Explain the difference between creditable and noncreditable nonbillable time.
- Calculate a billing in tenths of an hour.
- Complete a time sheet for billable and nonbillable time.
- Prepare management reports based on timekeeping records.
- Describe work on time sheets.
- Explain how coding is used on time sheets.
- Describe the various methods of timekeeping.
- Discuss timekeeping ethics.

INTRODUCTION

The knowledge and expertise of lawyers and paralegals are the products law firms sell to their clients. Time is the vehicle by which they deliver their products. Compare a manufacturing firm and a law firm. A manufacturing firm has a product: a widget. Salespeople sell widgets to customers. Sales produce orders for widgets. Orders result in accounts receivable, and accounts receivable result in money. A law firm's products are the knowledge and expertise of their lawyers and paralegals. Marketing activities result in clients. Clients order the time and expertise of the legal team, which results in work in progress. Work in progress results in accounts receivable, and accounts receivable result in money.

Unlike widgets that can be counted in inventory in a manufacturing firm, knowledge and expertise are not tangible products. As a result, lawyers and paralegals frequently have their own personal methods of recording their time. A firm that has minimal or no timekeeping policies gives lawyers and paralegals an enormous amount of personal discretion about what to bill a client, what not to bill a client, how to describe time, and how much time to record on a particular project. Without proper training in timekeeping, timekeepers produce inaccurate time records that result in inaccurate client billing and management reports. Inaccurate billing causes law firms to lose clients and client goodwill. Inaccurate management records cause management to make decisions on the basis of incorrect information. Therefore, comprehensive guidelines and timekeeping policies are essential for the success of a law firm.

Managing time is a skill that requires effort. Since time is the vehicle by which a law firm delivers its product, it must be documented before its value can be realized. If it is not documented, its value is lost, and a firm loses its product. Unlike a manufacturing firm that may produce more widgets, a law firm may never recover lost time.

Lawyers and paralegals are the primary timekeepers in a law office. A firm bills clients for their time, thereby obtaining its income. Other personnel, such as law clerks and secretaries, may also bill clients for their time, requiring them to keep time records. However, the main income producers for a firm are lawyers and paralegals.

Timekeeping is an essential element of a paralegal's job. Law firm management uses information derived from time records to bill clients, establish budgets, and prepare management reports. This chapter will prepare a student to develop timekeeping skills. The first section introduces the timekeeping requirements of most law firms and gives an overview of a firm's expectations. The second section explains how law firm management uses time records, and the third section discusses the elements of timekeeping and describes how to keep time records. The fourth section reviews various timekeeping methods. The fifth section discusses timekeeping ethics, and the last section gives pointers on accurate timekeeping.

TIMEKEEPING REQUIREMENTS

annual billable hours requirement
The number of hours a timekeeper is required to bill in a year.

Most law firms establish a minimum number of billable hours that must be produced by each timekeeper in a year. This is called an **annual billable hours requirement.** Since a firm bases its budget and financial forecasting on projected income produced by its timekeepers, it is very important that each timekeeper meet the annual requirement. In addition, a timekeeper's bonus, raise, or both may be based on whether an annual requirement is met. If it is exceeded, the timekeeper may expect a raise or bonus. If it is not, the timekeeper may not get a raise or bonus.

The number of annual billable hours required of a paralegal varies with each firm. The chart in Exhibit 7–1 indicates the number of hours one must bill a day to meet the indicated annual billable hours requirement, assuming a 236-day work year.

Studies indicate that paralegals are not required to bill as many hours as attorneys. According to a 2007 nationwide salary survey conducted by *Legal Assistant Today*- 48.5 percent of paralegals had an annual billable hour requirement.

HOURS A YEAR	HOURS A DAY
1,200	5
1,300	5.5
1,400	6
1,500	6.5
1,600	7
1,700	7.2
1,800	7.6
1,900	8
2,000	8.5

EXHIBIT 7–1 Annual Billable Hours a Day

NUMBER OF HOURS	LAT SURVEY
400–600	.9%
601–800	3.6%
801–1,000	1.8%
1001–1,200	2.7%
1201–1,400	6.4%
1401–1,600	20%
1601–1,800	10.9%
1801–2,000	1.8%
More than 2,000	1.8%

EXHIBIT 7–2   Paralegal Annual Billable Hours Requirement *(As seen in the March/April 2007 issue of Legal Assistant Today. Copyright 2007 James Publishing, Inc. Reprinted courtesy of Legal Assistant Today. For subscription information call 800-394-2626 or visit <http://www.legalassistanttoday.com>.)*

The majority of paralegals (20 percent) were required to bill from 1,401 to 1,600 hours per year, and 10.9 percent of the respondents were required to bill 1,601 to 1,800 hours a year. The results of that survey are reflected in Exhibit 7–2. Note that some paralegals are required to bill more than 1,800 per year, or 7.6 hours a day.

Billable and Nonbillable Hours

The hours of a workday are placed in two categories: billable and nonbillable. Billable hours are directly applied to clients' matters, while nonbillable hours are not applied to clients' matters. The average paralegal spends 75–85 percent of a day on billable projects. Two types of nonbillable hours exist: creditable and noncreditable, as shown in Exhibit 7–3.

CREDITABLE NONBILLABLE HOURS   Creditable nonbillable hours are credited toward an annual billable hours requirement and include time spent in the following five types of activities:

1. Duties in serving on law firm committees
2. Pro bono work, or work provided at no cost to a client

creditable nonbillable hours
The time that is applied to an annual billable hours requirement.

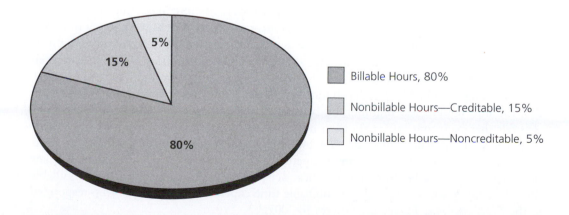

Billable Hours, 80%

Nonbillable Hours—Creditable, 15%

Nonbillable Hours—Noncreditable, 5%

EXHIBIT 7–3   Billable Hours and Creditable and Noncreditable Nonbillable Hours

3. Participation in management functions (e.g., completion of reports and attendance at law firm meetings)

4. Administrative functions

5. Training

noncreditable nonbillable hours
The time that is not applied to an annual billable hours requirement.

NONCREDITABLE NONBILLABLE HOURS   Noncreditable nonbillable hours are not credited toward an annual billable hours requirement and include time spent in the following three types of activities:

1. Educational activities, consisting of attendance at seminars, attendance at paralegal association conferences, and reading trade journals

2. Personal matters

3. Paralegal association work

Firms differ in their application of creditable and noncreditable time. Many firms do not consider nonbillable time as a firm expense, but it is. If a firm with ten attorneys and three paralegals had a 1-hour staff meeting each week, the annual cost to the firm is as follows:

$$\begin{aligned} 10 \text{ attorneys @ \$300/hr.} &= \$ \quad 3,000 \\ 3 \text{ paralegals @ \$100/hr.} &= \$ \quad\;\; 300 \\ \$3,300 \text{ per week} \times 50 \text{ weeks} &= \mathbf{\$165,000} \end{aligned}$$

ceiling
The maximum number of hours that may be spent on nonbillable projects.

Some firms put a **ceiling,** or maximum limit, on the number of creditable nonbillable hours to increase a timekeeper's billable hours. Others do not put a ceiling on creditable nonbillable hours if the time is spent on law firm business.

Some firms credit a paralegal's educational activities, and some do not. If the state bar requires continuing education hours for lawyers, most firms will credit a lawyer's educational activities to the annual billable hours requirement. A firm and ultimately a client indirectly benefit from hours spent in educational activities. Increasing the expertise of a timekeeper ultimately results in increased efficiency and services for a client. Crediting time spent in educational activities and paying for those activities are ways a firm encourages continuing education for its timekeepers. According to the *Legal Assistant Today* 2007 salary survey, 64.9 percent of firms pay for a paralegal's educational expenses, 15.6 percent shares the cost, and 19.5 percent do not pay educational costs.

Some firms may also credit hours spent by a paralegal on paralegal association work. If a paralegal holds an office in a paralegal association, some firms believe that it results in advertising for the firm. Firms that support networking of employees may encourage their employees to become involved in association work by crediting hours spent on association business.

Most firms give attorneys a higher allowance for creditable nonbillable hours than they do paralegals because attorneys are expected to participate in more marketing activities for a firm. For example, a lawyer would be given credit for such activities as working on pro bono cases, speaking at seminars, cultivating clients, and participating in community organizations. In addition, many lawyers must attend continuing legal education events to keep their license to practice law current.

pad
To expand in a fraudulent manner.

Recording nonbillable time has traditionally been neglected or not required. Firms felt that the information was unimportant because it was not used for billing purposes. They also felt that requiring information on nonbillable time offered opportunities for a timekeeper to **pad,** or fraudulently add time to, time sheets to make up for unproductive time. Since law firms have become more competitive, however, marketing and planning a law firm's resources have become crucial. These activities require management of nonbillable time. Exhibit 7–4 is a sampling of nonbillable time expended by paralegals who responded to the *Legal Assistant Today* salary survey in 2007.

The information that emerges from the nonbillable categories of a time sheet will tell law firm management a lot about the efforts being expended by a timekeeper on the firm's

% OF TIME SPENT ON NONBILLABLE TASKS	LAT SURVEY
0–5	9.5%
6–10	19.0%
11–20	19.0%
21–30	13.8%
31–40	12.1%
41–50	12.1%
More than 50	14.7%

EXHIBIT 7–4 Time Spent on Nonbillable Tasks *(As seen in the March/April 2007 issue of* Legal Assistant Today. *Copyright 2007 James Publishing, Inc. Reprinted courtesy of* Legal Assistant Today. *For subscription information call 800-394-2626 or visit <http://www.legalassistanttoday.com>.)*

behalf. These records are considered when an employee is evaluated and considered for a raise or bonus.

Calculation of a Billable Hour

Each firm differs on the method used to calculate billable hours. Some firms require time calculated in hours, quarters of an hour, or tenths of an hour. Other firms require time to be documented in minutes. The most common method used is tenths of an hour. Decimal time entries are easily input into a computer. A billable hour is divided into ten 6-minute increments, as shown in Exhibit 7–5.

TIME INCREMENT	DECIMAL ENTRY
1–6 minutes	0.1 hour
7–12 minutes	0.2 hour
13–18 minutes	0.3 hour
19–24 minutes	0.4 hour
25–30 minutes	0.5 hour
31–36 minutes	0.6 hour
37–42 minutes	0.7 hour
43–48 minutes	0.8 hour
49–54 minutes	0.9 hour
55–60 minutes	1.0 hour
61–66 minutes	1.1 hours
67–72 minutes	1.2 hours
73–78 minutes	1.3 hours
79–84 minutes	1.4 hours
85–90 minutes	1.5 hours
91–96 minutes	1.6 hours
97–102 minutes	1.7 hours
103–108 minutes	1.8 hours
109–114 minutes	1.9 hours
115–120 minutes	2.0 hours

EXHIBIT 7–5 Time Increments in Tenths of an Hour

Since it is difficult to work on a project in 6-minute intervals, accurate timekeeping is difficult with this method. A paralegal must become accustomed to watching the clock when a project begins and ends and also when the work is interrupted by a telephone call or coworker.

Minimum Charges

Most law firms have a minimum-charge policy, which is the minimum amount of time they will charge on any project or aspect of a project. The most commonly used minimum charge is 0.2 hour, or 12 minutes. However, some firms' minimum charge may be as much as 0.5 hour, or 30 minutes. For example, a paralegal makes a telephone call to opposing counsel. Opposing counsel is not available. The secretary takes the paralegal's telephone number and tells the paralegal that the attorney will return the call. The amount of time spent is approximately 1 to 2 minutes. The paralegal charges the client 0.2 hour, or 12 minutes, for that activity according to the minimum-charge policy.

An argument opposing this practice is that clients are being overcharged. An argument in favor of this policy is that it takes time for the timekeeper to make the transition from working on one file to working on another. When the paralegal hangs up the telephone, he or she must document the time spent making the call and document the file for which the call was made. The paralegal must retrieve the file of the next matter he or she will be working on and prepare his or her thoughts for the next matter. This time is covered by minimum charges, so a law firm does not lose money when timekeepers make the transition from one file to another.

CLIENT	BILLABLE TIME	ACTUAL TIME
A	0.2 hour	1 minute
B	0.2 hour	1 minute
C	0.2 hour	1 minute
D	0.2 hour	1 minute
E	0.2 hour	1 minute
Total	1.0 hour	5 minutes

EXHIBIT 7–6 Billable Hours versus Actual Hours for Five Phone Calls

TIME	DESCRIPTION	BILLABLE HOURS	ACTUAL HOURS
9:00 a.m.–9:30 a.m.	Search for Jones file		0.50
9:30 a.m.–10:00 a.m.	Research for Jones file	0.5	0.50
10:00 a.m.–12:00 p.m.	Equipment committee meeting		2.00
12:00 p.m.–1:00 p.m.	Lunch		1.00
1:00 p.m.–1:15 p.m.	Conference with Jones re file	0.3	0.25
1:15 p.m.–2:00 p.m.	Conference with new copier vendors		0.75
2:00 p.m.–2:10 p.m.	Conference with attorney re Jones file	0.2	0.20
2:10 p.m.–3:10 p.m.	Review of time sheets for billing		1.00
3:10 p.m.–4:00 p.m.	Paralegal staff meeting		0.80
4:00 p.m.–4:30 p.m.	Computer malfunction (tried to fix)		0.50
4:30 p.m.–5:00 p.m.	Interview with prospective secretary		0.50
Total hours		1.00	8.00

EXHIBIT 7–7 Billable Hours versus Actual Hours for a Paralegal's Day

Billable Hour versus Actual Hour

A billable hour is different from an actual hour. An actual hour contains 60 minutes. A **billable hour** may contain as little as 5 minutes or as much as 8 hours. For example, a paralegal must make five telephone calls to five different clients to inform them of hearing dates. Each telephone call takes a little over 1 minute, but each client is billed for 12 minutes—the 0.2-hour minimum charge. Therefore, the paralegal has 1 billable hour for 5 minutes' actual time spent, as shown in Exhibit 7–6.

A billable hour may also be as much as 8 actual hours because of nonbillable creditable or noncreditable time. For example, a paralegal spent her day as shown in Exhibit 7–7.

An example of a paralegal's time sheet that includes billable, creditable nonbillable, and noncreditable nonbillable time is given in Exhibit 7–8.

billable hour
Sixty minutes of time that are billed to a client.

(handwritten margin notes: 4.2 / 4.9 / 9.1)

Law Offices Of Black, White & Green

Name: Peggy McIntire   Date: March 22, 2007

TIME	DESCRIPTION	CREDITABLE BILLABLE HOURS	CREDITABLE NONBILLABLE HOURS	NONCREDITABLE NONBILLABLE HOURS	TOTAL HOURS
8:30–9:00	Administration—read office memos and correspondence		0.5		
9:00–10:00	*Smith v. Jones*—office conference w/client	1.0			
10:00–10:15	Education—read paralegal association news			0.3	
10:15–10:30	*Smith v. Jones*—draft memo to file re meeting	0.3			
10:30–11:00	*Shady Oak Corp. v. Industrial Metals*—review complaint	0.5			
11:00–12:00	Administration—staff meeting		1.0		
12:00–1:00	Lunch			1.0	
1:00–1:30	Phone call from daughter			0.5	
1:30–3:15	*Shady Oak Corp. v. Industrial Metals*—draft answer to complaint	1.8			
3:15–3:20	*Black v. Perry*—take call from client	0.2			
3:20–3:30	*Black v. Perry*—prepare memo to attorney re telephone call	0.2			
3:30–3:45	*Doss v. Frieholz*—review produced documents	0.3			
3:45–3:50	*Doss v. Frieholz*—make telephone call to client	0.2			
3:50–4:00	Call to Linda re paralegal meeting			0.2	
4:00–4:30	*Grey v. Rose*—look for file		0.5		
4:30–4:40	Telephone call from husband			0.2	
4:40–5:00	*Shady Oak Corp. v. Industrial Metals*—prepare continuance motion	0.4			
Total Hours		4.9	2.0	2.2	8.5

EXHIBIT 7–8   Time Sheet with Billable and Nonbillable Hours

TIMEKEEPING RECORDS AND REPORTS

Management uses time records for seven purposes:

1. Billing clients
2. Compensating hourly employees
3. Calculating employee productivity
4. Planning
5. Monitoring work in progress
6. Projecting profitability
7. Forecasting income

Billing Clients

Clients are billed according to the number of hours expended by a firm's timekeepers, unless they have a different fee arrangement, such as a flat fee or contingency fee. For cases that are billed hourly, computers generate bills on the basis of time records. Also, outside billing companies will prepare bills on the basis of time records.

Compensating Hourly Employees

Instead of having employees punch a time clock, law firms use time sheets to calculate an hourly employee's salary. A firm may also pay its nonemployees, such as freelance paralegals, according to the time sheets they turn in.

Calculating Employee Productivity

quota
An assigned goal.

Since law firms establish annual billable hours requirements, keeping track of the billable hours of each employee determines whether an employee will meet the **quota** set by a firm. By these records, management can determine whether an employee is productive.

In some firms, management will keep each timekeeper apprised of her or his creditable billable hours and give each timekeeper a report of billable hours monthly, quarterly, or biannually. These reports will allow a timekeeper to monitor accumulated billable hours to determine where she or he is in relation to her or his goal. For example, a paralegal with an annual billable hours requirement of 1,800 hours must bill as shown in Exhibit 7–9 to be on schedule.

Planning

Time records provide information regarding the activity of a firm by type of case. Firms that provide services in various areas of the law will be able to calculate how much business they are doing in each area. In large and medium-sized firms with departments established according to specialty, management can determine the activity of each department, as shown in the report in Exhibit 7–10. If management finds that a firm's bankruptcy department has increased its activity substantially, management may consider hiring another attorney and paralegal or distributing the increasing workload accordingly. If a firm's tax department has decreased its activity substantially, the firm may decide to transfer employees into another department or increase its marketing efforts toward tax clients. By comparing current figures with past years' figures, a firm can see its direction by the types of cases it is attracting. This type of information helps management direct the marketing efforts of a firm.

GOAL

1,800 Hours

December 31—1,800 Hours

September 30—1,350 Hours

June 30—900 Hours

March 31—450 Hours

EXHIBIT 7–9 Paralegal's Billable Hours Goal

Law Offices of Black, White & Greene

Quarterly Summary of Billable Hours by Department

DEPARTMENT	1st QTR ACTUAL	1st QTR PROJ.	2nd QTR ACTUAL	2nd QTR PROJ.	3rd QTR ACTUAL	3rd QTR PROJ.	4th QTR ACTUAL	4th QTR PROJ.
Antitrust	124.5	120.0	122.5	120.0	118.0	120.0	127.5	120.0
Litigation	860.0	950.0	875.0	950.0	980.0	950.0	989.0	950.0
Real Estate	320.0	300.0	313.5	300.0	290.0	300.0	304.0	300.0
Bankruptcy	560.0	400.0	523.0	400.0	497.5	400.0	560.0	400.0
Tax	125.0	350.0	164.0	350.0	112.0	350.0	243.5	350.0
Total	**1,989.5**	**2,120.0**	**1,998.0**	**2,120.0**	**1,997.5**	**2,120.0**	**2,224.0**	**2,120.0**

SUMMARY

QUARTER	ACTUAL	PROJECTED	VARIANCE
1	1,989.5	2,120.0	(130.5)
2	1,998.0	2,120.0	(122.0)
3	1,997.5	2,120.0	(122.5)
4	2,224.0	2,120.0	104.0

EXHIBIT 7–10 Departmental Management Report

Exhibit 7–11 is an example of a management report by type of case. Type-of-case reports provide management with information on the time it takes to complete a certain type of case. This helps management establish fees for flat-fee cases. For example, if a firm has records for the time spent on criminal cases for drunk driving defenses, it will average the time and apply the attorney's and paralegal's hourly rate to the average, thereby establishing

Law Offices of Black, White & Greene

Management Report of Drunk Driving Cases

CLIENT	TIME SPENT
A	10.3 hrs
B	11.8 hrs
C	16.2 hrs
D	14.7 hrs
E	13.5 hrs
Total	66.5 hrs

66.5 hrs ÷ 5 cases = 13.3 hrs for each case

13.3 hrs × $275 per hour = $3,657.50 set fee per case

EXHIBIT 7–11 Type-of-Case Report

a fixed fee. Time reports also monitor time spent on flat-fee cases to determine whether the fee is too low or too high so that an adjustment can be made if necessary.

Monitoring Work in Progress

Monitoring the time spent on each case will inform management where a firm's resources are and are not being spent. For example, if no activity has occurred on a file during a 60- or 90-day period, a report of the amount of time spent on each case will alert management to potential neglect of that case. The responsible attorney will be informed and the file reviewed. If a large amount of time is being spent on one case, management will consider obtaining additional staff for the case.

Time records also allow management to monitor the workload of attorneys and paralegals. These management reports give attorneys and paralegals a realistic idea of their caseload and allow management to allocate work accordingly.

Projecting Profitability

Time records allow management to project the productivity of its timekeepers. For example, if a paralegal is required to bill 1,500 hours a year, time sheets will reveal how close or how far the paralegal is from meeting the goal. If a firm allows a paralegal 20 percent of a day for nonbillable time, creditable and noncreditable, the time sheets will also reveal whether the paralegal spends too much time on nonbillable projects.

Forecasting Income

The number of billable hours projected for each timekeeper will determine the projected annual income of a law firm. A law firm budget is prepared from these projections. If the timekeepers meet their quotas and all fees are collected, a firm will receive its projected income. Exhibit 7–12 is an example of a firm's income projections.

Once a budget is prepared on the basis of anticipated income and expenses, management may plan for a firm's financial future. This planning includes retirement benefits, law firm investments, and long-term financial goals.

TIMEKEEPER	ANNUAL HOURS	HOURLY RATE	PROJECTED INCOME
Partner LuAnn Ephart	1,600	$200	$ 320,000
Partner Alex Webber	1,600	225	360,000
Associate Trevor Clarke	1,800	175	315,000
Associate Ina Davis	2,000	150	300,000
Paralegal Blake Rowan	1,800	100	180,000
Paralegal Wanda Lubovich	1,800	75	135,000
Total			$1,610,000

EXHIBIT 7–12 Income Projections

Amount of fees received			$12,000
Attorney's time	23 hrs. at $175	$4,025	
Paralegal's time	59 hrs. at $75	4,425	
Total			$ 8,450
Unexpected profit			$ 3,550

EXHIBIT 7–13 Contingency-Fee Case Report

If a timekeeper fails to meet the quota or exceeds the nonbillable time allowance, the firm's income will decrease, and the firm must plan accordingly. The firm may cut expenses, reduce the owners' profit, eliminate an employee benefit, or lay off employees. A timekeeper's mismanagement of time affects the firm's cash flow, therefore affecting the entire firm. Managing time is an important skill for paralegals.

A law firm also calculates the profitability of contingency cases by time records. When a contingency case has ended and a firm collects its fee, it calculates the profitability of the case by multiplying the amount of time spent on it by the attorney's and paralegal's hourly rates. If the fee is higher than the figure calculated, the case was profitable. If it is lower, the case was not profitable. Exhibit 7–13 is an example of a report on a contingency-fee case.

ELEMENTS OF TIMEKEEPING

Time sheets require the following eight pieces of information:

1. Name of timekeeper
2. Date
3. File name
4. Client number
5. File number
6. Amount of time expended, in tenths of an hour
7. Description of work performed
8. Name or initials of responsible attorney

Law Offices of BLACK, WHITE & GREENE
Time Record

Name: Peggy McIntire

Date: March 22, 2007

Client No.	File Name	Type	File No.	Description	Time	Attny
1001	*Dobmeyer v. Ferry*	102	1001-765	C/W Atty. Pflaum—R1–D1 answers to interrogs. T/C client re ans. to interrogs	2.3	DW
3014	*Shady Oak Corp. v. Industrial Metals*	104	3014-223	R2 from oppos. counsel—D3 memo to file	0.6	DW
2332	*In re Wilcox*	121	2332-405	P file for CH—summarize DP	1.5	DW
5667	*People v. Anderson*	133	5667-101	T/C client re CT	0.2	DW
3211	*Doss v. Frieholz*	105	3221-322	R negligent entrustment issue—D3 re research	2.4	DW
Firm	Paralegal committee	151		Paralegal committee meeting	1.0	DW
				Total	8.0	

EXHIBIT 7–14 Time Sheet

Firms may require three additional pieces of information:

1. Department code
2. Task-based code numbers, if applicable
3. Type-of-case code number

These entries will ensure that the appropriate client is billed for the time spent on the file and that management is supplied with appropriate information for its reports. An example of a time sheet is shown in Exhibit 7–14.

The date on a time sheet is used to inform a client of the date a service was rendered and also to inform management of the timekeeper's performance for that day. The client's number, file name, and file number are essential so that the correct client and case are billed, especially if a client has multiple cases with an office. Firms also require paralegals to insert the name or initials of their supervising attorney. This information is used in the event a discrepancy occurs as to the paralegal's assignment for a client. The description area is used to inform a client and management of the work performed. The amount of time spent on a matter is documented in the time area in tenths of an hour.

It is important to be as clear as possible when describing work, even if it takes more time. This information is entered on a client's bill so that the client will know what work was done and the cost of that work. Billing disputes are as likely to be caused by a client's irritation at the way time is described as by the amount of time spent. For example, a client may resist paying $250 for a paralegal's time spent "in conference with attorney" but would probably not resist paying for "planning trial strategy." Exhibit 7–15 gives examples of ineffective and effective descriptions.

INEFFECTIVE	EFFECTIVE
Work on case	Draft answers to third set of interrogatories
Review of file	Review first and second sets of answers to interrogatories for inconsistencies
Conference with attorney	Conference with attorney re client's deposition
Telephone call to counsel	Telephone call to counsel re setting deposition date

EXHIBIT 7–15 *Descriptive Entries Are Important*

Coding

To expedite the timekeeping process, law firms have developed codes for each function. A computer is programmed to pick up these codes and transform them into their proper meaning. Each firm develops its own coding system. An example of the types of codes used is shown in Exhibit 7–16.

Notice the column marked "Type" on the time sheet in Exhibit 7–14. This column is used for the type of case. Each type of case is given a specific number, and a computer is programmed to convert the numbers into the specific type of case. Exhibit 7–17 is an example of this type of coding.

Contingency Fee Law Firms

Time records are also important for law offices that do not bill clients by the hour. A firm working on personal injury cases on a contingency fee basis receives a percentage of the settlement at the end of a case. It needs time records to monitor the profitability of a case and monitor work in progress.

C/W	Conference with
CT	Court trial
CH	Court hearing
D1	Draft of pleadings
D2	Draft of correspondence
D3	Draft of memorandum
D4	Draft of other
DP	Deposition
N/C	Nonchargeable
P	Preparation of
R	Research of
R1	Review of pleadings
R2	Review of correspondence
R3	Review of memorandum
R4	Review of other
RV	Revision of
TC	Telephone conversation with

EXHIBIT 7–16 *Work Description Codes*

Litigation	
General	100
Real estate	101
Tort	102
Business	103
Corporate	104
Fraud	105
Domestic	
General	120
Uncontested	121
Contested	122
Custody	123
Adoption	124
Prenuptial	125
Name change	126
Criminal	
General	130
Misdemeanor	131
Felony	132
Driving while intoxicated (DWI)	133
Estate Planning	
General	140
Will	141
Trust	142
Probate	143
Litigation	144
Administration	
General	150
Attendance at meetings	151
Review of law firm correspondence	152
Continuing education	153
Law firm organization	154
Interviewing	155
Client development	156

EXHIBIT 7–17   *Type-of-Case Codes*

In addition, contingency attorneys are occasionally called on to produce time records. For example, if an attorney is terminated by a client, the attorney wants to be paid for work done to termination. If the case is a contingency case, the attorney is not paid until it is completed. The attorney may file a lien against the case, and to prepare the lien accurately, time records are essential. In court cases in which a former attorney has sued to recover a portion of a contingency fee, judges have requested time records to rule on the amount of the fee. Without these records, judges have difficulty evaluating the value of a former attorney's services to a client.

Time records are also valuable in fee disputes and other client complaints. They document an attorney's work on a case to disprove allegations of client abandonment or improper representation.

Another benefit of time records in contingency cases is in determining a case's settlement value. By keeping time records, attorneys are aware of the value of the time spent on a case. By comparing the time value multiplied by the timekeeper's hourly rates against settlement offers, an attorney can determine whether a settlement should be pursued. Exhibit 7–13 shows how profitability on a contingency case is calculated. It makes little economic sense to spend more time on a matter than the matter is worth. Through time records, contingency cases can be monitored to keep track of their value.

Corporate Legal Departments

Some corporate legal departments do not require time records from their attorneys and paralegals because the departments do not prepare billing statements. However, these legal departments are finding that their management reports are not as comprehensive as those from legal departments that require time records from their employees. Therefore, many corporate legal departments require their attorneys and paralegals to keep time records.

A corporate legal department services many departments of a corporation: finance, marketing, and sales. In addition, it may service subsidiaries of the corporation. These departments and subsidiaries are considered the legal department's clients.

Some corporate law departments bill each "client" for services rendered and are paid from that "client's" operating budget. Furthermore, documenting the time spent for each department or subsidiary gives management valuable information. When a legal department prepares its budget, time records are a valuable tool to justify additional staff or funding.

Corporate legal departments may be entitled to court-awarded legal fees if they prevail in litigation in addition to their outside counsel. A Delaware district court awarded Scott Paper Company in-house corporate counsel fees in a patent infringement case against Moore Business Forms (594 F. Supp. 1051 [D.Del 1984]). Scott's time records were evaluated when determining the fee award. Therefore, time records are essential to justify court-awarded legal fees.

Government Legal Offices

Timekeeping activities in government legal offices are becoming more common.

Time records for government agencies are valuable tools when preparing budget proposals and management reports. Management reports for a government office are usually very detailed to provide the government with statistics. In addition, lawyers employed by the U.S. government use timekeeping records for performance appraisals.

TIMEKEEPING SYSTEMS

Timekeepers have various methods of keeping track of time. Some track their time manually, and some use a computer or other devices. Manual time records are ultimately entered into a computer for billing and management reports. Each firm must examine the alternatives and select the appropriate system for its needs.

Although manual systems may be obsolete, familiarity with them provides a general understanding of the essential elements of timekeeping. In addition, many timekeepers keep their time records manually and then input them into the computer at the end of the day. This procedure may seem like preparing time sheets twice, but it ensures that the information put into the firm's computer system is accurate and complete. Furthermore, if a computer is not available because of a power failure or other reason, the timekeeper can keep time sheets up-to-date so that valuable time is not lost.

A time sheet is a permanent fixture of a timekeeper's desk. Entries are inserted on the time sheet daily or as a project is finished. In no situation should a timekeeper delay completing the time sheet, as delay causes information to be lost, resulting in lost revenue for the firm. If a paralegal who bills time at $75 an hour missed just one minimum-charge telephone call a day, the firm would lose $3,540 a year. Time sheets should be completed daily and, preferably, updated many times during the day. Timekeepers should never leave the office for the day without completing their time sheets. Legal consultants indicate that firms that require their timekeepers to keep an accurate accounting of their time make 15 to 30 percent more than those who do not.

It is recommended that timekeepers keep two types of time sheets: one for creditable projects and another for noncreditable projects. Paralegals who keep track of noncreditable time are better able to manage time because they can see where their time is going. This allows the timekeeper to see whether she or he is spending more than 5 percent of the day on noncreditable activities.

When completing time sheets, include billable and nonbillable creditable activities. Management needs this information to prepare management reports. In addition, the firm will have a permanent record of the time you spend on behalf of the firm, whether that time is for training an employee, looking for a file, or attending firm meetings. This information will be important when it comes time for a raise or bonus.

It is also beneficial to keep a separate time sheet documenting nonbillable noncreditable time. A written record of this time will help you develop your time management skills and monitor unproductive time. Five percent of your day (20 minutes in an 8-hour day) is allotted for nonbillable noncreditable time. Keeping track of it will alert you if you are exceeding this guideline.

There are two methods of manual timekeeping systems: the long method and the short method.

With the long method, you document each activity as you start and stop it. For example, you start the day working on the *ABC* case. Before you begin, you write the entry on your time sheet. You note the time you begin and describe your activity. After 30 minutes, you are interrupted by a telephone call from your client in the *Smith v. Jones* case. You note the time and complete your entry for the *ABC* case by inserting 0.5, indicating that you worked on the case for 30 minutes before the interruption. You then start a new entry for the *Smith v. Jones* case and insert the telephone call from your client. You speak to the client for 10 minutes. When you are finished, you document your time sheet for 0.2 hour and describe the telephone call. As you return to the *ABC* case, you make a new entry on your time sheet for the ABC case and describe your work again. You note the time and begin the clock running on the *ABC* assignment. Each time you stop working on a case, for whatever reason, you end your time sheet entry.

With the short method, you do not make a new entry each time you are interrupted. For example, you begin working on the *ABC* case and prepare your time sheet accordingly. After working on the case for 30 minutes, you are interrupted by a telephone call from your client in the *Smith v. Jones* case. You note the time and make an entry on your time sheet for the telephone call: *Smith v. Jones* case. You do not close out the first entry of the *ABC* case. The telephone call lasted 10 minutes, and you document your time sheet with the telephone call and note the time so you may start the clock running on the *ABC* case. You finish working on the *ABC* case an hour later. You have a total of 1.5 hours on the *ABC* case and document your time sheet entry for the ABC case with 1.5 hours. This method will give you one entry per case per day on your time sheet. When using the short method, be sure to describe all of your activities performed for that client. The short method is more concise and makes inputting the information into the computer easier.

Firms differ on their requirements for submitting time sheets. Some require that they be submitted daily, some weekly, and some monthly. Be sure to make copies of your time sheets before you submit them.

A paralegal works on the time sheet throughout the day. When it gets busy and there is a lot of activity, it is easy to overlook this very important task. Always have your time sheet handy. If you cannot complete an entry, at least write in the name of the case on which you worked and the time you started the activity. This entry will stimulate your memory of what transpired when you can complete your time sheet. You should never wait longer than the end of the day to complete your time sheet. It is the first task you do at the beginning of the day and the last task at the end of the day. Always end the day with a completed time sheet.

Of Interest . . .

ARE BONUSES CONNECTED TO BILLABLE HOURS?

A prominent New York law firm, LeBoeuf, Lamb, Greene & MacRae, reported that it gives its attorneys two types of bonuses: nondiscretionary and discretionary. A nondiscretionary bonus is based on a percentage of an attorney's base salary and is awarded if the attorney met his or her annual billable hours requirement. The discretionary bonus is awarded to attorneys who have made exceptional contributions to the firm. Attorneys are eligible for the discretionary bonus if they reported 2,200 creditable hours, including up to 200 hours of pro bono work. Among the attorneys who received the highest discretionary bonus were corporate and litigation associates who logged nearly 2,700 hours in one year. The amount of the discretionary bonus varied, but some associates earned as much as 25 percent of their base salaries.

Manual timekeeping systems are becoming obsolete as firms take advantage of timekeeping software products. Entering time information directly into a computer eliminates the need for data entry and saves the firm money. Management can produce daily reports more quickly than if data entry were required.

A timekeeper enters the essential information directly into a computer or submits completed time sheets to a data entry clerk who will code and enter the information. A computer can be programmed to accommodate a firm's coding system regarding type of case, type of work performed, and timekeeper. For management to receive the many different management reports, all necessary information must be "entered" into a computer.

The billing rates for each timekeeper are programmed into the system along with the firm's coding system. The program permits the firm to apply a markup or markdown of a particular bill. The computer automatically translates the codes into descriptive details of the services rendered, and client bills are automatically generated. The system tracks the time of each timekeeper and automatically apply each timekeeper's hourly rate to the charges. Software also tracks the productivity of fixed-fee and contingency matters. Software is available that accommodates task-based billing and check for conflicts. Some products allows entry from a PalmPilot, PDA, or portable PC. Exhibit 7–18 is an example of a time entry screen and calendar of billed time.

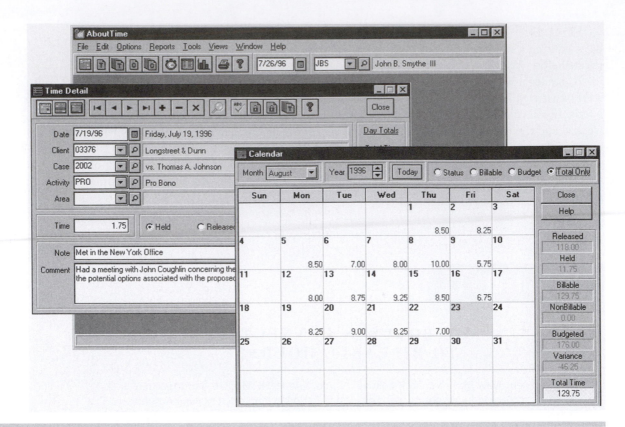

EXHIBIT 7–18   Example of Time Entry and Tracking Screen in Timekeeping Software *(Reprinted with permission of Versys Corporation.)*

TIMEKEEPING ETHICS

The ethical implications of accurate timekeeping cannot be overemphasized. When tracking time, be aware of the following ethical guidelines:

- *Do not bill clients for work not performed.* Billing clients for work not performed is stealing. When working on a client's file, be sure to note the exact time when you start and stop the work. If you should be interrupted by a telephone call from another client, note the time and stop the clock before you take the call. When you have finished the call and resume the previous client's project, note the time again. This will allow you to insert accurate time entries on your time sheet for both projects. Deduct the amount of time you spent on the telephone call from the time spent on the client's file.

- *Do not pad time sheets.* Be sure to insert accurate time entries for each client's case. Timekeepers with a heavy annual billable hours requirement may be tempted to include extra time on their time sheets, but should not give in to this temptation. If you completed a project in less time than anticipated, insert the correct time on your time sheet and bring it to the attorney's attention. If you think you spent more time than anticipated on a project, insert the correct time and, again, bring it to the attorney's attention. It is the attorney's responsibility to adjust the time entry if necessary. Padding time sheets is more prevalent than one would expect.

- *Do not bill a client for time spent on personal matters.* If you are working on a client's file when you receive a personal telephone call, note the time and deduct that time from the client's matter.

- *Do not double-bill.* If a paralegal works on two matters at once, the time must be split between the two matters. For example, a paralegal is traveling by air to another city to assist in a trial. The firm bills the client for travel time. While on the airplane, the paralegal works on a file for another client and bills both clients for the time spent on the airplane. Paralegals should work on the case for which she or he is being paid to travel.

- *Do not bill multiple clients for one activity.* If a paralegal is preparing interrogatories that will be used in two cases, you cannot bill both clients for the same time spent on the project. For example, spending 3 hours on an activity that benefits two clients does not equal 6 hours of billable time. The time should be split between both clients to total the actual time spent on the activity. The ABA ruled in its Formal Opinion 93-379 that attorneys who bill by the hour cannot double-bill for recycled work product. Other state bars have similar opinions.

- *Do not apply an attorney's hourly rate to the services of a paralegal.* Firms that bill an attorney's rate for paralegal time are committing fraud. Webster Hubbell, President Clinton's friend and right-hand man in the Justice Department, pled guilty to charging clients for work that was completed by associates. He spent 18 months in prison. If you discover that your firm is guilty of this practice, it should be brought to management's attention immediately.

Of Interest . . .

BURNING THE MIDNIGHT OIL

A partner in a respected Chicago law firm charged clients for 6,022 hours of work in 1993. This amounts to 16.5 billable hours a day, seven days a week, every week of the year. A review of his past billing record indicates that he billed about 5,000 hours a year for the previous 3 years at a billable rate of $350 an hour. Annual billings of 3,000 hours are extremely rare, and 5,000 hours of billing is virtually impossible.

An internal memorandum of this lawyer's firm specified that firm management, departmental, client relations, and general office matters are not billable. His colleagues described this lawyer as a tenacious litigator who regularly works long days and weekends, but they could not explain how he spent all the time that he was awake on billable matters.

Source: *Wall Street Journal,* May 1994.

COMMON TIMEKEEPING PROBLEMS

Each timekeeper will experience at least one of the following situations. These common problems should be discussed with the firm's management or supervising attorney for guidance on a firm's policies.

The Vanishing File   Finding files is an ongoing challenge for most law firms. Files have been found in the attorney's office, desk, briefcase, and car trunk— anywhere but in the file room.

Question: How does a paralegal document time spent looking for files? Should this time be creditable or noncreditable nonbillable hours?

Answer: The time should not be billed to the client. A paralegal's annual billable hours requirement should not be penalized because of a firm's mismanagement of files. Therefore, the time should be credited to the timekeeper's annual billable hours requirement as administrative time. If it is not creditable, the timekeeper would have to work extra hours to make up the time spent looking for files. It is an interesting exercise to keep track of time spent looking for files. Management would be surprised how much money file mismanagement costs a firm in unproductive time.

The Chatty Coworker   Every office has one. This employee tells coworkers her or his life story—twice—before starting work in the morning. Being polite to this coworker is important to develop a positive firm culture, but getting working done is also important.

Question: How does a paralegal handle this situation?

Answer: A paralegal can be both polite and assertive in this situation by commenting, for example, "Gee, I would love to hear all about this, but I must prepare this document by noon. Can we talk at lunch?" Also, subtle tactics, such as closing the office door, discourage a chatty coworker.

Time Constraints   Clients are becoming more cost-conscious, and many are requiring that a firm adhere to a budget for a case. Task-based billing projects require timekeepers to be especially aware of the amount of time spent on a matter.

Question: If a paralegal exceeds the allotted time for a project, how should she or he document the extra time?

Answer: The exact time spent on the matter should be included on the time sheet regardless of time restrictions. A note referencing the excessive time will alert management to the problem. Management or the attorney will catch the time and adjust the client's bill accordingly. Management monitors the time that each activity takes and uses this information to predict future charges. If in doubt, the timekeeper should consult management or the supervising attorney for guidance.

The Waiting Game   The paralegal has scheduled a meeting with the supervising attorney regarding a client's case. During the meeting, the supervising attorney takes telephone calls from other clients. The paralegal must wait for the attorney to finish before resuming the meeting.

Question: How should this time be documented?

Answer: The time the paralegal waits for the attorney to resume the meeting should not be charged to the client unless the timekeeper works on the case while waiting. The paralegal should consult management or the supervising attorney in this situation or leave the meeting until the attorney finishes the call.

Travel Time   Is travel time billable or nonbillable? The firm may bill some clients for travel time and not others. Others bill clients a reduced rate for travel time.

Question: If the firm bills a client for travel time, may the timekeeper work on another client's case while traveling?

Answer: No. If the timekeeper did so, she or he would be guilty of double billing.

Short Telephone Calls   A paralegal receives a series of short telephone calls on one case throughout the day.

Question: Are the calls billed at a minimum charge separately, or are they aggregated?

Answer: The paralegal must use her or his own judgment in this situation. The general rule is that if the calls occur while the paralegal is working on the case, the calls should be aggregated and included in the total time spent on the case. If the calls occur while the paralegal is working on another case, the calls should be billed at the minimum charge. The answer depends on the firm's policy, the type of client, and the circumstances involved.

Minimum Charges   Most firms have a minimum charge, usually 12 minutes, or .2 hour. On occasion, a paralegal may work on a matter for only 2 or 3 minutes. For example, a client calls and requests a copy of a document. The time it takes for the paralegal to take the call and retrieve the document to give it to the secretary for copying is 3 minutes.

Question: Should the paralegal bill the client for the minimum charge, or not document the charge?

Answer: Document the call. One solution is to document the charge as a minimum charge and attach a note to the supervising attorney that the matter took about 3 minutes. It is the supervising attorney's or management's responsibility to make the ultimate decision to charge or not charge the client.

TIMEKEEPING TIPS

Keep the Time Sheet Handy

Preparing a time sheet is the first thing a paralegal does in the morning. Completing a time sheet is the last thing a paralegal does in the evening. Since a paralegal works with time sheets constantly (whether a manual or an electronic time sheet), a time sheet must be accessible at all times. As a project is begun, the file name, client name and number, and description of the work are documented on the time sheet. The time is noted. When the project is finished, the time is noted. The time can then be calculated in tenths of an hour and entered on the time sheet. It is helpful to finish a project once it is started. However, if a paralegal is interrupted or must stop for another reason, the time is noted. The time the project is resumed is also noted. The interval time is deducted from the total amount of time for the project.

Record the Largest Amount of Time

When recording time in tenths of an hour, it is difficult to end a task on the exact 6-minute increment. If a paralegal worked on a project for 40 minutes, does he or she bill the client .6 hour (36 minutes) or .7 hour (42 minutes)? It is generally accepted to put down the largest amount of time.

Document the Time as a Project Is Finished

Timekeepers who wait until the end of a week to complete time sheets are costing their firms a lot of money. It is very easy to forget about many short telephone calls. Missing just one a day will add up to thousands of dollars by the end of a year.

Do Not Estimate Time

Timekeepers who wait until the end of a day to document time sheets usually estimate their time spent on a project. A timekeeper who thinks that he or she can accurately estimate time is fooling him- or herself and the firm. An experiment conducted by Altman, Weil & Pensa asked a number of attorneys to pick several files and estimate their time spent on each case. In every case, the attorney was either 50 percent too high or 40 percent too low. Other studies have consistently shown that timekeepers who estimate their time underestimate their time.

Be Accurate

If a paralegal feels that it took too much time to complete a project, he or she may be tempted to reduce the recorded amount of time spent on the project. This is a disservice to the paralegal. All time spent on a project must be recorded regardless of its billable nature. If a supervising attorney feels that the time spent on a project is not billable or is too high, it is the attorney's responsibility to reduce the cost to the client when the attorney reviews the bills.

If a paralegal feels that he or she completed a project too quickly and should have devoted more time to it, he or she may be tempted to add to the amount of time. A paralegal should not give in to this temptation. Each paralegal works at his or her own pace. What is speedy to one paralegal is average to another.

Be Descriptive and Concise

When describing time, a timekeeper should avoid using overly broad phrases such as "review of file" or "conference with lawyer." Descriptions should clearly identify the work performed, such as the reason a file was reviewed or the issues discussed at a conference. When describing telephone calls, include the name of the other party and the topic of conversation. Descriptions must be clear, brief, and concise.

Record All Nonbillable Time

If a firm does not require nonbillable time to be documented on time sheets, a paralegal should develop a "nonbillable time" time sheet and record all nonbillable activities on it. This will come in handy at evaluation time.

Develop "To-Do" Lists

Putting projects on a to-do list will help a paralegal give priority to projects and structure a day. Projects are placed in three categories: A, B, and C. A projects are urgent, B projects must be completed within a week, and C projects may be completed within a month. The list should be revised each week.

CONCLUSION

Timekeeping is a very important skill for all paralegals. Accurate timekeeping is especially important in view of the current economic conditions in which clients are pressured to keep legal fees down and law firms are pressured to maximize revenue.

SUMMARY

The knowledge and expertise of lawyers and paralegals are the products law firms sell to their clients. Time is the vehicle by which lawyers deliver their products. Managing time is a skill that requires effort. Since time is the vehicle by which a law firm delivers its product, it must be documented before its value can be realized. If it is not documented, its value is lost, and a firm loses its product.

Lawyers and paralegals are the primary timekeepers in a law office. Most law firms establish a minimum number of billable hours that must be produced by each timekeeper in a year. The number of annual billable hours required of a paralegal varies with each firm.

The hours of a workday are placed in two categories: billable and nonbillable. Billable hours are directly applied to clients' matters; nonbillable hours are not applied to clients' matters. Creditable nonbillable hours are credited toward an annual billable hours requirement, and noncreditable nonbillable hours are not credited toward an annual billable hours requirement.

Each firm differs on the method used to calculate billable hours. The most common method used is tenths of an hour, in which a billable hour is divided into ten 6-minute increments. Most law firms have a policy of charging a minimum of .2 hour, or 12 minutes, on any project or aspect of a project.

Law offices that do not bill clients by the hour need time records to monitor the profitability of a case and monitor work in progress. When the time comes for a government office or corporate legal department to prepare its budget, time records become a valuable tool to justify additional staff or funding.

The ethical implications of accurate timekeeping cannot be overemphasized. Timekeepers should not bill clients for work not performed or time spent on personal matters, pad time sheets, double-bill, or apply an attorney's hourly rate to a paralegal's services.

Preparing a time sheet is the first thing a paralegal does in the morning and the last thing a paralegal does in the evening. Time should be documented as a project is finished. Timekeepers who wait until the end of a day to document time sheets usually estimate their time spent on a project. A person who thinks she or he can accurately estimate time is fooling her- or himself and the firm.

CHAPTER ILLUSTRATION

Each attorney and paralegal at Black, White & Greene, LLP, has an annual billable hours requirement. Their annual requirements are as follows:

Robert Black	1,200 (the remainder of the time is spent managing the firm)
Dennis White	1,600
Grant Greene	1,600
Patrizia Boen	1,800
George Templeton	1,800
Milton Nollkamper	1,500
Julie Stockstill	1,500

The firm bills clients and prepares management reports on the basis of time sheet information. Each timekeeper prepares time sheets manually and gives them to the secretaries each Monday so that they can input the information into the computer system. They are comfortable with the system, and there are very few billing issues to resolve—except for Dennis.

Dennis has a problem getting used to documenting his time. He is disorganized by nature and forgets to write down important details about his work. He loses his time sheets, does not turn them in to Sandra on time, and forgets to write down his work. There are many times that the firm has had to delay billing because Dennis's time sheets were not turned in on time. Sandra, Dennis's secretary, is very frustrated with this problem.

The firm tried different techniques to help Dennis with his timekeeping. One method that seemed to work was the diary method. Dennis kept a large appointment book on his desk and was instructed to write down his work in the book. It would be easier for him to lose a time sheet than a large book. Sandra would then transfer the entries onto a time sheet and enter the information into the computer. However, Sandra noticed that essential work was not being documented. She had to remind Dennis that the work was done and ask him to estimate the time spent on the work. Dennis would estimate the time but could not ensure the accuracy of his time sheet. Robert and Tricia were concerned that the firm was not being compensated for some of Dennis's work. Dennis's quota was not being met, but he was working hard. It was a constant struggle that was affecting the firm's profitability.

As we saw in Chapter 6, the firm lost a client because it did not have the ability to offer task-based billing to its clients. Robert instructed Tricia to research timekeeping software that would enable the firm to offer task-based billing. Tricia did so, and the firm installed the software on its computer system. The new timekeeping system had to be developed, and each employee had to be trained on its use. The new system requires each timekeeper to be more detailed in her or his description of work. They had to implement a more complex coding system that would require more effort from the firm's timekeepers.

The attorneys and paralegals grumbled a bit, but Dennis had a fit. "I don't like to keep track of time anyway. This system is even worse than the old system! I don't have time to put down every little detail. And look at these codes. There are hundreds of codes to remember! It's just too much," he complained.

"Dennis," said Robert. "Last month we lost Technology Enterprises as a new client because we could not offer task-based billing to them. That client could have brought hundreds of thousands of dollars to the firm. You're one-third owner of this firm. How much money do you think you would have received if we would have landed that client?"

"Hmm," said Dennis. "I didn't think of that. Hundreds of thousands of dollars?"

"Yes," said Robert. "Smith & Jones got Technology because they were able to offer them task-based billing. There is a trend of the major corporations to require task-based billing from their outside counsel. I want us to be in a position to be competitive with other firms for their business. Implementing this timekeeping system is the first step. We must do it. Otherwise, we won't be able to compete for the big clients."

"Okay," said Dennis. "I'll learn the system. Sandra will have to help me. But if we can get a big corporate client with this system, it'll be worth the effort."

CHAPTER REVIEW

1. What is the annual billable hours requirement?
2. What activities are included in creditable nonbillable hours?
3. What is the difference between nonbillable creditable hours and nonbillable noncreditable hours?
4. Other than for billing clients, for what does management use time records?
5. How does law firm management use time records to establish flat fees?
6. How does law firm management use time records to determine an employee's productivity?
7. Why do firms keep time records on contingency cases?
8. Why do corporate legal departments keep time records?
9. Why do government offices keep time records?
10. What six timekeeping activities are unethical?

EXAMPLES FOR DISCUSSION

1. THE LOST FILE

Margaret Cleary is a paralegal who works for a law firm that requires her to bill clients 7 hours a day. One of Margaret's assignments was to prepare interrogatories on a real estate case. She entered the client's number, file name, file number, and date on her time sheet and went to the file room to retrieve the file. The file was not there. She spent 1.5 hours looking for the file, which was in the lawyer's brief case. If Margaret does not bill for that time, those 1.5 hours are lost time and she must stay an extra 1.5 hours to make them up.

1. How should Margaret bill this time?
2. If you were Margaret and the supervising attorney told you to bill the client for the time, what would you do?
3. If you were the law firm administrator, how would you remedy this situation?

2. OVERPRODUCTIVE COWORKER

Bill Seewich and John Carruthers work closely on a large litigation case. They come in at the same time and leave together in the evening. They eat lunch together and seldom work weekends. Bill had occasion to review the firm's billing summary for the month and noticed that John reported working at least 2 to 3 hours a day more than Bill. Bill suspects that John is padding his time sheet.

1. What should Bill do?
2. What should the law firm administrator do?

3. THE OPINION LETTER

Gay Keel is a real estate paralegal to Don Gonzales, the managing partner of a large law firm. Don told Gay to research a complex issue for Food Center Shopping Centers. Gay spent 5 hours researching the issue and gave Don a memo describing her findings. Don prepared an opinion letter for the client that was based on Gay's research. A week later, Gay discovered that Don had billed the client his hourly rate for the time Gay spent on the research.

1. If you were Gay, what would you do?
2. Suppose you informed Don of this problem and he did not resolve the problem, what would you do?
3. If you were the administrator for the firm, how would you handle the problem?

ASSIGNMENTS

1. Analyze Exhibit 7–8 and answer the following questions:
   a. Does a discrepancy exist between actual time spent and the total of billable time, creditable nonbillable time, and noncreditable nonbillable time? If so, why? Of how much?
   b. If this paralegal must have 1,500 billable creditable hours a year, has she met her quota for the day?
   c. Has this paralegal exceeded the average of spending 20 percent of her time on nonbillable items? If so, in what area?

2. You are the manager of a medium-sized law firm. The managing partner has asked for a report on the state of the departments in the firm. You run the departmental management report shown in Exhibit 7–10. After analyzing this report, answer the following questions:
   a. What is the financial condition of each department?
   b. Which departments are profitable? Which are not?
   c. What are the net results for each department?
   d. What are your recommendations for improving the firm's financial picture?
   e. What is the financial forecast for the firm for the year?

3. On blank time sheets provided on the accompanying CD, keep a record of your time for one week. Use tenths of an hour for each function and develop codes that apply to your situation. At the end of the week, answer these questions:
   a. How much of your time did you spend productively?
   b. How much of your time did you spend nonproductively?
   c. How much time did you spend studying for class?
   d. How much time did you lose?

4. Interview paralegals in your area who are required to keep time sheets. What are some common problems they encounter? What are their complaints about the timekeeping

system in their firm? What do they enjoy about timekeeping? How long did it take them to learn timekeeping methods?

5. For your law firm, describe the timekeeping procedures. If you do not work in a law firm, describe the timekeeping system used in Black, White & Greene. Assume that the firm uses a manual timekeeping system. Develop timekeeping policies and procedures. Develop a coding system and illustrate the system into your description. You may use the codes described in the text or develop your own. Describe what percentages of a timekeeper's time are billable and nonbillable time. Develop firm policies concerning nonbillable creditable and noncreditable time. Develop firm ethical guidelines regarding timekeeping. Describe your firm's policy concerning time spent looking for a file, traveling from one place to another, and minimum charges.

SELF TEST

How well did you grasp the material in the chapter? Test yourself by answering the following questions, and check your answers against the answers found in Appendix A.

1. What is a law firm's product, and how is it produced?
2. What do inaccurate time records produce?
3. Why must a timekeeper's time be documented?
4. Who are the primary timekeepers in a law office?
5. What is an annual billable hour requirement?
6. What are billable hours?
7. What are nonbillable hours?
8. What are the two types of nonbillable hours?
9. What are creditable nonbillable hours?
10. What are noncreditable nonbillable hours?
11. What are some ways a firm encourages continuing education?
12. Why do most firms give attorneys a higher creditable nonbillable hours allowance?
13. What are some activities that would be included in an attorney's creditable nonbillable hour allowance?
14. What information will management obtain from nonbillable hours?
15. What is the most common method of calculating time?
16. What is the most common minimum charge?
17. How is the billable hour different from an actual hour?
18. Name the seven most common management reports derived from time records.
19. How do time records assist management in its marketing efforts?
20. How do time records assist management in setting flat fees?
21. How do time records assist management in monitoring work in progress?
22. How do time records allow management to monitor the profitability of a timekeeper?
23. How do time records allow management to calculate the profitability of contingency cases?
24. How do time records assist management in making financial forecasts?
25. What are the eight elements contained in all time sheets?
26. What additional information may time sheets contain?
27. Why do firms use codes for each function?
28. Why do contingency law firms keep time records?
29. Why do corporate legal departments require time records?

30. Why do government legal offices use time records?
31. What are the six things a timekeeper may not do?
32. What is double billing?
33. What is padding time sheets?
34. How should a paralegal document personal telephone calls?
35. What is the first thing a paralegal does in the morning?
36. What is the last thing a paralegal does in the evening?
37. Why should you not wait until the end of the day to complete your time sheets?
38. Why should timekeepers not estimate their time?
39. Whose responsibility is it to reduce the cost of a project?
40. Why should a timekeeper record all nonbillable time?
41. Why should a paralegal maintain to-do lists?
42. When should a time sheet be completed?

Key Words

annual billable hours requirement	ceiling	pad
billable hour	creditable nonbillable hours	quota
	noncreditable nonbillable hours	

 Student CD-ROM
For additional materials, please go to the CD in this book.

 Online Companion™
For additional resources, please go to http://www.paralegal.delmar.cengage.com

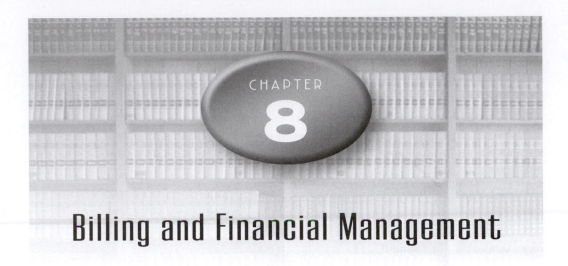

Billing and Financial Management

OBJECTIVES

After completion of this chapter, the student should be able to do the following:

- Explain the importance of good communication with a client.
- Describe the importance of documenting all client communication.
- Draft an engagement letter.
- Explain the importance of billing frequently.
- Understand the difference between descriptive and brief bills.
- Prepare a descriptive bill.
- List the steps involved in collection procedures.
- Prepare collection letters.
- Describe a firm's ethical responsibility concerning billing.
- Discuss some problems of the billing process.
- Describe the factors that affect a firm's profitability.
- Calculate an employee's realization rate.
- Identify the types of income and expenses in a law firm.
- Estimate projected law firm income and expenses.
- Calculate a firm's expense percentage and discuss the various ways it is used.

INTRODUCTION

Before the 1960s, lawyers had a reputation for casual billing practices. They billed their clients sporadically, some waiting as long as a year to bill for work done. Lawyers had few or no billing policies, and their incomes reflected this lack of policy.

Since the introduction of general business practices to law firms to encourage them to be more profitable, lawyers have realized the importance of appropriate and regular billing practices. As the practice of law becomes more competitive and expensive, firms can no longer afford to work for a client without receiving payment for their services on a regular basis.

Proper billing techniques result in bills being paid quickly, and improper billing techniques result in billing disputes that drain a firm's time and resources. Prompt payment of a firm's bills is important to the financial stability of the firm.

An administrator, managing attorney, or manager is responsible for setting billing policies and preparing timely bills. A paralegal's role in the billing process varies. A paralegal in a small firm may be directly responsible for calculating and preparing bills. A paralegal in a large firm may not be directly involved in the billing process. In every firm, however, a paralegal participates in the billing process by submitting time records.

This chapter will discuss the elements involved in effective billing techniques. It will also explain the billing process and billing reports and give examples of various styles of bills. It will describe procedures for collecting overdue bills as well as how a firm handles fee disputes. Finally, it will discuss ethical billing practices and some problems firms encounter with their billing procedures.

THE ART OF BILLING

The goal of a good billing practice is to get a firm's bills paid as promptly as possible. To do this, a firm must make a client aware of the value received for each dollar spent. The more valuable a client perceives a service, the more quickly the client will pay a bill.

The manner in which bills are prepared contributes to the speed of payment. A client who cannot understand the charges or who is unaware of the work performed will not promptly pay a bill.

The billing process has four essential elements: communication, documentation, regular and frequent billing, and descriptive bills.

Communication

The most important aspect of the billing process is communication. Communication begins at an initial client interview and continues throughout an attorney-client relationship until the relationship is terminated. The client should have a clear understanding of the fees involved at the beginning of the case.

INITIAL CLIENT INTERVIEW   A firm's fee structure is explained to a client at an initial client interview (see Exhibit 8–1). *A paralegal may not explain a fee agreement to a client.* It is the lawyer's responsibility to communicate a fee agreement to a client.

ETHICS
ALERT

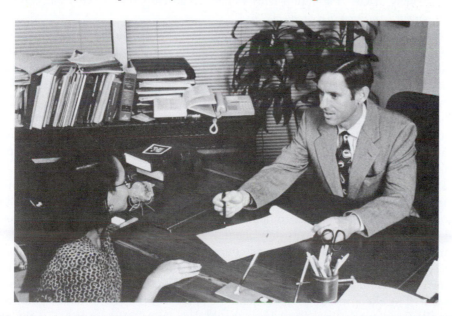

EXHIBIT 8–1   Explaining a Firm's Fee Structure and Billing Policies Is an Essential Element of the Initial Client Interview

A lawyer should also communicate expected hard and soft costs. Most clients do not realize that a flat fee does not include costs such as filing fees, photocopies, or other charges. A client's obligation for fees and costs should be clearly communicated and stated in a written fee agreement.

Although many attorneys discuss fees with clients, most do not inquire about a client's ability to pay. An attorney may discover that a prospective client mistakenly thinks that the opposing party will pay the fees or that the fees are payable out of the recovery. Knowledge of a client's ability to pay for legal services will enable an attorney to make an informed decision regarding acceptance of a matter. This can be a delicate area, and how it is handled affects an attorney-client relationship. If a case is a contingency or flat-fee case, the client's ability to pay is less critical.

ONGOING COMMUNICATION   A firm's communication responsibility does not end with the initial client interview. Communicating the cost of legal services to a client continues throughout an attorney-client relationship. An attorney is obligated to discuss steps of a client's case with the client. If a legal team informs a client of each aspect of a case, the client will not be surprised to see charges for those aspects on a bill. Many clients complain when they do not hear from their attorney for months and then receive a large bill. A client is surprised that a "simple matter" suddenly became complex. The client then blames the lawyer for making a simple matter complex to increase fees. Clients distrust their attorneys, causing an attorney-client relationship to deteriorate. This can be avoided by proper communication.

One way to keep clients informed is to send a client copies of all documents prepared or received on the client's behalf. An attorney often overlooks this function and relies on his staff to handle it. A paralegal can take the initiative and send a client copies of all documentation. A transmittal letter stating that the documents are for the client's information will go a long way in strengthening the attorney-client relationship. The attorney, as well as the client, will appreciate the extra time it takes to do this.

PARALEGAL COMMUNICATION   At times, a client may contact a paralegal with questions about a bill. These occasions give a paralegal the opportunity to participate in client relations by showing a client compassion and understanding of the client's concerns. A paralegal may discuss a situation with a client in an empathic manner *but may not give advice or suggest a solution to a problem.*

To help a client resolve a billing problem, all such calls should be directed to the attorney, a manager, or an administrator. If a client feels that charges are too high, only the responsible attorney or administrator has the authority to adjust the bill. If a client needs clarification on a bill, a paralegal may answer the client's questions if the paralegal knows the answers and the answers are within accepted parameters.

When communicating with clients, paralegals must be aware of the parameters within which they can work. *A paralegal may not discuss the duration of a case.* In other words, if a client asks a paralegal how long a case will take, the paralegal may not give an estimated amount of time. It is an attorney's responsibility to give the client this information. *A paralegal may not estimate the cost of a matter.* All fee quotes are an attorney's responsibility. In addition, *a paralegal may not give an opinion as to the possible outcome of a matter.* All client communication should be polite, compassionate, and professional. Every client should be treated as if he or she were a firm's only client.

Attorneys and paralegals have a good concept of the legal process, but most clients do not. Often, a client has no idea of the steps necessary for a successful resolution to a problem. The client should clearly understand the intricacies of a case and a lawyer's strategy for the case. The client must also understand the process of the case to have a good concept of what the fee is purchasing. The lawyer should describe all strategy and give the client a range of hours and discuss what could shorten or lengthen the amount of time. This will increase the client's understanding of the matter. However, it is important to remember that *a paralegal may not discuss strategy with a client.* A client's complete understanding of the fee structure will result in prompt payment of a firm's invoices.

ETHICS ALERT

Documentation

Documenting all communication concerning fees and billing matters is important, particularly if there is a fee dispute. Many firms start the documentation process by sending an engagement letter.

ENGAGEMENT LETTER   It is a good practice to send a new client an **engagement letter,** similar to the one shown in Exhibit 8–2, along with a copy of the fee agreement. This letter should be sent soon after the initial client interview. Often, during an initial interview, a client is upset or anxious about a case. Many clients sign fee agreements without taking the time to read or fully understand them. An engagement letter restates the terms of a representation as discussed in the interview. The client should sign a copy of the engagement letter and return it to the firm. American Bar Association (ABA) Model Rule 1.5(b) states:

> (b) The scope of the representation and the basis or rate of the fee and expenses for which the client will be responsible shall be communicated to the client, preferably in writing, before or within a reasonable time after commencing the representation, except when the lawyer will charge a regularly represented client on the same basis or rate. Any changes in the basis or rate of the fee or expenses shall also be communicated to the client.

DOCUMENTING COMMUNICATION   All client communications should be documented. If a client discusses a bill with a member of the legal team, the conversation must be documented by a memo to the file as soon as possible after the conversation takes place.

engagement letter
A letter summarizing the scope of representation and the fee agreement between a lawyer and a client.

Regular and Frequent Billing

Billing should be regular and frequent. Traditionally, lawyers have withheld billing until a substantial amount of time was spent on a case. With many law firms advancing costs, delaying the billing process was a very expensive practice. Lawyers were, in essence, lending interest-free money to their clients to finance a case. The cost of operating capital has forced lawyers to bill clients more frequently.

Monthly billing is the most common method of billing. Clients prefer to receive smaller monthly bills rather than larger infrequent bills. However, small firms and sole proprietors have difficulty meeting a monthly billing schedule, especially if a legal team is working hard to meet approaching deadlines. A sole proprietor preparing for trial is not thinking of billing. Nevertheless, small firms can least afford casual billing policies. A paralegal is in a good position to urge that billing be done in a timely fashion. A paralegal may suggest hiring temporary help in times of crisis so that billing can be prepared on time.

Billing a client as soon as possible after a matter is completed is a crucial element of a good billing policy. It is a good practice to send a bill with the final documents. A delay in billing will lower a client's perception of the value of services rendered, as shown in the chart in Exhibit 8–3.

Descriptive Bills

Firms disagree on how descriptive bills should be prepared. Some feel that extremely descriptive bills are confusing to clients, and others feel that they are essential. Bills in flat-fee cases need not be as descriptive as those in hourly cases. Bills should describe the service in a brief and concise manner.

An average bill has twelve basic elements:

1. Name of the case
2. Billing period

Black, White & Greene
Attorneys at Law
1212 Main St.
Anytown, IL

Date: June 1, 20XX

Lila Peterson
234 56th St.
Palo Alto, CA 90000

Re: *Peterson v. Johnson*

Dear Ms. Peterson:

We are very pleased you have retained us in connection with the matter of *Peterson v. Johnson*. The purpose of this letter is to confirm the terms by which this office will represent you.

The scope of our representation will include negotiating settlement of the dispute with Rita Johnson. If the dispute cannot be negotiated to your satisfaction, we will commence to file suit in the Superior Court and proceed to take the case to trial.

You have agreed to pay us $275 an hour for Dennis White's time and $225 an hour for Grant Greene's time. You have agreed to pay us $100 an hour for paralegal time and $75 an hour for law clerk time. You have also agreed to pay all costs incurred, which consist of filing fees if the suit is commenced ($120), service fees (approximately $50), and office costs. Office costs are $0.50 a copy for photocopies, the actual cost of long-distance telephone calls, and messenger costs, if needed. If the lawsuit proceeds to trial, there may be additional costs for discovery, such as motion fees, witness fees, and deposition costs. We will consult with you before incurring any discovery costs.

Ms. Peterson, it is very difficult to anticipate the total cost in a case such as yours. We expect, however, negotiation would take no more than 10 hours. Litigating this matter will be quite costly, possibly requiring as much as 100 hours to trial. We can give you the approximate cost of a trial as we approach the trial date.

You will be billed on the first of every month, for fees and costs incurred. You have agreed to pay our invoice within 15 days of receipt. If the invoice is not paid within 30 days, you have agreed to pay the firm 10 percent per annum interest on all past-due amounts.

Be assured we will do our best to serve you effectively. We cannot guarantee the success of your venture, but we will represent your interests professionally and efficiently. If at any time you should have any questions or concerns, please contact me.

If you disagree with the above, please contact me as soon as possible. If you agree, please sign and return the enclosed copy of this letter. Thank you for retaining our firm. I am sure you will be pleased with our service. We look forward to serving you.

Sincerely,

Black, White & Greene

Dennis White, Attorney

Agreed and accepted this _____ day of _____, 20XX.

_____
Lila Peterson

EXHIBIT 8–2   Engagement Letter

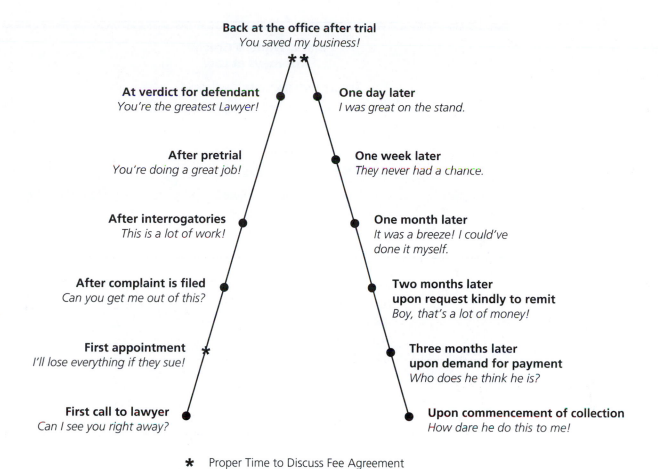

Back at the office after trial
You saved my business!
✱✱

At verdict for defendant
You're the greatest Lawyer!

One day later
I was great on the stand.

After pretrial
You're doing a great job!

One week later
They never had a chance.

After interrogatories
This is a lot of work!

One month later
It was a breeze! I could've done it myself.

After complaint is filed
Can you get me out of this?

Two months later
upon request kindly to remit
Boy, that's a lot of money!

First appointment
I'll lose everything if they sue!
✱

Three months later
upon demand for payment
Who does he think he is?

First call to lawyer
Can I see you right away?

Upon commencement of collection
How dare he do this to me!

✱   Proper Time to Discuss Fee Agreement

✱✱ Proper Time to Submit Final Bill

EXHIBIT 8–3   Client's Line of Gratitude

3. Date of the work
4. Description of the work performed
5. Time increment of the work
6. Name of the person who performed the work
7. Hourly rate of the person who performed the work
8. Cost of the work
9. Itemization of costs
10. Total costs
11. Total of fees and costs
12. Payment terms

THE BILLING PROCESS

Entries from time sheets are input into a computer. After the information is input, a **preliminary bill** is prepared. A lawyer reviews the preliminary bill and may add charges to or subtract charges from it. Often, paralegals are asked to assist an attorney in the review process.

The eight factors considered to determine the reasonableness of a fee are represented by the acronym TOCATPET (see page 227). A firm may be entitled to an increased fee if

preliminary bill
A bill prepared for an attorney's review and consideration for adjustment.

**Black, White & Greene
Attorneys at Law**

FEE ADJUSTMENT MEMORANDUM

Date: _____   Responsible Lawyer: Robert Black

Client: ABC Corp. v. Huntington Driving Range

File No: 45-456   Matter: Litigation

Final Bill _____ Interim Bill _____ Date from _____ to _____

Atty. Initials	Hours × Rate	= Time-Dollar Value
RB	15 × $275	$4,125
Total time-dollar value:		$4,125

Adjustments		Add	Deduct
a.	Novelty or skill	_____	_____
b.	Amount involved	_____	_____
c.	Loss of other employment	_____	_____
d.	Ability to pay	_____	_____
e.	Statutory limit	_____	_____
f.	Internal fee schedule of firm	_____	_____
g.	_____	_____	_____
	TOTALS	_____	_____
Final fee		$_____	

EXHIBIT 8–4   Fee Adjustment Memorandum

a case so warrants. If so, it is an attorney's responsibility to add these factors into the bill at the time of billing. In some cases, a decreased fee is appropriate. If the recovery for a client does not justify a large fee, an attorney may reduce it. An attorney may also reduce charges if he or she feels that they are too high.

To make adjustments to bills, many firms use a **fee adjustment memorandum.** The appropriate adjustments are made on the memorandum, and the memorandum is given to an administrator or billing manager, who will make the adjustments accordingly. An example of a fee adjustment memorandum is shown in Exhibit 8–4.

fee adjustment memorandum
A form used by an attorney to increase or decrease a client's bill as appropriate.

Interest Charges

Charging interest on past-due accounts is generally accepted. However, some states require a client's consent to charge interest, and some states require that the agreement be in writing. Other states require notice to a client with an opportunity to pay without interest. Interest is generally discussed in an initial client interview and documented in an engagement letter.

As a rule, interest is rarely collected. It has been only slightly successful in encouraging clients to pay bills. Firms have also found compliance with state and federal regulations burdensome and not worth the effort.

Credit and Credit Cards

Lawyers often extend credit to their clients. Credit has traditionally been extended to people on the basis of their ability to pay. Banks go through sophisticated procedures to determine whether a person has the ability to pay for credit. Very few lawyers, however, determine their clients' ability to pay their bill before they extend credit. This has caused law firms to have severe collection problems.

To ease the financial burden on firms, lawyers have offered clients two credit alternatives: loans and the use of credit cards. A firm will enter into an agreement with a local bank or lending institution. On approval of credit, the lending institution will buy a client's contract from an attorney at a 5 to 10 percent discount. The client then becomes obligated to the lending institution instead of the firm for the attorney's services.

Billing Systems

Law firms have computerized billing systems. There are hundreds of billing software packages available to law firms today, most of which are combined with their timekeeping systems. Some software packages are appropriate for the small firm, while others are developed for the large firm. Some large firms have developed their own billing software.

When a final bill is ready to be prepared for mailing, the software automatically prepares the bills and includes the date of the service, a description of the service, the initials of the timekeeper, the amount of time expended, and the costs. The bill is detailed and also includes payments received on the account.

Most software packages will bill for other forms of legal fees in addition to hourly fees. These include contingency, flat-fee, retainer, **fee allocation,** and split-fee billing. Some software will accommodate task-based billing, while others will not. Some software products allow a **cost recovery system** to be integrated with the firm's copier and telephone system. By programming the copier before copies are made, copy charges are automatically picked up by the billing system and inserted on the bill. Telephone charges are billed in the same manner.

In addition to billing clients, the software will track accounts payable and clients' funds trust account balances. Some programs will also do conflict checking and keep track of important due dates and appointments.

fee allocation
When a percentage of the bill is given to the originating or supervising attorney as compensation.

cost recovery system
A utility program that allows data to be transferred to a billing program by copier or telephone systems.

BILLING STYLES

Various billing styles are used by law firms. The style of a bill depends on the type of client, type of case, and policy of a firm. Some firms find long, detailed bills time-consuming and unnecessary. Other firms' clients demand detailed bills. Whenever a client questions a bill and contacts a firm for clarification, it delays payment of the bill. The rule of thumb is to be as descriptive as necessary to get a bill paid.

Billing an Hourly Fee Case

Two styles of hourly bills are used: detailed, shown in Exhibit 8–5, and brief, shown in Exhibit 8–6.

Billing a Flat-Fee Case

If a firm represents a client on a flat-fee basis, a detail of services performed is not necessary. However, some firms prefer to include a summary of services rendered to inform a client of the work done on a case. If the fee is paid before any work is done on the case, a bill is unnecessary, except for hard costs incurred. Normally, a flat fee includes all soft costs

Black, White & Greene
Attorneys at Law

Date

Valued Client
234 56th St.
Anytown, CA 90000

Re: Client v. Johnson, et al.

For legal services rendered from January 1, 20XX, through January 31, 20XX

Date	Initials	Description	Time	Cost
1/5/XX	RJB	Conference with opposing atty re discovery	.3	$ 90.00
1/6/XX	RJB	Draft and review interrogatories	1.5	135.00
1/6/XX	MN	Draft interrogatories	2.0	150.00
1/6/XX	MN	Conference with client re interrogatories	.3	22.50
1/15/XX	MN	Review request for production of docs	.4	30.00
1/16/XX	RJB	Review request for production	.3	90.00
1/18/XX	PB	Prepare for deposition	2.0	450.00
1/24/XX	PB	Attend deposition	4.0	900.00
1/25/XX	PB	Conference w/DAC re deposition	.5	112.50
1/25/XX	MN	Conference w/JKL re deposition	.5	37.50

Total Fees $2,017.50

Costs

Photocopies, 68 × .25	$17.00
Depositions	345.00
Long-distance telephone	6.50

Total Costs $368.50

TOTAL   **$2,386.00**

Billing code:

RJB	Robert J. Black, Senior Partner	$300.00 hr.
MN	Milton Nollkamper, Paralegal	75.00 hr.
PB	Patrizia Boen, Associate Attorney	225.00 hr.

Payment due within 15 days of receipt.

EXHIBIT 8–5   Example of Detailed Hourly Statement

incurred. An example of a descriptive flat-fee bill is shown in Exhibit 8–7; an example of a brief flat-fee bill is shown in Exhibit 8–8.

Billing a Contingency Fee Case

If a firm represents a client in a complex contingency case with high costs, the firm may periodically bill the client for costs or require the client to deposit money in an attorney's client funds trust account for payment of costs. It is preferable, however, to bill a client periodically for costs to keep a cost bill reasonable. If a client has prepaid costs, a statement should indicate the amount left in a client funds trust account after the costs are deducted. Some firms indicate the amount of time spent on a contingency case even though a client is not billed for the time. This time entry is made so that a client will know that a firm is working on a case. An example of a bill for costs in a contingency case is shown in Exhibit 8–9.

Black, White & Greene
Attorneys at Law

Date

Valued Client
234 56th St.
Anytown, CA 90000

Re: Client vs. Johnson, et al.

For legal services rendered from January 1, 20XX through January 31, 20XX

Professional services	8.5 hrs	$2,975.00
Costs		368.50
TOTAL DUE		**$3,343.50**

Payment due within 15 days of receipt.

EXHIBIT 8–6   Example of Brief Hourly Statement

Black, White & Greene
Attorneys at Law

Date

Valued Client
234 56th St.
Anytown, CA 9000

Re: Marriage of client

Initial client interview; conference with opposing attorney; prepare petition, summons
and order to show cause papers; prepare marital settlement agreement; negotiation with
opposing attorney; court hearings

Professional services		$3,000.00
Amount paid		1,000.00
Balance		**$2,000.00**
Costs		
Photocopies	$4.50	
Long-distance telephone	7.85	
Filing fee	120.00	
Total costs		132.35
Total due		**$2,132.35**

$1,000 and costs due within 15 days.
Balance due at the time of trial.

EXHIBIT 8–7   Example of Descriptive Flat-Fee Statement

Black, White & Greene
Attorneys at Law

Date

Valued Client
234 56th St.
Anytown, CA 90000

Re: Marriage of client

Professional services	$3,000.00
Amount paid	1,000.00
Balance	**$2,000.00**

Costs

Photocopies	$4.50	
Long-distance telephone	7.85	
Filing fee	120.00	
Total costs		132.35
Total due		**$2,132.35**

$1,000 and costs due within 15 days.
Balance due at the time of trial.

EXHIBIT 8–8   Example of Brief Flat-Fee Statement

Black, White & Greene
Attorneys at Law

Date

Valued Client
234 56th St.
Anytown, CA 90000

Re: Client v. General Motors

For costs incurred

Photocopies	$4.50	
Long-distance telephone	7.85	
Filing fee	120.00	
Total costs		132.35
Amount in client funds trust account		**$500.00**
Total due		**$132.35**
Balance of client funds trust account		**$367.65**

EXHIBIT 8–9   Contingency Statement for Costs

Most often, however, a firm will wait until the end of a contingency matter to give a client an accounting of fees and costs. The money from a judgment or settlement is deposited into an attorney's client funds account, also known as the trust account, and the funds disbursed therefrom. Exhibit 8–10 is an example of gross contingency fee accounting, and Exhibit 8–11 is an example of net contingency fee accounting.

E-Billing

The Internet is changing the way law firms do business, and the billing process is no exception. Electronic billing, or e-billing, is gaining popularity among corporate legal departments. However, e-billing is more complicated than merely e-mailing statements to clients. To bill electronically, special software is required for firms and clients. Firms and their clients must also use an outside vendor to implement the system. Some vendors are listed in the Cybersites section at the end of the chapter. Invoices are sent via the Internet, and clients can pay the firm via the Internet. The client logs on to a secure website and uploads

---

Black, White & Greene
Attorneys at Law

Date

Valued Client
234 56th St.
Anytown, CA 90000

Re: Client v. State Farm Insurance Co.

Gross recovery:		$15,000.00	
Less 33 ⅓% attorney's fee		5,000.00	
Balance			$10,000.00

Less Costs

1/4/XX	Filing fee	$120.00	
1/15/XX	Greg's Attorney Service, service fees	75.00	
1/26/XX	Mileage for interviewing witness	32.60	
2/5/XX	Private Eye Investigations	235.00	
2/8/XX	Wrecker Garage, storage of auto	532.00	
2/15/XX	The Photo Shop, photos	64.50	
3/15/XX	H. E. Sawitall, witness fees	22.50	
4/23/XX	Depo Service, depositions	321.00	
5/18/XX	Dr. Goode, medical report	175.00	
6/2/XX	Dr. Wright, medical report	125.00	
7/23/XX	Dr. Goode, medical lien	350.00	
9/15/XX	Speedy Messenger Service	45.00	
9/20/XX	Various long-distance telephone	27.50	
9/20/XX	Photocopies	68.30	
Total costs and disbursements			$2,193.40
TOTAL RECOVERY TO CLIENT			**$7,806.60**

EXHIBIT 8–10   Contingency Fee Accounting by Gross-Fee Method

---

Black, White & Greene
Attorneys at Law

Date

Valued Client
234 56th St.
Anytown, CA 90000

Re: Client v. State Farm Insurance Co.

Gross recovery: $15,000.00
Less costs

1/4/XX	Filing fee	$120.00	
1/15/XX	Greg's Attorney Service, service fees	75.00	
1/26/XX	Mileage for interviewing witness	32.60	
2/5/XX	Private Eye Investigations	235.00	
2/8/XX	Wrecker Garage, storage of auto	532.00	
2/15/XX	The Photo Shop, photos	64.50	
3/15/XX	H. E. Sawitall, witness fees	22.50	
4/23/XX	Depo Service, depositions	321.00	
5/18/XX	Dr. Goode, medical report	175.00	
6/2/XX	Dr. Wright, medical report	125.00	
7/23/XX	Dr. Goode, medical lien	350.00	
9/15/XX	Speedy Messenger Service	45.00	
9/20/XX	Various long-distance telephone	27.50	
9/20/XX	Photocopies	68.30	

Total costs and disbursements $ 2,193.40
Balance   12,806.60
Less 33 1/3% attorney's fee   4,268.87
Total recovery to client   **$8,537.73**

EXHIBIT 8–11 Contingency Fee Accounting by Net-Fee Method

the invoice. The client can review and approve the invoice and submit it for payment electronically. In addition, clients can generate a number of reports and statements based on electronic data submitted by the law firm with a click of a mouse. In 2007, 49 percent of legal departments used e-billing and 35 percent of legal departments required that their outside counsel offer e-billing.

E-billing requires extensive coding. At first, the Uniform Task-Based Management System (see Exhibit 6–4) was used, but this system did not provide a standard way of submitting and transmitting information. In 1998, Price Waterhouse Cooper helped develop the Legal Electronic Data Exchange Standard (LEDES), which provides a standardized format for electronic billing. The LEDES format was compatible with most billing software used by law firms and is the most popular format used today.

Once a law firm is set up to bill clients electronically, it takes time and resources to manage the system. The International Legal Technology Association reported in its e-billing survey that to set up a new client into the system required an average of 76 hours of work and an out-of-pocket expense of $711. In addition, electronic bills must be carefully reviewed for the correct coding structure. Some firms say e-billing actually adds time to their billing process rather than streamlining it. However, once the bill is properly submitted, firms report that they are paid more quickly.

COLLECTION

Most lawyers find collecting bills the most distasteful part of their job. However, collection activities are a necessary part of the overall operation of a firm. Once services have been rendered to a client, they cannot be repossessed and reused to benefit another client. The collection process usually begins with sending reminder letters and may advance through renegotiating a contract or withdrawing from the case to filing a lawsuit against a client or turning a matter over to a collection agency.

Sending Reminder Letters

Each firm has its own collection policy. Generally, accounts receivable are reviewed monthly, and collection activities begin when more than 30 days have passed since the last billing. At this time, a firm sends a client a mild reminder letter, such as the one shown in Exhibit 8–12.

If an account is 60 days past due, a more aggressive letter, such as the one shown in Exhibit 8–13, is sent, followed by a telephone call.

If payment is not received within 2 weeks of a 60-day letter, a firm's collection department will telephone the client. If the client is unable to pay the entire bill, the firm will make payment arrangements at this time. It is important that a firm's collection staff be aware of state and federal laws concerning proper telephone collection procedures, especially the Federal Fair Debt Collection Practices Act. Some states have enacted laws that prohibit

---

Black, White & Greene
Attorneys at Law

Date

Valued Client
1234 56th St.
Anytown, CA 90000

Re: Client v. Johnson

Dear Mr. Client:

Our records indicate that the attached invoice remains unpaid. If your payment has been mailed, please disregard this letter.

If you should have a problem with any aspect of the enclosed invoice, please contact me so we may discuss it. Otherwise, I look forward to receiving your check for $3,187.00 by return mail.

Thank you for your prompt attention to this matter.

Sincerely,

Tricia Bunnell
Administrator

EXHIBIT 8–12 Example of 30-Day Reminder Letter

Black, White & Greene
Attorneys at Law

Date

Valued Client
1234 56th St.
Anytown, CA 90000

Re: Client v. Johnson

Dear Mr. Client:

Your account with our firm is seriously past due.

Please remit $3,187.00 by return mail, or we will be forced to take further action on this account.

Your immediate attention to this matter is imperative.

Sincerely,

Tricia Bunnell
Administrator

EXHIBIT 8–13   Example of 60-Day Collection Letter

frequent or harassing telephone calls. An attorney may be disciplined and fined for the inappropriate collection techniques of staff members.

Renegotiating and Withdrawing

If a client still does not pay and an account is 90 days or more past due, a firm must decide on the correct collection procedure. At this point, the responsible lawyer becomes involved in the collection process. The lawyer will contact the client and discuss payment of the bill with the client. If a problem exists with the bill, the lawyer will try to work out the charges.

Each account is considered separately. If a client has been a very good client who has fallen on hard times, a firm may decide to give him or her more time, discount a bill, or even write it off completely. If a client has a case that is pending with the firm that is close to completion, the firm may decide to wait until the end of the case. In some cases, a firm will stop work for a client until a bill is paid or withdraw from a case completely.

Before a firm stops work or withdraws from a case, it must give careful consideration to an attorney's ethical responsibilities to a client. A lawyer may do nothing that would jeopardize a client's case. *If stopping all work on a case would jeopardize the case, a lawyer may not do so even though he may not be paid for his work.*

If a client fails to pay a fee, a lawyer may withdraw from a case if the withdrawal will not prejudice the client. Some states require a court's permission to withdraw from a case for nonpayment of fees. Even with a court's permission, an attorney must take steps to protect a client's interest. An attorney must give a client reasonable notice and time to employ a new attorney.

In some states, withdrawal is not justified if a client is unable to pay a fee, as long as the lawyer is able to continue. The ABA permits a lawyer to withdraw from a case in seven circumstances, one of which is nonpayment of fees. ABA Model Rule 1.16(b) and (c) states the requirements as follows:

> (b) Except as stated in paragraph (c), a lawyer may withdraw from representing a client if:
>
> (1) withdrawal can be accomplished without material adverse effect on the interests of the client;

(2) the client persists in a course of action involving the lawyer's services that the lawyer reasonably believes is criminal or fraudulent;

(3) the client has used the lawyer's services to perpetrate a crime or fraud;

(4) the client insists upon taking action that the lawyer considers repugnant or with which the lawyer has a fundamental disagreement;

(5) the client fails substantially to fulfill an obligation to the lawyer regarding the lawyer's services and has been given reasonable warning that the lawyer will withdraw unless the obligation is fulfilled;

(6) the representation will result in an unreasonable financial burden on the lawyer or has been rendered unreasonably difficult by the client; or

(7) other good cause for withdrawal exists.

(c) A lawyer must comply with applicable law requiring notice to or permission of a tribunal when terminating a representation. When ordered to do so by a tribunal, a lawyer shall continue representation notwithstanding good cause for terminating the representation.

Many states have passed ethical guidelines that prohibit a lawyer from withholding a client's property pending payment of fees. In addition, some states require attorneys to complete a case, even if fees have not been paid. For example, a lawyer may not wait until her fees are paid to file a final judgment in a divorce action. As discussed in Chapter 6, a lawyer may be entitled to a retaining lien on a final judgment but may not refuse to file the judgment. Nine issues should be considered before withdrawing from a case:

1. A client's financial condition at the beginning of the representation and whether the lawyer had knowledge of the client's ability to pay

2. A client's sophistication as a consumer of legal services

3. Whether the fees and expenses were explained fully to the client

4. Whether the lawyer offered several different fee arrangements and the client selected a payment option with knowledge of the consequences of the selection

5. Whether the client has received periodic notice about costs as they were incurred and whether the actual charges remained in the range predicted

6. How long the fee has been outstanding

7. Efforts the client has made to submit partial payment

8. Efforts of the lawyer to negotiate a more lenient fee payment schedule

9. Whether there is a dispute about the fee

Suing

If an account is past due by 90 days, a firm may decide to sue a client. If a firm sues a client, the firm has the burden of proving the extent of the services rendered and the reasonableness of the fee. If an attorney has no time records, he or she will have a difficult time proving the validity of a bill. *Furthermore, if a judge finds a suit to recover fees unjustified, a lawyer may be subject to disciplinary action.* Lawsuits against clients are disfavored by the courts. Model Code EC 2-23 states that

ETHICS ALERT

A lawyer should be zealous in his efforts to avoid controversy over fees with clients and should attempt to resolve amicably any differences on the subject. He should not sue a client for a fee unless necessary to prevent fraud or gross imposition by the client.

Suing a client should be the last resort. A high percentage of lawsuits for fees result in cross-claims for attorney malpractice. Some legal malpractice insurance companies prohibit their insureds from suing clients in court and demand that fee disputes be resolved in arbitration through a local or state bar association. An attorney will lose not only the goodwill of a client but also that of the client's friends and business associates.

Using a Collection Agency

The older an account, the more difficult it is to collect. A firm may decide to turn an account over to a collection agency. Most collection agencies operate on a contingency basis and are paid 50 percent or more of the amounts collected.

Most states allow lawyers to turn accounts over to a collection agency if all efforts by an attorney to collect a fee have failed. Other states prohibit the use of collection agencies because of their effect on an attorney-client relationship and on the profession's dignity.

Some states require an attorney to give notice to a client before turning an account over to a collection agency. It is standard practice for a firm to give a client at least 2 weeks' notice of collection agency involvement. This will give a client a chance to pay a bill before damaging the client's credit rating.

BILLING ETHICS

ETHICS ALERT

Lawyers are obligated under the code of professional responsibility of their states to deal honestly and fairly with clients. This admonition carries over to billing policies. Billing methods and disputes have contributed to the public's negative perception of lawyers. If clients cannot trust their lawyers to bill fairly and as agreed, they will not trust their lawyers' legal advice.

Four areas of unethical billing practices are the most common:

1. *Applying a client's funds to a disputed fee.* An attorney may not apply funds held in a client funds trust account to a disputed fee.

2. *Charging more than a client agreed to pay.* It is unethical to charge a client more than the client agreed to pay.

3. *Charging for services not rendered to a client.* It is unethical to charge a client for services not rendered to the client.

4. *Increasing a flat fee.* A firm that charges a flat fee at the outset cannot increase the fee if complications should arise, unless this possibility was discussed with the client and put into a fee agreement.

Legal fee agreements are held to a higher standard than other contracts because of the **fiduciary** relationship between an attorney and a client. This relationship exists whenever a person transacts business for another person and requires a great deal of confidence and trust from the second party and a high degree of good faith from the first. In a fee dispute, any ambiguity in a fee agreement will be construed against a lawyer. A lawyer who deviates from reasonable and acceptable billing practices is running the risk of disciplinary action.

fiduciary
Of, relating to, or involving great confidence and trust; a person who transacts business for another person, necessitating great confidence and trust by the second party and a high degree of good faith by the first.

Legal Auditors

The lack of ethical billing practices has resulted in a new type of service that began in the late 1980s: that of a legal auditor. Large corporations have hired independent auditing firms to review their outside law firm bills to find overbilling. Areas of concern include billing for more lawyers than are necessary for a project, vague service descriptions, billing a lawyer's time for work a paralegal could have performed, and unreasonable office expenses, or soft costs. The sad truth is that auditors often find enough overbilling to return a profit to their clients after their fee is paid. Some legal auditors charge a percentage of the overbilling they find. According to a survey of the 1,000 largest corporations published in *Corporate Counselor,* auditing legal bills was the third most popular method of controlling legal costs. If overbilling was not prevalent, legal auditors would be unnecessary.

Since the late 1990s, clients of legal auditors, usually large corporations and insurance companies, have been ending their legal auditing practices. They found that the use of outside auditors was damaging to their relationship with outside counsel. Outside counsel felt that legal auditors interfered with their professional judgment and tried to dictate how a case should be managed. Auditors routinely cut between 10 and 25 percent of lawyers' bills, and some lawyers say the cuts were not warranted.

Lawyers have successfully fought legal auditors by claiming that sharing their bills with outsiders violated attorney-client confidentiality. State ethics options, as well as court opinions, have ruled on this issue, most of which supported the lawyer's view.

Legal auditors saved St. Paul Companies tens of millions of dollars over 5 or 6 years. However, the savings came at the expense of the company's relationships with its outside counsel, so the company has stopped using auditors. Now, the company tracks its legal bills with software. It is expected that legal auditors will be replaced with tracking software in the near future.

PROFESSIONAL PROFILE 1

Examen Legal Cost Management Service, located in Sacramento, California, provides its clients with bill review services. Most of its clients are large corporate legal departments and insurance companies that submit their invoices from outside counsel for review.

When the invoices are received, Examen categorizes the entries by task. The categorization is similar to the Uniform Task Code and task-based billing (see Chapter 6). Examen then applies the client's billing policies and guidelines to the information and looks for compliance with them. The information is reviewed by an invoice analyst who notes any noncompliance with the client's billing policies. The information is also reviewed by a senior analyst and then by the company's quality control department, which makes sure that all the data are correct. A report is then sent to the client. A copy of the report may also be sent to the law firm at the client's request. If an entry is not in compliance with the company's guidelines, Examen may recommend that the entry not be paid or request follow-up information, depending on the client's billing guidelines.

For example, if a client's guidelines request that only one attorney attend a deposition without prior consultation, the invoice cannot contain an entry for two attorneys to attend the same deposition. If it does, the item is flagged and brought to the client's attention. If authorization was provided, the client will forward the authorization to Examen, who will note that on its report.

The company's primary function is to review law firm invoices for compliance with client guidelines and to provide its clients with a management report of legal services so that it can monitor their legal costs.

Examen employs attorneys, paralegals, and others. Paralegals are employed as invoice analysts. Examen also provides auditing software.

Common Billing Problems

Two of the major problems clients complain about are ambiguous bills and high legal costs. Sally King, manager of legal administration for General Electric Company, lists 14 problems as major contributors to ambiguous bills her company receives from law firms (reprinted with permission from the *National Law Journal*):

- *Vague Service Descriptions.* A description of the service performed must contain enough detail to allow the client to understand what was accomplished. Describing a service in a brief and concise manner can be difficult. A description that is too long and wordy can be ambiguous, and a description that is too short can be vague. An entry that describes a telephone conversation as "telephone conference with Attorney Smith" is inadequate. The entry should be "telephone conference with Attorney Smith re deposition."

- *Surprise Total.* Sometimes, a client is expecting an invoice for $10,000 and a $50,000 invoice arrives instead. Law firms should try to anticipate expectations and keep clients informed to avoid unpleasant surprises.

- *Perceived Poor Work.* Some in-house lawyers are forced to spend a considerable amount of time rewriting and improving a brief written by outside counsel, only to receive a bill for the full amount of time spent by counsel on an inadequate work product.

- *Team Churning.* In some firms, especially large ones, a legal team is constantly changing. This is called **team churning.** This means that additional time must be spent scaling the learning curve at the client's expense. The client is paying for the same service two or three times. It destroys any efficiency associated with the effects of experience.

- *Interoffice Conferences.* Clients frown on interoffice conferences between members of the legal team because they perceive the charge as paying for the legal team to chitchat. Law firms need to look closely at the proportion of conference time to the time spent on other activities as reflected in a bill.

- *Nickel-and-Dime Billing.* Some firms include line-item charges for postage, fax, and so on, amounting to less than $10 in a bill for tens of thousands of dollars. A variation on this theme may be a bill for $50,000, which is readily acceptable—followed a few days later with a "supplemental invoice" for a minimal amount.

- *Errors in Arithmetic.* Such errors reveal that no real billing review has been performed.

- *Other Glaring Errors.* Some bills indicate time billed to the wrong client or matter. Others may show that an attorney has worked 26 hours in one day. As in the previous point, mistakes such as these raise questions about an entire bill.

- *Bill Received Months after Work Is Completed.* When a bill is not timely, everyone who ever worked on, or was involved in, the matter has forgotten the complexity of the issues as well as the results obtained.

- *Bill Directed to Wrong Person.* The in-house lawyer who works on a matter may not be responsible for getting bills paid. A bill should go to the person charged with this responsibility. That person, often the administrator, will obtain all appropriate reviews and approvals.

- *Padding.* Charging a client for services not performed is fraudulent and illegal. It is important to be precise in entering the amount of time spent on a matter. If a new member of the legal team works on a matter, a task may take longer than if an experienced member does the work. Clients are increasingly intolerant of inexperience and less willing to pay for a person's training. The time of an inexperienced person should be billed at a lower rate.

- *Clerical Work.* Clients object to paying a paralegal for clerical work. Tasks such as typing, filing, photocopying, and indexing are generally considered clerical and part of the firm's overhead. From a management standpoint, a paralegal should not be performing clerical tasks because it is not a good use of the paralegal's time and training.

- *Review and Revision.* These terms are vague and ambiguous unless they are used with a more descriptive entry informing the client what was reviewed and why.

- *Block Billing.* **Block billing** is listing tasks in a one-block summary to avoid listing all the work done. An example of block billing would be an entry for 7 hours for "preparing for trial." Each activity of the trial preparation should be listed and the appropriate amount of time applied to each, as shown in Exhibit 8–14. Many courts do not permit block billing because it hinders them from applying lodestar to the task. A bankruptcy court completely disallowed blocked entries to determine lodestar in the case of *In re The Leonard Jed Company*, 103 B.R. 706 (Bankr. D. Md [1989]).

team churning
Making frequent changes in the legal team.

block billing
Charging a client for services rendered in one large block of time rather than itemizing the tasks performed in that period of time.

Block Billing—Improper

| 1/05/XX | Prepare summary judgment motion | 7.5 hrs. |

Block Billing—Proper

DATE	DESCRIPTION	TIME
1/05/XX	Review correspondence, discovery, pleadings, and evidence re summary judgment motion	2.0
1/05/XX	Legal research re liability issue	1.0
1/05/XX	Draft summary judgment motion and supporting brief re liability of independent contractors	2.5
1/05/XX	Telephone conference with attorney Smith re extension of time to file summary judgment motion	.2
1/05/XX	Telephone conference with Judge Jones re extension of time to file summary judgment motion	.2
1/05/XX	Complete summary judgment motion and supporting brief and memoranda	1.6

EXHIBIT 8–14   Example of Improper and Proper Block Billing

Client-Directed Billing Policies

Many large corporate legal departments and insurance companies have developed their own billing policies for their outside law firms to follow. These policies direct the law firms how to prepare their bills and inform them of unacceptable billing entries. Their policies indicate which soft costs are reimbursable. They also indicate the procedures to be followed before incurring hard costs and the parameters of acceptable charges.

Some law firms object to client-directed billing policies. They say that the policies illegally restrict their practice of law and are therefore contrary to the code of professional responsibility because they create a conflict of interest between the independence of outside counsel and their clients. Several state bar associations, including those of Tennessee and Kentucky, ruled that client-directed billing policies violate ethical codes. However, the majority of state bar associations see no ethical violations.

Fee Disputes and Arbitration

Most of the complaints received by bar associations are complaints of legal fees. The Michigan Attorney Grievance Commission estimates that 80 percent of complaints filed are fee disputes.

According to the Fair Credit Billing Act, once a firm has been advised of a dispute regarding a bill, the firm may not take steps to collect the amount. The firm may, however, send periodic statements informing the client of the amount of the bill. The firm may not send collection letters, telephone the client, or sue the client until the dispute has been resolved.

To keep fee disputes out of the court system, most state bar associations have developed **arbitration** programs to resolve them. In many states, state and local bar associations offer an arbitration service to resolve attorney-client disputes.

Most state arbitration programs are voluntary; in some states, however, arbitration is mandatory. Arbitration procedures must be exhausted before a court action is filed. All arbitration programs allow clients to begin an action, and some allow attorneys to begin an action. An arbitrator or arbitration panel hears a dispute and makes a ruling. In some states, the arbitration panel is comprised of lawyers, and in other states, the panel consists

arbitration
The resolution of a dispute without court involvement.

Of Interest . . .

TWELVE RED FLAGS IN LEGAL BILL REVIEW

Task descriptions. Are the task descriptions detailed and informative? Every task description should identify the activity with sufficient detail to assess its necessity and relevance to the project.

Inadequate time entries. Itemized time entries are preferable to block entries. Itemized time entries enable the reviewer to better ascertain the appropriateness of the time spent in relation to the significance and complexity of the task. All entries should include the date the work was performed.

Correspondent charge. Although most invoices will contain a total sum of the amount owed, there should be a charge after each particular task. This allows the firm to determine whether an overtime rate or inflated price was billed and to certify that the billing rates charged are those established at the inception of the case.

Timekeeper's identity. Identification of timekeepers should not be limited to three-letter initials unless they are identified elsewhere in the invoice. The entire name of the individual and title should appear on the bill along with the billing rate.

Appropriately staffed. Are there any unauthorized individuals billing time to the file? Are there too many professionals involved in the project? Overstaffing often lends to inefficiency and higher costs because of duplication of effort and time educating others.

Too much time? The time spent on an activity should be commensurate with the complexity and significance of the task.

Appropriate skill level. Are overqualified professionals performing tasks below their skill levels at standard billing rates? Examples include an associate charging for file organization or a senior partner billing for basic research.

Task justified? Excessive "file review" or other perfunctory phrases without stated reason should be further investigated to determine the purpose and necessity of task.

Interoffice conferences. Interoffice conferences are disliked by clients and should not be inserted on a bill.

Duplication of effort. Did two partners participate in a hearing when only one was needed? Did a paralegal attend all depositions unnecessarily? Did four associates contribute to one brief? Although such items may raise a red flag, at times they are justified. Be sure to communicate these events to the client.

Clerical charges. Charges for clerical tasks should not be on a bill.

Office expenses. Are office expenses authorized and appropriate? Be sure that office expenses are scrutinized and deleted when inappropriate.

SOURCE: Reprinted with permission of *Legal Assistant Today*.

of nonlawyers. Although clients have been reluctant to arbitrate fee disputes before a panel of lawyers, statistics have shown that many clients receive favorable results.

Each state differs in its arbitration procedures, although all arbitration procedures are similar. For example, the arbitration process starts with a client filing a request form with the secretary of the bar association's fee arbitration committee. The client must consent to be bound by the arbitration. To be sure the client understands the finality of the decision, the bar provides the client with an information booklet.

When a complaint is filed, the bar sends a questionnaire to the attorney, whose participation is mandatory. Besides asking the attorney to respond to the client's allegations, the bar asks for copies of the disputed bill as well as the fee agreement and time records.

Cases involving fees of $3,000 or more are heard by a panel with three members, usually two lawyers and one nonlawyer, who volunteer their time to the process. Smaller disputes are heard by a single arbitrator. Hearings are scheduled with at least 10 days' written notice. There is no

discovery, or acquisition of new information about acts or facts. All parties have the power of subpoena. No transcript of the proceeding is maintained because appeals are not allowed.

All proceedings are conducted in private. Rules of evidence are not observed. The burden of proof is on the attorney to show that the bill is reasonable. The eight factors determining the reasonableness of a fee (TOCATPET) are considered. A determination is mailed within 30 days.

The disciplinary board of the bar hears enforcement motions. If it finds that an attorney refused to comply with an arbitrator's ruling, it may ask the court or state bar association to suspend the attorney.

discovery
The acquisition of notice or knowledge of given acts or facts; that which was previously unknown.

FINANCIAL MANAGEMENT

The goal of every law firm is to be profitable. Whether a firm is profitable depends on management's methods of managing firm resources. Accounting systems play an important role in managing the firm to maximize profitability.

Every law firm employee contributes to law firm accounting functions. Timekeeping duties, keeping track of costs, and doing a probate accounting are examples of accounting functions. A general knowledge of law firm accounting is essential to a well-rounded knowledge of law firms in general.

Law Firm Profitability and Realization

To be profitable, law firm management must consider certain factors that contribute to profitability. These factors are called profitability factors. Law firm profits are the result of two types of profitability factors: direct and indirect.

DIRECT PROFITABILITY FACTORS   **Direct profitability factors** directly affect a firm's profitability in a short period, usually 1 year. Direct profitability factors consist of five elements: rates, utilization, leverage, expenses, and speed, the acronym for which is RULES.

direct profitability factors
Factors that affect a firm's profitability in a short period of time, usually 1 year.

Rates   Rates include the effective rates that are ultimately billed and collected, such as hourly fees and other types of fees. They are adjusted periodically to accommodate changes in the marketplace and to increase profitability, and they allow the firm to remain competitive.

A firm must give careful consideration when setting hourly rates. If the rate is too high, the firm may lose potential clients. If it is too low, the firm will lose income. Hourly rates should be competitive with the firm's geographic area but high enough for the firm to make a profit.

Utilization   Utilization includes the use of the chargeable hours of a firm's timekeepers and the ability to delegate responsibility to the lowest timekeeper. Law firms set the number of annual billable hours required of each timekeeper per year. It is important that each timekeeper meet the annual requirement because a firm estimates its income on annual billable hours expected from each timekeeper. If every timekeeper in a large firm produced 2 hours a week below the annual requirement, the firm would lose more than a million dollars of potential income per year.

Timekeepers in some firms also include law clerks and clerical staff. To be profitable, a task should be delegated to the least expensive employee capable of performing the task. A timekeeper's services are being effectively utilized if each is given adequate responsibility and challenge.

Leverage   Leverage is the number of profit contributors (associates and paralegals) for each owner. The more associates and paralegals for each owner, the higher the owner's income.

The leverage ratio of the number of profit contributors to owner differs in each firm. Some firms may have a 1 to 4 ratio (one profit contributor per four attorneys) or a 4 to 1 ratio (four profit contributors per attorney).

Expenses   Expenses directly affect a firm's profitability. To be profitable, management must control law firm expenses. Expenses eat up profits and can rapidly increase if management does not monitor them closely.

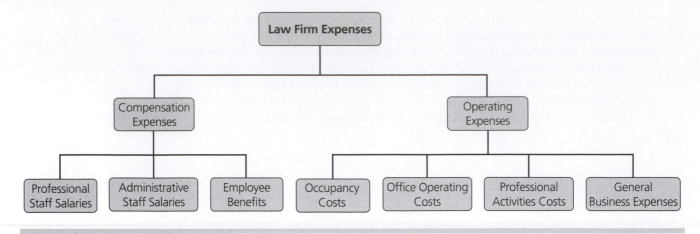

EXHIBIT 8–15 Law Firm Expenses

compensation expenses
Employee expenses,
including wages and
benefits.

operating expenses
Expenses other than
compensation expenses
that include occupancy
costs, office operating
costs, costs of professional
activities, and general
business expenses.

Expenses include staff salaries and benefits, supplies, and other costs of doing business. Expenses are the most flexible of the profitability factors. If expenses are too high, they are reduced. If expected income is not received, expenses are cut.

There are two types of expenses: compensation expenses and operating expenses, as shown in Exhibit 8–15. **Compensation expenses** include employees' compensation and are categorized into three categories: professional staff salaries; administrative staff salaries; and employee benefits. **Operating expenses** include all other expenses.

There are four categories of operating expenses: occupancy costs, office operating costs, costs of professional activities, and general business expenses. Occupancy costs include office rental, storage facilities, and utilities. Office operating costs include the day-to-day expenses involved in running the office, such as office equipment, computers, janitorial services, stationery, copying costs, and miscellaneous supplies. Professional activity costs include professional dues, continuing education, and client promotion. General business expenses include telephone costs, library costs, insurance, taxes, and interest expenses.

The cost of doing business continues to increase. Expenses increase faster than attorneys can increase their fees. To maintain profitability, management is continually seeking ways to manage expenses.

Speed   The time it takes to perform a task, bill for the service, and collect from the client contributes to a firm's profitability. If a bill is unpaid for 90 to 120 days, a firm's profitability for that project decreases. The sooner a bill is collected, the higher the firm's profitability.

indirect profitability factors
Factors that indirectly affect
a firm's profitability over a
longer period, more than
1 year.

INDIRECT PROFITABILITY FACTORS   **Indirect profitability factors** indirectly affect a firm's profitability over a longer period, more than 1 year. Indirect profitability factors consist of five elements: strategy, culture, organization, reward systems, and environment, the acronym for which is SCORE.

Strategy   Strategy includes the firm's plans for reaching its profitability goals. It also includes the type of clients the firm serves, the geographical area(s) in which the firm practices, and the areas of specialties of the firm. Management is constantly studying these factors and making changes as warranted. For example, if statistics indicate that more clients require legal services in the area of intellectual property, the firm will add that area of law to its specialties.

Culture   A firm's culture is the firm's environment, including intangible factors such as employee behavior patterns, social policies, and employees' values. It also includes how employees interact and dress and the way clients are treated. A positive culture creates a positive working environment that results in fewer position vacancies and more satisfied employees who maximize their contributions to a firm. A firm with a positive culture is more profitable than one with a negative culture.

Organization   Organization refers to a firm's organizational structure for managing its law practice as well as its business affairs. This includes the hierarchy of firm management and the structure of each department within the firm. A well-organized office is more profitable than a poorly organized office. The management structure, as discussed in Chapter 1, affects a firm's culture. An effective management structure increases a firm's profitability. An ineffective management structure is devastating to law firm profitability.

Reward system   Reward systems include compensation plans, bonus plans, and other professional and personal reward systems for motivating people to contribute to the firm's profitability. These reward systems include benefits, retirement programs, savings programs, and profit-sharing plans. Reward systems are carefully planned into the firm's financial forecast. A firm with a low profit margin cannot afford the luxury of generous reward systems for its employees.

Environment   Environment includes the office area, support staff, and technology that a firm provides its employees for enhancing their productivity and effectiveness. This is closely related to culture because it affects culture. The environment affects profitability because it affects a firm's employees. Employees must have a thriving environment within which to contribute their best effort. Without such an environment, employees are not productive, thereby affecting a firm's profitability.

Both direct and indirect profitability factors are responsible for a firm's profitability. If one factor is dysfunctional, a firm suffers economically. If a circumstance occurs that immediately affects the firm, such as a large client leaving the firm, direct factors are adjusted. For example, expenses are decreased, leverage is increased, and utilization is maximized. If a circumstance occurs that affects long-term goals, such as rapid growth, indirect factors are adjusted, for example, when the firm moves to a bigger building or creates an additional department.

The Realization Process

For a law firm to be successful, it must have strong **realization** policies. Realization is the process of turning time into cash. This begins when a firm accepts a client and consists of five steps: getting, doing, recording, billing, and collecting for the work, as shown in Exhibit 8–16.

realization
The process of turning time into cash.

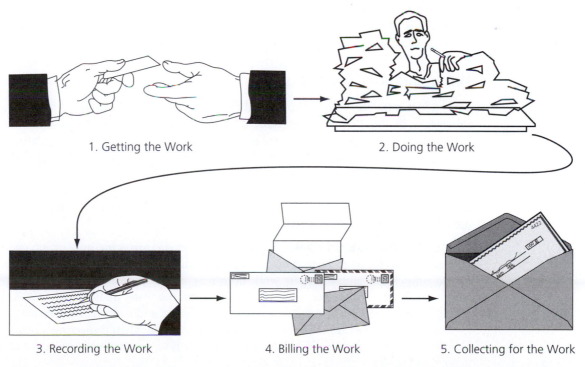

1. Getting the Work   2. Doing the Work

3. Recording the Work   4. Billing the Work   5. Collecting for the Work

EXHIBIT 8–16   The Realization Process Is the Process of Turning Time into Cash

When a new client retains the firm, the firm spends time on the client's matter. The firm bills for the work done, and the client pays for the service. The firm uses part of the money to obtain new clients, and the process repeats itself. There may be a difference between the amount billed and the amount collected. This difference is reflected in a percentage of the amount collected, known as a realization rate.

realization rate
The hourly rate of a timekeeper that the firm actually realizes when all accounts have been collected compared to the total amount billed.

REALIZATION RATE A **realization rate** is the rate that the firm actually receives for work done. This rate may be different from the timekeeper's hourly rate. For example, if a timekeeper's hourly rate is $100 an hour but the firm is unable to collect 10 percent of the timekeeper's bills, the realization rate is 90 percent of the hourly rate, or $90 an hour ($100 − $10 = $90). Management uses the realization rate to prepare the firm's budget. Anticipation of uncollectable debts is an important function of the budgeting process.

A number of factors affect the realization rate: nonbillable time, **write-ups, write-downs,** and **write-offs.**

write-up
An increase in the amount owed because of a premium.

As we discussed earlier in the chapter, a preliminary bill is prepared and given to the attorney for adjustment. A fee adjustment memorandum is prepared for some bills that need adjustment. A firm will write up a client's bill when the client receives a substantial benefit from the firm's work on the case and agrees to give the firm a premium. The timekeepers' realization rate is increased by the premium. A write-down is when some of the timekeeper's time is not billed to a client or is discounted. The timekeeper's realization rate is reduced. If a client's bill is uncollectable, or written off, the timekeeper's realization rate is further reduced.

write-down
A decrease in the amount owed because of a discount.

write-off
A credit for the total amount owed.

Management calculates a ratio of write-ups, write-downs, and write-offs from the fee adjustment memorandum. It strives for a 90 to 95 percent realization rate for each timekeeper, but an 80 percent realization rate is more common. To arrive at a timekeeper's realization rate, multiply the number of annual billable hours by the hourly rate and take 80 percent of that figure. A timekeeper with an annual billable hour requirement of 1,800 hours at $100 an hour would calculate the realization rate as follows:

$$\$100 \times 80\% = \$80 \text{ an hour}$$
$$1,800 \times \$80 = \$144,000$$

The firm estimates its income from that timekeeper at $144,000. If that income is not realized, the firm's profitability is decreased. If the income is exceeded, the firm's profitability is increased, and the paralegal may be entitled to a merit bonus.

The Budgeting Process

The budget is the key to law firm profitability. It contains guidelines that direct a firm's management in its financial decisions. It identifies how much money is needed to meet expenses. If an expense is underestimated, it will have an impact on the profitability of the firm. Studies have shown that firms that adhere to a budget are more profitable than those that do not.

A budget is prepared at the start of each year. Management uses one of two methods to prepare the budget: It may base its projections on the firm's activities of the previous year, or it may solicit input from the firm's employees. When developing a budget, a firm's management projects income, personnel costs, and operating expenses.

gross income
Income received before payment of expenses.

INCOME PROJECTION In order to project the **gross income,** or income received before expenses are paid, for the year, management must estimate the amount of work required for existing clients and anticipate work from new clients. Variables in determining income from new clients include the economic environment, the firm's marketing activities and strategic planning, past experience in producing new clients, and competitive pressures.

Income generated from each timekeeper is considered when projecting a firm's income. Factors considered are annual billable hours, hourly rate, and realization rate for each timekeeper, as follows:

Billable hours × Hourly rate × Realization rate = Gross income

Exhibit 8–17 shows an example of income projections.

Law Firm of Black, White & Greene

Projected Income for 20XX

Timekeeper	Billable Hours	Hourly Rate	Realization	Total
R Black, Esq.	1,600	450.00	90%	$648,000.00
D. White, Esq.	1,600	450.00	90%	648,000.00
G. Greene, Esq.	1,800	400.00	85%	612,000.00
P. Boen, Esq.	1,900	300.00	80%	456,000.00
G. Templeton, Esq.	1,900	300.00	80%	456,000.00
M. Nollkamper LA	1,800	100.00	85%	153,000.00
J. Stockstill	1,800	75.00	75%	101,250.00
Total Projected Gross Income				**$3,074,250.00**

EXHIBIT 8–17 Example Income Projections

PERSONNEL COSTS PROJECTION Budgeting for personnel costs requires management to anticipate personnel needs for the year. If management anticipates that fewer employees will be needed, the firm will **downsize,** and employees will be laid off. If additional personnel are anticipated, the cost thereof will be put into the budget. Budgeting for personnel costs requires management to anticipate associates' compensation, administrative staff salaries, employee benefit costs, and employee taxes.

If the firm is a sole proprietorship or partnership, the owners' salaries are not anticipated in personnel costs because they are paid out of the profits of the firm. If the firm is a professional corporation, the owners are employees of the corporation, and their salaries are included in personnel costs.

downsize
To reduce staff and expenses because of reduced income.

OPERATING EXPENSE PROJECTION Four categories are estimated when projecting operating expenses: occupancy costs, office operating expenses, professional activity costs, and general business expenses. These costs can be estimated from the previous year's expenses. Management will increase each category as needed. If a firm expects a 15 percent increase in new client work, it will increase the expenses accordingly. If it expects a 15 percent decrease in new client work, it will decrease the expenses accordingly. A sample budget is on the accompanying CD.

CALCULATING AN EXPENSE PERCENTAGE When the budget is prepared, management can calculate an expense percentage by dividing expenses by income as follows:

$$\text{Expenses} \div \text{Income} = \text{Expense percentage}$$
$$\$1,048,575 \div 1,886,500 = 56\%$$

Knowing the expense percentage will allow a firm to calculate the expenses it allocates to each timekeeper. This calculation is known as **per unit cost** and is used by businesses to determine how much it costs to produce a product or provide a service. For example, it costs the firm in Exhibit 8–18 $209,000 for timekeeper A to produce $380,000 in revenue and $37,125 for timekeeper H to produce $67,500 in revenue. Knowing the per unit cost of a timekeeper is helpful to calculate actual potential profits of each timekeeper. Actual profit expected is calculated by deducting the expense percentage of each timekeeper's gross fees, as shown in Exhibit 8–18.

per unit cost
The amount of money it costs to produce a product or provide a service.

Knowing the expense percentage of the firm has other uses. It is helpful when comparing the profitability of the firm with that of other firms. Management can also estimate partners' income without recalculating the expenses, as shown in Exhibit 8–19.

	BILLABLE HOURS	HOURLY RATE	REALIZATION RATE	TOTAL	EXPENSE (%)	TOTAL EXPENSE	NET PROFIT
A	1,600	$250	95%	$ 380,000	55%	$ 209,000	$171,000
B	1,600	250	90%	360,000	55%	198,000	162,000
C	1,800	200	85%	306,000	55%	168,300	137,700
D	1,900	175	80%	266,000	55%	146,300	119,700
E	1,900	175	80%	266,000	55%	146,300	119,700
F	1,800	100	85%	153,000	55%	84,150	68,850
G	1,800	75	80%	108,000	55%	59,400	48,600
H	1,800	50	75%	67,500	55%	37,125	30,375
	TOTAL			1,906,500		1,048,575	857,925

EXHIBIT 8–18 Net Profit Per Timekeeper

Law Firm of Black, White & Greene

Projected Partners' Income

Estimated income	$1,906,500.00
Less expenses 55%	1,048,575.00
Net distributable income	857,925.00
Distributable income per partner (3)	$ 285,975.00

EXHIBIT 8–19 Projected Partners' Income

The lower the expense percentage, the more profitable the firm. A typical expense percentage is between 40 and 70 percent, with an average of 60 percent. If the expense percentage is over 70 percent, management must take measures to either increase income or decrease expenses.

SUMMARY

For a law firm to be successful, it must have strong billing policies that quickly turn time into cash.

The goal of a good billing practice is to get a firm's bills paid as promptly as possible. The most important aspect of the billing process is communication. Communicating the cost of legal services to a client continues throughout an attorney-client relationship.

Paralegals are often asked to answer a client's questions regarding a bill. A paralegal should direct all inquiries to the attorney, the administrator, or an office manager. A paralegal may not negotiate a fee agreement. A paralegal also may not inform a client of the possible duration or outcome of a matter, or discuss strategy with a client. A paralegal should document all client communication.

Billing should be regular and frequent. Monthly billing is the most common method of billing. Billing a client as soon as possible after a matter is completed is a crucial element of a good billing policy.

In recent years, clients have demanded descriptive bills, and the trend is to be as descriptive as possible.

The billing process begins when entries from a time sheet are input into a computer and a preliminary bill is prepared. Charging interest on past-due accounts is generally accepted, and lawyers often extend credit to their clients. To ease the financial burden on firms, lawyers have offered clients two credit alternatives: loans and the use of credit cards. Law firms have computerized billing systems. Various styles of bills are used by law firms. The style of a bill depends on the type of client, the type of case, and the policy of a firm.

Each firm has its own policy for collecting accounts. Each account is considered separately. A lawyer may withdraw from a case if a client fails to pay a fee, if the withdrawal will not prejudice the client. Before a firm stops work or withdraws from a case, it must give careful consideration to an attorney's ethical responsibilities to a client. Suing a client should be the last resort.

To keep fee disputes out of the court system, most state bar associations have developed arbitration programs to resolve them. The ABA encourages lawyers to take advantage of bar-sponsored arbitration programs.

Legal fee agreements are held to a higher standard than other contracts because of the fiduciary relationship between an attorney and a client. Two of the major problems clients complain about are ambiguous bills and high legal costs. Most of the complaints received by bar associations are complaints of legal fees.

To be profitable, law firm management must consider certain factors that contribute to profitability. Two profitability factors are considered: direct profitability factors, consisting of rates, utilization, leverage, expenses, and speed; and indirect profitability factors, consisting of strategy, culture, organization, reward systems, and environment. A law firm's hourly rate for each timekeeper is an element of profitability. A timekeeper's realization rate is the amount of income the firm actually realizes from the timekeeper compared to the total amount billed.

The budget is the key to law firm profitability. A budget is prepared at the start of each year. In order to project the gross income for the year, management must estimate the amount of work required for existing clients and anticipate work from new clients. Income generated from each timekeeper is considered when projecting a firm's income.

There are four categories of operating expenses: occupancy costs, office operating expenses, professional activities, and general business expenses. Expenses are estimated to determine the expense percentage for the firm. Knowing the expense percentage of the firm will allow the firm to calculate the amount of expenses it allocates to each timekeeper. The lower the expense percentage, the more profitable the firm.

CHAPTER ILLUSTRATION

The budgeting process for Black, White & Greene begins in November of each year. In November, Tricia reviews various management reports to anticipate the firm's needs for the next year. Each attorney is involved in the process and is asked to project any major expenses. For example, the firm replaced Melvin when he was fired, so the firm does not expect to hire a new paralegal in the coming year. However, the firms needs an additional secretary, so Tricia increased the personnel cost projection accordingly. Dennis White was retained for a large contingency case and anticipates high litigation costs. Tricia increased the operating expenses projection accordingly.

The previous year, the firm's expense percentage was 55 percent of income, and its realization rate was 90 percent of total billings. This year, however, Patrizia Boen's realization rate is lower than last year, so Tricia expects a lower overall realization rate for the coming year. She calculated the realization rate for the firm at 85 percent for the new year. She made the adjustment in the income projection. She must also adjust the expenses for the firm to the lower income projection, so she reduced the expense projection 5 percent to maintain profitability. Tricia completed the new year's budget in December, and it was approved by Robert in January. The attorneys are expected to adhere to the budget and to report any extraordinary expenses so that they can be put into the budget.

Tricia handles the firm's finance function. The firm uses a popular time and billing software program that prepares descriptive, itemized bills for the clients. The software also includes an accounting function that tracks all the firm's accounts payable and accounts receivable. Tricia enters accounts payable information into the computer when she pays her bills. Each timekeeper enters his or her time directly into the computer. The computer prepares hourly bills, flat-fee bills, and contingency statements. Tricia recently upgraded the program to include task-based accounting functions. The computer is programmed to produce descriptive bills so that each client is aware of each service performed on his or her behalf.

The third week of the month, Tricia prepares preliminary bills on the basis of the timekeeping information input by the timekeepers. The preliminary bills are given to the responsible attorney for review. At times, mistakes are made that must be corrected. In addition, there are times when the attorney will increase or reduce a charge if he or she feels that the adjustment is warranted. The responsible attorney makes these corrections on a fee adjustment memorandum and submits it to Tricia, who makes the needed adjustments. The final bills are then prepared so that they can be mailed on the first of each month.

Tricia is never late with the billing. She knows that the sooner clients receive their bills, the sooner the firm will be paid. Prompt and regular billing is important for the firm to meet its commitments. If an account goes unpaid for 60 days, the computer is programmed to charge the client interest at a reasonable rate. Tricia prints out an aging report to determine the collection letters needed.

Black, White & Greene has a standard policy of explaining its charges to the client in the initial client interview. A fee agreement is prepared and executed for every case. An engagement letter is sent immediately after the initial client interview that summarizes the fee agreement. The client is expected to sign the engagement letter and return it to Tricia. On a few occasions, fee disputes have arisen, in which case the firm requires that the dispute be arbitrated by a fee arbitration panel of the local bar association.

George Templeton, the associate for the firm, represented Janine Jamison in her divorce case. He charged her a flat fee of $3,000 for the representation. She paid $1,000 at the beginning of the case, the remainder of which was due before the hearing. One week before the hearing, George called her to discuss the case and to request payment. She told George that she would give him a check the day before the hearing, but she did not. George considered continuing the hearing, but the opposing party, Janine's estranged husband, would not grant a continuance because he was anxious to remarry. George had no alternative but to appear at the hearing.

After the hearing, George asked Janine for payment. She told him that she was fired from her job and had no money. George completed her divorce and sent her collection letters to collect the fee. When Janine received the third collection letter, she called George and told him that she did not feel she should pay the remainder of the fee because she did not get the amount of child support she expected. She also accused George of conspiring against her with her ex-husband. George tried to explain to her that he did not conspire against her, but to no avail. Janine still refused to pay the remainder of the fee. George immediately submitted the dispute to the fee arbitration panel of his local bar association.

The bar association's fee dispute panel sent Janine a questionnaire to complete and asked her to describe her dispute. They also sent a questionnaire to George to complete and submit to them along with George's time records on the case. George asked Tricia for a client time report on the case. He sent the report with the questionnaire to the bar association, which set the matter for a hearing.

Both Janine and George appeared at the hearing and gave the panel their side of the story. Afterward, the panel ruled that George did not conspire against his client and that his representation of Janine was proper. They found, however, that he spent 8 hours on the case. Applying his hourly rate of $300 to the amount of time records (lodestar) totaled $2,400, so they deducted $600 from the remaining balance owed. Janine was ordered to pay $1,400 instead of $2,000. She sent a check the next week.

CHAPTER REVIEW

1. What is the main goal of a firm's billing policy?
2. What are the five steps of the realization process?
3. What is the most important aspect of the billing process?
4. What is an engagement letter?
5. When communicating with clients, what are the things a nonlawyer should not do?
6. Why is regular and frequent billing important?
7. What is a preliminary bill?
8. Describe the two methods lawyers use to extend credit to their clients.
9. What elements are contained in a descriptive hourly bill that are not contained in a brief hourly bill?
10. What is the difference between an hourly bill and a flat-fee bill?
11. What are the four most common unethical billing practices?
12. What is a legal auditor?
13. What are direct profitability factors?
14. What are indirect profitability factors?
15. What is a realization rate, and how is it calculated?
16. What are the three projections that management makes when preparing a budget?
17. What are the four types of operating expenses in a law firm?
18. What is an expense percentage, and how is it calculated?

EXAMPLES FOR DISCUSSION

1. UNITED STATES V. DELOREAN

In the 1984 white-collar criminal case of *United States v. DeLorean,* Howard L. Wietzman defended John DeLorean on charges of conspiring to possess and distribute cocaine. DeLorean was also prosecuted on fraud and racketeering charges. No fee agreement was made, and Wietzman kept no time records. He never quoted DeLorean a particular fee and waited 1 year to send DeLorean his first bill. He was known to "ballpark," or estimate, his fees. DeLorean paid Wietzman a total of $3.5 million.

At the time of DeLorean's acquittal, he was quoted as saying, "Without Mr. Weitzman, I would probably put my head in the oven." Later, however, a controversy arose over Wietzman's fee. Wietzman claims that DeLorean owes him an additional $683,392. DeLorean claims that Wietzman owes him a refund. When asked how he figured the additional fee that was due, Wietzman said, "How much would you pay to stay out of jail, pal? I owe him nothing. He owes me his life."

1. If you were the judge, how would you rule?
2. What are the issues in this case?
3. Are Wietzman's actions ethical?
4. What factors of reasonableness (TOCATPET) apply in this case?

2. THE SIXFOLD BILL

Geraldo Hernandez, a real estate developer, was sued by six separate parties in six cases resulting from a dispute about the same development project. Geraldo thought it would be advisable to have all six cases handled by Robert Valentino. The fee agreement between Geraldo and Robert stated that Robert would charge an hourly rate of $450.

Robert filed six answers that were essentially identical to one another. A few weeks later, Geraldo received a bill showing the same amount of time, and applying the same hourly rate, for the preparation of each answer. The amount of time shown on the bill suggested to Geraldo that he was being charged six times the actual number of hours worked.

When Geraldo called Robert about the bill, Robert stated that since one answer took one-half hour to prepare, the other answers have the same value.

1. If you were Geraldo, what would you do?
2. When discussing fees, what should Robert have done? What should Geraldo have done?
3. Was Robert's answer justified?
4. Were Robert's billing policies ethical?

3. THE MODIFIED AGREEMENT

Pete Moss retained Emily McGregor to negotiate a lease with Pete's landlord. Pete agreed to pay Emily $300 an hour. Emily sent Pete an engagement letter like the one shown on page 278.

As time elapsed, the negotiations with Pete's landlord became more complex. Because of the complexity, Emily felt that an increase in her hourly rate was warranted. She sent Pete a notice of fee increase that stated that her hourly fee was increased to $350 an hour because of the complexity of the issues. Pete refused to pay the increased fee, and Emily sued him for the difference.

1. Is the increased fee proper?
2. If you were the judge, how would you rule?
3. What is the basis of your ruling?
4. If you were the manager of Emily's firm, what would you do to prevent this situation from happening again?

4. HOURLY OR FLAT FEE?

You are the manager of a medium-sized law firm. The managing partner is concerned about the profitability of the domestic relations department consisting of three attorneys and one paralegal. The managing partner has asked you to prepare a report of the average cost and the average fee of each domestic relations case. He has also asked you to establish a flat fee for certain domestic cases and to recommend which cases should be on a flat-fee basis.

1. Where does information for your report come from?
2. How would you establish a flat fee?
3. What types of cases would be good candidates for a flat fee?

ASSIGNMENTS

1. From the records you kept for assignment 3 in Chapter 7, prepare a detailed hourly bill for your instructor for this class. Your hourly rate is $85 per hour. If you have spent any money for the class, such as for supplies or books, include them in the bill as costs. Follow the format on page 282 for a detailed hourly bill.

2. You are an administrator for a large law firm. The managing partner wants to start charging interest on all past-due accounts. He has asked you to research the applicable laws in your state concerning charging and collecting interest. He has asked you also to research the ethics opinions of the state bar concerning interest charges. Prepare a report of your findings that describes your firm's obligations and requirements concerning interest.

3. You are a dissatisfied client who disputes the fee charged by your lawyer. You want to arbitrate the dispute. Research the applicable arbitration programs in your area, and prepare a step-by-step procedural guide for arbitrating fee disputes in your state.

4. You are an administrator for a large corporate legal department. You want to implement e-billing and require your outside counsel to submit their bills in electronic format. Research e-billing software and vendor requirements and submit a report on the cost of implementing e-billing. Use the websites in the Cybersites section on page 308 for your research. Include the following:
   a. Vendor requirements and costs
   b. Software features and capabilities
   c. Ease of use
   d. Cost comparison
   e. Time commitments to implement the system

5. The law firm of Smith & Jones is a partnership owned by Steve Smith and Jerry Jones. In addition to the partners, the firm employs three associate attorneys and three paralegals. The partners are required to bill 1,800 hours at $450 an hour. They have a 90 percent realization rate. The associates are required to bill 2,000 hours at $300 an hour. They have an 85 percent realization rate. The paralegals are required to bill 1,800 hours. One paralegal's hourly rate is $85 an hour, and she has an 85 percent realization rate. The other two paralegals' hourly rate is $70 an hour. Paralegal number 2 has a realization rate of 80 percent, and paralegal number 3 has a realization rate of 75 percent. Calculate the firm's projected gross income for the year.

6. Smith & Jones has an expense percentage of 62 percent. On the basis of the projected income in question 5, calculate the firm's projected net income for the year.

7. On the basis of the projected income and expenses calculated in questions 5 and 6, calculate each partner's projected income for the year.

SELF TEST

How well did you grasp the material in the chapter? Test yourself by answering the following questions, and check your answers against the answers found in Appendix A.

1. What are the four essential elements of billing?
2. What is the most important aspect of the billing process?
3. Who has the responsibility to communicate the fee agreement to the client?
4. When discussing bills with clients, what may paralegals *not* do?
5. Who has authority to adjust a client's bill?
6. When communicating with clients, what may a paralegal *not* do?
7. When a paralegal has a communication with a client, what must a paralegal do?
8. How will a firm be rewarded for a client's complete understanding of the case?
9. What is an engagement letter?
10. Why should billing be regular and frequent?

11. What type of law firm has difficulty meeting a monthly billing schedule?
12. When should a client be billed?
13. What happens to a client's perception of legal services as time goes by?
14. What is the most common method of billing?
15. What are the 12 basic elements of an average bill?
16. What is a preliminary bill?
17. What is a fee adjustment memorandum?
18. What has caused law firms to experience collection problems?
19. What two methods do firms use to offer credit to clients?
20. What is fee allocation?
21. What is a cost recovery system?
22. What determines the style of a bill?
23. What is the rule of thumb of billing styles?
24. What are the two styles of hourly bills?
25. What is e-billing?
26. When do collection activities begin?
27. When does the lawyer become involved in collection activities?
28. If a lawyer withdraws from a case because of nonpayment of fees, what must the lawyer do?
29. What are the nine things to consider before withdrawing from the case?
30. If a firm sues a client, what must the firm prove?
31. When should a firm sue a client?
32. It is a standard practice to give a client at least _____ _____ notice of collection agency involvement.
33. What has contributed to society's negative perception of lawyers?
34. What are the four most common unethical billing practices?
35. Why are legal fee agreements held to a higher standard than other contracts?
36. What is a fiduciary?
37. If a fee agreement is ambiguous, how is it determined?
38. What is a legal auditor?
39. What do legal auditors do?
40. Why do companies resist using a legal auditor?
41. What are the two major problems clients complain about?
42. What are the 14 problems that are major contributors to ambiguous bills?
43. What are the majority of complaints received by bar associations?
44. What is team churning?
45. What is padding?
46. What is block billing?
47. What are client-directed billing policies?
48. Why do some attorneys object to client-directed billing policies?
49. If a fee is disputed, what must a firm do?
50. What have state bar associations done to keep disputes out of the court system?
51. What is arbitration?
52. What is discovery?
53. What determines the organization of a firm's finance function?

54. What are direct profitability factors?
55. Why should a task be delegated downward?
56. What is leverage?
57. What is a leverage ratio and how is it calculated?
58. What are the two types of expenses?
59. What are the three categories of compensation expenses? /
60. What are the four categories of operating expenses?
61. What do occupancy costs include?
62. What do office operating costs include?
63. What do professional activity costs include?
64. What do general business expenses include?
65. What are indirect profitability factors?
66. Of what elements does a law firm's culture consist?
67. What do reward systems consist of?
68. How does the environment affect a firm's profitability?
69. What is realization?
70. What are the five steps of the realization process?
71. What is a realization rate?
72. When is a realization rate used?
73. What factors affect a realization rate?
74. What is a write-up?
75. What is a write-down?
76. What is a write-off?
77. What is the most common realization rate?
78. How is a realization rate calculated?
79. What is they key to law firm profitability?
80. When developing a law firm budget, what does management do?
81. How does management project gross income?
82. What are the factors used to determine income from new clients?
83. What factors are considered when projecting firm income?
84. How does a firm budget for personnel?
85. How is an expense percentage calculated?
86. How is a firm's anticipated profit calculated?
87. What is the average expense percentage for law firms?

Key Words

arbitration	fee adjustment memorandum	preliminary bill
block billing	fee allocation	realization
compensation expenses	fiduciary	realization rate
cost recovery system	gross income	team churning
direct profitability factors	indirect profitability factors	write-down
discovery	operating expenses	write-off
downsize	per unit cost	write-up
engagement letter		

Cybersites

LEGAL AUDITORS

Lexis-Nexis Examen—<*http://www.examen.com*>
Lex Tech—<*http://www.lextechonline.com*>
Accountability Services—<*http://www.legalbills.com*>
Using Legal Auditors—<*http://www.quantilex.com/*>
Stuart Maue—<*http://www. stuartmaue.com*>

TIME AND BILLING SOFTWARE

Timeslips Deluxe: Sage U.S., Inc.—<*http://www.timeslips.com*>
Perfect Practice: ADC Legal Systems—<*http://www.adclegal.com*>
Legal Insight: Versys Corporation—<*http://www.versys.com*>
ASA Legal Systems: Rainmaker Legal Software—<*http://www.rainmakerlegal.com*>
Juris: Juris, Inc.—<*http://www.juris.com*>
Orion: Orion Law Management System—<*http://www.orionlaw.com*>
ProLaw: ProLaw Software—<*http://www.prolaw.com*>
RTG Bills: RTG Data Systems—<*http://www.rtgsoftware.com*>
Tabs 3: Practice Master—<*http://www. practicemaster.com*>
Abacus—<*http://www.abacuslaw.com*>

E-BILLING

CT Tymetrixv—<*http://www.cttymetrix.com*>
Serengeti—<*http://www.serengetilaw.com*>
E-billing Hub—<*http://www.ebillinghub.com*>
E-Billing—<*http://www.ebilling.org*>
Avolent—<*http://www.avolent.com*>

MISCELLANEOUS

Lawyer Billing Tips—<*http://www.lawyerbillingtips.com*>
Billing Express—<*http://www.xpressassistant.com*>
Legal Billing Services—<*http://www.slipsbillingpros.com*>

Student CD-ROM
For additional materials, please go to the CD in this book.

Online Companion™
For additional resources, please go to http://www.paralegal.delmar.cengage.com

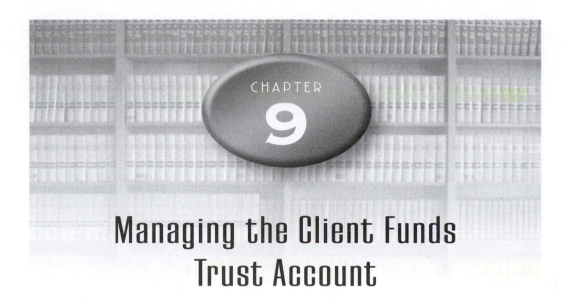

CHAPTER

9

Managing the Client Funds
Trust Account

OBJECTIVES

After completion of this chapter, the student should be able to do the following:

- Know the type of funds to be deposited in a trust account.
- Prepare a client ledger sheet.
- Document financial transactions in the cash receipts and cash payments journals.
- Document trust account transactions correctly.
- Disburse funds from the trust account.
- Prepare monthly trust account statements.
- Close a client's trust account.
- Guard against trust account abuse.
- Understand disciplinary actions for trust account abuses.

INTRODUCTION

The client funds trust account is a bank account established exclusively for clients' funds. It is separate from a firm's general or operating account. Almost every firm is called on to handle money for its clients, sometimes in large amounts. For example, a firm may handle a personal injury claim for a client. When the case is over, medical bills, costs, and other expenses are paid out of the proceeds of the case. Money derived from the proceeds of the case is deposited in, and disbursed from, the clients' funds trust account. The attorney holds the funds "in trust" for clients and acts as a fiduciary by maintaining control of the funds.

Each state's bar association has rules governing the client funds trust account. *The attorney and law firm are bound by state professional responsibility codes to keep client funds completely separate from office and personal bank accounts.* This principle is known as **segregation of cash.**

ABA Model Rule 1.15(a) states:

> (a) A lawyer shall hold property of clients or third persons that is in a lawyer's possession in connection with a representation separate from the lawyer's own property. Funds shall be kept in a separate account maintained in the state where the lawyer's office is situated, or

ETHICS ALERT

segregation of cash
Keeping clients' funds separate from law firm funds.

elsewhere with the consent of the client or third person. Other property shall be identifiable as such and appropriately safeguarded. Complete records of such account funds and other property shall be kept by the lawyer and shall be preserved for a period of 5 years after termination of the representation.

A firm usually has one account for the funds of all its clients. Opening a separate account for each client is cumbersome and discouraged by the American Bar Association (ABA). However, if a firm anticipates that a case will have many large transactions, the firm may open a separate trust account for that case only. Large probate cases commonly have their own trust account.

Examples of the types of funds held in the trust account are funds for costs and expenses, estate proceeds, escrow funds, settlements, judgment payments, fee advances, and funds in which a third party has an interest.

TYPES OF FUNDS HELD IN THE TRUST ACCOUNT

Costs and Expenses

When a client retains a firm, a firm normally requests a deposit of money for payment of costs of the case. Since the exact amount of the costs is unknown at the commencement of a case, a lump sum is requested and is deposited in the trust account. As the costs are incurred, they are paid directly from the trust account. For example, a client pays the firm a lump sum of $500 for payment of costs, and that sum is deposited in the trust account. A complaint is prepared and needs to be filed with the court. A check for the filing fee is drawn on the client's trust account and sent to the court with the complaint. The amount of the check is deducted from the $500 deposit.

Estate Proceeds

There are numerous financial transactions in a probate case. Expenses owed by the decedent before death must be paid, some of which must be paid immediately to preserve the assets of the estate. The heirs may deposit some money for payment of the expenses, or existing cash from the decedent's bank account may be used. If the decedent has income due at the time of death, the income is deposited in the estate trust account. In addition, the estate may receive periodic income from the sale of its assets that is used for the expenses of the estate. These transactions are managed from the estate's trust account.

Since there are many transactions in a probate case, it is more convenient for bookkeeping purposes to open a separate trust account for large estates. Meticulous records must be kept of each transaction. When the estate is closed and the assets are disbursed to the heirs, cash assets are disbursed from the trust account so that the firm has a permanent record of the disbursements. When all expenses have been paid, the law firm may pay itself from the cash in the trust account and return the remainder to the heirs. When all transactions are completed, the estate trust account is closed.

Escrow Funds

There are various reasons a firm will receive funds in escrow on behalf of a client. Law firms that handle real estate transactions will accept a down payment for the property and keep those funds in the trust account pending transfer of the property. Also, if the firm represents a client who is sued and owes payments to a creditor, the client deposits the money for the payment in the firm's trust account. The payments are paid from the law firm's trust account so that there is a record that the payments were made.

Another example of escrow funds is when a dispute arises regarding a debt. In this case, payments are made to the firm's trust account pending resolution of the dispute. For example, a client is a tenant of an apartment building and has a dispute with the landlord regarding the habitability of the apartment. The client refuses to pay the rent until the problems are fixed, but her obligation for the rent continues. The client pays the rent to the law firm's trust account instead of to the landlord. The attorney will transfer the rent when the repairs have been made. This procedure shows the tenant's good faith and ensures that the rent money will be available when repairs are made.

Settlements

When a case is settled, the trust account is used to accept the funds of settlement or judgment. Often, insurance companies make a check payable to the client and the lawyer. The client endorses the check, and the lawyer places the funds in the trust account. From these funds, costs and expenses are paid, as are the attorney's fees owed on the case. Other expenses, such as medical liens, are also paid directly from these funds. The client receives the balance after expenses are paid. Disbursing funds from the trust account creates a record that the payments were made.

Judgments

Judgments are normally paid to and from the attorneys' trust accounts. When a firm represents a judgment creditor, the firm receives the proceeds of the judgment from either the judgment debtor's attorney's trust account or directly from the judgment debtor. The payments are paid to the judgment creditor and the attorney so that the funds can be deposited into the judgment creditor's attorney's trust account. The funds are disbursed after deducting costs, expenses, and attorneys' fees. All payments are monitored by the attorneys so that if a dispute should arise, there are accurate records of each payment. In addition, most people prefer adversarial financial transactions to be completed with the assistance of an intermediary to eliminate misappropriation allegations. Attorneys' trust accounts are used for this purpose.

Fee Advances

There is a disagreement among bar associations regarding whether fee advances are to be deposited in the trust account or are the attorney's property. The majority of bar associations have taken the position that they are the property of the client and should be deposited in the trust account. *The attorney may not withdraw the funds until the fees are earned and a monthly accounting is sent to the client.* For example, a client pays an attorney an advanced fee of $3,000, which is prepayment for 10 hours of the attorney's time. The first month, the attorney spends 4 hours on the case. The attorney may withdraw $1,200 from the trust account after sending an invoice to the client indicating that the withdrawal was made and the services provided for the payment. *If the attorney withdraws the money before the usual billing period, the attorney may be violating the code of professional responsibility.*

ABA Model Rule 1.15 (c) states:

> (c) A lawyer shall deposit into a client trust account legal fees and expenses that have been paid in advance, to be withdrawn by the lawyer only as fees are earned or expenses incurred.

A nonrefundable nonchargeable retainer, or true retainer, is a fee that secures an attorney's availability. It may be deposited directly into the attorney's operating account. These funds are considered "earned on receipt" and are not considered prepayment for the attorney's services. Therefore, it is not necessary to deposit them in the trust account.

12:50

Funds in Which a Third Party Has an Interest

Funds in which an opposing party, or other person, has an interest are deposited into an attorney's trust account. These cases include domestic cases where there is a dispute as to the status of a community property asset. For example, husband and wife have a joint savings account. Husband claims that he deposited separate funds into the account, and therefore, wife is not entitled to them. Wife claims that the separate funds were a gift to the community. Until the judge determines the status of the funds, they are kept in the attorney's trust account for safekeeping.

ABA Model Rule 1.15(e) states:

> (e) When in the course of representation a lawyer is in possession of property in which two or more persons (one of whom may be the lawyer) claim interests, the property shall be kept separate by the lawyer until the dispute is resolved. The lawyer shall promptly distribute all portions of the property as to which the interests are not in dispute.

MAINTAINING THE TRUST ACCOUNT

Each law firm employee has the obligation to make sure that the client funds trust account is accurate and in compliance with the Code of Professional Responsibility. Paralegals are often given the responsibility of maintaining a trust account, especially in small firms.

Rules for maintaining a trust account vary from state to state. Some states have specific record-keeping requirements for the trust account and require lawyers to annually verify their compliance with the states' requirements. Legal malpractice insurance companies also have specific rules governing how trust accounts are maintained. Most billing and accounting software packages monitor trust accounts along with the firm's other accounting functions. Each software package has its own methods and features. However, it is important to check the applicable rules governing trust accounts before relying solely on the computer for trust account accounting functions. Some legal malpractice insurance companies require that manual records of the trust account be kept in addition to electronic records in case of computer failure, energy shortages, and other disasters.

The following sections outline the procedures used to maintain the client funds trust account. It is impossible to give precise instructions on the use of automated accounting programs because of the vast differences among software programs. It is recommended that manual procedures be followed in addition to computer records so that valuable information is not lost. The 10 steps outlined in the following sections are essential elements of proper trust fund accounting.

Opening a Trust Checking Account

State bar rules vary regarding establishing a trust account. All state bar associations require that every law firm that handles clients' funds must have a trust account. When opening a trust account, the following guidelines should be considered:

1. Some rules require that the trust account be established in a bank other than the bank where the firm has its general operating account. This acts as a precaution against accidentally depositing law firm funds into the client's funds accounts and vice versa.

2. Include the words *Trust Account* in the title of the account to adequately document the nature of the account.

3. Select checks of a different color from those of the operating account, and be sure to put the words *Trust Account* on each check. The numbering pattern of the account should begin with 1 or 100.

4. Deposit a reasonable, small amount of funds in the trust account to handle bank charges and check printing charges. Covering bank charges is the only time a firm may deposit its own funds into the trust account.

5. Depending on the state's requirement regarding IOLTA (Interest on Lawyers' Trust Account), discussed more fully later in the chapter, the account may or may not be an interest-bearing account. In all states, however, the trust account cannot be an interest-bearing account for the benefit of the lawyer or firm.

6. The bank or financial institution must file an overdraft notification agreement with the state's lawyer disciplinary agency or highest court agreeing to notify them in the event of an overdraft in the lawyer's trust account.

7. No overdraft protection loan can be placed on a trust account.

Preparing the Client Ledger Sheet

As soon as a client retains a firm, a client ledger sheet is prepared, such as the one shown in Exhibit 9–1. The client ledger sheet documents the amount of fees and costs billed, amount paid, and trust account funds received and disbursed. When the client is billed or pays the firm money, the transaction is documented on the client ledger card. If the client gives the firm money to deposit in the trust account, that transaction is also indicated on the client ledger card. *It is important that money deposited in the trust account be listed separately on the client ledger sheet* (see Exhibit 9–1).

Automated software programs automatically prepare a client ledger sheet after the client's information is input. These ledger sheets may also be maintained by hand, or a printout of each ledger sheet may be made each time a change is made. If a ledger sheet is printed after a change is made, the firm will always have a **hard copy** of current trust account information, which is important to maintain the integrity of the system.

Maintaining Journals

A **cash receipts journal** and a **cash payments journal** are maintained for the trust account, examples of which are shown in Exhibit 9–2. All money received for the trust account is entered in the cash receipts journal, and all checks written from the trust account are entered in the cash payments journal.

When manually entering information into the journals, the following information should be included:

- Date of transaction
- Name of payer
- Name of client
- Name of case
- Amount of transaction
- Check number
- Purpose and description of transaction (e.g., deposition of Harry Snow)

The cash receipts journal and cash payments journal are automatically generated by accounting software packages. The features of each package vary. Trust account software needs to be able to apply debits and credits to an individual client. Some programs require special setup procedures to accommodate the details necessary for trust account transactions.

The person responsible for the trust account must be very careful to enter all the information about the transaction into the system so that the computer can categorize the transactions correctly. When a check is written or a deposit made, the computer will require

ETHICS ALERT

hard copy
A copy of computer records on a sheet of paper.

cash receipts journal
Record of all deposits and cash received.

cash payments journal
Record of all checks written or cash disbursed.

Name Lila Peterson
Address 234 56th St., Palo Alto, CA 90000
Matter: *Peterson v. Johnson*

File No. 94-126R
Phone 555-1234

Date	Description	Chk. No.	FEES			COSTS			TRUST FUNDS		
			Charged	Rec'd.	Balance	Adv.	Rec'd.	Balance	Rec'd.	Paid	Balance
1/7/XX	Rec'd. from client	739							$1,500.00		$1,500.00
2/1/XX	Feb. billing		$465.00		$465.00	$ 56.92		$ 56.92			
2/1/XX	Payment of fees	840		$465.00	-0-		$ 56.92	-0-		$521.92	$ 978.08
3/1/XX	Mar. billing		$650.00		$650.00	$145.23		$145.23			
3/1/XX	Payment of fees	851		$650.00	-0-		$145.23	-0-		$795.23	$ 182.85
4/1/XX	Apr. billing		$295.00		$295.00	$ 31.90		$ 31.90			
4/1/XX	Payment of fees	863		$182.85	$112.15					$182.85	-0-

EXHIBIT 9–1 Client Ledger Sheet

Trust Account Receipts Journal

Month of _ January _ **20XX**

Date	Source	Person or Entity With Interest in Funds	Case or File No.	Amount	Total Daily Deposit
1/7/XX	Lila Peterson	Lila Peterson	94-126R	$1,500.00	$1,500.00

Trust Account Payments Journal

Month of _ March _ **20XX**

Date	Check No.	Payee	Purpose	Person or Entity With Interest in Funds	Case or File No.	Amount
3/1/XX	851	Firm	Fees & Costs	Lila Peterson	94-126R	$795.23
3/1/XX	852	Firm	Fees & Costs	Bob Jones	96-782	$361.86

EXHIBIT 9–2 Transactions Must Be Documented in the Trust Account Receipts Journal and the Trust Account Payments Journal

that a specific account be entered so that the entry will be posted to the correct account. How these entries are made is crucial. If they are not done correctly, the information will not be posted against the appropriate client's account. *This problem will cause the attorney to be subject to trust account abuse allegations.*

For example, client A deposited $500 in the trust account. The firm was filing a complaint on behalf of client A and required a filing fee from the trust account. When the check

ETHICS ALERT

Black, White & Greene Trust Account Receipts/Disbursements Control Sheet for the Year 20XX			
TRUST FUNDS			
Month	Received	Disbursed	Balance*
—	—	—	$
January	$	$	$
February			
March			
April			
May			
June			
July			
August			
September			
October			
November			
December			
Total			—

* This amount should agree with the trust account checkbook register's running balance.

EXHIBIT 9–3 Trust Account Receipts/Disbursements Control Sheet

was written, the computer asked for an account to apply the transaction against. If the transaction is applied to a "filing fees" account, it will not be debited against client A's funds unless the computer is specifically set up for this type of information. It would be very difficult to reconcile the trust account, especially when the trust account contains the funds of many clients.

At the end of every month, the total receipts and disbursements in the journals are totaled and inserted on a Trust Account Receipts/Disbursements Control Sheet, like the one illustrated in Exhibit 9–3. The client ledger sheets, cash receipts journal, and cash payments journal must balance with the total funds in the client funds trust account.

Communicating with Clients

Immediately upon receipt of the funds, the client must be notified that the funds were received. ABA Model Rule 1.15(d) states:

> (d) Upon receiving funds or other property in which a client or third person has an interest, a lawyer shall promptly notify the client or third person. Except as stated in this rule or otherwise permitted by law or by agreement with the client, a lawyer shall promptly deliver to the client or third person any funds or other property that the client or third person is entitled to receive and, upon request by the client or third person, shall promptly render a full accounting regarding such property.

Most codes of professional responsibility do not state a specific time period within which the client must be notified. They indicate only that it be immediately, or as soon as possible, after receipt. There have been many cases that have addressed the definition of *promptly*. This time period is subject to the court's, or state bar disciplinary tribunal's, interpretation on a case-by-case basis. A general rule that has been applied by some state bar associations is the next monthly reconciliation period, or within 30 days of receipt.

Lawyers have been disciplined for their delay in notifying clients of receipt of funds. It is a good management practice to notify the client in writing as soon as the property is received to avoid communication delay accusations.

In addition to informing a client when funds have been received, some states require that clients be informed before any funds can be withdrawn from the client funds trust account. Be sure to check your state's requirements.

Documenting Transactions

Often, checks for settlement of a case are made payable to both the client and the lawyer. If this is the case, the client must endorse the check before it can be deposited into the trust account for disbursement. If the client cannot come into the office to endorse the check, it should be sent to the client by certified mail and mailed back to the lawyer by certified mail. The lawyer then endorses the check and deposits the check into the trust account. If the lawyer endorses the check first and then mails the check to the client for endorsement, the endorsed, cashable check may be lost in the mail or subject to theft.

Before the check is deposited, copies of the deposit slip and the front and back of the check are made. A copy is filed in the client's file and a copy is filed in a trust account receipts file. A trust account receipts file is necessary in case of an account dispute and will come in handy when the account is reconciled. The deposit is then entered in the system on the client ledger sheet and journals. When entering the deposit, be sure to include the payer, check number, and exact date of deposit.

Disbursing Funds

A check must clear the bank before any funds are disbursed. Normally, the funds will clear the bank in 10 business days, but this time period varies with each bank. Some banks will make the funds immediately available pending clearance if prior arrangements have been made. If funds are disbursed before the check clears the bank, it is considered a violation of trust account rules.

When the check clears the bank, the funds may be disbursed. *The funds must be disbursed promptly after receipt to avoid allegations of commingling.* The exact meaning of *promptly* is determined on a case-by-case basis. All funds must be disbursed by check so that the firm will have a record that the check was negotiated. The responsible attorney or office manager signs each check.

All disbursements should have some written documentation describing what the payment is for. Payments for medical liens or other expenses should be accompanied by an invoice or a written statement. Disbursements for payment of attorney's fees and costs may be made after a statement is prepared for the client. If the disbursements are for settlement of a contingency case, the firm will prepare a contingency case accounting, which was illustrated in Chapter 8. The trust account check for fees and costs must be immediately prepared and deposited into the firm's general operating account. *Funds for payment of attorney's fees and costs must not be commingled with client funds.* Removing these funds as soon after billing as possible (after an accounting) will avoid allegations of commingling.

TRENDS

HOW PARALEGALS HELP ATTORNEYS MANAGE THE TRUST ACCOUNT

Paralegals help attorneys manage the client funds trust account by doing the following:

- Keeping the file organized to track expenses and receipts
- Maintaining a good file review system so each file is reviewed at least once a month
- Informing the attorney when a settlement check, or other money that is to be deposited into the trust account, is received
- When settlement checks come in, making sure they are deposited into the client funds trust account immediately
- Making sure all medical and other lienholders are paid from the proceeds of the case. Do not wait until directed to pay the liens. If there is a dispute as to the amount of a lien, all undisputed amounts must be paid. As soon as the dispute is resolved, the following appropriate accounting functions are performed:
  - Making sure the attorney's fee is deducted from the proceeds when funds are disbursed
  - Preparing an accounting for the client describing the transactions in the trust account
  - Making sure all client ledgers are accurate and up to date
  - Balancing the trust account as soon as the bank statement is received

Reconciling the Account

Each month, the bank sends the firm a statement of transactions of the account. The trust account must be reconciled to the bank statement immediately. The account must balance to the penny. If the account does not balance, it is important to determine the cause immediately. State bar associations may randomly audit trust accounts, and some may do so without notice. Keeping the trust account reconciled will ensure accurate record keeping of the account.

When the trust account bank statement is received, a form such as the Trust Account Reconciliation Sheet shown in Exhibit 9–4 is used to reconcile the account. The information on the Trust Account Receipts and Disbursements Control Sheet is used to balance the account. If the firm deposits money into the trust account to cover bank charges, the exact amount of the charges should be immediately deposited. Normally, firms wait until the exact bank charges are known before depositing this amount. Many banks will agree to waive their bank charges for trust accounts.

ABA Model Rule 1.15(b) states:

> (b) A lawyer may deposit the lawyer's own funds in a client trust account for the sole purpose of paying bank service charges on the account, but only in an amount necessary for that purpose.

In large firms, firm administrators or managers are responsible for reconciling the trust account. In small firms, paralegals are often given this responsibility. In many firms, outside accountants or CPAs balance the trust account. Some attorneys prefer to balance their own account because of the importance placed on trust accounts by bar associations. Attorneys

Black, White & Greene
Trust Account Reconciliation Sheet

As of the Month Ended_____, 20___

Trust Ledger Balances—Name of Client	Amount
	$_____
	_____
	_____
	_____
	_____
	_____
	_____
	_____
	_____
	_____
	_____

Total Trust Ledger Balances	$_____ *	
Receipts/Disbursements Control Sheet Balance	$_____ *	
Trust Account Checkbook Balance	$_____ *	
Bank Statement Balance	$_____	
Less: Outstanding checks	$_____	
Add: Outstanding checks	$_____	
Reconciled Bank Statement Balance	$_____ *	

* These amounts must be identical to each other.

EXHIBIT 9–4 Trust Account Reconciliation Sheet

have been disciplined for failing to regularly balance their trust accounts, so a high priority is placed on this function.

Preparing Monthly Statements

Each month, a statement must be sent to each client informing him or her of the status of their trust account. If the client is billed monthly, this statement can be included on his or her monthly bill. An example of a monthly statement of trust account status is shown in Exhibit 9–5.

Closing an Account

When a case has ended, whether by settlement or judgment, the client's trust account is ready to be closed. All the funds in the account must be disbursed before closing, and each transaction must be documented on the client ledger sheet. If there are any funds remaining in the account, they must be returned to the client. Most firms wait until all checks have cleared the bank before closing. Closing an account does not mean that the client funds trust account is closed, just that client's portion of the account. When an account is closed, the client ledger sheet must reflect a zero balance in the trust account section, as shown in Exhibit 9–6. A final accounting is prepared for the client and inserted into the client's file.

Black, White & Greene
Attorneys at Law

February 1, 20XX

Lila Peterson
234 56th St.
Anytown, CA 90000

Re: Peterson v. Johnson, et al.

Statement of Trust Account

January 1, 20XX to February 28, 20XX

Date	Description	Rec'd	Disbursed	Balance
1/7/XX	Received from client	$1,500.00		$1,500.00
2/1/XX	February attorneys' fees		$465.00	1,035.00
2/1/XX	February costs		56.92	978.08
Balance as of February 28, 20XX				**$978.08**

EXHIBIT 9–5   Statement of Trust Account

Keeping Records

Records of a trust account must be kept for auditing purposes or in the event of a malpractice claim. Individual state bar associations have their own trust account record retention schedules. Normally, trust account records should be kept for at least 5 years after the account is closed.

INTEREST ON LAWYERS' CLIENT FUNDS TRUST ACCOUNT

Lawyers who establish their trust accounts in an interest-bearing account do not receive interest on clients' funds. This interest is sent to state bar associations to fund legal programs for the indigent. The funds generating interest, when considered as an individual client's money, would not generate much interest if held in separate client accounts either because the amounts are too small or because the money is held for too short a time. However, the aggregate of all client funds held in a trust account can generate a substantial amount of interest.

The IOLTA (Interest on Lawyers' Trust Accounts) program began in England, Canada, and Australia in the 1960s. In the United States, it was introduced in Florida in 1981. States have been developing IOLTA programs since 1981, when Congress changed the banking laws to allow some checking accounts to bear interest.

IOLTA programs have funded legal services for indigent people through their funding of legal aid programs. In 1998, it was estimated that $1 billion in interest was paid to legal services organizations since 1981. Without IOLTA funds, these programs would not exist.

There are three types of IOLTA participation:

1. Mandatory: All lawyers in the state must participate in IOLTA.
2. Voluntary: All lawyers may choose whether to participate in IOLTA.
3. Opt-out: All lawyers must participate unless they affirmatively choose not to participate.

Name   Lila Peterson

Address   100 Park St., Palo Alto, CA 90000

Matter: *Peterson v. Johnson*

File No.   94-126R

Phone   555-1234

Date	Description	Chk. No.	FEES Charged	FEES Rec'd.	FEES Balance	COSTS Adv.	COSTS Rec'd.	COSTS Balance	TRUST FUNDS Rec'd.	TRUST FUNDS Paid	TRUST FUNDS Balance
1/7/XX	Rec'd. from client	739							$ 1,500.00		$ 1,500.00
2/1/XX	Feb. billing		$465.00		$465.00	$ 56.92		$ 56.92			
2/1/XX	Payment of fees	840		$465.00	-0-		$ 56.92	-0-		$ 521.92	$ 978.08
3/1/XX	Mar. billing		$650.00		$650.00	$145.23		$145.23			
3/1/XX	Payment of fees	851		$650.00	-0-		$145.23	-0-		$ 795.23	$ 182.85
4/1/XX	Apr. billing		$295.00		$295.00	$ 31.90		$ 31.90			
4/1/XX	Payment of fees	863		$182.85	$112.15					$ 182.85	-0-
5/1/XX	May billing		$540.00		$652.15	$ 86.50		$118.40			
6/1/XX	ABC Ins. Co.	2031							$15,000.00		$15,000.00
6/15/XX	Attorney's fees	901		$652.15	-0-		$118.40	-0-		$ 770.55	$14,229.45
6/15/XX	XYZ depositions	902								$ 245.00	$13,975.45
6/15/XX	Dr. Baker, M.D.	903								$ 675.00	$13,300.45
6/15/XX	Client	904								$13,300.45	-0-

EXHIBIT 9–6 Client Ledger Sheet 2

All 50 states, the District of Columbia, and the U.S. Virgin Islands operate IOLTA programs. As of January, 2008, 36 jurisdictions are mandatory, lawyers can opt out of participation in 14 others, and participation is voluntary in two others.

Of Interest . . .

GRANTEES OF IOLTA FUNDS

The Legal Services Corporation is perhaps the largest recipient of IOLTA funds. Other organizations and initiatives funded by IOLTA programs are listed below.

- Advocacy for Children in Oregon
- Minnesota's Disability Law Center
- New York Program to Aid Elderly
- Alabama's Miracle Riders Program
- Massachusetts Law Reform Institute: Making Public Housing Opportunities Accessible to All
- Legal Services of North Carolina
- Maine Project to Give Poor a Voice in Welfare Transition
- Washoe County CASA Program

Of Interest . . .

STATES' IOLTA PARTICIPATION

MANDATORY	OPT-OUT	VOLUNTARY
Alabama	Alaska	South Dakota
Arizona	Delaware	Virgin Islands
Arkansas	D.C.	
California	Idaho	
Colorado	Kansas	
Connecticut	Kentucky	
Florida	Nebraska	
Georgia	Nevada	
Hawaii	New Hampshire	
Illinois	New Mexico	
Indiana	Rhode Island	
Iowa	Tennessee	
Louisiana	Virginia	
Maine	Wyoming	
Maryland		
Massachusetts		

Of Interest . . . (Cont.)

MANDATORY	OPT-OUT	VOLUNTARY
Michigan		
Minnesota		
Mississippi		
Missouri		
Montana		
New Jersey		
New York		
North Carolina		
North Dakota		
Ohio		
Oklahoma		
Oregon		
Pennsylvania		
South Carolina		
Texas		
Utah		
Vermont		
Washington		
West Virginia		
Wisconsin		
36	**14**	**2**

The money received for interest is transferred to the state bar or state bar foundation to fund law-related public interest programs for the indigent, elderly, or disabled, including legal aid, victim assistance programs, and **client security funds.** A client security fund allows clients who have been damaged by an attorney's illegal use of trust account funds to be reimbursed for their losses. A client security fund was recommended by the ABA in 1959. Since that time, the majority of states have established a client security fund.

Opponents of IOLTA programs feel that interest on client funds should be paid to the client. They contend that technology exists today that easily calculates each client's share of the earned interest. Consequently, the legality of IOLTA programs was challenged in 1998 in the case of *Phillips v. Washington Legal Foundation* (524 U.S. 156, 118 S.Ct. 1925, 141 L.ed.2d 174), which was heard by the U.S. Supreme Court. The Court ruled that interest earned on client funds held in IOLTA accounts is the private property of the client. In the ruling, Chief Justice William H. Rehnquist said, "While the interest income at issue here may have no economically realizable value to its owner, possession, control and disposition are nonetheless valuable rights that inhere in the property."

This ruling caused a panic for IOLTA programs in the United States. IOLTA proponents feel that the ruling was logical but impractical. Since many people have small amounts in the trust account, the effort involved in providing the clients with a few pennies of interest and in eliminating IOLTA programs does not make sense. The National Association of IOLTA Programs (NAIP) secured the services of a law firm to address issues concerning the ruling. The Conference of State Supreme Court Chief Justices issued a unanimous resolution

client security fund
A fund established to reimburse clients who have been damaged because of their attorney's fraudulent abuse of the trust account.

urging "continued operation of IOLTA programs in every jurisdiction." In March 2003, the U.S. Supreme Court ruled in *Brown v. Legal Foundation of Washington* (538 U.S. 216) that IOLTA was not a taking of personal property and was constitutional.

Information about your state's IOLTA program can be found on the websites of various state bar associations. The Cybersites section at the end of the chapter lists some sites that have IOLTA information.

TRUST ACCOUNT ABUSES

ETHICS ALERT

The client funds trust account has been abused by lawyers who have used client funds without authorization. *Misuse of the client funds trust account is grounds for attorney discipline.*

It is because of past abuses that state bars closely monitor client funds trust accounts. Lawyers' trust accounts are under the jurisdiction of each state bar association that has authority to audit trust accounts. Each state bar association has its own procedures and requirements for auditing lawyers' trust accounts. In some states, the state bar may audit a firm's trust account at any time without provocation or reason, and other states audit only those accounts where abuse is suspected. The law firm must open its client funds account to the state bar on request. If the account is not found in proper order, the attorney or firm is subject to disciplinary proceedings. Most state bar associations require banks to automatically notify it of any trust account overdrafts or bounced checks, whether they were honored or not. An overdraft is an indication of mishandling a trust account.

Common trust account abuses include the following:

misappropriation
Using funds in the trust account for personal purposes.

- *Misappropriation.* **Misappropriation** includes writing personal checks from a trust account. If an attorney writes a personal check from the trust account, the attorney is essentially stealing clients' money. For example, an attorney represented a client in litigation against a school district. The attorney failed to file a complaint within the statutory time period. She was afraid of a legal malpractice lawsuit, so she did not inform the client of the missed deadline. Instead, she told the client that she settled the case for $10,000 and would send the client a check for $6,000 after deducting $4,000 for her attorney's fees. She sent the client a check from her trust account, thereby paying the client with other clients' funds. The attorney was disbarred for misappropriation of funds.

- *Paying office expenses with client funds.* Using funds from the trust account to cover business expenses, debts, or overhead.

- *Withdrawing funds from the trust account of one client to meet another client's trust account obligations.* For example, a client retained a lawyer to represent her in a lawsuit against her employer. She agreed to deposit $500 into the trust account for costs, but she could not pay the money for a month. Her complaint had to be filed immediately, so the lawyer wrote a check from the trust account to pay the filing fee, therefore using other clients' funds for payment of her expenses. The funds were reimbursed when the client made her payment. This activity is a violation of trust account rules.

check kiting
Using other clients' funds until a check clears the bank.

- *Check kiting.* **Check kiting** is when money is withdrawn from a recently deposited check before the check has cleared the bank, thereby using other clients' funds to cover the check. For example, a client retained a lawyer to represent her in a lawsuit that her neighbor filed against her. She paid $200 into the trust account for costs. However, her answer to the complaint had to be filed before her check cleared the bank. The lawyer wrote a check from the trust account to pay the filing fee for the answer, therefore using other clients' funds.

commingle
Mixing one person's funds with another person's funds.

- *Commingling.* **Commingling** includes mixing law firm funds with client funds. An attorney may not commingle client funds with law firm funds or personal funds. The only time an attorney may deposit firm funds into the clients' trust account is to cover monthly bank charges, such as service charges and check charges. If these expenses are incurred, the firm must deposit just enough money to cover those charges each month. If more money than is needed is deposited, the firm is commingling its funds with client funds. Many banks will waive the monthly charge for a clients' trust account.

- *Failure to promptly notify clients of receipt of funds.*   Clients must be notified as soon as funds are received on the client's behalf. Although the exact time period is not specifically indicated in rules of professional conduct, an average allowable time period is within 30 days.

- *Failure to promptly disburse funds.*   All expenses due to be paid from a trust account must be paid promptly. Failure to do so will subject the attorney to disciplinary proceedings. For example, a lawyer represents a client in her lawsuit against the city. The case settled for $30,000, and the lawyer deposited the funds in the trust account. The lawyer was obligated to pay medical liens from the proceeds. The lawyer deducted the liens and his attorney's fee and mailed the client a check for the balance. The lawyer deposited his attorney's fee in the firm's operating account. However, the lawyer did not pay the medical liens for 19 months. During that time, his trust account balance was under the total of the liens, indicating mishandling of client funds. The lawyer was disciplined (*Blair v. State Bar*, 47 Cal. 3d 448 [1988]).

- *Failure to provide clients with an accounting of trust account funds.*   Attorneys are obligated to provide periodic accountings of a client funds trust account. If there is activity on the account, an accounting should be sent monthly. If there is no activity on the account, an accounting may be sent quarterly, depending on the circumstances.

Although the attorney is ultimately responsible for the condition of the trust account, balancing the account is often delegated to a secretary or paralegal. *A paralegal not familiar with trust fund accounting principles may be exposing the firm to serious liability if allowed to maintain the firm's client funds trust account.*

If a client terminates the attorney–client relationship, all funds in the client's trust account that have not been earned must be immediately returned to the client. In most states, a lawyer must have a client's permission to apply funds in the trust account to an outstanding legal bill. If the bill is disputed, most states require that the attorney return the client's funds and take other action to collect the unpaid fee.

CONCLUSION

As this chapter illustrates, managing a client funds trust account correctly is extremely important. Attorneys who have abused their clients' trust funds have been severely disciplined by state bars. If an attorney who works for a law firm that is a partnership abuses the trust account, each partner may also be subject to disciplinary proceedings. ABA Model Rule 5.1 states:

> (a) A partner in a law firm, and a lawyer who individually or together with other lawyers possesses comparable managerial authority in a law firm, shall make reasonable efforts to ensure that the firm has in effect measures giving reasonable assurance that all lawyers in the firm conform to the Rules of Professional Conduct.
>
> (b) A lawyer having direct supervisory authority over another lawyer shall make reasonable efforts to ensure that the other lawyer conforms to the Rules of Professional Conduct.
>
> (c) A lawyer shall be responsible for another lawyer's violation of the Rules of Professional Conduct if:
>
> (1) the lawyer orders or, with knowledge of the specific conduct, ratifies the conduct involved; or
>
> (2) the lawyer is a partner or has comparable managerial authority in the law firm in which the other lawyer practices, or has direct supervisory authority over the other lawyer, and knows of the conduct at a time when its consequences can be avoided or mitigated but fails to take reasonable remedial action.

Managing the client funds trust account accurately has many benefits: reduced legal malpractice insurance costs, reduced ethics problems, reduced client complaints, and reduced stress and anxiety.

SUMMARY

The client funds trust account is a bank account established exclusively for clients' funds. The attorney and law firm are bound by professional codes of state bar associations to keep clients' funds completely separate from the office and personal bank accounts. A firm usually has one account for the funds of all its clients, except for large cases that require their own account. Examples of the types of funds held in the trust account are funds for costs and expenses, estate proceeds, escrow funds, settlements, judgment payments, fee advances, and property in which a third party has an interest.

Rules for maintaining a trust account vary from state to state. Ten steps are essential elements of proper trust fund accounting: opening a trust checking account, preparing a client ledger sheet, maintaining journals, communicating with clients, documenting transactions, disbursing funds, reconciling the account, preparing monthly statements, closing the account, and keeping accurate records.

The IOLTA program has been in effect for many years. Each state bar association determines its participation in IOLTA. The money received for interest is transferred to the state bar or state bar foundation to fund law-related public interest programs, such as legal aid, victim assistance programs, and client security funds.

The legality of IOLTA programs was challenged in 1998 in the case of *Phillips v. Washington Legal Foundation*, which was heard by the U.S. Supreme Court. The Court ruled that interest earned on client funds held in IOLTA accounts is the private property of the client. In *Brown v. Legal Foundation of Washington*, the Supreme Court upheld IOLTA'S constitutionality.

Attorneys' trust accounts have been abused, so state bar associations closely monitor them. The attorney may not misappropriate, pay office expenses or other clients' expenses with client funds, participate in check kiting, or commingle client funds with law firm funds. Furthermore, attorneys must promptly notify clients of receipt of funds and promptly disburse funds. They must also provide clients with an accounting of trust funds. If a client terminates an attorney-client relationship, all funds in the client funds account that have not been earned must be immediately returned to the client.

CHAPTER ILLUSTRATION

Tricia, the office manager for Black, White & Greene, is responsible for the financial management for the firm. She delegates the firm's banking functions to the secretary, Sandra Stinson. Sandra makes sure that all deposits are documented and that the bank accounts are reconciled.

Patrizia Boen, the attorney responsible for the firm's personal injury cases, settled a case for client Sheldon Goodman. She negotiated the settlement with Fred Hull, a claims adjuster for Good Hands Insurance Company. Before accepting the settlement offer, she discussed it with Sheldon, who agreed to the settlement figure. Fred told Patrizia that the settlement check would be mailed that day in the names of the client and the firm. Patrizia told her secretary, Sandra, to telephone the client to have him come into the office in 1 week to endorse the settlement check. She was sure that the check would be there in a couple of days and would surely be there in 1 week.

Before Sheldon's appointment, Patrizia asked Sandra whether the check had arrived. Sandra replied that she had seen it but did not know where it was. She looked all over for it but could not find it. It was not on her desk, on Patrizia's desk, or in the file. Patrizia called Fred and asked him whether the check had been mailed. Fred told her that it was mailed to the firm 1 week ago and verified that the check was mailed to the correct address. The check was somewhere in the office, and Patrizia told Sandra to find it.

Sandra was searching for the check when Sheldon arrived to endorse it. "Have you found that check yet?" asked Patrizia.

"No," said Sandra. "I've asked everybody. Kay (the file clerk) said she thought she saw a check come in when she was opening the mail, but she can't remember what case it was on. I'm having her go back through the daily logs for the week to find it."

"Okay. Sheldon is waiting in my office to sign the check. I'll have to tell him we are looking for it. This is very embarrassing. How can we lose a check for $45,000?"

Patrizia went back to her office to tell Sheldon the news. "The check has been misplaced. We are in the process of tracking it down. Normally, we are very organized and have systems in place to avoid this problem. I don't know what happened here. It may have been lost in the mail. I'll call you when we have the check. I'm sorry you made a trip down here for nothing."

"What! Can't find a check for $45,000? I took the morning off work to come here and missed an important meeting! Okay, I'll come back when you have the check."

Embarrassed, Patrizia apologized again and went into the file room, where Kay was searching the firm's daily mail logs. "Have you found that check?" asked Patrizia.

"I see here on the daily mail log that a check from Good Hands Insurance Company came in last Thursday. I've searched the file room, and it's not here. I'm sure I put it on your desk with the rest of the mail," said Kay.

"I've searched my office and Sandra's desk. It's nowhere to be found. Okay, let's go back over everything we did last Thursday and find that check!"

Sandra, Patrizia, and Kay spent hours tracing their activities on Thursday. They searched all files and finally found the check. It was in another file that Patrizia was working on that day. The check was picked up with other papers and put in the wrong file. Sandra called Sheldon back to come in and endorse the check. He was not happy about leaving work early to do so.

Sheldon endorsed the check. "When will I get my money?" asked Sheldon.

Patrizia answered, "We have to wait 10 business days for the check to clear before we disburse the funds."

"Ten business days? Boy, that's a long time. Why? Good Hands has millions. I'm sure the check is good. I need my money now!" said Sheldon.

"I know you're anxious for the money, Sheldon, but there's nothing I can do about it. The state bar has specific rules that require us to clear the check before disbursing funds from the trust account."

"Alright, I'll be in 2 weeks from today to pick up my check," said Sheldon.

Before Sandra left for the day, she prepared the check for deposit. She copied the front and back and entered the amount on the client ledger sheet and journals. She prepared the deposit slip and put the check in the mail pick-up area to go out in the morning mail.

Two weeks later, Sheldon arrived on time for his appointment to disburse the funds. Patrizia did an accounting of the disbursements and had the checks ready when Sheldon arrived. The accounting showed the amount of settlement, payment for Sheldon's medical expenses, payment for costs and expenses, and her attorney' fees. Sheldon was happy to get the check so that he could make a down payment on a new house he was purchasing.

Sandra mailed the checks for the medical liens and deposited the attorney' fees into the firm's general operating account. One week later, Patrizia received a call from Sheldon. He was very upset.

"What kind of law firm are you running over there anyway?" exclaimed Sheldon. "My check bounced! What the ——— is going on?"

"Bounced? Are you sure? That can't be. Good Hands has plenty of money. I'll look into it and call you back," said Patrizia.

In a panic, Patrizia called Sandra into her office. "Sheldon's trust account check bounced. Find out what's going on," Patrizia said.

Sandra called the bank and inquired about the trust account balance. She discovered that it was overdrawn.

"Are you sure you deposited the check?" Patrizia asked Sandra.

"Yes," responded Sandra. "I remember specifically depositing the check. I made copies and documented the ledger. I specifically remember because I had to stay late so it would be ready for the morning mail. It must have been lost in the mail," said Sandra.

"Mail rarely gets lost anymore," said Patrizia. "I'll check with Fred."

Patrizia called Fred and told him the problem. She asked Fred to cancel the check and issue another one. Fred checked his records and informed Patrizia that the check had already been cashed.

Patrizia was surprised. "Fax me a copy of the front and back of the check. Something's very wrong here."

"Okay," said Fred. "But it'll take a couple of weeks to get a copy from the accounting department."

"I can't wait 2 weeks!" said Patrizia angrily. "I have checks bouncing out of the trust account. I have an angry client who is ready to complain to the state bar. On top of that, I start a big trial on Friday. I need that check now!"

"Okay. I'll see what I can do," said Fred. That afternoon, Sandra received numerous telephone calls and complaints from Sheldon's doctors complaining that their checks bounced. The whole firm was in an uproar.

The next day, Fred faxed a copy of the check to Patrizia. "Oh no," said Patrizia as she went to Tricia's office. She showed Tricia the check. "Here's the problem. The check was deposited into the firm's operating account. Sandra used the wrong deposit slip. We need to get those funds out of there immediately! Write a check from the operating account for $45,000 and get it into the trust account right away."

Tricia wrote the check and took it to the bank personally. Patrizia called Sheldon and told him what happened. She apologized and told him that she would prepare new checks. She had Sandra call all the medical lienholders to apologize and tell them that they would receive new checks.

Patrizia issued new checks and had them ready when Sheldon came in. When Sheldon arrived, Patrizia handed him the check. "Thanks," said Sheldon. "Oh, by the way, I received this lien from my doctor yesterday. It took him 3 months to send it to me. I forgot to tell you about it. We need to send him a check also."

Patrizia looked at the lien and sighed. "Well, okay, we'll pay it, but we'll have to cancel all of these checks and recalculate the disbursement. We use the net fee accounting method, which means that my fee and your share are deducted after liens and costs. My fee has now changed, and your share is different now, too. Can you wait while I recalculate this and prepare a new statement?"

Patrizia prepared a new statement and new checks and gave Sheldon the check. "Are you sure this one won't bounce?" asked Sheldon. "I can't tell you the problems I've had with this. My house fell out of escrow, and I'm in a real mess. I think you should pay for all the extra expenses I've incurred because of this problem."

"I'm sure we can work something out," said Patrizia.

Patrizia was relieved that the settlement was completed. She instructed Sandra to close the trust account for Sheldon as soon as all the checks cleared the bank.

Three weeks later, Sandra received the bank statement for the trust account and was reconciling the account. She noticed that a check for a medical lien from one of Sheldon's doctors was not cashed, so she called to inquire about it. She learned that they did not receive the check. "It must have been lost in the mail," Sandra thought.

She went into Patrizia's office to tell her the news. She knew that Patrizia would not want to hear about this problem. As she walked in her office, Patrizia received a telephone call on her speaker phone. "Hello, Ms. Boen?"

"Yes," said Patrizia.

"This is Alice Verstegan from the state bar. We were informed by your bank that you had an overdraft in your trust account. . . ."

CHAPTER REVIEW

1. What is segregation of cash?
2. What types of funds are deposited in a client funds trust account?
3. Why would a client have a separate, individual trust account?
4. When a firm is paid an advanced fee, when is it paid?
5. What are the ten steps of maintaining a trust account?
6. Why must trust account records be kept after it is closed?
7. What is IOLTA?
8. What are the three types of IOLTA participation?
9. For what are IOLTA funds used?
10. What are the eight ways a client funds account is abused?

EXAMPLES FOR DISCUSSION

1. THE MONEY IS IN THE TRUST ACCOUNT

Ellen is the paralegal and office manager for Stephen Bristol, a sole proprietor. She was preparing a motion for client Fisher that had to be filed with the court that afternoon. A $25 filing fee had to accompany the motion. She prepared a check for the filing fee out of the office operating account and presented it to Mr. Bristol for signature. Mr. Bristol refused to sign the check, stating that payroll was due on Friday and that he was concerned there would not be enough money in the account to cover employee taxes. He instructed Ellen to take the money out of the trust account.

Ellen had checked the ledger card for client Fisher and informed Mr. Bristol that there was only $17 in Ms. Fisher's account. Mr. Bristol told Ellen that there was plenty of money in that account from other clients. He told Ellen to bill Ms. Fisher for the additional $8 and they could replace the money when she paid it.

1. Are Mr. Bristol's instructions ethical?
2. What should Ellen do?
3. What are some alternatives to the problem?

2. THOSE PESKY LITTLE DETAILS

Stephen Bristol, attorney for client Jane DeUlloa, settled her personal injury case for $45,000. The settlement check was made payable to Jane and Stephen. Stephen instructed Ellen, his paralegal, to contact Jane so that she could come into the office to sign the check. When she did, Jane told Ellen that she was on her way to the airport for a 3-week vacation to Europe and could not come into the office to endorse the check. Stephen was anxious to negotiate the check so that his attorney' fees could be paid as soon as possible. He needed the money to pay his state bar dues that were due next week. The check had to be deposited as soon as possible so that it would clear the bank in enough time to meet the deadline. He told Ellen to sign Jane's name to the back of the check and to deposit it. "Jane won't mind," he said. "She's as anxious as I am to obtain the funds."

1. Are Mr. Bristol's instructions ethical?
2. What should Ellen do?
3. What are some alternatives to the problem?

3. DOES INTEREST BELONG TO THE CLIENT?

In light of the U.S. Supreme Court's ruling regarding IOLTA funds, discuss the following:

1. Do you think clients should be paid interest on funds in an attorney's trust account? If so, why? If not, why not?
2. If interest is the client's property, what will happen to legal aid programs for the poor?
3. If IOLTA funds are not available to fund legal aid programs, what are some alternatives?

ASSIGNMENTS

1. Make a client ledger sheet for Lila Peterson like the one in Exhibit 9–6. A blank ledger card is on the accompanying CD. Document the following transactions on the client ledger sheet:

   a. 2/25/XX—Client retained firm and deposited $2,500.00 into the client funds account for advanced fees and costs. She used check number 2434.
   b. 3/1/XX—Billed client for $475.00 fees.
   c. 3/1/XX—Paid the firm for attorneys' fees owed with check number 467.
   d. 3/10/XX—Filed complaint—Filing fee $120.00 paid from trust account with check number 470.
   e. 4/1/XX—Billed client for $860.00 in fees and $145.00 in costs.
   f. 4/1/XX—Paid firm fees and costs with check number 474.
   g. 5/1/XX—Billed client for $525.00 in fees and $27.80 in costs.
   h. 5/1/XX—Paid firm for fees and costs with check number 482.
   i. 5/5/XX—Client deposited funds with check number 2564.
   j. 5/15/XX—Paid Fast Fingers Deposition Service $345.00 for deposition costs with check number 491.
   k. 6/1/XX—Billed client for $395.00 fees and $15.20 costs.
   l. 6/1/XX—Paid firm for fees and costs with check number 500.

   What is the balance of fees owed? Costs owed? What is the balance remaining in the trust account? Prepare a statement of account like the one illustrated in Exhibit 9–5.

2. Contact your state bar association and obtain a copy of its rules and requirements for trust accounts. Prepare a memorandum to your instructor about the rules and recommend trust account maintenance procedures accordingly.

3. Information about disciplined attorneys is often published in state bar association periodicals. Obtain your state bar's magazine or periodical and review the section on disciplined attorneys. Note the cases in which attorneys are disciplined for trust account abuses. Prepare a report for the class on the attorneys' abuses and the discipline imposed.

SELF TEST

How well did you grasp the material in the chapter? Test yourself by answering the following questions, and check your answers against the answers found in Appendix A.

1. For what purpose is a client funds trust account established?
2. What is a fiduciary?
3. Who makes the rules concerning a client funds trust account?
4. What is segregation of cash?

5. How many trust accounts do firms have for their clients?
6. When is an individual trust account established for just one client?
7. What types of funds are held in a trust account?
8. Why are escrow funds held in a trust account?
9. Why are expenses of a case paid from the trust account?
10. Why do people prefer that adversarial financial transactions be handled through a trust account?
11. When may an attorney withdraw advance fee funds from the trust account?
12. What type of retainer fees do not require to be deposited in the trust account?
13. Why are true retainer fees not required to be deposited in the trust account?
14. What entity may require that manual trust account records be maintained?
15. Why keep manual records of a trust account?
16. What are the ten steps of proper trust fund accounting?
17. What is a client ledger sheet?
18. How are trust fund monies indicated on the client ledger sheet?
19. What is a hard copy?
20. What is a cash receipts journal?
21. What is a cash payments journal?
22. What is a Trust Account Receipts/Disbursement Control Sheet?
23. What is a Trust Account Reconciliation Sheet?
24. What seven items must be entered into the journals?
25. With what must the client ledger sheet and journals be balanced?
26. When should a trust account be reconciled?
27. When must a client be notified of the receipt of funds?
28. If a check is made payable to the client and lawyer, who must endorse the check first? Why?
29. If the check is mailed to the client for endorsement, how should the check be mailed?
30. Before a check is deposited into the trust account, what must be done?
31. Where are copies of the check filed?
32. What is a trust account receipts file?
33. What information about a deposit is inserted on the client ledger sheet?
34. What must happen before a check may be written against a deposit?
35. When must funds be disbursed?
36. Who signs a trust account check?
37. What must each disbursement have?
38. When should payment for attorneys' fees be deposited in the firm's operating account?
39. When is a trust account reconciled with a bank statement?
40. How is accurate record keeping of the trust account ensured?
41. When should a firm send a trust account statement to a client?
42. When is a trust account closed?
43. What do most firms do before closing a trust account?
44. When a client's account is closed, how is it reflected on the client ledger sheet?
45. Why are trust account records kept?
46. For how long should trust account records be kept?
47. Who receives interest derived from trust accounts?
48. For what is interest used?
49. What does IOLTA stand for?

50. In what countries did IOLTA have its origin?

51. What state was the first state in the United States to have an IOLTA program?

52. What are the three types of IOLTA participation?

53. Who receives interest derived from attorneys' trust accounts?

54. What types of programs do IOLTA funds sponsor?

55. What is a client security fund?

56. What is the name of the case that challenged the legality of IOLTA programs?

57. What was the Supreme Court's ruling?

58. What did the Conference of State Supreme Court Chief Justices say?

59. What has happened to IOLTA programs since the Supreme Court's ruling?

60. What happens to an attorney who abuses the trust account?

61. Who audits attorneys' trust accounts?

62. When are trust accounts audited?

63. Some state bar associations require that banks notify them of what event?

64. An overdraft in a trust account is an indication of what?

65. What are the common abuses of the client funds trust account?

66. What is misappropriation?

67. If an attorney writes a personal check from the trust account, what is he or she doing?

68. What office expense may be paid from the trust account?

69. What is check kiting?

70. What is commingling?

71. When may an attorney deposit a firm's funds into the trust account?

72. Who is ultimately responsible for the trust account?

73. Why must a paralegal be familiar with trust account accounting principles?

74. If a client terminates the attorney-client relationship, what must be done with the funds in the trust account?

75. May an attorney apply funds in the trust account to an outstanding legal fee?

76. If an attorney in a partnership abuses the trust account, who may be subject to discipline?

77. What are the benefits of managing a trust account accurately and effectively?

Key Words

cash payments journal	client security fund	misappropriation
cash receipts journal	commingle	segregation of cash
check kiting	hard copy	

 # Cybersites

FINDING IOLTA INFORMATION ON THE WEB

Kentucky Bar Association—<*http://www.kybar.org*>

Maryland Legal Services Corporation—<*http://www.mlsc.org*>

Center for Civic Values—<*http://www.civicvalues.org*>

National Legal Aid and Defender Association—<*http://www.nlada.org*>

Minnesota Bar Association—<*http://www.mnbar.org*>

West Virginia Bar Association—<*http://www.wvbar.org*>

Arizona Bar Association—<*http://www.azbar.org*>

American Bar Association—<*http://www.abanet.org/legalservices/iolta*>

National Association of IOLTA Programs—<*http://www.iolta.org*>

GENERAL INFORMATION ABOUT TRUST ACCOUNTS

New York Guide to Trust Accounts—<*http://www.nylawfund.org/pubs/guide.shtml*>

Attorney Trust Account Depositories—<*http://www.judiciary.state.nj.us/notices/2005/n050207b.htm*>

 Student CD-ROM
For additional materials, please go to the CD in this book.

 Online Companion™
For additional resources, please go to http://www.paralegal.delmar.cengage.com

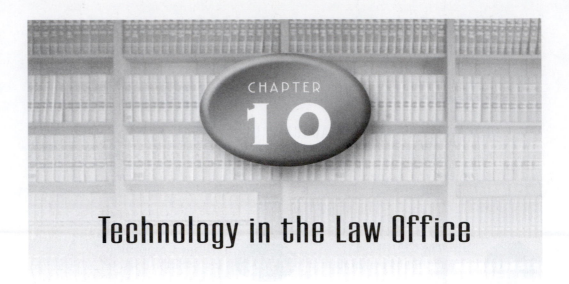

CHAPTER 10

Technology in the Law Office

OBJECTIVES

After completion of this chapter, the student should be able to do the following:

- Define the types of software most commonly used in a law office.
- Describe the origin of the Internet.
- Understand the essential elements of access to the Internet and the factors that contributed to its growth.
- Describe a website and its elements.
- Locate information on the Web.
- Search for information on the Web.
- Bookmark a website.
- Determine whether information on the Web is reliable.
- Know the features and benefits of an intranet and an extranet.
- Protect the confidentiality of information transmitted via the Internet.
- Participate in a blawg.
- Exhibit good e-mail netiquette.
- Write an appropriate e-mail message.
- Manage e-mail messages.
- Identify a potential ethical problem of a website.

INTRODUCTION

Technology is a tool that is used by legal professionals to deliver their product to a client. Effectively using this tool affects the quality of those services. It is necessary for lawyers and support staff to learn the tools and to learn them well. It is essential that all members of the legal team become proficient users of technology.

The technological advances made in the 1990s have transformed the average law office. The Internet and its technology have revolutionized the way law is practiced today. Before Internet technology, we were limited in our use of technology. Now, a wide variety of new technological opportunities are available to us. The future promises to excite us with even more technological advances.

The introduction of new technologies and rapid changes in existing technologies have been both a blessing and a curse. Upgrading existing technology and implementing new technology require a tremendous capital investment as well as trained computer specialists to manage a firm's technology. Although technology has streamlined many tasks and automated routine functions, it has placed new challenges on the legal team.

The primary challenge is keeping current with the latest technology. It is difficult for law firms, and for business in general, to keep up with the rapid changes in technology. New technologies are being developed faster than we can learn about them, and products become obsolete within months of their debut. As soon as one becomes proficient with a software product, it is upgraded to include new features that must be learned. This requires an investment of an employee's time and a firm's resources to train employees. To be trained adequately, employees must be trained often.

Another challenge is managing information. The legal team now has access to the information superhighway: the Internet. The Internet is exploding with information to enhance the practice of law. While access to this information enhances the delivery of legal services to a client, it has resulted in "information overload." The information must be managed properly in order for members of the legal team to be able to locate it. This has introduced new methods of information management of which all members of the legal team must be knowledgeable. Many legal professionals have difficulty implementing new methods of information management.

Internet technologies have also increased the speed with which we receive and process information. Information is transmitted in seconds rather than days, and this increases the pressures on the legal team. These pressures require increased competence of law firm employees. Clients are increasingly intolerant of delays and mistakes.

Paralegals must be familiar with the common software used in legal offices and are expected to be able to operate the firm's computer system. The 2007 Technology Survey conducted by *Legal Assistant Today* revealed that 52.2 percent of responding paralegals have input on technology decisions implemented by their firms.

This chapter will focus on the aspects of technology most frequently found in law offices. Since we are in the twenty-first century, it is assumed that the average person is knowledgeable about the basics of twentieth-century technology, such as computer hardware, software, and fax machines. First, this chapter will discuss the software most commonly found in law offices today, and then it will discuss the Internet and its impact on the legal profession. Next, this chapter will review intranets and extranets and how they are used in the law office. Finally, this chapter will discuss how emerging technologies have affected ethical rules and guidelines.

COMMON LAW OFFICE SOFTWARE

There are various types of software and thousands of software applications available in the legal marketplace to accommodate almost every aspect of a law office's functions, from specific practice areas to management tasks. Software applications can do almost anything, from assembling documents to helping a lawyer develop a trial strategy. As you are reading this, new software applications are being developed to further streamline legal tasks.

Software applications are developed specifically for the operating system used by a firm's computers. There are currently three major operating systems: Windows, Macintosh, and Unix.

Microsoft's Windows operating system is the most popular and widely used operating system used in law offices today. It has its origin in an operating system that was used in the 1970s and 1980s called MS-DOS (Microsoft Disk Operating System). Since Windows is based on the MS-DOS operating system, MS-DOS can be accessed from the Windows operating system. Most software in use today is designed for the Windows operating system.

The Macintosh operating system is used exclusively on Macintosh computers manufactured by Apple Computer. It was the first operating system to use a graphical user interface and "point and click" technology. For many years, it was the most user-friendly operating system available. The Windows operating system is very similar to the Macintosh operating system.

The Unix operating system was created for computer programmers developing software. It is not as easy to use as Windows and is generally used by very large computers and servers. Unix is not used in most law offices.

A new operating system, Linux, emerged in the late 1990s and is gaining prominence in the world of operating systems. Linux, distributed by Red Hat Software, was developed between 1991 and 1994 by Linus Torvalds, a student at the University of Helsinki. It is a variant of the Unix operating system and is used by some businesses as an alternative to the Windows operating system. It has been adopted primarily as a server platform.

Software applications are either custom or off-the-shelf. A custom software application is created exclusively for a law firm. It is created by computer programmers according to the parameters set by the firm's management. Employees using custom software are trained on its use by the software programmers. Off-the-shelf applications are created by software companies who market and distribute the software to the public. Training manuals are included with the software.

integrated software
A program that combines many different software applications into one program to make it easier to use.

Some software manufacturers have developed **integrated software** applications. Integrated software combines many software applications into one program. An advantage of an integrated system is that the commands in the software are uniform, making the program easy to use. A disadvantage to integrated systems is that the individual features are generally less powerful than an individual application.

Manufacturers also "bundle" software together in one package, called office suites. Office suites combine several separate software applications, such as word processing, spreadsheet, database, and presentation programs, into one package. The applications have similar interfaces that interact with one another, making them easily integrated. This reduces training time and makes the various features of the software easier to use. It is also less expensive than purchasing each application individually. A popular office suite manufactured by Microsoft, known as Office Professional 2007, consists of Microsoft Word (word processing), Excel (spreadsheet), Access (database), PowerPoint (presentation), Outlook (personal information manager), Accounting Express (accounting), and Publisher (desktop publishing). Office suites can also be purchased with just two or three of the applications rather than all the ones listed here.

Most law firms use off-the-shelf computer applications and office suites. There are standard software applications used in a law office. The most common applications are word processing, spreadsheet, database, time and billing, calendar and docket control, document management, and case/practice management systems.

Word Processing

Word processing software has been a standard application used in law firms since the 1960s. In the 1960s and 1970s, law firms had separate word processing departments that prepared only long, complicated documents, such as contracts and leases. In the 1980s, word processing programs became easier, eliminating the need for a separate department. Word processing tasks were given to clerical staff, mainly to secretaries. In the 1990s, all legal support staff were responsible for some word processing, and in the new millennium, everyone in the firm uses word processing in one way or another.

The two most popular word processing systems used in law offices today are Corel's WordPerfect and Microsoft's Word. Until the late 1990s, WordPerfect was the standard word processor for law firms, with 97 percent of small firms and 84 percent of large firms using it. Word was the standard for corporate legal departments and other businesses. Since that time, however, Microsoft Word has become the preferred word processing software. According to the 2007 *Legal Assistant Today* Technology Survey, 84.7 percent of respondents use Microsoft Word.

Software has been developed that adds features to the word processing program. This type of software is called **add-on** (or **plug-in**) software. An example of a popular add-on is HotDocs by Capsoft Development Corporation. HotDocs software consists of legal documents that are already prepared. The program uses the word processor's merge capabilities to create templates with customized prompt screens. This add-on allows routine documents to be produced by the word processor quickly and easily.

add-ons (plug-ins)
A software application that can be purchased to enhance the features of another software application.

Spreadsheets

A spreadsheet application, such as Microsoft Excel, is used to crunch numbers. It is used in cases in which long, complicated accountings are prepared, such as a probate case. A typical spreadsheet application can also be used to prepare charts, graphs, and reports on the basis of the data. A spreadsheet program has numerous other uses.

Database

A database application, such as Microsoft Access, is a powerful application used by law firms and other businesses to manage information. Law firms use a database for its client list, to log marketing efforts, and to manage its brief bank. Once the information is input into a database, it can be managed in a number of ways. A firm can search a client database to check for conflicts, search a brief bank to find a document, and sort the information into various groups. There are a number of other uses for a database.

Time and Billing

Time and billing software is used by all the timekeepers in a firm. It prepares timekeeping reports and numerous other management reports. The software contains a billing system so that client invoices can be automatically generated. It is a very powerful program and is essential to every law office. More specific aspects of the software are discussed in Chapters 7 and 8.

Of Interest . . .

TIME AND BILLING SOFTWARE

The following list includes the most popular time and billing software. The percentage number indicates the percentage of firms who use the software and responded to the *Legal Assistant Today* 2007 Technology Survey.

Carpe Diem—4.8 percent

Juris—6.6 percent

None—33.5 percent

PCLaw—4.8 percent

ProLaw—2.6 percent

QuickBooks—11.8 percent

TABS III—8.8 percent

Timeslips—13.2 percent

Calendar and Docket Control

Calendar software, also known as docket control software, is used to control calendars, monitor deadlines, and track essential law firm tasks. There are many calendaring software packages, each with different features. The software controls deadlines and calendar events critical to the effective management of a case. Deadlines found in court rules and civil procedure laws are programmed into the software and are automatically applied to a client's case. For example, 30 days after a complaint is served, an answer is due. The program automatically calculates the due date and enters it into the program. The program warns the legal team of the approaching deadline so that the answer can be prepared before the due date.

This automatic calendaring feature has many benefits. It guards against missed deadlines, reduces employee time to enter due dates, and is updatable if the rules are changed. The program prints various types of case management reports. It allows users to program dates that are far in the future, such as statutes of limitations. If an event is scheduled that conflicts with an earlier entry, the program will alert the user of a conflict. It also has other features, such as document assembly, filing, and conflicts-of-interest checking. Docket control software is more specifically described in Chapter 12.

Of Interest . . .

CALENDAR AND DOCKET
CONTROL SOFTWARE

The following list includes the most popular calendar and docket control software. The percentage number indicates the percentage of firms who use the software and responded to the *Legal Assistant Today* 2007 Technology Survey.

Abacus Law—5.3 percent

Amicus Attorney—5.3 percent

CaseTrack—3.3 percent

Elite Case Manager—2.4 percent

Needles—1.4 percent

None—57.4 percent

Practice Manager—1.4 percent

ProLaw—2.4 percent

Time Matters—6.2 percent

Document Management

Document management applications are used to manage complex litigation cases. This type of application keeps all necessary documents and information accessible for review, summarization, and organization, allowing the legal team to maintain control of various aspects of the case. It also allows information to be retrieved in many different ways that aid the lawyer in trial preparation and presentation. Document management systems follow an attorney into the courtroom where he or she can access all the information needed in seconds.

Complex litigation cases often involve thousands and sometimes millions of documents. These documents must be reviewed and organized in a manner that allows the legal team almost immediate access to them. By inputting each document into a litigation support database, the information can be screened, sorted, and located quickly.

There are four types of document management software: abstract, full-text retrieval, document imaging, and a combination thereof. A document abstract system prepares an abstract, or summary, of a document's contents. A full-text retrieval contains the entire document instead of a summary. Document imaging allows documents to be electronically **scanned** into the computer. A combination has at least two and perhaps all three features.

scanned
Entering text or graphics into a computer by electronically changing the characters into a computer-readable format.

Of Interest . . .

DOCUMENT MANAGEMENT SOFTWARE

The following list includes the most popular document management software. The percentage number indicates the percentage of firms who use the software and responded to the *Legal Assistant Today* 2007 Technology Survey.

Case Map—10.2 percent

Concordance—5.5 percent

Doculex—2.1 percent

DTSearch—.8 percent

E-Transcript Binder—3.8 percent

Live Note—3.8 percent

None—58.1 percent

Sanction—4.7 percent

Summation Blaze—16.1 percent

TimeMap—4.7 percent

Trial Director—4.2 percent

Case/Practice Management

Case/practice management applications, also known as legal specific software, are developed for use in specific areas of law. There are hundreds of software applications that aid a legal team in the practice of various areas of law. There is software that prepares a person's will or trust, prepares bankruptcy documents, manages collection cases, prepares family law documents, and prepares compliance forms.

For example, a bankruptcy software package guides the user in inserting all applicable information and will prepare the bankruptcy petition, schedules, and other required documents from the data. The forms are then printed on a laser printer or prepared for electronic filing. The software keeps all of the information about a case in one place.

THE INTERNET

The Internet is a tremendous tool for individuals and organizations. Through the Internet, we have access to vast amounts of information at any time of the day or night through our computers. The Internet has been responsible for the development of new technologies that have revolutionized the way we do business. Internet access is an essential tool for law firms.

History of the Internet

In 1958, President Dwight Eisenhower created the Advanced Research Projects Agency (ARPA—later Defense was added to the name, and it became DARPA) to safeguard the country's communications network in case of a nuclear attack. ARPA, headed by J. C. R.

Licklider, hired Lawrence Roberts to design and head the project. ARPA funded many U.S. university research labs and had a close relationship with leading industry labs, including Bolt Beranek and Newman, Computer Corporation of America, Rand, SRI, and Systems Development Corporation.

In 1969, the first **network,** ARPANET, was operational. It linked the scientific and research communities with U.S. defense contractors. The network could accommodate many different types of computers, and it grew quickly. It was designed to function even if one of its major components was destroyed or rendered inoperable.

In 1983, ARPANET split into two networks: ARPANET and MILNET. The Department of Defense turned ARPANET over to the National Science Foundation's Office of Advanced Scientific Computing. In 1985, the network became NSFNET, which was a "backbone" to which other networks were connected. Access to NSFNET was provided free to any U.S. research and educational institution for noncommercial purposes. It was used primarily by scientists, academics, and nonprofit organizations. At this time, regional networks were created to bring electronic traffic from individual institutions to the NSF backbone service. As the net grew, new software applications were created to make access easier. This was the beginning of the Internet, a worldwide cooperative network of networks. For more information regarding the history of the Internet, go to <http://www.livinginternet.com>.

Originally, the National Science Foundation (NSF) prohibited commercial use of NSFNET, but they lifted the restriction in 1991. Also in 1991, the National Research and Education Network (NREN) was approved by Congress. The NREN was a $2 billion project to upgrade the NSFNET backbone. It promised to increase the speed of data transfer on the Internet so that the entire *Encyclopaedia Britannica* could be transmitted electronically in one second.

No one "owns" the Internet. The networks that use the Internet are owned and maintained by their owners, and some are publicly traded companies, such as America Online, Inc.

To access the Internet, one must have **browser** software and an **Internet Service Provider (ISP).** ISPs maintain large computers known as **servers.** The ISP's server is connected either to larger regional networks or directly to the backbone sites that direct traffic on the Internet. An ISP is essentially a retailer of access to high-speed telephone or cable lines. They get their access from telephone and cable companies and charge a fee for their service.

network
Two or more computers connected to each other so they can share resources.

browser
A software program that allows viewing and interaction with various kinds of resources available on the Internet.

Internet Service Provider (ISP)
A private company that provides access to the Internet for a fee.

server
A large computer that contains a large amount of information and directs customers' inquiries to the Internet.

Of Interest . . .

THE INTERNET IN CHINA

The Chinese can access the Internet through cybercafes, which must be licensed by the government. Less than 25 percent of China's 200,000 cybercafes are licensed. Those that are licensed are expected to spy on customers and report anyone who accesses banned sites. China has the most sophisticated filtering system in the world. In order for cybercafes to remain open, they must install the filtering system on their computers, blocking about 500,000 banned sites. The banned sites contain content relating to Taiwanese independents, the Tiananmen Square incident, the Dalai Lama, and other political topics. Pornographic and religious sites are also banned.

In 2002, 25 people were killed when a pair of teens torched a Beijing cybercafe that had refused them entry. Consequently, Chinese authorities declared war on approximately 150,000 unlicensed cybercafes, comparing them to the opium dens where young men slowly destroyed themselves a century ago. In retaliation, a Declaration of Internet Users' Rights was signed and published by 18 dissidents calling for complete freedom of the Internet. They were jailed for their trouble. In June 2007, the number of Internet users in China was 162,000,000, and China has the largest number of Internet users in the world.

Protocols

A **protocol** is a set of rules that ensures that different network software products can work together. Protocols dictate how the various systems on the Internet operate. The very existence of the Internet depends on people voluntarily agreeing to configure their software to the protocol standard. It is the language computers use to communicate with each other.

Protocol standards are set by the Internet Engineering Task Force (IETF), a large international community of network designers, operators, vendors, and researchers concerned with the smooth operation of the Internet. Some Internet protocols include Internet Protocol (IP), which contains addressing information that enables packets to be routed; **File Transfer Protocol (FTP),** which allows entire files to be transferred between computers; and **Telnet,** a protocol that allows a computer to connect with a remote computer as if it were local.

Today, there are tens of thousands of networks from around the world connected to the Internet. America Online was among the first commercial networks. The Internet's growth is phenomenal. In 1998, the Internet grew at a staggering rate of 20 percent a month. In December 1995, there were 16 million Internet users. In September 2007, there were 1,245 million Internet users. Asia has the most Internet users.

The following five factors are attributed to the Internet's sudden growth and prominence:

1. Widespread use of personal computers and graphical user interfaces, such as the Windows operating system
2. Elimination of commercial use prohibitions
3. The creation of software applications specifically for use on the Internet
4. The existence of a large body of electronically stored data
5. Technological advances in computer hardware, such as modems and monitors

Domain Names

A **domain name** is a unique name that identifies an organization on the Internet. Domain names were created in 1986 by the NSF, AT&T, and Network Solutions, Inc. (NSI) through the InterNIC project. In 1993, the NSF turned over the registration and management of domain names to Network Solutions, Inc. In 2002, the government developed a private U.S. corporation to manage the domain name system. Known as the Internet Corporation for Assigned Names and Numbers (ICANN), it is comprised of an international group of Internet users. ICANN is responsible for creating new type identifiers, also known as top-level domains, and arbitrating domain name disputes.

Domain names consist of the organization's name (or specific designation) and a suffix that describes the type of organization, known as a **type identifier.** The type identifier places organizations on the Internet in ten categories, as shown in Exhibit 10–1. Type identifiers are used only for American organizations. Organizations outside of the United States have a country code to identify the country in which the organization is located, examples of which are illustrated in Exhibit 10–1.

The "first-come, first-served" system of registration of domain names has resulted in a host of disputes, ranging from traditional trademark infringement and dilution disputes to battles with a new breed of infringer—the **cybersquatter.** A cybersquatter registers domain names in an attempt to extort money from the trademark holder for transfer of the domain name. As NSI implemented its domain name policy, clever cybersquatters learned to add or change a letter in a registered trademark to circumvent the NSI dispute resolution policy, forcing a trademark holder to go to court to secure rights to the disputed domain name. This practice is known as **typosquatting.** Some typosquatters relied on a typo of a recognized name to direct people to their websites, which often contained numerous pop-up ads. Others registered the erroneous domain name to sell it to the trademark holder. Many

protocol
The set of rules that two computers use to communicate with each other.

File Transfer Protocol (FTP)
A protocol that allows files to be transferred between computers.

Telnet
A protocol that allows a computer to connect with a remote computer.

domain name
A unique name that identifies an Internet site.

type identifier
A suffix attached to a domain name that identifies the type of organization.

cybersquatter
A person who registers a trademarked domain name to extort money from the trademark holder.

typosquatter
Changing a letter in a trademark to circumvent the dispute resolution policy.

A suffix at the end of a domain name identifies the type of organization:

.com—commercial	.gov—government institution
.edu—educational institution	.biz—businesses
.org—nonprofit organizations	.info—unrestricted use
.mil—military organization	.name—individual registration
.net—network provider	.pro—professionals such as accountants, lawyers, and doctors

An additional extension identifies the country where the domain is located:

.au—Australia
.dk—Denmark
.ge—Germany
.uk—United Kingdom

EXHIBIT 10–1   Example of Domain Suffix and Country Codes

trademark holders found it easier to pay a few thousand dollars in exchange for the domain name than resort to expensive litigation.

To combat cybersquatters, the U.S. Congress enacted the Anti-cybersquatting Consumer Protection Act in 1999. The Anti-cybersquatting Consumer Protection Act amends Section 43 of the Trademark act to prohibit bad-faith registration of a domain name that is a registered trademark. The act provides for property-like actions where the domain name registrant cannot be located and prohibits registration of a domain name consisting of a living person's name with the specific intent to profit from that name. The act also extends to typosquatting. With the passage of this act, and an arbitration program offered by ICANN, cybersquatters and typosquatters have decreased substantially in the last decade.

Of Interest . . .

INTERNET FACTS

- The number of hosts to the Internet reached the one million mark in 1992.
- The phrase "surfing the Internet" was coined by Jean Armour Polly in 1992.
- NSFNET discontinued its function as the backbone of the Internet in 1995. It is now used solely for scientific research. The U.S. backbone now consists of interconnected network providers.
- Tim Berners-Lee coined the phrase "World Wide Web" in 1990.
- The first computer mouse was introduced in 1968 by Douglas Engelbart at the Fall Joint Computer Expo in San Francisco.
- Nam June Paik coined the phrase "information superhighway" in the early 1990s.
- Internet publications in New Zealand can be censored and seized.
- In 1997, the Chinese government arrested Lin Hai for inciting to overthrow state power because she provided a U.S. Internet magazine with 30,000 e-mail addresses.
- In 1997, domain names reached 2 million.

Of Interest . . . (Cont.)

- The first international connection to ARPANET was the University College of London and Royal Radar Establishment (Norway) in 1973.
- The first commercial presence on the Internet was The World (<http://www.world.std.com>) in 1991.
- The White House came online in 1993 (<http://www.whitehouse.gov>).
- The domain name "business.com" sold for $150,000.
- France sponsors an annual festival in recognition of the Internet: La Fete de l'Internet.

The World Wide Web

The World Wide Web (WWW, or Web) is not the Internet. It is only one of the protocols that operate via the Internet. It was developed by Tim Berners-Lee in 1990 at the European Laboratory for Particle Physics (CERN) in Switzerland. It is managed by the World Wide Web Consortium (W3C), also known as the World Wide Web Initiative (www.w3c.org). The W3C is run by the Massachusetts Institute of Technology (MIT), Keio University in Japan, and the European Research Consortium for Informatics and Mathematics, headquartered in France. The consortium has offices thoughout the world. It is funded by membership dues from a number of organizational members. The consortium's purpose is to promote the Web by developing specification and reference software that will be freely available to everyone.

The protocol used by the Web is called **Hypertext Transfer Protocol (HTTP).** The Web is actually the name given to all documents written in a specific software language known as **Hypertext Markup Language (HTML).** It allows documents to be downloaded via HTTP. In order for a computer to read the HTML language, it needs browser software.

Plug-in software adds features to a browser and allows a person to view documents, hear sound, and view video images on the Web. Plug-in software is often **shareware** or **freeware,** or software that is free to the user. Examples of plug-in software are Adobe Acrobat Viewer and Real Player for sound and video.

The Web delivers its information by **hyperlinks** to other pages or other areas on the Web. These hyperlinks enable readers to navigate through the Web. A collection of the linked pages, grouped together in an orderly manner, becomes a website.

Most websites contain levels. The number of levels in a website varies. Some contain as few as two levels, and some contain many levels. The levels are accessed through the first page of a website, known as the **home page.**

The Web has changed the way we do business and has enhanced our personal lives. We can do practically anything on the Web. We can bank, shop, gamble, play games, obtain a loan, and participate in an auction, and some of you may be taking this class via the Web. It offers numerous benefits to us, and new uses for the Web are being created.

The legal profession uses the Web for a number of functions. One is to publicize cases and manage the media in high-profile cases. For example, in the Unabomber case (*U.S. v. Theodore Kaczynski,* 154 F.3d 930.), the court clerk was inundated with requests for information by the media. He developed a section of the court's website that was devoted entirely to that case where he published dockets, pretrial depositions, trial transcripts, and evidence. The media consulted the website instead of the clerk, making the clerk's life a lot easier.

The September 11 tragedy in New York City caused law firms in the World Trade Center to lose valuable, essential data from their computer systems. This has caused attorneys

Hypertext Transfer Protocol (HTTP)
The protocol used by the World Wide Web.

Hypertext Markup Language (HTML)
A software language used by documents posted on the World Wide Web.

shareware
Software that is distributed without initial cost. If the user likes the software, a nominal payment is expected.

freeware
Free software.

hyperlinks
A connection to another page or site that allows a person to navigate the Web.

home page
The starting point of a Web presentation that contains a table of contents for the information that is available at the website, offering direct links to the different parts of the site.

to look to the Web to store their computer backup information. In the event of a disaster, the firm's information will be safe.

Another function of the Web is called e-bidding. While most people are familiar with online auctions such as eBay®, companies are using the Web to solicit bids for attorney services. Attorneys respond to the request and set a flat fee for their services. Attorneys with the lowest fee normally win the contract.

Web conferencing is another use of the Web. Companies offer conferencing websites that allow conference participants to log in to a conferencing website instead of traveling to a face-to-face meeting. Law firms also use this service for Web seminars for clients, known as webinars. Websites of conferencing companies are found in the Cybersites section. A law-related website is illustrated in Exhibit 10–2.

Locating Information on the Web

Before information on a website can be accessed, it must first be located. The Web contains millions of websites with hundreds of millions of pages of information. Finding the exact site can be tricky.

There are three basic ways to locate specific information on the Web: Uniform Resource Locator (URL), keyword search, and topical index.

Uniform Resource Locator (URL)
An address of a website that directs a person to the information.

UNIFORM RESOURCE LOCATOR Each website is given an address known as a **Uniform Resource Locator (URL).** A typical URL has four main elements:

1. Protocol
2. Address of server where the data are located
3. Domain name
4. Type identifier

A URL for the Web displays each element of the address as follows: http:// (protocol), www (server), .domainname (domain name), .com (type identifier) (e.g., <http://www.domainname.com>). To find the U.S. House of Representatives, you must first know its URL address. Many URLs can be found in periodicals and advertising materials. URL addresses are designed so that one can logically figure them out. The URL for the U.S. House of Representatives is <http://www.house.gov>. The "http" is the protocol, the "www" means World Wide Web, "house" is the domain name, and "gov" is the type identifier, which means that it is a government site (see Exhibit 10–1).

Almost all companies and corporations have websites ending with ".com," meaning that they are commercial sites. Most companies have secured a domain name that matches or closely resembles their name. To find a commercial website, enter its domain name after the protocol and "www," as follows: <http://www.microsoft.com>. Your school can be located on the Web in the same manner, only ending with ".edu" as the type identifier (e.g., <http://www.yourschool.edu>). To locate a website outside the United States, substitute the type identifier with the country code, as follows: <http://www.louvre.fr>. With these basics, it is not difficult to locate most of the major websites.

pathname
The URL address showing the path of where a certain document may be found on a website.

Most websites consist of many sections, or pages, and it is possible to go directly to the page that contains the information desired. Each page has its own URL indicating the name of the directory in which the document is stored. This is known as the **pathname.** Subsequent pages in a URL are separated by a forward slash, as follows: protocol://server.domainname/pathname/name of document (e.g., <http://www.microsoft.com/products/msword>).

Certain rules apply to all URLs. There are no spaces in a URL. Each word of a domain name is run together (although some words in a domain name may be connected by a dash or underscore). A forward slash (/) is always used instead of backward slash (\). Domain names are not capitalized but are entered in all lowercase letters.

FindLaw
en Español

Find a lawyer. Find answers.

Legal Professionals
click here ▸▸

Find a Lawyer

Search for a Local Lawyer

Legal Issue: (e.g., Bankruptcy)

Location: (e.g., Palo Alto, CA or 94306)

Guide Me
Name Search
Advanced Search

Have a Lawyer Contact You

Submit your legal issue and an attorney will contact you.

Step 1:  Choose Your Legal Issue ▾
Step 2: Tell us about your case
Step 3: Choose the attorney that's right for you

Get Help Now

FindLaw offers two services to find a lawyer for your legal issue.

Don't know where to start?

Get help now!

GREENBERG & STONE, P.A.
ATTORNEYS AT LAW • 305-595-2400

LOOKING FOR A LAWYER? OUR LAW FIRM HELPS INDIVIDUALS IN THEIR TIME OF NEED. LET US ASSIST YOU WITH YOUR CASE TODAY.

Browse Legal Information

View All Topics   Search FindLaw

 Accidents & Injuries
Personal Injury, Medical Malpractice, More...

 Dangerous Products
Asbestos, Benzene, Dangerous Drugs, More...

Immigration
Citizenship, Green Cards, Visas, More...

 Bankruptcy & Debt
New Bankruptcy Law, Debt Relief, More...

 Divorce & Family Law
Adoption, Child Custody, Child Support, Divorce

Real Estate
For Homeowners, Tenants, Landlords, Mold, More...

 Car Accidents
Truck Accidents, Motorcycle Accidents, More...

 DUI / DWI
State DUI Laws, DUI Resources, More...

Small Business
Incorporation, Forms & Contracts, Employment, More...

 Civil Rights
Employment, Housing, Laws, More...

 Employee Rights
Losing a Job, Wages, Harassment, More...

Traffic Violations
Tickets A to Z, State Traffic Law, DMVs, More...

 Criminal Law
Crimes A to Z, Your Rights, More...

 Estate Planning
Wills, Trusts, Living Wills, Probate, More...

? **Don't see what you're looking for?**
More Topics...

Stay Informed

Forms, Laws & More

Legal News

Economic Stimulus Act of 2008

Lenders Freeze Foreclosures

Feb. is Black History Month

Neb. Ct. Bans Electric Chair

Tainted Pet Food Indictments

New Border ID Rules in Effect

Today in Legal History

February 14, 1920 - League of Women Voters Formed

More Legal News | Commentary | Blog

Forms & Contracts

Business Forms, Living Wills, More...

State Laws

Business, Child Custody, Criminal, Divorce, DUI, Property, More...

Free Full-Text Books

Working Woman's Legal Guide, Social Security Handbook, More...

Guide to Hiring a Lawyer

Legal Dictionary

Feb. Spotlight: Marriage

2007 Webby
Award Winner

Time.com: 50 Coolest Websites 2005

Exhibit 10–2   Example of Law-Related Website

KEYWORD SEARCH   Each browser has a search feature that allows a keyword search. Enter the keyword of the desired site or information, and the browser will retrieve the websites that contain information about the words inserted. At times, there may be thousands of websites that contain the keywords, and it may take some time to review all of them before you find the one you want. For example, say you want information about the U.S. House of Representatives. In the keyword search area of the browser, you enter "House of Representatives." The browser will retrieve all websites that contain the words "House" and "Representatives," including state houses of representatives. You will find the U.S. House of Representatives after reviewing the choices available. Clicking on the appropriate site will take you there.

Boolean search
A method of defining search criteria.

Proximity searching, or **Boolean search,** creates sets of words so that a search engine can narrow the search. It gives a search engine parameters within which to conduct the search, narrowing the outcome of a search. Boolean searches are constructed using the words *and, or,* and *not* with your keywords. Connectors are also used, such as "w/5" to indicate "within five words" or "adj15" to indicate that the search words must be adjacent within 15 words. An example of this concept is shown in Exhibit 10–3.

Searching for the URL of the House of Representatives in a search engine will return thousands of possible URLs because it will return all the sites that contain the word *house* and all the sites that contain the word *representative*, as follows:

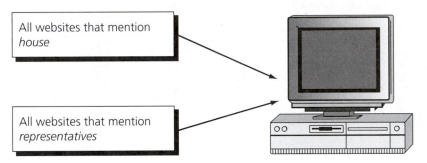

By inserting the word *AND* between House and Representatives, it instructs the computer to locate only those sites that contain both words, as follows:

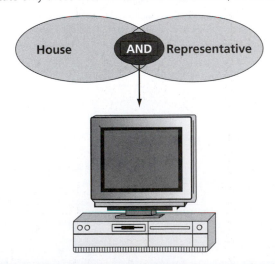

EXHIBIT 10–3   Example of Boolean Search

Of Interest . . .

WHY IS IT CALLED "BOOLEAN?"

The term "Boolean" is named after George Boole (1815–1864), an English mathematician who studied theories of logic. His theories of mathematical set creation formed the basis of modern computerized text searching.

TOPICAL INDEX   Various Internet indexing companies exist that have categorized Internet sites into groupings of related fields, such as government, law, judiciary, and so on. There are many indexing companies, which are also known as **search engines,** some of which are listed in Exhibit 10–4.

Search engines are a popular method for searching the Web. However, no search engine works exactly like another. For example, Google indexes legal topics under *Society* while Yahoo! categorizes them with *Government*. No search engine will give a researcher comprehensive results. Websites can be marked by a browser. This activity is known as **bookmarking.** When you bookmark a site, the URL is inserted in the Bookmarks section of the browser. To return to the website, access the list of bookmarked sites and choose the desired site. The browser will take you directly to the site.

search engine
An independent company that has indexed Internet sites and categorized them so that they can be found easily.

bookmarking
A part of browser software that marks a website so that its URL is accessible without searching for it.

Reliability of Information on Websites

Websites are created by commercial companies, organizations, associations, universities, the government, and individuals. You can find anything you want on the Web, but not all information is reliable. Verifying the accuracy of data on the Web is a problem. Commercial websites of reputable companies warrant their accuracy, as do those created by law librarians and archivists, but not all entities offer such warranties.

Alta Vista—<http://www.altavista.com>
Excite—<http://www.excite.com>
Go.com—<http://www.go.com>
Google—<http://www.google.com>
Google, Advanced—<http://www.google.com/advanced_search>
HotBot—<http://www.hotbot.com>
Lycos—<http://www.lycos.com>
MSN Search—<http://www.search.msn.com>
Northern Light—<http://www.northernlight.com>
WebCrawler—<http://www.webcrawler.com>
Yahoo—<http://www.yahoo.com>

Specialty Search Engines

Google U.S. Government—<http://www.google.com/unclesam>
Pandia Newsfinder—<http://www.pandia.com/news>
SearchEdu.com—<http://www.searchedu.com>
Search Gov—<http://www.searchgov.com>
SearchMil.com—<http://www.searchmil.com>

EXHIBIT 10–4   Example List of Search Engines

Anyone can post information on the Web regardless of age, background, and mental health. Almost all the websites created by the government and its agencies are reliable. Law school and university websites are also generally reliable. Some websites, especially those containing information about single subjects, are created by individuals who may lack the knowledge and background necessary to rely on their information. In addition, they may lack the resources necessary to update and maintain the website adequately, and so the information may be wrong, incomplete, or outdated.

There are certain things to look for when investigating the legitimacy of a website:

- Check to see whether the author of the website is identified.
- Determine the purpose of the website. Is it for the reader's benefit or the author's benefit?
- Do not judge a website by its home page. Home pages can look professional but may promote quack remedies or illegal activities.
- Look for the date of the last update. If one is not available, the site may be outdated.
- Look at the site's links. If some have disappeared, it is a clue that the site is outdated.
- Verify the information elsewhere. Some experts recommend verifying information by two other sources.
- Consult website review guides, some of which are listed in the Cybersites section.

Of Interest . . .

WHAT IS SPAM?

The term *spam* refers to promotional material sent by e-mail to thousands, perhaps millions, of people over the Internet. The term is not taken from a lunch meat product. It comes from a *Monty Python's Flying Circus* skit titled "The King of Spam" by S. Garfunkel. One of the most famous examples of spamming occurred in 1994 when an immigration lawyer advertised his services to members of about 5,000 listservs without regard for the subject of the listserv. He received over 30,000 replies, mostly flames that caused his ISP's server to crash. The ISP revoked his access rights, and he received a 1-year suspension from the Arizona Supreme Court.

In November 2007, the University of California at Irvine reported that it rejected 108,117,179 spam messages in one month. It accepted 8,078,030 legitimate messages. This works out to 3,603,905 spam messages per day, and 2,502 spam messages per minute.

Examples of spam follow:

- Unsolicited commercial messages
- Messages from individuals where the sender has not participated in the topical discussions of the list and the message is a commercial advertisement
- Messages that do not offer direct content to the topic being discussed
- Messages that have nothing in common with the topic of the list
- Messages like any of the above that are cross-posted to multiple mailing lists

INTRANETS AND EXTRANETS

Internet technology has been the foundation of new systems and software products, among them intranet and extranet programs. This technology, known as web-based technology, uses the www protocol, which is easy to use and understand. Law firms have taken advantage of this technology to create intranets and extranets.

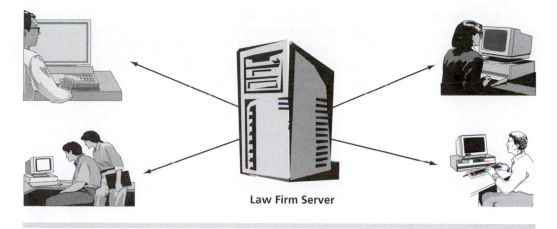

EXHIBIT 10–5   Example of Law Firm Intranet

Intranets

An **intranet** is a law firm's internal information distribution system that is based on Web technology. It differs from the Web because it is private and is accessible only by designated individuals, normally firm employees. It provides employees of a firm with the ability to access a variety of resources through one source.

Each person's computer is connected to the firm's server that stores the information. In order to accommodate the various types of information stored on an intranet, an intranet search engine is used. An intranet also uses specialized software, known as **groupware,** or software created specifically for use by groups. An index page directs the user to the information desired. The information is accessible from each person's individual workstation, as shown in Exhibit 10–5. Employees use their Internet browser software to access the information. The user just clicks on the desired subject matter. All of the information is in one place, is easy to find, and can be searched easily.

Intranets are custom made and designed according to a firm's specifications by professional intranet designers or in-house computer specialists. They generally have four or five levels that branch out from the top down:

Level 1: The home page

Level 2: Firm departments

Level 3: Links within a department

Level 4: Documents or databases to retrieve information

Level 5: Forms, documents, or pages that contain the desired material.

Examples of the types of uses for an intranet follow:

- *Law firm calendar.* Law firm employees have their calendars posted to the intranet so that they are accessible to the entire firm. This facilitates scheduling events and locating an employee. Case management software is accessed from this area.

- *Continuing legal education.* Notices of upcoming educational seminars and workshops are posted or distributed to specific practice groups. Law firm employees can also access legal courses that are offered through the Internet, and can take the course online at their convenience.

- *Client information.* Law firm records pertaining to clients including client lists, matter lists, contact information, billing information, outstanding invoices, and the status of the client's case, can be accessed. Client information, which is essential for conflict-of-interest checks, is displayed immediately without searching through files and records.

intranet
A private collection of information that is viewed by Internet Web browser software and is accessible only to authorized members of a private network; a private Internet site.

groupware
Software created for and used by an intranet or extranet.

- *Training.* Keeping employees informed about new features of a firm's software is a constant challenge for a law firm's management. Software manuals are accessed through an intranet, as is additional training on firm-specific systems. An employee can learn and be trained directly from the intranet according to the employee's schedule, and training is available immediately as the need arises.
- *Discussion groups.* The firm can create discussion groups for the entire firm, firm management, individual practice areas, or case-specific groups. This feature reduces in-person meetings and keeps all interested persons abreast of the status of a case or changes in specific practice areas.
- *Internal directory.* A directory of all firm employees is accessed from the intranet. The directory may contain telephone, address, home phone, cell phone, and department information. An employee can be located quickly if needed.
- *Brief bank.* A **brief bank** consists of form documents, such as letters, agreements, pleadings, and other documents that are used frequently. It also consists of legal research memoranda and briefs. These documents are used as a **template** to prepare new documents. Documents are prepared quickly without having to prepare them from scratch, saving the firm time and the client money.
- *Library resources.* Research materials, including WESTLAW and Lexis-Nexis materials, are accessed from the intranet. Other research resources, such as legal research search engines or law-related websites, are also accessed from this location.
- *Management and firm policies.* Management memoranda are distributed through the intranet, informing employees of new policies, firm announcements, employee benefits, and other firm news. The firm's employee manual is also posted. Vacation planning forms or other management forms are readily available when needed and can be downloaded and printed from the intranet. If the firm is recruiting new employees, a prospective employee can download an employment application from the firm's website and submit it via e-mail.
- *Practice area information and forms.* Whenever there is a change in the law, the employees in the applicable practice area can be immediately informed. If there is a change in a judicial form, the form is posted so that it is immediately available to anyone needing the form. This ensures that the firm has updated information at all times.
- *Time and billing.* A user's timesheets are completed through the intranet and submitted to management from the intranet. Preliminary bills are also reviewed from the responsible attorney's workstation. The firm's time and billing software is accessed in this area.
- *Access to courts.* Courts that accept electronic filing are accessed through the intranet. Documents are filed electronically through an individual workstation. Updated court information, such as calendars, dockets, and rules, are just a click away.
- *Marketing.* The intranet contains all the firm's marketing brochures and mailings, press releases, and advertisements. These materials can be incorporated into word processing documents.

Intranets require constant maintenance and updating. A firm's investment to produce, install, and maintain an intranet will come back to the firm quickly after implementation. A study conducted by International Data Corporation of Framingham, Massachusetts, concluded that a firm will realize a return of 1,000 percent on its investment in an intranet.

Extranets

An **extranet** is a Web-based interface to a private network. It is a separate area of an intranet that is intended for private use by its members and selected outside entities. Larger than an intranet, extranets operate on the same Web-based platform.

brief bank
A collection of documents that are used as templates to prepare new documents.

template
A form document used as a guide to prepare new documents.

extranet
A Web-based interface to a private network; used to communicate directly with clients.

An extranet is a private network that is accessible by a number of organizations, including selected firm employees, clients, outside counsel, and others who work together. An extranet offers the same benefits as an intranet: efficiency, improved quality of work, and enhancement of communication among people working together. An extranet also offers such features as access to calendars, scheduling, collaborative document drafting and editing, and distribution of messages to specific groups.

The difference between an intranet and an extranet is that an extranet is directed to different people and has different uses. Among the uses are direct client access and multijurisdictional litigation management.

DIRECT CLIENT ACCESS   A law firm creates an extranet connection to its clients, especially large, corporate clients. Some firms may have more than one extranet, connecting multiple clients. Some firms have one extranet with many areas for various clients. This connection is a separate system developed exclusively for the client and the client's cases. A firm provides the client with information regarding the client's cases to which the client has constant access. The client can also view its financial account with the firm as well as other information as needed. A firm can transmit documents, edit documents simultaneously, communicate via e-mail, and directly collaborate on a case. This type of extranet is known as a firm-centered extranet and is shown in Exhibit 10–6.

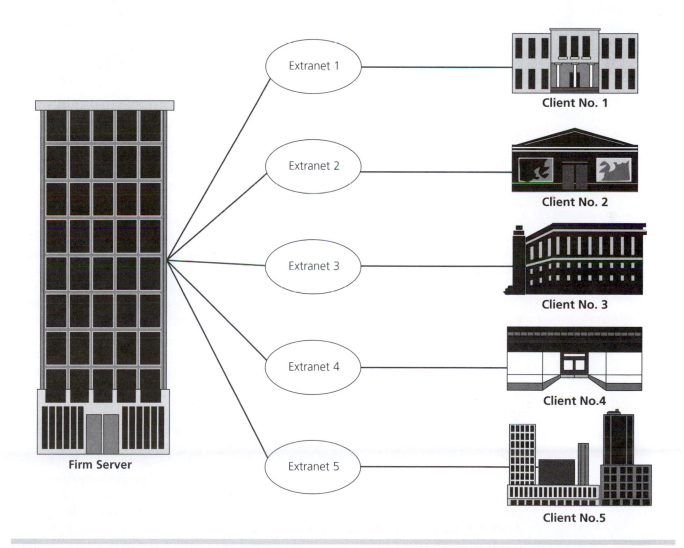

EXHIBIT 10–6   Example of Firm-Centered Extranet

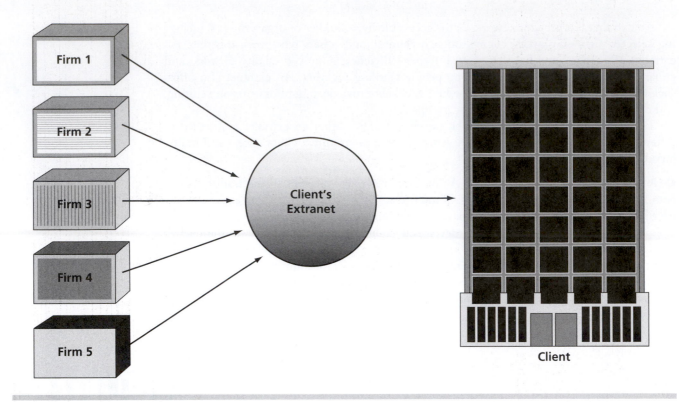

EXHIBIT 10–7   Example of Client-Centered Extranet

Clients also provide law firms with an extranet. Large corporations that use many law firms to handle their legal work provide their many outside counsels with an extranet to facilitate communication. This is especially helpful when preparing a case and handling the corporation's legal affairs. Responding to discovery requests often requires answers to technical questions that only the client can provide. Before extranets, the firm would request the information from the client, who would search through the records, prepare the information, and send it back to the firm. This was done several times for several cases. Sometimes the responses were complete, and other times they were not, resulting in delay. Providing this information on an extranet allows many different firms immediate access to the information from their individual computers. This saves both the client and the firm time and money. An example of this type of extranet is shown in Exhibit 10–7.

Another advantage of an extranet is communicating with clients from another part of the world. Trying to communicate through time zones is difficult and causes delays. For example, with an extranet, a Japanese client has immediate access to the information provided by its New York law firm and communicates with the firm regardless of the time of day or night. Extranets also reduce travel costs to attend strategy meetings with clients in another state or country.

MULTIJURISDICTIONAL LITIGATION   It is not uncommon for 40 or more law firms to join together on large class-action cases. A law firm involved in complex, multijurisdictional litigation uses an extranet to communicate with other counsel in the litigation. Attorneys share information through the extranet, such as witness lists, discovery, legal research, and so on. Sharing this information ensures that all parties have current and complete information and reduces duplication of effort. Each counsel involved with an extranet has access to pertinent information of the others, allowing the case to be prepared more completely and efficiently and in less time.

Attorney Charles Renfrew, partner at Leboef, Lamb, Greene & MacRae, said, "At times outside counsel find themselves reinventing the wheel—doing research that others have

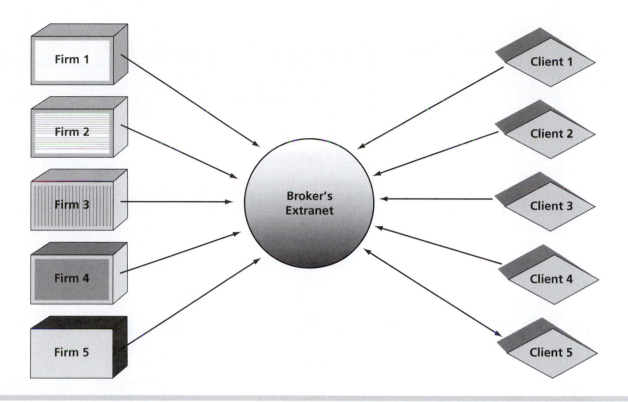

EXHIBIT 10–8   Example of Brokered Extranet

done for the client or work that the firm itself had done—but no one is easily able to locate the work, so it is easier to start from scratch than look through the files [to find it]" *National Law Journal,* "Clients Force Technology on Firms to Trim Costs," April 14, 1997.

Extranets can be developed by using an outside extranet vendor, called an extranet broker. A broker provides a network server through which interested parties can connect. A number of firms can manage a complex case without the expense of implementing their own extranet. This type of extranet is known as a brokered extranet and is shown in Exhibit 10–8. According to the 2007 Technology Survey conducted by *Legal Assistant Today*, almost 40 percent of respondents had an extranet.

EXTRANET SECURITY   Since extranets contain sensitive, confidential information, they must be secure so that unauthorized individuals cannot access the information. In addition, because extranets are connected to a firm's intranet, the private part of the firm's intranet must be protected. There are two types of security risks with an extranet: restricting access so that unauthorized persons do not have access to the system and protecting information in transit to and from other members in the extranet.

There are several access control methods used to secure access to an extranet. A **firewall** is an electronic barrier erected around the firm's network that will not allow an unauthorized person to get through to protected areas. It serves as a buffer between a firm's internal network and a number of external networks, including the Internet.

Perhaps the easiest security method to implement is to place the extranet in an undisclosed address on the Web. A private website can be hidden from search engines and its address provided only to those persons entitled to it. The address can be changed periodically so that unauthorized persons cannot find the site. The new address is given only to those entitled to it.

The most common security method is to require each user to use a special ID and password to gain entry to the extranet. A second-level password is required on some sites for additional protection. A second-level password can be changed or rotated according

firewall
A protective electronic barrier constructed around a network so that unauthorized persons cannot get through.

to a prearranged schedule. A company called SecurID has taken the ID/password security one step further. It issues a special card, similar to an ATM card, that displays a six-digit number. An ID, a password, and a card are required to access a system protected with SecurID.

digital ID
A personal ID number that is encrypted and can be read only by the extranet.

Another security measure is a **digital ID.** A digital ID is a personal identification number or word issued to an individual or organization by an independent certifying authority. A digital ID solves the problem of losing a password or having a password stolen. A digital signature tells the recipient of the message or document that the person sending it is the correct person. It also verifies that the message or document sent has not been altered.

Users with digital IDs can obtain certificates from an outside vendor, Verisign, which will certify that the user is who he or she purports to be. To obtain a certificate, the user must provide personal identification that is validated by a credit bureau. Verisign is not the only vendor that issues certificates after verifying identity. Law firms may issue their own certificates to authorized persons. To issue identification certificates, a firm needs a certificate server, available from Microsoft, Netscape, Xcert, Entrust, and GTE.

It is important that the third-party vendor issuing certificates be reliable. As such, the regulation of digital signatures has been proposed. The Information Security Committee of the Science and Technology Section of the ABA published digital signature guidelines in 1997. Some states have also enacted some form of legislation pertaining to the use of digital signatures, some of which used the ABA guidelines as a model.

cryptography
The method of scrambling information so that it is unreadable except by the person who holds the key to unscramble the information.

encrypt
A way of coding the information so that if it is intercepted by a third party, it cannot be read.

decrypt
A way of decoding information so that it may be read.

There are many software products that protect information in transit from one computer to another. These software products use **cryptography** to **encrypt** and **decrypt** data. Cryptography is the process of securing private information that is passed through public networks by mathematically scrambling (encrypting) it in a way that makes it unreadable to anyone except the person holding the mathematical key that can unscramble (decrypt) it. Cryptography is not new technology; it was developed by the government many years ago as a method of keeping espionage activities secret. There are two types of cryptography that are in use today: same key and public key.

With same-key cryptography, a message is encrypted and decrypted using the same key, which is passed along from one party to another. A more secure method is public-key cryptography, which uses a pair of different keys (one public, one private). A message encrypted with one key can be decrypted only with the other key and vice versa.

Members of an extranet own a unique pair of keys. The public key is widely distributed among the extranet network and is used for encoding messages. The private key is held by one member of the network and is used to decrypt the incoming message, making it safe from interception. Controlling access to the encryption keys is important and requires close monitoring.

Other security methods are being developed every day. A New York company, Finger/Matrix, offers Check/One, which is a single finger scanner that limits access to the computer's data to individuals whose fingerprints identify them. Another security system scans an individual's retinas before granting access to the system.

ELECTRONIC MAIL

Electronic mail (e-mail) is an electronic message system that allows communication from one person to another through their computers. It is one of the most commonly used features of technology law firms. In addition to receiving messages, a person can receive attachments to a message, such as documents, files, graphics, and computer programs. People can communicate with other people from around the world at any time of the day or night in seconds through e-mail. In 2006, 22,000 billion e-mail messages were sent.

E-mails that are damaging to an employer are common in U.S. lawsuits. Almost 10 percent of U.S. companies have been ordered by courts to produce employee e-mail, and have battled sexual harassment claims stemming from employee e-mail and/or Internet use. The Federal Electronic Communications Privacy Act (ECPA) gives employers the right to monitor all e-mail and Internet activity of the company's computers. According to the 2001 Electronic Policies and Practices Survey conducted by the American Management Association, the ePolicy Institute, and *U.S. News and World Report,* employers are exercising their rights under the ECPA. Of the 435 respondents to the survey, 61.6 percent monitor employees' e-mail and Internet activity. Among the employers who monitor, 63 percent cite reducing legal liability as the primary reason.

E-mail passes to its destination through servers. To receive e-mail, one must have access to a server. An ISP provides each customer with an e-mail address that allows the customer to use the ISP's server. Like snail mail, each e-mail must contain an address so that the server will know where to deliver the e-mail. Each individual has his or her own e-mail address.

One must be alert to fraudulent e-mail scams known as **phishing.** Phishing is a form of fraud designed to steal a person's identity. It seeks to get people to disclose personal information, such as credit and debit card numbers, account passwords, or Social Security numbers. The e-mail claims to be from a well-known company and is connected to a **spoof site,** a fraudulent website that looks like the well-known site. The "From" line may include an official-looking e-mail address that may actually be copied from a genuine one. The e-mail address can easily be altered—it is not an indication of the validity of any e-mail communication. Reputable, well-known companies will not ask for personal information such as credit card numbers, bank account numbers, e-mail addresses, or passwords.

phishing
Fraudulent e-mail scams that are designed to steal a person's identity.

Spoof site
A fraudulent website that looks like a website from a large, reputable company.

E-Mail Addresses

E-mail addresses normally have three main parts: username, domain name, and type identifier.

The username is the name of the person to whom the e-mail is sent. The same principles discussed in the World Wide Web section of this chapter apply to e-mail addresses. An e-mail address contains no spaces. Therefore, a username is not a person's actual name consisting of a first name and a surname. A username consists of a number of variations of the person's name, as follows: surname only (e.g., smith), or first initial and surname (e.g., jsmith), or first name and surname (e.g., johnsmith), or first name and surname separated by an underscore or hyphen (e.g., john_smith). A person's username may also be a nickname (e.g., cuddles). However, nicknames are rarely used in an office environment.

The second part of the e-mail address is the domain name. The domain name is the name of the organization that contains the server that transmits the e-mail. The username and domain name are separated by the axon symbol (@), which symbolizes the word *at.* For private e-mail accounts, the domain name is the name of the ISP (e.g., jsmith@aol.com). For work-related e-mail accounts, the domain name is the name of the company (e.g., jsmith@ microsoft.com).

The third part of the e-mail is the type identifier. It is separated from the first two parts of the e-mail address by a dot or period (.) and is generally considered a part of the domain name (e.g., .com).

E-mail addresses are always in lowercase letters. However, e-mail addresses are not **case sensitive.** This means that you can send an e-mail to Jsmith@Microsoft.com, JSMITH@ MICROSOFT.COM, or Jsmith@MICROSOFT.com, and it will be delivered to the correct destination: jsmith@microsoft.com. However, some Internet addresses are case sensitive, and URLs are partially case sensitive. Therefore, it is good practice to get used to entering all addresses in the correct case. E-mail addresses, as well as Web addresses, should be in all lowercase letters.

case sensitive
Requiring that all letters be in a specific case. If a letter is the wrong case, the information cannot be read.

As of this writing, there is no comprehensive directory of e-mail or Internet addresses. However, there are several resources that are used to locate a person, some of which are listed in the Cybersites section. If you cannot find a person in a directory, it is not difficult to figure out a person's e-mail address if you know the domain name of his or her place of work. Assume that his or her username is the first initial and surname.

E-mail addresses and Web addresses are different. For example, if you wanted to locate the White House on the Web, you would locate it through its URL: <http://www.white-house.gov>. If you wanted to send the president an e-mail message, you would do so by the president's e-mail address: president@whitehouse.gov.

Listservs and Discussion Groups

listserv
A group of people who exchange information about a particular topic on the Internet.

There are thousands of groups and organizations that have their own discussion groups on the Internet. These groups exchange information and communicate with one another via e-mail. There are two types of discussion groups: newsgroups and mailing lists, which are also known as **listservs.** Newsgroups are public discussions on topics of general interest in which anyone with newsreader software can participate. A listserv contains a mailing list of e-mail addresses of people interested in the same subject. A member sends a message to a common e-mail address, and it is then distributed to everyone on the list. When someone replies to the message, the reply goes to everyone on the list. One need not participate in the discussion to be a member of a listserv. One may just read the material being posted without responding. This activity (or lack thereof) is called **lurking.**

lurking
Not responding to messages posted on a listserv.

Listservs are either public or private and consist of two types: announcement type and discussion type. With an announcement-type list, you receive messages but cannot respond to the message. With a discussion-type list, every member can participate in the discussion. In addition, listservs are either moderated or unmoderated. In a moderated list, all messages are sent to a list moderator, who reviews them and makes a determination of whether it is appropriate to be distributed to the group. In an unmoderated list, each message is automatically sent to the group regardless of content.

There are thousands of law-related listservs, including many listservs for paralegals. The NFPA's website (<http://www.paralegals.org>) as well as *Legal Assistant Today* (<http://www.legalassistanttoday.com>) have links to paralegal listservs. If you want to find a listserv on a specific topic and do not have a Web address, you can search the catalog of listserv lists. Catalist is a catalog of listserv lists and can be found at <http://www.lsoft.com/catalist.html>.

Web Logs

Web log (blog)
Web page consisting of frequently updated, chronological entries on a particular topic.

A Web log (blog) is a Web page consisting of entries from the blog owner and visitors regarding a specific topic. It provides a forum to share ideas, opinions, and information. Pictures, audio, and video files are also posted on a blog. A blog is different from a regular Web page because of **permalinks** that are created and assigned to each individual blog entry, making it accessible to all readers who access the blog. The Pew Internet & American Life Project estimated that 12 million Americans maintained a blog in 2006, and the number of blogs doubles every 6 months. According to Technorati, the leading search engine for blogs, there were 83.6 million blogs worldwide as of June 2007. Technorati also estimated that approximately 75,000 new blogs were launched each day.

permalink
Permanent URLs connected to a Web log post.

Blogs that focus on the legal profession are known as **blawgs.** Law firms and legal professionals use blawgs to stay current on changes in the law, to monitor legal trends, and to keep clients up-to-date on changes in the law and other information. Some law firms use blawgs in addition to their regular website to market their services. A well-written blawg that is kept current can establish the blawger as an expert in his or her field, leading to business

blawgs
Web logs focused on topics of interest to the legal profession.

referrals and connections. For many students, maintaining a professional blawg has led to employment opportunities.

To be good cybercitizens, it is suggested that each listserv or blog participant become familiar with e-mail etiquette, known as netiquette.

Netiquette

Netiquette is a form of online etiquette. It is an informal code of conduct that governs the acceptable way for users to interact with one another through e-mail. The guidelines were informally developed by many different people on the Internet. There is no one authority or governing agency that makes and enforces the rules. The rules are enforced by the people using them. A disregard of the rules is considered rude and improper. Some people will only know you from how you portray yourself over the Internet.

Some people receive hundreds of e-mails a day. Researchers have estimated that professionals spend 40 percent of their day reading and producing e-mails. It's easy to be inundated with an overflowing inbox. Adhering to netiquette guidelines will make the process of managing e-mails easier for everyone. The following are rules to follow when communicating by e-mail:

- *Do not assume that your e-mail is private.* Do not send an e-mail that contains material that you would not want everyone at work to see. The firm's system administrator has access to e-mails to maintain the system, and e-mails are easily forwarded to others.
- *Never give your user ID or password to another person.* Another person can wreak havoc with your e-mail account. Since your e-mails can be viewed by the system administrator, all e-mails containing your user ID and password are presumed to be written by you.
- *Keep messages short and to the point.* Most busy people resent long e-mails that contain information not relevant to the subject matter.
- *Edit quotations.* Quotations should be edited to include only the relevant material to keep messages short.
- *Limit each message to one subject.* An e-mail should be limited to one subject, and that subject should be clearly indicated in the subject section of the e-mail.
- *Include your signature at the bottom of the e-mail.* A signature footer should include your name, position, affiliation, and e-mail address. It should not exceed four lines. A telephone number can be included.
- *Do not use words in all uppercase.* Words in all uppercase are considered shouting. If you want to capitalize a word to emphasize it, do so sparingly.
- *Never send chain letters.* Chain letters clutter the system.
- *Spell out dates.* Because of the international nature of the Internet, understanding dates can be confusing. Do not list dates by the numbers (12/21/YY). Always spell out the month to avoid confusion: Dec 21, 2009, or 21 Dec 09.
- *Be careful what you say about others.* E-mails are easily forwarded, and a derogatory remark may come back to haunt you. An angry or a derogatory e-mail is known as a **flame.** Responding angrily to a flame will result in a flame war, which is unpleasant for everyone.
- *Do not forward personal mail.* It is considered extremely rude to forward a personal e-mail to members of a listserv without the original author's permission.
- *Be careful with humor.* Without verbal communication and body language it can be difficult for others to detect your intent, and e-mails can be misinterpreted. Use **emoticons** to express your feelings. Commonly used emoticons are shown in Exhibit 10–9. Jokes may not be appreciated by coworkers and should not be distributed through an office's e-mail system. In 1998, two employees sued New York's Morgan Stanley for $30 million

netiquette
An informal code of conduct that governs e-mail communication.

flame
An angry or a derogatory e-mail message.

emoticons
Symbols used to express feelings in written e-mail communication.

:-) Happy	:-(Sad	:-o Surprised
:-I Indifferent	:-e Disappointed	:-<Mad
;-) Winking	:-& Tongue-tied	:- Lips are sealed
:-|| Really angry	:-@ Screaming	:-] Grinning
:-D Laughing	:-(o) Yelling	:-] Smirk
8-) Wide-eyed	:-| Apathetic	:'-(Crying
:-[Sad sarcasm	;-(Feel like crying	:-\ Undecided
%-) Happy but confused	:-* Kiss	:->Sarcastic smile
8-o Shocked	:-/ Skeptical	>:-) Devilish
;^) Smirking smile	X-(Brain dead	
O:-) Angelic	:-P Sticking tongue out	

EXHIBIT 10–9   Emoticons

because of an offensive joke that was distributed by e-mail throughout the company. Employees have sued their employers for a hostile work environment because of offensive e-mails intended as jokes (*Daniels v. WorldCom*, Civ A.3:97-CV-0721-P, 1998 WL. 91261 [N.D. Texas 1998] and *Schwenn v. Anheuser-Busch, Inc.*, Civ A.95-CV-716- WL. 166845 [N.D. New York 1998]).

- *Use acronyms.* Acronyms shorten messages and should be used whenever possible. Make sure, however, that the recipient will understand the acronyms. Commonly used acronyms are shown in Exhibit 10–10.

- *Know your firm's e-mail policy.* In-house e-mails (e-mails sent to persons within the firm) are subject to a firm's e-mail policy. In-house e-mails should be regarded as memoranda used for office business. Personal e-mails should be kept to a minimum. There have been many controversies about personal e-mails sent at the office being the private property of the employee. Since e-mails at work are created on company time using company equipment, employers feel that e-mails are no different than letters and memos on company letterhead. Employees claim a right to privacy. Courts have agreed

<BRB> Be right back	<BTW> By the way
<CUL> See you later	<F2F> Face to face
<FWIW> For what it's worth	<FYA> For your amusement
<FYI> For your information	<GMTA> Great minds think alike
<HHOK> Ha ha only kidding	<IMHO> In my humble opinion
<IOW> In other words	<LOL> Laughing out loud
<OIC> Oh, I see	<ROTFL> Rolling on the floor laughing
<SO> Significant other	<TIA> Thanks in advance
<TNX> Thanks	<WB> Welcome back
<WRT> With respect to	<WTG> Way to go
<BFN> Bye for now	<G> Grin
<HTH> Hope this helps	<IJWTK> I just want to know
	<OTOH> On the other hand

EXHIBIT 10–10   Common E-Mail Acronyms

with the employer and have ruled that an e-mail sent at work, regardless of its nature, is the property of the employer.

- *Clearly identify yourself.* When communicating with clients or others regarding a case, it is important that each e-mail clearly states your status and that you are not an attorney. All e-mails should also state your full name, title, firm name, and return address.

- *Check e-mail daily.* Important information comes through e-mail that requires an immediate response. In addition, e-mails can pile up, making review and response a time-consuming activity.

- *Request a return receipt.* Most e-mail software has the capability to request a receipt verifying when the message was viewed by the recipient. This can be important information, especially when notifying a party of important dates or events in a litigation or case. Return receipts for case information should be used as a matter of policy and the receipts retained.

- *Do not promote or advertise a product or service to a listserv.* Sending e-mails that contain promotional material or advertisements to a group, such as a listserv, is known as **spamming** and is unlawful. There are federal and state laws that prohibit using a computer to send unsolicited advertisements. A person who sends illegal junk e-mails may be fined $500 per e-mail sent.

- *Send ccs and bccs only when necessary.* Do not "reply to all" unless absolutely necessary. Do not unsubscribe to the entire listserv.

- *Use punctuation sparingly.* Be careful with punctuation. Many periods can separate thoughts (. . . . .), but the use of many exclamation marks looks like anger (!!!!!). Many question marks also signify strong emotion (?????).

- *Use the spell-check feature.* Because e-mails are quick, they tend to be sloppy.

- *Use correct grammar.* Be sure to always use correct grammar, syntax, and sentence structure.

- *Develop e-mail templates.* Templates will make writing standard e-mails faster. Be sure that the template has no grammatical or spelling errors.

- *Be brief.* Studies have shown that people read from computer screens about 25 percent more slowly than they do from paper. They also do not like to scroll to get to the end of an e-mail. They tend to look only at the first few sentences and scan e-mail messages. Therefore, make sure your message is brief.

spamming (spam)
To send unsolicited commercial e-mail messages to large numbers of people on the Internet on an indiscriminate basis.

Managing E-Mail

Managing e-mail is a time-consuming process, especially if one participates in a number of listservs. E-mails should be considered documents, such as memoranda or letters. E-mails are no longer a casual mode of communication. They are an essential element of a law firm's communication system. Preserving the integrity of the system is important for all employees of a firm. Some people receive hundreds of e-mails a day. Netiquette helps, but many people have difficulty managing their e-mails.

An e-mail that requires a reply should be responded to immediately on receipt. E-mails that are unimportant and require no response should be deleted immediately. Old e-mails should be deleted from the system periodically. However, not all e-mails should be deleted, and discretion should be used to identify which e-mails should be retained and which should be deleted.

Some e-mails that contain important information should not be deleted but should be stored permanently on the firm's server or printed and put in the file. Software that automatically manages e-mails is known as an **e-mail filter.** The software will automatically discard e-mails that contain profanity or sexually explicit material. It is also used to keep confidential e-mails confidential by not allowing them to be disseminated over a network. The software can be programmed to filter e-mails from a certain person who sends e-mails

e-mail filters
Software that manages e-mail and that can be programmed to delete e-mails that contain profanity or offensive material.

for harassment or flaming purposes. It also can be programmed to automatically delete old e-mails. E-mails are placed in three categories: the first category is permanently stored and not deleted, the second category is automatically deleted monthly, and the last category is automatically deleted weekly. Using an automatic system is convenient if e-mails are categorized correctly.

Of Interest . . .

WHAT DOES THE > SYMBOL MEAN IN E-MAILS?

The > symbol is commonly seen in e-mails. It is called an annotate feature, and it is offered by individual software packages. Some software annotates a message automatically, and others have it as an option. When a user replys to an e-mail, the original message is repeated and enclosed in the > symbol. This allows the person responding to the message to view it while responding. A number of > symbols displays the number of times the message has been answered. For example, a message with >>> before it means that the message has been answered three times. When replying to a long message, delete the parts of the original message that are not applicable to the response.

Keeping E-Mail Confidential

E-mails that contain legal advice and are sent to clients must be kept confidential to protect attorney-client privilege. An e-mail that is sent to a client is subject to interception by others over the Internet. In addition, if the e-mail is sent to the client's work, others, such as the employer, may have access to the client's e-mail, waiving attorney-client privilege. If they are not secured, attorney-client privilege may be lost.

The ABA Standing Committee on Ethics and Professional Responsibility issued its formal opinion 99–413 addressing the confidentiality problem with e-mail. The opinion stated that a lawyer may transmit information to a client via e-mail without violating the Model Rules of Professional Conduct. It further stated that e-mail affords a reasonable expectation of privacy without the necessity of encryption. However, the ABA guidelines include a strong recommendation that lawyers use encrypted e-mails in highly sensitive matters. According to the 2007 Legal Technology Report, only 17 percent of respondents use encryption when sending e-mails.

National and state bar associations are developing rules and guidelines pertaining to e-mail. Some states have considered the confidentiality problem and have created a varying degree of rules that pertain to e-mail. Some states require clients to acknowledge that they understand the confidentiality risks associated with e-mails. Other states, including Vermont and Illinois, have ruled that there is a reasonable expectation of privacy with e-mail.

Courts have considered whether the use of e-mail waives attorney-client privilege. Under most court decisions, if a lawyer takes reasonable precautions to protect confidentiality, attorney-client privilege will not be damaged even if eavesdropping occurs. Many people believe that encryption is the only method that ensures security in e-mail communication. In addition, an e-mail from a lawyer to a client should contain the following warning:

This message is intended for the use of the individual or entity to whom or which it is addressed and may contain information that is privileged, confidential, and exempt from disclosure under applicable law. If the reader of this message is not the intended recipient or the agent responsible for delivering the message to the intended recipient, you are hereby notified that any dissemination, distribution, or copying of this communication is strictly prohibited. If you have received this transmission in error, please notify us immediately.

TECHNOLOGY ETHICS

The prominence of the Internet has created new ethical considerations that have caused existing ethical rules and guidelines to be reexamined. The 3-year period of 1995 through 1998 saw the Internet emerge in nearly every major law firm in the United States. The speed with which the Internet has become an integral part of law offices has caused an immediate demand for ethical rules specifically directed to cyberspace, especially in the area of client development.

As we learned in Chapter 4, both national and state bar associations have rules pertaining to client development. When the ABA's rules were developed in 1983, the Internet was not used for lawyer advertising or client development. Even though the rules have been amended since 1983, none of the changes have specifically addressed advertising issues in cyberspace. In the absence of specific cyberspace rules, the ABA applies its current rules to cyberspace, causing conflicts about defining what activity constitutes compliance and what activity does not, resulting in more questions than answers.

Some states have issued rules that specifically address the ethics of new technologies, and others are in the process of developing them. All state bar associations that have considered the subject of lawyers advertising on the Web have concluded that advertising legal services on the Web is an ethical activity as long as the lawyers comply with other advertising rules.

Advertising

Most of the nation's attorneys have websites, which has posed a question to bar associations. Are websites considered advertising? Most states say yes as more and more law firms promote their firm via the Web. The global nature of the Internet raises ethical issues regarding application of a state's legal advertising guidelines. If an attorney from state A advertises over the Web in a manner that violates state B's advertising rules, can state B prosecute the offender? Since state B cannot impose its rules on a lawyer who practices in another state, how does the presence of a website in state B affect the rules? State B could complain to state A's bar association, who could investigate the lawyer's advertising practices, but state A could impose discipline only if the advertising violates its rules, not state B's rules.

The ABA and state bar associations apply their existing rules to the Web. As was discussed in Chapter 4, the ABA applies its Model Rule 7.1 to websites, which states the following prohibitions of advertising material in general:

- It cannot contain a misrepresentation.
- It cannot contain an omission of fact, making a statement misleading.
- It cannot create an unjustified expectation about the results the lawyer can achieve.
- It cannot compare the lawyer's services with those of other lawyers.

These rules are generally accepted restrictions on a law firm's advertisements, including its website. What is uncertain, however, is how the rule is applied to links contained on a firm's website. For example, phrases such as "expert," "best lawyers in town," and so on are considered a comparison with other lawyers' services and are therefore prohibited. Suppose a client writes a newspaper or magazine article that discusses a firm's expertise and labels its lawyers "great lawyers." Would a link to the article on a firm's website be an ethical violation? If a website links to a nonlegal website for which a nonlawyer is responsible, must that person adhere to the advertising guidelines? Can a firm use links without being held responsible for the content of those links?

Another uncertain aspect of Web page advertising is its use of multimedia, such as video and sound. As you learned in Chapter 4, the ABA and state bar associations have strict rules regarding media advertisements on radio and television. Would websites that have multimedia features fall under the current media advertising restrictions?

Another question of Web advertising is if it constitutes solicitation. As you learned in Chapter 4, solicitation of clients is an area forbidden to lawyers. Many legal websites tell visitors about the firm and areas of practice. Some offer to send a visitor more information about the firm. Is the website guilty of soliciting? The ABA and many state bar associations require that an attorney's advertisement be labeled as such at the top of the advertisement. Does a firm's website have to have the word *ADVERTISEMENT* at the top of the Web page? Many state bar associations have ruled that, since a website is not sent to or directed to a single entity, it need not contain the word *advertisement* at the top.

The construction of a website may violate ethical rules. Professional Web page designers encourage the use of pictures on a website to make it appealing, and many legal websites contain pictures. However, some pictures may be misleading. For example, a website that has a picture of a lawyer in a courtroom may be misleading if the lawyer lacks trial experience.

Domain Names

A firm's domain name is subject to ethical rules. Most firms choose a domain name that is similar to, or an acronym of, the firm name. Others, however, choose a domain name that communicates its expertise, such as "quickdivorce.com," "drunkdriving.com," and so on. Since most individuals search for a subject through a search engine by keywords, such as *divorce, bankruptcy,* and *drunk driving,* firms with these domain names are easily located through a search engine. If the domain name is used as a locator only, is it proper and subject to ethics rules? Does the domain name "bestlawyers.com" constitute a comparison and therefore violate Model Rule 7.1?

E-Mail

ETHICS ALERT

E-mail presents an ethical problem not covered by current ethical rules. The ethical prohibition against client solicitation has been applied to e-mail. Many lawyers subscribe to listservs and maintain blawgs, some of which do so to promote their law practice. If a member of a listserv asks a lawyer a legal question and the lawyer responds, is it solicitation? *Lawyers have been accused of solicitation for listserv activities.*

Some firms' e-mails contain disclaimers to avoid solicitation allegations. An example of a disclaimer is as follows:

> Participation in a discussion of ideas and issues of common interest with respect to the various subjects covered on this listserv should not be construed as creating an attorney-client relationship between attorney and the participants. Nothing in this e-mail should be construed as legal advice or legal opinion. Participation in the discussions is not confidential or privileged, and any material submitted or comments made shall not be deemed to be confidential or privileged.

In 1988, the U.S. Supreme Court held that lawyers could send direct-mail advertisements to those persons known to be in need of legal services (discussed in Chapter 4). Some argue that e-mail falls under direct-mail guidelines. Others argue that e-mails are direct communication, not written communication, and are therefore subject to solicitation accusations. Some court rulings have stated that participation on a listserv constitutes solicitation. Others have ruled that it is not solicitation, but a response to a potential client's request for information. Spamming is a clear violation of ethical rules, but there is no agreement as to what other e-mail activities are ethical violations.

Unauthorized Practice of Law

ETHICS ALERT

The Web has many opportunities for the unauthorized practice of law. Lawyers must be licensed to practice law in their state. Giving legal advice is practicing law. *Giving legal advice to a person in another state could be unauthorized if the lawyer is not licensed in that state.*

Nonlawyers are portraying themselves as lawyers and giving bogus legal advice over the Internet. The unauthorized practice of law is defined as a crime in most states, and its definitions and elements are set forth in the statutes of the state. It is very difficult to prosecute these people because most states require that a defendant in a matter related to the unauthorized practice of law be physically present in the state while engaged in the unauthorized activity. If the act did not occur in the state, the state would have no jurisdiction over the perpetrator. California has closed this gap in jurisdiction by holding that one engages in the unauthorized practice of law if there is significant contact with someone in California. In this case, the defendant's physical appearance may not be required to prosecute for the crime.

CONCLUSION

Technology has affected every aspect of our lives: the government, the manufacture and delivery of products, the economy, our households, transportation, communication systems, and business. We can now communicate with computers as we do with one another—through speech. It will not be long before computers will develop the capability to process information and to use logic to make decisions for us. Technology is a two-edged sword. While offering us numerous benefits, it also creates some challenges. As new technology is mastered, there will be others to give us new opportunities and new challenges.

SUMMARY

Technology is a tool that is used by legal professionals to deliver their products to clients. The technological advances made in the 1990s have transformed the average law office. The introduction of new technologies and the rapid changes in existing technologies have been both a blessing and a curse. The primary challenge is keeping current with the latest technology. Another challenge is managing information. Paralegals must be familiar with technology and the common software used in law offices.

There are various types of software and thousands of software applications available in the legal marketplace to accommodate almost every aspect of a law office's functions, from specific practice areas to management tasks. Software applications are developed specifically for the operating system used by the firm's computers. There are currently three major operating systems: Windows, Macintosh, and Unix. Microsoft's Windows operating system is the most popular and widely used operating system used in law offices today.

Software applications are either custom or off-the-shelf. Some software manufacturers have developed integrated software applications. Manufacturers also bundle software together in one package, called office suites. Most law firms use off-the-shelf computer applications and office suites. The most common law office software applications are word processing, spreadsheet, database, time and billing, calendar and docket control, document management, and case/practice management systems. Add-on, or plug-in, software has been developed that adds features to software programs.

The Internet is a tremendous tool for individuals and organizations and is an essential tool for law firms. The Internet is a worldwide cooperative network of networks. No one owns the Internet. The networks that use the Internet are owned and maintained by their owners, and some are publicly traded companies. Today, there are tens of thousands of networks from around the world connected to the Internet.

To access the Internet, one must have browser software and an Internet Service Provider (ISP). A protocol is a set of rules that ensures that different network software products can work together. Protocol standards are set by the Internet Engineering Task Force (IETF), a large international community of network designers, operators, vendors, and researchers concerned with the smooth operation of the Internet.

A domain name is needed to be located on the Internet. It is a unique name that identifies an organization on the Internet. Domain names consist of the organization's name (or specific designation) and a suffix that describes the type of organization, known as a type identifier.

The World Wide Web (WWW, or Web) is not the Internet. It is only one of the protocols that operate via the Internet. The protocol used by the Web is called Hypertext Transfer Protocol (HTTP). The Web is actually the name given to all documents written in a specific software language, known as Hypertext Markup Language (HTML). The Web delivers its information by hyperlinks to other pages or other areas on the Web. The organization of these links constitutes a website. Most websites contain levels. The levels are accessed through the first page of a website, known as the home page. The Web offers us numerous benefits.

Before information on a website can be accessed, it must be located. There are three basic ways to locate specific information on the Internet: Uniform Resource Locator (URL), keyword search, and topical index. Almost all companies and corporations have websites ending with ".com"; these are commercial sites. Most websites consist of many sections, or pages, and it is possible to go directly to the page that contains the information desired by its URL. Certain rules apply to all URLs.

Keyword searching, or Boolean searching, gives a search engine parameters within which to conduct the search, thus narrowing the outcome of a search.

Various Internet indexing companies have categorized Internet sites into groupings of related fields, such as government, law, judiciary, and so on. Websites can be marked by a browser. This activity is known as bookmarking.

You can find anything you want on the Web, but not all information is reliable. Anyone can post information on the Web regardless of age, background, or mental health. The federal government is the largest contributor of material on the Web. Websites are accessible from other websites by links.

Internet technology has been the foundation of new systems and software products, among them intranet and extranet programs. An intranet is a law firm's internal information distribution system that is based on Web technology. Each person's computer is connected to the firm's server that stores the information. An intranet also uses specialized software, known as groupware, or software created specifically for use by groups. Intranets are custom made and designed according to a firm's specifications by professional intranet designers or in-house computer specialists. An intranet has many uses but requires constant maintenance and updating. Law firms, especially large firms, realize a number of benefits to distributing information electronically via an intranet.

An extranet is a Web-based interface to a private network; it is a network accessible by a number of organizations, including selected firm employees, clients, outside counsel, and others who work together. The difference between an intranet and an extranet is that an extranet is directed to different people and has different uses. Among the uses are direct client access and multi-jurisdictional litigation management. Since extranets contain sensitive, confidential information, they must be secure so that unauthorized individuals cannot access the information. There are two types of security risks with an extranet: restricting access so that unauthorized persons cannot access the system and protecting information in transit to and from other members in the extranet.

Electronic mail, known as e-mail, is an electronic message system that allows communication from one person to another through their computers. E-mail passes to its destination through servers. E-mail addresses normally have three main parts: username, domain name, and type identifier. E-mail addresses and Web addresses are different.

There are thousands of groups and organizations that have their own discussion groups on the Internet. There are two types of discussion groups: newsgroups and mailing lists, which are also known as listservs. Newsgroups are public discussions on topics of general interest in which anyone with newsreader software can participate. A listserv contains a mailing list of e-mail addresses of people interested in the same subject. Listservs are either public or private and consist of two types: announcement type and discussion type. There are thousands of law-related listservs, including many listservs for paralegals.

Web logs, also known as blogs, are Web pages consisting of entries from the blog owner and visitors regarding a specific topic. Blogs focused on the legal profession are known as blawgs. Blogs and blawgs have many uses for law firms and individuals.

To be good cybercitizens, it is suggested that each listserv participant become familiar with e-mail etiquette, known as netiquette. Netiquette is a form of online etiquette. It is an informal code of conduct that governs the acceptable way for users to interact with one another through e-mail.

Managing e-mail is a time-consuming process, especially if one participates in a number of listservs. An e-mail that requires a reply should be responded to immediately on receipt. Some e-mails that contain important information should not be deleted but should be stored permanently on the firm's server or printed and put in the file. E-mails that contain legal advice and that are sent to clients must be kept confidential to protect attorney-client privilege. National and state bar associations are developing rules and guidelines pertaining to e-mail. Under most court decisions, if a lawyer takes reasonable precautions to protect confidentiality, attorney-client privilege will not be damaged even if eavesdropping occurs.

The prominence of the Internet has created new ethical considerations that have caused existing ethical rules and guidelines to be reexamined. The speed with which the Internet has become an integral part of law offices has caused an immediate demand for ethical rules specifically directed to cyberspace, especially in the area of client development. In the absence of specific cyberspace rules, the ABA applies its current rules to cyberspace, causing conflicts about defining what activity constitutes compliance and what activity does not, which results in more questions than answers. Some states have issued rules that specifically address the ethics of new technologies, and others are in the process of developing them.

Are websites considered advertising? Most states say yes as more law firms promote themselves via the Web. What is uncertain, however, is how the rules are applied to a firm's website. Another uncertain aspect of website advertising is its use of multimedia, such as video and sound. Another question of Web advertising is whether it constitutes solicitation. The construction of a website may violate ethical rules. A firm's domain name is subject to ethical rules. E-mail presents an ethical problem not covered by current ethical rules. Spamming is a clear violation of ethical rules, but there is no agreement as to what other e-mail activities are ethical violations.

While offering us numerous benefits, technology also creates some challenges.

CHAPTER ILLUSTRATION

Part of Black, White & Greene's marketing budget for the year was dedicated to developing the firm's website. Robert directed Tricia to begin the process. Tricia called a number of website design firms and obtained estimates. She chose Web Page Design, Inc. The firm's consultant, Jim Parks, owner of Web Page Design, Inc., determined that the first step was to obtain a domain name for the firm. He said that the domain name blackwhitegreene.com was available, so he registered it. When he received confirmation of the registration, he proceeded to develop the site.

After consultation with Tricia and the attorneys in the firm, it was decided that the website would contain the following information:

- The firm's brochure
- A biography of the attorneys, including their pictures
- The firm's practice areas
- A list of news items about the firm and its cases
- An e-mail link
- A blawg of business topics of interest to the business community
- The firm's newsletter

Jim worked with Sandra to post the firm's newsletter and obtained all the information needed for the site. In a month, the website was completed, and it looked great. It contained a picture of the outside of the firm's building and a map showing directions to get to the firm. The firm brochure described the history of the firm and listed the attorneys in the firm. The name of each attorney linked to that attorney's biographical information, which showed a current picture of him or her, the date he or she graduated from law school, and his or her area of expertise. It also listed each attorney's professional accomplishments. Each page of biographical information contained a link to that attorney's e-mail address so that the attorney could be contacted directly.

Since Grant's expertise was tax, the site's blawg focused on tax issues and discussed recent changes in tax law.

Robert, the managing partner, was concerned about the ethical implications of the website. He was concerned about potential problems with communications being unsecured and potential solicitation accusations. After researching the state's ethical rules concerning websites, he decided that the site should contain a disclaimer. He called Jim and had the following disclaimer put on the site:

> This website is intended to supply general information to the public. It is not intended to be advertising, solicitation, or provide legal advice. The legal information provided at this site is general and not specific. The reader should not assume that the legal information at this site applies to his or her specific situation without consulting competent counsel in his or her state. We cannot guarantee the accuracy of information contained on websites to which this site is linked. We do not intend the links on this website to be referrals or endorsements of any kind. This website is not an invitation for an attorney-client relationship. We do not wish to represent anyone from another state unless the party has a valid claim in this state. We do not guarantee that the e-mail to the firm will be secure. Do not send confidential or sensitive information over this e-mail system.

The website was posted to the Web. Tricia directed that the firm's website address, <http://www.blackwhitegreene.com>, be inserted on the firm's stationery and business cards. Tricia could now concentrate on the next technology upgrade for the firm: an intranet.

Tricia called TrialNet, a company that installs intranets for law firms, and hired them to install an intranet for the firm. TrialNet obtained intranet groupware that linked everyone's computer with the firm's server. When it was completed, the firm's employees had direct access to the firm's server. The intranet contained the firm's client list, calendar, brief bank, law library resources, Internet, policy manual, time and billing program, newsletter and marketing materials, and management forms, such as check requests, new client matter sheets, and personal leave requests. Each practice area had its own area for access to information and materials that pertain only to that specific practice area.

Everyone at the firm was extremely pleased with the intranet. They commented that it saved them a lot of time. Everything they needed was at their fingertips, and the intranet was easy to use. When all employees learned to use the intranet effectively, Tricia noticed that the firm's billing increased. Tricia credited the increase in profitability to the intranet because it increased employees' productivity.

It was a policy of the firm that employees check their e-mail daily. One day, Patrizia noticed that she had received three e-mails from the same person—someone called sexymale@ aol.com. She read the first e-mail message. It said that he was surfing the Internet and saw her picture on the firm's website. He told her that he thought she was beautiful and wanted to meet her. The other two e-mails relayed the same message. Patrizia was amused but did not respond.

Each day that Patrizia checked her e-mail, there was at least three e-mails from sexymale. Each day, the e-mails from sexymale became more intense. Sexymale professed his undying love and affection for Patrizia and was very anxious to meet her. He pleaded with her to meet him and respond to his e-mail.

Patrizia decided to respond to let him know that she was not interested in meeting him and had no intention of continuing a communication with him. Her response was nice but straightforward.

Sexymale would not accept Patrizia's rejection. He threatened to come to the office to meet her regardless of her disinterest. His e-mails became more frequent and threatening. Patrizia became concerned. "Who is this nut?" she thought to herself.

Sexymale's e-mails began to flood Patrizia's e-mail box with sexually graphic material. Since the firm's website contained a map, sexymale could easily find his way to the office. Patrizia was frightened. She called the police and alerted the firm of the problem.

The police came out to the firm and took a police report. Patrizia told police detective Ryan, "I am frightened that this person may be stalking me. What can you do to protect me?"

"Do you have reason to believe that he is stalking you?" asked detective Ryan.

"No, but he knows where I work. He even has a map to the office from our website," said Patrizia.

Detective Ryan responded, "We can't do much without more evidence of actual stalking. We don't know who this guy is or where he lives. He may live in Timbuktu for all we know. If he is from another state, the matter is out of our jurisdiction. We will assign an investigator to the problem and do what we can to get him to stop. The investigator assigned to these types of cases gets hundreds of e-mail-related complaints a week. We just don't have the resources to thoroughly investigate them all."

When detective Ryan left, Patrizia submitted a complaint to America Online, sexymale's ISP. America Online said that it would investigate the matter but that the only thing it can do is give the perpetrator's identity to the police and cancel the person's account.

Tricia quickly installed an e-mail filter that blocked all e-mails from sexymale@aol.com. The e-mail filter program automatically sends a responding e-mail to sexymale that Patrizia does not accept e-mail from his address and to immediately cease sending further e-mails to her. The firm also installed a security system at the receptionist's desk that will alert police of an unauthorized visitor. The door between the reception area and the rest of the offices was kept locked and opened only to those authorized to get through.

Tricia called Jim Parks at Web Page Design and instructed him to take the attorneys' pictures off of the website immediately. She also told him to remove the map. Patrizia also took security precautions. She made sure that she was escorted out of the office by one of the other attorneys each evening and that her husband drove her to work each day. The atmosphere in the firm was tense.

Two weeks later, Patrizia received a telephone call from the police investigator assigned to her case. He told her that sexymale was a fifteen-year-old boy who lived in California with no criminal record. He said that he posed no threat to her or the firm. The investigator referred the case to juvenile authorities in California for further action. Patrizia was relieved. She e-mailed everyone in the firm about the update. Everyone in the firm was glad that the crisis was over and that the firm could get back to normal.

CHAPTER REVIEW

1. What is the difference between custom computer applications and off-the-shelf computer applications?
2. What are add-on software applications, and what do they do?
3. What is a case/practice management software application?
4. What is a protocol, and for what is it used?
5. Who manages the Web, and what is its purpose?
6. What are the four main elements of a URL?
7. What is a Boolean search, and what is its purpose?
8. What is an intranet, and for what is it used?
9. What is an extranet, and for what is it used?
10. What is a firewall, and what is its purpose?
11. What is cryptography, and what is its purpose?
12. What are the three main parts of an e-mail address?
13. What is a listserv, and how does it differ from a newsgroup?
14. What is netiquette, and who enforces it?
15. Why must e-mails to clients be kept confidential?

EXAMPLES FOR DISCUSSION

1. Does the domain name "never-lose-a-case.com" violate ABA Model Rule 7.1? If so, why? If not, why not?
2. Do you have experience with any of the most common software applications used in a law office? If so, which one(s)? Discuss your experiences with the features of each. What do you like and dislike about them?
3. Does your place of employment have an intranet or an extranet? If so, how is it used? What features does it contain? Has it improved your productivity? If so, how?

ASSIGNMENTS

1. The law firm of Black, White & Greene is replacing its computer applications because its current software is outdated. Your group has been given the responsibility of researching software applications for the firm. You are to research the software applications for word processing, spreadsheets, database, time and billing, calendar and docket control, document management, and case/practice management. One group member is assigned to one type of application. Research the features, requirements, functionality, and cost of each product. Write a report to the managing partner, Robert Black, about each program researched, do a cost comparison, and make your recommendations. Your report should include the reason(s) you chose the product for the firm.

2. Conduct a search of lawyers' websites. Search by legal practice area. Note the domain names. Are any improper?

3. What are the cyberspace ethical guidelines for your state? Consult the legal ethics website (<http://www.legalethics.com>). Research the following areas for your state:
   a. Solicitation through Web pages, blawgs, and listservs
   b. Requirements for e-mail confidentiality
   c. Advertising guidelines for websites
   d. Activities that constitute UPL in cyberspace

4. Go to <http://www.blawg.com>, choose Paralegals, and note the blawgs available for paralegals. Choose each of the blawgs listed and review them. Answer the following questions:

   a. Who is the writer of each blawg?

   b. What is the author's position and paralegal qualifications?

   c. What is the topic of each blawg?

   d. Which blawg did you like the best? Why?

   e. Write a short summary of each blawg.

5. Examine a software program or demo disk of a program that automates a law office administrative or practice area (e.g., case management, time and billing, document management, or case/practice management application). Describe the function the program intends to automate, and evaluate the effectiveness of the program.

6. Interview an information manager at a large law firm in your area. Prepare a report that describes his or her duties and responsibilities.

SELF TEST

How well did you grasp the material in the chapter? Test yourself by answering the following questions and check your answers against the answers found in Appendix A.

1. What is the primary challenge of new technology?
2. How has access to the Internet created a challenge for the legal team?
3. For what are software applications specifically developed?
4. What are the three major operating systems?
5. What operating system is most commonly found in law offices?
6. In what operating system does the Windows operating system have its origin?
7. For what operating system is most software designed?
8. Which operating system was the first to use a graphical user interface?
9. For what is the Unix operating system used?
10. What is a custom software application?
11. What are off-the-shelf computer applications?
12. What is an integrated software application?
13. What is an advantage to an integrated software application?
14. What is a disadvantage to an integrated software application?
15. What are office suites?
16. What are some advantages to an office suite?
17. What type of computer applications do most law offices use?
18. What software application has been used in law offices since the 1960s?
19. What are the two most popular word processing applications?
20. What are add-on (or plug-in) software applications?
21. What does add-on software do?
22. For what is a spreadsheet application used?
23. For what is a database used?
24. For what type of tasks do law firms use a database?
25. What is time and billing software?
26. For what is calendar and docket control software used?
27. What are the benefits of a calendar and docket control application?
28. For what is document management software used?

29. How are documents in a litigation case managed by document management software?
30. What are the four types of document management software?
31. What is a document abstract system?
32. What is a full-text retrieval system?
33. What is scanning?
34. What are case/practice management applications?
35. What is the Internet?
36. Who designed the Internet?
37. For what government agency was the Internet designed?
38. For what purpose was the Internet designed?
39. What was the name of the first Internet?
40. For what does the name of the first Internet stand?
41. In 1983, the first Internet split into what two networks?
42. What government agencies controlled the two networks?
43. What was the name of the second Internet?
44. Who had access to NSFNET?
45. Who used NSFNET?
46. When was commercial use of the Internet allowed?
47. What does NREN stand for?
48. What is NREN?
49. Who owns the Internet?
50. To access the Internet, what two things must one have?
51. What is an ISP?
52. What are an ISP's computers called?
53. To what is an ISP connected?
54. From what does an ISP get its access?
55. What is a protocol?
56. What does a protocol do?
57. Who establishes protocol standards?
58. What is an FTP protocol?
59. What is a Telnet protocol?
60. What five factors are responsible for the Internet's sudden growth?
61. What is a domain name?
62. Who created domain names?
63. What was the name of the domain name project?
64. What is the name of the private U.S. corporation that manages domain name registration?
65. What is a type identifier?
66. What are the 10 categories of type identifiers?
67. How are countries outside the United States identified on the Internet?
68. What is a cybersquatter?
69. What is the name of the law that outlaws cybersquatting?
70. What is the World Wide Web?
71. Who developed the Web?
72. Who manages the Web?
73. Who runs the W3C?

74. Who funds the W3C?
75. What is the W3C's purpose?
76. What is the protocol used by the Web?
77. What is the software language used by all documents on the Web?
78. What does a computer need to read the HTML language?
79. What is shareware?
80. What is a hyperlink?
81. For what are hyperlinks used?
82. What is a collection of hyperlinks called?
83. What is the first page of a website called?
84. How does the legal profession use the Web to publicize and manage the media in high-profile cases?
85. What are the three basic ways to locate information on the Internet?
86. What is a Uniform Resource Locator?
87. What are the four main elements of a URL?
88. What type identifier do most companies use?
89. What does ".com" mean?
90. How do you locate a website that is outside the United States?
91. What is a pathname?
92. How are pages in a URL separated?
93. What are the rules that apply to URLs?
94. What is a keyword search?
95. What is a Boolean search?
96. What does a Boolean search do?
97. What is a search engine?
98. What does a search engine do?
99. What is bookmarking?
100. Who warrants the accuracy of their websites?
101. What seven things can you do to verify the accuracy of information on a website?
102. Who is the largest contributor of material on the Web?
103. What is an intranet?
104. What is Web-based technology?
105. How does an intranet differ from the Web?
106. What is groupware?
107. How is an intranet designed?
108. For what is an intranet used?
109. What is a brief bank?
110. What is a template?
111. What is an extranet?
112. What are the benefits of an extranet?
113. What is the difference between an intranet and an extranet?
114. What is a firm-centered extranet?
115. What is a client-centered extranet?
116. What is the difference between a firm-centered extranet and a client-centered extranet?
117. What is a brokered extranet?
118. What are the two types of security risks with an extranet?

119. What is a firewall?
120. What is the easiest security method to implement for an extranet?
121. What is the most common security method for an extranet?
122. What is a digital ID?
123. What is a digital ID certificate?
124. What is cryptography?
125. What does cryptography do?
126. What are the two types of cryptography?
127. What is same-key cryptography?
128. What is public-key cryptography?
129. What is e-mail?
130. How does e-mail reach its destination?
131. Who provides a person with an e-mail address?
132. What are the three main parts of an e-mail address?
133. An e-mail username contains no _____ and no _____.
134. What word does the axon symbol mean?
135. In what case are e-mail addresses?
136. What does case sensitive mean?
137. How are e-mail addresses and Web addresses different?
138. What is a listserv?
139. What is the difference between a listserv and a newsgroup?
140. What is lurking?
141. What are the two types of listservs?
142. What is an announcement-type listserv?
143. What is a discussion-type listserv?
144. What is a moderated listserv?
145. What is an unmoderated listserv?
146. What is netiquette?
147. Who enforces netiquette rules?
148. Why should you not assume that your e-mail is private?
149. Why should you not give your ID or password to another person?
150. Why should you keep e-mail messages short?
151. Why should you edit quotations?
152. Why should e-mail messages contain only one subject?
153. What information should be contained in your e-mail signature?
154. Why should you not use all caps in e-mail messages?
155. Why should you never send chain letters via e-mail?
156. Why should you spell out dates in an e-mail message?
157. What is a flame?
158. Why should you not forward personal e-mail messages to a listserv?
159. What is an emoticon and how is it used?
160. Why should you be careful with sending jokes via e-mail?
161. Why use acronyms in an e-mail message?
162. Why is it important to know your firm's e-mail policy?
163. Why should you clearly identify yourself when sending an e-mail to a client?
164. Why should you check your e-mail daily?

165. What is spam?
166. Why should you use punctuation sparingly?
167. When should an e-mail be permanently stored?
168. What is an e-mail filter?
169. Why should e-mail messages to clients be secured?
170. What is one method that ensures confidential e-mail messages?
171. Are websites considered advertising?
172. What four advertising prohibitions apply to websites?
173. Why have lawyers been accused of solicitation for Web activities?

Key Words

add-ons (plug-ins)
blawgs
bookmarking
Boolean search
brief bank
browser
case sensitive
cryptography
cybersquatter
decrypt
digital ID
domain name
e-mail filters
emoticons
encrypt
extranet
File Transfer Protocol (FTP)

firewall
flame
freeware
groupware
home page
hyperlinks
Hypertext Markup Language (HTML)
Hypertext Transfer Protocol (HTTP)
integrated software
Internet Service Provider (ISP)
intranet
listserv
lurking
netiquette
network

pathname
permalink
phishing
protocol
scanned
search engine
server
shareware
spamming (spam)
Spoof site
Telnet
template
type identifier
typosquatter
Uniform Resource Locator (URL)
Web log (blog)

Cybersites

E-MAIL WEBSITES

For information concerning e-mail, try the following sites:

Software for e-mail management—<*http://www.mailstart.com*>

General information and e-mail listservs—<*http://www.emailman.com*>

Website that contains e-mail tips, netiquette, and software information— <*http://email.about.com*>

Internet Mail Consortium—<*http://www.imc.org*>

How e-mail works—<*http://www.howstuffworks.com/email.htm*>

THE INTERNET

The Living Internet—<*http://www.livinginternet.com*>
Learning the Internet—<*http://www.learnthenet.com*>
Internet Terms—<*http://www.netlingo.com*>
Internet News—<*http://www.internet.com*>
Internet Public Library—<*http://www.ipl.org*>
The Public Library of Law—<*http://www.plol.org*>

BLAWGS

Listing of legal blawgs—<*http://www.blawg.com*>
Blawg design—<*http://blog.justia.com*>
Blawg Republic—<*http://www.blawgrepublic.com*>
Blawg Review—<*http://www.blawgreview.blogspot.com*>
List of recently updated blogs—<*http://www.weblogs.com*>
Search engine for blogs—<*http://www.blogsearch.google.com*>; <*http://www.technorati.com*>
Legal Guide for bloggers—<*http://www.eff.org/bloggers/lg*>
Paralegal blawg—<*http://paralegalgateway.typepad.com/my_weblog/*>

INTRANETS AND EXTRANETS

Intranet Journal—<*http://www.intranetjournal.com*>
Recommended Intranet Resources—<*http://www.strom.com/places*>
Intranet Solutions—<*http://www.intranet.org*>
Extranet News—<*http://www.extranetnews.com*>
Legal Extranet Blog—<*http://legalextranet.blogspot.com*>
Intranet and Extranet Collaboration Software—<*http://www.trichys.com*>

ETHICS ON THE WORLD WIDE WEB

The Web contains many websites that are devoted to legal ethics and advertising on the Internet. Among them are the following:
The American legal Ethics Library—<*http://www.law.cornell.edu/ethics*>
Legal Ethics—<*http://www.legalethics.com*>
Texas Center for Legal Ethics and Professionalism—<*http://www.txethics.org*>
ABA Center for Professional Responsibility—<*http://www.abanet.org/cpr*>
Lawyer's Advertising on the Internet—<*http://www.bodi.com/papers/advertising/toc.htm*>
Legal Site Check—<*http://www.legalsitecheck.com*>

Student CD-ROM
For additional materials, please go to the CD in this book.

Online Companion™
For additional resources, please go to http://www.paralegal.delmar.cengage.com

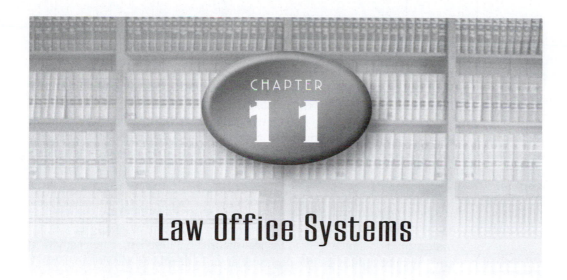

CHAPTER

11

Law Office Systems

OBJECTIVES

After completion of this chapter, the student should be able to do the following:

- Define the goals and purpose of systems in a law office.
- Describe the four types of systems and how they function.
- Identify the components of the four stages of systems development.
- Explain the difference between administrative and substantive microsystems.
- Develop a system, including forms, checklists, and written instructions.
- Discuss common problems with systems development.
- Explain how systems evolve.
- Describe third-party systems.

INTRODUCTION

Law offices, or any business for that matter, must have systems in order to function in an organized manner. A law office is a collection of systems working together to achieve its goals. Systems contribute to the orderly performance of legal work. Without them, confusion and chaos would occur. Paralegals not only participate in a law office's systems but are also involved with systems development and implementation.

This chapter will discuss the general concept of systems to provide an overall understanding of systems. It will then describe different types of systems, illustrate how systems are developed, explain systems evolvement, and examine third-party systems. A paralegal will often use the skill of developing and implementing a system and will find this skill useful in any type of law firm.

WHAT IS A SYSTEM?

The *Oxford English Dictionary* defines a system as a "set or assemblage of things connected, or interdependent, so as to form a complex unity; a whole composed of parts in orderly arrangement according to some scheme or plan." Roberta Ramo, author of *How to Create a System for the Law Office*, defines a law office system as "a documented logical method or way of handling transactions, procedures, or work flow in a law office so as to minimize waste, conserve professional time, and optimize productivity."

The purpose of a system is to streamline a task so that members of a legal team do not do unnecessary work, waste law firm resources, or make mistakes. As a result of a good system, a legal team will become more efficient, reduce costs to a client, reduce costs to a firm, increase client satisfaction, and increase profits for a firm.

The goals of a system are to maximize productivity, minimize waste, conserve resources, reduce errors, and produce high-quality work. Systems play a vital role in increasing employee efficiency. If there were no systems, there would be no organization of efforts, and chaos would result.

Systems are tools used to do the following:

- *Guarantee that a firm's products maintain their excellence.* Missed deadlines are common malpractice claims against lawyers, and it is embarrassing to inform a client that a court would not accept a document because it was incorrect. These errors are costly to a client and a firm. Systems reduce the possibility of error in deadlines and documents.

- *Guarantee that a firm's commodity—time—is used to its maximum potential.* A disorganized office wastes employees' time, and wasted time costs a firm money. Systems save time and increase the efficiency of their users. This results in increased profits for a firm.

- *Give each member of a legal team the benefit of the experience of another.* Each person involved in a system contributes his or her knowledge, experience, and know-how. Less experienced team members learn from the contributions of others. This increases the expertise of each team member.

- *Substitute for recollection.* Undocumented systems are stored in the heads or memories of their users. This does not benefit a firm or other team members. Memory is known to fail, especially when pressing matters occupy its space. A system will relieve the necessity of storing many facts in a person's memory, thereby reducing the amount of stress on the individual.

- *Improve language and legal skills.* Preparing standard documents enhances a user's language skills. Using a systematic approach to projects increases legal skills.

- *Promote delegation.* A system encourages delegation of tasks. A systems review highlights areas to be delegated downward. Without a system, delegation could be overlooked.

- *Preserve methods.* A system is documentation of a procedure that was successful in the past. As paralegals gain experience in an area of law, they learn the right way to do a task and the wrong way to do a task. Documenting the right way preserves this experience for other paralegals.

- *Systems save time and resources.* Using a system saves the firm's employees' time, making them more efficient. Increased efficiency results in increased profits for the firm. In addition, systems decrease the potential for a legal malpractice claim, saving the firm money.

TYPES OF SYSTEMS

Four types of systems exist: macrosystems, microsystems, minisystems, and subsystems (see Exhibit 11–1). A macrosystem is a large system within which microsystems are contained. A microsystem functions within a macrosystem and contains minisystems. A minisystem functions within a microsystem and contains subsystems. A subsystem is a small system that functions within a minisystem. All are interrelated and depend on one another. Each part relies on the other parts to accomplish its goals. A macrosystem cannot be successful without good microsystems, and microsystems cannot be successful without good minisystems.

A law firm comprises one macrosystem, two types of microsystems (substantive and administrative), many minisystems, and many subsystems.

SYSTEMS STRUCTURE

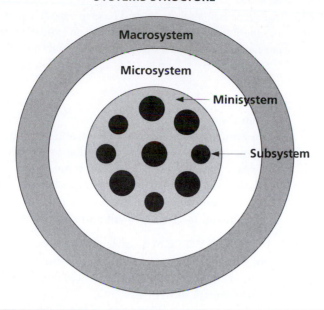

EXHIBIT 11–1 Systems Structure

Macrosystems

The definition of the Greek word *macro* is "large." Therefore, we may define the term *macrosystem* as "a large system." A firm's macrosystem consists of affiliated industries within which the firm must operate. An example of a part of a law firm's macrosystem is the U.S. court system.

Many elements affect a firm's macrosystem: technology, economy (U.S. and local), and government laws and regulations. When a change occurs in one of those elements, the firm's macrosystem feels its repercussions. These elements change often, and a firm must change with them.

TECHNOLOGY   Technology has changed the way in which we conduct business. E-mail, unheard of in the early 1980s, is a major source of communication in law firms today, and many firms are connecting their e-mail systems to those of their clients. This benefits the communication process and eliminates frustrating **telephone tag**, which occurs when someone calls a person who is unavailable, leaves a message, and then is unavailable when the person returns the call. With the use of computers, law firms can deliver legal services in a more expeditious manner. As computer technology continues to streamline many legal tasks, systems must change to take advantage of this resource.

ECONOMY   Eventually, the economy affects everyone—from a large corporation to a day laborer. In a recession, budgets are cut. Businesses cut budgets by reducing the amount of work given to their lawyers. People who cannot afford legal services find alternatives to their legal problems or go without legal representation. This eventually affects law firms, which must also cut their budgets. People are laid off because of lack of work—and the cycle continues.

When the economy changes, firms must also change to remain competitive. In a recession, firms may restructure their leadership and management policies to maintain their profitability. In addition, a firm may merge with another firm and change its entire macrosystem and its microsystems.

GOVERNMENT LAWS AND REGULATIONS   A firm whose clients are among highly regulated industries, such as public utilities, will have a different macrosystem than a firm whose clients are part of an unregulated industry. For example, some states impose state inheritance

telephone tag
A situation in which someone leaves a message for a person who is unavailable, and then is unavailable when the person returns the call.

taxes on their citizens. These states establish inheritance tax agencies to collect the taxes, and law firms must interact with these agencies in probate cases. These agencies are part of a firm's macrosystem. If a state abolishes an inheritance tax or changes its laws and regulations, this affects a firm's system of completing probate cases and affects its macrosystem and substantive microsystem.

Microsystems

As we learned in previous chapters, a law firm has three goals: (1) to provide quality legal services to clients, (2) to attain growth and profit for the firm, and (3) to provide growth and satisfaction for employees. A microsystem is a firm's methodology for reaching its goals.

substantive microsystem
A system of providing legal services to a client.

administrative microsystem
A system relating to the management of a firm.

A law office has two types of microsystems: administrative and substantive. These microsystems function together. A **substantive microsystem** supports goal 1, to provide quality legal services to clients. An **administrative microsystem** supports goals 2 and 3, to attain growth and profit for a firm and to attain growth and satisfaction for employees.

ADMINISTRATIVE MICROSYSTEMS   Management develops and implements an administrative microsystem. The administrative microsystem consists of the firm's goals and objectives, resources, culture, and management style. Each of these microsystems contains minisystems, and the minisystems may contain subsystems.

There are many administrative minisystems. These minisystems include a firm's management policies and methods of implementing them. For example, a minisystem may be a firm's policy regarding employee vacations. A subsystem of that minisystem is the procedure for requesting a vacation, including preparing the required forms. Management's receipt of the form starts the second step in the minisystem: securing a replacement for the vacationing employee.

Many administrative minisystems are automated, such as conflict-of-interest checking, time sheet preparation, and others. For firms with an intranet (discussed in Chapter 10), the administrative minisystems are located on the firm's server and accessed from the employee's computer. Instructions for the minisystems can also be found on a firm's intranet.

SUBSTANTIVE MICROSYSTEMS   A firm's substantive microsystem is responsible for delivering legal services to a client. This system relates solely to the practice of law. It is specifically designed to contribute to greater efficiency in providing legal services. The lawyers and paralegals who use substantive systems increase their productivity significantly.

The number of substantive microsystems in a firm varies according to the areas of law in which the firm practices. A small boutique firm specializing in one area of law will have one substantive microsystem and several minisystems. A large firm with many specialties and departments will have many substantive microsystems and minisystems, as shown in Exhibit 11–2.

Many substantive microsystems consist of software products specifically designed for a particular area of law. There are hundreds of such software packages on the market today. These products were discussed in Chapter 10.

Three methods are used to acquire a substantive microsystem: developing, evolving, and buying. Each of these methods is discussed later in this chapter.

Minisystems and Subsystems

A minisystem is a system within a microsystem. It is an intregal part of a microsystem. The type and number of minisystems depend on individual system users and the efforts of a firm to develop systems. Some minisystems die early, and others survive for as long as a firm exists.

Minisystems are constantly changing. Parts of a minisystem are improved, expanded, or changed as the law changes and as its users become more experienced. If a system is developed to the complete satisfaction of its users, changes, such as changes in the law, may still occur to a firm's macrosystem, which will affect the system. Therefore, minisystems are never fixed and permanent.

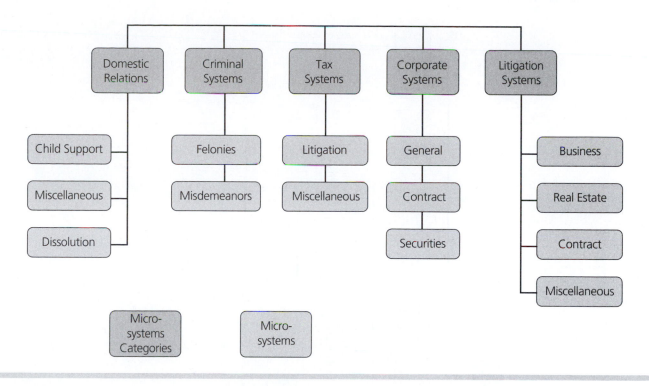

EXHIBIT 11–2 Substantive Microsystem and Minisystems for a Large Firm

A minisystem must operate within substantive and administrative microsystems. For example, the number of paralegals and secretaries per attorney—the legal team—is considered an administrative minisystem. A substantive minisystem must function within this administrative minisystem. An administrative minisystem affects a substantive minisystem's development and the delegation of tasks within the substantive system.

Minisystems make the way a firm manages cases consistent. Each minisystem contains steps to complete a case. Each step is considered a subsystem. The number of subsystems in a minisystem depends on the procedural aspects of a case.

For example, an average business litigation case is a microsystem that consists of eight activities, or minisystems, as shown in Exhibit 11–3.

1. Initial client interview
2. Prepare complaint
3. File complaint
4. Serve complaint
5. Commence discovery
6. Prepare for trial
7. Trial or disposition
8. Close file

Each minisystem can be broken down into tasks, or subsystems. For example, in the third minisystem (file complaint), it is the secretary's or paralegal's responsibility to prepare the documents for court filing. Eight tasks (or subsystems) are involved in this minisystem.

1. Check spelling of all names
2. Check to see whether the original is signed
3. Put documents in correct order
4. Photocopy documents

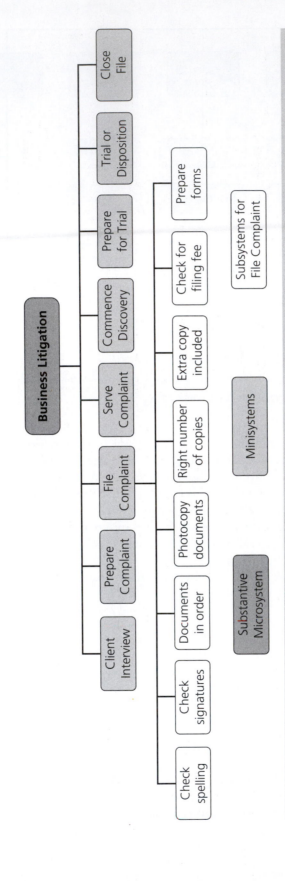

EXHIBIT 11–3 Example of a Substantive Microsystem, Including Minisystems and Subsystems

5. Include appropriate number of copies for court or prepare documents for electronic filing

6. Include additional copy to conform if filing conventionally

7. Include check for filing fee

8. Prepare attorney service instruction form for service of process

Once all eight tasks, or subsystems, are completed, the minisystem (file complaint) is complete, and the documents are ready to file with the court. If one of the tasks is overlooked, the documents will be filed incorrectly and rejected by a court clerk. This will result in delay and inefficiency. Each step of a subsystem is important to the success of a minisystem.

SYSTEMS DEVELOPMENT

Systems development is nothing more than the process of thinking through and documenting in detail the way to get a job done. How logically the steps are thought out and organized makes the difference between a good system and a poor system.

Paralegals take an active role in systems implementation and development. They are often asked to assume the development process. *A lawyer must, however, supervise the work of a paralegal and take ultimate responsibility for the supervision and management of a system.*

ETHICS ALERT

Paralegals must be familiar with the requirements of a case before they can develop a substantive minisystem. Only through experience will paralegals know the procedures of a case well enough to anticipate the next step. With experience, paralegals become familiar with a case's standard documents and delegation of duties. Paralegals also become familiar with the best methods to complete a task. They must also be familiar with a firm's administrative microsystem, and they must structure substantive minisystems to work within that microsystem. It takes time to gain complete knowledge of a firm's administrative micro- and minisystems. It normally takes about 6 months for an employee to become familiar with a firm's systems, procedures, and style.

Systems development involves choosing candidates, completing four stages (analysis, synthesis, organization, and finalization), and storing the system. It requires special skills and poses unique problems.

Candidate Selection

Certain areas of law are especially appropriate for systems development because they involve a series of routine tasks that are similar in each case. Those areas include the following:

Litigation	Dissolution of marriage
Adoption	Name change
Probate	Estate planning
Workers' compensation	Subrogation
Collection	Real estate
Corporate	Bankruptcy

Once a type of case is chosen, three questions must be answered:

1. Can this project be simplified?

2. Can this project be streamlined?

3. Can this project be improved to better serve the client?

If the answer to any of these three questions is yes, the project is a good candidate for a system. However, systems take time and effort to develop, and the effort should not be expended unless a system will be used. A hastily developed system will be more a hindrance than a help. A paralegal must choose system candidates carefully. If a paralegal occasionally works on probate cases, perhaps one or two a year, it would not be an effective use of the paralegal's time to develop a comprehensive probate system. On the other hand, if a paralegal works on probate cases 50 percent of the time, a firm would benefit from a probate system.

To develop the first system, a paralegal should choose something that is easy and familiar, such as a routine project. If an office has established systems, a paralegal may use them as a guide. Systems development consists of four stages:

1. Analyze
2. Synthesize
3. Organize
4. Finalize

Stage 1: Analyze

Analyzing a system has four steps: review, separate, evaluate, and communicate.

REVIEW   The project chosen for systems development must be reviewed to determine whether it warrants the time and expense of systems development. If an existing system is being revised, it must be determined whether the system can be improved considerably. If revision would result in a slight improvement, a complete system revision should not be done; only necessary changes within the existing system should be made. Once the decision to develop a system has been made, all components must be reviewed to be sure all the necessary elements are available for analysis.

SEPARATE   For a system to be analyzed adequately, each step must be separated from the others. All the major activities are listed and broken down into smaller tasks and then steps. Writing down each step in a system gives a paralegal the opportunity to see it. Seeing each step gives the paralegal insight into ways to make the system better. Steps taken for granted are seen in the context of the entire system and therefore are better understood.

The first major activity in a substantive project is an initial client interview. This activity can be broken down into smaller increments, or tasks, and each task can be broken into smaller increments, or steps. After the steps have been broken into their smallest increments, the responsible team member for each task is listed. Exhibit 11–4 shows an organization chart that documents this breakdown.

EVALUATE   Each step is now ready to be evaluated. For each step, the following questions are asked:

- Is it necessary?
- Could the step be delegated downward?
- Could this step be done more easily?
- Could this step be done in less time? If so, how?
- Have problems occurred with this step in the past?
- Could the forms be made simpler?
- Could this step be combined with another?

Answers to these questions are written on an evaluation sheet in a comments section after each step, as shown in Exhibit 11–5.

Coding each step will allow a paralegal to identify the status of each step quickly. Each step is coded by number or color. If coding is by number, each step is assigned a number according to importance, as follows:

1 = very important

2 = important

3 = somewhat important

4 = not important

TASK	STEP	WHO
1. Make appointment.	Check attorney's calendar and enter appointment.	Secretary
	Check paralegal's calendar and enter appointment.	Secretary
	Send confirming letter.	Secretary
	Give copies of letter to paralegal.	Secretary
	Give copies of letter to attorney.	Secretary
2. Conduct initial consultation with paralegal.	Give introduction.	Paralegal
	Complete questionnaire.	Paralegal
	Give overview of case.	Paralegal
3. Conduct initial consultation with attorney.	Introduce attorney.	Paralegal
	Review questionnaire.	Attorney
	Give overview of case.	Attorney
	Discuss strategy.	Attorney
	Discuss fees.	Attorney
	Check conflicts.	Paralegal
4. Sign retainer agreement.	Prepare agreement.	Paralegal
	Review agreement.	Attorney
	Sign agreement.	Attorney
5. Set up file.	Give questionnaire to secretary.	Paralegal
	Input client data.	Secretary
	Set up client ledger.	Secretary
	Incorporate file into filing system.	Secretary

EXHIBIT 11–4   Initial Client Interview Task Breakdown

Initial Client Interview

STEP	WHO	COMMENTS
Check attorney's calendar and enter appointment.	Secretary	OK
Check paralegal's calendar and enter appointment.	Secretary	OK
Send confirming letter.	Secretary	OK
Give copies of letter to paralegal.	Secretary	Could be elimiated
Give copies of letter to attorney.	Secretary	Could be eliminated
Give introduction.	Paralegal	OK
Complete questionnaire.	Paralegal	OK
Give overview of case.	Paralegal	Could be eliminated
Introduce attorney.	Paralegal	OK
Review questionnaire.	Attorney	OK
Give overview of case.	Attorney	OK
Discuss strategy.	Attorney	OK
Discuss fees.	Attorney	OK
Check conflicts.	Paralegal	Could be done by secretary
Prepare agreement.	Paralegal	Could be done by secretary
Review agreement.	Attorney	OK
Sign agreement.	Attorney	OK
Give questionnaire to secretary.	Paralegal	OK
Input client data.	Secretary	OK
Set up client ledger.	Secretary	OK
Incorporate file into filing system.	Secretary	OK

EXHIBIT 11–5   Evaluation Sheet

If coding is by color, each step is highlighted with a different color highlighter, as follows:

Yellow = very important

Green = important

Pink = somewhat important

Orange = not important

Coding each step will save time when communicating the steps of a system to other team members and will give a paralegal an overall view of how many steps in the system need to be changed.

COMMUNICATE After each step has been evaluated, it is time to identify other members of the team who will participate in the system. Each step should be discussed with them. It is better to call a meeting, as shown in Exhibit 11–6, than to discuss the system with them when they are in the middle of other projects. It is important to get their opinions of each step of the system that they will be expected to perform. Each team member should evaluate each step in order of importance. A paralegal will then have their perception of each step in writing, which will be valuable information in the next step of systems development. Each team member should be asked the following questions:

• How would you rate each step in order of importance?
• Have you encountered problems with any of the steps? If so, what are they?
• What are your suggestions to correct the problems?
• Can any of the steps be delegated downward?
• Can any steps be eliminated?
• Must new steps be added?
• What can we do to make the system better?

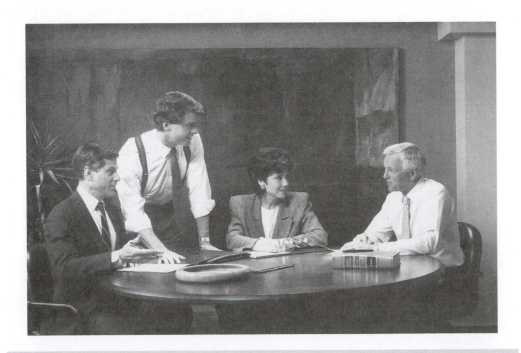

EXHIBIT 11–6 Legal Team in Conference
Each step of the system should be discussed with team members who will use the system. It is preferable to call a meeting for this purpose.

Stage 2: Synthesize

Synthesize means "to make up by combining parts or elements." The synthesis stage has three steps: eliminate, delegate, and consolidate.

ELIMINATE   The first step in the synthesis stage is to eliminate all steps determined to be unnecessary. The effect of eliminating a step on the entire system is considered, and if it is minimal, the step should be eliminated.

DELEGATE   When all unnecessary steps have been eliminated, the remaining steps are reviewed to determine which ones can be delegated downward. For example, in Exhibits 11–4 and 11–5, the paralegal prepares a retainer agreement for the attorney's review. This is a necessary step in the initial interview process. Can this function be delegated to the secretary? If so, the appropriate changes for each function should be made.

ETHICS
ALERT

When delegating functions, it is important to understand the limits within which support staff can operate. A systems developer must have a clear understanding of what a paralegal can and cannot do. For example, it is recommended that paralegals not quote fees. Case law has determined that quoting fees to a client requires an attorney's judgment and analysis of the issues. Therefore, a systems developer cannot delegate this function to anyone other than an attorney.

Delegating tasks is a skill. Delegating too much responsibility or too many tasks results in frustration and work overload, and delegating too little results in a lack of motivation. Effective delegation develops employees and allows them to grow professionally. Successful delegators know that an employee needs increased responsibilities to grow professionally. They also know that mistakes are common in the learning process and understand that how these mistakes are handled affect the growth process.

In order to delegate successfully, the delegator must have a clear understanding of the delegatee's abilities and trust the delegatee to perform at an acceptable level. A poor performer will receive fewer opportunities for increased responsibilities. To delegate over the person's abilities will have disastrous effects. The delegatee will become frustrated and lose confidence in her or his abilities. Delegating under a person's abilities sends a message of a lack of confidence in one's abilities, resulting in a lack of motivation.

Communication is the key to effective delegation. The duties and responsibilities must be clearly communicated, preferably in writing so there is no misunderstanding. After the task is communicated, the communication door must be left open for direction on each step of the process. When the task is finished, it is the delegator's responsibility to give feedback, whether it be constructive criticism, suggestions for improvement, or praise for a job well done.

Another, often overlooked aspect of delegation is authority and accountability. Many times, responsibility is delegated, but the authority necessary to adequately perform the task is withheld, resulting in failure. The person accepting the responsibility must also be held accountable for its success or failure. The responsible employee can then delight in an accomplishment or learn from mistakes made.

CONSOLIDATE   Consolidation is combining the new elements. A new document that incorporates the changes is prepared, as shown in Exhibit 11–7.

Notice that some steps were eliminated, new steps were incorporated, and some steps were delegated downward. The material is now ready to be organized.

Stage 3: Organize

The two steps of the organization stage are establishing a chronological sequence and developing a master task list.

Initial Client Interview

TASK	STEP	WHO
1. Make Appointment	Check attorney's and paralegal's calendar and enter appointment.	Secretary
	Send client confirming letter.	Secretary
2. Initial Consultations	Introduction and client questionnaire.	Paralegal
	Introduce attorney.	Paralegal
	Review questionnaire. Give overview of case. Discuss fees.	Attorney
3. Retainer Agreement	Check for conflicts. Prepare agreement.	Secretary
	Review and sign agreement.	Attorney
4. File Setup	Give questionnaire to secretary.	Paralegal
	Input client data, set up client ledger.	Secretary
	Incorporate into filing system.	Secretary

Exhibit 11–7   Steps of an Initial Client Interview after Consolidation

CHRONOLOGICAL SEQUENCE   After each step of a task has been consolidated, the steps are organized in chronological order. The following questions must be asked after this is done:

- Does the task flow?
- Does the sequence make sense?
- Should one step be completed before another?
- If the steps were reorganized, would it expedite the process?

Now, necessary changes are made in the organization of the steps.

DEVELOP A MASTER TASK LIST   When each step has been put in its proper order, it is inserted on a master task list. This list is the skeleton from which a system will be developed. Each step is listed in chronological order. A master task list will do the following:

- Give a description of each task.
- Describe specifically when each task is due.
- Indicate the documents required to complete each task.
- List the person responsible for completing each task and preparing the documents.
- Give the order in which each task is to be completed.
- List all actions to be taken.
- Include telephone calls or court appearances.
- Direct each team member to the appropriate checklist.

A master task list should be self-explanatory, inclusive, and descriptive. It is reviewed with other members of a legal team for their opinions and suggestions. If other team members do not accept the organization of a project, it may be necessary to reorganize the project or make other changes.

Exhibit 11–8 is an example of a master task list for civil litigation. When the final reorganization has been approved, a project is ready to go on to the final stage of systems development: finalization.

Civil Litigation

TASK	WHO	WHEN/HOW	√
1. Make appointment.	Secretary	When client calls	A
A. Check calendars.	Secretary	Before client hangs up	A
B. Send confirming letter.	Secretary	Same day appointment is made	A
C. Send questionnaire—D–1.	Secretary	Enclose with letter—L-1	A
2. Conduct initial interview with paralegal.			
A. Review and complete questionnaire.	Paralegal	During interview	A
B. Introduce attorney.	Paralegal	After paralegal interview	A
3. Conduct initial interview with attorney.			
A. Review questionnaire.	Attorney	During interview	A
B. Discuss strategy.	Attorney	During interview	A
C. Discuss fees.	Attorney	During interview	A
4. Sign retainer agreement.			
A. Prepare agreement A-1.	Secretary	When instructed by attorney	A
B. Review agreement.	Attorney	When completed, during interview	A
C. Sign agreement.	Attorney	At end of interview	A
5. Set up file.			
A. Give questionnaire to secretary.	Paralegal	After reviewed	A
B. Input client data.	Secretary	After receipt of questionnaire	A
C. Set up client ledger.	Secretary	After data input	A
D. Open file.	Secretary	After ledger setup	A
6. Prepare documents.			
A. Draft summons and complaint P-1.	Paralegal	As soon after interview as possible	B
B. Give to attorney for review.	Paralegal	When draft is completed	B
C. Approve draft complaint.	Attorney	As soon as possible	B
D. Prepare final summons and complaint.	Paralegal	As soon as possible	B
E. Give to attorney for review.	Paralegal	When final is completed	B
F. Approve final summons and complaint.	Attorney	As soon as possible	B
G. Give to client for approval.	Paralegal	After attorney approval	B
H. Send cover letter.	Secretary	After client approval—form L-1	B
I. Sign complaint.	Attorney	Upon approval	B
7. File complaint.			
A. Check spelling of names.	Secretary	When complaint is received	C
B. Make six copies of summons and complaint.	Secretary	After complaint is checked	C
C. Obtain check for filing fee.	Secretary	After complaint is photocopied/use check request form M-45	C
D. Send original and four copies to court.	Secretary	When check is received/use L-2	C
E. Insert one copy in file.	Secretary	During process	C
F. Send copy to client with cover letter.	Secretary	During process/use form L-3	C

(Note: √column directs the reader to the appropriate checklist: A, B, or C.)

EXHIBIT 11–8   Master Task List

Stage 4: Finalize

The finalization stage is the most time-consuming aspect of systems development. This stage has four steps:

1. Preparing forms and checklists
2. Writing instructions
3. Checking the system and following up
4. Revising the system

if clause
A clause inserted in a form document alerting the preparer to insert the appropriate paragraph.

PREPARE FORMS AND CHECKLISTS   Forms consist of form letters, court documents, agreements, and other documents. Documents of prior cases are reviewed to determine whether variations of the same document exist. If a document can be standardized, a form is developed with information pertinent to each case left blank, such as client name and date. If special paragraphs should be inserted in certain circumstances, this is indicated by an **if clause:** "If corporation, insert paragraph A. If individual, insert paragraph B." The paragraphs are stored in a computer and are easily inserted into a document.

If a court document requires standard language, a form can be developed to insert information pertinent to each case. Each form can be used in every case of its type. By having these forms on a computer, it is a simple matter to insert a case caption and other pertinent information. A document is then ready for an attorney's signature. Exhibits 11–9 and 11–10 show a sample form pleading and a sample form letter, respectively.

Insert caption

Complaint for Personal Injuries

1. Plaintiff is a citizen of the State of Florida (or corporation with its principal place of business in the State of Florida) and Defendant is a citizen of the State of ***Insert state*** (or corporation organized under the laws of the State of ***Insert state*** having its principal place of business in ***Insert state***). The matter in controversy exceeds, exclusive of interest and costs, the sum of $50,000.00.

2. On or about ***Insert date*** on a public highway called ***Insert name of street*** in the city of ***Insert city and state***, Defendant drove his/her motor vehicle in such a negligent manner so as to strike Plaintiff as he/she was crossing said street.

3. As a result of the negligence of Defendant, Plaintiff was injured. Plaintiff has been prevented from transacting his/her business, suffered great pain of body and mind, and incurred expenses for medical attention at ***Insert name of hospital*** in a sum in excess of $50,000.

WHEREFORE, Plaintiff requests judgment against Defendant as follows:

1. For special damages in a sum in excess of $50,000;

2. For general damages in a sum in excess of $500,000;

3. For such other and further relief as the court may deem just and proper.

Dated: ***Insert date***

Law Offices of Black, White & Greene

_____

Robert L. Black, Esq.

Doc.P-45 Rev.9/04

EXHIBIT 11–9   Form Pleading

Note: The document number, Doc. P-45 Rev.9/04, identifies the form and the date it was developed or revised.

Black, White & Greene
2121 Broadway
Palo Alto, CA 90000
(555)123-4567

Insert date

Insert client name and address

Re: ***Insert case name***

Dear ***Insert client name***

Enclosed is the completed Complaint in the above matter.

Please review it carefully. If the Complaint requires correction, please contact Ms. Bunnell, Mr. Black's legal assistant, and inform her of the changes. If the Complaint meets with your approval, please sign in the appropriate place and return it to this office in the enclosed envelope. We will proceed to file it as soon as possible after receipt.

If you should have any questions or comments, please contact Ms. Bunnell or Mr. Black. Thank you for your prompt attention to this matter.

Sincerely,

Black, White & Greene

Name, Secretary

sb

Encls.:

Doc.L-3, Rev.9/04

EXHIBIT 11–10   Form Letter

The documents are reviewed and analyzed considering applicable laws and regulations. Whenever possible, terms such as *plaintiff, defendant,* or *debtor* should be used when developing forms. This will avoid the "he or she" differences and streamline the form. Lines or a specific "insert here" code are inserted to alert a user to enter the appropriate information in a form document. These codes can be **blind inserts,** which are entries that are seen on a computer screen but not printed and are available in most word processing software packages. *It is a lawyer's responsibility to proof and check all documents.* Approval of all form documents must be obtained before implementation.

Checklists are vital to the success of a system and are simple to create. Each step of a system is listed and includes the name of the responsible team member. Places for the completion date and the team member's initials are also included. The responsible team member dates and initials the checklist as each task is completed. By doing this, each member of the team will be able to monitor each aspect of the project by looking at the checklist. If a question arises, the checklist will show the date a step was completed and the person who completed the step. Exhibit 11–11 is an example checklist.

Checklists should contain a descriptive notation of when a step must be completed. If a document must be filed within 10 days, is it 10 days from the date of mailing? Date of receipt? Date of hearing? Is it 10 calendar days? Ten business days? It is important to be specific.

Checklists are maintained in a computer so that they may be changed easily. Some firms have found that keeping master checklists in a computer reduces storage problems. When a checklist is needed, a hard copy is printed. The hard copy is usually kept in a client's file and is readily accessible to anyone working on the file.

When form and checklist documents are completed, they must be incorporated into a firm's computer system. Each one must be **cross-indexed** on the computer and identified to the system. To be easily located in a computer system, each form or checklist document

blind insert
An entry in a form document alerting the preparer to insert material; seen on the computer screen but not printed.

ETHICS ALERT

cross-index
To mark a document so that it can be easily found in a system.

Initial Client Interview

STEP	WHO	DATE COMPLETED	INITIALS
Check attorney's calendar and enter appointment.	Secretary	_____	_____
Check paralegal's calendar and enter appointment.	Secretary	_____	_____
Send confirming letter.	Secretary	_____	_____
Give introduction.	Paralegal	_____	_____
Complete questionnaire.	Paralegal	_____	_____
Give overview of case.	Paralegal	_____	_____
Introduce attorney.	Paralegal	_____	_____
Review questionnaire.	Attorney	_____	_____
Give overview of case.	Attorney	_____	_____
Discuss strategy.	Attorney	_____	_____
Discuss fees.	Attorney	_____	_____
Prepare agreement.	Secretary	_____	_____
Review agreement.	Attorney	_____	_____
Sign agreement.	Attorney	_____	_____
Give questionnaire to secretary.	Paralegal	_____	_____
Input client data.	Secretary	_____	
Set up client ledger.	Secretary	_____	_____
Incorporate file into filing system.	Secretary	_____	_____
Doc.C-1, Rev.9/04			

EXHIBIT 11–11   Example Checklist

must have an identifying number in the footer, usually in the order it will be used. The footer should also contain the revision date of the form. Each document may be lettered and numbered to indicate the type of document and the use sequence, as follows:

L-1	First letter
P-1	First pleading
C-1	First checklist
A-1	First agreement

The document coding system must be developed so that the system may be expanded. For example, if all letters were coded 1 through 10, all pleadings 11 through 20, and all checklists 21 through 30, there would be room for only 10 documents in each section. Adding an 11th document would require completely renumbering the documents, changing the master task list, and rewriting the instructions. The letter-and-number coding illustrated here will allow unlimited expansion of each section.

The master task list can be finalized at this point (see Exhibit 11–8).

WRITE INSTRUCTIONS   Each system must have written instructions that explain how to use the system. Instructions are absolutely necessary and are often neglected. Many people will not take the time to prepare instructions when developing a system; this is a disservice to the system. As new people come into the firm and use the system, they must read the instructions to understand the system. A lack of written instructions will cause frustration and a lack of enthusiasm about the system.

Information for instructions is derived from the final master task list. This list is used as a guide. The first draft of the written instructions is prepared on the computer so that it may be revised easily. The written instructions are divided into four sections: information, requirements, instructions, and examples of forms and checklists.

The information section contains information about the goal and purpose of the system and the specific area of law for which the system was developed. If the system has limits, the reader is informed of them in this section. It is a good idea to refer the reader to additional sources of information.

All of a system's requirements are listed in the requirements section. These include the following:

- Software, including version
- Titles of team members using the system
- Outside services, such as attorney service or courier
- Other supplies and requirements

The instruction section is the largest section. Written instructions are the basis of a system's evaluation. Without them, it would be difficult to determine whether a system was successful. They are also vital to a firm's training program.

The master task list is the beginning of the instructions section. The instructions should inform the reader when to use the system, how to use the system, and explain each step of the system. They should be as specific as possible. If there is a doubt about whether to include some information, it should be included; it is better to over-explain a step than to under-explain a step. Each form and checklist should be referenced, with instructions on how to complete it.

Instructions should include a section for special circumstances. No system can anticipate every situation that will arise in a case. The circumstances that a system will not accommodate should be indicated and the reader told what to do in those circumstances.

The forms and checklists section should include a hard copy, or printed copy, of every form and checklist. Each document should be presented in the order in which it is used. Each document must include the document number and a detailed description of where it can be found in the computer system. It should also contain the date it was developed or revised (see Exhibit 11–9). Whenever a form is revised, this information must be updated.

When a first draft of the instructions' four sections is completed, it is given to other team members for their review and approval. Management should review and approve all systems. Documents and instructions may be finalized when final approval is received.

CHECK THE SYSTEM AND FOLLOW UP   As a system is tested, necessary changes are noted. Any changes in the law that will affect the system must be incorporated by the attorney. Other team members are involved in this process. Problems or missed steps are noted. Depending on the area of law of the system, it is a good idea to complete one case using the new system before making a final determination of the success of the system. After the problems have been evaluated, the system is revised to eliminate those problems.

REVISE THE SYSTEM   The revision step consists of the entire system's development process but on a smaller scale. Only one or two areas may need revision. Once the revised material has been analyzed, synthesized, and organized, the system is finalized by preparing a final draft of the forms, checklists, and written instructions. The system may now be implemented.

When a system is implemented, it will grow and evolve over time. As more people use the system, suggestions will be made to improve the system. The system must be flexible in order to be effective. The four stages of systems development are shown in Exhibit 11–12.

Systems Storage

Systems are normally stored on the computer for easy access and revision. The system will be backed up in the firm's regular backup process. However, it is recommended that a hard copy of the system instructions and documents be kept in case of computer failure. A system in a hard-copy format can be reviewed easily.

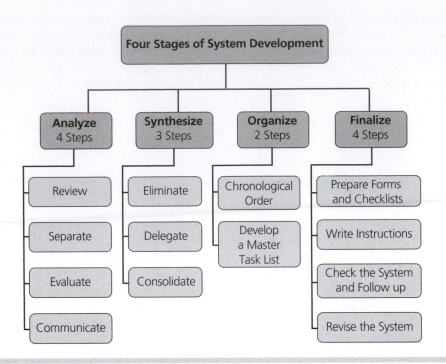

EXHIBIT 11–12   Four Stages of Systems Development

The best method of storing a hard copy of the system is in a three-ring binder, in which individual documents and sections of the system can be easily updated and changed by page. If a system requires more than one binder, the same size and color of binder should be used for each section of the system. A 1 1/2 inch binder usually works well. A smaller binder may cramp the documents, and a larger binder would be too heavy to handle if placed on a high shelf.

The binder should have a label holder on its spine to mark its contents. Putting a label on the spine with transparent tape is not a good way to mark the binder.

Tabbed dividers should be used in the binder to separate sections of the system. The dividers should be made of sturdy, heavy stock. Each tabbed divider should be marked with the section of the system to which it relates: information, requirements, written instructions, forms, and checklists.

The front of the binder should contain a table of contents with corresponding page numbers. This will direct a user to the desired information with little effort. The table of contents should be replaced when the contents have been updated. A revision date in the footer of the index will reflect a revision date.

The binder will contain copies of all documents and checklists. The checklists for each phase of a case are stored in the client's file and are completed as a task is completed. As a paralegal proceeds to the next stage of a case, the appropriate checklist for that stage is copied or printed from the system and inserted in the client's file.

An extra copy of a system is made and stored in the library. It is not necessary that each member of a team have a copy of the system as long as they know where the master original is located and it is accessible to them at all times. In many firms, storage is a problem and space is at a premium. One master copy plus a **backup** copy are all that is needed and will make a system easier to update. In addition, since people are becoming conscious of our natural resources, unnecessary copies of documents are discouraged. A backup of the entire system must be made and stored in a safe place.

backup
Substitute; in computer systems, a copy of a system on a different disk.

Essential Skills for Systems Development

Sharp analytical skills are essential to produce a good system. No matter how well a system is developed, it is only as good as its users. If users will not properly use a system, the system is wasted. One member of a team not participating in a system can cause the system to bog down and grind to a stop.

No matter how much time and expertise have been programmed into a system, the person using the system must have knowledge in the area of law and good work habits in order to use it properly. A good system will not compensate for poor work habits. A checklist can prompt a user when a document is due, but it cannot produce the document on time. Good planning and scheduling are required. Each member of a legal team must be a good time manager.

Developing a system is time-consuming: The average systems development project takes about 3 months to complete. However, if planned and analyzed carefully, a good system is a tremendous asset to a firm. The system must be manageable, easy to use, and save users' time. If all the steps are followed, a system will benefit its users for many years.

Common Problems with Systems Development

It is difficult to develop a system that will satisfy each member of a team, especially when each member participates in its development. What works well for one person may not work well for another. One person will want more steps in a system, and another will want fewer steps. It is a challenge to accommodate each person's needs. Other problems arise as a system ages and updates are not performed. It is also a problem when users look to a system as a source of law or procedure.

DESIRE FOR MORE STEPS   A person who feels that more steps should be added may want to cover every conceivable occurrence in a case. It is impossible to develop a system so comprehensive that it will accommodate every contingency of a case; the system would be too complicated to use. In addition, the time it would take to develop such a system would be prohibitive. Lawyers are good at playing the "what-if" game. This game is appropriate when developing systems, but one must know when to quit.

A good rule to follow is the 90 percent rule: If a situation can be expected to happen 90 percent of the time, it should be included; if a situation is expected to happen infrequently, it should be excluded. For example, suppose an attorney wants additional steps to a Chapter 11 bankruptcy system to include cases that involve individuals with an annual income of $1,000,000 or more. Chances are there will be few such cases. Therefore, it would not be practical to include such steps in the system. A good system is a simple system.

DESIRE FOR FEWER STEPS   When functions in a system are divided among team members—secretary, paralegal, and attorney—it is easy for a team member to underestimate the importance of another's tasks. Because she or he does not fully understand the importance of a function outside her or his own domain, she or he may eliminate a function as unnecessary. For this reason, it is vital to receive feedback from each member of a legal team working with a system. If the responsible team member considers a function important, it should not be eliminated. To do so would decrease the system's effectiveness.

If a team member suggests eliminating a step, the step should be carefully evaluated before it is deleted. If it is found to be "somewhat important," it should be eliminated during the trial period of the system. If a problem occurs, the step can be reinstated. The system will be more successful if it is streamlined.

NEED FOR UPDATES   Once a system has been operating successfully for some time, changes may occur that affect the system. The firm may change its software, which will affect the system, or the law may change, requiring changes in the forms or procedures. The system should be reviewed periodically and updated accordingly.

A major problem with a system's success is that written instructions may not be updated to reflect changes in the system. The system's users are familiar with the system, so they may make periodic changes without referring to written material. Therefore, the written material is not updated and becomes outdated. If a new person uses the system, the written instructions are incorrect, so the system is of no use to them. A system's written instructions must be updated with all revisions.

USE AS AN INFORMATION SOURCE   A system should never be used as a source of law or procedure. It may be tempting for a paralegal to consult a system for the answer to a procedural question instead of doing research in the library. Since a system was not developed to cover every contingency in a case, it is a poor source of information on a question concerning that area of law. Systems are not alternatives to learning but can help a user learn.

SYSTEMS EVOLVEMENT

Not all systems are developed from scratch; some systems evolve. As paralegals work in an area of law, they become familiar with procedures in that area. They gain experience in the essential elements required. Most paralegals keep an extra copy of each document they prepare to use as a form to prepare future documents.

Most paralegals keep these sample documents in form files, also known as brief banks (discussed in Chapter 10). As they collect these documents, they have the beginning of a system. During the course of a case, paralegals develop their own personal checklists or have a checklist in their mind of projects to do. Eventually, paralegals have the documents portion of a system developed on an "as-you-go" basis.

Putting together a formal system from existing documents, checklists, and methods that evolve over time involves the same four areas of systems development: analysis, synthesis, organization, and finalization. However, a systems developer will save a considerable amount of time in document preparation. Since all sample documents are prepared, all that is needed is to standardize them.

THIRD-PARTY SYSTEMS

Substantive minisystems can be purchased from several companies. These commercial systems are developed to accommodate many specialized areas of law. The first commercial systems on the market consisted of form letters, checklists, and written instructions. Now, commercial systems consist of computerized documents, written instructions, and some electronically filed documents.

When purchasing a commercial system, it is important to realize that the system was developed by someone's analysis of the necessary components of the system. This other person's logic composed the sequence of events and essential parts of the system. The method of analysis the author used should be reviewed to determine whether the system's divisions and subdivisions are adequate for the firm. Sample letters and documents should also be reviewed to determine whether they fit the firm's style.

Management needs to look for a couple of specific things when purchasing a system. First, is the system current? Outdated law or forms make a system obsolete. Second, can the system be changed or expanded? This is especially important as the law changes. Some companies offer updates to a system to accommodate these changes. Sometimes, the purchase price of a system is a small portion of its total cost; updates could make the system cost-prohibitive. Third, can the system be expanded to include firm-specific documents and information? If a system cannot be expanded, it will soon become obsolete.

It is important that the forms in a system comply with a court's requirements. Each jurisdiction has different requirements for documents. For example, some federal district courts have their own local forms to use in lieu of official forms.

Computerized commercial substantive legal systems can save a lot of time and be a valuable asset to a firm. These systems are programmed so that information entered on a master information sheet or initial client interview sheet is automatically inserted in the correct place on a form. This is done automatically by a computer rather than by a lawyer or paralegal. Commercial management systems offer the same feature. Information entered from a new-client form is automatically inserted on a client's ledger, a responsible attorney client list, and other management documents. Therefore, a secretary enters the information into the computer once rather than several times. The money a firm saves in employee time greatly justifies the cost of the system.

CONCLUSION

Whatever the method used to obtain a system, paralegals will be asked to participate in law firm systems. If a paralegal spots an area in a system that can be improved, she or he should be assertive and bring it to the management's attention. The use of systems streamlines the practice of law and is essential for an organized, efficient law firm.

SUMMARY

Systems are tools used to streamline a task so that a legal team does not do unnecessary work, waste law firm resources, or make a mistake.

Four types of systems are used: macrosystems, microsystems, minisystems, and subsystems. A law firm comprises one macrosystem, two types of microsystems (substantive and administrative), minisystems, and subsystems.

Systems development is nothing more than the process of thinking through and documenting in detail the way to get a job done. It consists of four stages: analysis, synthesis, organization, and finalization.

Analyzing a current or new system has four steps: review, separate, evaluate, and communicate. The synthesis stage has three steps: eliminate, delegate, and consolidate. Organizing has two steps: establishing a chronological sequence and developing a master task list. Four steps constitute the finalization stage: preparing forms and checklists, writing instructions, checking the system and following up, and revising the system.

Each system must have written instructions that explain how to use the system. Information for written instructions is derived from a final master task list. Written instructions are divided into four sections: information, requirements, instructions, and examples of forms and checklists.

It is difficult to develop a system that will satisfy each member of a team, especially when each member participates in its development. It is impossible to develop a system so comprehensive that it will accommodate every contingency of a case. A good rule to follow is the 90 percent rule.

Once a system has been operating successfully for some time, changes may occur that affect the system. A major problem with a system's success is that written instructions may not be updated to reflect changes in the system. A system should never be used as a source of law or procedure.

Not all systems are developed from scratch; some systems evolve. Developing a formal system from existing documents, checklists, and methods that evolve over time involves the same four areas of systems development: analysis, synthesis, organization, and finalization.

Sharp analytical skills of a system's developer are essential to produce a good system. No matter how much time and expertise have been programmed into a system, the person using the system must have knowledge in the area of law and good work habits in order to use it properly. If all the steps of development are followed, a system will benefit its users for many years.

CHAPTER ILLUSTRATION

Dennis White—Black, White & Greene's litigation attorney—represents Secluded Homes Corporation in a very large business litigation case. The company is a large real estate developer in the area. It is being sued by the Washington County Home Owners' Association for construction defects found in their homes. The homes in the Washington County development are having problems with water and sewer drainage, and some homes' foundations are cracking. The case is expected to involve many parties and will generate thousands of documents to manage.

Since the case is expected to be so large, Dennis needs to hire a freelance paralegal to work exclusively on the case. The firm called the local paralegal association, and Dennis had many referrals, one of whom he decided to hire. Judy Tuttle is an experienced litigation paralegal with 5 years of experience. She has experience with large litigation cases and accepted the position. She will work exclusively on the case and will end her association with the firm when the case is finished.

Dennis called a meeting with Judy and Sandra, his secretary, to discuss the case. The client was just served with a complaint that they must answer in 30 days. He wants to file a cross-complaint against 45 subcontractors. Dennis's case strategy needs a system that will organize the case from the beginning so that the team can manage it. He asked Sandra and Judy to develop a system for the case.

The first step in the process is to research the marketplace for software that will accommodate the case. Sandra and Judy received literature on 10 document management software packages, each with similar features. Judy mentioned that she had experience working with the CaseMap software package and that it was a good program. She felt that it would be perfect for the case. Tricia ordered the software, which they received 10 days later.

Judy then went to work to develop the system. The first step was to make a list of tasks that needed to be done for the case. She consulted with Dennis and Sandra and came up with an overview of the major tasks of the litigation. She incorporated the major tasks into the software and asked Sandra to prepare the software for the case. The parties had to be entered, as did the dates on which the complaints and cross-complaints were filed. Sandra did the necessary formatting, and Judy went to work dividing each task into segments. She developed a master task list of the essential elements of the case.

Judy reviewed the master task list with Dennis and Sandra for their input. Dennis noted that some of the tasks that Judy was to be responsible for could be delegated to Sandra. Sandra also suggested some revisions to the list. After revision, the master task list was approved.

The next step of the development process was developing forms and checklists. This was a time-consuming process for Judy, but the case management software helped her because it contained sample forms that she could revise for use. She knew that some forms, such as form letters, would have to be changed as the need arose, and she made provision for it.

The largest area of the system was the discovery process, as they expected thousands of documents to be produced in the case. Judy developed a system that would organize the documents, gather essential information from them, and monitor them. The case management software is a full-text retrieval system that allows for all the information in the documents to be input into the computer. The documents can then be searched for their content and the information separated into categories. All information pertaining to one subject matter could then be found together. The system will allow the information to be organized in other ways, such as chronologically or by party.

When the discovery phase began and they received discovery documents, Judy gave each document an identifying number. The number was put on each document in a bar code that also contained other information, such as producing party, date of input, and other information. The document was then scanned into the case management system. Sandra was responsible for storing the hard copy of each document. She organized each document chronologically by its identifying number and stored them in a fireproof filing cabinet that was kept locked. The software automatically created a cross-reference to each document's location so it could be easily found.

Judy prepared written instructions for each phase of the system. She asked Sandra for help in preparing the instructions. Sandra wrote down each step of the system for which she was responsible and inserted how she accomplished each step. Judy did the same and then integrated the instructions into one document.

When the system was completed, Judy printed out the instructions and cross-referenced the instructions with the applicable form and checklist. She inserted clear instructions on each form and checklist on how they should be completed. All members of the team reviewed the system and were very pleased with it. The system was finished, just in time for all its aspects to be tested. While there were a couple of things that needed revision, most of the system worked very well.

The firm had the entire case organized. When Dennis took depositions of opposing parties, he took the system with him on his laptop computer. He had all the information about the case with him so that he could pinpoint his questions. When his client was deposed, Dennis was able to quickly counter tough questions with copies of the exact document that substantiated his point. Opposing attorneys on the case were very impressed with the system. Some felt intimidated by how organized and efficient Dennis was, considering the complexity of the case.

The system made preparing for trial very easy for Dennis. While opposing attorneys on the case struggled with managing the complex issues and thousands of documents, Dennis and Judy prepared the case quickly and easily.

Two weeks before trial, the parties attended a settlement conference. Dennis was ready. He could tell that the other attorneys did not want to try the case because of the magnitude of it. He also knew that he had the upper hand because he had such good control over the issues and evidence. He started settlement negotiations, and eventually the case was settled. The client was very pleased with the outcome of the matter. Dennis was also pleased. He knew that the system helped him greatly with the case.

Because the case settled, Judy was ending her contract with the firm. Dennis saw Judy as an integral part of his team and wanted her stay with the firm to work on some other projects with him. He offered her a position as a full-time paralegal to him, and Judy accepted. The system Judy developed was used as the system for other large litigation cases the firm handled.

CHAPTER REVIEW

1. What are the five basic goals of a system?
2. What are the four types of systems, and how do they function together?
3. What types of systems are found in a law firm?
4. What are the four stages of systems development?
5. Describe the four steps of stage 1, analysis.
6. Describe the three steps of stage 2, synthesis.
7. Describe the two steps of stage 3, organization.
8. Describe the four steps of stage 4, finalization.
9. What skills must a paralegal have to develop a system?
10. How do systems evolve?
11. What should management consider when purchasing a third-party system?

EXAMPLES FOR DISCUSSION

1. WHAT HAPPENED?

Most people have encountered a service or business that seems totally disorganized. Disorganization usually means the lack of an effective system. Discuss with class members your experience with a business or service that did not function well and the possible reasons for the malfunction. Could a system have improved the service? What elements of systems planning were missing? What needed to be done to improve the system?

2. THE WRONG FORM

Brad Longstreet, a paralegal at the firm of Henderson & Ruohniemi, created a system for dissolutions of marriage. It was a good system with written system requirements, instructions, and forms and checklists. Brad became ill and was replaced with a temporary paralegal, Brenda Engstrom. Brenda followed the system and completed the documents for a simple dissolution and filed the documents with the court. When Brad returned, he discovered that the court had rejected the documents because one document was prepared on an outdated form. Brad was aware of the change in the form and tried to determine how Brenda could have filed the wrong form.

1. What step in the systems process was overlooked?
2. What must Brad do to keep the problem from happening again?
3. Should another step be added to Brad's system? If so, what step?

ASSIGNMENTS

1. Analyze your place of employment, home, or organization and answer these questions:
   a. What does the macrosystem consist of?
   b. How many microsystems are there?
   c. How many minisystems can you identify?
   d. How many subsystems are there?

2. Prepare a checklist for a task you do often at work or home.

3. Prepare a form or a document you use often at work or school.

4. Choose an established system at your place of employment, home, or organization and answer the following questions:
   a. What are the problems of the system?
   b. How do these problems affect your work? The work of others? The final work product? The environment?
   c. What are your suggestions to improve the system?

5. Prepare a master task list of the system you have chosen and do the following:
   a. Analyze its components. What could you do to make the system better? What resources would you need? How would you delegate the tasks?
   b. Incorporate your changes and revisions in a new master task list. Is the system better?
   c. Present your final master task list to your employer, your family, or the head of your organization and report any comments to the class.

6. Prepare written instructions for the system you chose in assignment 4.

7. Research case/practice management software programs. Compare the features of three programs and answer the following questions:
   a. What are the differences?
   b. What are the similarities?
   c. What tasks are automated?

8. For the law firm of Black, White & Greene, describe the following:
   a. Macrosystem
   b. Minisystems
   c. Administrative minisystems including number of attorneys, paralegals, and secretaries per attorney
   d. Substantive minisystems
   e. Procedures to keep systems updated

SELF TEST

How well did you grasp the material in the chapter? Test yourself by answering the following questions, and check your answers against the answers found in Appendix A.

1. What is the purpose of a system?
2. What are a system's goals?
3. What seven things are systems used for?
4. What are the four types of systems?
5. What is a macrosystem?
6. What types of systems are found in law firms?
7. What does a law firm's macrosystem consist of?
8. What are the three main elements that affect a firm's macrosystem?
9. How many microsystems does a law firm have?
10. What are the two microsystems in a law firm?
11. What does a law firm's administrative microsystem consist of?
12. What is the purpose of a firm's substantive microsystem?
13. What determines the number of substantive microsystems in a law firm?
14. What are the three methods of acquiring substantive microsystems?
15. What is a minisystem?
16. What determines the type and number of substantive minisystems in a law firm?
17. Why are a firm's minisystems constantly changing?
18. What is a subsystem?
19. What determines the number of subsystems in a minisystem?
20. What is systems development?
21. Who has ultimate responsibility for the management and supervision of a system?
22. What are the four stages of systems development?
23. What are the four steps of systems analysis?
24. What are the advantages of coding each step?
25. Why is it important to discuss each step of the system with coworkers?
26. What are the three steps of the synthesis process?
27. What is important to remember when delegating functions?
28. How does a systems developer consolidate?
29. What are the two steps of the organization process?
30. What is the master task list?
31. What is the purpose of a master task list?
32. What are the four steps of the finalization process?
33. What is a form letter?
34. What is a blind insert?

35. What is a checklist?
36. Why are checklists maintained in a computer?
37. Why are form documents numbered?
38. Why are written instructions important for a system?
39. Where is information for written instructions obtained?
40. What are the four sections to the system's written instructions?
41. What does the information section of written instructions contain?
42. What does the requirements section of written instructions contain?
43. What is the purpose of the instructions section?
44. What is the beginning of the instructions section?
45. What is the basis of system evaluation?
46. What does the forms and checklist section of the written instructions contain?
47. How does you follow up on a system once it has been developed?
48. How is a system revised?
49. What is the best method to store a system?
50. How is a system divided into sections?
51. How many copies of the system should there be?
52. What are the essential skills you must have for systems development?
53. What are the four common problems of systems development?
54. How do systems evolve?
55. What is a commercial substantive minisystem?
56. What does a person look for when purchasing a system?

Key Words

administrative microsystem	cross-index	substantive microsystem
backup	if clause	telephone tag
blind insert		

Student CD-ROM
For additional materials, please go to the CD in this book.

Online Companion™
For additional resources, please go to http://www.paralegal.delmar.cengage.com

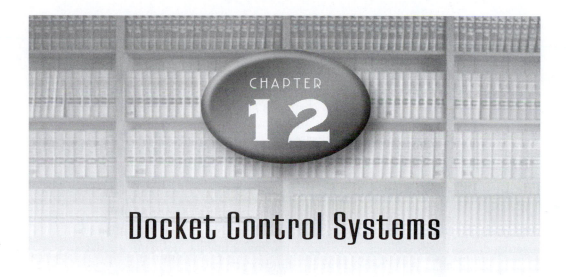

Docket Control Systems

OBJECTIVES

After completion of this chapter, the student should be able to do the following:

- List the elements of a docket control system.
- Explain what information is placed on a master calendar.
- Describe primary and secondary information.
- Explain how to maintain a tickler system.
- Explain how to tickle various types of due dates.
- Explain how to tickle statutes of limitations.
- Explain how to manage reminder dates.
- Describe the difference between a static and an automated computerized docket system.
- Explain the major features of automated docket control software.
- Set up a manual tickler system.
- Discuss the various forms and reports used in docket control systems.
- Describe file review.

INTRODUCTION

Scheduling a law firm's obligations is a great challenge for law firms, government agencies, and corporate legal departments. There are many deadlines in a law office, and a firm must have a scheduling system that controls those deadlines, allocates work so that projects are completed on time, and ensures that nothing is overlooked. An overlooked deadline can result in a legal malpractice suit, disciplinary proceedings, damage to a firm's reputation, or all of these.

To meet this challenge, every firm relies on a **docket** control system. A docket control system is perhaps the most important system in a law office. The system is so important that professional liability insurance companies require applicants to describe their docket control systems on application forms in order to obtain legal malpractice insurance. According to the ABA's Profile of Legal Malpractice Claims, calendaring errors are the leading cause of legal malpractice claims. A firm with no docket control system will not qualify for professional liability insurance.

Each member of a legal team takes an active role in a firm's docket control system and works with it every day. Secretaries and paralegals in small firms may have total responsibility for the docket system. In larger firms, maintaining a firm's docket is the responsibility of docket

docket
An abstract or brief entry of an event or deadline.

coordinators or docket clerks. Since a paralegal is responsible for the day-to-day maintenance of a case, the skill of controlling deadlines is essential. Every paralegal and legal secretary must have knowledge of docket control systems.

This chapter will detail the essential elements of a docket control system and thoroughly explain and illustrate each element. It will examine calendaring systems, tickler systems, and file review systems. After reading this chapter, a student should be familiar enough with docket control systems to develop the skill of maintaining a firm's docket and be familiar with the features of docket control software.

ELEMENTS OF A DOCKET CONTROL SYSTEM

A good docket control system contains trial dates, court and hearing dates, deposition dates, meeting dates, filing deadlines, follow-up dates, appointments, and reminder dates.

A good, reliable system will perform six functions:

1. Meet time requirements
2. Expedite the completion of tasks
3. Promote good client relations
4. Ensure that professional liability insurance requirements are satisfied
5. Reduce stress
6. Avoid financial loss by reducing malpractice claims

The characteristics of a good system are as follows:

- Provides immediate and automatic calendaring
- Provides a double-check of entries
- Allows sufficient lead time for completion of tasks
- Provides for follow-up to ensure actual performance of work
- Is easily maintained and operated

The type and sophistication of a docket control system varies according to the size of a firm, the type of firm, and the specialty of a firm. A firm's docket control system consists of a calendaring system, a tickler system, a file review system, and computerized docketing systems.

CALENDARING SYSTEMS

A firm's calendar is a key component of the smooth operation of a law office. It is imperative that all members of the legal team manage their calendars correctly. Calendars come in two forms: computerized and manual. Calendaring skills are among the most important skills a paralegal will learn. Mastery of calendaring skills is important to a paralegal's success.

Two types of calendars are used in most law offices—master calendar and personal calendar. The calendars are categorized by the type of information inserted in the calendar.

Master Calendar

master calendar
A calendar that contains hearing and deposition dates for each attorney in the firm.

Firms vary by what information is inserted on a **master calendar.** However, all master calendars contain trial dates, hearing dates, and deposition dates for each attorney in a firm. The purpose of a master calendar is to locate an attorney and to schedule future events.

A master calendar varies in size and format. Most firms have a computerized calendar program that provides a master calendar. A printout of the master calendar is distributed regularly to each member of a law firm. Large firms normally distribute a master calendar daily. A small firm that has few changes in the master calendar distributes it less often, normally weekly. Firms with an intranet do not distribute hard copies of the master calendar. These employees have immediate access to the most recent changes to the master calendar on their desktops. As a staff member makes changes or enters new information into the master calendar, it is immediately updated and accessible to all other firm employees.

Essential information on a master calendar includes the following:

- *Attorney.* First initial and last name of the attorney, or initials of the attorney.
- *Type of matter (trial, hearing, deposition).* If a trial or hearing is expected to last many days, a line or other designation is drawn through those days. If it is a motion, the type of motion is indicated. It is appropriate to use abbreviations.
- *Date and time.* If an event consists of several days, those days are included on the master calendar.
- *Name of case.* The case name is inserted on the master calendar. A client's surname is always indicated as the first name of a case, for example, *Client v. Name of Defendant* if the client is a plaintiff or *Client adv. Name of Plaintiff* if the client is a defendant.
- *Location.* If the matter is a trial or hearing, the court and the courtroom are indicated. If it is a deposition, the address of where it will be held is indicated.

Exhibit 12–1 is an example of a master calendar.

Master Calendar				
MONDAY	**TUESDAY**	**WEDNESDAY**	**THURSDAY**	**FRIDAY**
1 J FH—9:00 Trial, Black v. Claridge, Sup. Ct. D-56 - - - - - ERN—9:00 Trial— Gardner v. Larson, Cir. Ct D-87 * * * *	2 * * * * * * * * * * * PDF—10:00 Dep., Brown v. Redd, 346 Capitol St. LA, #787	3 * * * * * * * * * *} BSD—9:00 Hrg. Motion to compel, Sand v. Waters, Sup. Ct. D12	4 WAC—10:00 Dep., Jacks v. Yawl, here REN—2:00 Dep., Tru v. Falz, here	5 PDF 9:00 Motion to quash, Pert v. Yerl, Cir. Ct., D-5
8	9 LCN—9:00 Disso Marriage of Yale, Sup. Ct. D-33	10 xxxxxxxxxxxxxxxxxxxxxxxxx BSD—10:00 Dep., Young v. Osterholm 1600 Main St., LA	11 xxxxxxxxxxxxx} NAD—1:00 Hrg. Luther v. Ti, Tax Ct., Rm. 9	12 ++++++++++++++++++++
15 ++++++++++++} 2:00 REN Dep., Tooly v. Hale, here ^^^^^^^^^	16 ^^^^^^^^^^^^^^^^^^^	17 - - - - -] ^^^^^^^^^^^^^^^^^^^^^^^^^^^	18 ^^^^^^^^^^^^^^^^^^}	19
22 HOLIDAY	23	24	25	26

EXHIBIT 12–1 Sample Master Calendar

personal calendar
An individual's calendar that contains the same information as a master calendar but also includes appointment dates, follow-updates, deadlines, and personal information.

statute of limitations
The time period after an offense within which a lawsuit must be filed.

ETHICS ALERT

Personal Calendar

Each member of the legal team has a **personal calendar.** A personal calendar contains two types of information: primary and secondary.

Primary information includes all of the information inserted on the master calendar (court hearings, trials, and depositions). These dates are included in a personal calendar as well as the master calendar to ensure that the information is not missed. It is also necessary that the information be in front of the attorney and paralegal at all times for scheduling purposes.

Primary information also includes the **statute of limitations** for each case for which the legal team is responsible. Statutes of limitations are entered in the personal calendar in red or in bold. *It is very important that statutes of limitations are not missed.* If a statute of limitation is missed, the client is barred from filing the action. The attorney becomes liable to the client for damages that may result in a legal malpractice lawsuit, disciplinary proceedings, or both. As an extra precaution, statutes of limitations are also entered in a tickler system (discussed later in this chapter).

Secondary information includes the following:

* Dates and times of appointments with clients
* Dates and times of conferences
* Other dates, such as bar association luncheons or continuing education obligations
* Personal reminders, such as birthdays and vacations dates
* Deadlines and reminder dates

Some people combine primary and secondary information into one personal calendar. Others have a separate calendar for secondary information. Most personal calendars are computerized and are part of a firm's docket control software program, as shown in Exhibit 12–2. However, manual calendars, or calendars that are maintained by hand, are an important element of a firm's calendaring policy in the event of computer malfunction.

Changing days
Move ahead or back one day by clicking the right (ahead) or left (back) arrow.

Schedule conflicts
Shown in red.

Event duration
Blocked out time is shown in color.

Entering events
Double-click the desired time. The New Event dialog appears.

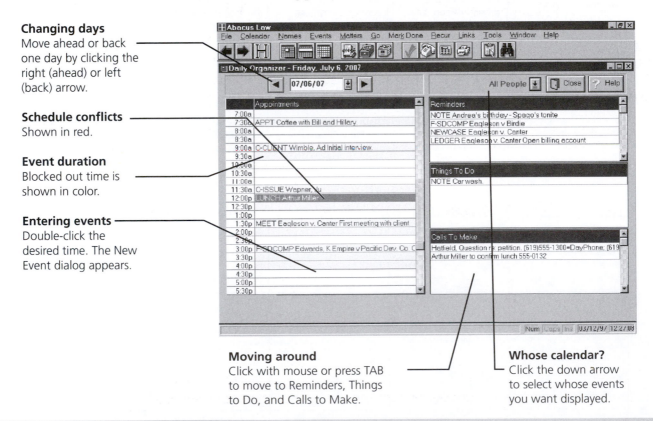

Moving around
Click with mouse or press TAB to move to Reminders, Things to Do, and Calls to Make.

Whose calendar?
Click the down arrow to select whose events you want displayed.

EXHIBIT 12–2 Sample Personal Calendar *(Reprinted with permission of Abacus Data Systems, Inc.)*

A paralegal's personal calendar is a duplicate of the attorney's personal calendar. If a paralegal reports to more than one attorney, the paralegal's personal calendar will contain information for each of those attorneys. These duplicate calendars are used to schedule events for the attorney. For this reason, it is important to update personal calendars daily. A personal calendar may also contain a tickler system, as discussed later in this chapter.

Most professional liability insurance companies recommend that each attorney maintain a manual calendar in addition to a computerized calendar as a backup in the event the computerized system is not available. This backup system will ensure that valuable information is not lost. It is also a method of double-checking entries.

A manual calendar consisting of primary and secondary information may be a large appointment book, small appointment book, desk calendar, or an electronic calendar device. It may also be a hard copy of the information stored in the computer. Some attorneys use all three: an electronic calendar to transport to court, a large appointment book for the person in charge of scheduling, and a desk calendar for the attorney's office. Paralegals often use desk calendars for their personal schedules and have a separate calendar that is a duplicate of the attorney's calendar book.

Calendaring Procedures

Events are calendared as soon as possible after they are discovered. Waiting too long could have disastrous consequences. Documents from opposing parties that require a response or other action are entered into the docket system as they are received. Each document is stamped or initialed (or both) indicating that the event was docketed, and then the document is delivered to the appropriate attorney or paralegal. The absence of the initials or stamp of a docket clerk on any document containing a hearing or deposition date indicates that the date was not docketed. In many firms, the pertinent file is pulled, the document put on top of the file, and the file delivered to the appropriate attorney so that the document can be reviewed with the file.

Events that require an action and are generated within the firm must also be calendared as soon as possible after they are discovered. The person responsible for maintaining the calendar enters the events into the system.

Regular calendar meetings, at least once or twice a week, should be set with the attorney, paralegal, and legal secretary. Calendar meetings are often short, informal meetings. If a secretary or paralegal is responsible for the calendars of more than one attorney, calendar meetings should be held more often than for those who work for just one attorney. Calendars should be updated daily, and the updated information should be shared with other members of the legal team. This will ensure that everyone has updated calendars.

Many medium and large firms have a docketing department that handles their docket. A **docket coordinator** is in charge of the docketing process. This is known as a centralized docketing system. A legal secretary or paralegal instructs the docket coordinator to insert an event on the docket by completing a docket request sheet, such as the one shown in Exhibit 12–3.

docket coordinator
A person in charge of a firm's docketing process.

Black, White & Greene

Docket Request Sheet

Requesting party _____   Responsible atty/LA _____

Case name _____ File no. _____

Event _____

Date _____ Time _____

Place _____

Reminder _____ Urging _____ Warning _____ Alert _____

Docketed on _____ [date] _____ By _____ [name or initials]

EXHIBIT 12–3   Sample Docket Request Sheet

Everyone in a firm should be familiar with a docket request sheet and should know how to use it. A docket request sheet contains the following information:

- Name or initials of the person requesting the docket entry
- Responsible attorney
- Name of case and file number
- Type of matter (e.g., trial or deposition)
- Date and time
- Place (if court, indicate courtroom)
- Reminder dates
- Date the event was docketed
- Signature or initials of docket clerk indicating completion

Many different docket request sheets are used. These sheets are either purchased from a legal supply company or developed by the firm and printed on multipart, multicolored paper. Each docket request sheet should have an original and three copies, with each page a different color (e.g., white, blue, pink, and yellow). As a secretary or paralegal completes the top white sheet, three copies of the information are automatically made. The requesting party keeps the bottom pink sheet as a record that the request was made. The remaining original and two copies are transferred to the docket coordinator. A docket clerk enters the information and signs and dates the docket sheet. The docket coordinator keeps the yellow sheet and returns the white original and blue copy to the requesting party, indicating that the docket entry was made. The secretary or paralegal keeps the white original as a record that the event was docketed and as a reminder to enter the information into the manual calendars. The blue copy is given to the attorney so that he or she can enter the information into a manual calendar. This docketing process is shown in Exhibit 12–4.

A calendar request may also be e-mailed to the person responsible for the calendar. In many cases, this is the attorney's secretary or paralegal. An acknowledgment that the e-mail was received and the event was calendared is essential. The requesting party must have a system in place to monitor acknowledgments to calendar requests. This may be a reply to the calendar request that the event was calendared. The reply e-mail may then be filed in a separate calendar request file.

If a firm has an intranet, an updated calendar is instantly available to all employees. However, if manual calendars are kept, it is the secretary's responsibility to ensure that the information is inserted in the manual calendars.

In a small office, docketing is handled by a secretary or paralegal, and the procedures are less formal. A secretary or paralegal enters the docketing information directly into the firm's computer. A docket request sheet is used to inform other members of the legal team that an event was docketed so that they can insert the information into their calendars. This can be by e-mail or hard copy. A docket request sheet consisting of an original and two copies is usually sufficient. The original is a record that the matter was docketed, one copy is given to the paralegal to enter the information into a personal calendar, and the other copy is given to the attorney to enter the information into a personal calendar. It is preferable to e-mail the information rather than use a hard copy. It is easy for slips of paper to get lost on the recipient's desk. As stated above, an acknowledgment of the receipt of the information is important.

Calendaring Ethics

ETHICS ALERT

Members of a legal team consult their calendars many times throughout the day. Their calendars should always be handy so that they can be reviewed and revised easily. The calendars are usually kept on each person's desk. *It is important to keep all calendars, whether they are computerized or manual, out of the view of clients.* If there is a possibility that a client will visit

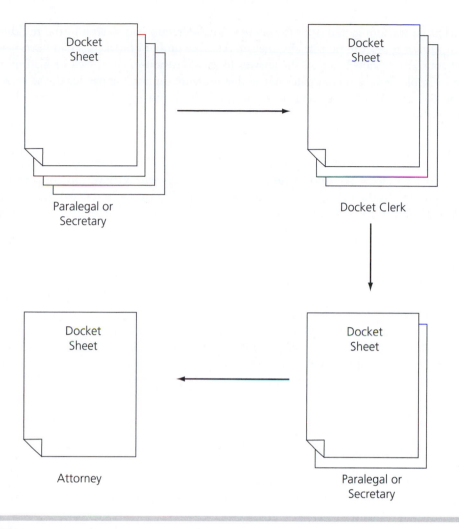

EXHIBIT 12–4 Route of a Docket Request Sheet

your office, remove your calendars from view. Calendars contain names of other clients. To ensure the confidentiality of clients' cases, always keep calendars private.

TICKLER SYSTEMS

A tickler system, also known as a come-up system, is a method of controlling deadlines. It is used as a reminder and follow-up system. Documents must be filed with the court on time, and the filing of some documents triggers the clock to run on other deadlines. Every law firm has a system to control these deadlines. If no reminder system were implemented, a legal team would be in a constant state of panic.

For example, Jane Gavin was notified that her client, Flo Nygun, was served with a summons and complaint on June 1. Flo had 30 days in which to answer the complaint, which was due on July 1. Flo notified Jane of the service on June 3, which means that the complaint had to be answered within 27 days. Jane entered July 1 into her calendar as the due date for the answer, without any additional reminders. On July 1, Jane directed her paralegal, Jack Schrantz, to stop what he was doing and immediately draft an answer to Flo's complaint, which was due that day. Jack, already working on a rush project for Jane, had to drop what he was doing and draft the answer. The secretary had to stop in the middle of a very important project to prepare the answer. After a number of revisions had been made, a special courier was called to rush the answer to the courthouse. Jane's lack of planning and failure to implement reminder dates put undue pressure on her, the paralegal, the secretary, and the courier. A tickler system uses reminder dates and specific tickler procedures to eliminate this pressure.

The basic rule of a tickler system is that no item is removed from the system until it is completed. The system will keep a matter active until completed. Each morning, a secretary, or other member of the legal team, retrieves the tickler information and gives the attorney and paralegal the information. Some secretaries will retrieve the appropriate file to correspond with the tickler entries and give it to the attorney or paralegal. *An attorney or paralegal should never be verbally reminded of tickler information.* If the information is verbally communicated, chances are that the information will get lost in myriad other matters on the minds of the attorney and paralegal. It is important that an attorney and paralegal have written notification of reminder date information. Tickler reports are usually put on the attorney's or paralegal's desk so they are reminded whenever they look at it.

Tickler systems are both manual and automated. Most law firms have an electronic calendaring system, and most legal malpractice insurance companies require use of an electronic calendaring system. However, knowing how to manually enter deadlines and due dates is a skill that offers many benefits for the paralegal. A proper docket control system must have two separate calendars so that scheduling errors are avoided. A computerized system and a manual system are recommended so that important data is not lost in case of computer failure.

Manual Tickler Systems

A manual tickler system can still be found in law offices as a backup to a computerized system. Compared to an automated system, manual tickler systems are less reliable, more time-consuming, and error prone.

The manual system that has been used by law offices since 1915 is the basic system. It has been so successful that no changes have been made to it since that time. To set up a basic tickler system, the following materials are needed:

1. A tin or wood box 3-1/2 inches deep
2. One set of monthly divider cards, 3 × 5 inches
3. Three sets of daily reminder cards, numbered 1 through 31
4. Yearly divider cards, 3 × 5 inches, for 3 years
5. Docket Request Sheets, plain 3 × 5-inch cards, or paper in four different colors.

All materials can be purchased from any stationery store and are inexpensive. The monthly index cards are placed in the box in sequence. The three sets of daily reminder cards are placed behind the current month's divider, and the next month's divider. The yearly cards are placed behind the monthly cards. Exhibit 12–5 is an example of a basic manual tickler system.

A docket request sheet, like the one shown in Exhibit 12–3, is used with this system. A docket request sheet can be developed on 3 × 5-inch cards or slips of different color paper. The sheets can also be purchased from a legal supply store. They come in multipart sets with each page a different color. If docket request sheets are purchased from a legal supply store, they must have at least four pages in different colors. The original white page is for the due date, the pink slip for the warning date, the blue slip for the urging date, and the yellow slip for the reminder date (or other color-coding scheme as the firm may choose). When a docket request sheet is completed, each page is inserted behind the corresponding date. Each morning, the tickler slips are pulled and the appropriate actions taken.

ETHICS ALERT

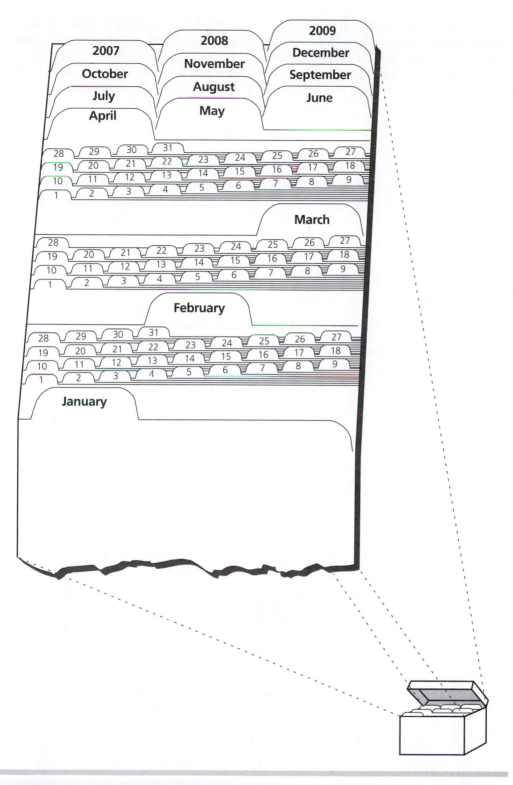

EXHIBIT 12–5   Sample Manual Tickler System

When the current month ends, there should be no tickler sheets left behind any daily dividers in that month. The daily divider cards in the current month are then transferred to the first month without daily divider cards. Tickler slips behind that month are then put behind the appropriate daily divider. Yearly index cards are used for long-range dates for such events as judgment renewal dates, stockholder meetings, tax return dates, statutes of limitations, and review dates for wills and contracts.

To be effective, a manual system must be maintained. Nothing should be overlooked. A method should be devised to identify weekend and holiday dates so no reminder sheets will be inserted behind that date. Colored sticker dots can be put on those cards that represent weekend and holiday dates. When the daily cards are moved to the back of the system, the colored sticker dots are removed and inserted on the holiday and weekend dates of the current month.

Tickler Procedures

A tickler system is integrated into the calendaring system because it is preferable for scheduling purposes to have all information in one place—a calendar. Each member of the team can see the entire day's activities at a glance and plan accordingly. Each office has its own methods.

For example, in a manual system that combines calendar and tickler dates, a paralegal enters calendar information on the left side of his or her personal calendar as follows:

8:30 Meeting with Dave re calendar review

12:00 Paralegal Assn. meeting—Jack's Restaurant

2:00 Conference with client Sanders re interrogatories

3:30 Deposition of N. Nelson re *Davis v. Nelson,* here

On the right side of the personal calendar, the paralegal enters tickler information as follows:

Warning: *Smith v. Johnson* interrogs due 6/27*

Reminder: Galt v. Lowe Response to motion to compel due 7/3*

Due date: Answer of P. Lang due today, *Anderson v. Lang*

Due date: Answer to interrogatories due from Reed, *Reed v. Jackson*

(*Note:* The asterisk [*] indicates documents to be prepared by the firm. Entries with no asterisk concern documents due from opposing parties.)

Exhibit 12–6 is an example of a desk calendar with the calendar information on one side, and tickler information on the other.

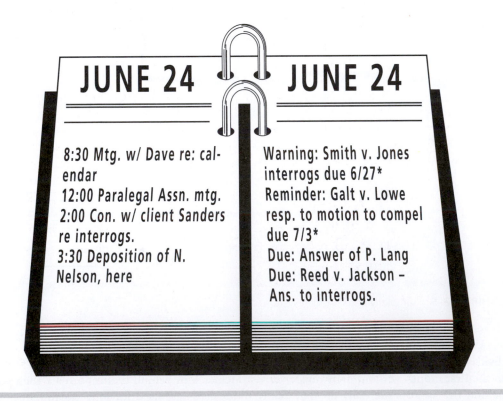

EXHIBIT 12–6 Sample Manual Desk Calendar

DETERMINING DUE DATES Before you can enter reminder dates, you must first determine the due date. Three dates are considered when determining due dates.

1. *Trigger date.* The **trigger date** starts the clock running on an event. It is the date a document was served or delivered or the date it was mailed as indicated on a **proof of service by mail** form. In the previous example, the trigger date is the date that Flo Nygun was served with a summons and complaint, June 1. It started the 30-day countdown to the deadline for the answer.

[handwritten: Do not Count]

2. *Due date.* The due date is the day a document is due. If a due date falls on a holiday or weekend day, the due date is the next business day. In the previous example, the due date for Flo's answer was July 1, 30 days after she was served with the summons and complaint. If July 1 is a Saturday, the due date is the next business day, July 3.

3. *Mail date.* The mail date is the date a document must be mailed to reach its destination by the due date. The exact number of days that should be set aside for mailing is determined by statute. For state court cases, the state statute is applied. For federal court cases, the federal statute is applied. Be sure to check the statute to determine the time period that should be set aside for the mail date. The federal statute requires that 3 days be set aside for mailing. In the previous example, assume that Flo Nygun's case is a federal case and that Jane Gavin will mail the answer to the court. To reach the court on the due date, Flo's answer must be mailed 3 days before the due date: June 28 (July 1 is counted as the third day).

[handwritten: Mail box rule]

If the document is served by e-mail (must have written consent of all parties in a federal case), the 3-day mail time applies. A document is deemed mailed when it is deposited in a mail box, picked up by a mail carrier, or transmitted electronically.

When counting days to determine the due date of a document, the first day is *excluded* and the last day is *included*. In other words, the trigger date is not counted. The first day after the trigger date, including holidays and weekends, is the first day counted, and the due date is the last day counted. If the due date falls on a holiday or weekend, the due date is the next business day.

In a federal case, weekends and holidays are counted except when a due date is less than 11 days after the trigger date, at which time holidays and weekends are not counted. For state court cases, each state has different requirements. Check your state's statutes regarding mail time.

For example, a firm received a cross-complaint that required an answer from a client in 30 days. The proof of service by mail indicated that the document was mailed on November 15. Calculate the due date as follows: You did not receive the cross-complaint on November 15 because that is the date it was mailed. Federal law allows you to add 3 days to November 15 for mailing (November 18). November 18 is the date you begin counting days, regardless of the actual date you received the cross-complaint. November 18 is not included in the count. Count 30 days with day 1 starting on November 19. December 18 is the 30th day and is therefore the due date. If you are going to mail the answer to the court, subtract 3 days to allow for mail time to arrive at the mail date: December 15. To be timely, the answer to the cross-complaint must be completed and mailed on December 15.

A simpler method of counting days is to eliminate the two sets of 3 days for mailing because, in essence, they cancel each other out. Instead of adding 3 mailing days to the date of mailing as shown on the proof of service form, count 30 days from the date the document was mailed as shown on the proof of service form. You will arrive at the same due date that you would by adding and subtracting the mailing time (30 + 3 − 3 = 30). Mailing dates are important when determining due dates and are an essential element of calculating due dates. Be sure to check your state's rule regarding the number of days allowed for mailing.

trigger date
The date of an event that starts the clock running on a deadline.

proof of service by mail
A document that informs the recipient of the date the attached document was mailed.

Of Interest . . .

DOCKET CONTROL CHECKLIST

- ☒ Double-check all entries.
- ☒ When setting reminders, provide enough lead time to allow a task to be completed.
- ☒ Have regular calendar meetings.
- ☒ Train all employees how to use the system effectively.
- ☒ Always insert follow-up dates.
- ☒ Screen incoming mail for calendaring needs.
- ☒ Have procedures for handling deadlines in case of absence.
- ☒ Do not procrastinate.
- ☒ Do not leave projects to be completed on the due date.
- ☒ Always check statutes and rules.
- ☒ Do not assume anything.

DETERMINING REMINDER DATES For documents to be completed on time, reminder dates must be integrated into a docket system to remind an attorney and a paralegal that action is required on a file. In addition, reminder dates must be integrated into the system to alert the legal team when a statute of limitations is due to expire, when documents are due from an opposing party, and when other important events are scheduled to take place. The lawyer and support staff should work together to determine the reminder dates that are entered prior to the deadline. Normally, there are four reminder dates.

1. *Reminder date.* A reminder date is the first of a series of reminders that a deadline is approaching. It is the least urgent of the reminders.
2. *Urging date.* An urging date is the second in a series of reminders that a deadline is approaching. It signifies that a deadline is getting very close and urges the legal team to take action on a matter.
3. *Warning date.* A warning date is the third and last reminder that a deadline is approaching. It is a warning that action must be taken or else a deadline may be missed. It signifies that no further reminders will be given before the due date.
4. *Alert date.* An alert date is an optional reminder date that is used when three reminders are not enough for a project to be completed.

The time intervals between these dates depend on the type of deadline imposed, the type of project, and where holidays and weekends fall on a calendar. The exact time intervals between reminder dates vary from a day to a year in some cases. State and federal statutes determine the time periods within which an event must happen, and reminder dates must work within these time frames. Establishing reminder date guidelines is subject to the discretion of firm management.

The accompanying CD provides a Docket Calculation Chart to help you calculate due dates and reminder dates.

ENTERING REMINDER DATES Reminder dates are used to manage projects. They keep a legal team on schedule by alerting them to the next step in a project. Placing reminder dates at the appropriate interval gives a legal team the necessary time to complete a project.

Placing reminder dates in the correct time intervals requires knowledge of the requirements of each type of project. Lengthy projects require four and sometimes more reminder dates, and short-term projects require only one or two reminders. For most projects, three reminders are sufficient. Anticipating the need for reminders is essential so that the correct number of reminders will be inserted into the system. The more experience you gain with various calendaring projects, the better you can anticipate a project's tickler needs. Each reminder date signifies completion of a part of a project, as follows:

- Reminder date—10 days before due date: do research and review information to prepare document
- Urging date—7 days before due date: prepare draft document
- Warning date—3 days before due date: finalize document
- Due date—file document

There are no specific rules that govern reminder date intervals. These time intervals are general guidelines and are very flexible. Some firms may set the reminder date for 15 days before the due date instead of 10. Time intervals between reminder dates must be adjustable to accommodate holidays, weekends, and other events. Although it is a simple matter to count back 3 or 4 days from a due date, attention must be given to holidays and weekends. A reminder date cannot be a weekend or holiday date. A docket clerk or secretary must know on what dates holidays and weekends fall so that reminder dates are not entered on those dates. If a matter is inadvertently calendared for a holiday or weekend date, it is likely to be overlooked.

For example, suppose that the 10th day before a due date is a Sunday. A reminder date cannot be entered there. Therefore, it would have to be entered on the next business day, Monday, which is the 9th day before the due date, or it could be entered on the Friday before, which is the 12th day before the due date. This adjustment would require that all reminder dates be adjusted accordingly:

- Reminder date—9 days before due date
- Urging date—6 days before due date
- Warning date—2 or 3 days before due date

Most computer tickler systems will let a docket clerk or secretary see what dates are holidays or weekends and will alert the docket clerk if an entry is inserted on a weekend date. Some software programs will automatically reject an entry on a holiday or weekend. Law firm holidays, retreats, or other events for which an office will be closed can be programmed into the computer so that no entries are made on those dates. Another example of tickling reminder dates around weekends and holidays is found in Exhibit 12–7.

Statutes of Limitations   Monitoring statutes of limitations is extremely important. As noted previously, if a statute of limitations is missed, a client is prohibited from proceeding. Statute of limitations dates are entered into the calendar as well as into the tickler system. Statutes of limitations are set by state and federal law. There are different statutes of limitations for different types of actions, and they vary by state. For example, a breach of written contract may have a 4-year statute of limitations and a personal injury action a 1-year statute of limitations. *Before calendaring reminder dates for a statute of limitations, always check the statute to determine the exact time period.*

ETHICS ALERT

For a 1-year statute of limitation, four dates are entered:

1. Reminder date—120 days before due date
2. Urging date—60 days before due date
3. Warning date—30 days before due date
4. Due date—5 days before actual due date (just to be sure the statute is not missed; if a document is mailed, the due date is the mail date)

Suppose a document is due 30 days from November 26, on December 26, which is a Sunday as shown on the following calendar. The due date will be December 27, and the answer will be calendared as follows:

December						
Sun	Mon	Tues	Wed	Thur	Fri	Sat
			1	2	3	4
5	6	7	8	9	10	11
12	13	14	15	16	17	18
19	20	21	22	23	24	25
26	27	28	29	30	31	

1. December 15—Reminder date—do research and compile information to prepare answer.
2. December 20—Urging date—draft answer—December 18 and 19 would be inappropriate urging dates because they are weekend dates.
3. December 23—Warning date—finalize answer. Since 3 days before the due date is Christmas Eve, chances are the office will close early. Therefore, Christmas Eve would be an inappropriate warning date.
4. December 27—Due date—file answer.

EXHIBIT 12–7   Sample Tickler System for 30-Day Deadline

For a 4-year statute of limitations, five dates are entered:

1. Reminder date—1 year before due date
2. Alert date—120 days before due date
3. Urging date—60 days before due date
4. Warning date—30 days before due date
5. Due date—5 days before actual due date (just to be sure the statute is not missed; if a document is mailed, the due date is the mail date)

Litigation and Case Documents   Litigation cases have many deadlines, the majority of which are 30 days. Normally, a standard 30-day deadline has three reminder dates:

1. Reminder date—10 days before the due date
2. Urging date—7 days before the due date
3. Warning date—3 days before the due date

If a document will be mailed, the reminder dates for a 30-day deadline are as follows:

1. Reminder date—10 days before the mail date
2. Urging date—7 days before the mail date
3. Warning date—3 days before the mail date
4. Mail date—3 days before due date (in federal cases, but subject to state statute)
5. Due date—actual due date

In the previous example, Jane should have tickled the due date and entered three reminder dates:

1. June 21—reminder date: get information together to prepare answer
2. June 24—urging date: draft answer
3. June 28—warning date: finalize answer
4. July 1—due date: last day to file answer

If Jane was going to mail the answer to the court, she would have tickled the mail date and entered three reminder dates:

1. June 18—reminder date: get information together to prepare answer
2. June 22—urging date: draft answer
3. June 25—warning date: finalize answer
4. June 28—mail date: mail answer to the court
5. July 1—due date: court receives answer

For a document that must be filed within 15 days, such as a response to a motion, two reminders are sufficient. For example, a response that has a due date of June 23 needs two reminders:

1. June 16—reminder date, 7 days before due date: draft response
2. June 20—warning date, 3 days before due date: finalize response
3. June 23—due date: file response

Reminder Dates of Opposing Parties   A document that is due from an opposing party must be documented to alert an attorney of a possible **default,** or failure to respond. When entering the due dates of opposing parties, it is not necessary to have reminders; one entry is sufficient. A method should be devised to differentiate between due dates of clients and due dates of opposing parties. Various methods are used to differentiate between the two. If a computerized system is used, a client's information can be entered in italics, bold, or color. If a manual system is used, the information may be entered in red for a client and black for an opposing party, or an asterisk (*) may be inserted by information concerning a client, or a "C" for a client, and an "O" for an opposing party can be entered. Whatever method is chosen, it is important to be consistent.

Other Reminder Dates   Paralegals and attorneys use a tickler system to remind them of several important dates and events. If a paralegal requests that a client send documents, the paralegal must have a reminder system to follow up. The circumstances of each event will dictate the dates of the reminders. If a paralegal mails court documents to a client for approval or signature, enough time must be allowed for mailing and for the review of the documents. This will require additional tickler dates. In the previous example, if Jane sent the answer to Flo for her approval and signature, the tickler dates for the answer would be as follows:

1. June 15—reminder date: get information together for answer
2. June 20—urging date: draft answer
3. June 21—alert date: complete answer
4. June 22—mail date: send answer to client for approval and signature
5. June 27—alert date: receive answer from client
6. June 28—warning date: finalize answer
7. July 1—due date: file answer

If a document mailed to a client does not require filing with a court or is not subject to other deadlines, an entry must be made in a paralegal's tickler system if the document is expected back. If an entry is not made, the event may be overlooked. The timing of the entry is subject to the paralegal's judgment but should give the client enough time to review the document and return it to the paralegal. If a client is a corporation and a document must be

default
Failure to respond within the required time.

approved by corporate officers, the paralegal must allow the client more time. An example of tickler entries for return of documents that were mailed on June 4 is as follows:

1. June 14—reminder date: interrogatories back from client Jeffries?
2. June 21—warning date: interrogatories back from client Jeffries? (mailed 6/4)

When the entry comes up on the paralegal's tickler system on June 14, if the documents were received, the paralegal eliminates the June 21 entry from the tickler system. If the documents were not received, the reminder date tag tells the paralegal that a warning date will follow. The paralegal then decides whether follow-up should be immediate or whether it can wait until the warning date. When the warning date comes up on June 21, the paralegal contacts the client by mail, e-mail, or telephone and inquires about the status of the documents. If a letter is sent, a reply must also be tickled for about a week in the future. If a deadline is put in the letter, the paralegal must insert that date into the tickler system and follow up as necessary.

Another area of use for the tickler system is to track verbal and office commitments. If a client, opposing counsel, or other person agrees to provide a paralegal with information on a certain date, an entry is made to a tickler system to remind the paralegal that the information is coming. If a paralegal is scheduled to give a report at a law firm meeting, an entry is made in the paralegal's tickler system to allow the paralegal enough time to prepare the report.

Tickler systems are also used to complete work of an absent attorney or paralegal. If an attorney is unexpectedly ill and must be out of the office for a period of time, the tickler system is consulted by other attorneys in the office who will temporarily take over the absent attorney's workload. This ensures that no project or deadline is overlooked in the attorney's absence.

Tickler systems schedule tasks to distribute work without undue stress and pressure on a legal team. Allowing sufficient time to complete a project eliminates frustration caused by the absence of employees who are essential to the completion of the project or other unforeseen circumstances.

Docketing due dates and reminder dates correctly is only half the battle; getting the job done is the other half. The best docketing system in the world will not put the words down on paper. It is essential that each member of the legal team understand the importance of docketing procedures. Docket meetings with the attorney, paralegal, and secretary should be priority meetings held at least once a week and preferably more often. Detailed to-do lists should be kept current and reviewed.

Of Interest . . .

$750,000 A DAY

A calendaring error can be very expensive. The Los Angeles firm of Latham & Watkins learned the importance of accurate calendaring the hard way.

First Los Angeles Bank filed a legal malpractice suit in L.A. Superior Court that named Latham and Watkins. The bank complains that when the firm was defending it against an irate bank patron, Latham's miscalculation caused the firm to miss a deadline by 1 day, which resulted in a $750,000 liability, including interest against its client, First Bank. The underlying case concerns a customer, Patricia Teitel, who sued the bank for dishonoring her outstanding checks when her boss accused her of forgery.

A jury awarded Ms. Teitel $509,000 against the bank, $500,000 of which was punitive damages. The bank's efforts to get the amount reduced or win a new trial got mixed results during two trips to the California Second District Court of Appeal. The bank says it had a chance to win until its attorney gave the court the wrong date to issue an order, so the initial award became final.

COMPUTERIZED DOCKETING SYSTEMS

There are three types of computerized docketing systems: static calendar programs, automated docketing programs, and online calendaring services. Computerized docketing programs are found in most law firms today. Manual systems still exist in some areas, but they are being replaced by computerized systems.

Computerized docket control software programs combine calendar and tickler systems. In other words, the calendar contains both calendar and tickler information. Many law firms use docket control software to manage their calendars. There are hundreds of docket control software packages available for the legal marketplace. Some packages are directed to large firms, and others are more conducive to small firms.

Static Calendar Programs

A **static calendar program** allows the user to enter dates into the program, and the event will be noted on a specific date of the calendar. Both primary and secondary information are entered, along with tickler dates. The program can compile reports for printing, as shown in Exhibit 12–8. All dates, including tickler dates, are inserted manually. These programs are also known as Personal Information Managers (PIMs). Most static systems are not specifically

static calendar programs
A calendar program that requires entries to be made manually.

Black, White & Greene

For week of May 1, 20XX, to May 5, 20XX

DATE	ATTY/LA	TYPE	CASE	TASK
5/1/XX	White	Reminder	Hopewell v. Miller	Answer of Jenkins
5/1/XX	Greene	Due date	ABC Corp.	Notice of annual mtg.
5/1/XX	Greene	Reminder	XYZ Corp.	File articles of incorp.
5/1/XX	Boen	Reminder	Goldberg Agmt.	Agmt. rec'd from client
5/1/XX	White	Due date	Reed v. Taylor	Req. for prod. of doc.*
5/1/XX	Boen	Due date	Keel v. Davis	Resp. to interogs. (Keel)*
5/2/XX	White	Reminder	DEF Corp.	Prep. contract
5/2/XX	White	Warning	Baxter v. Hemstreet	Trial brief*
5/2/XX	White	Urging	Hedfer v. Marine Co.	Answer of Dell*
5/2/XX	Boen	Warning	Tazmanian v. Yuan	Ans. to Yuan interogs.*
5/2/XX	Greene	Warning	Travel Time v. AA	Judgment expires 5/10
5/3/XX	Black	Due date	Estate of Pride	Final accounting*
5/3/XX	White	Due date	Beil Ins. Co.	File tax return
5/3/XX	Black	Reminder	Est. of Harold	File petition
5/4/XX	White	Urging	Hopewell v. Miller	Answer of Jenkins
5/4/XX	Boen	Warning	Noel v. Granger	Verification from Noel?
5/4/XX	Boen	Reminder	Allway v. Wier	Req. for prod. of docs.*
5/4/XX	Greene	Urging	XYZ Corp.	File articles of incorp.
5/4/XX	White	Due date	Sand v. See	Res. motion to compel*
5/4/XX	Black	Urging	Est. of Capp	Letters testamentary*
5/5/XX	White	Urging	DEF Corp.	Prep. contract
5/5/XX	White	Due date	Baxter v. Hemstreet	Trial brief

EXHIBIT 12–8 Sample Static Calendar System Tickler Report

designed for a law office. An example of a static calendar system is Microsoft Outlook. Mark Bassingthwaighte, Risk Management Coordinator for Attorney Liability Protection Society, stated in 2003: "About half of the law firms I've visited are using Microsoft Outlook—and many of them are still missing deadlines, big time!"

Static calendar programs are very similar to manual, handwritten systems. The only difference is that a computer, rather than a desk calendar or appointment book, is used to generate the information. Therefore, they are prone to error. For example, when a software program permits operators to enter case names, they may inadvertently schedule events for a single case under numerous different case names. Data entered for a case named American International Parts Corp. might have events scheduled for it under American International Parts, American Parts Corp., AIP Corp., or American International. When a report is generated for it, only information entered for American International Parts Corp. or American Parts Corp. will be generated, resulting in essential information entered under the other names being excluded and therefore missed.

Since tickler dates are calculated manually, it is possible for an entry to be scheduled for a holiday or weekend, resulting in lost information. Further consistency problems arise when more than one person manages the calendar program. Static calendar systems are found in small firms and are not recommended for medium or large firms, especially those with heavy trial schedules. An example of a static calendar is shown in Exhibit 12–9.

Automated Docketing Programs

Automated docketing programs are designed specifically for law firms. Two areas of automated docketing software set them apart from static calendaring programs: (1) they prevent users from entering data incorrectly, (2) they apply preprogrammed court rules to schedule events. Such programs automatically calculate and schedule important dates, including tickler dates, and insert them on a calendar. These programs are very powerful and provide the most accurate calculation of dates, warn users of approaching deadlines, and provide the best protection against missed deadlines.

Legal malpractice insurance companies are so impressed with automated docketing programs that some require their insureds to use one. In addition, some insurance companies offer their insureds a discount on their premiums of up to 10 percent if they implement an automated docketing program. Insurance companies, such as Virginia Surety Insurance Corporation, will not insure a law firm that does not have this type of software in place.

Some consider automated docketing programs an essential tool for all law firms. Scheduling deadlines can be a complicated, time-consuming task. Law firms must adhere to many statutes regarding deadline rules. There are deadline rules for federal courts, federal appellate courts, the U.S. Supreme Court, state trial courts, state appellate courts, and state supreme courts, and there are also specialty-specific rules (e.g., bankruptcy rules, local rules of state courts, and local rules of federal courts). It is a monumental task to know all these rules to determine due dates correctly. Automated docketing programs contain databases that are preprogrammed with docketing rules so that the correct rule and its time frame are automatically applied to a client's matter. Software with preprogrammed court rules is called **court rules-based calendaring software.**

court rules-based calendaring software
Calendaring software that has state, federal, and local court rules programmed into it.

Court rules-based calendaring software has federal, state, and local court rules programmed into it. When a trigger date is entered, all other dates are automatically calculated based on the law. This feature reduces scheduling errors dramatically. If a statute or rule should change, the system automatically recalculates the dates for all cases in the system. This feature is very valuable to a firm with a heavy trial schedule. Going through the entire calendar to adjust dates because of a rule change would take a very long time. Most court rules-based calendaring software vendors update their software quarterly. A firm ran into this rule change problem in the case of *Laffit Pincay, et al v. Vincent S. Andrews, et al.* A copy of the case is found on the accompanying CD.

Daily Calendar/To Do	Wednesday, September 12, 2007	Untitled

August 2007	September 2007	October 2007

◷ Calendar

Time	Description
8 00	
15	
30	
45	
9 00	Hearing: People vs. Jones. Superior Court. Dept. 4
15	
30	
45	
10 00	
15	
30	
45	
11 00	
15	
30	
45	
12 PM	Lunch w/Fred – Fancy chicken Restaurant
15	
30	
45	
1 00	
15	
30	
45	
2 00	
15	
30	
45	
3 00	William Rogers – Appt. re will
15	
30	
45	
4 00	Staff Meeting
15	
30	
45	
5 00	
15	
30	
45	
6 00	
15	
30	
45	

☑ To Do

S	P	Category Description
F	1	DUE DATE: Gray vs. Addington – Statute of Limitations expires TODAY
F	2	WARNING: Jenkins vs. Brown – File complaint by 9/15
F	3	REMINDER: Neal vs. Armstrong – Start research for opposing to the motion to dismiss
F	3	Jones, adv. Smith – Client Jones to return information re Interrogatories

©1999 Lotus Development Corp.   4/24/99 at 3:44 PM   SaStatus PaPriority   Page 1

EXHIBIT 12–9   Sample Static Calendar System

Automated docketing systems are integrated into case management software, discussed in Chapters 10 and 11. The software does more than calendaring; it manages case files, performs conflict checks, and prepares legal documents. It generates management reports and to-do lists. Some software integrates with the firm's e-mail program and provides remote access to the system from anywhere in the world. Some software integrates with a firm's time and billing software programs.

A number of different scheduling reports are automatically generated. A report that is handy for a firm's management to guard against files being overlooked is a malpractice alert report. This report lists all cases that have no activity scheduled for them. A firm's management can easily spot files that may be neglected or lost in the system. This report prevents cases from "slipping through the cracks" of a firm's filing system.

Experts agree that an automated docketing program should contain some key features to make it an effective program, including the following:

- *Preprogrammed court rules.* The program applies preprogrammed court rules to a scheduling event. Court rules from the Federal Rules of Civil Procedure and each state's Rules of Civil Procedure are programmed into the computer and automatically applied to a specific case. It is important that the court rules be specific to the firm's jurisdiction and include all the courts in which the attorneys practice. It is also important that the rules be current and an update service is available to keep the rules current. Some rules, such as those of administrative agencies, may not be available for purchase, so the system must be able to allow the user to program it with additional rules. This custom rule programming feature allows other rules, such as firm-specific rules, to be programmed into it. For example, when a deposition is set, it triggers certain events, such as preparing a notice, serving the notice, scheduling a court reporter, reserving a conference room, and preparing for the deposition. Although some of these tasks are not contained in a statute or court rule, they can be programmed into the system to be implemented as needed. The system automatically reminds each member of the legal team of their step of the process. An example of this feature is found in Exhibit 12–10.

- *Automatic date scheduling.* This feature allows a user to enter a key event date, such as a trigger date, and the due date and reminder dates are automatically calculated and scheduled. The system automatically applies applicable court rules to the due dates and will not schedule a reminder on a holiday or weekend. This process, if done manually, can be very complex. For example, when a case is set for trial, entering the trial date can trigger as many as 50 deadlines, such as discovery cutoff, witness lists, jury fees, settlement conferences, and so on. The system must be able to handle a complex scheduling process that considers the many variables involved.

- *Automatic reminders.* The program automatically generates reminders that an event is approaching. It automatically enters a reminder date, urging date, warning date, and alert date. This feature must be flexible so that intervals between reminder dates can be adjusted according to the needs of the firm. An example of this feature is shown in Exhibit 12–11.

data validation
A feature in automated docket control software that will not allow an incorrect entry.

- *Data validation.* The program will automatically validate client matters so that an incorrect entry cannot be made. This **data validation** feature prevents the possibility that two schedules are prepared for one client. For example, if a user attempted to enter

Add a rule
Click **Add**, a notice appears, click **OK**, and the Add Rule dialog appears as shown.

Rule name
Enter FILECOMP for this example and click **OK**.

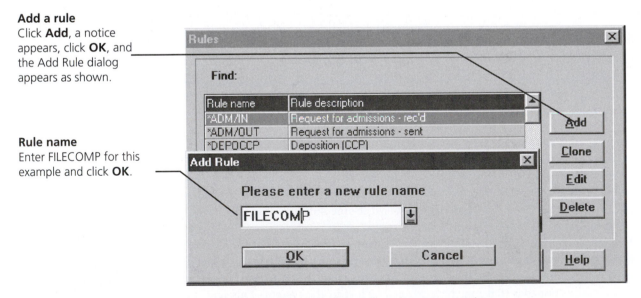

1. Click **Add** in the Rules window. An information window appears that tells you the name of the rule will automatically be added to the What Codes list. Click **OK** and the Add Rule window appears.

EXHIBIT 12–10 Example of Software that Preprograms Court Rules in a Docket Program *(Reprinted with permission of Abacus Data Systems, Inc.)*

2. Type FILECOMP in the Add Rule window. Every rule is simply a series of What codes that are linked according to the rule. Because FILECOMP is not already set up as a What code, a New What Code window appears.

Add the What codes
Every step in a rule must have a valid What code for the event. You can add it on-the-fly!

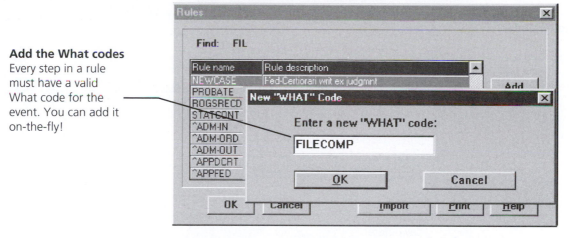

3. The Rule event editing window appears. In *What* enter SERVCOMP, in *Interval* enter 60, and in *Relative to event* enter 0.

What's next
Enter the What code for the next event in the rule.

Interval
Enter the days to be added (minus for subtracted) in calculating the date of this event.

Relative to event
The first event in a rule is always relative to event #0, the trigger event.

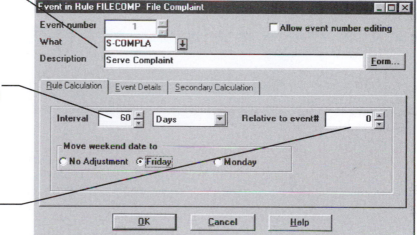

4. Our rule has one event, SERVCOMP, that will be automatically calendared 60 days after FILECOMP. Whenever you calendar an event with FILECOMP in the What field, *ABACUS LAW* will ask you if you want to add the other events from the Rule.

EXHIBIT 12–10   *(Continued)*

information for American International Parts Corp. by inserting the name of the client as American Parts, the system would not accept the information and would direct the user to the correct name: American International Parts Corp. This feature will not tolerate errors in data entry and protects the integrity of the system.

• *Holiday scheduling.* Most docketing software programs come preprogrammed with a few of the most commonly observed national holidays, such as Thanksgiving and Christmas. To be effective, this feature must be flexible to allow the user to insert other holidays that may be jurisdiction specific. For example, some courts close to observe Martin Luther King Jr.'s birthday, and others do not. In addition, the system must be able to recognize other days a firm may be closed, such as days for a firm's retreats, the

First reminder
In the first Reminder field enter 1 to create a reminder on the day before.

Second reminder
In the second Reminder field enter negative seven (-7) to create a reminder to follow up a week later.

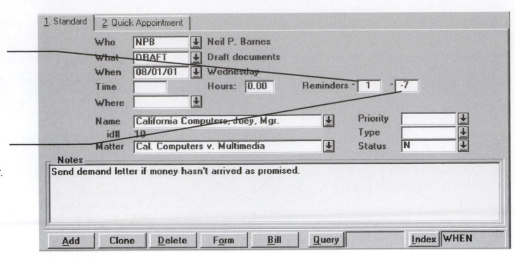

View linked events
See the reminders in the Linked Events window!

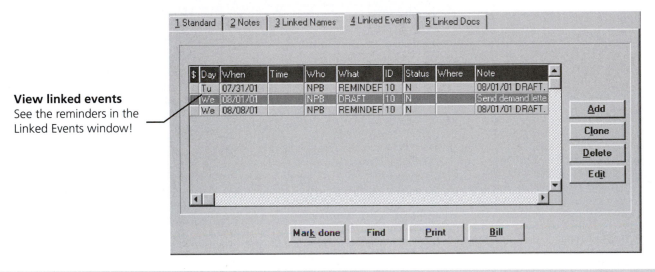

2. In Who enter NPB, in What enter DRAFT, then enter:
   - a 1 in the first Reminder field (to create a reminder for the day before)
   - a -7 (negative 7) in the second Reminder field (to create a reminder to follow up a week later

3. Click *Save* and select *Links/Events* from the Menu Bar. The following window appears.

EXHIBIT 12–11 Example of Software that Automatically Generates Reminder Dates *(Reprinted with permission of Abacus Data Systems, Inc.)*

founding partner's birthday, or other nonworkdays. Programming the software with these holidays ensures that reminder dates will not be inserted on those days.

- *Retroactive event recalculation.* **Retroactive event recalculation** allows entries to be recalculated if a rule or event changes. For example, if a court changes a rule that goes into effect on June 1, the program automatically recalculates entries made pursuant to the old rule and updates them to the new rule. This feature is also used if a trigger date changes or a matter is continued. It will automatically recalculate all dates attached to that event and adjust them to the new information.

- *Group scheduling.* The program provides for group scheduling, which is used by medium and large firms. For example, if a legal team consisting of three attorneys and two paralegals is working on a specific case, the system provides all members of a legal team

retroactive event recalculation
A feature in automated docketing software programs that automatically recalculates dates in the event of a change in a corresponding date.

Black, White & Greene
Tickler List
Hopewell v. Miller

For week of May 1, 20XX, to May 5, 20XX

DATE	ATTY/LA	TYPE	CASE	TASK
5/1/xx	White	Reminder	Hopewell v. Miller	Answer of Miller
5/4/xx	White	Urging	Hopewell v. Miller	Answer of Miller
5/4/xx	White	Due date	Rec'd docs from Miller?	

EXHIBIT 12–12 Sample Scheduling Report by Case

with scheduling information regarding that case. Whenever an event is scheduled for the case, each member of the team receives the information in his or her calendars.

- *Scheduling reports.* The program provides a number of scheduling reports. Examples of scheduling reports are those categorized by case, as shown in Exhibit 12–12; by day, event, or team, as shown in Exhibit 12–13; or by some other desired topic. If this feature is not available, a hard copy of a large firm's calendar may be as large as 50 or more pages, making review cumbersome and wasting resources.

The information in an automated system is displayed in a calendar that resembles a personal calendar. It can be displayed in a number of different calendar formats: daily, weekly, or

Black, White & Greene
Tickler List for Attny White and Paralegal Stockstill

For week of May 1, 20XX, to May 5, 20XX

DATE	ATTY/LA	TYPE	CASE	TASK
5/1/XX	White	Reminder	Hopewell v. Miller	Answer of Jenkins
5/1/XX	Stockstill	Reminder	Goldberg Agmt.	Agmt rec'd from client
5/1/XX	Stockstill	Due date	Keel v. Davis	Resp. to interogs. (Keel)*
5/2/XX	Stockstill	Warning	Baxter v. Hemstreet	Trial brief*
5/2/XX	White	Urging	Hedfer v. Marine Co.	Answer of Dell*
5/2/XX	Stockstill	Warning	Tazmanian v. Yuan	Ans. to Yuan interogs.*
5/4/XX	White	Urging	Hopewell v. Miller	Answer of Jenkins
5/4/XX	Stockstill	Warning	Noel v. Granger	Verification from Noel?
5/4/XX	Stockstill	Reminder	Allway v. Wier	Req. for prod. of docs.*
5/4/XX	White	Due date	Sand v. See	Res. motion to compel*
5/5/XX	White	Due date	Baxter v. Hemstreet	Trial brief
5/5/XX	White	Warning	Hedfer v. Marine	Answer of Dell*
5/5/XX	Stockstill	Due date	Tazmanian v. Yuan	Yuan's ans. to interogs.*
5/5/XX	Stockstill	Reminder	Quick Print v. Elkins	File stipulation*

EXHIBIT 12–13 Sample Scheduling Report by Legal Team

monthly, as shown in Exhibit 12–14. Court hearings and appointments are separated from reminder entries, with hearings and appointments on the left and tickler entries on the right, as in manual and static calendar systems.

There are many advantages to an automated docketing program. It increases accuracy and productivity, thereby causing a firm's profits to increase. An automated docket control program will pay for itself by way of reduced malpractice premiums and claims. It also contributes to positive client relations by increasing the efficiency of each member of the legal team. An example of some docketing software products are listed in the Cybersites section.

Your Weekly Calendar

Jump to organizer
Double-click on any day column header.

Drag and drop
Reschedule your week by dragging events to different times and days.

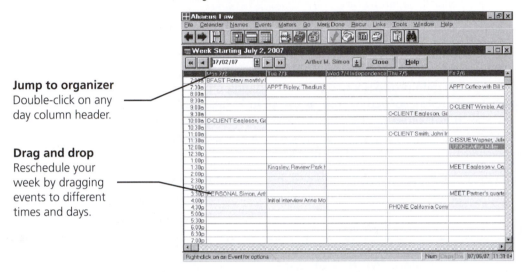

Your Monthly Calendar

Jump to Organizer
Double-click on any day to see your Daily Organizer.

Highlights/counters
Set up counters and highlights for priority events from *File/Setup/Calendar/Queries.*

Change months/years
Use the double arrows to change years, the single arrows to change months.

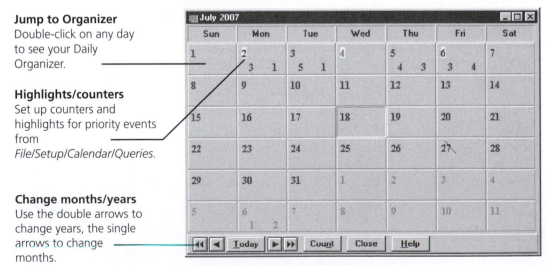

Tip: You can jump to another date by typing D and entering the date.

EXHIBIT 12–14 Example of Automated Docket System Calendars *(Reprinted with permission of Abacus Data Systems, Inc.)*

Your Daily Calendar

Change the date
Display the Organizer for 08/06/07 and the sample data should look like this.

Highlight the appt.
Click once to highlight.

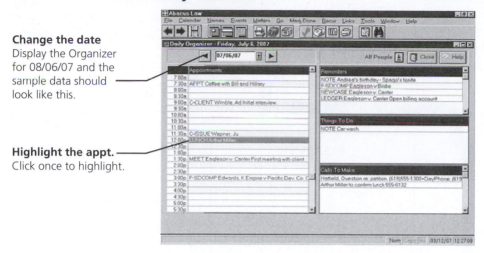

Highlight the 1:00 P.M. appointment with George Eagleson and click the Rolodex on the Tool Bar. Your contacts list appears with George Eagleson's name highlighted. Click OK to display George's name record.

EXHIBIT 12–14   *(Continued)*

Online Calendaring Systems

You can do anything on the Internet—even calculate deadlines. Online deadline calculation technology provides law firms with an alternative to expensive software packages. Online service companies will provide **online calendaring systems** to calculate deadlines for a fee, ranging from $5.00 to $99.00 per calculation.

Online calendaring service companies have court rules databases for all state and federal courts. This service comes in handy for law firms with an out-of-state case. Instead of investing in a court rules database for another state, the firm can pay for the service from an online calendaring service company. The customer enters the area of law, court location, and the date of an event (such as a trial). They get back a list of deadlines and corresponding authorities. The information may be exported directly into the firm's calendaring program, both static and automated. If a change in a rule occurs, the service will notify its customer of the rule change by e-mail.

online calendaring system
A service that will calculate deadlines from the Internet.

A FILE REVIEW SYSTEM

File review is another aspect of docket control systems. It is easy for an attorney who is responsible for many files to inadvertently ignore a file. A system must be devised in which a file cannot be ignored. Professional liability insurance companies require that a file review system be implemented.

As a general rule, every file should be reviewed monthly. A busy attorney with many files often finds file review a burdensome but necessary task. It may be tempting for an attorney to postpone file review until a more convenient time (which never comes), but efforts should be made not to do so. Postponing file review defeats its purpose and results in loose habits. File review procedures should be strictly enforced.

Often, an attorney will delegate file review to an experienced paralegal. Files that require no activity are calendared for the next month's review. This ensures that no file will be overlooked or lost in the system. It is also a method of double-checking when documents are due.

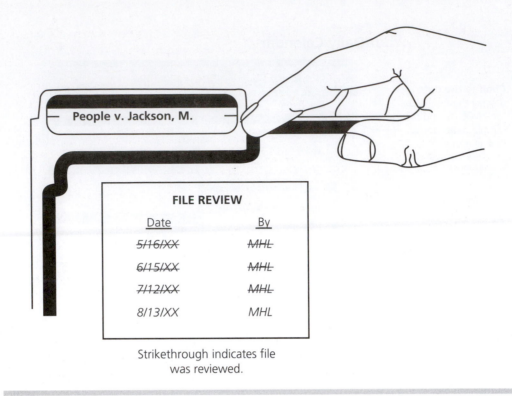

People v. Jackson, M.

FILE REVIEW

Date	By
~~5/16/XX~~	~~MHL~~
~~6/15/XX~~	~~MHL~~
~~7/12/XX~~	~~MHL~~
8/13/XX	MHL

Strikethrough indicates file
was reviewed.

EXHIBIT 12–15   Sample File Review

When a file is reviewed, it must be documented as such. This is done by computer, or by inserting the review date on a file review sheet, which is inserted in the file or taped to the cover of the file folder. When the file is reviewed, the review date is crossed out and a new date inserted, about 30 days from the current review date, as shown in Exhibit 12–15.

The docketing coordinator or secretary inserts the name of the file and the name of the attorney and/or paralegal scheduled to review that file into the firm's docketing computer system. The computer inserts the date for file review on the attorney's or paralegal's calendar, along with any pertinent notes for the next file review. Each morning, the docket coordinator or secretary pulls the files listed on the file review section of the calendar for that day and gives them to the attorney or paralegal for review. When the file has been reviewed, a new review date is put into the system, usually for 30 days in the future, and the cycle continues.

Reviewing clients' files creates a good opportunity to promote positive client relations. One major complaint that clients have about their attorneys is that attorneys do not inform them of the status of their cases. Months go by without any communication from an attorney. An attorney or paralegal may review the file each month, but unless the client knows this, the client is unaware of the efforts made on his or her behalf. Statistics have shown that clients who are regularly kept apprised of the status of their cases are satisfied clients. Statistics have also shown that regular contact with clients reduces the number of client telephone calls to an attorney or a paralegal.

A short informational letter should be sent to a client each time a file is reviewed to report the status of a case. If no activity has occurred on the file in the past 30 days, the client should be told this. If activity has occurred within the last 30 days, the client should be informed what the activity was and the status of the event.

Client relations is an area in which paralegals can become valuable to a firm by taking the responsibility to prepare short informational letters for either the attorney's or the paralegal's signature. Attorneys can easily delegate this task to a paralegal. If an attorney does not delegate this task, a paralegal can take the initiative and prepare a letter without being formally told to do so, *as long as the attorney reviews the letter before it is mailed.* Goodwill letters, such as those

ETHICS
ALERT

found in Chapter 5 on pages 178 and 179, can be put in the computer system and quickly prepared. A firm will reap great rewards in good client relations from this small effort.

CONCLUSION

Being efficient in docket control systems and procedures requires time and experience. The time that a paralegal or other legal support staff member devotes to learning effective docketing skills will reward them with an essential, marketable skill.

SUMMARY

There are many deadlines in a law office, and a firm must have a scheduling system that controls deadlines, allocates work so that projects are completed on time, and ensures that nothing is overlooked. A docket control system is perhaps the most important system in a law office. Each member of a legal team takes an active role in a firm's docket control system and works with it every day.

A good docket control system contains all trial dates, court and hearing dates, deposition dates, meeting dates, filing deadlines, reminder dates, follow-up dates, appointments, and personal and professional reminders. The type and sophistication of a docket control system varies according to the size of the firm, the type of firm, and the specialty of the firm.

A firm's calendar is a key component of the smooth operation of a law office. Two calendars are used in most law offices: a master calendar and a personal calendar. Each member of the legal team has a personal calendar. A paralegal's personal calendar is a duplicate of the attorney's personal calendar.

Events are docketed as soon as possible after they occur. Regular meetings, at least once or twice a week, should be set with the attorney, paralegal, and legal secretary to review calendars.

A tickler system, also known as a come-up system, is a method of controlling deadlines. Every law firm has a system to control deadlines called a tickler system that consists of due dates and reminder dates. The basic rule of a tickler system is that no item is removed from the system until it is completed. A manual tickler system can still be found in law offices as a backup to a computerized system. The manual system used by law offices since 1915 is the basic system. A docket request sheet is used with this system.

Three dates are considered when determining due dates: the trigger date, mail date, and due date. When counting days to determine the due date of a document, the first day is *excluded* and the last day is *included*. In most jurisdictions, weekends and holidays are counted except when a due date is within 11 days or less of the trigger date, at which time holidays and weekends are not counted. One must consider the time necessary to mail a document to determine a mail date.

For documents to be completed on time, reminder dates must be integrated into a docket system to remind an attorney and a paralegal that action is required on the file. The time intervals between these dates depend on the type of deadline imposed, the type of project, and where holidays and weekends fall on a calendar. Placing reminder dates in the correct time intervals requires knowledge of the requirements of each type of project. There are no specific rules that govern reminder date intervals.

Paralegals and attorneys use a tickler system to remind them of several important dates and events. Monitoring statutes of limitations is extremely important. Litigation cases have many deadlines that must be monitored. A document that is due from an opposing party must be documented to alert an attorney of a possible default or failure to respond.

Other uses for a tickler system are to track verbal and office commitments, to complete the work of an absent attorney or paralegal, and to schedule tasks to distribute work. Docketing due dates and reminder dates correctly is only half the battle; getting the job done is the other half.

There are three types of computerized docketing systems used by law firms: static calendar programs, automated docketing programs, and online calendaring services. A static calendar program allows the user to enter dates into the program, and the event will be noted on a specific date of the calendar. Static calendar programs are very similar to manual, handwritten systems. Tickler dates are calculated manually, so it is possible for an entry to be scheduled for a holiday or weekend, resulting in lost information.

Automated docketing programs are designed specifically for law firms. Experts agree that an automated docketing program should contain key features that make it an effective program. The information in an automated system is displayed in a calendar that resembles a personal calendar. Software with preprogramed court rules is called court rules-based calendaring software. There are many advantages to a court rules-based calendaring program. Calendaring functions may also be performed by an online calendaring service.

File review is another aspect of a docket control system. Every file should be reviewed monthly. Often, an attorney will delegate file review to an experienced paralegal. Reviewing clients' files creates a good opportunity to promote positive client relations. A short informational letter should be sent to a client each time a file is reviewed to report the status of a case.

Client relations is an area in which paralegals can be valuable to a firm by taking the responsibility to prepare short informational letters. Being efficient in docket control systems and procedures requires time and experience, but it is an essential skill for paralegals.

CHAPTER ILLUSTRATION

Before Black, White & Greene installed their intranet, they used a static calendar system. The system consisted of a calendar program that displayed the calendar information in a number of formats: by day, by week, and by month. It also generated a to-do list that was posted to a specific date. Reminder information was manually put in the to-do list, and the date was entered so that the information would be displayed on the appropriate date. The program automatically blocked out the duration of a matter. For example, if an attorney was scheduled to attend a hearing for 3 hours, that information was inserted into the entry, and nothing could be inserted for that time period without a warning coming up on the screen.

Each secretary was responsible for her attorney's calendar. Sandra was responsible for Dennis's and George's calendars, Pam was responsible for Patrizia's and Grant's calendars, and Tricia was responsible for Robert's calendar. Kay Bowen, the file clerk, was responsible for the master calendar and duplicating tickler information.

When the mail was delivered, the mail would be routed to the secretary for the attorney to whom the mail was directed. If a pleading or other document that required calendaring came in, the following procedures would be followed:

- The secretary calculates the due date and tickler dates.
- The secretary inserts the due date and tickler dates into the calendar system.
- The secretary completes a docket request sheet and inserts her initials; attorney's initials; name of the case; description of the event; date, time, and place of the event; and reminder dates, if applicable.
- The secretary keeps the bottom yellow copy and puts it in a docket-pending file. The original and remaining three copies are given to Kay for her to put into the master calendar and duplicate tickler system.
- When Kay receives a docket request sheet, she puts all primary information on the firm's master calendar. She puts secondary information, such as the reminder dates, on a separate firm follow-up calendar. Kay does not insert all secondary information into the follow-up calendar, such as appointments with clients, professional meetings, or personal information. The secretaries monitor that information and do not give them

to her. Kay initials the docket request sheet, inserts the date the information was docketed, and retains the bottom blue copy as a record that the event was docketed. She returns the remaining original and two copies to the secretary.

• When the secretary receives the completed docket request sheet from Kay, she removes the slip from the docket-pending file. She gives the green copy to the attorney so that the attorney can insert the information into his or her calendar, and she gives the pink copy to the paralegal to insert the information into his or her calendar. The original docket slip is inserted into the completed docket request file.

Each Monday morning, Kay prints the master calendar and distributes it to everyone in the firm. She also prepares a follow-up report of the reminder dates scheduled for each legal team and distributes it to the team's secretary. The secretary compares Kay's master calendar and follow-up report with hers to make sure that all reminder dates are inserted. When the reports are received, the secretary schedules a calendar meeting with the attorney and paralegal. Each team schedules its own meeting around the attorney's availability and court schedule. At the calendar meetings, all three calendars are compared so that each team member has all the necessary information.

The firm also requires its attorneys to review each file monthly so that a file is not neglected. Each morning, the secretary retrieves all the files that need to be reviewed that day and puts them on the attorney's desk. When a file is reviewed, the date and the attorney's initials are put on the outside of the file folder. A new file review date for the next month is inserted. The attorney then gives the file to the secretary, who inserts the file review date into the calendar and returns the file to the file room.

Sandra has difficulty setting calendar meetings with Dennis. He either has a court hearing or is too busy to meet with her and Judy, the paralegal. When she sets a calendar meeting, Dennis often cancels it because of a rush project. Dennis often schedules appointments with clients or continues a hearing without informing her of the changes, making their calendar meetings critical. She has asked him to send her a quick calendar note when he does this, but to no avail. She has tried scheduling luncheon calendar meetings or meetings after work. Sometimes her efforts are successful, and sometimes they are not. There are times when 2 or 3 weeks may go by without a calendar meeting.

There have been many times that she schedules a meeting with a client or potential client at times that conflict with an appointment Dennis made without telling her. One time, the client showed up for an appointment, only to find that Dennis had a court hearing of which he had not informed Sandra. This instance was embarrassing to her. This problem really frustrates Sandra and Judy because they are unable to rely on the calendar to schedule appointments, motions, and depositions.

The calendar problem is not the only problem that frustrates Sandra. Dennis has a problem performing his file review duties. He says that he is too busy to review the files and that he will do it on the weekend. He has good intentions to do it, and he works most Saturdays. However, other priorities interfere with file review, and it does not get done. Files are piled up in his office for review. He has an area in his office for these files: against the wall in piles 4 feet high. Many times, he has three or four piles of files to review. Whenever Sandra cannot find a file, she knows exactly where to look—in Dennis's office against the wall.

One Monday morning, Sandra tried to schedule a calendar meeting with Dennis. "Can we meet for 20 minutes around 10:00 this morning for calendar review?" asked Sandra.

"No," replied Dennis. "I have that settlement conference on the Acme Products case this afternoon at 1:00. We have to put the finishing touches on the settlement brief. How is it coming?"

"I don't know," replied Sandra. "I'll check with Judy."

Sandra checked the calendar and saw that the settlement conference was not on the schedule for that day. It was scheduled for Wednesday of next week. She wondered whether she had made a mistake in the calendar and checked with Judy.

"I have the Acme Products settlement conference scheduled for next Wednesday also," said Judy. "I have research on the brief scheduled for tomorrow. Dennis's calendar must be wrong. Let's find out."

They went into Dennis's office and asked about the conference. "We have the Acme settlement conference scheduled for next Wednesday. I haven't started on it yet," said Judy.

Dennis replied, "It was scheduled for next Wednesday, but we had to move it up a week. It is this afternoon at 1:00. You haven't started on it yet? We have to get the brief done by noon today!"

"What?" exclaimed Judy. "You didn't tell us it was moved up a week. There is no way we can get it done in 3 hours!"

"We have to. Here's the file. Use the Backus Car Agency case's settlement brief as a guide and plug in the figures in the file."

"But . . . ," stammered Judy. "No buts. Get started," said Dennis. Both Sandra and Judy went to work on the brief right away. The phone was ringing off the hook. Both Dennis and Judy instructed Sandra that they could not accept telephone calls, so Sandra took messages for them. She finally asked Pam to cover the phones for her until they got the settlement brief done, and Pam complied. It was 12:30. They were not finished. Dennis had to leave for court.

"How long until it's done?" asked Dennis. "I need to put in information regarding the fraud allegation," said Judy. "To do it right, I need a few hours of research. The other parts of the brief can be done in an hour. What should I do?"

"Forget the fraud allegation," said Dennis. "I have to leave now to be there on time. As soon as you're finished, bring it to court. I'll be in Department 17."

"Okay," said Judy.

Judy completed the brief at 1:30 and rushed it to the courthouse. The freeway was jammed. It took her an hour to reach the courthouse, only to find the parking lot full. She had to park on a side street, blocks from the courthouse. She ran to the courthouse and got to the courtroom at 3:00. When Dennis saw her, he breathed a sigh of relief.

"The freeway was jammed, and I couldn't find a parking place," said Judy breathlessly.

"Thank God you made it," said Dennis as he took the brief. "I'll see you back at the office."

Sandra and Judy were at their wits' end. Sandra scheduled a meeting with Tricia and Robert to discuss the calendaring problems. She was hoping that Tricia and Robert could give her a suggestion to fix the problems. At the meeting, Tricia and Robert told her that they were aware of the file review problem but did not know there were calendaring problems.

"What can I do?" asked Sandra.

Tricia said, "We are currently installing an intranet that will centralize all our systems. One of the systems that will be centralized is the calendar system. We are purchasing an automated docketing program that will automatically do the calendaring for us. Everyone's calendar will be on the system and they will all be integrated with one another. A current master calendar and tickler system will always be available on everyone's computer. When you calendar something, it will automatically show up on Dennis's and Judy's calendars. Whenever Dennis calendars something, it will automatically be put on your and Judy's calendars, so you won't have to worry about him not telling you about changes anymore. And the system will automatically recalculate reminder dates if a date changes. This new system should solve this calendar problem."

"Wow, great!" said Sandra. "When will we get the system?"

"We've ordered it," said Robert. "It should be installed in about 2 weeks. But it will need to be set up, and we will need to input all our case data into it. This should take at least a month. We've made arrangements with Data Specialists to come in and set up the systems at night and on weekends so they won't interfere with regular business. Then, everyone will need to be trained on the system."

"I think we should have the system up and running in a couple of months. Just hang in there until then." "Okay," said Sandra. "Now, about file review."

CHAPTER REVIEW

1. What are the five characteristics of a good docket control system?
2. What are the three main areas of a docket control system?
3. What information is considered primary information?
4. What information is considered secondary information?
5. How are events placed on a calendar in a large firm? In a small firm?
6. Why would a firm maintain a manual calendar?
7. What three dates are considered when determining due dates?
8. What are the four reminder dates used in a tickler system?
9. How are the time intervals between reminder dates determined?
10. What is the basic rule of a tickler system?
11. What is a static computerized calendar system?
12. What is an automated docket control program, and what features are considered important for this system?
13. Why is a file review system important for good client relations?

EXAMPLES FOR DISCUSSION

1. **RELUCTANT FILE REVIEW**

   Richard Everett is a busy trial attorney specializing in personal injury cases. The medium-sized firm for which he works has a monthly review for all files and sends a monthly status letter to clients. Richard's files do not get reviewed, however, and they pile up in his office, the walls of which are lined with stacks of files. Whenever a file is missing from the file room, the firm's employees know where to find it—in Richard's office. Richard says that he does not have time to review all the files, with his heavy trial schedule, and files are becoming neglected.

   1. You are the law firm's manager. What would you do to remedy the problem?
   2. If Richard's files were given to a paralegal to review, is it fair to the other attorneys who review their own files? Why or why not?
   3. Should a paralegal or other person selected to review the files have any special training or qualifications? If so, what?

2. **WEEKEND AND HOLIDAY PROJECTS**

   Sandy Esmay is the manager of a small firm. She hired a new secretary who is responsible for maintaining a static computerized and manual tickler system for the firm. The secretary was instructed in the proper method of maintaining the tickler system. After 6 weeks had passed, an attorney approached Sandy in a panic and reported that he had missed a very important deadline. He accused the new secretary of not putting the information in the tickler system. The secretary insists that she inserted the information. Sandy suspects that the information was inserted on a weekend day.

   1. What could have happened here?
   2. Where could Sandy go to determine whether the secretary inserted the information on a weekend day?
   3. You are the manager of the law firm. What procedures would you put in place so that the situation would not happen again?

3. **AUTOMATED SYSTEMS**

   Do any students in the class have experience with a docket control system? If so, what type of system? What are the advantages and disadvantages of the system? Would any of the features of an automated docket control system described on pages 418 to 423 improve the system? Discuss how a law firm could benefit from an automated docket control system.

4. CALENDAR MEETINGS AND FILE REVIEW PROBLEMS

Calendar meetings are an important aspect of docket control. As we saw in the Chapter Illustration section, Sandra had problems scheduling calendar meetings with Dennis. There were also problems with Dennis performing his file review duties. If you were Sandra, how would you handle these problems? Do you think that Sandra was right in discussing the problems with Robert and Tricia? What are some possible solutions to the file review problem? Do you think that Dennis will be upset with Sandra for discussing the problems with Robert and Tricia? Why or why not?

ASSIGNMENTS

1. Robert Black, the managing partner, has assigned you to recommend an automated docket control software program for Black, White & Greene. Research the available programs in the Cybersites section and write a report about your findings. Compare features, capabilities, requirements, and price. Choose the product that you would recommend, and state the reasons that you chose that product.

2. Make up a manual tickler system as described on pages 408–409. Enter your class assignments into the system, scheduling your time to complete the assignments on time. Include reminder dates and follow-up dates. Also include any personal or professional obligations into the system.

3. Use the following calendars to determine the due dates and mail dates for the following scenarios. Use the federal 3-day mail allowance. Blank tickler sheets are on the accompanying CD. Copy the form as needed. *Note*: Holidays are November 23 and 24 and December 25.

October

Sun	Mon	Tues	Wed	Thur	Fri	Sat
1	2	3	4	5	6	7
8	9	10	11	12	13	14
15	16	17	18	19	20	21
22	23	24	25	26	27	28
29	30	31				

November

Sun	Mon	Tues	Wed	Thur	Fri	Sat
			1	2	3	4
5	6	7	8	9	10	11
12	13	14	15	16	17	18
19	20	21	22	23	24	25
26	27	28	29	30		

December

Sun	Mon	Tues	Wed	Thur	Fri	Sat
					1	2
3	4	5	6	7	8	9
10	11	12	13	14	15	16
17	18	19	20	21	22	23
24	25	26	27	28	29	30
31						

a. Your client, Leona Ledford, was personally served with a summons and complaint on October 23 in the case of *Masters v. Ledford*. Her answer is due in 30 days. What are the due date, mail date, and reminder dates?

b. In the case of *Brozowski vs. Thrifty Drugs,* your client, Rose Brozowski, was served with a cross-complaint by mail. The proof of service by mail form indicated that it was mailed on October 25. Her answer is due in 30 days. You will mail the answer to the court. What are the due date, mail date, and reminder dates?

c. In the case of *Masters vs. Ledford*, your client, Leona Ledford, was served with interrogatories by mail. The proof of service by mail form indicates that it was mailed on November 21. Her response is due in 30 days. You will mail a draft to the client for her review before finalizing the document. You will mail the response to the opposing party. What are the due date, mail date, and reminder dates?

d. The trial of *Stacy v. Pinkerton* is scheduled for December 18. A trial brief must be filed 10 days before trial. The brief contains many complex issues. It will be mailed to the court and opposing counsel. What are the due date, mail date, and reminder dates?

e. In the case of *Fullbright v. Kanner*, you received a motion to compel further answers to interrogatories of your client, Ron Kanner. The proof of service by mail form indicates that the motion was mailed on November 13, and a response is due in 15 days. You will personally deliver the response to the court and opposing party. What are the due date and reminder dates?

f. In the case of *People v. Gates*, your client wants to file an appeal. The verdict was rendered on October 3 and a Notice of Appeal was filed on October 17. Your appellate brief is due 30 days after the notice of appeal is filed, and the reply brief of the opposing part is due 30 days after the date your brief is due. You will mail your brief to the court. What are the due date, mail date, and reminder dates? When is the reply brief of the opposing party due?

g. In the case of *Fullbright v. Kanner*, you mailed the opposing party a request for production of documents on November 3. A response is due in 30 days. What is the due date?

h. The trial of *Stacy v. Pinkerton* is scheduled for December 18. Subpoenas must be prepared and personally served on eight witnesses 15 days before the trial. What is the last day the subpoenas may be served? What are the reminder dates?

4. Your firm represents ABC Company in the case of *ABC Company v. XYZ Company*. The attorneys for XYZ Company filed a Motion for Summary Judgment with a hearing date of December 8. Your opposition to the motion must be filed with the court no later than 14 days before the date of the hearing. When is the due date of the response? You will mail the response to the court. On what date must it be mailed to reach the court by the due date? The brief contains many complex issues. How would you enter reminder dates?

5. Your firm represents Ms. Grace in a slip-and-fall matter against Lucky Market. Her accident occurred on December 23 of last year. The statute of limitations is 1 year. How would you tickle the statute of limitations for her case?

6. In the case of *Johnson v. Mandle*, your client's brief in opposition to a motion is due within 10 days after receipt of the motion. The proof of service by mail form indicates that the motion was mailed on October 26. What is the due date? What is the mail date? How many reminders would you enter for the response?

SELF TEST

How well did you grasp the material in the chapter? Test yourself by answering the following questions, and check your answers against the answers found in Appendix A.

1. According to the ABA, what is the leading cause of legal malpractice claims?
2. Who has responsibility for a docket system in a small firm?
3. Who has responsibility for a docket system in a large firm?
4. Why must a paralegal have knowledge of docketing procedures?

5. What types of information are contained in a docket control system?

6. How can a missed deadline have disastrous consequences for a firm?

7. What are the six functions of a good docket control system?

8. What are the characteristics of a good docket control system?

9. What are the two types of calendars used in a law office?

10. What information is contained on a master calendar?

11. What is the purpose of a master calendar?

12. How often do large firms distribute master calendars to employees?

13. How often do small firms distribute master calendars to employees?

14. How do firms with an intranet distribute their master calendars?

15. What essential information does a master calendar contain?

16. What two types of information does a personal calendar contain?

17. What does primary information include?

18. What is a statute of limitations?

19. What does secondary information include?

20. Why are manual calendars an essential element of a firm's calendaring policy?

21. Describe the various types of manual calendars.

22. Who is responsible for keeping calendars current?

23. When should personal calendars be updated?

24. When are events docketed?

25. When are documents from opposing parties docketed?

26. What does a stamp or an initial on a document mean?

27. What does the absence of a stamp or an initial on a document mean?

28. Describe a calendar meeting.

29. What is a docket coordinator?

30. What is a docket request sheet, and for what purpose is it used?

31. What information is contained on a docket request sheet?

32. How many pages does a docket request sheet contain?

33. How are the copies of the docket request sheet used?

34. What is used to inform other members of the legal team that an event was docketed?

35. Why is it important to keep all calendars out of the view of clients?

36. What is a tickler system?

37. What would happen if a firm had no tickler system?

38. What is an integrated tickler system?

39. What type of information is inserted on the left side of a personal calendar?

40. What type of information is inserted on the right side of a personal calendar?

41. What three dates are considered when determining due dates?

42. What is a trigger date?

43. What is a due date?

44. If a due date falls on a holiday or weekend, when is the due date?

45. What is a mail date?

46. How does one determine the number of days that should be set aside for mailing?

47. When counting days to determine a document's due date, what is excluded?

48. When counting days to determine a document's due date, what is included?

49. What day is counted as the first day when determining due dates?

50. Are weekends and holidays counted when determining due dates?

51. When are weekends and holidays excluded from the day count?
52. Where would you find out a state's requirements for including weekends and holidays in a due-date calculation?
53. How do you compensate for mail time when determining due dates?
54. What are the four reminder dates?
55. How are the time intervals between reminder dates determined?
56. What governs the time intervals between reminder dates?
57. Why must time intervals between reminder dates be adjustable and flexible?
58. Why is it important to monitor statutes of limitations?
59. How many reminder dates does a 1-year statute of limitations require?
60. How many reminder dates does a 4-year statute of limitations require?
61. How many reminder dates does a 30-day deadline require?
62. How many reminder dates does a 15-day deadline require?
63. What is a default?
64. How many reminder dates does a document that is due from opposing parties have?
65. What methods are used to differentiate between tickler entries for a firm's documents and those of opposing parties?
66. If a letter is sent that requires a reply, how is it tickled?
67. How is a tickler system used to track verbal and office commitments?
68. How is a tickler system used to complete the work of an absent attorney or paralegal?
69. What is the basic rule of a tickler system?
70. Why should an attorney or a paralegal never be verbally reminded of tickler information?
71. Docketing due dates and reminders is half the battle. What is the other half?
72. What are the two types of computerized docket systems?
73. What is a static calendar program?
74. What types of information are put into a static calendar program?
75. How are dates inserted into a static calendar system?
76. Static calendar programs are similar to what type of system?
77. How accurate are static calendar programs?
78. In what size of firm are static calendar programs found?
79. What are the two areas that set automated docketing software programs apart from static calendar programs?
80. Court rules-based docketing programs contain databases that contain what information?
81. What does a malpractice alert report contain?
82. What are the key features of an automated docketing program?
83. What is automatic date scheduling?
84. What is data validation?
85. Why must the holiday scheduling feature be flexible?
86. What is retroactive event recalculation?
87. Why is the group scheduling feature important?
88. How is information in an automated docketing system displayed?
89. What are the advantages to an automated docketing program?
90. What is an online calendaring service?
91. When would it be convenient for a firm to use an online calendaring service?
92. How is a manual tickler system used?
93. What type of method can be implemented into a manual tickler system that will identify weekend or holiday dates?

94. What is a file review system?
95. How often should each file be reviewed?
96. Why should an attorney not postpone file review?
97. How are files documented for file review?
98. How does file review promote good client relations?

Key Words

court rules-based calendaring software	docket coordinator	retroactive event recalculation
data validation	master calendar	static calendar programs
default	online calendaring system	statute of limitations
docket	personal calendar	trigger date
	proof of service by mail	

 # Cybersites

STATIC CALENDAR PROGRAMS

The following is a sample of related software:
Lotus Notes: Lotus—*<http://www.lotus.com>*
Microsoft Outlook: Microsoft—*<http://www.microsoft.com>*

DOCKET AND CALENDAR CONTROL SOFTWARE

Abacus Law: Abacus Data Systems, Inc.—*<http://www.abacuslaw.com>*
CompulawVision: Compulaw—*<http://www.compulaw.com>*
PerfectLaw: Perfect Law Software—*<http://www.perfectlaw.com>*
Thomson Elite: ProLaw Software—*<http://www.elite.com>*
Time Matters: Lexis-Nexis—*<http://www.timematters.com>*

MISCELLANEOUS

Online Calendaring Service Deadlines on Demand —*<http://www.deadlines.com>*
Legal Malpractice Blog —*<http://www.illinoislegalmal.com>*

 Student CD-ROM
For additional materials, please go to the CD in this book.

 Online Companion™
For additional resources, please go to http://www.paralegal.delmar.cengage.com

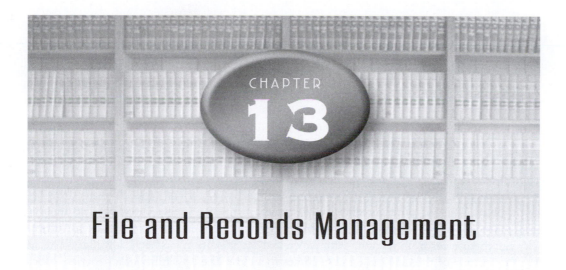

CHAPTER

13

File and Records Management

OBJECTIVES

After completion of this chapter, the student should be able to do the following:
- Organize a legal file.
- Maintain a legal file.
- Open a legal file.
- Perform a conflict-of-interest check.
- Discuss file organization procedures.
- Prepare a file for closing and retention.
- Discuss file retrieval procedures.
- Prune a file for closing and schedule it for destruction.
- Discuss essential documents used in a law firm.
- Explain when to keep or discard a document.
- Explain how filing systems are categorized.
- Categorize subjects.
- Discuss the various types of coding systems for files.

INTRODUCTION

A firm's file and records system is the nerve center of a law office. It is an active and vital part of the firm and must be properly managed and maintained. Every paralegal will interact with a law firm's file and records system regardless of employer. An overview of a firm's file and records system will prepare legal staff members for employment in the legal marketplace by giving them an understanding of the rules and requirements necessary to maintain a system and to keep it running smoothly.

This chapter will instruct the paralegal student of proper file-management procedures to create professional, well-managed files. File-maintenance concepts will be discussed, as will file-retention and file-destruction procedures. It will also discuss each element of a records management system and will give the student knowledge of the various filing systems used in today's law office. This knowledge will prepare the student to participate in a firm's file and records management system. The paralegal student will be able to take this knowledge into any law firm and display excellent organizational skills.

FILING SYSTEMS

The management and organization of a firm's filing system are essential to the smooth operation of a law firm. Each firm uses a different filing system, usually customized to the needs of the office. For a system to be effective, it must consist of a logical division of categories of records, and it must use a logical, efficient coding method.

The beginning of the computer revolution promised a "paperless" office. However, this has not evolved. The computer generated more paper. Firms run longer, more detailed reports, and computers allow for multiple revisions of documents. It has taken a decade for offices to wean themselves from working with paper, and the transition has been slow. However, as the first decade of the new millennium comes to a close, the possibility of a paperless office becomes more real. Office workers are becoming accustomed to working with digital files. However, paper documents are still the standard in law offices. All documents, paper or electronic, must be organized and maintained in a well-structured filing system.

Types of Filing Systems

There are three types of filing systems: centralized, decentralized, and automated.

CENTRALIZED   A centralized filing system has all the files located in one area and is normally managed by a file coordinator or clerk. A large firm and many medium-sized firms have a centralized system. The files are stored in a centralized area and are maintained and controlled by one or more individuals, known as file clerks or file coordinators. In a centralized system, there is **controlled access,** which means that no one can remove a file without notifying the file clerk. When a file is needed, it is checked out of the file area and returned by the end of the day.

DECENTRALIZED   A decentralized system has files located in various areas, usually near the responsible attorney's office. Generally, a small firm will have a decentralized system. The files are stored in or near the responsible attorney's work area, and each attorney is responsible for maintaining his or her own files.

There are few totally centralized filing systems. Most lawyers like to keep their most active files in their work areas for easy retrieval as they are needed rather than returning them to a central file area at the end of the day. If this is the case, a system must be in place that documents the location of each file. This is known as **central file control** and is implemented for both centralized and decentralized systems.

AUTOMATED RECORDS MANAGEMENT   Firms are moving toward a paperless office by use of automated records management software programs. An automated records management program classifies files and folders in the same way a manual system does. Records management software tracks a file from its opening through its destruction. It assigns closed-file numbers and a file location in the inactive storage area. It has the capability of running numerous file reports.

Filing System Classification

A filing system, whether centralized, decentralized, or automated, consists of a logical division of categories of records. Dividing records into categories is known as **classification.** A good classification system increases accessibility and reduces complexity. The categories chosen will depend on a firm's size and specialties. A boutique law office specializing in one area of law will have fewer categories than a large firm practicing in many areas of law.

---

controlled access
The access and retrieval of a firm's files are controlled by a specific system.

central file control
A system that documents the location of each file.

classification
The process of separating items into categories.

Records are divided into categories that have a logical connection to one another. There are four major categories for most law firm files: function, subject, topic, and subtopic. First, their function is identified, then they can be categorized further by subject, topic, and subtopic. Knowing a record's function is essential before it can be located.

FUNCTION CATEGORIES The first step in categorizing documents is to identify their function. After their function is identified, records are divided into subjects, and the subjects are further divided into topics.

Clients' files (function)
 Criminal cases (subject)
  Burglary (topic)
Personnel records (function)
 Performance evaluations (subject)
  Performance appraisals, June 2009 (topic)

SUBJECT CATEGORIES Functions are divided into subjects.

 I. Clients (function)
  A. Individual clients (subject)
  B. Business clients (subject)
 II. Area of law (function)
  A. Probate (subject)
  B. Real estate (subject)
  C. Corporate (subject)

TOPIC CATEGORIES Subjects are further divided into topics.

 I. Clients (function)
  A. Individual clients (subject)
   1. Adams, Alice (topic)
   2. Benson, Bernadette (topic)
   3. Springer, David (topic)
  B. Business clients (subject)
   1. Quick Sell Real Estate (topic)
   2. Zono's Restaurant (topic)
   3. Velco Tire Company (topic)

SUBTOPIC CATEGORIES Topics may be further divided into subtopics.

 I. Clients (function)
  A. Individual clients (subject)
   1. Adams, Alice (topic)
    a. In re Marriage of Adams (subtopic)
    b. Bankruptcy of Alice Adams (subtopic)
    c. Star Financial Services v. Adams (subtopic)
   2. Benson, Bernadette (topic)
    a. Estate of Benson (subtopic)
    b. Name change of Benson (subtopic)
   3. Springer, David (topic)
    a. People v. Springer (subtopic)
    b. Marriage of Springer (subtopic)
    c. Springer v. Fedco (subtopic)

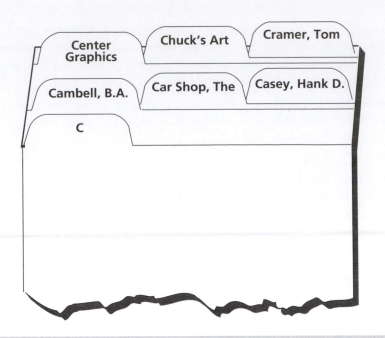

EXHIBIT 13–1   Alphabetical Client Files

Coding Systems

A coding system is a method used to store files in a specified sequence. The sequence must be logical, follow a set of rules, and be simple to use. There are three methods of coding files: alphabetic, numeric, and alphanumeric.

ALPHABETICAL CODING SYSTEMS   An alphabetical coding system, also known as a direct coding system, is the most common coding system used by small firms. A number of consultants feel that an alphabetical coding system is outdated, but small firms continue to use it because it is the easiest coding system to establish and maintain. In this system, a law firm's business records are arranged in alphabetical order by function, such as accounts receivable, accounts payable, and personnel.

Client files are arranged in alphabetical order according to a client's surname, as shown in Exhibit 13–1.

Each file title or name is comprised of units, and each word is considered a unit. When filing, unit 1 is considered before unit 2, and unit 2 is considered before unit 3.

Unit 1	Unit 2	Unit 3
Brown	John	T.
Great	Lakes	Realty

Although an alphabetical coding system seems easy, problems occur when employees have not been instructed in its rules. For the system to run smoothly, users must strictly adhere to the following alphabetical coding rules.

Rule 1   Always use the surname of an individual client as the first unit, as follows:

Unit 1	Unit 2	Unit 3
Brown	John	T.

If the client is a business, the first name of the business is the first unit, as follows:

Unit 1	Unit 2	Unit 3	Unit 4	Unit 5
John	T.	Brown	Tire	Company

John T. Brown's file is filed under "B," and John T. Brown Tire Company is filed under "J."

Rule 2   File nothing before something. For example, Jane Roberts is filed before Jane Robertson, as follows:

Roberts, Jane A.

Robertson, Jane M.

Rule 3   Consider each unit when filing documents. If a firm has two clients named Jane Roberts, the third unit—middle name or initials—is considered:

Roberts, Jane

Roberts, Jane A.

Roberts, Jane E.

Roberts, Jane Michelle

Units include prepositions, conjunctions, and articles. Note that when the word *the* is used to begin a title, it is always the last unit:

Unit 1	*Unit 2*	*Unit 3*	*Unit 4*
Children's	Shop,	The	
A	Formidable	Feast	Restaurant

A Formidable Feast Restaurant is filed under "A," and The Children's Shop is filed under "C."

Rule 4   Ignore all punctuation and symbols when alphabetizing, and drop punctuation to determine a unit:

	Unit 1	*Unit 2*	*Unit 3*
A-1 Business Service	A1	Business	Service
A.A.A. Glass Co.	AAA	Glass	Co.
B&B Barbecue Equipment	BB	Barbecue	Equipment

Rule 5   Arabic and roman numerals are filed sequentially before alphabetic letters. Arabic numerals precede roman numerals. They are filed according to their number rather than the word that spells the number. For example, the first unit for The 21 Club is 21 instead of twenty-one:

Unit 1	*Unit 2*	*Unit 3*
21	Club	The
42nd	Street	Restaurant
IV	Brigade	The

Rule 6   Radio and television station call letters are identified as one unit, as follows:

Unit 1	*Unit 2*
KNBC	Television
WGN	Radio

Rule 7   File a record under its most commonly used name or title and cross-reference it under other names that might be used:

File Under	*Cross-Reference Under*
American Telephone and Telegraph	ATT
Internal Revenue Service	IRS

Rule 8   Always file under the client's name, regardless of his or her status in a case. If the client is the sole plaintiff, his or her name will always be first in the case. For example, in *Jones v. White,* if your firm represents the plaintiff, the case will be filed under J for Jones:

Jones, Stanley T. v. White, Mary L.

If your firm represents the defendant, list your client first and insert "adv." (adverse) instead of "v." (versus) to indicate that the client is the defendant:

White, Mary L. adv. Jones, Stanley T.

In this case, *Jones v. White* is filed under the client's surname: "W" for White.

---

primary case name
The name used to identify a case, consisting of the first-named plaintiff and the first-named defendant.

In lawsuits with many plaintiffs and defendants, only the names of the first plaintiff and first defendant are used as the **primary case name,** which is the name used to identify a case. All parties are not included in the primary case name because the name would be too long. If a client's name is not in the primary case name, the primary case name is included on the client's file label, as follows:

Snow, Harry M. (Jones, Stanley T. v. White, Mary L.)

A cross-reference is required to refer the user to Harry Snow when a document is received concerning the *Jones v. White* case. If no index is available, a person searching for the *Jones v. White* case would be unable to find it because it is filed under the client's name: Snow, Harry M.

In an insurance defense firm or a corporate legal department with only one client, the client's name is not indicated on the label, as that name is the same for each file. Only the other party's name is indicated on the file label in such a case.

A firm may also have clients' files arranged alphabetically by subject, as shown in Exhibit 13–2. Subjects for clients' files are by area of law or responsible attorney. This method is more difficult than straight alphabetical coding because a user must know the subject before a file is accessible. A case may involve multiple areas of law, or a user may know that a client has a case with the firm but cannot remember the subject matter of the case. Firms that code files by subject must cross-index the case in an alphabetical listing by a client's name to locate the files.

For practice in applying alphabetizing rules, complete the two alphabetizing exercises on the accompanying CD.

NUMERIC CODING SYSTEMS   Files coded with numerical coding are arranged in numeric order according to a particular numbering pattern. Various numbering patterns are used, with management determining the one for a particular system. Management determines the order and progression in which the numbers or parts of numbers will be read.

Six different types of numeric systems are used: straight, coded, calendar, standard, account, and combination.

Straight Numbering   Straight numbering is consecutive numbering: 1, 2, 3, 4. A firm assigns a file number to each new matter as a file is opened. This is the least complicated

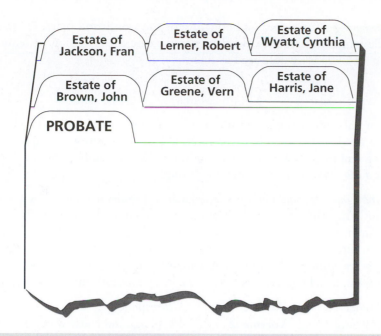

EXHIBIT 13–2   Clients' Files by Subject

numeric numbering system. By using this numbering system, a firm keeps track of the number of cases it represents from the beginning of its operation. Numbering normally begins at 100.

In this type of system, a client with many cases will have files scattered throughout a filing system. A user must rely on an alphabetical index to find the proper file.

Coded Numbering   Coded numbering combines numbers with letters of the alphabet. Letters preceding the file number are used to further categorize files. The letters may be a responsible attorney's initials or the initials of a branch office or type of case. The file numbers are assigned sequentially:

AS 123	Al Simpson's case, case no. 123
LA 567	Los Angeles branch, case no. 567
LIT 865	Litigation case, case no. 865

Coded numbering allows all of one attorney's files to be filed together, all the cases of the same type to be filed together, or the all cases of a branch office to be filed together. Color-coded file labels are used to further categorize files. Exhibit 13–3 shows an example of coded numbering with color coding.

Color of file label indicates type of case

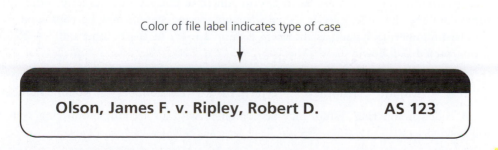

Olson, James F. v. Ripley, Robert D.   AS 123

EXHIBIT 13–3   Coded Numbering

Calendar Numbering Calendar numbering inserts the month and year a file was opened as part of the file number. After the calendar code, the case file is numbered sequentially. For example, case no. 0903341 would read as follows:

09	03	341
Year	Month (March)	File number

Calendar numbering will keep all files opened in one year together. It tells a firm how many files are opened in a year and in a month. This information is important for long-range planning and marketing projects. In addition, the file number tells a user the age of a case and that a case may be a candidate for closing.

Standard Numbering Standard numbering separates categories of numbers by a space, comma, period, or dash. Any number of considerations can be given the number. With a standard numbering system, a user gains information just by reading the file number.

Some firms further categorize case documents by separating documents by their type. These subfiles are known as volumes. A volume may have its own categorization and number. For example, a litigation case may have its own classification system as follows:

Folder 1	Volume .1	Correspondence
Folder 2	Volume .2	Pleadings and court documents
Folder 3	Volume .3	Medical records
Folder 4	Volume .4	Discovery
Folder 5	Volume .5	Legal research
Folder 6	Volume .6	Miscellaneous notes and reports

Each section may have up to 10 volumes in each section. If a second correspondence volume is opened, that file would be volume .11. The third discovery volume would be volume .42.

For example, the file number 4/23-321.2 tells the user the responsible attorney, type of case, file number, and volume:

4	23	321	.2
Attorney's number	Type of case	File number	Volume number

When documents are logically categorized and consistent, all members of a legal team will know that volume .5 contains legal research and that volume .3 contains medical records. This system expedites retrieval of a document by directing a user to the subject matter of the document requested. For example, if a paralegal needed to retrieve a medical report for the *Olson v. Ripley* case, he or she would retrieve file number 4/23-321.3.

Account Numbering Account numbering gives each client a permanent number, and all subsequent cases are filed with that account number. Each case is given a sequential number after the account number, normally starting with 100. Client number 862's fourth case would be numbered 862-104. This type of coding system is used by firms that represent clients with a large number of cases, such as collection cases for a large department store.

Combination Coding It is not necessary to adhere to one style of numeric coding; many firms combine the coding styles. A calendar numbering system may be combined with a standard numbering system, as shown in Exhibit 13–4. The file number 0907-4-23.321/3 is interpreted as follows:

09	07	4	23	.321	/3
Year	Month	Attorney	Type of case	File number	Volume number

A coded numbering system may be combined with an account numbering system as follows:

LA	862	123
Attorney	Client number	File number

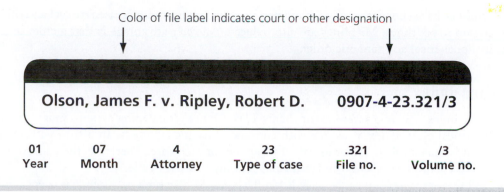

Color of file label indicates court or other designation

01	07	4	23	.321	/3
Year	**Month**	**Attorney**	**Type of case**	**File no.**	**Volume no.**

EXHIBIT 13–4   Combination Coding

In addition, a firm may combine standard, calendar, and account numbering systems: The number 0907-4-23.867/341/3 is interpreted as follows:

09	07	4	23	.867	341	/3
Year	Month	Attorney	Type of case	Client	File number	Volume number

ALPHANUMERIC CODING   An alphanumeric coding system is a numeric system that codes files alphabetically. A number is assigned to each letter of the alphabet, and each file is given a number that corresponds to the surname of a client. Files are then filed in alphabetical and numeric order:

A = 1	I = 9	Q = 17	Y = 25
B = 2	J = 10	R = 18	Z = 26
C = 3	K = 11	S = 19	
D = 4	L = 12	T = 20	
E = 5	M = 13	U = 21	
F = 6	N = 14	V = 22	
G = 7	O = 15	W = 23	
H = 8	P = 16	X = 24	

The first four or five letters of a client's surname are assigned a number according to their numeric value:

Abrams, E.	A-B-R-A-M	1-2-18-1-13
Ackerman, D.	A-C-K-E-R	1-3-11-5-18
Adams, N.	A-D-A-M-S	1-4-1-13-19
Aggate, P.	A-G-G-A-T	1-7-7-1-20
Ahart, Y.	A-H-A-R-T	1-8-1-18-20

The cases are filed in numeric order but retain their alphabetical value. Therefore, when a new file is opened, it is given a number that pertains to its alphabetical value. For example, when Renee Aggerty's case is opened, her file would be given the number 1-7-7-5-18 (A=1, G=7, G=7, E=5, R=18). The file would be filed between Aggate and Ahart according to its numeric value as follows:

Abrams, E.	1-2-18-1-13
Ackerman, D.	1-3-11-5-18
Adams, N.	1-4-1-13-19
Aggate, P.	1-7-7-1-20
Aggerty, R.	**1-7-7-5-18**
Ahart, Y.	1-8-1-18-20

Note that the file is in both numeric and alphabetical order.

Studies have shown that an alphanumeric coding system can increase retrieval and filing speed up to six times. Misfilings are also reduced. Another advantage is that a cross-index is in alphabetical and numeric order.

Cross-Index

A cross-index is a cross-reference of clients' files. All numeric coding systems must have an alphabetical cross-index of clients with corresponding file numbers. In a firm with many cases, it is impossible to remember the file number of each case. Therefore, the name of the case and client must be cross-indexed alphabetically to locate a file.

All files and subfiles must be included in the index. Whenever a new subfile is opened, it is given a number and included on a cross-index. For example, a case has a combination numbering system, and a subfile is opened for each aspect of a litigation, as shown on page 444. All medical records are given the volume number of .3. As a file expands, new volumes are opened. The second medical records file is volume .31, and the third medical records file is .32. These new volumes must be inserted on a cross-index as they are opened, or no one will know they exist.

A **numeric index** must also be maintained. This index will inform the person assigning file numbers of the next number in the sequence to be assigned. As a number is assigned to a file, the file name is inserted on the index. This index ensures that no two files will have the same file number. Most records management software packages perform this feature automatically.

numeric index
An index in numeric order that lists files and the date opened. The purpose is to inform the file clerk of the next number in the sequence when opening files.

Color Coding

Color coding is a common method of categorizing files. The use of color can categorize files according to a number of designations. Examples include type of case, type of document, responsible attorney, branch office, area of law, and year a file was opened. A user can quickly see the correct file by looking at the color of the file label or folder.

One problem with an alphabetical filing system is that retrieval time is increased if a client has many files. A user will have to go through each file before a specific file is found. This problem is solved with the use of colored file folders, colored file labels, colored stickers, or colored numbers.

A color is assigned to a particular area of law and may be a colored label or file folder as follows:

Litigation: Red

Probate: Black

Corporate: Blue

Real estate: Brown

Tax: Orange

Domestic: White

Criminal: Purple

Agency: Green

If a paralegal was looking for John Brown's criminal case, she or he would look for a file with purple coding. If she or he were looking for John Brown's marriage dissolution file, she or he would look for a file with white coding.

In an office with more than one or two attorneys, color may be used to differentiate one attorney's files from another's as follows:

Morland Fischer's cases: Red

Loretta Ferro's cases: Blue

James Duncan's cases: Green

Michelle Gordon's cases: Yellow

EXHIBIT 13–5   Example of Colored Number Labels *(Reprinted with permission of Smead Manufacturing Company.)*

A colored dot or sticker may also be added to the label to add additional information as follows:

Superior court case: Red dot

Appeals court case: Green dot

Federal court case: Yellow dot

Companies offer colored alphabetic and numeric labels. The numbers or letters are inserted on the edge or top of a file folder so that they can be easily seen. When numbers are given a color, misfilings are easily spotted because a file with the contrasting color "pops out" from the rest of the files, as shown in Exhibit 13–5.

Some records managers maintain that color coding increases speed and accuracy in filing. Others claim that color coding is a waste of money and creates visual confusion. The answer is determined by the management of a firm. Each member of a legal team must know the meaning of each color before a system is effective. If too many colors are used, the system is too complicated.

Color may be applied to any system and may be used for paper or computer records. The many purposes that color has to offer a records management system is limited only by management's creativity and imagination.

File Retrieval

More than 900 million documents are created each day in the United States. According to statistics, about 3 percent (or 2,700,000) are misfiled. If finding each misfiled document costs $100 (a conservative estimate), the cost associated with misfiling documents and files is astronomical. A file retrieval system must allow for easy access to files. It must also reduce the possibility of lost or misplaced documents and files. Procedures must be developed to facilitate file retrieval, and these procedures must be followed by each member of a legal team. Noncompliance with retrieval procedures results in lost files.

Firms employ file personnel who are responsible for maintaining a retrieval system. In small firms, a secretary or paralegal may be responsible for file system maintenance in addition to other duties. In large firms, file clerks or file coordinators whose sole responsibility is to maintain the system are employed. An efficient system has a central person who is responsible for maintaining a system's procedures.

File name _____	File no. _____
Requestor _____	Dept. _____
Date of request _____	Date required _____
Date file to be returned _____
Date file delivered _____
Follow-up dates _____

EXHIBIT 13–6   Sample File Requisition Form

Requests for files from a centralized system are initiated by a requisition form similar to the one shown in Exhibit 13–6. The requisition form is completed and transferred to a file clerk, who retrieves and delivers the file. A written request has one important advantage over an oral request: It provides a record that the request was made. A requisition form is also used to monitor a file's location.

A file must be accessible before it is retrieved. If management has established an understandable and precise coding system for a file, the file should be readily accessible. However, files may be in a location other than a file room for various reasons, including the following:

- An attorney is reviewing it.
- A paralegal is working on it.
- A secretary is working on it.
- A law clerk doing research has it in the library.
- It is in the copy center having documents copied.

When a file is removed from the file area, its location must be traceable and monitored. Without a tracking system, time is wasted by searching an entire office for a file. A system used by firms for many years is an "out-card" system, which is similar to the out-card system used in law libraries. Bar code technology is also used to manage and retrieve files. The newest technology for file retrieval is radio frequency identification (RFID).

OUT-CARD SYSTEM   An out card is the size of a file folder, made of heavy vinyl, and has lines on the front on which to put names and dates, as shown in Exhibit 13–7. When a file is removed from the filing area, the responsible party inserts his or her name or initials and the date on the out card, which is then placed in the location of the removed file. The person requesting the file knows the location of the file by looking at the last name on the out card.

Advantages to the out-card system include the following:

- It shows that the file is being used and has not been misplaced.
- It enables a user to know the location of files at all times.
- It acts as a marker to indicate the proper place for a file.

This sounds like a simple and effective system. However, problems occur when employees do not put their names on the out card or do not use an out card. Many firms have problems getting staff to adhere to this simple procedure, so efforts are made to simplify the system further. Out cards are made to accommodate business cards or requisition slips of the firm's employees: Instead of writing his or her name, all the person has to do is insert a business card or requisition slip into the slot in the out card.

Out folders are also used. These are the same as out cards, except they will allow for documents to be inserted in them. This is convenient for a file clerk who is waiting for a file to be returned to file documents. A clerk can file documents into the out folder until the absent file is returned.

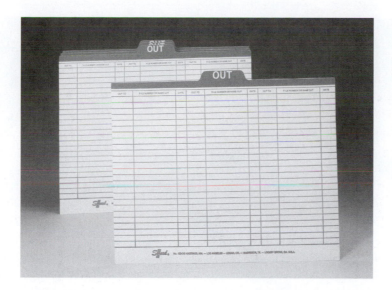

EXHIBIT 13–7   Example of an Out-Card System *(Reprinted with permission of Smead Manufacturing Company.)*

BAR CODING   Bar codes are a fast, easy, and accurate data entry method used in a process known as **automatic data collection.** Bar coding appeared in the food industry in the early 1970s and has evolved into an effective and popular tool used in most businesses today. A number of bar code standards have been developed and refined over the years into accepted languages called **symbologies.** Bar codes are used as we check out of the grocery store or have a package delivered.

Bar coding technology is used by universities and libraries to manage circulation of books and journals. It is also used by businesses to manage inventory. Courts use bar code technology in their records management systems. Law offices have discovered that bar coding is excellent for managing records.

A bar coding system automates records management. Documents, files, books, and furniture may be bar coded. Firms using bar codes have reported that the system provides firms with more efficient document handling, an automated rather than a manual master index, a more accurate index of files stored off site, and decreased retrieval time.

A bar code is put on a label that is attached to a file, as shown in Exhibit 13–8. Whenever a file is removed from a central filing area, its bar code label is scanned by a portable data entry terminal that communicates its information back to the firm's computer via radio frequency. The file's new location is inserted into the computer, and the file database is automatically updated. As a file moves around the office, its location can be determined by using a portable bar code scanner. An office is easily inventoried using this system. A bar code is also read by other computerized programs, such as a time and billing program. When a timekeeper begins work on a file, the bar code is scanned, and the information is automatically entered into the timekeeping system. Medium and large firms especially benefit from using bar code technology for their files.

Six benefits to using bar code technology follow:

1. *Accuracy.* Bar codes are more accurate than manual data entry. Studies show that the entry and read error rates for bar code technology are about one error in one million characters versus one error in 300 characters in manual key entry.
2. *Ease of use.* Bar codes are easy to use and understand.
3. *Uniform data collection.* Bar code symbologies are universally understood and accepted.
4. *Timely feedback.* Information entered into a system is available immediately to a law firm's personnel.

automatic data collection
The data entry method used in bar code technology.

symbologies
Language used in bar code technology.

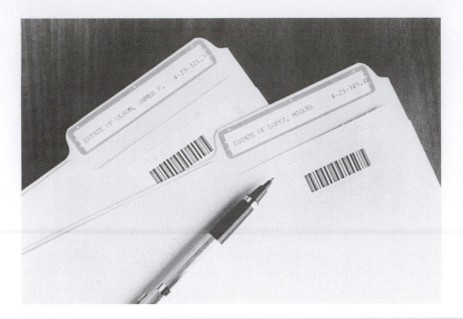

EXHIBIT 13–8 Bar Coded Files

5. *Improved productivity*. Bar codes automate tasks, enabling a law firm's personnel to devote their time to other projects.

6. *Increased profitability*. Using bar code technology increases the efficiency of a firm's filing system. This results in increased employee efficiency, resulting in increased profitability.

radio frequency identification
A generic term for technologies that use radio waves to identify people or objects.

RADIO FREQUENCY IDENTIFICATION **Radio frequency identification** may eventually replace bar codes for a file retrieval system. It is a generic term for technologies that use radio waves to identify people or objects. RFID technology has been around since World War II and is in use all around us. We insert an RFID tag in our pets to locate them if they are lost, we insert RFIDs in transponders for toll road access, and we attach them to merchandise in the event of theft.

RFID tags
Microchips encoded with a file's information.

It works by placing special microchips, called **RFID tags,** in the file. RFID tags come in a variety of shapes and sizes. A tag's memory size varies according to application requirements and can contain as much as one megabyte of memory. The microchip contains information about the file and has an antenna on it. The antenna enables the chip to transmit the identification information to a reader. The reader converts the radio waves from the RFID tag into digital information that is then passed on to computers, as shown in Exhibit 13–9.

The big difference between RFID and bar codes is that a bar code is a "line-of-sight" technology. That is, a scanner has to "see" the bar code to read it, which means people usually have to orient the bar code toward a scanner for it to be read. RFID doesn't require line of sight. RFID tags can be read as long as they are within range of a reader, which is as much as 100 feet or more depending on its power output and the radio frequency used. RFID data can be read through the human body and nonmetallic materials.

Electronic Files

Law firms are moving to electronic files that are accessible to each member of the legal team from their desktops. Not only do electronic files save valuable space, but file retrieval is easy. Paper documents are scanned into the computer and filed in electronic file folders. Electronic file folders use the same coding systems discussed earlier in this chapter. Whenever a document is needed, it can be accessed from the computer. Each member of the legal team has access to the same file simultaneously, thus reducing unproductive employee time spent looking for files. Software products offering document management are listed in the Cybersites section.

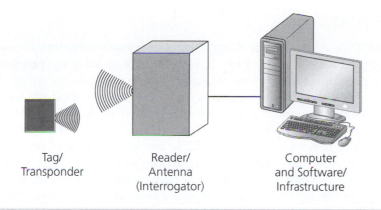

Tag/
Transponder

Reader/
Antenna
(Interrogator)

Computer
and Software/
Infrastructure

EXHIBIT 13–9   Example of Radio Frequency Identification *(Reprinted with permission of Datamax®.)*

More than 90 percent of all new information is created and stored in electronic form. Electronic records management is the number-one priority of records and information managers. In order to deal with the influx of electronic records, law firms must invest in sophisticated records management technology to manage a wide variety of electronic records, including e-mails, attachments, electronic documents, Web pages, database output, digital images and recordings, and instant messaging.

Electronic files will not replace paper files, however. Paper files are necessary for the following reasons:

- Computers can and do crash without adequate backup storage.
- Many clients and third parties require paper documents.
- Software becomes obsolete quickly. Backup files are useless if they cannot be read by current software.
- Paper documents contain original signatures.

Law office filing systems are as varied as the examples in this section. Whatever system is used, it is important to learn the system quickly and satisfactorily. One member of a legal team not adhering to the rules of a system can cause documents or files to be lost. Lost documents and files mean lost information and potential liability for a firm.

Of Interest . . .

TRACING LOST FILES

In 1987, Todd Brockman, a student at the University of Southern California, was doing an internship at Sun Microsystems. An attorney in the office kept losing his files. Brockman attached bar codes to the attorney's files and developed a device that consisted of a bar code generator and portable bar code scanner. Whenever the attorney lost a file, he simply walked through the office waving the magic scanner. When it beeped, he found the missing file. Brockman programmed the device so that it would display where the file was supposed to be, even down to the exact filing cabinet. The device, now called The Tracker, is sold by Todd's new technology company, CCG. It can also be used to find other lost items, such as keys and office supplies.

FILE OPENING ★

File opening consists of opening two types of files: preclient files and client files.

Preclient Files

preclient
A person who consults an attorney but does not formally retain the services of the attorney.

preclient file
A file containing notes of interview or consultation to be retrieved if the client retains the firm.

Not all potential clients retain a firm. Some interview many attorneys before choosing a lawyer, and some just need some quick legal advice. These matters are known as **preclient** matters.

A firm keeps information about each person who consults with an attorney. If a lawyer or paralegal takes notes during an initial interview, the notes are inserted into a **preclient file.** If a potential client returns to retain the firm, the notes are retrieved from the preclient file, and a client file is opened. A client file is not opened unless a client formally retains a firm. Normally, preclient files are coded alphabetically and kept for at least one year. However, each law firm has its own retention period and coding method for preclient files.

As you learned in Chapter 4, an attorney-client relationship is formed whenever an attorney gives a person legal advice. Even though a client does not formerly retain a firm, *if a person consults a lawyer about a matter, that person would be considered a client in many states.* As such, a preclient's information must be entered into a firm's conflict-checking system and the system must be checked before accepting representation of a client. If there is a conflict of interest with a preclient, an attorney may not represent the person.

File-Opening Procedures

new case memorandum
A form used to provide information about a case so that a file may be opened.

A client file is opened immediately after a client retains a firm. A **new case memorandum** form, similar to the one shown in Exhibit 13–10, is completed by an attorney or paralegal and given to a secretary or file clerk. The secretary or file clerk opens a file from the information provided on the new case memorandum form.

When a clerk or secretary receives a new case memorandum, the first step is to do a conflict check. Once a client has been cleared for conflicts, a client file is ready to be opened.

CONFLICT CHECK Each new client must be checked for a possible conflict of interest. If *a firm represented an adverse party at any time in the past or has another conflict, as described in Chapter 4, the firm has a conflict of interest in representing the new client.* A firm must reject a new client unless the conflicting client consents to the representation, although states vary on this requirement.

A database is maintained with clients' names and the names of all parties to a matter in which the firm was involved. The database must be searched before a file is opened. *If a new client has a dispute with a previous client, the firm has a conflict in representing that client* (see Chapter 4). *If a new client was an opposing party in a case and the new matter does not involve the firm's client, a firm must have written permission from the client in the previous matter to represent the new client in the new matter, although this requirement also varies by state.* Careful attention must be given to this most important aspect of opening a file. Firms have been disciplined for conflict-of-interest violations.

A conflict check is the most important aspect of file-opening procedures but is not limited to file opening. Each time a party makes an appearance in a case, a firm's client database must be checked to determine the new party's relationship to the firm, if any.

Most firms require some type of written record that a conflict check was made. As you can see in Exhibit 13–10, there is an area on the new case memorandum that must be completed when a conflict search is completed. *If the person conducting the conflict search suspects that there may be a problem with the representation, the attorney or manager must be notified immediately.*

file-number index
An index containing sequential file numbers and case names indicating the next available file number.

CLIENT FILE OPENING If a firm has no conflict of interest in representing a client, a client file may be opened. Each firm has different requirements for opening files. If a firm uses a numeric system, a clerk must consult a **file-number index** to determine the next number for the file, unless an automated system is used. The file number is inserted on the new case memorandum form, and the file labels are prepared. If a firm uses a color-coding system, a clerk prepares the file accordingly.

It is difficult to anticipate the size of a case when opening a file. Some firms open one main file and expand to additional files as the case develops. Other firms prepare one file

Date_____Responsible attorney_____

CLIENT INFORMATION

Name _____ New ☐ Old ☐
Address _____
City, State, Zip _____
Phone: Home _____ Work _____
Place of employment _____
Address _____
Department _____ Position _____

CASE INFORMATION

Matter name _____
Type of matter _____
Other party name _____
Address _____
Phone _____
Statute of limitations _____

FEE AND BILLING INFORMATION

Deposit received $ _____ for Retainer ☐ Costs ☐ Fee ☐
Fee to be billed   ☐ Hourly   ☐ Contingency _____% Fixed fee of $_____
Payable _____

INSTRUCTIONS

_____
_____

Conflict check made by _____ on _____
File opened _____ File no. _____ By _____

EXHIBIT 13–10 New Case Memorandum Form

folder for each area of the case, such as a folder for correspondence, a folder for pleadings, a folder for discovery, and so on. Each category may be given a different colored folder or label to quickly identify it. Files with multiple folders are stored in an expandable accordion file with the file numbers inserted on the outside of the file, as shown in Exhibit 13–11.

A file clerk or secretary uses a new case memorandum as a checklist to complete file-opening procedures. Many firms use an automated system that will guide a clerk to enter specific information into a firm's computer. Most automated systems are connected to other programs, such as timekeeping, billing, and docket programs, and will automatically insert the required information into them when the information from a new client is input. This integration saves a clerk time because the information is entered into the system only once. Many automated software packages create file folder labels, print request slips, and prepare filing-opening reports. Common entries of both automated and manual systems include the following:

ETHICS ALERT

- *Conflict status*. The results of the conflict check are inserted on the new case memorandum. *If a direct or potential conflict exists, the attorney or manager must be informed immediately.* File-opening procedures cease until the conflict has been cleared. If no conflict exists, file-opening procedures may resume. The person performing the conflict search inserts his or her initials on the new case memorandum form as verification that the search was made.

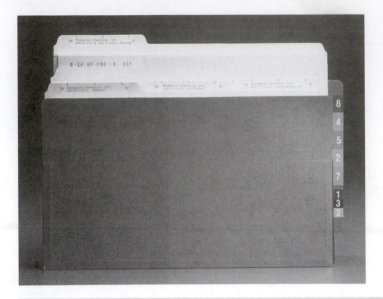

EXHIBIT 13–11 Client File that Contains Multiple Folders *(Reprinted with permission of Smead Manufacturing Company.)*

ETHICS ALERT

- *Statute of limitations.* Some firms put the statute of limitations date on the outside of the folder in bold, red ink. *The date the statute of limitations expires must be put in the firm's tickler system to monitor it.* This information is integrated into a docket system.
- *Client information.* The client's name, address, telephone and fax numbers, and e-mail address(es) are needed.
- *Subject matter.* The subject matter of the case is inserted.
- *Opposing parties.* The name, address, and telephone numbers of opposing parties are inserted. This information is important for future conflict searches and is put into the conflict database.
- *Responsible attorney.* The responsible attorney is inserted into the system. This ties the case to the responsible attorney for time and billing purposes. If a team is assigned, the names of all team members are inserted.
- *Date.* The date a file is opened is inserted. Some automated systems automatically put a file on the firm's case review schedule.
- *Billing information.* The type of fee charged, the amount, and billing instructions are inserted. The billing cycle is also inserted, such as monthly, quarterly, or contingency. This information is automatically integrated with the billing program in an automated system.
- *Name of referring party.* The name of the person who referred the client to the firm is inserted. This prompts the firm to send an acknowledgment or thank you to the referring party. Preparing and sending this acknowledgment is part of the file-opening procedures.
- *Type of case.* The type of case is inserted. This information is used by a law firm's management for statistics and marketing information. It also allows the computer to track time spent on various types of cases.

The original new case memorandum is inserted into the client's file. Some firms keep a copy of it in a separate binder in alphabetical order according to the client's name or in a file on the computer. This binder is used as a cross-reference for numeric cases in the event that the computer is not available. A new case report is circulated among the attorneys to inform them of the new client and the parties involved. This acts as a double-check against direct or potential conflicts of interest.

A firm's management may have other file-opening requirements, such as inserting the client's name, address, and telephone number on the attorney's and paralegal's client list or telephone directory. It is important that file-opening procedures and information be accurate. Since the information is used in timekeeping, billing, and docketing programs, any errors at the file-opening stage will affect other programs. Incorrect preliminary information results in incorrect reports, records, and other essential documents.

FILE MAINTENANCE

A paralegal is responsible for keeping clients' files in good order. The paralegal may not be responsible for doing the actual clerical work involved, but the paralegal most often directs that the clerical work is to be done accurately.

How files are maintained is changing with new technological advances. Before computers, a document was a sheet of paper. Now, documents consist of electronic documents, e-mails, photographs, video clips, digital images, diskettes, and CD-ROMs. Document management is moving toward image-based documents, called **rich media.** The Web is responsible for this transition because it is visual. As a result, there has been a shift from text-based to image-based media that is one of the biggest changes facing records management today. These innovations will continue to change the way that files and documents are managed.

rich media
Image-based technology that is visual rather than text oriented.

Document Categories

The first step in file maintenance is categorizing its documents. Documents are inserted into a file by category. For example, all correspondence is filed together in chronological order with the most recent on top, all notes are filed together in chronological order with the most recent on top, and so on. Filing correspondence, notes, pleadings, and court documents together results in messy, disorganized files.

Correspondence, pleadings, notes, and all other documents are filed in chronological order unless the case is large. In a small case, correspondence is inserted on the left side of the folder, and pleadings and other documents are inserted on the right side in chronological order with the most recent on top. A number of file folder products are available to help organize files. File partitions and folders that have sections built into them, as shown in Exhibit 13–12, may be purchased. With a partitioned folder, categorizing documents is easier.

In a large or complex case, correspondence documents are further categorized by type, that is, by year or subject matter. They are filed chronologically within each group. Pleadings and discovery documents may be categorized by type as follows:

File 1: Pleadings
    Section I: Complaints
    Section II: Cross-complaints
    Section III: Answers

EXHIBIT 13–12 Partitioned File Folder

File 2: Discovery
  Section I: Interrogatories
  Section II: Requests for admissions
  Section III: Requests for production of documents
  Section IV: Deposition summaries

Case Cover Sheets

Case cover sheets are used to monitor the status of a case. They provide a synopsis of the events of a case. By looking at a case cover sheet, the attorney or paralegal can see the current status of a case. A case cover sheet, such as the one shown in Exhibit 13–13, has been credited for saving valuable time searching the file for information. An example of a Case Cover Sheet is on the accompanying CD.

Case _____ No. _____

Attorney _____ S/L _____ Type of case _____

PLEADINGS

Complaint: Filed _____ Served _____ Ans. due _____ Ans. rec'd. _____
X Complaint: Served _____ Ans. due _____ Ans. filed _____

DISCOVERY

Int./RA propounded by _____ to _____
Served _____ Ans. due _____ Ans. rec'd. _____
Int./RA propounded by _____ to _____
Served _____ Ans. due _____ Ans. rec'd. _____
Int./RA propounded by _____ to _____
Served _____ Ans. due _____ Ans. rec'd. _____
Deposition of _____ Set for _____
by _____ Reporter _____ Depo. rec'd. _____
Deposition of _____ Set for _____
by _____ Reporter _____ Depo. rec'd. _____
Deposition of _____ Set for _____
by _____ Reporter _____ Depo. rec'd. _____
Prod. of docs. by _____ to _____
Served _____ Ans. due _____ Ans. rec'd. _____
Prod. of docs. by _____ to _____
Served _____ Ans. due _____ Ans. rec'd. _____
Prod. of docs. by _____ to _____
Served _____ Ans. due _____ Ans. rec'd. _____
Prod. of docs. by _____ to _____
Served _____ Ans. due _____ Ans. rec'd. _____

TRIAL

Trial date _____ Jury requested by _____ Fees posted _____
Settlement conference dates _____
Continuances _____ Requested by _____ to _____

EXHIBIT 13–13 Example of a Case Cover Sheet

Many docket control software programs automatically generate a case cover sheet that indicates due dates, tickler dates, and the date a task was completed. A case cover sheet may be put on top of a folder or in a file so that it can be viewed immediately on opening the file. Some firms keep case cover sheets or copies of them in a binder or on a computer so the status of each case can be updated and available without pulling the file from the file room. If a paralegal needs to know when an answer to a complaint is due, she or he looks on the cover sheet instead of going through a file to find a certificate of service of the complaint. It takes a little time to maintain a case cover sheet, but the time it will save in searching files for information is worth it.

Indexes

As a case grows and documents are categorized, indexes, such as the one shown in Exhibit 13–14, are used to direct a person to a document's exact location in a file. For example, as pleadings and court documents are received, they are filed chronologically in a small case. Each document is given a number that is put on a tab so that it can be found quickly. The tab is then inserted on a divider sheet and protrudes so that it can be seen easily. It is important not to put a tab on the actual document; tabs must be put on a separate divider sheet. Tabs may be purchased alone, or divider sheets may be purchased with tabbed numbers on them. Many indexing products are available.

A document is inserted behind its divider so that it can be located by lifting up the tabbed divider. As a new document is received, it is put on top of the previous document's divider sheet and given the next number in sequence.

The number, title of document, date, and party are inserted on an index sheet, which is placed on top of the applicable section. A specific document can be located quickly and easily. The use of cover sheets and indexes will keep files organized and decrease the time it takes to retrieve a document.

Tabs and indexes can be modified further to accommodate categorization of documents. For example, a file may be separated by sections as follows:

Section I: Pleadings (complaints, cross-complaints, and answers)

Section II: Discovery documents

Section III: Medical reports

Section IV: Other documents

Case: Smith, John J. v. Brown, Janis L. File no. 2003-596

No.	Description of Document	Date	Party
1	Summons and complaint for personal injuries	3/4/XX	Plaintiff
2	Proof of service of complaint	3/10/XX	Plaintiff
3	Answer to complaint	4/9/XX	Defendant
4	Cross-complaint	4/9/XX	Defendant
5	Answer to cross-complaint	5/7/XX	Plaintiff

EXHIBIT 13–14 Example Pleadings Index

Case: Smith, John J. v. Brown, Janis L.		File no. 200203-596	
No.	**Description of Document**	**Date**	**Amount**
1	St. Jude Hospital	2/4/XX	$16,785.30
2	Dr. Fredericks, orthopedic surgeon	1/10/XX	4,521.70
3	Dr. Maynard, anesthesiologist	1/10/XX	987.00
4	Dr. Bunnell, physical therapist	1/19/XX	2,117.50

EXHIBIT 13–15 Example Medical Expenses Index

Each document is numbered sequentially within each section as follows:

Document I-1: Plaintiff's complaint

Document II-1: Interrogatories

Document III-1: Medical report of Dr. Gunn, date June 10, 2008

Indexes should be developed for every category of file except correspondence and miscellaneous notes. Exhibits 13–15 and 13–16 show examples of medical expenses and research indexes, respectively. No loose papers should be in a file. Every document, regardless of size, must be secured by file fasteners. Systems can be developed to accommodate any type of document. For small pieces of paper, such as telephone messages, an envelope can be inserted in a file. Photographs should be put on a piece of paper or put in an envelope that is attached to the file with fasteners.

Document Management

Documents are generated in a law office in one of two ways: They are developed or received. A paralegal will encounter many different types of documents and must make decisions regarding each document. Choosing which document to retain or discard requires judgment that is developed with time and experience.

Case: Smith, John J. v. Brown, Janis L.		File no. 200303-596	
No.	**Case Name**	**Date**	**Subject**
1	Grand Trucking v. Henry, Gloria	2/4/XX	Liability
2	Sanchez v. Bell Laboratories	11/15/XX	Liability
3	ABC, Inc. v. VBF Corp.	6/8/XX	Liability

EXHIBIT 13–16 Example Research Index

LIFE CYCLE OF A DOCUMENT   Every document has a life cycle and lives only as long as it serves its purpose. Since each document has a different purpose, each document has a different life cycle. Pleadings live as long as a litigation case, and correspondence may have a shorter life. Determining the life cycle of a document is vital to effective records and file management. Exhibit 13–17 shows a document's life cycle.

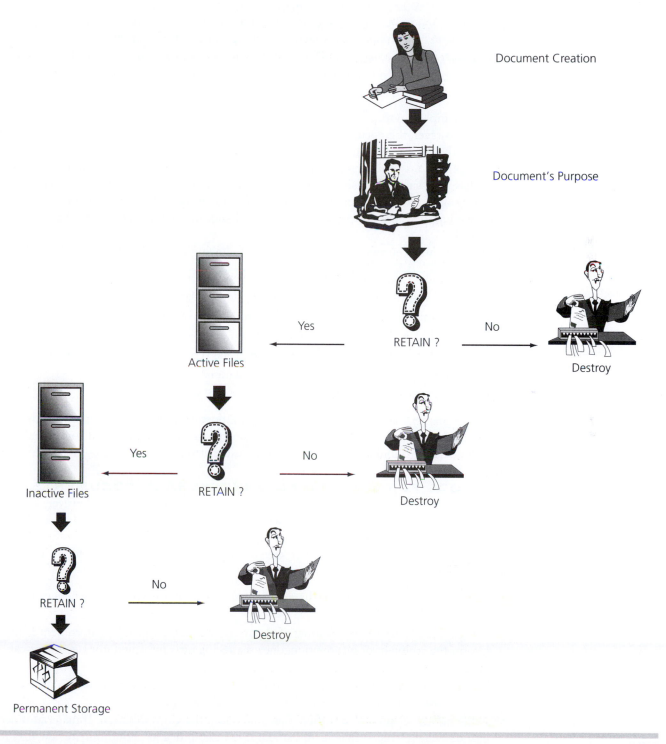

EXHIBIT 13–17   Life Cycle of a Document

To determine the life cycle of a document, one must first identify a document's value. Three value determinations are used.

1. *Operational value.* This refers to whether a document or information is needed on a day-to-day basis. A document that is referred to at least once a month has high operational value, while a document that is referred to less than once a month has low operational value. An example of a document with high operational value is an index of a firm's clients or cases.

2. *Technical value.* This refers to whether a document or information has technical or procedural importance. An example of a document with technical value is instructions on how to operate a system or a change in court procedure.

3. *Legal value.* This refers to whether a document or information is covered by a statute or regulation. An example of a document with legal value is a pleading or corporate minutes.

For example, a notice of shareholders meeting has no operational value after the meeting is held. However, the document has legal value because it shows that the meeting was held and that the legal requirement of notice was accomplished. A letter confirming an extension of time to answer interrogatories has no operational value after the deadline has passed, but it has legal value because it shows that the extension was given and may be evidence in a hearing on a motion to compel answers. A document describing a change in procedural rules of filing petitions for probate has technical and operational value until the procedure is learned.

To determine the value of a document, the following questions should be asked:

- Why would anyone refer to this document again?
- To what degree is this document needed for day-to-day business?
- When will the information in this document lose its validity? Two weeks? One month?
- Will this document be referred to often?
- Will this document be helpful information in the type of law in which I am working?
- Is this document covered by a statute or regulation?
- Has the statute of limitations expired on this document?

There are certain points in the life cycle of a document when a decision regarding its future must be made. These periods vary according to the type of document considered. The ultimate decision should be made by the responsible attorney.

METHODS FOR DISCARDING UNNECESSARY DOCUMENTS The decision to dispose of a document is a difficult one for most people. However, keeping unnecessary documents is a waste of space and therefore costly for a firm. It also clutters files and makes files less manageable.

When making a decision to either keep or dispose of a document, the following questions should be asked:

- Is the document available elsewhere? Is it in the computer or on a disk where it is readily available?
- Is the material strictly for informational purposes? If the purpose of a document is to inform the recipient of information, once the recipient is informed, the document can be discarded.
- When would this information be needed? If there is no immediate answer and there is no legal reason to keep it, it is probably not worth saving.
- Is the information current? Often, files contain outdated information. If material is not part of a client's file, it may be discarded. It is a good idea to periodically review files to **purge**, or clear, them of outdated information.

purge
To clear or discard.

Time management experts advise that document management decisions should be made as soon as a document is received. A document should be handled only once to efficiently manage time. However, if you cannot decide what to do with a document after asking yourself the previous questions, put the document in a "decision file" and review the document in one week. The office manager or supervising attorney can also give you guidance in this area.

Among the documents found in a typical law office are the following:

- Correspondence (client correspondence, law firm business correspondence, promotional mail and advertisements, and miscellaneous correspondence)
- Clients' case documents, such as pleadings
- Interoffice memos and reports
- Photocopies
- Meeting notes (notes from client conferences, law firm business meetings, and miscellaneous meetings, such as educational seminars)
- Rough drafts
- Articles and newspaper clippings

Correspondence   Filing experts have estimated that correspondence constitutes most of the documents received. However, not all correspondence is vital. All correspondence pertaining to a client's case must be filed in the client's file. If a document was faxed, the fax cover sheet must also be saved to show the date and origin of the fax. All incoming correspondence is **date stamped,** or marked with the date it was received, even fax cover sheets. Date-stamping correspondence when it arrives makes it easier to respond to a document in a timely manner and eliminates paper glut. Envelopes need not be saved unless the correspondence was mailed certified or special delivery or unless the postmark or return address is important to a client's case. Some law firms have a policy to save all envelopes.

Promotional documents are a form of correspondence. If promotional material concerns a product or service that interests the recipient or someone else in the office, it should be saved or passed to an interested person. If the material is of no interest to anyone in the firm, it may be discarded.

The person to whom correspondence is sent is responsible for deciding whether to keep the material. If a decision is made to keep the material, it is filed in the appropriate file.

Clients' Case Documents   No document pertaining to a client's case may be discarded. Each document must be appropriately filed. If a document's importance or validity to a case is unclear, the responsible attorney should be consulted.

Interoffice Memos and Reports   Interoffice memos are important communication vehicles between a firm and its employees. A memo announcing an event or activity may be discarded after the event or activity has occurred. Memos regarding firm policies or systems are kept for future reference. All documents pertaining to employment reviews or benefits are retained. Memos regarding a client's case are filed in the client's file.

Photocopies   Excess photocopies cause files to bulge. A survey of a national records management organization found that the average office makes 19 copies of each document. Thirty-seven percent of these are unnecessary, 45 percent of the documents are duplicates, and 85 percent of the records are never referred to again after they are created. If an original document is in a file, additional copies are unnecessary and should not be made. If a photocopy contains notes or highlighting that makes it different from the original, it should be retained. If a copy of a document is used often, as with a form, a photocopy should be made as it is needed. The original document should be marked to alert employees to make a copy of it instead of using the original. Placing the original in a sheet protector will discourage employees from using the original rather than a copy.

A **courtesy copy** is a copy of a document sent to a person as a courtesy, or for informational purposes only. The recipient is considered a **secondary recipient,** and the person to

date stamp
To stamp a document with the date it was received.

courtesy copy
A document that is sent to a person for informational purposes only.

secondary recipient
A person to whom a document is sent for informational purposes only.

primary recipient
A person to whom a
document is directed or
addressed.

whom the memo is sent is considered the **primary recipient.** A secondary recipient has no responsibility to retain the document but does have the responsibility of deciding what to do with the information. If the author of the document was within the organization, an official original will be filed in the appropriate file, so filing the courtesy copy is not necessary in most instances.

Meeting Notes   Notes taken in a meeting with a client or on a client's behalf are always retained. If there is a misunderstanding of a meeting's discussions, the notes will be valuable documentation of the meeting's substance. For a law firm's meetings, pages of notes are often generated that are never referred to again. The decision to keep or discard the notes of a law firm's meeting depends on the notetaker's level of involvement in the meeting. If the notetaker was in charge of the meeting, was required to report on the meeting, or was required to do something as a result of the meeting, the notes are retained.

Rough Draft   Rough drafts of documents pose difficulties in deciding whether to retain them. As the terms of a contract are negotiated, many drafts are generated. As provisions are negotiated, they are modified. Rough drafts of agreements are important documents when negotiating a contract. A draft is written by one party to the contract and given to the other party for approval. Changes that are made are highlighted and marked to indicate the party who made them. Rough drafts are numbered as to the author of the changes, such as Party No. 1's Draft No. 1, Party No. 2's Draft No. 2, and so on. No rough draft of a contract is destroyed until the agreement has been fully negotiated and signed. Some law firms have a policy to retain all rough drafts of contracts in the event of future litigation. If the importance of the draft is unclear, the responsible attorney should be consulted.

Rough drafts of correspondence or pleadings are destroyed when the final document is completed. However, some firms may have a policy to determine the destruction of rough drafts on a case-by-case basis. Be sure to have a solid understanding of your firm's policy before discarding rough drafts.

Articles and Newspaper Clippings   Various types of articles and newspaper clippings are of interest to a law office. A high-profile case will receive publicity, and a firm should keep all articles pertaining to a client's case.

Case law and changes in statutory law are often publicized when they occur. An article in a legal publication may be directly related to a client's case. An attorney or paralegal may choose to keep the article for future reference as an aid in legal research.

When magazine and newspaper articles are kept, they should be clipped rather than retaining the entire magazine or newspaper. The name, volume number, and date of an article's source must be indicated on the article. The rest of the magazine or newspaper may be discarded or filed.

If it is beneficial to retain each issue of a particular magazine, firms file these in magazine files that require little space and help keep an office uncluttered. Some firms put periodicals on microfilm. However, before magazines are saved, a firm's librarian should be consulted to make sure that duplicate issues are not retained.

Managing Electronic Records

When is a message considered a record? The U.S. National Archives and Records Administration (NARA) defines a message as a record if it is "made or received in connection with the transaction of the organization's business, or it is preserved by the organization, or is appropriate for preservation." Managing electronic documents is similar to managing paper documents, with the exception that they require less space to store. After you have read a document, you make a decision to do one or more of the following: copy it, file it, write comments on it, forward it to someone in the firm, or dispose of it. These same actions are taken with an electronic document.

The files and subfiles into which electronic documents are stored must be similar in structure to the filing system for paper documents. Electronic documents are classified in the same manner as shown on page 439. The first step is to determine function categories. Then subject, topic, and subtopic categories can be identified. This hierarchy of folders is duplicated on the computer for electronic documents. For example, an e-mail regarding firm business, such as health benefits, should be filed in an electronic file as follows:

Firm policy (function)
   Benefits (subject)
      Health (topic)
         Corres 2009 (type and year of document) (subtopic)

It is important to protect your electronic documents. After finalizing documents, you can move them to a similar directory structure in another part of the network where the directory is marked for "read only" access. This allows documents to be accessible to others in the firm but protects them from alteration. Electronic documents should be backed up each day to preserve them. Most firms have backup systems in place.

Of Interest . . .

MANAGING E-MAILS

An informal study conducted in 1997 within a large government organization looked at the e-mail activity of a typical user. One hundred forty-nine e-mail messages sent to a typical user revealed:

- 16 career opportunities
- 25 promotional or advertising e-mails
- 7 miscellaneous messages
- 33 message-received confirmations
- 68 valid work-related messages

The user was asked to identify the messages appropriate for filing. The user filed 35 messages. After filing, a records manager evaluated them and determined that only 10 of them were worthy of preserving. You need to decide which e-mail messages are worthy of retaining. Some unofficial guidelines to help you decide follow:

- Was the message developed in preparing reports, papers, or documents?
- Does the message reflect official actions taken?
- Does the message convey information on programs, policies, or decisions?
- Does the message convey statements of official policy or rationale for official decisions?
- Does the message document oral exchanges where official decisions were discussed?

In other words, retain the e-mail if it

- Contains a decision or discussion of a decision.
- Calls for a reply or action.
- Concerns official business about a case.
- Involves a significant member of your firm or your client.

Just as with paper documents, electronic documents must be managed according to a well-planned system. Some people may file an electronic document that was prepared for a client in the client's electronic file. Others may file it in an electronic folder by type of document.

Others may have no destination for the electronic document and save it wherever the document may end up in the system. A lack of planning causes confusion in the system.

A law office must have naming and saving rules for its electronic documents. Filing systems for electronic documents are similar to those for paper documents, with more complex cases requiring more classification of documents and more folders than are required for smaller cases. Everyone in a firm should adhere to the rules; otherwise, a system will fail. A good system is easy to use, easy to remember, and is universally accepted by all employees.

A good document-naming system makes it easy for a person to determine the document's contents by its name. A popular electronic filing system that is used in some law firms is to give each client an electronic file on the firm's computer system. As a document is prepared for a client, it is saved with a name that contains three components: the first four or five letters of the client's name or surname, the date of the document, and a code that indicates the type of document (e.g., CMP = complaint, ANS = answer, INT = interrogatories, LTR = letter). For example, a letter written for client Smith on June 14, 2008, would be named SMITH.080614.LTR. A complaint for client Johnson prepared the same day would be named JOHNS.080614.CMP. The document is saved in the applicable client's file, which lists all the documents in the folder in chronological order. One can look at the name of the document and get an idea of the document's contents.

Just as paper documents are stored on site until they are no longer needed for current business, electronic documents remain on the network's hard drive until they are no longer needed, until they can be disposed of, or until the need to recoup hard drive space occurs. Electronic documents can be transferred to digital storage media for continued retention. A list of documents on disks can be created, showing the locations of the documents on diskette or other media. Document management software makes this process easy.

Document Retrieval

Documents should never be removed from a file. When documents are removed from their files, they are likely to get lost. If a specific document is needed from a file, the entire file should be requested. If a paralegal needs a copy of a document, the document should be copied and immediately returned to its correct location in the file.

Automated Document Management

A recent survey reported that for 90 percent of the paper documents found in a law firm's files, one could find an electronic copy on the firm's computer system. Electronic documents have many advantages: They are stored in less space, are accessible, and are easily edited. There are also disadvantages: They are difficult to manage, are easily lost without a good filing system in place, and are difficult to search and review without opening the file. Many large and medium-sized firms found help managing their electronic documents from document management software programs.

Automated document management software applications are multiuser, shared workgroup products that hook into the Open and Save commands of word processing or other application software. This software allows a user to complete a profile of a document and to store the document on the firm's network or intranet. It stores the profile information in a central database where it controls user access. The document's profile is updated automatically every time it is retrieved, edited, printed, archived, or deleted. It keeps track of clients, cases, authors, keywords, and other relevant information. A user can search the database for a document.

An automated document management system has other functions, including the following:

- Locates any document
- Calculates how much time attorneys, paralegals, and secretaries spend editing documents, and automatically enters that information into the billing system

- Moves seldom-used documents to remote storage
- Provides extra copies of documents in case the system fails
- Archives documents after a prearranged retention period is determined
- Keeps track of versions of documents
- Calculates the number of keystrokes typed and the number of pages printed for each document, and automatically transfers the information to a time and billing system
- Makes a backup copy of the document

A document management software system tracks and manages every legal document created in a law office. Such a system is beneficial to firms because it helps employees locate information, ultimately saving a firm money.

Various software packages exist that help prepare legal documents. These software programs consist of a database of standard clauses used in standard contracts, leases, letters, memos, and other legal documents. They assist the document preparer by allowing a choice as to which clauses should be inserted into a document, and then prompt the preparer for variable information, such as the party's name, address, and other fill-in-the-blank information. The software automatically assembles the document and opens it directly into the firm's word processing program.

Once prepared, the document is saved on the firm's network or intranet. The software can track multiple versions of a document, perform document comparisons, and save the document's criteria. The software contains a library of legal documents that can be accessed by all a firm's personnel. The library can be searched by a variety of search methods: full-text, Boolean, and proximity.

There are other uses for this software. If an attorney wants to check on your productivity for a day, he searches for the documents that you prepared on a particular day and will get a list of all those documents. If a client calls and wants an immediate update, the system will search for all documents prepared for that client and list all the documents in the case. Because of this search capability, no document can be lost in the system.

Document management software that contains documents directed to specific legal practice areas can be purchased. Most packages are integrated with a firm's word processing system and can be integrated with other software applications, such as docketing and calendar programs, e-mail, and spreadsheet programs. Documents from the library may be "checked out" for use outside the network or intranet.

FILE CLOSING, RETENTION, AND DESTRUCTION

How a file is managed after the case is closed is just as important as when the case was active. Files must be accessible after they are closed in the event of an audit, reactivation, or noncompliance with a judgment or agreement. There are thousands of laws, both state and federal, that mandate how long a file must be retained after closure. Implementing sound file-closing procedures ensures that closed files are easily located.

File-Closing Procedures

When a case is completed, certain procedures must be followed before a file is a candidate for closing:

- A file must be reviewed to make sure that all final documents have been completed.
- The final bill must be paid.
- A disengagement letter must be sent to the client.
- Unnecessary documents must be discarded from the file, a procedure known as **pruning** a file.

pruning
To discard unnecessary documents from a file.

- The status of a file must be changed from active to inactive.
- Valuable original documents must be returned to the client.
- Any electronic records of the case must be deleted from the firm's computer system.

FINAL DOCUMENTATION When a case has been completed, a file must be double-checked to ensure that all documents have been completed and filed. If they have not, a file must remain active. Just because there has been no activity on a case for some time, it does not mean that it is completed. A case may not have been entered in the file review system, or a final document may have not been calendared. The final documentation, such as a final judgment or dismissal, may have been overlooked. It is important to carefully review a file before considering the file a candidate for closing. This is often an attorney's responsibility but may be delegated to an experienced, senior paralegal.

If the appeal period has not expired, a case may not be closed. It is often a paralegal's responsibility to calculate the appeal period or to know the status of a judgment. For example, if a judgment has not been completely satisfied, the file may not be closed until it is. If a judgment has been satisfied, final documentation must be filed with the court, indicating that the case is closed and that the judgment has been satisfied. If payments on a judgment have taken a long time, final documentation may have been overlooked.

FINAL BILLING A client's final bill must be paid before a case is closed. Paralegals should double-check with management to ensure that the final bill has been paid before proceeding with file-closing procedures. If the bill has been recently paid, final closing procedures should be delayed to allow a client's check to clear.

DISENGAGEMENT LETTER Some firms send a disengagement letter with a final bill, while others wait until the bill has been paid. A disengagement letter promotes client relations and also substantiates that the client's perception of the status of the case is the same as the attorney's. It is often a paralegal's responsibility to draft a disengagement letter for an attorney's signature. It is advisable to wait a couple of weeks after the letter is sent before closing a file. An example disengagement letter is shown in Chapter 4.

PRUNING Pruning a file eliminates unnecessary documents and compacts a file for storage. There are four considerations of pruning a file for closure. First, if the document is vital to the client, such as an original will or a deed, it must be returned to the client. Second, if a document pertains to an attorney's fiduciary duties to the client, it must be retained. Third, information that the firm needs to check for future conflicts of interest must remain in the file. Fourth, if the firm suspects that there may be a problem with the representation, such as legal malpractice, fee dispute, or state bar action, all documents should be retained as evidence of the representation.

It is often a paralegal's or secretary's responsibility to prune files. The person responsible for pruning files should be familiar with the case so that important documents are not discarded. Some experts recommend that the person pruning the file do so with the responsible attorney so that nothing is overlooked. Other experts say that an attorney reviewing files for closing is a waste of the attorney's time and therefore too costly for a firm.

All documents that are not essential to a case are either returned to the client or destroyed. However, some firms will not allow anything in a file to be discarded. In most cases, cover letters, extra copies (unless a copy is altered in some way), phone messages, drafts, and miscellaneous notes can be eliminated. All original documents, such as wills and deeds, are returned to the client by certified mail, return receipt requested. Some firms discard pleadings since they can be retrieved from court records. Each firm has specific pruning policies for its closed files.

master client list
A list of active clients; does not include closed files.

closed-file list
A list of closed files by name, number, and closed-file number.

ETHICS
ALERT

STATUS CHANGE Changing the status of a case from active to inactive involves changing the **master client list** and inserting the case on a **closed-file list.** *The conflicts-of-interest database should be double-checked to determine whether all parties are in it.* The file is given a closed-file number, and its retention period is determined (see "Records Retention" later in this chapter). Each firm has its own procedures for changing the status of a file.

Paralegals are often responsible for determining the retention period, but other file-closing tasks are usually delegated to a secretary.

DOCUMENTS RETURNED TO THE CLIENT   Original documents that are vital to a client, such as a will or deed, should be returned to the client. Some firms keep original wills for their clients. Normally, they are stored in a safe-deposit box or other secure area. If a firm retains original wills, they should be removed from the file and stored in the will storage area. As noted previously, other records are a client's property and are returned to the client. An inventory of the items returned should be maintained in the file. Some firms require that a copy be made of all important items that are sent to a client and the copies inserted in the closed file.

Case law and state bar opinions have ruled that materials in a client's file belong to the client. These materials include correspondence, pleadings, deposition transcripts, exhibits, experts' reports, and physical evidence. Opinions differ on whether a firm must give a client its work product, such as research memoranda, opinion letters, and notes. The case of *Sage Realty Corp. v. Mendelson*, 97 N.Y. Int. 0208 (1997), ruled that an entire file, including the attorney's work product, belongs to a client except for certain internal law firm memoranda. However, in some states, an attorney's work product need not be returned to the client. Be sure to check your state's rules and regulations before returning or destroying any documents.

DELETE ELECTRONIC RECORDS   Electronic documents that are stored in a client's file on the firm's computer system are deleted from the system. Before doing so, they should be reviewed to determine if they should be put into a firm's form files and knowledge bank (see Chapter 14). The electronic documents are put on a CD-ROM and the CD is inserted in the closed file. Some firms keep an extra CD of a closed file in the office for future reference. To ensure future readability of documents, the documents should be stored in a nonproprietary format, such as plain text or image. If stored in a proprietary format, such as MS Word, the firm must have MS Word to open the file in the future. A firm may have other filing procedures for storage of clients' electronic documents.

FILE-CLOSING MEMORANDUM   A file-closing memorandum, such as the one shown in Exhibit 13–18, is prepared and acts as a checklist for file-closing procedures. A file-closing memorandum is inserted into the closed file when the procedures are completed. A copy of it is stored in a closed-file binder for future reference.

Black, White & Greene, LLP

FILE-CLOSING MEMORANDUM

Open file no. *98-03-2043*	Closed file no. *C2004.326.05*
File name: *Jackson v. Holiday Inn*	Responsible attorney: *Robert Black*
Client: *Sarah Jackson*	Date file opened: *03/09/98*
Type of matter: *Personal injury*	Date file closed: *07/19/04*
Locator code: *Box 704-16 off site*	Destruction date: *07/19/14*

FUNCTION	INITIAL	DATE
Approval to close by responsible attorney	*RLB*	*7/10/04*
File purged	*TB & RLB*	*7/10/04*
Authorization that account balance is paid	*TB*	*7/08/04*
Client documents returned	*ALE*	*7/21/04*
All parties entered in conflict-of-interest database	*ALE*	*7/19/04*
Electronic documents deleted from computer system	*ALE*	*7/26/04*

EXHIBIT 13–18   Example File-Closing Memorandum

Inactive Records Storage

Inactive records are records that are seldom needed for the business of an office. They include office records that may be needed only once or twice a year and closed clients' files. Inactive records should not be stored in the main filing area because they waste valuable floor and filing space. A law firm's management provides a less costly storage area for these records. Some firms put their documents on electronic media for storage and destroy the hard copies, if the hard copies are not essential documents. Whatever storage method is used, a firm must employ an indexing system to locate and retrieve inactive files and records.

Inactive records are usually stored in filing cabinets or storage boxes outside the main storage area. Storage equipment and facilities must allow for the safety of the files so that they are not damaged by fire, water, or other natural elements. Each container, whether a cabinet or box, must be properly marked and labeled. Storage areas include a basement, back storage room, or off-site storage facility. Inactive files are also stored by micrographics and imaging technology.

MICROGRAPHICS   An alternative method for storing inactive files is to microfilm them. Microfilm has been used in firms for many years and is especially useful for firms that store a large quantity of records.

Large and medium-sized firms may microfilm their inactive records, but sole proprietors and small firms with smaller storage needs often cannot justify the expense. When justifying the expense of micrographics, management considers space savings, durability, safety, and speed of reference.

IMAGING   An imaging system is also used by large firms to store its closed files. This system consists of a control unit with a monitor, scanner, and printer; CD-ROM storage unit; and software. The documents are scanned into the system, and an image of each document is saved on CD-ROMs, which will hold as many as 250,000 documents on one disk. The disks are stored in a **jukebox,** which is a device that can hold many CD-ROMs. The imaging software will generate an index of all documents and identify the CD-ROM on which a document is found. In the event a document must be retrieved, it can be easily found and printed. Digital images are also saved on portable hard drives, which can hold a lot of data.

jukebox
A device that contains many CD-ROMs and allows retrieval of a document on request.

best evidence rule
The requirement that courts must admit the best evidence that is available to a party and procurable under the existing situation.

BEST EVIDENCE RULE   The **best evidence rule,** which requires a court to admit the best evidence that is available to a party under the existing situation, directly applies to micrographics and imaged records. Congress has expanded the basic concepts of this rule by the enactment of two statutes that pertain to these records: the Uniform Photographic Copies of Business and Public Records as Evidence Act of 1949 (UPA) and the Uniform Rules of Evidence Act of 1974. These statutes permit the introduction of a microfilmed or imaged duplicate as evidence if the original document has been lost or destroyed, and if certain conditions are met. However, other regulations have mandated the retention of certain original documents, such as contracts. If a question exists concerning the admissibility of an imaged or microfilmed document, statutes and state regulations should be consulted.

INACTIVE STORAGE INDEXING SYSTEMS   When inactive records are stored, they still must be accessible for retrieval. Therefore, all stored records are numbered and their storage media labeled. The closed-file number and location are inserted on a closed-file index for retrieval purposes. Firms use various systems to locate an inactive file.

Closed–File Coding   Most firms have a separate coding system for closed files. Firms that use an alphabetical coding system find that storing closed files alphabetically requires frequent reorganization. For example, a firm's closed files A–C are filed in one box or file drawer. As additional A–C files are closed, the box or drawer becomes too small, so the files must be moved to the next box or drawer. Putting C files in the D–F box will make that box or drawer too small, so each box or drawer must be reorganized.

To eliminate box and file drawer shuffling, closed files are arranged numerically. Calendar numbering is the preferred method for coding closed files. The calendar numeric code refers to the date a case is closed or the date a file is scheduled for destruction. With calendar coding, a file's age is quickly recognized.

Some firms that use numeric coding for active files change the file number when the file is closed. Others just insert a *C* before the number to indicate that the file is closed. Whatever coding method is used, it is imperative to keep an index of all closed files.

Closed-File Index   A closed-file index is kept on the computer, and a hard copy is maintained as a backup in case of computer failure. The information should be in alphabetical order according to the client's surname and should include the location of all files.

The following information should be inserted on a closed-file index:

- File name
- Active-file number, if a numeric coding system
- Closed-file number
- Date file was opened
- Date file was closed
- Location of file in storage (box or cabinet number or, if in microfilm or electronic format, the information pertaining to the location of the file)
- Short description of the disposition of the matter
- Date the file may be destroyed.

Information for a closed-file index is obtained from a closed-file index form, such as the one shown in Exhibit 13–19. This form is completed by the person responsible for closing files. The form is inserted in the file or taped to the front of the file folder. A copy of the form can be used as a closed-file index log.

Records Retention

Records retention is the time period during which records must be maintained by an organization because they may be needed for legal, operational, historical, or other purposes. These time periods are established by state and federal law. There are thousands of laws that pertain to records retention. *It is necessary that an organization develop a retention schedule that complies with the law.*

A retention schedule is a list of retention periods categorized according to type of document or case, as shown in Exhibit 13–20. Every firm should have an updated retention schedule and procedures for the retention of records. Many things must be considered when determining the retention period for documents. Research has shown that 95 percent of all references to

Name _____
Active file no. _____ Closed file no. _____
Date opened _____ Date closed _____
Location _____
Description _____
_____
File destruction date _____
_____

EXHIBIT 13–19   Sample of Closed-File Index Form

TYPE	PERIOD	COMMENCING FROM
Contract action	4 years	End of contract
Dissolution	5 years	Entry of final judgment or date when marital settlement agreement is no longer effective
Dissolution, child	5 years	Date children reach age of majority
Bankruptcy	5 years	Discharge
Probate	10 years	Final judgment
Estate planning	Permanent	
Tort claims	5 years	Collection of final judgment or dismissal
Tort, minor	5 years	Date child reaches age of majority
Real estate	5 years	Completion of transaction
Real estate contract	Permanent	
Leases	5 years	Termination of lease
Product liability	5 years	Judgment
Tax	10 years	Completion

Note: This schedule is for example only; each state has different guidelines.

EXHIBIT 13–20   Example of Retention Schedule

closed files occur within the first two years of closing. The responsibility for setting a retention period rests with management after researching legal requirements. Considerations vary, depending on whether a document is a business record or a client record.

When a file is closed, its retention period is indicated on the folder and inserted into a closed-file index. This will help a file clerk determine the destruction date for the file. Records may be destroyed after the retention period expires. However, some records and files should be permanently retained. Courts and government agencies have imposed heavy fines for the inappropriate destruction of records.

A retention schedule integrated into a firm's computer system will automatically calculate a file's retention period. The computer will keep track of each file's location and the date each file is scheduled to be destroyed. However, no firm should rely on an automated retention schedule. Paralegals must review a file before establishing a file's retention period. For example, a dissolution of marriage may have a retention period of 5 years after the dissolution is final. However, tax records must be retained for 10 years. If the dissolution contained tax issues, it must be retained for 10, instead of 5, years. In addition, if the matter involved minor children, records must be maintained until the child reaches the age of majority. The exact number of years the records must be maintained after the child has reached the age of majority varies by jurisdiction. A computerized system may not pick up all aspects of a case. Human interaction is essential before a file is scheduled for destruction. If a paralegal is uncertain of a retention period, management or the responsible attorney should be consulted.

BUSINESS RECORDS   For business records, management must consider statutes and regulations, any future need for the records, and the statute of limitations.

Statutes and Regulations   The law sets retention periods for business records as follows:

- The Internal Revenue Service may audit a tax return for 3 years after the return is filed. Therefore, it is prudent to keep income and expense records substantiating a tax return for at least 3 years.
- Personnel records are subject to many federal statutes. Various aspects of an employment relationship are the subject of different regulations. For example, payroll records should be kept for 4 years to meet the requirements of the Federal Insurance and Contributions Act (FICA) and the Federal Unemployment Tax Act (FUTA). Records

of an employee's injury on the job should be kept for 5 years after the date of termination. An employee's medical records should be retained for 30 years after termination.

- Corporate records are permanent records and should not be destroyed.

Future Need for Records   The future need for business records is determined by a firm's management.

Statute of Limitations   The statutes of limitations for lawsuits are set by each state. For example, in California, a breach-of-contract action must be brought within 4 years of the breach. Therefore, contracts should be retained for 4 years after the term of the contract expires.

CLIENT RECORDS   Considerations for the retention period for clients' records are statutes and regulations, any future need for records, the statute of limitations, the applicable age of majority if minors are involved, the appeal period, and malpractice concerns.

Statutes and Regulations   Very few legal requirements affect the retention of client records unless the records are kept in a **custodial** or fiduciary capacity.

Future Need for Records   The future need for records can be anticipated by the responsible attorney. Paralegals should always consult with the responsible attorney regarding the future need for client records.

Statute of Limitations   Records should be kept for as long as a statute is running. For example, if a judgment was obtained but was uncollectible, the judgment is good for 10 years in some states and may then be renewed for another 10-year period. The file should not be destroyed until the judgment has been collected or the statute has expired.

Applicable Age of Majority   The statute of limitations on a minor's action begins to run when the child has reached the age of majority. If an action involves a 4-year-old child, the child will reach age 18 in 14 years. If the statute of limitations is 4 years, the file should be retained for another 4 years. The total retention period is 18 years after the case is closed.

Appeal Period   A file should not be closed until the time period for an appeal has expired.

Malpractice Concerns   The statute of limitations for professional liability varies by state. It ranges from 6 months to 10 years after the firm's last contact with a client. A file should be retained for the appropriate time period pertaining to professional responsibility.

custodial
Relating to a person who has custody of another person or thing and is expected to act in its best interests.

Records Destruction

When a file's retention period has expired, the file and its contents are destroyed by following established procedures. *To ensure confidentiality, records should never be disposed of in the trash can.* They must be destroyed.

In the past, businesses destroyed records by burning them. Today, however, environmental concerns discourage burning. Today documents are shredded in a shredder machine. Shredders are cost-effective, environmentally safe, and meet most business needs.

Before records can be shredded, they must be properly prepared. All clamps, paper clips, staples, and plastic covers must be removed. For very large amounts of shredding, a commercial disposal company provides "witnessed" destruction. The disposal company will haul the records off site and destroy them in the presence of a supervisor. A supervisor will certify that the confidentiality of the records was preserved during destruction. This certification becomes a permanent record of the destruction process.

For smaller shredding projects, a firm shreds the documents. It is important that the shredding process be supervised. It is inappropriate to leave a shredder unattended because the confidentiality of the documents will not be protected.

Some firms make it a practice to recycle as much of their disposable records as possible. Preparing records for recycling requires extra effort. Only white paper is recyclable. Glossy paper and colored paper cannot be mixed with white paper. Some dealers will not take

ETHICS ALERT

cardboard. All documents must be sorted, and staples, clips, and covers must be removed before the shredding process. After the white paper is shredded, it is taken to a recycling center.

Some state bar associations require that attorneys notify their clients by letter before destroying their files. A notification letter contains the following information:

- The date the file is scheduled for destruction
- The client's right to obtain or inspect the file
- Notice to the client that if he or she chooses to preserve the file, he or she is responsible for the cost thereof

Some firms insert their file-closing and-destruction policies in their retainer agreements. If a firm informs a client of its file-destruction policy in its retainer agreement, it does not have to notify the client before destroying the file.

FILE AND RECORDS MANAGEMENT ETHICS

Law firm personnel must be aware of five ethical considerations when managing files and records: Preserve a client's property, diligently perform conflict-of-interest checks, promptly return a client's property, retain records according to government regulations, and preserve a client's confidentiality.

Preserve Client's Property

An attorney is a client's agent and acts in a fiduciary capacity. *As such, the attorney must preserve a client's property and records in a safe environment and guard them against theft and damage.* Many firms require that clients' files be maintained in locked filing cabinets.

American Bar Association (ABA) Model Rule 1.15(a) states:

> (a) A lawyer shall hold property of clients or third persons that is in a lawyer's possession in connection with a representation separate from the lawyer's own property. . . . [P]roperty shall be identified as such and appropriately safeguarded. Complete records of such . . . property shall be kept by the lawyer and shall be preserved for a period of five years after termination of the representation.

A law firm's personnel should be cautioned not to remove a file from the office. Some attorneys and paralegals want to take files home to work on them in the evening, but they should be discouraged from doing so. There have been many files lost or damaged while in transit from the office to home. Some firms require that a file be copied and that only copies of necessary documents may be removed from the office.

Perform Conflict-of-Interest Checks

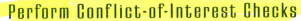

It is imperative that conflict checks be performed often. It is not just a file-opening procedure. Each time a new party makes an appearance, the new party must be entered into the conflicts database. *Each time a potential client makes an appointment with an attorney, the database must be checked for conflicts.* The attorney must be informed of a potential conflict immediately.

Promptly Return File to the Client

If a client should terminate the attorney-client relationship, the file must be returned to the client promptly so that the client can obtain legal representation elsewhere. Some firms hold the file pending payment of an invoice. Most state bar associations prohibit this activity and require attorneys to return the file regardless of the status of the client's account.

When a matter has been completed, the client is entitled to the original documents in his or her file. *Case law has ruled that all materials in the file, with the exception of certain internal memoranda, belong to the client.* Many firms duplicate the necessary documents and return the originals to the client. The duplicates are stored in inactive-file storage, on microfilm, or on CD-ROMs to comply with a firm's retention schedule.

Retain Records

A firm must comply with records retention regulations set by state and federal governments. There are thousands of records retention laws and regulations, some of which conflict with one another. Once a schedule is established, it must be reviewed and approved by an attorney and be strictly adhered to. *A file must not be destroyed until its retention period has expired.* To do so would expose the firm to sanctions and/or fines.

The 5-year period mentioned in Model Rule 1.15a covers most legal malpractice statutes of limitations. However, some government regulations may require a longer period of retention. Whenever a rule conflicts, the record should be retained for the longer period.

Preserve Confidentiality

All clients' records and documents must be kept confidential. This was discussed in detail in Chapters 4 and 5, but the concept cannot be overemphasized. When closing and destroying clients' files, be sure to take steps to ensure their confidentiality. Some ethics authorities have rendered opinions that confidentiality must be safeguarded when storing clients' closed files. They suggest that the files be stored in a secure facility with controls over access to the files.

CONCLUSION

File and records management procedures are important to the smooth operation of a law office. Understanding and complying with these procedures takes effort, but the effort will contribute to a paralegal's success.

SUMMARY

A firm's filing and records system is the nerve center of a law office. The management and organization of a firm's filing system are essential to the smooth operation of a law firm.

There are three types of filing systems: centralized, decentralized, and automated. A centralized filing system has all the files located in one area and is normally managed by a file coordinator or clerk. A decentralized system has files located in various areas, usually near the responsible attorney's office. An automated filing system electronically stores files and records.

A filing system, whether centralized, decentralized, or automated, consists of a logical division of categories of records. Records are divided into categories that have a logical connection to one another. A coding system is a method used to store files in a specified sequence.

An alphabetical coding system is the most common coding system used by small firms. In this system, a law firm's records are arranged in alphabetical order according to a client's surname. Although this coding system seems easy, problems occur when employees have not been instructed in its rules.

Files may also be coded with numeric coding according to a particular numbering pattern. Six different types of numeric systems are used: straight, coded, calendar, standard, account, and combination. An alphanumeric system is also used, which is a combination of an alphabetical and numeric system.

A cross-index is a cross-reference of records. All files and subfiles must be included on a cross-index. A numeric index must also be maintained.

Color coding is a common method of categorizing files. Some records managers maintain that color coding increases speed and accuracy in filing. Color may be applied to any system and may be used for paper or computer records.

A file retrieval system must allow for easy access to files. Firms employ file personnel who are responsible for maintaining a retrieval system. File requests are initiated by a requisition form.

A file must be accessible before it is retrieved. When a file is removed from a filing system, its location must be traceable and monitored. One method used to trace files is an "out card." An out card is the size of a file folder, made of heavy vinyl, and has lines on the front on which to put names and dates. Whenever someone removes a file, an out card is inserted in its place. Out folders are also used.

Bar codes are used to monitor files. Bar codes are a fast, easy, and accurate data entry method used in the process known as automatic data collection. Bar coding technology is used by universities and libraries to manage the circulation of books and journals. A bar coding system automates records management. A bar code is put on a label that is attached to a file. Large and medium-sized firms especially benefit from using bar code technology for their files.

Radio frequency identification is a generic term for technologies that use radio waves to identify people or objects. It may eventually replace bar code technology for records management. The big difference between RFID and bar codes is that a bar code is a "line of sight" technology.

Not all potential clients retain a firm: Some interview many attorneys before choosing a lawyer, and some just need some quick legal advice. A firm keeps information about each person who consults with an attorney. As we learned in Chapter 4, an attorney-client relationship is formed whenever an attorney gives a person legal advice. A client file is opened immediately after a client retains a firm.

When a clerk or secretary opens a file, she or he must do a conflict check for a possible conflict of interest. A database is maintained that includes the names of clients and all parties to a proceeding in which a firm was involved. A conflict check is the most important aspect of file-opening procedures but is not limited to file opening. A conflict check must be performed as each new party enters a case. Most firms require some type of written record that a conflict check was made. If a firm has no conflict of interest in representing a client, a client file may be opened.

A paralegal is responsible for maintaining clients' files in good order. The first step in file maintenance is categorizing the documents. Correspondence, pleadings, notes, and all other documents are filed in chronological order unless the case is large. In a large case, documents are further categorized by type. Case cover sheets are used to monitor the status of a case.

Indexes are used to direct a person to a document's exact location in a file. Each document is given a number that is put on a tab so that it can be found quickly. A document is inserted behind its divider so that it can be located by lifting up the tabbed divider. The number, title of document, date, and party are inserted on an index sheet that is placed on top of the divider sheets. Indexes should be developed for every category of a case, except correspondence and miscellaneous notes.

Every document has a life cycle and lives only as long as it serves its purpose. To determine the life cycle of a document, one must first identify the document's value. After its value has been determined, a decision regarding its future must be made. Time management experts advise that document management decisions be made as soon as a document is received.

Filing experts have estimated that correspondence constitutes most of the documents received. Promotional documents are a form of correspondence. The person to whom correspondence is sent is responsible for deciding whether to keep the material. No document pertaining to a client's case may be discarded. Notes taken in a meeting with a client or on a client's behalf are always retained.

Complex agreements require many drafts that should be retained until the final agreement is signed. Some firms have a policy to keep all rough drafts of agreements. Rough drafts of correspondence or pleadings are destroyed when the final document is completed.

When magazine and newspaper articles are kept, they should be clipped rather than retaining the entire magazine or newspaper. If it is beneficial to retain each issue of a particular magazine, firms then file these in magazine files.

There are many types of documents: e-mail, word processing, spreadsheets, graphics, video clips, voice mail, and document images. After you have read an electronic document such as e-mail, you make a decision to do one or more of the following: copy it, file it, write comments on it, forward it to someone in the firm, or dispose of it. The files and subfiles into which electronic documents are stored must be similar in structure to the filing system for paper documents. Electronic documents remain on the network's hard drive until they are no longer needed, until they can be disposed of, or until the need to recoup hard drive space occurs.

An automated document management system is an electronic filing system containing a database of documents that is updated automatically every time a document is created, retrieved, edited, printed, archived, or deleted. A document management system tracks and manages every legal document created in a law office. Once prepared, a document is saved on the firm's network or intranet.

When a case is completed, certain procedures must be followed before a file is a candidate for closing. When a case has been completed, a file must be double-checked to ensure that all documents have been completed and filed. If the appeal period has not expired, a case may not be closed. The final bill must be paid before a case is closed. Some firms send a disengagement letter with the final bill, and others wait until the bill has been paid. Pruning a file prepares a file for closing by eliminating unnecessary documents. Each firm has specific pruning policies for closed files.

Changing the status of a case from active to inactive involves changing a master client list and inserting the file on a closed-file list. Original documents that are vital to a client, such as a will or deed, should be returned to the client. Electronic documents that are stored in a client's file on the firm's computer system are deleted from the system. A file-closing memorandum is prepared and acts as a checklist for file-closing procedures.

Inactive records are records that are seldom needed for the business of an office. Inactive records are usually stored in filing cabinets or storage boxes outside the main storage area.

An alternative method for storing inactive files is to microfilm or image them. Large and medium-sized firms may image or microfilm their inactive records, but sole proprietors and small firms with smaller storage needs often cannot justify the expense. The best evidence rule, which requires a court to admit the best evidence that is available to a party under the existing situation, directly applies to imaged and microfilmed records.

When inactive records are stored, they still must be accessible for retrieval. Most firms have a separate coding system for closed files. Some firms that use numeric coding for active files change the file number when the file is closed. A closed-file index is kept on the computer, and a hard copy closed-file index log is maintained as a backup in case of computer failure. Information for the closed-file index is obtained from a closed-file index form.

Records retention is the time period during which records must be maintained by an organization because they may be needed for legal, operational, historical, or other purposes. A retention schedule is a list of retention periods categorized according to type of document or case. A retention schedule integrated into a firm's computer system will automatically calculate a file's retention period. However, human involvement is necessary to establish a file's retention period.

For business records, management must consider statutes and regulations, any future need for the records, and the statute of limitations. Considerations for the retention period for clients' records are statutes and regulations, any future need for the records, statute of limitations if minors are involved, applicable age of majority, appeal period, and malpractice and business concerns.

When a file's retention period has expired, the file and its contents are destroyed by following established procedures. Today, documents are shredded in a shredder machine. Before records can be shredded, they must be properly prepared. Some state bar associations require that attorneys notify their clients by letter before destroying their files. Some firms insert their file-closing and destruction policy into their retainer agreement.

A law firm's personnel must be aware of five ethical considerations when managing files and records: preserve a client's property, diligently perform conflict-of-interest checks, promptly return a client's property, retain records according to government regulations, and preserve a client's confidentiality.

CHAPTER ILLUSTRATION

When Black, White & Greene started their law firm, they had a decentralized filing system. Each attorney's files were stored in a filing cabinet in his or her secretary's area close to his or her office. Each secretary was responsible for opening files, and each paralegal was responsible for maintaining the files. The secretaries were responsible for filing documents and keeping the files organized and indexed. Each attorney had his or her own file preferences: Robert and Dennis used partitioned folders, Grant used regular folders, and George used a folder for each type of document in a case. The firm used an alphabetical coding system for all files. Just one attorney, Patrizia, used color-coded labels to identify the file by type of case.

As the firm grew and the support staff grew busier, the secretaries had a problem keeping up with their filing duties. They did not like to file, so they would leave the filing until they completed their other, more pressing work. Consequently, the filing did not get done, and each secretary had a large pile of filing to do.

The secretaries handled this filing problem in different ways. Sandra came in on Saturdays to catch up on her filing. Pam just threw the documents in the file without putting them in the proper order or placing them on an index sheet. Tricia collected the documents in a pile on her desk and watched the pile grow higher each day.

This filing backlog caused problems for the firm. When an attorney needed a document, it was not in the file. It was in the filing pile, and the paralegal or secretary would have to search the pile to find it. George and Grant, Pam's attorneys, always had messy files. They spent a lot of time going through loose documents to find the information they needed. They would give the messy files to Milton to organize and put the documents on index sheets. Milton resented this and felt that it was Pam's responsibility to keep the files in order.

When Tricia did her human resource audit (discussed in Chapter 3), she found that filing interfered with the secretaries' productivity. She also found that the current filing system was fragmented and disorganized. It had no uniformity, which was important for the firm. She decided to overhaul the system to a centralized system, and she hired Kay Bowen as the firm's file clerk.

All the files were moved to a central area, and the secretaries were relieved from their filing responsibilities. Kay was responsible for filing documents. She changed the coding for clients' files from alphabetical coding to a standard numeric system. This coding system allowed for file volumes, which would satisfy George's preference for separate folders for each type of document. The system also accommodated files that had no volumes. Each attorney was given a number that was the first number in the code, as follows:

2	45	321	.1
Attorney	Type of case	File number	Volume number

With this coding system, each attorney's files were filed together. Within each attorney's files, all cases of the same type were filed together. In addition, Tricia developed a color code that identified the year in which each case was opened. All files opened in 2008, for example, had the same color label. The age of the case was easily identified by looking at the file label.

Secretaries were responsible for opening a file. The attorney or paralegal completed a new case memorandum and gave it to the secretary. Each secretary checked the conflicts database for a conflict of interest and, if there were no conflicts, opened the file. To determine the file number, the secretary consulted the new file index, which gave the next number in sequence for each attorney. She entered the file number on the new case memorandum and makes a copy of it. The original memorandum was filed in the client's file, and the copy was filed in an alphabetical binder, which was used as a backup to the cross-index of clients' files. Once all file-opening procedures were completed, the secretary prepared a new client memorandum and distributed it among the staff. The file was then given to Kay, who filed it in the file room.

Kay was responsible for filing all documents and tracking the location of each file. If a file was needed, a file requisition slip was completed and given to Kay, who retrieved the file and inserted the person's name on an out folder. She then put the out folder in the file's position in the file drawer. She signed and dated the file requisition form as evidence that the request was completed. The file requisition slip was stored in a "files out" file. As a file was returned, the requisition slip was removed from the files out file and inserted in a binder for future reference. If a file was not returned in a day or two, Kay knew where to find it.

When a file was ready to be closed, the attorney reviewed it to make sure that all documentation has been completed. A file-closing memorandum was signed by the responsible attorney, who transfered the file to Tricia, the office manager. Tricia checked to see whether the final bill was paid. If it was paid, she initials the file-closing memorandum and transfered it and the file to the paralegal. Paralegals were responsible for file-closing procedures.

When Julie received the file, she first checked the conflicts database to verify that all parties were listed. Then the file is reviewed for any original documents that were to be returned to the client. After she made a copy, she returns the original documents to the client with a disengagement letter that contained a notice informing the client that he or she was entitled to documents from the file. She gave the client 30 days to respond to the notice. If she did not hear from the client, she proceeded with file-closing procedures.

She began pruning the file and discarded all unnecessary documents. Then she changes the status of the case from active to inactive. She removes the case from the active-files list and inserted it on the closed-files list. She gives it a closed-file number, which is a combination of calendar and straight coding systems. The first part of the number is the date the file is closed, and the second part of the number is the length of time the file must be retained according to the firm's retention schedule: 0903.10 means that the file was closed in March 2009 and must be retained for 10 years. She calendars the file for destruction for March 2019 and inserts the file into a numbered container. She inserts the number of the container, its location, and all other information on the file-closing memorandum and in the computer system. She then deletes the electronic file from the computer system after putting the electronic files on a CD. The closed-file container was then transferred to storage, where the firm's inactive files were stored.

The new system was a definite improvement over the old system, but it was not without its problems. Some attorneys, especially Dennis, did not return files to the file room. He liked the convenience of having his files where he could get to them quickly. When Kay would came into his office looking for the files, he always told her that he was not through with them. Files piled up in his office, along with his files to be reviewed. Robert and Tricia talked to Dennis about the importance of all employees following the rules of a filing system, but to no avail.

When the firm got an intranet (discussed in Chapter 10), Robert and Tricia realized that many aspects of the filing process could be automated. They researched records management programs and decided that they were not ready to transfer all their paper documents to electronic documents. However, they liked some of the features offered, such as automated file tracking, integrated conflict database, and file-closing indexing and processing. They found a software package with these features. They purchased it and began the implementation process.

The first thing that had to be done was to put all their existing cases in the system. When a file was input, the system prepared a bar code label for the file that transferred the information to the firm's time and billing system and automatically assigned a file number. The system was programmed with the firm's file-coding system, and it automatically prepared a cross-index, list of cases, conflicts database, and file label. When a file was needed, the requester would e-mail the file requisition slip to Kay, who would scan the bar code, and the new location of the file would automatically be put into the database. Each member of the firm could access the database from the firm's intranet.

It took a long time to completely implement the automated system. An outside temporary service was called in to help Kay input all the files. After the files were in the system, each person had to be trained on the system. The secretaries, paralegals, and some of the attorneys loved the system. The other attorneys had difficulty adjusting to the "high tech" nature of the system. However, as they grew accustomed to it, they found the system very convenient and easy to use.

The firm could now boast of its state-of-the-art filing system. Now, if Dennis would just return all those bar coded files he kept in his office, in his car, in his briefcase, and in his home!

CHAPTER REVIEW

1. Describe the three types of filing systems.
2. Describe the classification of documents.
3. Describe the six types of numeric coding systems.
4. What is alphanumeric coding?
5. How are bar codes used in filing systems?
6. What is a preclient file?
7. Why is it important to do a conflict check for new clients?
8. When organizing a small file, how is correspondence filed?
9. What is the function of a case cover sheet?
10. What are the three value determinations for a document?
11. When may a document pertaining to a client's case be discarded?
12. What functions must be completed before a file is closed?
13. What is file pruning?
14. What is a closed-file index?
15. What is a records retention schedule, and how is it developed?
16. What are the five ethical considerations of file and records management?

EXAMPLES FOR DISCUSSION

1. ALPHABETICAL CLIENT FILES BY SUBJECT

The law firm of Smith & Jones utilizes a subject alphabetical system and separates client files by area of law: bankruptcy, criminal, domestic, litigation, probate, and real estate. Litigation was commenced on real property in Thomas Nelson's case. Sharon, the paralegal, was given an assignment on the case and must retrieve the file. She knows that Thomas Nelson is deceased, and a case was opened.

1. If you were Sharon, in which category would you look for the file?
2. Do you see any problems with this coding system? What are they?
3. What are your suggestions for improving the system?

2. MISSING FILES

Julie is a paralegal for a medium-sized firm. She is having problems finding files in the office. The files are never in the central filing area, and out cards are not inserted where the missing files should be filed. After hours of searching, one attorney, the managing partner, is always found to be responsible for removing the files without placing out cards in their places. The files are buried in his office, in the trunk of his car, or at his home.

1. What are the problems with the system?
2. What could be done about this problem?
3. What would you do about this problem?

3. TOO MANY FILES

Darrel Horsted is a paralegal for a small boutique firm specializing in personal injury cases. The firm has a policy to prepare five file folders per case as follows:

- Correspondence
- Pleadings
- Discovery
- Medical records
- Research

At the beginning of a case, there are few or no documents in many of the files. When Darrel must retrieve the file, he must retrieve all five files. Some employees retrieve only the file folder they need at the moment, causing the master file to be fragmented and disbursed all over the law firm. The system is fine for large cases, but most of the cases are small. Darrel is very frustrated with the system and has been asked to develop new file-maintenance procedures.

1. How should Darrel change the file-opening procedures?
2. What new file-maintenance procedures should he recommend?
3. What file-retrieval procedures should he recommend?

4. AN EMBARRASSING MOMENT

Patrizia Boen, associate of Black, White & Greene, was in trial on a complicated real estate litigation matter. She was in the process of cross-examination when the opposing party gave a different answer than he stated in his interrogatories. Ms. Boen, in an attempt to impeach his testimony, indicated that his interrogatory answers were contrary to his current testimony. She grabbed the file to find the interrogatories. The file was neither indexed nor organized, and Ms. Boen could not find the interrogatories. Five minutes passed as Ms. Boen thumbed through the file. The judge and jury watched her in silence. She stated that the interrogatories must be in another file and picked up another file to search for the interrogatories. As she did, 20 to 30 small phone message slips fell out of the file and scattered all over the courtroom floor. The judge and jury watched as she picked them up off the floor and then continued to search the file for the interrogatories. Needless to say, the judge, jury, and her client were not impressed.

1. If you were the judge, what would be your impression of Ms. Boen?
2. If you were on the jury, what would be your impression of Ms. Boen?
3. If you were Ms. Boen's client, how would you feel?
4. Do you think this disorganized file reflected on Ms. Boen's capability? How?
5. What needs to be done to improve the situation?

5. **WHAT ABOUT THE CLOSED FILES?**

Smith & Jones law firm merged with Black & White law firm to form a new firm: Smith, Jones, Black & White. Before the merger, two attorneys from Smith & Jones, Bob Jackson and Sharon Fields, left the firm to form their own firm. The firm of Smith, Jones, Black & White have all of Smith & Jones' closed files, including the files of Bob and Sharon, who left the firm prior to the merger.

1. What is Smith, Jones, Black & White's obligation with regard to the closed files of Bob Jackson and Sharon Fields?
2. May they destroy the files? If not, why not? If they may, how?
3. If you were the managing partner of Smith, Jones, Black & White, what would you do with Bob and Sharon's files?

ASSIGNMENTS

1. You are a probate paralegal for a large firm. Three of the attorneys in the probate and estate planning department want to quit the firm and start their own boutique firm specializing in probate and estate planning. They want you to go with them and be the office manager for the new firm. You must set up the new firm's filing system. They have asked for a report that includes a descriptive report of the filing system. In your report:
   a. Describe the type of filing system you would choose and explain your choice.
   b. Describe the type of coding system you would choose and explain your choice.
   c. Include a list of materials needed to implement the system.
   d. Describe file-opening procedures.
   e. Describe file-maintenance procedures.
   f. Describe file-closing procedures.
   g. Describe the storage and destruction of closed files.

2. Review the records management system at your place of employment. Write a report about the system and describe the following:
   a. What type of system is it?
   b. Do the system's users think the system is adequate? Inadequate? Why?
   c. How could the system be improved?

3. Set up files for all your school assignments. You may use regular file folders, partitioned file folders, or three-ring binders. Classify the assignments by function, subject, topic, and subtopic by establishing categories of documents, such as notes, quizzes, exams, and homework. Prepare an index sheet and tabbed dividers for each category. Choose a coding system for your files and use color where appropriate. Index sheets are on the accompanying CD.

4. Create a class cover sheet similar to the case cover sheet in Exhibit 13–13. Insert data from your course syllabus and include your grades received on all assignments, quizzes, and exams. Insert it in front of your class file mentioned in assignment 3. A sample case cover sheet is on the accompanying CD. You may change it to suit your needs.

5. Your boss has asked you to research automated records management software. Choose three automated records management software products listed in the Cybersites section on page 487 and write a report comparing the software. In your report:
   a. List the common features of the software.
   b. Identify the hardware requirements of the software.
   c. Explain how the firm can benefit from the software.

d. Analyze the cost factor of the software.

e. List any problems of the software.

f. Make your recommendation for the firm to purchase one product.

6. File management is one of a paralegal's main responsibilities and an area in which paralegals and legal secretaries can demonstrate excellent organizational skills. A file is a package that contains a firm's product. The condition of the package communicates to the world a firm's perception of its product. The image that files communicate to the world can be one of excellence and professionalism, or one of sloppiness and neglect. Good file management skills will help create a reputation of excellence for a firm. After completing this chapter, you will increase your organizational skills so you can accept the responsibility of file management with confidence. This very important skill will make you a valuable asset to any law office. Have you ever worked in an office with messy, disorganized files? If so:

a. What was your perception of the organization?

b. How much time was wasted finding the information you needed?

c. What did the organization communicate by its files?

d. What could have been done to eliminate the problem?

7. Create file and records management procedures for Black, White & Greene. Include the following:

a. Procedures to retrieve a file

b. Preclient files

c. File-opening procedures

d. File organization

e. File-closing procedures

f. File storage

g. File-storage procedures

h. File destruction

i. Alphabetical or numerical filing system

j. How documents are filed in each client's file

SELF TEST

How well did you grasp the material in the chapter? Test yourself by answering the following questions, and check your answers against the answers found in Appendix A.

1. What are the three types of filing systems?

2. What is a centralized filing system?

3. Who manages a centralized filing system?

4. What type of firm uses a centralized filing system?

5. What is controlled access?

6. What is a decentralized filing system?

7. Who manages a decentralized filing system?

8. What type of firm uses a decentralized filing system?

9. What is an automated filing system?

10. What are the three parts of an automated filing system?

11. What is imaging?

12. What can a user do with an automated filing system?

13. What is classification?

14. What does a good classification system do?
15. What are the four major categories for most law firm files?
16. Before a document can be located, what must first be known?
17. After the function of a record is identified, what is it divided into?
18. After the subject is identified, what is it divided into?
19. What is a subtopic?
20. What is a coding system?
21. What are three coding methods?
22. What is the most common coding method used by small firms?
23. What coding system is the easiest to establish and maintain?
24. When a client's records are arranged in alphabetical order, what name is used?
25. What is the first unit of an individual client's file called?
26. What is the first unit of a business client's file name called?
27. File _____ before _____.
28. The word *the* is always considered as the _____ unit.
29. When alphabetizing records, what do you do with all punctuation and symbols?
30. Where are arabic and roman numerals filed in an alphabetical system?
31. The call letters of a television station are considered _____ unit(s).
32. What is cross-referencing?
33. If the client is the sole plaintiff in a case, his or her name would be the _____ name in a case name.
34. If the client is the defendant, his or her name would be the _____ name in the case name.
35. What does *adversus* (adv.) mean?
36. What is a primary case name?
37. In a corporate legal department or other firm with just one client, when is the client's name mentioned in the case name?
38. Why is subject alphabetical coding more difficult than straight alphabetical coding?
39. What must be used if a firm codes files by subject?
40. What are the six types of numeric coding systems?
41. What is straight numbering?
42. What numeric coding system is the least complicated?
43. Straight numbering normally begins at what number?
44. What is coded numbering?
45. How are files with a coded numbering system filed?
46. What is calendar numbering?
47. How are files with a calendar numbering system filed?
48. The file number in a calendar numbering system gives the user what information?
49. What is standard numbering?
50. What type of information does a standard numbering system convey?
51. What is a volume?
52. What is account numbering?
53. How are files with an account numbering system filed?
54. How are numbering systems combined?
55. What is alphanumeric coding?
56. How are files in an alphanumeric coding system filed?
57. What are the advantages to an alphanumeric coding system?

58. What is a cross-index, and how is it used?
59. What is a numeric index, and how is it used?
60. For what is color coding used?
61. What types of information can color coding convey?
62. For what purpose is a colored dot or sticker used?
63. How are misfilings reduced by giving file numbers a color?
64. According to statistics, what percentage of documents are misfiled?
65. What does noncompliance with retrieval procedures result in?
66. In a small firm, who is responsible for file system maintenance?
67. In a large firm, who is responsible for file system maintenance?
68. What does an efficient system have?
69. How is a file requested from a centralized filing system?
70. What advantage does a written request for a file have over an oral request?
71. For what reasons would a file not be available in a file room?
72. What is an out-card system, and how is it used?
73. What are the advantages to an out-card system?
74. When do problems occur with an out-card system?
75. What is an out folder, and how is it used?
76. What is bar coding, and how is it used?
77. What is automatic data collection?
78. What are symbologies?
79. What are the advantages to bar coding?
80. How is bar code information communicated back to a firm's computer?
81. What is used to determine a file's location?
82. What type of firm benefits from using bar code technology?
83. What are the six benefits of using bar code technology?
84. What is radio frequency identification?
85. How does RFID work?
86. What is the main difference between RFID and bar code technology?
87. What is a preclient?
88. When is a client's file formally opened?
89. What is a conflict check, and why is it necessary?
90. What information does a conflict-check database contain?
91. What is the most important aspect of file-opening procedures?
92. In addition to file opening, when must a conflict check be performed?
93. If there is a potential conflict of interest, what must be done?
94. What is a file-number index, and for what is it used?
95. What is used as a checklist to complete file-opening procedures?
96. When opening a file, what is done with the statute of limitations?
97. When opening a file, where does a clerk obtain billing information?
98. How is referral information used in file opening procedures?
99. How is type-of-case information used by a law firm's management?
100. What acts as a double-check against direct or potential conflicts of interest?
101. Why is it important that information generated when opening a file be accurate?
102. Who is responsible for maintaining clients' files in good order?
103. What are now considered documents?

104. What is rich media?

105. What is one of the biggest changes facing records management today?

106. What is the first step in file maintenance?

107. How is correspondence filed?

108. How are notes and pleadings filed in a small case?

109. Where is correspondence inserted in the folder in a small case?

110. Where are pleadings inserted in the folder in a small case?

111. How are documents categorized in a large case?

112. What is a case cover sheet, and how is it used?

113. Where is a case cover sheet located in a file?

114. Why do some firms keep an extra copy of a case cover sheet in a separate binder?

115. What is an index, and for what is it used?

116. How are indexing tabs used?

117. Where is a document inserted in an indexed system?

118. What information is inserted on an index sheet?

119. What categories of documents do not require an index?

120. How are photographs inserted into a file?

121. What are the two ways documents are generated in a law office?

122. What must be determined to identify a document's life cycle?

123. What are a document's three value determinations?

124. What is operational value?

125. What is considered high operational value?

126. What is technical value?

127. What is legal value?

128. How does one determine the value of a document?

129. Why should unnecessary documents not be kept?

130. What does it mean to purge a file?

131. When do time management experts advise that document decisions be made?

132. What types of documents are found in a typical law office?

133. Most of the documents received are what type of document?

134. What should be done with a fax cover sheet?

135. What is date stamping?

136. Why are documents date stamped?

137. When should envelopes be retained?

138. Who is responsible for deciding whether to keep or discard a document?

139. What document pertaining to a client's case may be discarded?

140. Who should be consulted if a document's importance is unclear?

141. What type of interoffice memo is always retained?

142. When should a photocopy of an original document be retained?

143. What is a courtesy copy of a document?

144. What is a secondary recipient?

145. What is a primary recipient?

146. What type of recipient has no responsibility to retain a document?

147. When are notes of a meeting with a client discarded?

148. When must a note taker in a law firm meeting retain notes of the meeting?

149. When is a rough draft of an agreement discarded?

150. When are rough drafts of correspondence and pleadings discarded?

151. What information is inserted in a magazine or newspaper article?

152. The files and subfiles into which electronic documents are stored must have what structure?

153. What is "read only" access?

154. Why are documents not removed from a file?

155. What are the advantages of electronic documents?

156. What are the disadvantages of electronic documents?

157. What are the functions of an automated document management system?

158. Most automated document management programs are integrated into what systems?

159. Where is an electronic document that has been prepared for a client filed?

160. What type of rules must a firm have for electronic documents?

161. How will a filing system for electronic documents fail?

162. What are the characteristics of a good system?

163. A popular system that is used for saving electronic documents contains what three components?

164. Using the three components in answer 163 gives an electronic filing system what advantage?

165. What procedures must be followed before a file can be closed?

166. What is a disengagement letter?

167. What is pruning a file?

168. What is a file-closing memorandum?

169. To determine whether a file is a candidate for closing, the file must be reviewed for what purpose?

170. What must be paid before a file is closed?

171. Who is responsible for drafting a disengagement letter?

172. Who has the responsibility for pruning files?

173. Why should an attorney review a file for closing?

174. Why do some experts recommend that an attorney not review files for closing?

175. When a file is closed, it changes its status from what to what?

176. Why should a conflict-of-interest database be checked when a file is closed?

177. What must be determined when a file is closed?

178. Who is usually responsible for file-closing procedures?

179. If a firm retains a client's original will, where is it stored?

180. What happens to a client's electronic documents when a file is closed?

181. Why should inactive records not be stored in the active filing area?

182. What is used to locate and retrieve inactive files and records?

183. Where are inactive records stored?

184. What must be done to each inactive records container?

185. Storage areas include what three things?

186. What is micrographics?

187. What type of firm benefits from using micrographics to store records?

188. Why do smaller firms not use micrographics to store their inactive files?

189. What is imaging?

190. What items does an image system include?
191. How many documents will a CD-ROM hold?
192. What is a jukebox?
193. How is an imaged document located?
194. What is the best evidence rule?
195. What are the names of the two statutes that pertain to imaged records?
196. A closed file's number is listed on what?
197. Why do closed files with an alphabetical coding system create storage problems?
198. What is the preferred coding method for closed files?
199. What is a closed-file index?
200. In what order should information be inserted on a closed-file index?
201. What information should a closed-file index contain?
202. From where is the information for a closed-file index obtained?
203. Who completes the closed-file index form?
204. What is done with a completed closed-file index form?
205. What is records retention?
206. How are records-retention time periods established?
207. For what purposes may an organization need inactive records?
208. When may records be destroyed?
209. When do 95 percent of all references to closed files occur?
210. Who is responsible for setting a retention period?
211. What is a retention schedule?
212. Why should a paralegal not rely on an automated retention schedule?
213. When determining the retention period for business records, what three things are considered?
214. Who determines the future need for business records?
215. What are the six considerations for retaining client records?
216. Who determines the future need for client records?
217. When does the statute of limitations begin on a minor's action?
218. Why should records be shredded instead of disposing of them in the trash can?
219. What must be done to prepare records for shredding?
220. What is witnessed records destruction?
221. How are small shredding projects performed?
222. Why must a shredding project be supervised and not be left unattended?
223. What type of paper is recyclable?
224. Who requires that an attorney notify the client before a file is destroyed?
225. What information does a notification letter regarding file destruction contain?
226. Some firms are notifying clients of their file-destruction policy in what document?
227. Why should files not be removed from the office?
228. When should conflict-of-interest checks be performed?
229. If a client terminates the attorney-client relationship, when should a file be returned to a client?
230. Who must approve a records retention schedule?
231. Why must a file not be destroyed until the expiration of the retention period?
232. Why is knowledge of file and records management procedures important?

Key Words

automatic data collection	file-number index	pruning
best evidence rule	jukebox	purge
central file control	master client list	radio frequency identification
classification	new case memorandum	RFID tags
closed-file list	numeric index	rich media
controlled access	preclient	secondary recipient
courtesy copy	preclient file	symbologies
custodial	primary case name	
date stamp	primary recipient	

Cybersites

DOCUMENT MANAGEMENT SOFTWARE PROGRAM

Legal Key Records Management: Open Text—<*http://www.opentext.com*>
GroupWise: Novell—<*http://www.novell.com*>
Legal Files Case Management: Legal Files—<*http://www.legalfiles.com*>
Hot Docs: LexisNexis—<*http://www.hotdocs.com*>
Worldox: World Software Corp.—<*http://www.worldox.com*>
IPRO Tech: IPRO Tech—<*http://www.iprocorp.com*>

GENERAL RECORDS MANAGEMENT INFORMATION

The Paper Tiger: Monticello Enterprises, Inc. —<*http://www.thepapertiger.com*>
Record Management Association: Arma International—<*http://www.arma.org*>
Records Management Educational Program: Gatlin Education Services—<*http://www.gatllineducation.com*>
Microsoft Records Management Team Blog—<*http://blogs.msdn.com/recman*>

RECORDS SERVICE COMPANIES

Nova Records Management LLC—<*http://www.novarecordsmgmt.com*>
Iron Mountain—<*http://www.ironmountain.com*>

RECORDS STORAGE COMPANIES

Penn Records Management—<*http://www.pennrecords.com*>
Archive America—<*http://www.archiveamerica.com*>
Cor-o-van Record Storage—<*http://www.corovan.com*>

BAR CODING AND RADIO FREQUENCY IDENTIFICATION

Worth Data—<*http://www.barcodehq.com*>
File Tracking Software—<*http://www.filetrackingsoftware.com*>
List of bar code suppliers—<*http://www.isbn.org/*>
RFID Organization—<*http://www.rfid.org*>

RFID Journal—<*http://www.rfidjournal.com*>

RFID Tags: Beyond Bar Codes: Wired—<*http://www.wired.com/*>

Association for Automatic Identification and Mobility—<*http://www.aimglobal.org*>

FILING GENERAL INFORMATION

Retrieval Business Systems, Inc.—<*http://www.retrieval1.net*>

Designing and Effective System: Blu Fish—<*http://www.theblufish.com/*>

Color Coding: Color Flex—<*http://www.colorflex.com/*>

The Library of Virginia: Filing Practices—<*http://www.lva.lib.va.us/whatwedo/*>

 Student CD-ROM
For additional materials, please go to the CD in this book.

 Online Companion™
For additional resources, please go to http://www.paralegal.delmar.cengage.com

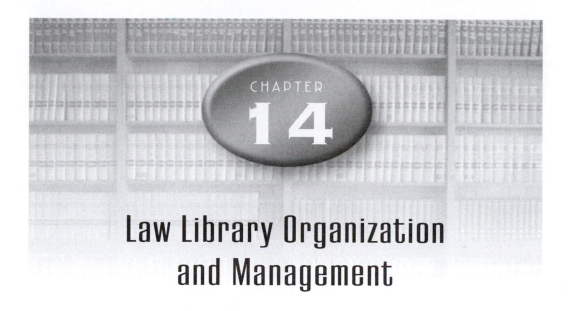

CHAPTER

14

Law Library Organization and Management

OBJECTIVES

After completion of this chapter, the student should be able to do the following:

- Describe the nature of law.
- Explain how laws are classified.
- Discuss the various types of law libraries.
- Discuss library organization.
- Describe the importance of updating.
- Discuss library technology.
- Identify the function of each book in the library.
- Explain how knowledge banks and form files are used.
- Find legal research sites on the Internet.
- Cite a case found on the Internet.
- Describe the duties of a law librarian.
- Update a law library.

INTRODUCTION

The law library has served as a symbol of the practice of law for centuries. Libraries are used as the background for a law firm's photographs and are displayed in the background of television commercials as attorneys advertise their services. Library shelves neatly lined with impressive, leather-bound law books greet clients as they enter a law firm, communicating a message of an attorney's expertise and knowledge of the law.

Two types of knowledge exist: knowledge we have about a subject and knowledge of where to find information about a subject. A law library is where attorneys and paralegals obtain knowledge. Every law library is different. Each encompasses a world of knowledge that forms our society and documents the evolution of the United States. It is a place of excitement and frustration. It is a place where a paralegal views a part of other people's lives. It is a place of continuing education. It is a legal professional's most valuable tool.

Millions of laws are in effect today. The United States is governed by the U.S. Constitution, the highest law in the land. Each state has a state constitution, the highest law in that state. Federal laws are enacted by Congress. Each federal agency, such as the Federal Drug Administration (FDA) and the Federal Aviation Administration (FAA), has laws that govern it. Each state has its own laws and laws that govern state agencies. In addition, each county and city have laws and ordinances that govern them. Each individual in the country is bound by the U.S. Constitution, state constitution, federal law, federal agency law, state law, state agency law, county ordinances, and city ordinances. At this moment, the federal and state legislatures are busy enacting more laws. Organizing laws in an orderly manner so that each law is easily found is a huge undertaking.

Entering a large law library that contains thousands of books can be intimidating, to say the least. A paralegal must be comfortable in a library setting because success as a paralegal depends on it. Acquiring knowledge of libraries is the first step in understanding a law library. The second step is gaining knowledge of the contents of a law library. A paralegal need not read every book in a library but should understand the function of each book.

The purpose of this chapter is to familiarize a prospective paralegal with library management. Being familiar with this important tool is the beginning of using it effectively. The first section of the chapter will review the nature and classes of law. The second section will discuss law libraries and their maintenance. The third section will discuss law library technology. Finally, the chapter will discuss law librarians and their role in law library management.

THE NATURE OF LAW

Law has been defined as follows: "Law consists of enforceable rules governing the relationships between individuals and their relationships to society." Professor Holland, in *Elements of Jurisprudence,* defines law as "a general rule of external human action enforced by a sovereign political authority." Our legal system is based on a combination of civil law and common law.

Civil law is derived from Roman law and is based on a series of written laws. In advanced countries, laws were written as early as 2100 BCE. Cases were decided by applying written law to them. There are two main sources of written law: constitutions and statutes.

Common law, also known as case law, evolved in England, where there were no written laws. During the reign of Edward I (1272–1307), some people, perhaps student lawyers, attended trials and reported what was said. Their accounts were later compiled into a series called the Yearbooks. Courts would consult the Yearbooks when making a ruling, establishing the doctrine of **stare decisis,** or standing by decisions. Cases were adjudicated by stare decisis, or following precedent, that is, following previous court decisions.

stare decisis
The legal principle that a court will follow the decision of another court in a similar case.

codify
To arrange laws by subject.

The U.S. legal system utilizes both written law and case law. Most laws of the United States originated from English common law and were **codified,** or arranged, into written laws. In addition to establishing case law, U.S. courts interpret the statutes, and that interpretation sets a precedent.

Law Classification

One of the most important aspects of legal editorial work is classifying the law. The classification process entails placing law into categories. It is very similar to the classification process we learned in Chapter 13 when we classified documents so that they could be located quickly. Classification of the law was introduced in England in 1490. A man named Statham produced a subject-key index to all the cases in the Yearbooks, titled *Abridgment of the Yearbooks.* This was the first legal index published. Today, we place laws into categories, and this helps us find them quickly. Laws are categorized according to function. When the function of a law is identified, it is categorized by subject. When the subject is identified, it is further categorized by topic and then subtopic, as we learned in Chapter 13. For example, statutes are classified by function: civil and criminal.

> Civil statutes (function)
> > Bankruptcy (subject)
> > > Chapter 7 (topic)
> > > > Stockbroker liquidation (subtopic)
> Criminal statutes (function)
> > Felony (subject)
> > > Murder (topic)
> > > > First degree (subtopic)

There are millions of case laws, and 45,000 to 50,000 court decisions are made each year. If these decisions were not classified, it would be extremely difficult, if not impossible, to find a case. To eliminate this problem, case law is classified according to its subject matter. For example, a case dealing with probate is classified under the title "probate." A case regarding corporations is classified under the title "corporations." Understanding this classification process is important to understanding the law library.

There are four functions of law: type of action (civil or criminal), individuals involved (public or private), nature of the law (substantive or procedural), and source of the law (constitutions, statutes, and cases). This breakdown is shown in Exhibit 14–1.

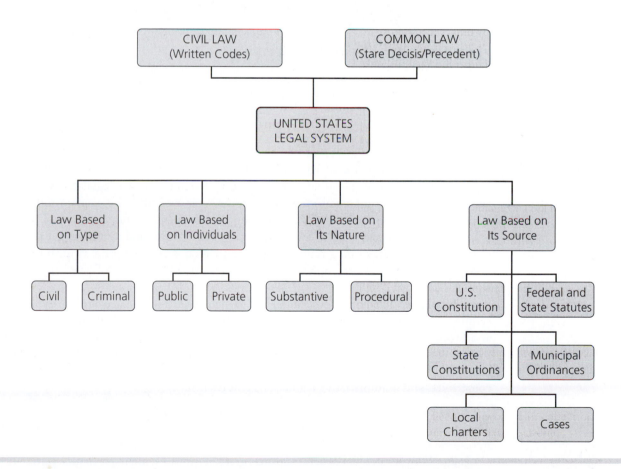

EXHIBIT 14–1   The Four Functions of Law *(Copyright 1987 by West Publishing Co. All rights reserved. Reprinted with permission from the National Association of Legal Secretaries [International], The Career Legal Secretary, rev. ed.)*

TYPE OF LEGAL ACTION   Two types of legal actions are filed: civil and criminal. In a criminal action, the government, state or federal, is the plaintiff in the action. The victim of a crime does not prosecute a criminal; crimes are considered an injury to society, so they are prosecuted by the government. A civil action is brought by one party against another party. Two types of remedies are available in a civil case: monetary relief and equitable relief. **Monetary relief** is compensation that consists of money that is paid to a party for an injury. **Equitable relief** is compensation other than money that is given to a party for an injury, such as the return of a person's property that was wrongfully taken.

INDIVIDUALS INVOLVED   Two types of laws apply to individuals: public laws and private laws. Public laws apply to everyone. Private laws apply only to individuals who fall under the jurisdiction of a law by circumstance. For example, property tax laws apply only to people who own property.

NATURE OF LAW   A law can be either substantive or procedural in nature. **Substantive laws** are laws that govern society. They create, define, and regulate rights. If a substantive law is broken, the injured party is entitled to **damages,** or compensation for the injuries. How does one go about recovering damages? This question is answered in **procedural law,** which sets forth methods to enforce a person's rights and tells a person how to obtain relief.

SOURCE OF LAW   A law is categorized by its source. Constitutional law encompasses the U.S. Constitution and the constitution of each state. Federal statutory law encompasses laws passed by the U.S. Congress. State statutory law encompasses laws passed by the state legislatures and local governments. Case law encompasses court decisions resulting from legal controversies.

CLASSES AND AUTHORITY OF LAW

There are three classes of law: primary authority, secondary authority, and search tools.

Primary Authority

Primary authority consists of laws made by the three branches of government: executive, legislative, and judicial. These are laws enacted by federal and state legislatures and administrative agencies. Primary authority is given the most weight and consideration in a case. Some disputes arise concerning the meaning or intent of a statute, or both. The judicial branch of the government, the courts, interprets the statutes and applies them to the facts of a dispute. A court's ruling results in case law, which is also the primary authority. In the U.S. legal system, a court's opinion constitutes a precedent to be followed in subsequent similar cases.

A legislature also enacts procedural law, which consist of laws governing the legal procedure used to redress wrong or injury. The judicial branch creates laws governing the rules and procedures of the court system. In addition, each court creates rules, called **local rules,** to be followed in that court only. These procedural laws and court rules are also primary authority. Therefore, primary authority consists of constitutions, statutes, judicial opinions, court rules, and administrative regulations and decisions.

STATUTES   The most commonly used statutes are organized according to subject matter. The U.S. Code is categorized into 50 titles, each title being a separate topic. Each title is divided into sections.

Large libraries contain federal statutes, state statutes for their particular state, and the statutes of other states. Small libraries contain state statutes for their particular state and may or may not contain federal statutes.

---

monetary relief
Compensation by money for an injury.

equitable relief
Compensation other than money for an injury.

substantive law
A law that creates, defines, or regulates rights.

damages
Compensation for a wrong or an injury.

procedural law
A law that defines procedures of a lawsuit.

local rules
Rules created by an individual court that apply in that court only.

Statutes may be either **annotated** or **unannotated.** Annotated statutes contain historical information concerning amendments and additions to a statute, citations to judicial opinions interpreting a statute, and references to secondary sources that are relevant to a statute. Unannotated statutes contain a statute, delete repealed statutes, and insert all amendments and additions to a statute.

In a library, annotated statutes are placed where they are most accessible. Statutes that apply to a firm's jurisdiction are given priority over other state statutes. In large firms, more than one set of state statutes may be provided to accommodate a firm's employees. Placing statutes on a high shelf is not a good idea. Unannotated statutes are often placed in an attorney's or a paralegal's office so that they are accessible whenever needed.

As new laws are passed, it is essential to have immediate access to them. Legal publishing companies provide an update service called Advance Legislative Service. New laws are published in **pocket parts,** which are additions that are inserted into a pocket inside the back cover of the applicable volume. A pocket part uses the same numbering system as the bound volume. It brings a law current to the beginning of the year. Every 5 or 6 years, a new edition of the U.S. Code is published with supplements being incorporated into the new volumes.

Pocket parts must be inserted into the back of the applicable volumes as soon as they are received. They should not be allowed to accumulate because employees will not have the most recent law at their disposal.

JUDICIAL OPINIONS   Books called **reporters** contain the text of judicial opinions as they are made. Federal reporters report federal judicial opinions, and state reporters report state judicial opinions.

Thousands of volumes of reporters are published, and the volumes of each reporter are numbered consecutively. Since a reporter has hundreds of volumes, it may have more than one **series,** or set. When the volumes reach a high number, a publisher will name a new series and begin numbering its volumes from 1. For example, West's California Reporter has three series: California Reporter, 1960–1991; California Reporter, 2nd series, 1991–2003; California Reporter, 3rd series, 2003–present.

Reporters contain hundreds of volumes and occupy a lot of shelf space in a library. They are placed in numeric order according to series, starting with the first series. Some libraries, especially small libraries, do not contain a first series because it is outdated and the library's space is limited. Other libraries may have a first series on microfilm or CD-ROM.

When an opinion is first printed, it is known as a **slip opinion.** Most law libraries do not receive slip opinions as they are made unless they are specifically requested. About 4 weeks after a slip opinion is printed, it is published in an **advance sheet,** which is a pamphlet that contains the **full text** of opinions released in the same time period. Advance sheets are sent to law libraries weekly and are placed at the end of a reporter set. After a period of time, the cases reported in the advance sheets are accumulated and bound together in a new volume. Once a new volume is received, the advance sheets may be discarded and the new volume placed at the end of the set. The case citations do not change.

COURT RULES   Every law library contains court rules, which were first developed by the Judiciary Act of 1789, passed at the first session of Congress. They are court procedures that must be followed in cases before that court. They relate to such matters as filing papers, pretrial procedures, pretrial requirements, filing fees, and so on.

Court rules have three purposes:

1. To aid the court in expediting the business that comes before it
2. To establish uniform procedures for the conduct of a court's business
3. To provide parties to a lawsuit with procedural information and instructions on bringing the matter before a court

In addition to court rules governing federal and state courts, each federal and state court creates local rules. Local rules may be different from court rules of general application.

---

annotated
Referring to a publication that contains a law and other pertinent information about the law.

unannotated
Referring to a publication that contains the text of a law only.

pocket part
An addition to a book that updates its contents.

reporter
A published volume of court decisions.

series
A set of reporters in numeric order.

slip opinion
A printed copy of a judicial opinion that is distributed soon after the decision is rendered.

advance sheet
A softcover book of decisions that is circulated soon after a decision is rendered.

full text
Consisting of a verbatim text that allows every word in a document to be retrieved by a researcher.

The U.S. Supreme Court has rule-making authority over other federal courts. It has created rules for use in the federal district courts. In addition to these rules, individual lower federal courts have created rules that govern an individual court only. Every law library must have court rules for each court in which an attorney practices.

Court rules are placed in a library where they can be retrieved quickly. Large firms may have more than one copy of court rules to accommodate many employees.

Court rules are updated by a publisher or the particular court. Most often, they are contained in a three-ring binder to facilitate updating. When the updates are received, they must be quickly inserted into a volume. Many courts now publish their local rules on their websites, which makes locating them convenient. Always check a court's website to keep abreast of changes in the court's local rules.

ADMINISTRATIVE REGULATIONS AND DECISIONS Administrative law governs the powers and procedures of administrative agencies. Administrative agencies are established by Congress and are government entities (other than a court or legislative body) that affect the rights of people through their rules and decisions. Agencies make rules, adjudicate issues, provide licenses, distribute money, investigate matters, prosecute violators, mediate disputes, and exercise whatever other powers a legislature mandates. Agency regulations look very much like statutes.

There is no reporter of agency decisions, such as the West Reporter System for Federal Courts. Some agencies publish their own opinions. A few private publishers publish administrative and judicial opinions on particular subjects, such as the *United States Patents Quarterly*.

Many state administrative agencies exist. State agency administrative regulations and decisions are published chronologically, although some states codify their regulations. Some state administrative rulings are privately published in loose-leaf reports or by services. State administrative agency rulings are not as uniformly published as federal administrative rulings.

Only large libraries contain administrative rulings. Since these rulings are very specialized, they should be accessible by the attorneys and paralegals who use them. Administrative rulings are updated in the same manner as are reporters. In other words, many agencies provide a subscription service for their rulings.

Secondary Authority

Secondary authority is anything other than primary authority that aids a court in reaching a decision. At some point, primary source material reached such voluminous proportions that it was necessary to provide aids in identifying and explaining the law; secondary authority was developed for this purpose. Secondary authority is used to persuade. It is not considered in lieu of primary authority but is used in addition to primary authority.

Secondary authority includes commentary material written by legal scholars or experts in a particular field. It encompasses treatises, periodicals, dictionaries, and encyclopedias.

Treatises are legal commentaries on various subjects of law. Their purpose is to simplify and explain the law. Treatises can be either federal or state in nature.

Periodicals are booklets concerning articles about the law. The articles describe and analyze the law and, in some cases, make recommendations for changes in the law. To provide access to all the articles published in a legal periodical, indexes are published. The most established index service is the *Index to Legal Periodicals*, which dates back to 1908.

Every law library has a legal dictionary, and large libraries may contain more than one. Dictionaries do not restate the law or act as sources of the law. They are reference tools. However, if the meaning of a word is in dispute, the definition in a legal dictionary is quoted and is considered secondary authority.

Encyclopedias are volumes that contain statements on principles of law and are organized alphabetically by subject matter. They are categorized into broad topics that are subdivided into narrower topics and act as an index and guide to the law. Some states have encyclopedias devoted to their own laws.

Large libraries contain many volumes of secondary authority. Small libraries contain legal dictionaries and some periodicals but have very few treatises and encyclopedias. Volumes of secondary authority are placed according to their numeric order. Dictionaries are usually placed in a central area of a library.

As the law changes, editors will write some annotations to commentaries of treatises that supersede older annotations. Many treatises are updated by pocket parts, **restatements** are rewritten, and the new material is contained in an updated series. Other treatises are updated as the law changes.

The *Current Law Index* is published monthly. Most indexes are published quarterly and are accumulated to provide a new volume each year. Encyclopedia volumes have pocket parts and replacement volumes issued periodically. Legal dictionaries are not updated, but it is a good practice to replace them with a new volume every 7 to 10 years. Secondary authority is shown in Exhibit 14–2.

restatement
A series of volumes authored by legal scholars that describe the law, its changes, and future direction of the law.

Search Tools and Form Books

Search tools help a researcher find primary authority. Form books help prepare a case. Search tools and form books are never cited as a source of law; they are tools only. Most libraries contain both.

Search tools consist of digests and citators. **Digests** are commonly used search tools that list case citations that pertain to a particular subject or statute. The main body of a digest is arranged by topic like an encyclopedia. Each topic is divided into subtopics. An example of a digest is shown in Exhibit 14–3.

A **citator** is a valuable addition to a law library. Citators give a researcher the current status of a law. Statutes are often **repealed,** or revoked, and case law is often **overruled.** It is important to know the status of a law before quoting it. A citator will inform a researcher whether a case was **affirmed** (confirmed), overruled, or mentioned in another case. A citator also provides a list of references to sources that were cited in a case. Each statute and case must be checked in a citator.

One main function of attorneys and paralegals is drafting legal documents. Many types of legal documents are used: pleadings, contracts, wills, trusts, and deeds, to name a few. Form books contain samples of documents that attorneys have used successfully in the past. The forms are not comprehensive enough to be used in all situations, but they act as a guide. They are valuable tools for preparing documents. A variety of form books are available for each state.

digest
A collection embodying the chief matter of numerous books, articles, court decisions, and so on, usually arranged alphabetically.

citator
A set of books that provide the judicial history and interpretation of reported decisions.

repeal
To abrogate or annul an existing law by the enactment of a statute that declares the former law revoked.

overrule
To reject or supersede an existing judicial opinion; to invalidate.

affirm
To confirm an existing judicial opinion.

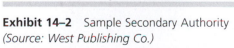

Exhibit 14–2   Sample Secondary Authority
(Source: West Publishing Co.)

Exhibit 14–3   Sample Digest
(Source: West Publishing Co.)

LAW LIBRARY ORGANIZATION AND PROCEDURES

Every law office, corporate legal department, and government agency has a library or access to a law library. Some libraries consist of very few books, and others contain thousands of books. Most libraries contain electronic resources. The manner in which these resources are managed determines a library's organization.

Maintaining a library is extremely important. Every paralegal should understand how a library is maintained. A comprehension of law library maintenance requires knowledge of its technology and systems. While no two law libraries are alike, they all have common elements.

Library Size

Law libraries are described according to size. A library's size depends on the size, specialties, and resources of a firm. A sole practitioner or a small firm in general practice may need a large library but may not be able to afford it. A small boutique firm with one specialty does not need a large library and will find a very small library sufficient.

Small libraries that contain only the books essential for the lawyers' needs are called **skeletal libraries.** These consist of state statutes, case reporters for a specific jurisdiction in which the lawyers practice, form books, and a legal dictionary. A skeletal library may also contain a treatise in a particular area of law. If more in-depth research is necessary, a researcher must go to a nearby county library or law school library or use an online legal database. Some libraries give the public access to the entire library and others only to certain sections of the library. Some law schools forbid public access, and others charge for library use.

Libraries that contain a comprehensive collection of the laws of the country are called **complete libraries.** These are very rare because of their cost. Complete law libraries are found in large law schools, some large agencies, courthouses, and major city libraries. A complete law library has over 300,000 hardcover volumes, microform, CD-ROMs, and access to legal and nonlegal databases. The largest complete law library in the United States is the Library of Congress in Washington DC, with more than 134 million items. Harvard Law School Library contains over 1,500,000 volumes. Large law libraries, such as the one shown in Exhibit 14–4, are found in large law firms, law schools, courthouses, and

skeletal library
A small library containing only essential material.

complete library
A library containing a comprehensive collection of material.

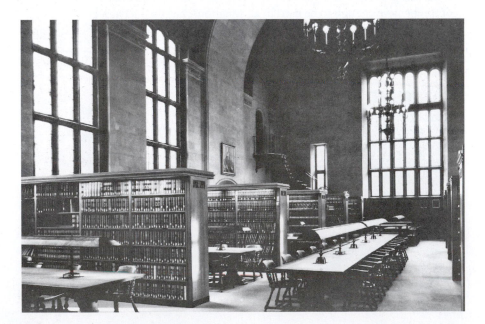

EXHIBIT 14–4 A Large Law Library

administrative agencies. An average large library contains about 50,000 volumes, microform, CD-ROMs, and access to legal and nonlegal databases.

Types of Library Organization

Three types of library organization are used: centralized, decentralized, and satellite.

CENTRALIZED ORGANIZATION   A centralized library is found in one location that has been set aside by a firm. All library materials are found in one location. A centralized library provides a work area for those using the library, usually one seat for every five attorneys. A small firm with a centralized library may combine the library with the conference room. This combination creates problems by making the library inaccessible when a conference is being held. A large firm that occupies several floors of a building may designate one full floor as the library, depending on the size of the library. Most large firms have a centralized library.

Sole practitioners and small firms that cannot afford large libraries often pool their resources and form a **library cooperative.** These firms are located in the same building or close to each other. A portion of a floor is dedicated to a centralized library for the participating lawyers. Each lawyer pays his or her proportionate share of the cost of the library. This arrangement works well for sole practitioners.

library cooperative
A group organized to pool library resources for the benefit of the group.

DECENTRALIZED ORGANIZATION   A decentralized library is distributed throughout a firm. The books are placed on bookshelves lining the office walls in the same location as the attorneys using them. For example, books used by a tax attorney are placed near the tax attorney's office. Corporate law books are placed near the corporate attorney's office. There is no library work area in a decentralized library. Attorneys and paralegals use the books in their individual offices. Sole practitioners and small firms may have decentralized libraries.

Scattering a library throughout an office has three advantages:

1. The books are close to the attorneys and the paralegals using them.
2. The books are decorative and give the office a nice appearance.
3. The books act as a noise buffer to keep an office quieter. For example, lining the walls of a copy room with books reduces noise from the copy machine.

The disadvantages of a decentralized library are that books may not be readily accessible when needed, they are often misplaced, and they are kept in offices and not returned to the shelf.

SATELLITE ORGANIZATION   Satellite libraries are found in large firms with a large centralized library. A large firm that occupies several floors of a building locates a library in the brightest location, usually on the top floor. The attorneys and paralegals must use the elevator and walk a distance to reach the library. Going back and forth to the library many times a day may be inconvenient. Some firms will remove specialty books from a central library and put a satellite library close to the employees using these books.

Tax and labor libraries are the most common satellite libraries. Satellite libraries are convenient for attorneys and paralegals using the books, but are difficult to maintain and control. In addition, other employees of a firm do not have convenient access to the books in a satellite library.

Law Library Maintenance

A law library must be maintained so that it is always current. The status of the law is of utmost importance to judges, lawyers, and clients. *The outcome of a client's case may depend on thorough legal research.* A California attorney was sued by a client for not adequately researching the issues of a case. In that case, the court awarded the client $100,000 (*Smith v. Lewis,* 13 Cal. 3d 349 [1975]). In another California case, an attorney was sanctioned for incorrectly citing a case.

ETHICS ALERT

update service
A service that keeps books
current.

Because the law is changing and new cases are being decided daily, updated research may mean the difference between winning and losing a case.

Legal publishers provide an **update service** with their products. As new laws are made and enacted, they are automatically sent to subscribers. Supplemental material should be inserted into the proper books as soon as possible so that the attorneys and paralegals have current law at their disposal. The outcome of a client's case may depend on the timelines of this function.

Law books must be updated constantly. In small and medium-sized firms that do not employ a full-time librarian, it is often a paralegal's duty to maintain a library. Library update services are also available. These are private companies that employ paralegals or other personnel to go into legal offices and update their libraries for a fee.

Firms have a substantial investment in their library. The cost of maintaining a law library is very high. It is also expensive to keep the books and electronic resources current. Ninety percent of a law library's budget is spent to update law resources. Law firms are constantly challenged to maintain an adequate library and to keep costs down.

Library Checkout Systems

All libraries, whether centralized, decentralized, or satellite, must have a system that will locate every book in them. The system must reduce the possibility of lost or misplaced books. Books often leave the library for use in individual offices, are taken home, or are taken to court. It is easy for a book to be lost or misplaced. A misplaced book results in areas of the law not being accessible when needed. Paralegals spend many frustrating hours looking for lost books.

A library checkout system consists of procedures to locate library materials. These procedures must be followed by each member of a legal team. Noncompliance with retrieval procedures results in lost library materials. A system is effective only if all employees participate in it.

The three most common systems used in law firm libraries are the out card, the bar code, and the library card system.

OUT CARD   A library out-card system is used like an out-card system for files described in Chapter 13. An out-card system is inexpensive and easy to set up and maintain. However, problems arise when employees do not take the time to write their names on the card or the cards fall off the shelf or are out of place. Library out cards also tend to cause a library to look messy.

BAR CODE   Some firms have bar codes placed on their books, and the system is used like the one described in Chapter 13 for bar coded files. Bar coding makes it easy to check out books, maintains an accurate location of all books at all times, and is easy to operate. However, problems arise if the computer is down or the equipment is inoperable.

LIBRARY CARD   A popular checkout system for library books is the library card system. Each book has a library card placed in a pocket on the inside cover of the book. A library card contains the book's name, author, and other pertinent information about the book. As the book leaves the library, the library card is placed into a card box or card holder behind the person's name taking the book. When the book is returned, the person replaces the card in the book. This system is fast and easy for law firm employees and requires little effort to maintain. However, cards may be misplaced or lost, and books may be replaced without their cards being inserted.

LAW LIBRARY TECHNOLOGY

Technology has had a great effect on the traditional law library. Law libraries are no longer book depositories; they are now considered information management and transfer centers. Just as technology promised a paperless office, it now promises a bookless library. Some experts predict that an electronic library will be here soon. Others say that an electronic library is somewhere in the distant future. Technology has become a vital part of the law library but will not completely replace books until sometime in the future.

People, including attorneys, love books. Humans have been trained to absorb information from print media, and that is not likely to change soon. Recent sales figures from Amazon.com attest to this fact. However, law libraries are getting smaller because they are implementing technology by combining it with law books. Fewer books and more technology are being purchased.

Five types of technology are used in law libraries:

1. Online legal and nonlegal databases
2. Microform
3. CD-ROM
4. E-mail and telefacsimile (fax) transmissions
5. The Internet

Online Legal and Nonlegal Databases

Online legal and nonlegal databases are the most common type of technology found in law offices today. An online legal database is a database of laws compiled by a publisher who charges customers to use it. Legal research conducted with an online legal database is called **computer-assisted legal research** (CALR). Full-text copies of statutes, court opinions, regulations, agency rulings, and other material are available. They are accessed by the internet. When a case or statute is found and a user desires a hard copy of a document, the database materials are downloaded from the internet to the user's computer. The central computer and the user's personal computer "talk" to each other when sending and receiving information.

> **computer-assisted legal research**
> Legal research on a legal database accessed by computer.

The two primary CALR systems are WESTLAW, from IT Thomson's West Group, and LexisNexis, from Reed Elsevier, both of which provide access to full-text legal documents through a computer. Other online legal databases provide an **abstract system,** which does not provide the full text of a decision but instead provides an abstract, or summary, of a law.

> **abstract system**
> A collection of abstracted, or summarized, documents.

Information may be quickly retrieved with a legal database. Learning to use CALR takes practice, training, and patience. One must know how to search a database and how to use the proprietary software necessary to access a database. One must learn how to conduct a search and how to narrow a search for faster results. Many law firms use CALR with book research for more comprehensive research projects.

Nonlegal databases operate the same as legal databases but contain nonlegal information. Many law firms subscribe to nonlegal databases and find them useful in cases that are technical in nature or that require specific information. For example, if a case involves the construction of a complex electrical plant, a lawyer may need the answer to a technical engineering question; or in a personal injury or medical malpractice case, a lawyer may need a definition of a certain type of injury or medical treatment. Among the nonlegal databases used by law firms are Dun & Bradstreet's credit ratings, Standard & Poor's company profiles, and databases that provide economic statistics and stock market data.

WESTLAW is found at <http://www.westlaw.com> and LEXIS Nexis at <http://www.lexis.com>. To access a database from the Internet, one needs an account and a password and must pay the requisite fees. Accessing a database from the Internet requires no specialized software (except a browser) and can be accessed from an individual computer. It is convenient for traveling attorneys and paralegals.

Microform

Microform is the process of storing information photographically in reduced form. It involves printing miniature images of documents on film or paper and consists of microfilm and **microfiche.** Microfilm is 35-millimeter film that stores a large number of pages that run

> **microform**
> The process of storing information photographically.

> **microfiche**
> Sheets of film on which documents are photographed.

continuously in sequence and that need no alteration. Microfiche is a sheet of microfilm that comes in the form of a card that is used to store a small number of pages. One 100-foot roll of microfilm contains five large books. Six microfiche cards are needed to photograph one book. The new generation of microfiche, called ultrafiche, will hold more data than microfiche.

microfilm
Film on which documents are photographed.

Microfilm is the most popular method of microform in law libraries. Volumes of books can be put on microfilm and stored in a small desk drawer. After documents have been photographed, the film is inserted into a reader/printer that enlarges the document on a screen for viewing. Each microform image can be converted into a hard copy if desired.

Microform is not new technology. Miniaturization of documents on paper has been used since the 1830s. Banks have been photographing records, mostly canceled checks, for storage purposes since 1930. Libraries began to use microform in the 1950s. The use of microform expanded into the legal profession in the 1960s and has been a popular method of storing records and documents. Law libraries are adding more microform than hard-copy volumes to their libraries because microform is less expensive to purchase, store, and catalog.

Microform is especially useful for preserving volumes of out-of-print law books. Many books printed after 1850 were printed on acidic paper, and the pages are now crumbling into dust on library shelves. Since these books cannot be replaced, they are being put on microfilm. Microfilm will last about 200 years, so long-term preservation of the material is ensured.

CD-ROM

CD-ROM
Compact disk read-only memory. A computer disk that stores a large amount of data.

CD-ROM (compact disk read-only memory) disks can be found in our homes and offices and can contain software, text, music, or movies. In a law library, a single 4.25-inch disk, 1/32 of an inch thick, stores about 300,000 manuscript pages, or 250 large law books. It is the equivalent of 1,500 conventional diskettes, or 600 **megabytes** (about 600 million characters) of data. CD-ROMs are found in most law libraries. A library can expand without the necessity of acquiring more library space and can be accessible to traveling lawyers away from the office. Books that are not frequently used can be replaced by CD-ROMs, freeing valuable library shelf space.

megabyte
A computer term used to measure data: one megabyte contains about one million characters.

Legal publishers make material found in law books available on CD-ROM and sell the disks to their customers. CD-ROMs are available for every area of law, both federal and state. An example of a legal CD-ROM is West's *Federal Taxation Library,* which contains statutes, legal history, regulations, judicial decisions, administrative materials, and a digest of judicial decisions and administrative materials pertaining to federal taxation.

CD-ROM drive
A device that is connected to a computer and reads CD-ROMs.

A **CD-ROM drive,** found on most personal computers today, is needed to access the material, which is displayed on a computer screen. CD-ROMs allow faster and more precise access to the information. A researcher can search the contents of a disk (250 law books) faster than through an online database. If a firm has a network or intranet, a CD-ROM drive is not necessary for each computer. Users can access the information from their computers through the network or the intranet. Firms use CD-ROM jukeboxes (Chapter 13) to make many disks available to users through a network or an intranet. A jukebox is a CD-ROM storage device that can hold as few as six and as many as 500 disks. With all of a firm's library material contained in a jukebox, lost or misplaced materials are a thing of the past.

With CD-ROMs, a large law firm with a centralized library can make portions of its library available to other areas of the firm, making access to the library more convenient. However, unless a firm has many CD-ROMs of the same title, only one person at a time has access to the information in 250 books rather than 250 people using 250 books.

One problem with CD-ROMs is that their data are often not current. As laws change, a disk must be updated by its publisher. Since laws change daily, providing current material has been a challenge for legal CD-ROM publishers. Because of the time and processes needed to produce and ship them, they are out of date when they are received. It is difficult to tell how current the material is on a CD-ROM or what changes have been made from a previous edition. In addition, CD-ROMs contain only recent statutes. If a paralegal needed to know what the law was 20 years ago, the information would not be available on CD-ROM.

Law firms have been reluctant to replace law books with CD-ROMs and have had problems with CD-ROM technology. Each legal publisher's CD-ROMs operate differently because of their unique **user interface,** or screen methods of operation. They also use different search protocols, and this has caused training difficulties. With multiple CD-ROMs from different vendors, a user's ability to effectively use the products is reduced. Some CD-ROMs are not easily installed on networks and are not compatible with basic word processing programs.

It was forecast that CD-ROM technology would someday replace microform, but law firms have been reluctant to do so. The lifetime of a CD-ROM is currently 10 to 30 years—not long enough to replace microform's longevity. Many people see CD-ROM technology as transitional until information contained on them is moved to the Internet. It has been predicted that CD-ROMs will become obsolete in the near future.

user interface
The method of operation developed by a legal publisher for its CD-ROM products.

E-Mail and Telefacsimile (Fax) Transmissions

Telefacsimile (fax) machines send documents from one location to another electronically over telephone lines. E-mail and fax machines are standard equipment in law firms and in large law and bar association libraries. They give attorneys and paralegals immediate access to materials not otherwise readily available to them.

As law firm libraries are stepping into their role of information centers, they must have access to a variety of information that may be needed by researchers.

Bar association libraries that provide library services to their members deliver materials by e-mail or fax. Previously, paralegals and other law firm personnel had to go to a library to copy materials. As cities become more congested, the time it takes to travel from one end of a city to another is a cost factor in obtaining the material. In addition, a library was inaccessible to firms a long distance away. E-mail and fax machines have solved these problems and have increased the accessibility of information.

Large firms with large libraries often lend materials to other firms and provide library materials to their branch offices. With the use of a fax machine, a book or document is sent over the telephone wires and need not leave the library, eliminating the need to monitor a book's or document's location. The fax machine has reduced the number of lost materials considerably.

telefacsimile
A system of transmitting documents over telephone wires.

The Internet

The Internet is the information superhighway that is absorbing other legal media types, such as print, CD-ROM, and online database services. Access to the information superhighway has put small firms on par with large law firms that have large libraries and therefore offer more resources to a client. According to the 2007 Technology Survey conducted by *Legal Assistant Today,* 82.4 percent of the respondents conduct legal research on the Internet.

Access to federal and state statutes and court decisions is available on the Internet for free. Access to this information is partially due to the assertive position of government agencies in placing their information on the Internet and to entrepreneurs who seek to bring viewers to their legal websites. These legal websites put the Internet in a position to be a serious research tool.

However, as of this writing, the Internet is not a better research tool than other, conventional types of technology used in law libraries. It is a myth that everything is on the internet and is available for free. A great deal of information that lawyers and librarians need is not available from the Internet, such as secondary authority material. It is estimated that less than 20 percent of legal information is committed to the Internet, with the remainder found in books and on CD-ROM. In addition, the credibility of the source of the information is uncertain, and the current nature of the material is questionable. Websites that require a fee, such as WESTLAW and LexisNexis, have an advantage because their publishers guarantee the reliability of the information.

Another problem with conducting legal research on the Web is its poor classification system, which makes correct legal information difficult to locate. The question is not whether the information is available on the Internet but how to find it. According to a recent Gartner Group study, typical computer users spend up to 50 percent of their time searching for the information they need. The results from queries on a search engine are often so vast that it takes longer to do research on the Internet. For example, if a person searched for law regarding stockbroker bankruptcies, he or she may get hundreds of results that would have to be reviewed before the desired information is found.

The Internet is an important medium of gathering and disseminating information in new and powerful ways. Each year, more legal material will be available on the Internet, which will provide numerous benefits to law firm personnel.

Electronic Citation

The emergence of electronic legal research has created the need for new methods of citing the material. Traditional legal cites refer to the volume and page number of a law book, but if a case was not found in a law book, how is it cited?

The *Harvard Blue Book: A Uniform System of Citation* is used as a guide to legal citation. With reference to citing electronic documents, it states in rule 10.8.1(a):

> When a case is unreported and available on a widely used electronic database, then it may be cited to that database. Provide the case name, docket number, database identifier, court name, and full date of the most recent major disposition of the case. The database identifier must contain enough information to enable a reader to identify the database and find the case. If the database has identifying codes or numbers that uniquely identify the case (as do Lexis-Nexis and Westlaw after 1986), these must be given. Screen or page numbers, if assigned, should be preceded by an asterisk. . . . Cases that have not been assigned unique database identifiers should provide all relevant information.

The American Association of Law Libraries (AALL) recognized the need for a new citation format for electronic materials and recommended that a legal cite include the case name, year of the decision, specific court, a consecutively assigned case number, and paragraph number for the exact location of the quote. The case number is a consecutive number that refers to the number of decisions in a year. For example, the following case was the 235th decision in 1996:

Smith v. Jones	1996	6th Cir.	235	15
Case name	Year	Court	Number	Paragraph

In 1996, the ABA adopted the AALL's recommendation but suggested that the traditional cite be included as follows:

Smith v. Jones	1996	6th Cir.	235	15	22 F. 3d 955
Case name	Year	Court	Number	Paragraph	Traditional cite

Many other groups have made recommendations for citing electronic documents, including the American Psychological Association and the Modern Language Association of America (MLA). While each group has slightly different recommendations, all seem to emphasize this basic format: name of author, title of document in quotes, version, date of document or last revision, protocol and address, and access path or directories. The MLA recommends that a website be cited as shown below.

For a professional site, name of page, host of page, date of last revision of site (if known), and URL (see Chapter 10) are cited as follows:

Portuguese Language Page. U of Chicago. 1 May 1997. http://humanities.uchicago.edu/romance/port

The *Brief Guide to Citing Government Publications* by the Government Publications Department recommends the following citation format:

Name of law, code designation, date of law, URL, last revision date

For the Federal Register:

"Protection of Historic Properties." 59 Federal Register (3 Oct. 1994). ONLINE. Available: telnet://swais.access.gpo.gov [26 Feb. 1996].

For the Congressional Record:

Ford, Rep. [TN]. "Tribute to Rhodes College Mock Trial Team." Congressional Record ONLINE 25 May 1995. GPO Access. Available: http://bubba.ucc.okstate.edu/wais/ GPOAccess [3 March 1996].

For Congressional bills:

U.S. House. 104th Congress, 1st Session. H.R. 1950, Newborns' and Mothers' Health Protection Act of 1995. ONLINE. GPO Access. Available: http://www.lib.ncsu .edu/stacks/gpo/ <104th Congress> [8 June 1995].

For GAO reports:

U.S. General Accounting Office. U.S. Vietnam Relations: Issues and Implications. ONLINE. GPO Access. 1995. Available: http://bubba.ucc.okstate.edu/wais/ GPOAccess GAO "Blue Book" Reports [30 Dec. 1995].

For statutes:

U.S. Code: Abandoned Shipwrecks (1995). Title 43 U.S. Code, Ch. 39 ONLINE. GPO Access. Available: telnet://swais.access.gpo.gov. [1 Feb. 1996]. CO Rev Stat § 1-40-107 (1996 through 2nd Reg Sess, 60th Gen Ass).

For microform:

American Statistics Index (ASI*)*: U.S. Department of Health and Human Services. 1992 AFDC Recipient Characteristics Study. Washington: The Department, 1994 (1994 ASI microfiche 4584-7).

Statistical Reference Index (*SRI*): Delaware. Department of Labor. Snapshot Delaware 93. Newark: Delaware Department of Labor, 1994 (1994 SRI Microfiche S1405-4).

No universally accepted citation system for electronic documents exists. The trend is for states to adopt the recommendations of the American Bar Association (ABA). It will be interesting to watch the evolution of this important area. The websites listed in the Cybersites section will help you monitor this issue.

COURT FORMS, FORM FILES, AND KNOWLEDGE BANKS

Court forms, form files, and knowledge banks are found in law libraries. Each employee in a law office must have access to court forms and knowledge banks.

Court forms are forms that are used in specific courts. Knowledge banks, also known as brief banks, are copies of work previously completed that may be used again or used as a guide to complete new projects.

Court Forms

Every law office must have an adequate supply of court forms, which are form documents used in a specific court. Each federal and state court has specific forms used by that particular court. Federal court forms and state court forms are available. Some court forms are used throughout all state courts, and others are used in a specific court only. Law offices use hundreds of court forms.

Court forms must be located quickly. All forms relating to a specific court must be clearly identifiable. In addition, court forms change often. Therefore, a library has a system to keep all forms current and up to date.

There are four methods of storing court forms: manually, as masters that are photocopied, by using computer programs, and the internet.

Court forms that are stored manually are filed in filing cabinets. These forms are rarely filed alphabetically by title. A paralegal looking for wage garnishment forms would have a difficult time locating them in that type of an alphabetical system; for example, an affidavit for writ of garnishment would be found at the beginning of the alphabet, and a writ of garnishment would be found at the end of the alphabet. A paralegal would have to look through hundreds of forms to find the correct forms that apply to a specific case and would also need to know the exact name of all the necessary forms to find them. If all wage garnishment forms were found in one place, it would save a paralegal's time.

Court forms are normally organized alphabetically by subject matter. All forms relating to a particular subject will then be found in one place. Some firms store court forms by a numeric filing system. Each form is given a number, and each number gives the user information regarding a form, including subject and applicable court. File folders and labels may be color coded in a numeric system to further identify a form.

Photocopier-created forms are stored in three-ring binders to save space. The binders are indexed and divided into subjects. Only one copy of each form, the master form, is inserted into a binder. That form is photocopied when it is needed. Everyone using the form must understand the importance of returning the original form to the binder after photocopying. It is frustrating to not have access to the correct form.

Problems with storage, access to, and updating court forms are solved with computer-generated forms. There are software programs that provide court forms and assist a user in completing them. They are printed after completion. Computer-generated forms are convenient and save space. All software containing court forms must be updatable to accommodate frequent changes in the forms. If an outdated form is used, a court may reject the document. Before using computer-generated forms, check with the court to determine its policy. Some courts require that a form be a specific color and will not allow printed forms unless they are produced on the correct color of paper. Some courts undertake responsibility for distributing new court forms via their website. Some courts, however, do not want to be burdened with this responsibility and so delegate it to a printing company, court form software company, or court form service. The legal industry supports many court form service companies that will distribute forms to their subscribers. They will automatically send new and updated forms when these forms become effective. Automated court form software is updated by the publisher. This service saves a firm a lot of time in updating court forms.

Court forms may also be found on the internet. Courts that have their own forms post them on their websites for download.

Form Files

Forms other than court forms are used by a law office. These forms include deeds, corporate forms, and forms required by government agencies. These forms may be integrated into a firm's court form filing system or have their own filing system by subject.

Knowledge Banks

The knowledge of employees is a firm's most valuable asset. Managing this knowledge to its maximum potential is a challenge. One method used is a knowledge bank, which consists of samples of research and documents prepared by a firm and used in the same manner as form books. If used effectively, a knowledge bank will provide a firm with many benefits.

A knowledge bank contains briefs, research memoranda, opinion letters, pleadings, discovery requests, contracts, leases, and articles that may be useful in a future case. Eighty percent of work done in most law firms is not new. The work of attorneys and paralegals is often similar to a previous case. If a firm can realize increased efficiencies on 80 percent of its work, it will increase productivity, resulting in increased profits. Keeping copies of briefs and research memorandums regarding an issue or subject saves employees' time in researching that issue again should a similar case arise. A knowledge bank helps ensure effective use of a firm's investment in its research, and it benefits clients by helping to provide better-quality, more efficient legal services at the lowest possible rates. Firms that keep copies of their work product in knowledge banks are generally more efficient than firms that do not.

When paralegals and attorneys prepare a complex document or do comprehensive research on a subject, a copy of the document or research is deposited in the firm's knowledge bank. Some firms require their employees to look for law in a knowledge bank before doing research on a topic. However, legal professionals should be cautioned to always check the law in a previous document to make sure the law hasn't changed and that case law is still current.

Before a knowledge bank is useful, its contents must be accessible. A work-product retrieval system is used to retrieve its information. There are two types of work-product retrieval systems: manual and automated.

A manual system is used by small firms. With a manual system, documents in a knowledge bank are filed alphabetically by subject to allow searchers to locate a document quickly. However, many firms use a numeric coding system for their knowledge banks. A comprehensive index is required to locate the appropriate document. The index is prepared alphabetically by subject matter and contains the law or rule to which the document applies. If there is more than one subject matter, the document is cross-referenced to other topics. When a document is inserted into a knowledge bank, it is incorporated into the system by a research index memorandum form, such as the one shown in Exhibit 14–5.

A manual knowledge bank may also be kept in three-ring binders, with one binder containing documents for one subject. The subject is labeled on the outside of the binder, and the binders are organized in alphabetical order; or a paralegal may organize a knowledge bank according to type of document, such as complaints, answers, interrogatories, and so on. Each binder is indexed just as files are, as shown in Chapter 13. Tabbed dividers are used with a document behind it to facilitate locating the appropriate document. An index, such as the one shown in Exhibit 14–6, is placed at the beginning of the form file so that its contents can be viewed easily. Each document in the bank should be given a reference number when

---

Research Index Memorandum

Name of case: _____

Type of document: _____

Author: _____

Year prepared: _____

Topic(s): _____

_____

Statutes and rules involved: _____

_____

Summary of material: _____

_____

_____

Index number: _____

Location: _____

EXHIBIT 14–5 Sample Research Index Memorandum Form

Complaint Knowledge Bank

TAB NO.	DESCRIPTION
1.	Complaint for personal injuries (auto accident)
2.	Complaint for personal injuries (slip and fall)
3.	Complaint for personal injuries (assault)
4.	Complaint for personal injuries (negligence)
5.	Complaint for medical malpractice
6.	Complaint for breach of contract
7.	Complaint for fraud
8.	
9.	
10.	

EXHIBIT 14–6   Sample Index Sheet for a Knowledge Bank

it is indexed, and the index should contain a short summary of each document's contents. The number and manner of coding the materials vary.

Automated work-product retrieval systems are used by large and medium-sized firms that have large knowledge banks. A large knowledge bank must be automated to manage the high number of documents in it. Many document management software products are used for knowledge banks and were discussed in Chapter 13.

There are four types of automated work-product retrieval systems: full-text, index, abstracts, and a combination of these. A full-text system provides word-by-word search capabilities that will review the entire text of document to find the desired subject. An index system searches for documents by fields that are customized by a firm. An abstract system searches an abstract, or summary, of a document.

An automated system allows a user to search a knowledge bank database according to a number of parameters, including author, date, client, type, and subject. If a paralegal is looking for a document that an attorney drafted for a particular client but cannot recall the date and name of the document, a search would list every document created by that attorney for that client. If a paralegal knows that research was conducted on a particular subject but cannot remember who conducted it or the date it was conducted, a search would list all documents prepared on a particular subject.

An automated system on a firm's network or intranet makes a knowledge bank available from each person's computer terminal. Attorneys and paralegals locate a document on a computer and either view or print it without leaving their desk. Without a network, a knowledge bank is found on a dedicated computer in the library. Many librarians periodically circulate a list of the contents of a knowledge bank to inform attorneys and paralegals of changes and additions to the bank.

Documents in knowledge banks become obsolete with changes in the law. Pruning a knowledge bank is an important but often overlooked task. When a change is made in the law or in the procedure of a case, obsolete documents must be removed from the system and replaced with a current document. The index must also be updated when a knowledge bank is pruned. An attorney relying on outdated law or a paralegal drafting an incorrect document have grave consequences for a firm and a client. A document's date should be inserted on the document before inserting it into the knowledge bank. If a change occurs, the outdated nature of the document can be determined quickly and the document replaced with a current one.

Many paralegals create and maintain their own knowledge banks. A personal knowledge bank is very helpful and saves a paralegal time. Some paralegals prepare a personal knowledge bank as samples of their work to show prospective employers and to take with them if they should leave a firm. Before so doing, however, a paralegal should have explicit permission from the employer, preferably in writing. *Work that was created while employed belongs to the employer.* To keep a personal knowledge bank useful, a paralegal must be diligent about pruning the knowledge bank and discarding obsolete documents to keep it updated.

THE LAW LIBRARIAN

The role of a law librarian is changing with the information explosion. The trend in hiring law firm librarians has coincided with the increased use of technology. As information becomes more accessible, a manager is needed to handle it. A librarian is this manager. With the advent of technology, a librarian's role is changing into that of an information manager. As such, a librarian must be familiar with a firm's network and software programs. As more firms market their services on the Internet through a website, many librarians are considered a firm's Web master, who is responsible for designing, updating, and monitoring a firm's website. As the role of the librarian changes with technological changes, some have changed their title from librarian to information manager.

As libraries become smaller with the use of electronic resources, attorneys who are not familiar with electronic research resources depend on a librarian for their electronic research needs. Librarians who do research projects for a firm charge a client for their time. A librarian's billing rate is lower than an attorney's but higher than a paralegal's. An assistant librarian also bills a client for research. An assistant librarian's billing rate is usually the same as that of a paralegal.

Among the duties of a law librarian are the following:

- *Research.* Provide research services to attorneys and paralegals. Most librarians are generalists and are familiar with most areas of law. However, librarians increasingly tend to specialize in a particular area of law.
- *Collection development.* Acquire, retain, and preserve library materials. The American Library Association defines collection development as "the process of planning, building and maintaining a library's information resources in a cost-effective and user-relevant manner."
- *Library maintenance.* File supplements and pocket parts, shelve books, and organize library materials, including CD-ROMs. Library maintenance is a daily function of a law librarian.
- *Indexing.* Develop and maintain a catalog and index of all library materials.
- *Establish library policy.* Establish loan policies and procedures and monitor a firm's library loan program.
- *Organization.* Manage and organize the court form files and knowledge bank.
- *Training.* Train the firm's employees on the use of a library and the firm's computer programs to keep attorneys and paralegals informed of library acquisitions.
- *Management.* Manage the financial aspects of a library, such as accounts payable and budgets.
- *Personnel management.* Manage library staff, such as assistant librarians.
- *Planning.* Plan for library growth.
- *Web maintenance.* Manage the firm's website and keep it updated.

In addition, some librarians have duties outside the library, such as managing paralegal or secretarial staff. Some librarians may also manage a central filing area.

A law librarian devotes full time to a firm's library and is found in large firms with large libraries. Most librarians in large firms have a master of library science degree, and some have a law degree. In small and medium-sized firms, paralegals and experienced legal secretaries act as librarians. Many paralegals are finding the librarian profession an exciting and challenging adjunct to their paralegal education. Paralegals are excellent candidates for the position of librarian, as discussed in the Professional Profile.

The twenty-first century offers exciting innovations to existing law library resources available through technology. We will also see changes to the manner in which we use the library. These changes will require us to develop new research and organizational skills to manage the information.

PROFESSIONAL PROFILE 1

Melonia Nixon had no particular interest in libraries and was somewhat disappointed in her first job. After earning her paralegal certificate from Davidson County Community College, she was hired as a librarian and part-time receptionist at Womble, Carlyle, Sandridge & Rise in Winston-Salem, North Carolina.

"In those early days, there weren't many law firms in North Carolina that used legal assistants," she says. "Womble Carlyle needed a librarian. I'd had a legal bibliography course in my legal assistant program, and I'd written a manual on library procedures for it. Plus, I could do research, and they liked that."

The library at Womble Carlyle was relatively well organized when Nixon took over. She did the updating and filed all the library material in addition to taking over for the receptionist during lunch and breaks. But Nixon soon was faced with managing a library for a firm that was experiencing phenomenal growth. Within 2 years, she was working in the library full time.

The firm's size increased from about 30 lawyers in one office to over 140 attorneys with offices in Winston-Salem, Raleigh, and Charlotte. Nixon manages the library operations for all three offices.

Nixon now has two full-time and two part-time assistants on her staff in the Winston-Salem office who file loose-leaf services, handle photocopying requests, and shelve. Library assistants manage the libraries in each of the branch offices under Nixon's direction.

Nixon handles all the administrative work of the 15,000-volume main library and the two branch office libraries. She helps attorneys with research, including computer-assisted research. Lately, she has concentrated her efforts on automating the library and research operations. "Systems that worked for a small- and medium-sized firm don't work for us now that we are so large," says Nixon. "Automation is a necessity."

"I've attended computer training courses to learn how to build databases and general reports to make managing the library more efficient and effective," she says. "I want to use the new technology to the fullest to continue building the library into an information resource for the attorneys and other employees."

Over the years, Nixon has learned a lot from other librarians by attending the American Association of Law Libraries (AALL) conventions and meetings of the Southeastern Chapter of AALL. "My job is not the same as it was 10 years ago," she says. "The best advice I can give to others who manage law libraries is to plan for growth and change."

"I never thought I'd be in this career," she says, "but now I wouldn't trade what I do for anything."

SOURCE: Adapted by permission of James Publishing Company and *Legal Assistant Today*, September/October 1988.

CONCLUSION

Law firm libraries are getting smaller. As attorneys are becoming comfortable with online reference materials and electronic libraries, volumes of books are being replaced by electronic data. Additionally, as electronic research services, such as WESTLAW, become more affordable, more legal professionals find that source materials are more conveniently located through them. Soon, law firm' libraries will be **virtual libraries.**

A virtual library is an electronic library without regard to physical space or location. A virtual library may include CD-ROMs, Internet subscriptions, lists of annotated Web links, internal work products (such as brief banks), proprietary databases (such as LexisNexis or WESTLAW), and even Web spiders or push technology that deliver targeted research to the user. There are advantages and disadvantages to a virtual library.

An obvious disadvantage is that a virtual library requires power to operate. If there is no power, there is no library. Another disadvantage is that legal professionals are still more comfortable with books. As a new generation of legal professionals comes into the workplace, this comfort level will switch to electronic media. Until then, law libraries will continue to be a carefully planned mix of electronic and paper resources.

virtual library
A virtual library is an electronic library without regard to physical space or location.

SUMMARY

The law library has served as a symbol of the practice of law for centuries and as a symbol of an attorney's knowledge. Two types of knowledge exist: knowledge we have about a subject and knowledge of where to find information about a subject. A law library is where attorneys and paralegals obtain knowledge.

Millions of laws are in effect today. Organizing laws in an orderly manner so that each law is easily found is a huge undertaking. Library management is a function of law office management.

The U.S. legal system consists of two types of law: written law and common law. Civil law is derived from Roman law and is based on a series of written laws. There are two main sources of written law: constitutions and statutes. Common law, also known as case law, evolved in England, where there were no written laws. The U.S. legal system uses both written law and case law, with the exception of a few states.

One of the most important aspects of legal editorial work is classifying the law, which is placing laws into categories. This helps us find laws quickly. If decisions were not classified, it would be extremely difficult, if not impossible, to find a case.

There are four areas of law: type of action, laws that apply to individuals, nature of law, and source of law. There are two types of legal actions: civil and criminal. Two types of laws apply to individuals: public laws and private laws. A law can be either substantive or procedural in nature, and a law is categorized by its source.

There are three classes of law: primary authority, secondary authority, and search tools. Primary authority consists of laws made by the three branches of government: executive, legislative, and judicial. A legislature also enacts procedural law, which consists of laws governing the legal procedure used to redress wrong or injury. Primary authority consists of constitutions, statutes, judicial opinions, court rules, and administrative regulations and decisions.

The most commonly used statutes are organized according to subject matter. Statutes may be either annotated or unannotated. In a library, annotated statutes are placed where they are most accessible.

As new laws are passed, it is essential to have immediate access to them. Pocket parts must be inserted into the back of the applicable volumes as soon as they are received to keep laws updated.

Books called reporters contain the text of judicial opinions as they are made. Thousands of volumes of reporters are published, and the volumes of each reporter are numbered consecutively. When an opinion is first printed, it is known as a slip opinion. Reporters contain hundreds of volumes and occupy a lot of shelf space in a library.

Every law library contains court rules. In addition to court rules governing federal and state courts, each federal and state court creates local rules. Court rules are placed in the library, where they can be accessible quickly. Court rules are updated by a publisher or the particular court.

Administrative law governs the powers and procedures of administrative agencies. There is no reporter of agency decisions, such as the West Reporter System for Federal Courts. State agency administrative regulations and decisions are published chronologically, although some states codify their regulations. Only large libraries will contain administrative rulings.

Secondary authority is anything other than primary authority that aids a court in reaching a decision. Secondary authority includes commentary material written by legal scholars or experts in a particular field. Treatises are legal commentaries on various subjects of law. Periodicals are booklets concerning articles about the law. Every law library has a legal dictionary, and large libraries may contain more than one legal dictionary. Encyclopedias are volumes that contain statements on principles of law and are organized alphabetically by subject matter. Large libraries contain many volumes of secondary authority. As the law changes, editors will write some annotations to commentaries of treatises that supersede older annotations.

Search books help a researcher find a primary authority. Search tools consist of digests and citators. A citator is a valuable addition to a law library.

Every law office, corporate legal department, and government agency has a library or access to a law library. Law libraries are described according to size. Small libraries that contain only the books essential for the lawyers' needs are called skeletal libraries. Libraries that contain a comprehensive collection of the laws are called complete libraries.

Three types of library organization are used: centralized, decentralized, and satellite. A centralized library is found in one location that has been set aside by a firm. A decentralized library is distributed throughout a firm. Satellite libraries are found in large firms with a large centralized library. Tax and labor libraries are the most common satellite libraries.

All libraries, whether centralized, decentralized, or satellite, must have a system that will locate every book in them. A library checkout system consists of procedures to locate library materials. The three most common checkout systems used in law firm libraries are the out-card, bar code, and library card systems. A library out-card system is used like an out-card system for files, which is described in Chapter 13. Some firms have bar codes placed on their books, and the system is used like the one described in Chapter 13 for bar coded files. A popular checkout system for library books is the library card system.

Technology has had a great effect on the traditional law library. Five types of technology are used in law libraries. Online legal and nonlegal databases are the most common type of technology found in law offices today. Information may be quickly retrieved through a legal database. Nonlegal databases operate the same as legal databases but contain nonlegal information. Legal and nonlegal databases may also be accessed from the Internet.

Microform is the process of storing information photographically in reduced form. Microfilm is the most popular method of microform in law libraries. Microform is especially useful for preserving volumes of out-of-print law books.

CD-ROMs can be found in our homes and offices and contain software, text, music, or movies. Legal publishers make material found in law books available on CD-ROMs and sell the disks to their customers. With CD-ROMs, a large law firm with a centralized library can make portions of its library available to other areas of the firm, making access to the library more convenient. One problem with CD-ROMs is that their data are often not current. Law firms have been reluctant to replace law books with CD-ROMs and have had problems with CD-ROM technology.

Telefacsimile (fax) machines send documents from one location to another electronically over telephone lines. As law firm libraries are stepping into their role of information centers, they must have access to a variety of information that may be needed by researchers. Large firms with large libraries often lend materials to other firms and provide library materials to their branch offices via e-mail and fax machines.

The Internet is the information superhighway that is absorbing other legal media types, such as print, CD-ROM, and online database services. Access to federal and state statutes and court decisions is available on the Internet for free. However, as of this writing, the Internet is not a better research tool than other, conventional types of technology used in law libraries. However, the Internet is an important medium of gathering and disseminating information in new and powerful ways.

The emergence of electronic legal research has created the need for new methods of citing the material. The American Association of Law Libraries (AALL) recognized the need for a new citation format for these materials and recommended that an electronic legal cite include the case name, year of the decision, specific court, a consecutively assigned case number, and paragraph number for the exact location of the quote. Many other groups have also made recommendations for citing electronic documents, including the American Psychological Association and the Modern Language Association of America (MLA). As of 2007, no universally accepted citation system for electronic documents exists.

Court forms, form files, and knowledge banks are found in law libraries. Every law office must have an adequate supply of court forms, which are form documents used in a specific court. Court forms must be located quickly. There are three methods of storing court forms: manually, as masters that are photocopied, and by using computer programs. Court forms are normally organized alphabetically by subject matter. Problems with storage and access to court forms are solved with computer-generated forms. Forms other than court forms are also used by a law office.

The knowledge of employees is a firm's most valuable asset and must be gathered into a knowledge bank. A knowledge bank contains briefs, research memoranda, opinion letters, pleadings, discovery requests, contracts, leases, and articles that may be useful in a future case. When paralegals and attorneys prepare a complex document or do comprehensive research on a subject, a copy of the document or research is deposited in the firm's knowledge bank.

Before a knowledge bank is useful, its contents must be accessible. There are two types of work retrieval systems: manual and automated. A manual system is used by small firms and consists of documents kept in three-ring binders, with one binder containing documents for one subject. Automated work retrieval systems are used by large and medium-sized firms that have large knowledge banks.

There are four types of automated work retrieval systems: full-text, index, abstracts, and a combination of these. An automated system allows a user to search a knowledge bank database according to a number of parameters, including author, date, client, type, and subject. An automated system on a firm's network or intranet makes a knowledge bank available from each person's computer terminal. Documents in knowledge banks become obsolete with changes in the law and must be updated periodically.

The role of a law librarian is changing with the information explosion. With the advent of technology, a librarian's role is changing into that of an information manager. Among the duties of a law librarian are research, collection development, library maintenance, indexing, establishing library policy, organization, training, management, personnel management, planning, and Web maintenance. In addition, some librarians have additional duties outside the library, such as managing paralegals or secretarial staff. A law librarian devotes full time to a firm's library and is found in large firms with large libraries.

Law firm libraries are getting smaller. Soon, law firm' libraries will be virtual libraries. A virtual library is an electronic library without regard to physical space or location. Legal professionals are still more comfortable with books. As a new generation of legal professionals comes into the workplace, this comfort level will switch to electronic media. Until then, law libraries will continue to be a carefully planned mix of electronic and paper resources.

CHAPTER ILLUSTRATION

The law firm of Black, White & Greene has a skeletal library consisting of state statutes, state reporters, court rules, and some form books. The firm also has a set of tax codes and books relating to tax law for Grant. The library is decentralized throughout the office. Shelves of library books line the office walls. Employees retrieve the books they need and use them in their individual offices. If a person needs more room for research, she or he uses the conference room.

The conference room is used more for research than for conferences. The employees refer to it as the "war room" because stacks of books and papers are scattered all over the conference room table. If the conference room is needed for a conference, at least 2 hours' notice is required so that it can be cleaned up.

Tricia, as office manager, was responsible for maintaining the library. As pocket parts and advance sheets would come in, they would pile up in Tricia's office until she had time to update the library. However, she never had the time, and the updating got way behind. The attorneys started to complain about the condition of the library, so Tricia delegated library maintenance to Kay, the file clerk.

"That's an easy job," said Kay, cheerfully. "Sure, I'll do it. It shouldn't take much time."

Kay accepted her new responsibility with a smile. As pocket parts and advance sheets would come in, Kay would insert them in the books. Tricia was impressed that Kay did not allow the library updates to get behind.

One day, as Robert retrieved the court rules, he noticed that it would not close completely. He then noticed a pocket part in the court rules. He showed the book to Tricia. "What's going on here?" he asked. "There are pocket parts in the court rules and advance sheets in the statutes."

"Oh no!" said Tricia. "I'll talk to Kay about it to find out what's going on."

Tricia approached Kay and asked her how she was updating the library. "Fine," said Kay. "Is there a problem?"

"Yes." Tricia said. "The problem is that pocket parts are put in the court rules, and advance sheets are inserted in the statutes!" exclaimed Tricia.

"What's a pocket part?" asked Kay. "I've never heard of an advance sheet."

"What? You said this would be an easy assignment when I gave it to you," said Tricia. "I assumed you knew how a law library was updated."

"It was easy," said Kay. "I watched you do it, and it looked easy. I didn't know they had to be put in specific books. I'm sorry, Tricia," said Kay.

"Don't worry about it, Kay," said Tricia. "We'll fix it. By the way, you don't have to worry about updating the library anymore."

Every book in the entire library had to be reviewed and updated. No one in the firm had time to do it, so Tricia called Law Library Services, a company that comes to law firms to maintain their libraries. The library consultants came in and updated the entire law library. They also agreed to come to the firm once a month to take care of the library updates and to make sure that the library was in good order.

Tricia received a request from George for a set of restatements that he thought would help him with a case he was working on. Tricia checked her library budget and approved the order. The firm was quickly running out of library space to store the new volumes of statutes and reporters that were delivered each month. When the restatements arrived, there was not enough shelf space to store them. The only space available for the restatements was in George's office. Tricia contacted a cabinetmaker to build new shelves in George's office for the restatements, as this was the only space left in the office for books. The firm had no room left for new volumes or updates.

At the monthly management meeting, Tricia discussed the library space problem and told the attorneys that soon there would be no space left to store new volumes of reporters as they came in. Patrizia recommended that the firm consider using CD-ROMs for their reporters, replacing the books with the CDs.

"Just think of the shelf space we would save," said Patrizia. "One whole section of books, 250 of them, can be put on one CD. We could put the CD on the intranet and everyone in the firm would have access to it simultaneously. It is really fast and convenient. As changes are made, we get a new CD replacing the outdated one. It's really nifty."

"Yes," said George. "Some firms have a lot of volumes on CDs. Some have hundreds of CDs instead of thousands of books. It's the wave of the future. They store all these CDs in a jukebox, which is accessible from the firm's network. Everyone has access to the library from their computers. There're no books to put away, no lost books, no books to look for, and, uh, the conference room is always clean!"

"How much does it cost?" asked Tricia. "I'm not real sure," said George. "I think the cost of CDs is comparable to the cost of books. I read somewhere that legal publishers have package deals where you can get discounts if you're an established customer."

"I heard that the Internet was the wave of the future," said Dennis. "You can find all the statutes on the Internet. And, it's free."

"Yeah," said George, "but you can't find all the cases. As of now, case law on the Internet goes back only to 1960 or so. I think all the federal statutes are on the Internet, but I'm not sure about all the state statutes."

Patrizia responded, "My problem with the Internet is that it's hard to know how reliable it is. It's hard to know if a website can be trusted to be accurate and current. Government and university websites are reliable, but I don't know about the rest. If you want to do research on the Internet, what about an online legal database such as WESTLAW? It costs a fee, but they guarantee that their information is current and accurate."

Robert chimed in, "Hey, let me tell you about Internet research. I had to find a law regarding interstate trucking licensing requirements, so I did a search on the Web. I put the words "interstate trucking license" into a search engine and got 43,768 results. It took me hours to weed them out to find the information I needed. There's no way I can charge the client for all the time I spent. The Internet may be free, but it's very expensive in terms of time."

Tricia said, "I can see that we have a lot of options to expand our library without expanding our space requirements. I'll do a cost analysis to find out what is best and submit my report to you at the next meeting."

At the next meeting, Tricia reported her findings. The attorneys agreed that the firm will establish an account with WESTLAW, which will give them access to all the law they will need. The legal database will be put on the firm's intranet and be accessible by everyone in the firm from their computers.

"My research indicates that most firms charge their clients for the cost of online legal research," said Tricia. "Therefore, the service should pay for itself."

"Sounds good," said George. "Now, I can hold my conferences in the conference room!"

CHAPTER REVIEW

1. What are the four categories of laws?
2. What are the three classes of law?
3. What is a skeletal library, and what type of attorneys utilize a skeletal library?
4. What is the difference between a complete library and a large library?
5. Describe the three types of library organization.
6. Describe the three types of library checkout systems.
7. Describe the five types of library technology.
8. Describe how court forms are organized.
9. How is a manual knowledge bank organized?
10. What are the four types of automated work retrieval systems?
11. What are the duties of a law librarian?

EXAMPLES FOR DISCUSSION

1. THE MISMANAGED LIBRARY

The law firm of Smith & Jones is a medium-sized firm located in Cincinnati. It has an average-sized centralized library that contains a large worktable in the center of the library. The attorneys and paralegals do research at the table as well as in their individual offices. The firm has no law librarian and has delegated the function of library maintenance to a paralegal, Cindy Anderson, with the help of the receptionist, Marion Malloy.

The library is a constant mess. Books are left on the table in piles and are missing from the shelves and cannot be found. Boxes of new pocket parts, updates, and supplements have been stacked to the ceiling for months. The attorneys and paralegals constantly complain to Cindy that they cannot find the information they need to complete their projects. Cindy is assigned to a very large case that is going to trial soon. There is a lot of work to do on the case and very little time to complete her projects. She is under constant pressure.

Cindy has stayed late and come in on Saturdays to maintain the library. However, she spends most of her time looking for books that are scattered all over the firm. Once the books are put away, the day is gone. Marion tries to help Cindy, but as soon as she goes into the library, the phone rings. She cannot get away from her desk. New updates keep coming in. Cindy is at her wits' end.

1. What are the problems with this library?
2. If you were the manager, what would you do to remedy the problem?
3. Assume there is no money for a librarian's salary. What systems and controls would you implement?
4. If you were Cindy, how would you handle the problem?
5. How could technology help this situation?

2. THE PROBLEM ATTORNEY

Dennis Vaughan is the librarian for a large firm in Chicago. He has implemented a library card checkout system for the library. Each attorney, paralegal, and law clerk has a box in which library cards are placed if a book leaves the library.

Dennis has had great success with this system. Most of the firm's employees are diligent about using the system when they check out books. One attorney, however, refuses to use the system. She removes books from the library without placing the library cards in her box. She often takes books home and to court, and Dennis spends hours trying to locate them. Dennis has talked to her many times about complying with the system's requirements, but to no avail.

1. If you were Dennis, how would you remedy this problem?
2. Would you change the checkout system? If so, how? With no additional funds in the library budget? With unlimited funds in the library budget?
3. How could technology help this problem?

3. THE VIRTUAL LIBRARY

This chapter discusses the various types of technology used in law libraries. Do you foresee a bookless library? If so, why? If not, why not? Describe what technology would be the dominant technology in a virtual (bookless) library. Is it the Internet? If so, what are the advantages and disadvantages to an Internet virtual library? A CD-ROM virtual library? How would a virtual library affect the practice of law?

ASSIGNMENTS

1. Go to a library near you and ask to use its microfilm to find an article on a subject that interests you. Note how to place the microfilm in the reader. Print a copy of the article

and bring it to your instructor. Write a procedural manual informing other students how to use microfilm.

2. Tour law libraries in your area. Tour a large centralized library, a scattered library, and a satellite library. Write a descriptive report of your tour and include the following:

   a. How the library materials are organized and distributed

   b. The checkout procedures

   c. The advantages and disadvantages of each style of organization

   d. Whether each library has a librarian (if so, describe the duties of the librarian; if not, report who is responsible for maintaining the library and describe their duties)

   e. Whether the libraries use technology (if so, report what type)

3. You are the librarian for a large firm with a large library. On a piece of graph paper, illustrate how you would organize the library. Include placement of the following:

   a. Statutes

   b. Reporters

   c. Treatises

   d. Encyclopedias

   e. Dictionaries

   f. Knowledge bank

   g. Form files

4. You are the librarian for a large firm. The managing partner wants to purchase an additional set of your state's statutes and asked you to prepare a cost analysis of acquiring an additional set of statutes. Research the cost of the statutes, including update service. Consider CD-ROM and online legal databases in your analysis. Make a recommendation at the end of your report. Also include a yearly budget for the cost of the statutes.

5. Go to the Internet sites listed in the Cybersites section and research the current status of electronic citation recommendations of the various groups. Prepare a report to the class and include your opinion as to which system is the best.

SELF TEST

How well did you grasp the material in the chapter? Test yourself by answering the following questions, and check your answers against the answers found in Appendix A.

1. How has a law library been a symbol of the practice of law?

2. What does a law library symbolize?

3. What are the two types of knowledge?

4. What is the highest law in the land?

5. What is the highest law in a state?

6. How are federal laws created?

7. By what laws is each individual governed?

8. Why should a paralegal be comfortable in a law library?

9. What is the first step in understanding a law library?

10. What is the second step in understanding a law library?

11. Who maintains a library in a small firm?

12. On what two types of law is our legal system based?

13. On what is civil law based?

14. From what was civil law derived?

15. How early were laws written?
16. What are the two main sources of written law?
17. What is common law?
18. Where did common law originate?
19. Reports of court decisions were first compiled into what?
20. What is stare decisis?
21. How was stare decisis established?
22. Where did most laws of the United States originate?
23. What does codify mean?
24. What is the classification of law?
25. When and where was the classification process introduced?
26. What was the name of the first legal index?
27. Why are laws categorized?
28. How are laws categorized?
29. How many laws are made each year?
30. How is case law classified?
31. What are the four functions of law?
32. What are the two types of legal actions filed?
33. Who is the plaintiff in a criminal action?
34. Why are criminal cases prosecuted by the government?
35. What are the two types of remedies available in a civil case?
36. What is monetary relief?
37. What is equitable relief?
38. What are the two types of laws that apply to individuals?
39. What are public laws?
40. What are private laws?
41. What are the two natures of law?
42. What are substantive laws?
43. What are damages?
44. What are procedural laws?
45. What are the sources of law?
46. What are the three classes of law?
47. Of what does primary authority consist?
48. Who enacts primary authority?
49. Who enacts procedural law?
50. Who creates laws governing the rules and procedures of the court system?
51. What are local rules?
52. What types of law is primary authority?
53. How are statutes organized?
54. What do large libraries contain?
55. What are annotated statutes?
56. What are unannotated statutes?
57. Where are annotated statutes placed in a library?
58. Where are unannotated statutes placed?
59. How are new laws published?
60. What is a pocket part?

61. What numbering system does a pocket part use?
62. How often is a new edition of the statutes published?
63. Where are pocket parts placed in a book?
64. Why should pocket parts not be allowed to accumulate?
65. What are books that contain judicial opinions called?
66. How are the volumes of a report numbered?
67. What is a series?
68. When does a publisher produce a new series of reporters?
69. How are reporters placed in a library?
70. Why do many libraries not contain the first series in a reporter set?
71. What is a slip opinion?
72. What is an advance sheet?
73. When are advance sheets sent to law libraries?
74. Where are advance sheets placed in a library?
75. What is done with advance sheets when a new volume has been printed?
76. When were court rules first developed?
77. What are court rules?
78. What are the three purposes of court rules?
79. What are local rules?
80. Where are court rules placed in a library?
81. Who updates court rules?
82. Who establishes an administrative agency?
83. Who publishes opinions from administrative agencies?
84. How are state agency administrative regulations and decisions published?
85. What type of library contains administrative rulings?
86. What is secondary authority?
87. Why was secondary authority developed?
88. How is secondary authority used?
89. What types of documents does secondary authority include?
90. What is a treatise, and what is its purpose?
91. What are periodicals, and what is their purpose?
92. Why are indexes published?
93. What is the name of the most established index service?
94. What is a legal dictionary?
95. What are encyclopedias, and how are they organized?
96. How are encyclopedias categorized?
97. How are the volumes of secondary authority placed in a library?
98. Where is a dictionary placed in a library?
99. When are treatises updated?
100. What is the purpose of search tools?
101. When are search tools cited?
102. What is a digest?
103. How is a digest arranged?
104. What is a citator?
105. What happens when a statute is repealed?
106. What are form books?

107. What determines a library's organization?
108. How are law libraries described?
109. What is a skeletal library?
110. What does a skeletal library contain?
111. What are complete law libraries?
112. Where are complete law libraries found?
113. What is the largest complete law library in the United States?
114. What are the three types of library organization?
115. What is a centralized library?
116. What size firm has a centralized library?
117. What is a library cooperative?
118. What is a decentralized library?
119. Where do attorneys and paralegals use the books in a decentralized library?
120. What types of firms have decentralized libraries?
121. What are the three advantages to a decentralized library?
122. What are the disadvantages to a decentralized library?
123. What is a satellite library?
124. What type of firm has a satellite library?
125. Where are satellite libraries located?
126. What are the most common satellite libraries?
127. Why must a library be maintained so that it is always current?
128. What is an update service?
129. When should law books be updated?
130. Where is most of a law library's budget spent?
131. What are the three most common checkout systems used in law libraries?
132. What are some problems with an out-card system?
133. What is a bar code system?
134. What is a library card system?
135. How are law libraries getting smaller?
136. What are the five types of technology used in law libraries?
137. What is an online legal database?
138. What is computer-assisted legal research (CALR)?
139. What does "full text" mean?
140. What are the two primary CALR systems?
141. What is an abstract system?
142. What is a nonlegal database?
143. How can a legal database be accessed from the Internet?
144. What is microform?
145. What is microfilm?
146. What is microfiche?
147. How many books does a 100-foot roll of microfilm contain?
148. How many microfiche cards are needed to photograph one book?
149. After documents are put on microfilm, how is it viewed?
150. Why is microform useful for preserving volumes of books?
151. What is the lifetime of microfilm?
152. What does "CD-ROM" stand for?

153. How many books can a CD-ROM store?
154. What is a megabyte?
155. How is material on a CD-ROM accessed?
156. What is a jukebox?
157. How many CD-ROMs does a jukebox hold?
158. Why are CD-ROMs not current?
159. What is a user interface?
160. What is the lifetime of a CD?
161. How have e-mail and the fax machine reduced the number of lost library materials?
162. According to the 2007 Technology Survey conducted by *Legal Assistant Today*, what percentage of responding paralegals conducted research on the Internet?
163. What factors contributed to law being put on the Internet?
164. What type of information is not found on the Internet?
165. What is a problem with conducting research over the Internet?
166. Why does it take longer to do research on the Internet?
167. What book is used as a guide to legal citations?
168. What electronic citation system did the AALL recommend?
169. What electronic citation system did the ABA recommend?
170. What electronic citation system is universally accepted?
171. For what are court forms used?
172. What are the three methods of storing court forms?
173. Where are manual court forms stored, and how are they filed?
174. Where are photocopier-created court forms stored?
175. What are computer-generated court forms?
176. Who is responsible for distributing new court forms?
177. What does a knowledge bank contain?
178. How does using a knowledge bank increase efficiency?
179. What are the two types of work-product retrieval systems?
180. What type of firm uses a manual work-product retrieval system?
181. How are documents filed in a manual system?
182. What is required to locate a document in a manual system?
183. How is an index prepared?
184. How is the document indexed if it has more than one subject matter?
185. What is a research index memorandum form, and what is its purpose?
186. What type of firm uses an automated work-product retrieval system?
187. Why must a large knowledge bank be automated?
188. What are the four types of automated work-product retrieval systems?
189. What is required for a knowledge bank to be available on each employee's computer system?
190. Where are knowledge banks found if a firm does not have a network?
191. What has been responsible for the changing role of the law librarian?
192. What are the duties of a law librarian?
193. What additional duties may a law librarian have outside of the library?
194. In what type of law firm may a law librarian be found?
195. What type of degree do most librarians in a large firm have?
196. What is a virtual library?
197. What does a virtual library contain?

Key Words

abstract system	full text	reporter
advance sheet	library cooperative	restatement
affirm	local rules	series
annotated	megabyte	skeletal library
CD-ROM	microfiche	slip opinion
CD-ROM drive	microfilm	stare decisis
citator	microform	substantive law
codify	monetary relief	telefacsimile
complete library	overrule	unannotated
computer-assisted legal research	pocket part	update service
damages	procedural law	user interface
digest	repeal	virtual library
equitable relief		

Cybersites

FINDING LEGAL RESEARCH SITES ON THE WEB

Findlaw—<*http://www.findlaw.com*>

Court Rules—<*http://www.llrx.com*>

General Regulations—<*http://www.access.gpo.gov*>

Tech Legislation—<*http://www.techlawjournal.com*>

State Legislative Reports—<*http://www.statenet.com*>

Library of Congress Thomas—<*http://www.thomas.loc.gov*>

Fast Search—<*http://www.fastsearch.com*>

Search Engine—<*http://www.dogpile.com*>

Legal Ethics—<*http://www.legalethics.com*>

Attorney Finders—<*http://www.martindale.com*>

Expert Witnesses—<*http://www.expertwitness.com*>

Legal Research Service VersusLaw—<*http://www.versuslaw.com*>

Law Guru—<*http://www.lawguru.com*>

WESTLAW—<*http://www.westlaw.com*>

Index of legal and governmental indexes—<*http://www.catalaw.com*>

Internet Legal Research Group—<*http://www.ilrg.com*>

Online dictionary—<*http://www.thefreedictionary.com*>

The Public Library of Law—<*http://www.plol.org*>

FINDING ELECTRONIC CITATION RULES ON THE WEB

Citation of Legal and Non-Legal Electronic Database Information, by Candace Person—<*http://www.michbar.org/publicationscitation.cfm*>

Developing a Standard for Legal Citation—<*http://www.murdoch.edu.au/elaw/*>

How to Cite Electronic Sources—<*http://www.law.cornell.edu/citation/2_100.htm*>

LAW LIBRARIES

American Association of Law Libraries—<*http://www.aallnet.org*>
Integrated Library System Reports—<*http://www.ilsr.com*>
Law Library Resource Exchange—<*http://www.llrx.com*>

MICROFORM

Microform Information—<*http://www.microform.com*>
Law Library Microform Consortium—<*http://www.llmc.com*>

 Student CD-ROM
For additional materials, please go to the CD in this book.

 Online Companion™
For additional resources, please go to http://www.paralegal.delmar.cengage.com

Chapter 1

The Legal Marketplace

1. The four things that determine the structure and organization of a law office are size, specialty, management style, and form.
2. The size of a law office is measured by the number of attorneys employed by that office and includes branch offices.
3. The geographic location of the office determines the size differential of a law office.
4. The majority of lawyers prefer to practice in small firms.
5. The four types of large law firms are local, regional, national, and international.
6. A mega firm employs 1,000 or more attorneys and has branch offices all over the world.
7. The complexity of the law has forced attorneys to specialize.
8. Specialty areas determine the firm's clientele and its need for staff, equipment, and resources.
9. A law office's culture is its working environment. It consists of intangible elements, such as the social environment, employee relationships, and attitudes.
10. The five management styles are autocratic, democratic, managing partner, committees, and combination.
11. An autocratic form of governance is one in which one attorney is responsible for all management and decision-making responsibilities.
12. The two types of the democratic form of governance are those in which all attorneys in the firm have a vote on management policy and those in which only owners of the law firm have a vote in management policy.
13. A legal administrator is an experienced manager who is hired to manage a law firm and has the authority of a managing partner.
14. An office manager is a person hired to assist a managing partner or legal administrator with the management functions of a firm.
15. The managing partner is the most common management style.
16. The managing partner is encouraged to practice law in addition to management duties to increase the firm's revenues and keep his or her skills sharp.
17. An executive committee is composed of heads of various committees.
18. A combination management style is a combination of the following management styles: autocratic, democratic, managing partner, and committee.
19. The two forms of management are centralized and decentralized.
20. A sole proprietor is one attorney who owns the law firm.
21. A general practitioner is an attorney who does not specialize in a particular area of law.
22. The five most common specialties for sole proprietors are family law, real estate, torts and personal injury, criminal defense, and probate and estate planning.
23. Contract attorneys work only for other attorneys.
24. The three classes of attorneys that work in a partnership are partners, associates, and nontraditional.
25. Only attorneys may be shareholders of a professional legal corporation.
26. The board of directors of a professional corporation is elected by its shareholders and is the policymaking body of the corporation.
27. An LLC is a limited liability company formed to shield its owners and their assets from liability arising from the misconduct of other owners or employees.
28. A boutique firm is a small firm in which the attorneys specialize in one area of law.
29. The two types of office-sharing arrangements are the suite concept and the firm concept.

30. Cost control motivates an attorney to seek an office-sharing arrangement.
31. Legal clinics are legal offices formed for the purpose of providing low-income people with free or low-cost legal services.
32. Legal clinics receive funding from federal and state grants, private contributions, and fundraising events.
33. Some legal clinics may take litigation cases, but most of their cases are family issues, landlord-tenant, immigration, public benefits, and contracts.
34. An outside counsel is an attorney retained by a corporation.
35. Preventative law avoids legal problems before they occur.
36. A corporate legal department functions as a part of the whole corporation around the projects of the corporation.
37. The head attorney in a corporate legal department is called general counsel.
38. In-house counsel are attorneys employed by the corporation.
39. Some of the areas in private industry that paralegals have utilized their paralegal training are the following:
    i. Insurance underwriter
    ii. Recruiting coordinator
    iii. Rehabilitation counselor
    iv. Consultant
    v. Sales representative
    vi. Employee benefits manager
    vii. Law firm administrator
    viii. Law firm marketing specialist
    ix. Corporate personnel director
    x. Commercial arbitrator
    xi. Corporate bond department manager
    xii. Association manager
    xiii. Writer
    xiv. Career counselor
    xv. Sales marketer
    xvi. Convention marketer
    xvii. Teacher
    xviii. Litigation consultant
    xix. Environmental specialist
    xx. Paralegal program director
    xxi. Editor
    xxii. Legal software trainer
    xxiii. Politician
    xxiv. Negotiator
    xxv. Investigator
    xxvi. Real estate broker
    xxvii. Civil rights analyst
    xxviii. Stockbroker
    xxix. Computer-related careers
    xxx. Law librarian
40. A freelance paralegal service provides services to firms on a contract basis. The paralegals are not firm employees.

41. An independent paralegal is a person who does law-related work for the general public without the supervision of an attorney.
42. Freelance paralegals may work in the attorney's office, rent their own offices, or work out of their homes.
43. A freelance paralegal should have at least 5 years of experience because the majority of attorneys utilizing freelance paralegals are new sole practitioners. They are not experienced enough to supervise a new paralegal adequately.
44. The four types of government agencies that employ paralegals are federal agencies, state agencies, county agencies, and local agencies.
45. The three largest employers of paralegals in the federal government are the Department of Health and Human Services, the Department of Justice, and the Department of Treasury.
46. The General Schedule is the government's largest white-collar pay system that lists paralegal positions.
47. The legal clerk/technician is a stepping-stone to a paralegal specialist position.
48. Among the opportunities at the county level are county counsel (who represents the county when the county is sued), district attorney offices, public defender offices, public administrator, and court clerk.
49. A paralegal specialist is classified under GS-950.
50. A multidisciplinary law practice is made up of a lawyer and a member of another profession who practice together to provide both legal and nonlegal services to a client.
51. Nonlegal subsidiaries are related, nonlegal businesses owned by attorneys.
52. Prepaid group legal plans are insurance plans that give their members low-cost legal services.

Chapter 2
The Legal Team

1. The advent of the paralegal and legal administrator has changed the traditional law firm.
2. The paralegal and legal administrator professions were created to increase lawyers' efficiency and incomes.
3. Paralegals perform routine tasks and legal administrators perform management duties. This relieves the attorney to practice law, which has increased a lawyer's efficiency.
4. The factors contributing to the growth of the paralegal profession are the following:
    i. Promotion by bar associations
    ii. Growth of paralegal education
    iii. Organization of paralegals and managers
    iv. Restructuring of other professions
5. The size and specialty of the firm determines the firm's need for personnel.

6. The four categories of attorneys are the following:
   i. Rainmakers
   ii. Owners
   iii. Associates and senior associates
   iv. Nontraditional

7. Rainmakers bring in the clients that provide the firm with work.

8. Associates do the work. Senior associates supervise junior associates.

9. Leveraging is making a profit on the work of others.

10. A leverage ratio is the number of attorneys and paralegals (income producers) per owner.

11. A permanent associate is an employed attorney who is not eligible for an ownership interest in a firm.

12. A staff attorney is an employee of a law firm who has no advancement opportunities.

13. Of-counsel refers to an attorney affiliated with a firm on a part-time basis.

14. A legal administrator is responsible for the management of the law firm.

15. The administrator is responsible for making major business decisions for the firm. An office manager is under the direction of the legal administrator or managing partner and does not have the authority of the administrator.

16. The three major differences between an administrator and office manager are the following:
   i. The administrator attends all partnership or committee meetings, although the administrator has no right to vote on issues.
   ii. An administrator has authority to hire and discharge staff personnel and administer salaries within approved guidelines.
   iii. An administrator has authority to make major purchases of furniture and equipment and make financial decisions for the firm.

17. A legal administrator in a large firm enjoys the same status and compensation as an attorney.

18. The legal administrator may be referred to as the chief operating officer or executive director.

19. In a small firm, the legal administrator has the same responsibilities as an administrator in a large firm, but on a smaller scale. This person may have other duties in addition to management duties, such as paralegal or accounting work.

20. The eight main areas of an administrator's responsibilities are the following:
   i. Financial management
   ii. Personnel management
   iii. Systems management
   iv. Facilities management
   v. General management
   vi. Practice management
   vii. Marketing
   viii. Leadership

21. The size of the firm and the amount of authority given the administrator determine the administrator's responsibilities.

22. Other types of law office managers are the following:
   i. Financial manager
   ii. Personnel manager
   iii. Administrative manager
   iv. Facilities manager
   v. Marketing manager
   vi. Paralegal manager

23. A paralegal manager's responsibilities are the following:
   i. Direct paralegal personnel matters and act as a liaison between legal assistants and firm management
   ii. Supervise paralegals
   iii. Coordinate paralegal workload and assign responsibilities
   iv. Train paralegals
   v. Verify that paralegal duties are performed in accordance with the attorney's instructions and act as a liaison between the paralegals and attorneys
   vi. Evaluate paralegals' performance
   vii. Oversee the firm's paralegal program
   viii. Establish policies and guidelines relating to the effective utilization of paralegals
   ix. Recruit and interview new paralegals
   x. Conduct orientation and training for new paralegals
   xi. Maintain paralegal personnel records.

24. A tiered paralegal program provides upward mobility for the paralegal by establishing categories of paralegal positions.

25. Paralegals advance by demonstrating abilities.

26. The majority of paralegals specialize in litigation.

27. A law clerk is a law student who works in a law office on a temporary basis.

28. Some firms have elaborate programs to attract the best law students from the best law schools. They want to establish a relationship with the student so that the student will consider being employed by that firm on graduation.

29. The law clerk's duties are legal research, writing memorandum of law, and case briefs.

30. The differences between a law clerk and a paralegal are the following:
   i. Law clerks are temporary employees of the firm.
   ii. A clerk's time may or may not be billed to the client.
   iii. Law clerks will not make a career of clerking.
   iv. Law clerks generally work part time while attending law school.

31. Legal secretaries are responsible for clerical tasks.

32. Receptionists are responsible for answering the telephone and greeting clients.

33. Law librarians manage information and the firm's library. They also do research projects.

34. Investigators investigate cases and interview witnesses.
35. Messengers run errands for the firm.
36. Recruiters recruit new attorneys and law clerks.
37. Process servers are responsible for service of process.
38. Case coordinators have the responsibility for the successful management of a case.
39. Outsourcing is the use of outside service companies for support staff functions.
40. An attorney service picks up documents from the firm and files them with the court. It also does service of process and other services.
41. Paralegal services work for attorneys on a contract basis.

Chapter 3

Personnel Relations

1. A firm's personnel are its most important resource.
2. Finding the right place to work is important for personal character building, self-esteem, and overall happiness in life.
3. A manager's performance can be measured by two characteristics: effectiveness and efficiency.
4. The three main objectives of a law firm are the following:
   i. Provide quality legal services to the client
   ii. Provide growth and profit for the firm
   iii. Provide growth and satisfaction of the employees
5. The three main objectives of a government office are the following:
   i. Provide quality legal services to the government or the people
   ii. Operate within the budget set by the government
   iii. Provide growth and satisfaction of the employees
6. The three main objectives of a corporate legal department are the following:
   i. Provide quality legal services to the corporation
   ii. Keep outside legal costs low and operate within the budget set by the corporation
   iii. Provide growth and satisfaction of the employees
7. External conditions that affect management consist of economic conditions, government regulations, and laws.
8. Internal conditions that affect management include the nature and structure of the firm, the nature of the work, and the nature of the employees.
9. The five functions of a personnel manager, or law office manager responsible for personnel relations, are the following:
   i. Planning
   ii. Controlling
   iii. Organizing
   iv. Leading
   v. Staffing

10. Forecasting includes strategic planning and long-range planning for the firm.
11. The four areas of human resource planning are the following:
    i. Establishing human resource objectives
    ii. Assessing current human resource conditions
    iii. Designing and evaluating human resource activities
    iv. Monitoring and evaluating the results of activities
12. The goal of human resource planning is to develop personnel policies and programs that will achieve the firm's objectives.
13. Controlling can be defined as the process of ensuring that actions conform to the plans.
14. The three main elements of control are the following:
    i. Establishing standards of performance
    ii. Measuring current performance and comparing it to established standards
    iii. Taking action to correct performance that does not meet established standards
15. If standards are set too high, employee frustration develops.
16. If standards are set too low, employees will not be challenged by their work.
17. The consequences of win-lose management are the following:
    i. The atmosphere in the office becomes competitive and hostile.
    ii. Time and energy are diverted from the main issues.
    iii. Creativity, sensitivity, and empathy are eliminated from the office environment.
    iv. Authority conflicts become more frequent and bitter.
    v. Important organizational decisions are increasingly made by an isolated, elitist group.
    vi. New ideas are discouraged.
    vii. Deadlocks are created and decisions are delayed.
    viii. Nonaggressive people are discouraged from participation.
18. The organization function requires the manager to coordinate the resources of the firm to maximize productivity and effectiveness.
19. Leadership involves determining what is to be accomplished and how to accomplish it.
20. Staffing includes such functions as recruitment, screening, interviewing, testing, hiring, firing, job analysis, job description, and keeping personnel records.
21. The four steps in the hiring process are the following:
    i. Planning
    ii. Recruitment
    iii. Selection
    iv. Training
22. Four advantages of promoting from within the firm are the following:
    i. Costs: The selection cost of hiring a new employee is eliminated.

ii. Productivity: The employee already knows the structure and procedures of the firm, so loss in productivity is reduced.

iii. Loyalty: Promotions encourage employee loyalty.

iv. Morale: The promoted employee receives recognition, which increases employee morale.

23. Prospective employees are recruited through employment agencies, newspaper advertising, paralegal associations, word of mouth, and the Internet.

24. Questions on the application that pertain to an applicant's age, sex, race, height, or weight violate federal regulations.

25. The ouch formula is an acronym for proper interview questions. Questions must be the following:
    i. Objective
    ii. Uniform
    iii. Consistent
    iv. Have job relatedness

26. Casual conversation at the beginning of an interview is one method of giving an applicant the opportunity to relax.

27. Some danger signs a manager should look for when interviewing an applicant are the following:
    i. Job hopping
    ii. Distance from home
    iii. Health
    iv. Improper termination notice to previous employer
    v. Reasons for leaving
    vi. Poor relationship with previous employer

28. The CEMEC principle is an acronym that describes employee expectations, as follows:
    i. Communication
    ii. Education
    iii. Motivation
    iv. Evaluation
    v. Compensation

29. Fear is the inhibiting factor of open communication: fear of rejection, fear of looking stupid, and fear of losing the respect of coworkers.

30. The buddy system is used when the firm pairs a new employee with another employee in the same job capacity for training purposes.

31. A mentor is an experienced paralegal or attorney from whom the new paralegal can learn.

32. Poor working conditions increase turnover and decrease efficiency.

33. Good working conditions decrease turnover and increase efficiency.

34. Good working conditions consist of the following:
    i. Policy: reasonable office policies fully set forth in an office manual with grievance procedures and appeal process established and explained
    ii. Health and safety: good lighting and a clean, comfortable environment with regulated heating and air conditioning
    iii. Tools: updated tools and equipment

35. The two types of evaluation are the following:
    i. Formal evaluation
    ii. Informal evaluation

36. Formal evaluation is in writing and is followed by a performance interview with the employee and evaluators.

37. Informal evaluation occurs daily when employees' mistakes are corrected or they are told that they did a good job on a project.

38. Some of the areas considered in a formal performance evaluation are the following:
    i. Courtesy to clients
    ii. Punctuality
    iii. Dependability
    iv. Communication skills
    v. Leadership capabilities
    vi. Initiative
    vii. Work habits
    viii. Willingness to work overtime
    ix. Skills rating
    x. Job performance

39. If a paralegal is unhappy with the formal performance evaluation, the paralegal should contact the firm's administrator to determine what steps can be taken to remedy the situation.

40. To establish a basic compensation structure, firms consider the following:
    i. The marketplace: what other firms in the area pay their employees
    ii. Job analysis: a study of the job activities, duties, and responsibilities of each job
    iii. Job description: a detailed description of the job and the skills required to perform the job
    iv. Job evaluation: establishes the value of the job and puts a monetary value on the job

41. Raises are based on the consumer price index and merit, tenure, incentives, base salary, or employer's discretion.

42. Bonuses are based on merit, tenure, incentive, base salary, and/or employer's discretion.

43. When calculating raises, the consumer price index is often considered.

44. Merit raises and bonuses acknowledge above-average quality and quantity of work.

45. Raises and bonuses based on tenure occur when an employee is rewarded for longevity with the firm.

46. A small firm usually offers fewer benefits than does a large firm.

47. FLSA stands for the Federal Labor Standards Act.

48. The Federal Labor Standards Act (FLSA) designates the parameters within which an employee may be designated exempt or nonexempt and eligible for overtime compensation.

49. Employees who are exempt are paid an annual or monthly salary and are not entitled to overtime pay.

50. Employees who are nonexempt are paid by the hour and are entitled to overtime pay for all hours worked in excess of 40 per week.

51. The basic theory behind the team approach is as follows: By aligning the organization's needs with the needs of the employees, the organization will benefit from employees' personal motivation, energy, and drive as well as benefiting employees by being a vehicle by which they can achieve their personal goals.

52. Studies have shown that the team approach plays an important role in the following:
    i. The personal satisfaction of employees
    ii. The success of the enterprise
    iii. Good service to the client

53. The five Cs of the team approach are the following:
    i. Commitment
    ii. Competency
    iii. Constructive feedback
    iv. Creativity
    v. Cooperation

54. Each employee should be committed to the following:
    i. Providing quality legal services to the client
    ii. Contributing to the profitability of the firm
    iii. Deriving personal satisfaction and growth from work

55. Making a commitment requires trust in the organization and trust in the people.

56. Education, experience, on-the-job training, and continuing education are the keys to competency.

57. Continuing legal education is essential to keep abreast of changes in the law.

58. The following attributes increase creativity:
    i. An open mind
    ii. Curiosity
    iii. Ability to concentrate
    iv. Persistence
    v. Cooperation

59. The business of law is more stressful than other industries because of the constant deadlines and needs of clients.

60. The basis of most personality conflicts is lack of communication.

61. If a paralegal observes unethical behavior, the paralegal should bring the situation to the attention of the perpetrator or the office manager.

Chapter 4

The Attorney-Client Relationship

1. The following four things have affected the traditional attorney-client relationship:
   i. Economics
   ii. The demand for varied specialties
   iii. Marketing
   iv. Business management changes

2. A state bar's Code of Professional Responsibility provides a joint-venture approach to the attorney-client relationship and provides a model in which the responsibilities in any representation are allocated between the attorney and the client.

3. The American Bar Association (ABA) adopted rules of ethics known as the Model Rules of Professional Conduct (Model Rules).

4. As a client's representative, a lawyer performs the following three functions—the three As:
   i. Advisor
   ii. Advocate
   iii. Agent

5. As an adviser to the client, the lawyer will do the following:
   i. Exercise independent judgment for the client
   ii. Be candid no matter how unpleasant the advice may be
   iii. Discourage illegal or fraudulent conduct
   iv. Inform the client of adverse consequences
   v. Apprise the client of the proposed course of action

6. As a client's advocate, the lawyer will do the following:
   i. Represent a client before a court or tribunal
   ii. Make reasonable efforts to expedite litigation consistent with the interest of the client
   iii. Not bring a claim that has no basis in fact to harass another

7. The eight duties the ABA Model rules impose on an attorney as an advocate are to:
   i. Expedite litigation in the interests of the client
   ii. Be truthful to the court or tribunal
   iii. Be fair and honest to the opposing party and do nothing to obstruct his or her case
   iv. Engage in conduct intended to disrupt a court
   v. Make a statement to the media that will be prejudicial to the proceeding
   vi. Be an advocate in a case in which the attorney is a witness
   vii. Not prosecute a criminal matter that is not supported by probable cause
   viii. Meet disclosure requirements when representing a client in an administrative hearing or legislative body

8. As a client's agent, the lawyer will do the following:
   i. Seek results advantageous to the client while being honest and fair with others
   ii. Be a spokesperson for the client
   iii. Negotiate on the client's behalf
   iv. Abide by the client's decision after informing the client of the issues of the case and ramifications of the client's decision

9. The attorney is ultimately responsible for the attorney-client relationship.

10. The attorney is responsible for the paralegal's actions.

11. Paralegals are not bound by the Rules of Professional Responsibility of state bar associations.
12. Paralegals are considered lawyers' agents.
13. The four factors clients want most from attorneys are:
    i. Commitment (most important)
    ii. Integrity
    iii. Commentary
    iv. Fairness in fees
14. Satisfied clients are the best source of new clients for the firm.
15. A firm's marketing activities are stated in a marketing plan.
16. Positioning a law firm is where the marketing manager analyzes the information from client surveys to determine the firm's strengths, weaknesses, opportunities, and roadblocks.
17. A target market is a group the firm wants to attract as clients.
18. Advertising was banned by the ABA to avoid "extravagant, artful, self-laudatory brashness" that could mislead laypersons and cause public distrust of the legal system. It was also considered demeaning and was believed that advertising had a negative effect on society.
19. The U.S. Supreme Court ruled that the ban on lawyer advertising was a violation of First Amendment guarantees of a lawyer's right to advertise.
20. Yellow Page ads are the most common method of lawyer advertising.
21. The key consideration in evaluating the content of lawyer television advertising is that it not be false, misleading, or deceptive.
22. "Issues advertising" is television advertising that directly targets people with a specific problem.
23. Netvertising is advertising products or services on the Internet.
24. A firm's website is considered its most valuable marketing tool.
25. Model Rule 7.1 applies to Netvertising.
26. Some problems associated with advertising on the Internet include applying each state's Code of Professional Responsibility to multistate advertising and monitoring misleading information.
27. False and misleading information and attorney comparisons are prohibited in attorney's Internet advertising.
28. The term blog is short for Web log. A Web log is a journal (or newsletter) that contains Internet links and is intended for public consumption and participation.
29. Large firms are most likely to sponsor seminars for their clients.
30. Seminars keep corporate clients informed and create a personal rapport with clients.
31. A firm newsletter can help a firm attain a variety of goals, including the following:
    i. Reminding clients of their obligation to file reports with government agencies

    ii. Informing clients about new developments in the law
    iii. Informing clients about services available from the firm
32. A combination of four different trends has contributed to the success of the law firm newsletter:
    i. Desktop publishing and laser printers
    ii. Increased usage of personal computers in law firms
    iii. The awareness of increasing demands for technical support
    iv. The spread of multiple offices that are connected to a computer network
33. Public relations is developing and maintaining a favorable public image between the law firm and the community.
34. Public relations has more credibility than advertising because its source is presumably objective and non-biased.
35. The general rule against soliciting is that a lawyer may not solicit legal business from a potential client to whom he or she is not related or with whom he or she has had no prior professional relationship when the solicitation is for the lawyer's monetary gain.
36. The justification for the prohibition against first contact is that lawyers are trained in the art of persuasion and people in need of legal services may be emotionally vulnerable and subject to overreaching.
37. The U.S. Supreme Court ruled in *Shapero v. Kentucky Bar Association* that direct mail solicitation is constitutionally protected free speech.
38. Spam is the indiscriminate posting of e-mail messages promoting a product or service. A Phoenix lawyer was suspended for spamming.
39. A capper is paid to get business for an attorney.
40. Exempt from solicitation accusations are the following:
    i. Public defenders and district attorneys because they are employed by a county or state government and receive a salary from taxpayer dollars
    ii. Sponsored attorney referral services
    iii. Attorneys employed by prepaid legal insurance plans
    iv. Attorneys who communicate directly with a family member, current or former client, or pro bono client regarding legal services
    v. Lawyers who provide information to a potential client at their request
41. Types of potential cappers include insurance adjusters, medical personnel, and police officers.
42. An attorney may inform a potential client of services if no financial benefits will be gained, except if the case is a high-profile case.
43. A problem occurs if the employee is compensated for the referral.
44. It is considered improper for an attorney to try to persuade clients to leave the firm with the attorney

because clients belong to a firm, not to an individual attorney. However, it is the client's decision to choose the attorney or the firm.

45. The five Cs are competence, commitment, communication, conflict of interest, and confidentiality.

46. Case law determines when the attorney-client relationship begins.

47. The Iowa Supreme Court used three factors to test when an attorney-client relationship exists:
    i. The client sought legal advice.
    ii. The advice sought was within areas of a lawyer's competence.
    iii. The lawyer gave, or agreed to give, the advice sought.

48. Paying a fee is not essential to create an attorney-client relationship.

49. Four things are required to represent the client competently:
    i. Legal knowledge
    ii. Legal skill
    iii. Thoroughness
    iv. Preparation

50. Legal skills include technical skills such as the ability to draft documents, review documents, conduct research, and perform administrative tasks such as record keeping.

51. The standard of "thoroughness" as required by the ABA Model Rules is the degree of thoroughness ordinarily employed by lawyers undertaking similar matters.

52. Adequate preparation requires necessary legal research and investigation of the facts of the case.

53. If the attorney is inexperienced in an area of law before accepting a client's case, the attorney need not decline the case if the attorney makes an effort to become knowledgeable in that area without jeopardizing the client's case.

54. A lawyer who knows that he or she does not have the necessary skills to undertake a complex matter is bound by the Code of Professional Responsibility to either decline the case or associate another attorney on the case that is competent in the subject matter.

55. If a lawyer chooses to associate another lawyer on a case, the lawyer must have the client's consent.

56. No. The fees charged the client cannot be increased because of the involvement of the additional lawyer.

57. Commitment to a client's case forbids a lawyer to neglect the case.

58. Some examples of a lack of commitment to a client's case follow:
    i. Failure to begin an action
    ii. Failure to appear at a hearing
    iii. Failure to file pleadings
    iv. Filing carelessly drafted pleadings
    v. Failure to respond to interrogatories
    vi. Failure to respond to correspondence from opposing counsel
    vii. Failure to correct a known defect in a case
    viii. Failure to notify clients of a lawyer's new office address or telephone number

59. The term *zeal* suggests the frame of mind appropriate in advocacy but not appropriate in the lawyer's role as advisor.

60. Attorney's failure to communicate with clients is the most common complaint clients have about attorneys.

61. A lawyer can keep clients informed by doing the following:
    i. Advising them of the status of their affairs
    ii. Responding to their requests for information
    iii. Responding to letters sent by clients
    iv. Notifying clients of changes in a lawyer's address and telephone number
    v. Apprising clients of any reason why the lawyer cannot provide them with diligent representation
    vi. Advising clients of the proper course of action and the risks involved and possible alternative action
    vii. Informing clients of their rights, especially in criminal cases
    viii. Advising clients on both the legal and practical aspects of a matter
    ix. Providing clients with copies of all documents received or prepared in their cases

62. Providing the client with information relates to two areas of the client's case: informing the client of the status of the case and advising the client of the law to allow the client to make informed decisions concerning the case.

63. A lawyer may not represent one client whose interests are adverse to another client, even if the two representations are unrelated, unless the client consents and the lawyer believes the representation will not adversely affect a client.

64. It is generally agreed that a greater obligation is owed to a former client than a potential client.

65. Two attorneys in the same firm cannot represent two sides of a dispute because to do so would be a conflict of interest.

66. A direct conflict of interest is when an attorney or firm has a relationship with a person who may be involved in the conflict or if the attorney or firm has a financial interest in an entity involved in the conflict.

67. A potential conflict arises when an attorney has an indirect relationship with a person who may be involved in the conflict.

68. A positional conflict arises when an attorney or firm represents a client's competition.

69. One of the major factors that differentiates a law firm from other industries is the requirement that all matters within that office be kept confidential.

70. The primary justification for the strict rules on confidentiality is the desirability of complete candor

between client and lawyer. Confidentiality not only facilitates the full development of facts essential to proper representation, but also encourages people to seek legal assistance at an early stage.

71. The exceptions to the confidentiality rule follow:
    i. A client may consent to a lawyer's divulging confidential information, but only after full disclosure and consultation.
    ii. A lawyer may reveal a client's intentions to commit a crime and the information necessary to prevent a crime.
    iii. If the client commits perjury, the attorney has an obligation to reveal the perjury. Perjury is a fraud on the court, and the Model Code requires total candor with the court. The Model Code further forbids lawyers to "knowingly use perjured testimony or false evidence" or to "knowingly make a false statement of law or fact." It is the lawyer's obligation to encourage the client to rectify the fraud and reveal the fraud to the court.
    iv. If a law or a court order requires the lawyer to disclose otherwise confidential information, the lawyer may do so.
    v. A lawyer may reveal a client's confidences to collect fees and defend him- or herself against claims of criminal or unethical conduct arising out of the lawyer's representation of the client.

72. The attorney-client privilege permits a client to refuse to testify and to keep an attorney from testifying in a legal proceeding about communications made between the two in strict confidence.

73. In order for a communication between an attorney and client to be privileged, three factors must be present:
    i. Communication must be made in confidence.
    ii. Communication must be to obtain legal advice.
    iii. Communication must be with an attorney.

74. The differences between confidentiality and the attorney-client privilege follow:
    i. The attorney-client privilege protects only information covered by attorney-client communication. It does not protect the facts generating the confidences nor the knowledge of the client.
    ii. Information that is open to the public is not covered by the attorney-client privilege. However, the lawyer's obligation to keep information confidential includes information that is public.
    iii. The attorney-client privilege includes information that the lawyer obtains from the client only. Confidentiality includes all information "relating to the representation of a client," regardless of its source.
    iv. The attorney-client privilege prevents disclosure in the litigation process.
    v. Confidentiality prevents disclosure anywhere at any time, even after the death of the client.

75. One such exception is when a client questions the attorney's professional competence through criminal charges or a malpractice suit. Also, when an attorney represents two clients who later become adversaries, privileged matters relating to the joint matter are waived. Confidential disclosure about a future crime is not protected because lawyers are required to reveal such information to enforcement officials.

76. The attorney work-product doctrine requires that information the attorney learns in representation of a client be kept confidential and may not be revealed to third parties.

77. Some examples of paralegals' work product that are subject to the work-product doctrine include:
    i. Interoffice memoranda discussing case status or case strategy
    ii. Telephone memos of conversations with clients, witnesses, and relating to investigation
    iii. Notes of meetings with clients
    iv. Document screening and site inspection notes
    v. Investigation memos and interview notes
    vi. Document production notes
    vii. Case memoranda and task assignment documents
    viii. E-mails

78. A client may end the relationship with the lawyer at any time without justifying the termination.

79. If a lawyer wants to end the relationship with a client and the client will not release the lawyer from the obligation, in most cases, the lawyer must have the court's permission.

80. Under the ABA Model Rules, a lawyer may terminate the attorney-client relationship if any of the following are true:
    i. The client insists upon a claim or defense that cannot be supported by a good-faith argument on existing law
    ii. The client acts unlawfully or insists that the lawyer do so
    iii. The client makes it unreasonably difficult for the lawyer to be effective
    iv. Before a case goes to court, the client insists that the lawyer act contrary to the lawyer's judgment and advice
    v. The client deliberately disregards an agreement with the lawyer as to fees or expenses
    vi. The lawyer's continued employment is likely to result in a violation of an ethics rule
    vii. The lawyer is unable to work with co-counsel to the detriment of his or her client's interest
    viii. The lawyer has physical or mental problems that make it difficult to provide the client with an effective representation
    ix. The client consents to the withdrawal
    x. Any other reason found by the court to be good cause for withdrawal

81. A lawyer must still protect the client's interest even after the lawyer has either withdrawn or been terminated from the case.

82. The state bar or other agency may impose discipline on the lawyer in any one of five ways:
    i. Admonition
    ii. Reprimand
    iii. Probation
    iv. Suspension
    v. Disbarment

83. An admonition is the least severe form of discipline. The state bar or other attorney disciplinary agency will declare the attorney's conduct improper, but will keep the information private.

84. A reprimand is a form of public discipline that publicly declares the attorney's conduct improper. The state bar or other attorney disciplinary agency will publish the name of the attorney, the facts surrounding the discipline, and the form of reprimand in newspapers, magazines, journals, and other publications.

85. When an attorney is on probation, the state bar or disciplinary agency will impose certain conditions that must be met in order for the lawyer to continue to practice law. Probation may be ordered alone, or with an admonition or reprimand. Probation also may be imposed as a condition upon reinstatement of a suspended or disbarred attorney.

86. A more severe form of discipline, suspension means that an attorney may not practice law for a specific period of time, usually from 6 months to 3 years.

87. Disbarment, the most drastic of attorney's discipline, terminates the lawyer's status as a lawyer and cancels the attorney's license to practice law.

88. Some state bar associations do not have the ultimate authority to disbar an attorney. Since disbarment has a devastating effect on the attorney's livelihood that directly affects the attorney's ability to make a living, some states require that all disbarment proceedings be appealed or reviewed by the state's high court.

89. Disbarment is not always permanent. An attorney may apply for reinstatement after a sufficient amount of time has elapsed (usually about 5 years).

90. The following are other forms of discipline:
    i. Restitution (if the lawyer steals a client's funds)
    ii. Payment of costs
    iii. Limitation on practice
    iv. Requirement that the lawyer take the professional responsibility exam
    v. Resignation

91. If the attorney fails to act competently or represent a client diligently, the client may sue the attorney for malpractice.

92. If an attorney is negligent, the attorney may be sued for malpractice.

93. Personal injury plaintiff firms are sued for malpractice most often.

94. Client satisfaction is the basis for measuring a law firm's performance.

95. The survey identified three areas that contributed to client dissatisfaction:
    i. Not keeping up with changing client needs
    ii. Doing a poor job of articulating and delivering value
    iii. Poor communication

Chapter 5
Paralegal Ethics and Client Relations

1. Family, friends, religious upbringing, education, environment, and past experiences contribute to our ethical values.

2. The *Living Webster Encyclopedic Dictionary* defines ethics as "the principles of morality, or the field of study of morals or right conduct."

3. Ethics cannot be defined as honest versus dishonest, right versus wrong, or good versus bad because there are many gray areas in between.

4. Our personal characteristics influence the degree to which we can recognize ethical issues.

5. People with good intentions sometimes violate ethical standards because they are unaware of ethical boundaries or do not give their actions serious thought.

6. The foundation of ethical standards is established through education and knowledge of ethics and professional responsibility.

7. National and state bar associations; national, state, and local paralegal associations; and the courts have developed ethical guidelines for paralegals to follow.

8. Paralegals are not lawyers and are therefore not bound by the attorney's state bar code of ethics, by which attorneys must abide.

9. Paralegals are lawyers' agents.

10. A paralegal cannot be prosecuted by a state bar or governing agency for unethical behavior.

11. The client and employing firm or attorney suffer from a paralegal's unethical conduct.

12. Paralegals comply with ethical codes to protect their employers from liability.

13. The paralegal profession was born in the 1960s out of concern for the legal profession as it was structured.

14. A study conducted by the ABA in the early 1960s revealed that lawyers' businesses were not as profitable as those of other professionals, such as doctors, dentists, and architects.

15. Other professions were professionally managed and used assistants.

16. The ABA considered the use of paralegals and determined that it would do three things:
    i. Increase lawyers' efficiency
    ii. Decrease costs to the client
    iii. Increase the attorney's profitability
17. The ABA established a committee on paralegals in 1968, now called the ABA Standing Committee on Paralegals.
18. The first formal paralegal educational programs were established in the early 1970s.
19. The ABA began its approval process of paralegal programs in 1975.
20. The three national paralegal associations are (1) The National Federation of Paralegal Associations (NFPA), (2) The National Association of Legal Assistants (NALA), and (3) The American Alliance of Paralegals, Inc.
21. A national, state, or local paralegal association may impose any of the following sanctions for violation of its code of ethics:
    i. Letter of reprimand
    ii. Counseling
    iii. Attendance at an ethics course approved by committee
    iv. Probation
    v. Suspension of authority to practice
    vi. Revocation of authority to practice
    vii. Imposition of a fine
    viii. Assessment of costs
    ix. Referral to the appropriate authority if criminal activity is found
22. It has been a problem to monitor adherence to the organization's ethics code because unless a violation is reported, the association is unaware of the violation.
23. The five Cs of client relations follow:
    i. Competence
    ii. Commitment
    iii. Communication
    iv. Conflict of interest
    v. Confidentiality
24. The four aspects of a lawyer's competency that apply to paralegals are legal knowledge, skill, thoroughness, and preparation.
25. Legal knowledge is acquired in school, by experience, and through continuing legal education.
26. Skill is created by applying that knowledge to clients' cases.
27. Knowledge and skill are increased by experience and continuing legal education.
28. Thoroughness is developed by adequate preparation.
29. Laziness and failing to prepare a document correctly or being sloppy in work habits affect thoroughness.
30. Technology has been responsible for a lack in thoroughness because a task can be accomplished faster, and it is easy to rely on technology to be thorough for us. We tend to be lazy in the details.

31. The eight areas that indicate a lack of commitment to a client's case are the following:
    i. Failure to begin an action
    ii. Failure to appear at a hearing
    iii. Failure to file pleadings
    iv. Filing carelessly drafted pleadings
    v. Failure to respond to interrogatories
    vi. Failure to respond to correspondence from opposing counsel
    vii. Failure to correct a known defect in a case
    viii. Failure to notify clients of a lawyer's new office address or telephone number
32. Paralegals can greatly assist an attorney in communicating with clients by answering a client's request for information about a case, easing a client's concerns, and responding to a client's correspondence or request for a status report.
33. A goodwill letter is a letter written to create rapport and good relations.
34. Only an attorney may give legal advice to a client.
35. A general guideline for legal advice is this: If a paralegal applies knowledge of the law to the facts of a case and renders an opinion, it is legal advice.
36. The following activities constitute legal advice:
    i. Recommending a course of conduct or action to a client
    ii. Evaluating a case and predicting the possible outcome
    iii. Evaluating a case and suggesting a course of action
    iv. Explaining the client's rights or obligations to a client
    v. Independently interpreting statutes, decisions, or legal documents to a client
37. The prohibition against giving legal advice is difficult for experienced paralegals because they know the law and the answers to questions. The line between giving information and giving legal advice is confusing.
38. If a paralegal is asked a question that requires legal advice, she or he must ask the attorney for the answer even though she or he may know the answer.
39. No. A paralegal may draft the letter for the attorney's approval and signature, but the paralegal may not sign the letter.
40. A "jailhouse lawyer" may give legal advice, and a paralegal may give legal advice to a client she or he is representing at an administrative hearing, if the administrative agency allows nonattorney representation.
41. The case of *Johnson v. Avery*, 393 U.S. 484 (1969), created the "jailhouse lawyer."
42. When communicating with clients, a paralegal must always identify him or herself as a paralegal so that the client understands that the paralegal is not an attorney. This will ensure that no one is confused as to the paralegal's status.

43. A paralegal may not accept a case, because accepting a case creates an attorney-client relationship, for which the attorney is responsible.

44. Nonlawyer conflict of interest is when a paralegal learns of confidential information about a case during employment with one firm and then goes to work for the opposing firm.

45. A Chinese wall prohibits a person from working on or discussing a case.

46. A Chinese wall prohibits a paralegal from working on any case with the paralegal's former employer and imposes the following restrictions:
    i. The firm must educate all employees about the importance of the Chinese wall.
    ii. The isolated person may not discuss the case with others or be near others who are working on the case. All firm employees must be aware of the wall that is constructed around the employee.
    iii. The isolated person may not have access to files and documents of the case. The subject case files must be "flagged" in a manner that is identifiable from a distance and is obvious to all who see the file that it is subject to a Chinese wall.
    iv. The client must be notified of the potential conflict and of the firm's efforts to isolate the person from those working on the case.

47. A freelance paralegal must keep a list of cases she or he has worked on, because if a freelance paralegal worked on a case for one firm, she or he may not work on the same case for another firm.

48. A paralegal keeps a client's matter confidential by doing the following:
    i. Not discussing the case outside the office
    ii. Making sure that the surroundings are private when discussing a case with a coworker
    iii. Concealing a client's file from others outside the office
    iv. Making sure that a client's e-mail is not subject to the view of others
    v. Not accepting a telephone call from a client while in conference with another client
    vi. Not exposing client documents on a computer screen

49. An e-mail must be sent to a client on a secure server to protect confidentiality.

50. The activities that constitute the unauthorized practice of law are subject to legislation, regulation, and case law interpretation of each state.

51. The three activities that have been determined to be the unauthorized practice of law by a paralegal are the following:
    i. Representing clients in court or government agency proceedings
    ii. Preparing legal documents without supervision of an attorney
    iii. Giving legal advice

52. Paralegals may represent clients before many federal or state administrative agencies if the agency allows nonattorney representation.

53. No. While paralegals may attend depositions with their supervising attorney, they may not ask the deponent questions.

54. In many states, unauthorized practice of law occurs when legal documents are prepared without the attorney's direct supervision.

55. Unbundled legal services are when an attorney breaks a legal representation into tasks that are performed by a lawyer and nonlawyer.

56. Courts have ruled that completing a court form for a client requires knowledge obtained by a law school education and constitutes giving legal advice. There have been other court rulings that said that even informing a person what form to use is an unauthorized practice of law.

57. Many courts have a program to help pro se parties complete their paperwork, consisting of legal forms for dissolutions, restraining orders, and small-claims cases.

58. Courts employ nonattorneys to help people complete their paperwork because wrong and incomplete forms are filed, causing delays in the court system.

59. A paralegal may not sign a pleading (except in emergency situations in North Carolina).

60. An attorney must sign a pleading because the attorney's signature is verification that the attorney read and knows the contents of the document.

61. In the *Dacey* case, the court ruled that publication of forms and instructions on how to complete the forms did not constitute legal advice if the instructions were directed toward the public and not individual clients.

62. Legal kits contain the requisite forms for a particular area, such as wills, trusts, and dissolutions of marriage, along with instructions on how to complete the forms.

63. The courts ruled that the legal kits did not constitute the unauthorized practice of law because they are directed to the public rather than to an individual client.

64. Legal kits for dissolution of marriage, bankruptcy, and will preparation are available in most stationery stores.

65. Independent paralegals provide legal services directly to the public in areas such as divorce, bankruptcy, immigration, and landlord-tenant matters at reduced rates.

66. Freelance paralegals work for attorneys on an independent contractor basis under their direct supervision.

67. Independent paralegals provide legal services to the public, and freelance paralegals provide legal services to attorneys.

68. The Wave Project was a chain of do-it-yourself divorce centers.

69. Wave centers provided independent paralegal services and offered typing and information services to the public.

70. Rosemary Furman was convicted of the unauthorized practice of law for giving her clients legal advice on the correct information to insert on legal forms and was prohibited from helping customers complete the forms. The court eventually imposed a jail sentence on her for failing to abide by its order.

71. Rosemary Furman's jail sentence was commuted after she agreed to close her business.

72. In late 1998, California enacted SB 1418, which allows paralegals to do "scrivener-type" services for the public if they register with their county.

73. Independent paralegals may make legal information available to customers but may not offer legal advice.

74. Independent paralegals are identified as "Legal Document Assistants" and "Unlawful Detainer Assistants" under SB 1418.

75. Bankruptcy Petition Preparers are disfavored by trustees and bankruptcy courts because some are making serious mistakes that have caused chaos in the court system.

76. HALT stands for Help Abolish Legal Tyranny.

77. Traditional paralegals work under the direct supervision of an attorney.

78. Traditional paralegals object to the title "legal document assistants" because it is too close to the title "legal assistant." CAPA stated that independent paralegal activities are scrivener-type work, and it sees the role of paralegals as much more substantive.

79. Other terms for independent paralegals are *legal technician, legal document assistant, public paralegal,* and *limited law advisers.*

80. The case that identifies activities that are not considered to constitute the unauthorized practice of law is *People v. Landlords Professional Services,* 215 Cal. App. 3d 1599; 264 Cal. Rptr. 548 (1989).

81. The lack of regulation of the paralegal profession, especially independent paralegal services, has created problems for the paralegal profession as a whole.

82. "Fly-by-night" paralegal programs and services are programs or independent paralegal services that are unqualified and damage their customers and the paralegal profession.

83. "Fly-by-night" paralegal programs and services are dangerous because the public has no way of knowing whether the independent paralegal service is operated by a knowledgeable, experienced paralegal or one with no paralegal training.

84. The lack of regulation allows unqualified paralegals to proliferate.

85. To ensure professionalism, paralegals must be committed to the following:
    i. Public service
    ii. Education
    iii. High standards of ethical conduct
    iv. Excellence
    v. Strong work ethic
    vi. Integrity and honor
    vii. Development of the whole person
    viii. Exercising good judgment, common sense, and communication skills.

Chapter 6
Legal Fees

1. At the time of the Roman republic, legal services were free of charge—rendered for the honor and personal satisfaction the advocate received by providing the service.

2. The different types of fees are the following:
   i. Retainer fees
   ii. Hourly fees
   iii. Flat (fixed) fees
   iv. Task-based fees
   v. Contingency fees
   vi. Statutory fees
   vii. Referral fees
   viii. Premiums
   ix. Value-based fees
   x. Combination fees

3. The four types of retainer fees are the following:
   i. True retainer
   ii. Nonrefundable chargeable retainer
   iii. Nonrefundable nonchargeable retainer
   iv. Refundable retainer

4. A true retainer fee is paid to the law firm to ensure the firm's availability to the client.

5. A true retainer fee is used to secure a firm's loyalty to a client.

6. A nonrefundable chargeable retainer fee is paid in advance of representation and is not refundable to the client in most circumstances. It is applied to the client's bill.

7. A nonrefundable nonchargeable retainer fee is paid to the firm at the beginning of the case and is not applied to the client's bill. It is not refundable if the firm is discharged.

8. Many firms use nonrefundable retainers to ensure client loyalty to the firm and to test a client's commitment to the case.

9. A refundable retainer fee is applied to the total fee and is refundable if the client terminates the attorney-client relationship.

10. Hourly fees are when clients are charged by the hour for each hour or portion of an hour spent on the case.

11. Hourly rates vary according to specialty, geographic area, and the lawyer's years of experience.

12. A blended hourly rate is the average hourly rate of the people working on the case.

13. The six factors used to determine hourly rates are the following:
    i. Planned or budgeted expenses, excluding partner or shareholder compensation and benefits
    ii. Anticipated billable time by a partner, an associate, or a paralegal
    iii. Desired profit percentage
    iv. Reasonable allocation of expenses by a partner, an associate, or a paralegal
    v. Firm collection rate—billings divided by cash receipts
    vi. Billing rate—work-in-progress billable time versus past billed hours

14. An hourly fee is the most common fee found in law offices.

15. A flat (fixed) fee is a set fee for a service rendered.

16. A per diem flat fee is a fee charged by the attorney for a day's work.

17. Minimum/maximum flat fees are based on the outcome of the matter. If the outcome of the matter is extremely satisfying for the client, the maximum fee is charged. If the outcome is not as the client had hoped, the minimum fee is charged.

18. A law firm knows by experience about how long it takes to complete a certain type of case. The attorney's and paralegal's time are estimated, and the attorney's and paralegal's hourly rates are applied to the time estimate for completion of the case.

19. Each phase of a case contains a list of tasks, and each task contains activities. Each task is given a specific fee or hourly rate that is appropriate to the level of complexity of the task.

20. A contingency fee is a fee based on a percentage of the client's recovery in a case.

21. The two methods of calculating the attorney's fee are the gross-fee method and the net-fee method.

22. The difference between the gross-fee method and net-fee method of calculation is that the attorney's fee is deducted before the costs in the gross-fee method. In the net-fee method, the attorney's fee is calculated after deducting costs.

23. A client receives more money when a contingency fee is calculated by the net-fee method.

24. In a modified contingency fee case, the lawyer is paid a percentage of the difference between the amount at issue and the amount of the final judgment.

25. The four considerations in taking a case on a contingency basis are the following (RISC):
    i. Risk
    ii. Inflation
    iii. Significant expense
    iv. Cash flow

26. Several states have put limits on contingency fees because they felt that doing so would discourage lawsuits.

27. Statutory fees are fees set by state statute.

28. According to Model Rule 1.5(e), the three occasions when a lawyer may divide a fee with another lawyer are the following:
    i. If the division is in proportion to the services rendered by the lawyer or by written agreement with the client
    ii. If the client agrees to the division
    iii. If the total fee is reasonable

29. According to Model Rule 5.4, the three occasions when a lawyer may divide a fee with a nonlawyer are the following:
    i. It is payment to a lawyer's widow or widower after the lawyer's death
    ii. A lawyer purchases a law practice of a deceased or disabled lawyer
    iii. The firm has a profit-sharing or retirement plan for employees

30. Lawyers are prohibited from fee splitting with nonlawyers because it may allow the lawyer's independent judgment to be controlled by a nonlawyer who is interested in his or her own profit rather than the legal needs of the client. It also discourages nonlawyers from engaging in the unauthorized practice of law and referring clients to the lawyer for a percentage of the fee, known as capping.

31. According to Model Rule 7.2(c), the three occasions when an attorney may pay a referral fee are the following:
    i. For advertising purposes
    ii. For a lawyer referral service
    iii. For payment of a law practice.

32. The four arguments against referral fees are the following:
    i. The fee may increase the client's bill.
    ii. Referral fees have a damaging effect on a lawyer's image.
    iii. Most clients are offended by referral fees.
    iv. Referral fees are beneath the dignity of the profession.

33. The two arguments for referral fees are the following:
    i. Clients benefit by being referred to the most competent attorney.
    ii. Clients are protected from increased fees by other rules of professional conduct.

34. Premiums can be best described as tips. If the attorney obtains an especially favorable result for the client, the client will give the firm a premium fee in addition to the usual attorney's fee, whether it is a contingency fee, flat fee, or hourly rate.

35. Value-based fees are paid according to the value of the outcome to the client.

36. Combination fees are a combination of all the types of fees.

37. Hard costs (also called direct costs) are directly attributable to the client's case, such as filing fees, service fees, deposition expenses, and so on.

38. Costs are recoverable by the prevailing party in some cases, and expenses are not recoverable.

39. Modern-day reasoning for not allowing attorneys to pay for the expenses of litigation is to discourage lawyers from putting their own recovery before that of the client and therefore creating a conflict of interest.

40. Soft costs (also known as indirect costs) cannot be directly attributable to a client's case until applied to the client's case.

41. Examples of soft costs include the following:
    i. Photocopies
    ii. Attorney's time in preparing forms or other multiple-use documents
    iii. Use of conference rooms
    iv. Use of substantive systems
    v. Local and long-distance telephone charges
    vi. Meals and transportation on occasions of overtime
    vii. Telex and fax
    viii. Supplies
    ix. Storage of documents
    x. Use of computer and computer database
    xi. Destruction of documents
    xii. Housekeeping services for meetings and depositions
    xiii. Interest on accounts receivable
    xiv. Outside services
    xv. Document production
    xvi. Postage

42. The ABA established rules and guidelines concerning legal fees (1) to preserve the effectiveness, integrity, and independence of the profession, and (2) to give society reasonable access to the legal system.

43. The eight considerations of determining a reasonable fee are the following:
    i. Time and labor required
    ii. Other employment opportunities
    iii. Customary fees in community
    iv. Amount involved and results obtained
    v. Time limitations
    vi. Professional relationship with client
    vii. Experience, reputation, and ability of lawyer
    viii. Type of fee: fixed or contingent

44. Calculation of a lodestar equation is accomplished by determining the number of hours reasonably spent in a case and applying the attorney's hourly rate thereto to arrive at a reasonable fee.

45. If the court determines that lodestar does not adequately compensate an attorney for all factors of the case, the court may apply a multiplier to the lodestar figure, thereby increasing the fee. Multipliers are additional fees.

46. The two types of liens that a lawyer may place on a case are a charging lien and a retaining lien.

47. A charging lien is placed on a client's judgment that the lawyer obtained for the client.

48. A retaining lien allows a lawyer to retain papers, money, or other property received from a client until the lawyer is paid the fee.

49. In addition to a charging and a retaining lien, an attorney may secure payment of fees by having the client sign a promissory note secured by a deed on the client's property. Lawyers also may obtain a security interest in client's property, such as a car.

50. The lawyer has full responsibility for a client's fee.

51. Paralegals must comply with attorneys' guidelines concerning fees because they are agents of the attorney.

52. Case law has ruled that a person must have a law school education to quote fees.

53. Attorneys or law firm management have the responsibility to set fees.

54. The case of *Missouri v. Jenkins,* 109 S. Ct. 2463 (1989), ruled that paralegal fees are recoverable.

55. A misunderstanding about fees is frequently a source of disputes between a client and a lawyer and erodes the attorney-client relationship.

56. All fee agreements should be in writing.

57. According to Model Rule 1.5(c), all contingency fee agreements must be in writing.

58. Written fee agreements are desirable for the following reasons:
    i. They prevent misunderstandings.
    ii. They enhance the attorney-client relationship.
    iii. They provide protection for the lawyer in case of a fee dispute.

Chapter 7

Timekeeping

1. The knowledge and expertise of lawyers and paralegals are the products that law firms sell to their clients. Time is the vehicle by which the product is produced.

2. Inaccurate time records result in inaccurate client billing and management reports. Inaccurate billing causes law firms to lose clients and client goodwill. Inaccurate management records cause management to make decisions on the basis of incorrect information.

3. If time is not documented, its value is lost, and the firm loses its product.

4. Lawyers and paralegals are the primary timekeepers in a law office.

5. The annual billable hour requirement is the minimum number of billable hours that must be produced by each timekeeper per year.

6. Billable hours are hours directly applied to clients' matters.

7. Nonbillable hours are not applied to clients' matters.

8. The two types of nonbillable hours are creditable and noncreditable.

9. Creditable nonbillable hours are credited toward the annual billable hours requirements and include the following:
    i. Time spent serving on firm committees
    ii. Pro bono work
    iii. Participating in management functions (i.e., completing reports, firm meetings, and so on)
    iv. Administrative functions
    v. Training

10. Noncreditable nonbillable hours are not credited toward the annual billable hours requirement and include the following:
    i. Educational activities, consisting of attending seminars, attending paralegal association conferences, and reading trade journals
    ii. Time spent on personal matters
    iii. Paralegal association work

11. Crediting time spent in educational activities and paying for educational activities are ways a firm encourages continuing education for its timekeepers.

12. Most firms give attorneys a higher creditable nonbillable hours allowance than paralegals because attorneys are expected to participate in more marketing activities for the firm. Many lawyers are also required to attend continuing legal education events to keep their license to practice law current.

13. Some activities included in an attorney's creditable nonbillable hour allowance are the following:
    i. Working on pro bono cases
    ii. Speaking at seminars
    iii. Cultivating clients
    iv. Participating in community organizations

14. Nonbillable hour information will tell law firm management about the efforts being expended by the timekeeper on the firm's behalf. These records are considered when an employee is evaluated and considered for a raise or bonus.

15. The most common method of calculating time is tenths of an hour.

16. The most commonly used minimum charge is 0.2 of an hour.

17. The billable hour is different from an actual hour in that the actual hour contains 60 minutes, while a billable hour may contain as little as 5 minutes or as much as 8 hours.

18. Management uses time records for the following seven purposes:
    i. Billing clients
    ii. Compensating hourly employees
    iii. Calculating employee productivity
    iv. Planning
    v. Monitoring work in progress
    vi. Projecting profitability
    vii. Forecasting income

19. Time records assist management in its marketing activities by determining what types of cases the firm is attracting.

20. Type-of-case reports derived from time records provide management with information on the time it takes to complete a certain type of case. A set fee can then be established.

21. Work-in-progress reports derived from time records give attorneys and paralegals a realistic idea of their caseload and allow management to allocate work accordingly.

22. Time records allow management to project a timekeeper's profitability by checking to see whether a timekeeper is meeting her or his quota.

23. A firm calculates the profitability of the contingency case by multiplying the amount of time spent on the case by the attorney's and paralegal's hourly rate and comparing that figure with the amount of money received on the case.

24. Management forecasts its income on the basis of projected income derived by timekeepers meeting their annual billable hour quotas.

25. The seven elements of time sheets are the following:
    i. Name of timekeeper
    ii. Date
    iii. File name
    iv. Client number
    v. File number
    vi. Amount of time expended in tenths of an hour
    vii. Description of work performed

26. Firms may require the following additional information on time sheets:
    i. Department code
    ii. Name of supervising attorney
    iii. Type of case code number

27. Firms developed codes for each function to expedite the timekeeping process.

28. Contingency law firms keep time records to monitor the profitability of the case and monitor work in progress. Time records are also important if the attorney must file a lien or prove that time was spent on a case. Time records also assist attorneys in determining a case's settlement value.

29. Corporate legal departments require time records to prepare management reports, keep track of departmental use of the legal services, and prepare departmental budgets.

30. Government legal offices use time records for budget proposals and management reports.

31. A timekeeper may not do the following six things:
    i. Bill clients for work not performed
    ii. Pad time sheets
    iii. Bill a client for time spent on personal matters
    iv. Double-bill
    v. Bill multiple clients for one activity
    vi. Apply an attorney's hourly rate to a paralegal's services

32. Double billing is working on two matters at the same time and billing each client separately for the time.

33. Padding time sheets is fraudulently adding time to a client's matter that was not spent.

34. Personal telephone calls are considered nonbillable noncreditable time.
35. Preparing the time sheet is the first thing a paralegal does in the morning.
36. Completing the time sheet is the last thing a paralegal does in the evening.
37. A paralegal should not wait until the end of the day to complete time sheets because many short activities will be forgotten and lost.
38. Timekeepers should not estimate their time because surveys have shown that timekeepers underestimate their time when time is estimated.
39. It is the attorney's responsibility to reduce the cost of a project.
40. A timekeeper should record all nonbillable time to show the firm's management that time was spent on the firm's activities and not wasted. It is also a good method of determining whether time was spent productively. By monitoring all nonbillable time, a timekeeper can determine whether she or he exceeded the time allowed for nonbillable matters and adjust her or his activities accordingly.
41. Listing projects on a to-do list will help the paralegal prioritize time and structure the day.
42. A time sheet should be completed when an activity is completed. If a paralegal is working on one project that exceeds one day, a time sheet should be completed at the end of each day.

Chapter 8
Billing and Financial Management

1. The four essential elements of the billing process are communication, documentation, regular and frequent billing, and descriptive bills.
2. The most important aspect of the billing process is communication.
3. It is the lawyer's responsibility to communicate the fee agreement to the client.
4. The paralegal may discuss the situation with the client in an empathic manner, but may not give advice or suggest a solution to the problem.
5. The responsible attorney or administrator has the authority to adjust a client's bill.
6. When communicating with clients, a paralegal may not discuss the duration of a case, estimate the cost of a matter, give an opinion as to the possible outcome of a matter, or discuss the lawyer's strategy.
7. When a paralegal has a communication with a client, the paralegal must document that the conversation took place and the contents of the conversation.
8. A client's complete understanding of the case will reward a firm in prompt payment of the firm's invoices.

9. An engagement letter is a letter that summarizes the scope of representation and the fee agreement between a lawyer and a client.
10. Billing should be regular and frequent because delaying the billing process is very costly for a firm.
11. Small firms and sole proprietors have difficulty meeting a monthly billing schedule, especially if the legal team is working hard to meet approaching deadlines.
12. A client should be billed as soon as possible after the matter is completed.
13. As time goes by, a client's perception of legal services decreases.
14. Monthly billing is the most common method of billing.
15. The elements of an average bill are the following:
    i. Name of case
    ii. Billing period
    iii. Date of work
    iv. Description of work performed
    v. Time increment of the work
    vi. Who performed the work
    vii. Hourly rate of person performing work
    viii. Cost of work
    ix. Itemization of costs
    x. Total costs
    xi. Total of fees and costs
    xii. Payment terms
16. A preliminary bill is prepared for the attorney's review and consideration for adjustment.
17. A fee adjustment memorandum is a form used by an attorney to increase or decrease a client's bill.
18. Traditionally, attorneys do not determine their clients' ability to pay legal fees, and this has caused firms to experience collection problems.
19. The two methods used by firms to extend credit to clients are bank loans and credit cards.
20. Fee allocation is a percentage of a bill that is given to the originating or supervising attorney as compensation.
21. A cost recovery system is a utility program that allows data to be transferred to a billing program by a copier or telephone system.
22. The style of the bill depends on the type of client, the type of case, and the policy of the firm.
23. The rule of thumb is to be as descriptive as necessary to get the bill paid.
24. The two styles of hourly bills are detailed and brief.
25. E-billing is sending an electronic bill to a client.
26. Collection activities begin when an account is 30 days past due.
27. A lawyer will become involved in collection activities when the account is 90 days past due.
28. If an attorney withdraws from a case because of nonpayment of fees, the attorney must take steps to protect the client's interest. The attorney must give the client reasonable notice and time to employ a new attorney.

29. The nine things a lawyer must consider before withdrawing from a case are the following:
    i. The client's financial condition at the beginning of the representation and whether the lawyer had knowledge of the client's ability to pay
    ii. The client's sophistication as a consumer of legal services
    iii. Whether the fees and expenses were explained fully to the client
    iv. Whether the lawyer offered several different fee arrangements and the client selected a payment option with knowledge of the consequences of the selection
    v. Whether the client has received periodic notice about costs as they were incurred and whether the actual charges remained in the range predicted
    vi. How long the fee has been outstanding
    vii. Efforts the client has made to submit partial payment
    viii. Efforts of the lawyer to negotiate a more lenient fee payment schedule
    ix. Whether there is a dispute about the fee

30. If a firm sues the client, the firm has the burden of proving the extent of the services rendered and the reasonableness of the fee.

31. Suing a client should be the last resort.

32. It is standard practice for a firm to give a client at least two weeks' notice of collection agency involvement.

33. Billing methods and disputes have contributed to the public's negative perception of lawyers.

34. The four most common areas of unethical billing practices are the following:
    i. Applying a client's funds to a disputed fee
    ii. Charging more than the client agreed to pay
    iii. Charging for services not rendered to the client
    iv. Increasing a flat fee

35. Legal fee agreements are held to a higher standard than other contracts because of the fiduciary relationship between attorney and client.

36. A fiduciary is a person who transacts business for another person, necessitating great confidence and trust by one party and a high degree of good faith by the other party.

37. Any ambiguity in a fee agreement will be determined against the lawyer.

38. A legal auditor is a person or company that audits legal bills.

39. A legal auditor is paid to find discrepancies in a law firm's bill.

40. Companies resist using a legal auditor because it may damage its relationship with outside counsel.

41. The two major problems clients complain about are ambiguous bills and high legal costs.

42. The following 14 problems are major contributors to ambiguous bills:
    i. Vague service descriptions
    ii. Surprise total
    iii. Perceived poor work
    iv. Team churning
    v. Too much interoffice conference time
    vi. Nickel-and-dime billing
    vii. Errors in arithmetic
    viii. Other glaring errors
    ix. Bill received months after work is completed
    x. Bill directed to wrong person
    xi. Padding
    xii. Paying paralegal rates for clerical work
    xiii. Review and revision charges
    xiv. Block billing

43. Of the complaints received by bar associations, most of them are complaints about legal fees.

44. Team churning is making frequent changes in the legal team and charging the client for the new team member's education about the case.

45. Padding is fraudulently increasing a bill when the fee is not warranted.

46. Block billing is charging a client for services rendered in one large block of time rather than itemizing the tasks performed in that period of time.

47. Client-directed billing policies are when clients, usually large corporations and insurance companies, have developed their own billing policies for their attorneys to follow.

48. Some attorneys object to client-directed billing because they say that the policies illegally restrict their practice of law. They say they are contrary to the code of professional responsibility and create a conflict of interest between the independence of outside counsel and their clients.

49. Once a firm has been advised of a dispute regarding a bill, a firm may not take steps to collect the amount. The firm may not send collection letters, telephone the client, or sue the client until the dispute has been resolved.

50. To keep fee disputes out of the court system, most state bar associations have developed arbitration programs to resolve fee disputes.

51. Arbitration is a process of dispute resolution in which a neutral third party (arbitrator) renders a decision after a hearing at which both parties have an opportunity to be heard.

52. Discovery is the acquisition or knowledge of facts or that which was previously unknown.

53. The organization of a firm's finance function depends on the size of the firm.

54. Direct profitability factors are factors that affect a firm's profitability in a short period of time, usually 1 year.

55. To be profitable, a task should be delegated to the least expensive employee capable of performing the task.

56. Leveraging is the ability to make money from the work of others.

57. A leverage ratio is a formula used to identify the number of leveraged income earners per partner.

Some firms may have a 1-to-4 ratio (one profit contributor per four attorneys) or a 4-to-1 ratio (four profit contributors per attorney).

58. The two types of expenses are compensation expenses and operating expenses.

59. Compensation expenses include employees' compensation and are categorized into three categories: associates' and paralegals' compensation, administrative staff salaries, and employee benefits.

60. The four categories of operating expenses are occupancy costs, office operating costs, costs of professional activities, and general business expenses.

61. Occupancy costs include office rental, storage facilities, and utilities.

62. Office operating costs include the day-to-day expenses involved in running the office, such as office equipment, computers, janitorial services, stationery, copying costs, and miscellaneous supplies.

63. Professional activity costs include professional dues, continuing education, and client promotion.

64. General business expenses include telephone costs, library costs, insurance, taxes, and interest expenses.

65. Indirect profitability factors are factors that indirectly affect a firm's profitability over a long period, more than 1 year.

66. A law firm's culture is the firm's environment, including intangible factors such as employee behavior patterns, social policies, and employees' values.

67. Reward systems include compensation plans, bonus plans, and other professional and personal reward systems for motivating people to contribute to the firm's profitability.

68. The environment affects profitability because it affects a firm's employees. Employees must have a thriving environment within which to contribute their best effort. Without such an environment, employees are not productive, therefore affecting a firm's profitability.

69. Realization is the process of turning time into cash.

70. The five steps of the realization process are getting, doing, recording, billing, and collecting for the work.

71. A realization rate is the rate that the firm actually receives for work done.

72. Management uses the realization rate to prepare the firm's budget.

73. A number of factors affect the realization rate: nonbillable time, write-ups, write-downs, and write-offs.

74. A firm will write up a client's bill when the client receives a substantial benefit from the firm's work on the case and agrees to give the firm a premium.

75. A firm will write down a client's bill when some of the timekeeper's time is not billed to the client or is discounted.

76. A write-off is when a firm credits an account for the total amount owed.

77. An 80 percent realization rate is common in a law firm.

78. To arrive at a timekeeper's realization rate, multiply the number of annual billable hours by the hourly rate and take the realization percentage of that figure.

79. A budget is the key to a law firm's profitability.

80. When developing a budget, a firm's management projects income, personnel costs, and operating expenses.

81. To project a firm's gross income for the year, management must estimate the amount of work required for existing clients and anticipate work from new clients.

82. Factors used to determine income from new clients include the economic environment, the firm's marketing activities and strategic planning, past experience in producing new clients, and competitive pressures.

83. Factors considered when projecting a firm's income are income generated from each timekeeper, annual billable hours, hourly rate, and realization rate for each timekeeper.

84. Budgeting for personnel costs requires management to anticipate associates' compensation, administrative staff salaries, employee benefit costs, and employee taxes.

85. Management calculates an expense percentage by dividing expenses by income.

86. A firm's anticipated profit is calculated by deducting the expense percentage of each timekeeper's gross fees.

87. The average expense percentage is 60 percent.

Chapter 9
Managing the Client Funds Trust Account

1. The client funds trust account is a bank account established exclusively for client funds.

2. A fiduciary is a person who holds the character of a trustee.

3. Each state's bar association has rules governing the client funds trust account.

4. Segregation of cash is keeping client funds completely separate from office and personal bank accounts.

5. A firm usually has one account for the funds of all its clients.

6. If a firm anticipates that a case will have many large transactions, the firm may open a separate trust account for that case only.

7. The type of funds held in the trust account are funds for estate proceeds, escrow funds, settlements, judgment payments, advanced fees and costs, and funds in which third persons have an interest.

8. Law firms that handle real estate transactions will accept a down payment for the property and keep those funds in the trust account pending transfer of the property.

9. The payments are paid from the law firm's trust account so that there is a record that the payment was made.

10. People prefer adversarial financial transactions to be completed with the assistance of an intermediary to eliminate misappropriation allegations.

11. An attorney may not withdraw the funds until the fees are earned and a monthly accounting is sent to the client.

12. Nonrefundable nonchargeable, or true retainer, fees that secure an attorney's availability may be deposited directly into the attorney's operating account.

13. True retainer fees are not required to be deposited directly into the trust account because they are considered "earned on receipt" and are not considered prepayment for the attorney's services.

14. Some legal malpractice insurance companies require that manual records of the trust account be kept in addition to electronic records.

15. Manual records are necessary in case of computer failure, energy shortages, and other disasters.

16. The nine steps of proper trust fund accounting follow:
    i. Preparing the client ledger sheet
    ii. Maintaining journals
    iii. Communicating with clients
    iv. Documenting transactions
    v. Disbursing funds
    vi. Reconciling the account
    vii. Preparing monthly statements
    viii. Closing an account
    ix. Keeping records

17. The client ledger sheet documents the amount of fees and costs billed, amount paid, and trust account funds received and disbursed.

18. If the client gives the firm money to deposit in the trust account, that transaction is listed separately on the client ledger card.

19. A hard copy is a copy of computer records on a sheet of paper.

20. All money received for the trust account is entered in the cash receipts journal.

21. All checks written from the trust account are entered in the cash payments journal.

22. A Trust Account Receipts/Disbursement Control Sheet monitors each activity in the trust account.

23. A Trust Account Reconciliation Sheet is used when reconciling the trust account with the bank statement.

24. The following seven items must be entered into the journals:
    i. Date of transaction
    ii. Name of payer
    iii. Name of client
    iv. Name of case
    v. Amount of transaction
    vi. Check number
    vii. Purpose and description of transaction (e.g., deposition of Harry Snow)

25. The client ledger sheets, cash receipts journal, and cash payments journal must balance with the clients' funds trust account.

26. When trust account bank statements are received each month, the statement must be reconciled immediately.

27. A client must be notified that funds were received immediately on receipt of the funds.

28. If a check is made payable to both the client and lawyer, the client must endorse the check first so it can be deposited into the trust account for disbursement.

29. If the client cannot come into the office to endorse the check, it should be sent to the client by certified mail and mailed back to the lawyer by certified mail.

30. Before a check is deposited into the trust account, copies of the deposit slip and the front and back of the check are made.

31. The copies of the check are filed in the client's file, and a copy is filed in a trust account receipts file.

32. A trust account receipts file is a file of copies of checks deposited in the trust account.

33. When entering a deposit on a client ledger sheet, include the payer, check number, and exact date of deposit.

34. A check must clear the bank before any funds are disbursed.

35. Funds must be disbursed promptly after receipt to avoid allegations of commingling.

36. The responsible attorney or office manager signs a trust account check.

37. All disbursements should have some written documentation describing what the payment is for.

38. Disbursements for payment of attorneys' fees and costs may be made after a statement is prepared for the client.

39. The trust account must be reconciled to the bank statement immediately after receipt of the statement.

40. The account must balance to the penny.

41. A statement must be sent to each client informing him or her of the status of his or her trust account each month there is activity in the account.

42. A client's trust account is ready to be closed when a case has ended and all checks have cleared the bank.

43. Most firms wait until all checks have cleared the bank before closing a client's trust account.

44. All the funds in the account must be disbursed before closing, and each transaction must be documented on the client ledger sheet.

45. Records of a trust account must be kept for auditing purposes or in the event of a malpractice claim.

46. Trust account records should be kept for at least 5 years after the account is closed.

47. Interest on trust accounts is sent to state bar associations to fund indigent legal programs.

48. The funds are used to fund legal programs for the indigent.

49. IOLTA stands for Interest on Lawyers' Trust Accounts.
50. The IOLTA program was begun in England, Canada, and Australia in the 1960s.
51. Florida was the first state in the United States to adopt an IOLTA program.
52. The three types of IOLTA participation follow:
    i. Mandatory: All lawyers in the state must participate in IOLTA.
    ii. Voluntary: All lawyers may choose whether to participate in IOLTA.
    iii. Opt-out: All lawyers must participate unless they affirmatively choose not to participate.
53. The money received for interest is transferred to the state bar or state bar foundation.
54. The IOLTA funds sponsor law-related public interest programs for the indigent, elderly, or disabled, including legal aid, victim assistance programs, and client security funds.
55. A client security fund is a fund established to reimburse clients who have been damaged because of their attorney's fraudulent abuse of the trust account.
56. The legality of IOLTA programs was challenged in the 1998 case of *Phillips v. Washington Legal Foundation* (96-1578).
57. The U.S. Supreme Court ruled that interest earned on client funds held in IOLTA accounts is the private property of the client.
58. The Conference of State Supreme Court Chief Justices issued a unanimous resolution urging "continued operation of IOLTA programs in every jurisdiction."
59. IOLTA programs continue to function as usual since the Supreme Court's ruling, because the constitutionality of their programs was upheld.
60. Attorneys who abuse their trust accounts may be disciplined by the state bar association.
61. The state bar association audits attorneys' trust accounts.
62. In some states, the state bar may audit a firm's trust account at any time without provocation or reason, and other states audit only those accounts where abuse is suspected.
63. Some state bar associations require banks to automatically notify it of any trust account overdrafts or bounced checks, whether they were honored or not.
64. An overdraft is an indication of mishandling a trust account.
65. Common abuses of the client funds account include the following:
    i. Misappropriation
    ii. Using client funds to cover office expenses
    iii. Withdrawing funds from the trust account of one client to meet another client's trust account obligations
    iv. Check kiting

    v. Commingling funds
    vi. Failure to promptly notify clients of receipt of funds
    vii. Failure to promptly disburse funds
    viii. Failure to provide clients with an accounting of trust account funds
66. Misappropriation is writing personal checks from a trust account.
67. If an attorney writes a personal check from the trust account, the attorney is essentially stealing the client's money.
68. No office expense may be paid from the trust account, except bank charges for the trust account.
69. Check kiting is when money is withdrawn from a recently deposited check before the check has cleared the bank, thereby using other clients' funds to cover the check.
70. Commingling is mixing law firm funds with client funds.
71. The only time an attorney may deposit a firm's funds into the clients' trust account is to cover monthly bank charges, such as service charges and check charges.
72. The attorney is ultimately responsible for the condition of the trust account.
73. A paralegal not familiar with trust funds accounting principles may be exposing the firm to serious liability if allowed to maintain the firm's client funds account.
74. If a client terminates the attorney-client relationship, all funds in the client funds account that have not been earned must be immediately returned to the client.
75. In most states, a lawyer must have a client's permission to apply funds in the trust account to an outstanding legal bill.
76. If an attorney who works for a law firm that is a partnership abuses the trust account, each partner may also be subject to disciplinary proceedings.
77. Managing the client funds account accurately has the following benefits:
    i. Reduced legal malpractice insurance costs
    ii. Reduced ethics problems
    iii. Reduced client complaints
    iv. Reduced stress and anxiety

Chapter 10

Technology in the Law Office

1. The primary challenge is keeping current with the latest technology.
2. Access to the Internet has resulted in information overload. Information must be managed properly in order for members of the legal team to be able to locate it.
3. Software applications are developed specifically for the operating system used by the firm's computers.

4. There are currently three major operating systems: Windows, Macintosh, and Unix.

5. Microsofts Windows operating system is the most popular and widely used operating system used in law offices today.

6. The Windows operation system has its origin in an operating system that was used in the 1970s and 1980s called MS-DOS (Microsoft Disk Operating System).

7. Most software in use today is designed for the Windows operating system.

8. The Macintosh operating system was the first to use a graphical user interface.

9. The Unix operating system was created for computer programmers developing software, and is generally used by very large computers and servers.

10. A custom software application is created exclusively for the law firm.

11. Off-the-shelf applications are created by software companies that market and distribute the software to the public.

12. Integrated software applications combine many software applications into one program.

13. An advantage of an integrated system is that the commands in the software are uniform, making the program easy to use.

14. A disadvantage to an integrated system is that the individual features are generally less powerful than an individual application.

15. Office suites combine several separate software applications, such as word processing, spreadsheet, database, and presentation programs, into one package.

16. Some advantages to an office suite are that the applications have similar interfaces that interact with one another, making them easily integrated. Training time is reduced, and the features of the software are easier to use. It is also less expensive than purchasing each application individually.

17. Most law firms use off-the-shelf computer applications and office suites.

18. Word processing software has been a standard application used in law firms since the 1960s.

19. The two most popular word processing systems used in law offices today are Corel's WordPerfect and Microsofts MS Word.

20. Add-ons (or plug-ins) are software created to enhance the features of other software and are used in conjunction with other software.

21. Add-on software adds features to other applications.

22. A spreadsheet application is used to crunch numbers.

23. A database application is a powerful application used by law firms and other businesses to manage information.

24. Law firms use a database for its client list, to log marketing efforts, and to manage its brief bank.

25. Time and billing software prepares timekeeping reports, prepares invoices, and prepares numerous management reports.

26. Calendar and docket control software is used to control calendars, monitor deadlines, and track essential law firm tasks.

27. The benefits of a calendar and docket control application are guarding against missed deadlines, reducing employee time to enter due dates, and updating rules when rules are changed.

28. Document management software manages a complex litigation case.

29. Complex litigation cases often involve thousands and sometimes millions of documents. These documents must be reviewed and organized in a manner that allows the legal team fast access to them. By inputting each document into a document management database, the information can be screened, sorted, and located quickly.

30. There are four types of document management software: abstract, full-text retrieval, document imaging, and a combination of these.

31. A document abstract system prepares an abstract, or summary, of a document's contents.

32. A full-text retrieval contains the entire document instead of a summary.

33. Scanning is entering text or graphics into a computer by electronically changing the characters into a computer-readable format.

34. Case/practice management software is developed for use in a specific area of law.

35. The Internet is a worldwide cooperative network of networks.

36. The Internet was designed by the Advanced Research Projects Agency headed by Lawrence Roberts.

37. The Internet was designed for the U.S. Department of Defense in the 1960s.

38. The Internet's purpose was to be a means of communication that would withstand nuclear war or other disaster.

39. The name of the first Internet was ARPANET.

40. ARPANET stands for the Advanced Research Projects Agency of the Department of Defense, which funded it.

41. In 1983, ARPANET split into two networks: ARPANET and MILNET.

42. The Department of Defense controlled MILNET, and the National Science Foundation controlled ARPANET.

43. The name of the second Internet became NSFNET.

44. Access to NSFNET was provided free to any U.S. research and educational institution for noncommercial purposes.

45. NSFNET was used primarily by scientists, academics, and nonprofit organizations.

46. Commercial use of NSFNET was allowed in 1991.

47. NREN stands for the National Research and Education Network.

48. NREN was a $2 billion project approved by Congress to upgrade the NSFNET backbone.

49. No one owns the Internet.

50. The two things needed to access the Internet are browser software and an Internet Service Provider (ISP).

51. An Internet Service Provider (ISP) is a private company that provides access to the Internet for a fee.

52. An ISP's computers are known as servers.

53. The ISP's server is connected either to larger regional networks or directly to the backbone sites that direct traffic on the Internet.

54. An ISP gets its access from telephone and cable companies and charges a fee for its service.

55. A protocol is a set of rules that ensures that different network software products can work together.

56. Protocols dictate how the various systems on the Internet operate.

57. Protocol standards are set by the Internet Engineering Task Force (IETF).

58. An FTP, or File Transfer Protocol, is a protocol that allows files to be transferred between computers.

59. Telnet protocol is a protocol that allows a computer to connect with a remote computer as if it were local.

60. The five factors that attributed to the Internet's sudden growth and prominence are the following:
    i. Widespread use of personal computers and graphical user interfaces, such as the Windows operating system
    ii. Elimination of commercial use prohibitions
    iii. The creation of software applications specifically for use on the Internet
    iv. The existence of a large body of electronically stored data
    v. Technological advances in computer hardware, such as modems and monitors

61. A domain name is a unique name that identifies an organization on the Internet.

62. Domain names were created in 1986 by the National Science Foundation (NSF), AT&T, and Network Solutions, Inc. (NSI).

63. The domain name project was called the InterNIC project.

64. The name of the private company that manages domain name registration is the Internet Corporation for Assigned Names and Numbers (ICANN).

65. A type identifier is a suffix at the end of a domain name that describes the type of organization.

66. The 10 categories of type identifiers are commercial, educational institution, nonprofit organization, military organization, network provider, government institution, business, information, individual name, and professional.

67. Countries are identified on the Internet by an additional extension after their domain name identifying the country.

68. A cybersquatter registers domain names to extort money from the trademark holder.

69. The Anti-cybersquatting Consumer Protection Act of 1999 outlaws cybersquatting.

70. The World Wide Web (WWW, or Web) is one of the protocols that operate via the Internet.

71. The Web was developed by Tim Berners-Lee in 1990 at the European Laboratory for Particle Physics (CERN) in Switzerland.

72. The Web is managed by the World Wide Web Consortium (W3C), also known as the World Wide Web Initiative (<http://www.w3c.org>).

73. The W3C is run by the Massachusetts Institute of Technology (MIT), Keio University, and the European Research consortium for Informatics and Mathematics in France.

74. The W3C is funded by membership dues from organizational members.

75. The W3C's purpose is to promote the Web by developing specification and reference software that will be freely available to everyone.

76. The protocol used by the Web is called Hypertext Transfer Protocol (HTTP).

77. The specific software language used by all documents on the Web is Hypertext Markup Language (HTML).

78. In order for a computer to read the HTML language, it needs browser software.

79. Shareware is software that is distributed without initial cost. If the user likes the software, a nominal payment is expected.

80. A hyperlink is a connection to another page or site that allows a person to navigate the Web.

81. Hyperlinks enable readers to navigate through the Web.

82. A collection of hyperlinks, grouped together in an orderly manner, is called a website.

83. The first page of a website is known as the home page.

84. The legal profession uses the Web to publicize cases and manage the media in high-profile cases by posting exhibits and other information on the Web.

85. The three basic ways to locate specific information on the Internet are the following:
    i. Uniform Resource Locator (URL)
    ii. Keyword search
    iii. Topical index

86. A Uniform Resource Locator (URL) is an address of a website that directs a person to the information.

87. The four main elements of a URL are the following:
    i. Protocol
    ii. Address of server where the data are located
    iii. Domain name
    iv. Type identifier

88. Almost all companies and corporations use a ".com" identifier.

89. The ".com" identifier means that it is a commercial site.

90. To locate a website outside the United States, substitute the type identifier with the country code, as follows: <http://www.louvre.fr>.

91. A pathname is the URL address showing the path of where a certain document may be found on a website.

92. Pages in a URL are separated by a forward slash, as follows: Protocol://server.domainname/pathname/name of document (<http://www.microsoft.com/products/msword>).

93. Certain rules apply to all URLs. There are no spaces in a URL. Each word of a domain name is run together (except some words in a domain name may be connected by a dash). A forward slash (/) is always used instead of a backward slash (\). Domain names are not uppercase but are entered in all lowercase letters.

94. Each browser has a search feature that allows a keyword search. Enter the keyword of the desired site or information, and the browser will retrieve the websites that contain information about the words inserted.

95. A Boolean search is a method of defining search criteria.

96. A Boolean search creates sets of words so that a search engine can narrow the search.

97. A search engine is an independent company that has indexed Internet sites and categorized them so that they can be found easily.

98. A search engine categorizes Internet sites into groupings of related fields, such as government, law, judiciary, and so on.

99. Bookmarking is a part of browser software that marks a website so that its URL is accessible without searching for it.

100. Commercial websites of reputable companies warrant the accuracy of their websites, as do most created by law librarians and archivists.

101. The seven things you can do to verify the accuracy of a website are the following:
    i. Check to see whether the author of the website is identified.
    ii. Determine the purpose of the website. Is it for the reader's benefit or the author's benefit?
    iii. Do not judge a website by its home page. Home pages can be professional looking but may promote quack remedies or illegal activities.
    iv. Look for the date of the last update. If one is not available, the site may be outdated.
    v. Look at the site's links. If some have disappeared, it is a clue that the site is outdated.
    vi. Verify the information elsewhere. Some experts recommend verifying information by two other sources.
    vii. Consult website review guides.

102. The federal government is the largest contributor of material on the Web.

103. An intranet is a law firm's internal information distribution system that is based on Web technology.

104. Web-based technology is Internetlike software applications.

105. An intranet differs from the Web because it is private and is accessible only by designated individuals, normally firm employees.

106. Groupware is software created for and used by an intranet and an extranet.

107. Intranets are custom made and designed according to a firm's specifications by professional intranet designers or in-house computer specialists.

108. An intranet is used to distribute information electronically to its members.

109. A brief bank is a collection of documents that are used as templates to prepare new documents.

110. A template is a form document used as a guide to prepare new documents.

111. An extranet is a Web-based interface to a private network.

112. An extranet offers the same benefits as an intranet: efficiency, improved quality of work, and enhancement of communication among people working together.

113. The difference between an intranet and an extranet is that an extranet is directed to different people and has different uses.

114. A firm-centered extranet is where a law firm creates an extranet connection to its clients, especially large corporate clients.

115. A client-centered extranet is where a client provides its law firm(s) with an extranet.

116. The difference between a firm-centered and a client-centered extranet is that a firm-centered extranet gives a firm control over its content and access, and a client-centered extranet gives a client control of its content and access.

117. A brokered extranet is where a third party provides access to an extranet for a fee.

118. The two types of security risks with an extranet are restricting access so that unauthorized persons cannot access the system and protecting information in transit to and from other members in the extranet.

119. A firewall is a protective electronic barrier constructed around a network so that unauthorized persons cannot get through.

120. The easiest security method to implement is to place the extranet in an undisclosed address on the Web.

121. The most common security method is to require each user to use a special ID and password to gain entry to the extranet.

122. A digital ID is a personal ID number that is encrypted and can be read only by the extranet.

123. Users with digital IDs can obtain certificates from an outside vendor that will certify that the user is who he or she purports to be.

124. Cryptography is the process of securing private information that is passed through public networks.

125. Cryptography mathematically scrambles information in a way that makes it unreadable to anyone except

the person holding the mathematical key that can unscramble it.

126. The two types of cryptography that are in use today are same key and public key.

127. Same-key cryptography is when a message is encrypted and decrypted using the same key, which is passed along from one party to another.

128. Public-key cryptography uses a pair of different keys (one public, one private). A message encrypted with one key can be decrypted only with the other key and vice versa.

129. Electronic mail (e-mail) is an electronic message sent from one person to another through their computers.

130. E-mail passes to its destination through servers.

131. An ISP provides each customer with an e-mail address that allows the customer to use the ISP's server.

132. The three main parts of an e-mail address are username, domain name, and type identifier.

133. A username contains no spaces and no uppercase letters.

134. The username and domain name are separated by an axon symbol (@), which symbolizes the word *at*.

135. E-mail addresses arc always in lowercase letters.

136. "Case sensitive" means that all letters must be in a specific case. If a letter is the wrong case, the information cannot be read.

137. E-mail addresses and Web addresses are different. A Web address has a URL, and an e-mail message is sent to a section of the URL.

138. A listserv is a group of people who exchange information about a particular topic on the Internet.

139. Newsgroups are public discussions on topics of general interest in which anyone with newsreader software can participate. A listserv contains a mailing list of e-mail addresses of people interested in the same subject.

140. Lurking is reading but not responding to messages posted on a listserv.

141. Listservs are either public or private and consist of two types: announcement-type and discussion-type.

142. An announcement-type listserv allows you to receive messages, but you cannot respond to the messages.

143. A discussion-type listserv allows every member to participate in the discussion.

144. A moderated listserv allows all messages to be sent to a list moderator who reviews them and makes a determination of whether it is appropriate to be distributed to the group.

145. An unmoderated listserv does not review each message, which is automatically sent to the group regardless of content.

146. Netiquette is an informal code of conduct that governs e-mail communication.

147. Netiquette rules are enforced by the people using them.

148. You should not assume that your e-mail is private because a firm's system administrator has access to

e-mails to maintain the system, and e-mails are easily forwarded to others.

149. You should never give your user ID or password to another person because another person can wreak havoc with your e-mail account.

150. You should keep messages short and to the point because most busy people resent long e-mails that contain information not relevant to the subject matter.

151. Quotations should be edited to include only the relevant material to keep messages short.

152. An e-mail should be limited to one subject to keep e-mails short.

153. A signature footer should include your name, position, affiliation, and e-mail address. It should not exceed four lines. A telephone number can be included.

154. You should not use words in all caps because it is considered shouting.

155. Never send chain letters because they clutter the system.

156. Spell out dates because of the international nature of the Internet. Do not list dates by the numbers (12/21/YY). Always spell out the month to avoid confusion: Dec 24, 2009, or 24 Dec 09.

157. A flame is an angry or derogatory e-mail message.

158. You should not forward personal e-mail because it is considered extremely rude to forward a personal e-mail to members of a listserv without the original author's permission.

159. An emoticon is a symbol used to express feelings in e-mail.

160. Be careful with humor because without verbal communication and body language that can communicate your intent, e-mails can be misinterpreted.

161. Use acronyms to keep e-mail messages short.

162. You should know your firm's e-mail policy because e-mail sent to persons within the firm are subject to the firm's e-mail policy.

163. You must clearly identify yourself when communicating with clients or others regarding a case because it is important that your status indicates that you are not an attorney.

164. You should check your e-mail daily because important information requires an immediate response, and e-mails can pile up, making review and response a time-consuming activity.

165. Spam is junk e-mail that is unsolicited. Spamming is the practice of promoting a product or service by e-mail to a group of people.

166. You should use punctuation sparingly. Many periods can separate thoughts (.....), but the use of many exclamation marks looks like anger (!!!!!). Many question marks also signify strong emotion (?????).

167. E-mails that contain important information should not be deleted but should be stored permanently on the firm's server or printed and put in the appropriate file.

168. An e-mail filter is software that manages e-mail and that can be programmed to delete e-mails that contain profanity or offensive material.
169. E-mail messages sent to clients that contain legal advice must be kept confidential to protect attorney-client privilege.
170. One method that ensures an e-mail message is kept confidential is encryption.
171. Most states say that websites are advertising.
172. The four advertising prohibitions that apply to websites are the following:
    i. It cannot contain a misrepresentation.
    ii. It cannot contain an omission of fact, making a statement misleading.
    iii. It cannot create an unjustified expectation about the results the lawyer can achieve.
    iv. It cannot compare the lawyer's services with those of other lawyers.
173. Attorneys have been accused of soliciting if their websites are considered misleading.

Chapter 11

Law Office Systems

1. The purpose of a system is to streamline a task so that members of the legal team do not do unnecessary work, waste firm resources, or make a mistake.
2. The goals of a system are to maximize productivity, minimize waste, conserve resources, reduce errors, and produce high-quality work.
3. Systems are used to do the following seven things:
    i. Guarantee that the firm's products maintain their excellence
    ii. Guarantee that the firm's commodity (time) is used to its maximum potential
    iii. Give each member of the legal team the benefit of the experience of another
    iv. Substitute for recollection
    v. Improve language and legal skills
    vi. Promote delegation
    vii. Preserve methods
4. The four types of systems are macrosystems, microsystems, minisystems, and subsystems.
5. A macrosystem is a large system within which microsystems are contained.
6. A law firm is comprised of a macrosystem, two microsystems (substantive and administrative), many minisystems, and many subsystems.
7. A firm's macrosystem consists of affiliated industries within which a firm must operate.
8. The three main elements that affect a firm's macrosystem are technology, the economy (U.S. and local), and government laws and regulations.

9. A law firm has two microsystems.
10. The two microsystems in a law firm are administrative and substantive.
11. The administrative microsystem consists of the firm's goals and objectives, resources, culture, and management style.
12. A firm's substantive microsystem is responsible for delivering legal services to the client.
13. The number of substantive microsystems in a firm varies according to the areas of law in which the firm practices.
14. The three methods of acquiring substantive microsystems are to develop the system, to evolve the system, and to buy the system.
15. A minisystem is a system within the microsystem.
16. The type and number of minisystems depend on the individual system users and the efforts of the firm to develop systems.
17. Minisystems are constantly changing because parts of the minisystem are improved, expanded, or changed as the law changes and as its users become more experienced.
18. Each step in a minisystem is considered a subsystem.
19. The number of subsystems in a minisystem depends on the procedural aspects of the case.
20. Systems development is thinking through and documenting in detail the way to get the job done.
21. The lawyer has ultimate responsibility for the management and supervision of a system.
22. The four stages of systems development are analyze, synthesize, organize, and finalize.
23. The four steps of system analysis are review, separate, evaluate, and communicate.
24. Coding each step allows the paralegal to identify the status of each step quickly.
25. It is important to discuss each step of the system with coworkers because they will be expected to participate in the system.
26. The three steps of the synthesis process are eliminate, delegate, and consolidate.
27. When delegating functions, it is important to understand the limits within which support staff can function.
28. A systems developer consolidates by combining the new elements.
29. The two steps of the organization process are chronological sequencing and developing a master task list.
30. The master task list is the skeleton from which the system will be developed.
31. The purpose of a master task list is to do the following:
    i. Give a description of each task.
    ii. Describe specifically when each task is due.
    iii. Indicate the documents required to complete the task.
    iv. List the person responsible for completing the task and preparing the documents.

v. Give the order in which each task is to be completed.

vi. List all actions to be taken (e.g., telephone client).

vii. Include telephone calls or court appearances.

viii. Direct the person to the appropriate checklist.

32. The four steps of the finalization process are forms and checklists, written instructions, system checks and follow-up, and revision.

33. A form letter is a letter that contains standardized language and can be customized for a particular case.

34. A blind insert is an entry in a form document alerting the preparer to insert material. It is seen on the computer screen but is not printed.

35. A checklist includes each step of the system and lists the responsible team member.

36. Checklists are maintained in the computer so that they may be changed easily.

37. Form documents are numbered so that they are easily identified.

38. Written instructions are important because they explain how to use a system.

39. Information for written instructions is obtained from the final master task list.

40. The four sections to the written instructions are information, requirements, instructions, and examples of forms and checklists.

41. The information section of written instructions contains information about the goal and purpose of the system and the specific area of law for which the system was developed.

42. All the system's requirements are listed in the requirements section and include the following:

i. Software used (including version)

ii. Titles of team members using the system

iii. Outside services, such as attorney service and courier

iv. Other supplies and requirements necessary

43. The instructions section should inform the reader when to use the system and how to use the system, and provide an explanation of each step of the system.

44. The master task list is the beginning of the instructions section.

45. Written instructions are the basis of the system's evaluation.

46. The forms and checklist section contains a hard copy of all forms and checklists in the order they are used.

47. As the system is tested, necessary changes are noted.

48. The revision process consists of the entire systems development process but on a smaller scale.

49. The best method of storing a system is in a three-ring binder.

50. A system is divided into sections by tabbed dividers to separate sections of the system.

51. There should be an original and one copy of a system.

52. Essential skills for systems development are sharp analytical skills, good work habits, good planning and scheduling skills, and good time management skills.

53. The four common problems of systems development are desire for more steps, desire for fewer steps, need for updates, and use of the system as an information source.

54. During the course of working in a particular area of law, checklists, form documents, and form files are developed. These are the beginning of a system.

55. A commercial substantive minisystem is one that is purchased from an outside company.

56. When purchasing a system, a person must be sure that the system is current and expandable. It is also important that the forms in the system comply with the court's requirements.

Chapter 12

Docket Control Systems

1. According to the ABA, calendaring errors are the leading cause of legal malpractice claims.

2. Secretaries and/or paralegals in small firms may have total responsibility for the docket system.

3. In large firms, maintaining a firm's docket is the responsibility of docket coordinators or docket clerks.

4. A paralegal must have knowledge of docket control systems because she or he is responsible for the day-to-day maintenance of a case.

5. A docket control system contains trial dates, court and hearing dates, deposition dates, meeting dates, filing deadlines, follow-up dates, appointments, and reminder dates.

6. A missed deadline can result in a legal malpractice suit, disciplinary proceedings, and/or damage to a firm's reputation.

7. The six functions of a good docket control system are the following:

i. Meet time requirements

ii. Expedite completion of tasks

iii. Promote good client relations

iv. Ensure that professional liability insurance requirements are satisfied

v. Reduce stress

vi. Avoid financial loss by reducing malpractice claims

8. The characteristics of a good docket control system are the following:

i. Provides immediate and automatic calendaring

ii. Provides a double-check of entries

iii. Allows sufficient lead time in advance for completion of tasks

iv. Provides for follow-up to ensure actual performance of work

v. Is easily maintained and operated

9. The two types of calendars used in a law office are master and personal.

10. The master calendar contains trial dates, hearing dates, and deposition dates for each attorney in the firm.

11. The purpose of the master calendar is to be able to locate the attorney in case of an emergency and for future scheduling.

12. Large firms normally distribute master calendars daily.

13. A small firm that has few changes in the master calendar distributes it less often, normally weekly.

14. Firms with an intranet do not distribute hard copies of master calendars because employees have immediate access to the most recent changes to the calendars on their desktops.

15. Essential information on a master calendar includes the following:
    i. The first initial and last name of the attorney or the initials of the attorney
    ii. Type of matter (trial, hearing, deposition)
    iii. Time
    iv. Name of case
    v. Location

16. A personal calendar contains two types of information: primary and secondary.

17. Primary information includes court trials and hearings, depositions, and statutes of limitations.

18. A statute of limitations is the time period within which an action must be commenced.

19. Secondary information includes the following:
    i. Dates and times of appointments with clients
    ii. Dates and times of conferences
    iii. Other dates, such as bar association luncheons or continuing education obligations
    iv. Personal reminders, such as birthdays and vacations
    v. Deadlines and reminder dates

20. It is recommended that a manual system be used, in addition to a computerized system, as a backup in the event that the computer system should be unavailable for some reason and to double-check against missed deadlines.

21. A manual calendar consisting of primary and secondary information may be a large appointment book, a small appointment book, or a desk calendar. It may also be a hard copy of the information stored in the computer.

22. A legal secretary is usually given the responsibility for keeping the calendars current.

23. Personal calendars should be updated daily, and the updated information should be shared with other members of the legal team.

24. Events are docketed as soon as they occur.

25. Documents from opposing parties that require a response or other action are entered into the docket system as they are received.

26. A stamp or an initial on a document means that the event was docketed.

27. The absence of a stamp or an initial on a document means that the event was not docketed.

28. A calendar meeting is often a short, informal meeting.

29. A docket coordinator is a person in charge of a firm's docketing process.

30. A docket request sheet is a form that contains docketing information that is directed to a docketing coordinator for insertion into a firm's docket system.

31. A docket request sheet contains the following information:
    i. Name or initials of person requesting the docket entry
    ii. Responsible attorney
    iii. Name of case and file number, if applicable
    iv. Type of matter (trial, deposition)
    v. Date and time
    vi. Place (if court, indicate courtroom)
    vii. Reminder dates
    viii. Date the event was docketed
    ix. Signature or initials of docket clerk indicating completion

32. Each docket request sheet should have an original and three copies, with each page a different color (e.g., white, blue, pink, and yellow).

33. As a secretary or paralegal completes the top white sheet, three copies of the information are automatically made. The requesting party keeps the bottom pink sheet as a record that the request was made. The remaining original and two copies are transferred to the docket coordinator. A docket clerk enters the information and signs and dates the docket sheet. The docket coordinator keeps the yellow sheet and returns the white (original) and blue copies to the requesting party, indicating that the docket entry was made. The secretary or paralegal keeps the white original as a record that the event was docketed and as a reminder to enter the information into the manual calendars. The blue copy is given to the attorney so that he or she can enter the information into a manual calendar.

34. A docket request sheet is used to inform other members of the legal team that an event was docketed so that they can insert the information into their personal calendars.

35. It is important to keep all calendars, whether they are computerized or manual, out of the view of clients to protect the confidentiality of the information.

36. A tickler system is a method of controlling deadlines.

37. If no tickler system is implemented, a legal team would have no method to control deadlines.

38. An integrated tickler system is combined with the firm's calendar.

39. A paralegal enters the daily schedule on the left side of a personal calendar.

40. A paralegal enters tickler dates on the right side of a personal calendar.
41. The three dates considered when determining due dates are the trigger date, the due date, and the mail date.
42. A trigger date begins the clock running on an event.
43. A due date is the date a document is due, which is also known as the drop-dead date.
44. If a due date falls on a holiday or weekend day, the due date is the next business day.
45. A mail date is the date a document must be mailed to reach its destination by the due date.
46. The exact number of days that should be set aside for mailing is determined by statute.
47. When counting days to determine the due date of a document, the first day is excluded.
48. When counting days to determine the due date of a document, the last day is included.
49. The first day after the trigger date, including holidays and weekend days, is the first day counted (the due date is the last day counted).
50. Weekends and holidays are counted when determining due dates.
51. Weekends and holidays are not counted when a response is due in a federal case in 11 days or less of the trigger date.
52. A state's requirements for counting weekend and holiday dates are found in statutes.
53. You compensate for mail time when determining due dates by adding the correct number of days for mailing.
54. The four reminder dates are reminder, urging, warning, and due date.
55. The time intervals between reminder dates are flexible.
56. The time intervals between reminder dates are determined by the firm's management or responsible attorney.
57. Time intervals between reminder dates must be adjustable and flexible to accommodate holidays, weekends, and other events.
58. Monitoring statutes of limitations is extremely important because if a statute of limitations is missed, a client is prohibited from proceeding.
59. A 1-year statute of limitation has four reminder dates.
60. A 4-year statute of limitations has five reminder dates.
61. A standard 30-day deadline has three reminder dates.
62. For a document that must be filed within 15 days, two reminders are sufficient.
63. A default is a failure to respond within the required time.
64. When entering the due dates of opposing parties, only the due date is entered.
65. Various methods are used to differentiate the due dates of opposing parties. If a computerized system is used, clients' information can be entered in italics, bold, or color. If a manual system is used, the information may be entered in red for a client and black for an opposing party, or an asterisk (*) may be inserted beside information concerning a client, and a *C* for a client and *O* for an opposing party.
66. If a document is mailed to a client and is subject to other deadlines, an entry must be made in a paralegal's tickler system when the document is expected back.
67. If a client, opposing counsel, or other person agrees to provide a paralegal with verbal information on a certain date, an entry is made to a tickler system to remind the paralegal that the information is coming.
68. If an attorney is unexpectedly ill and must be out of the office for a period of time, the tickler system is consulted by other attorneys in the office who will temporarily take over the absent attorney's workload.
69. The basic rule of a tickler system is that no item is removed from the system until it is completed.
70. If information is verbally communicated, chances are that the information will get lost in myriad other matters on the minds of the attorney and paralegal.
71. Docketing due dates and reminder dates correctly is only half the battle; getting the job done is the other half.
72. The two types of computerized docketing systems are static calendar programs and automated docketing programs.
73. A static calendar program is a calendar program that requires entries to be made manually.
74. Both primary and secondary information are entered into a static calendar program.
75. All dates, including tickler dates, are inserted manually into a static calendar program.
76. Static calendar programs are similar to manual, handwritten systems.
77. Static calendar programs are prone to error.
78. Static calendar programs are found in small firms.
79. Two areas of automated docketing software set them apart from static calendaring programs: they prevent users from entering data incorrectly, and they apply preprogrammed court rules to schedule events.
80. Court rules-based docketing programs contain databases that are preprogrammed with court rules so that the correct rule and its time frame are automatically applied to a client's matter.
81. A malpractice alert report lists all cases that have no activity scheduled for them.
82. The key features of an automated docketing program are the following:
    i. Preprogrammed court rules
    ii. Automatic date scheduling
    iii. Automatic reminders
    iv. Data validation
    v. Holiday scheduling
    vi. Retroactive event recalculation
    vii. Group scheduling
    viii. Scheduling reports

83. Automatic date scheduling allows a user to enter a key event date such as a trigger date, and the due date and reminder dates are automatically calculated and scheduled.
84. The data validation feature will automatically validate client matters so that an incorrect entry cannot be made. This feature prevents the possibility that two schedules are prepared for one client.
85. The holiday scheduling feature must be flexible to allow the user to insert other holidays that may be jurisdiction specific.
86. The retroactive event recalculation feature allows entries to be recalculated if a rule changes.
87. The group scheduling feature is important so that all members of the team receive important information relating to the group in their calendars.
88. The information in an automated docketing system is displayed in a calendar that resembles a personal calendar.
89. The advantages to an automated docketing program are that it will increase accuracy, thereby increasing productivity and thus the firm's profits.
90. An online calendaring service calculates due dates and reminder dates online and sends their customer the information via e-mail.
91. It would be convenient for a law firm to use an online calendaring service when it needs access to out-of-state court rules information.
92. A docket request sheet is used with a manual tickler system. These sheets come in multipart sets, with each page a different color. If docket request sheets are purchased from a legal supply store, they must have at least four pages in different colors. The original white page is for the due date, the pink slip for the warning date, the blue slip for the urging date, and the yellow slip for the reminder date (or other color-coding scheme as the firm may choose). When a docket request sheet is completed, each page is inserted behind its corresponding date. Each morning, the tickler slips are pulled, and the appropriate action is taken. When the current month ends, there should be no tickler sheets left behind any daily divider in that month. The daily divider cards in the current month are then transferred to the first month without daily divider cards. Tickler slips behind that month are then put behind the appropriate daily divider. Yearly index cards are used for long-range dates for events such as judgment renewal dates, stockholder meetings, tax return dates, statute of limitations, and review dates for wills and contracts.
93. Red sticker dots can be put on those cards that represent weekend or holiday dates.
94. A file review system is a system in which a file cannot be ignored or lost.
95. Each file should be reviewed monthly.
96. An attorney should not postpone a file review because doing so defeats its purpose and results in loose habits.
97. When a file is reviewed, the review date is inserted into the system and on a file review sheet, which is inserted into the file or taped to the cover of the file folder.
98. File review promotes good client relations because it gives the firm an opportunity to communicate with a client.

Chapter 13

File and Records Management

1. The three types of filing systems are centralized, decentralized, and automated.
2. A centralized filing system has all files in one location.
3. A centralized filing system is managed by a file coordinator or clerk.
4. Large firms and many medium-sized firms use centralized filing systems.
5. Controlled access is access and retrieval of a firm's files that is controlled by a specific system.
6. A decentralized filing system has files in different locations, usually divided by department or category.
7. The files are stored in or near the responsible attorney's work area, and each attorney is responsible for maintaining his or her own files.
8. A small firm will have a decentralized system.
9. An automated filing system uses the computer to classify files and folders in the same way a manual system does.
10. The three parts of an automated filing system are document entry, scanning, and retrieval.
11. Imaging is the process of scanning a paper document into a computer system.
12. A user may search the database to find a file. The system will display the files that match the criteria and will display the documents in the file. A user can review, print, or fax documents directly from the system.
13. Classification is the process of separating items into categories.
14. A good classification system increases accessibility and reduces complexity.
15. The four major categories for most law firm files are function, subject, topic, and subtopic.
16. Before a document can be found, the function of its file must be known.
17. After the function is identified, records are divided into subjects.
18. After the subject is identified, it is further divided into topics.
19. Topics may be further divided into subtopics.
20. A coding system is a method used to store files in a specified sequence.

21. The three methods of coding files are alphabetical, numeric, and alphanumeric.

22. An alphabetical coding system is the most common coding system used by sole proprietors and small firms. Corporate legal departments will also use an alphabetical coding system.

23. An alphabetical coding system is the easiest coding system to maintain.

24. An alphabetical coding system files a client's files alphabetically by the surname of the client.

25. The first unit of an individual client's file is his or her surname.

26. The first unit of a business client's file name is the first word of the business name (except the word "the").

27. File nothing before something.

28. The word *the* is always considered the last unit.

29. Ignore all punctuation and symbols when alphabetizing.

30. Arabic and roman numerals are filed sequentially before alphabetical letters.

31. The call letters of a television station are considered one unit.

32. Cross-referencing a file is documenting other names that might be used and directing the reader to the appropriate file.

33. If a client is the sole plaintiff in a case, his or her name would be the first name in a case name.

34. If a client is the defendant, his or her name would be the second name in the case name.

35. "Adversus," as opposed to "versus," indicates that the client is a defendant.

36. A primary case name is the name used to identify a case. It consists of the first-named plaintiff and the first-named defendant.

37. In an insurance defense firm or corporate legal department with only one client, the client's name is not indicated on the label since that name is the same for each file.

38. Subject alphabetical coding for clients' files is more difficult than straight alphabetical coding because a user must know the subject before a file is accessible.

39. Firms that code files by subject must cross-index the case in an alphabetical listing by a client's name to locate the files.

40. The six types of numeric systems are the following:
    i. Straight numbering
    ii. Coded numbering
    iii. Calendar numbering
    iv. Standard numbering
    v. Account numbering
    vi. Combination numbering

41. Straight numbering is consecutive numbering: 1, 2, 3, 4.

42. Straight numbering is the least complicated numeric numbering system.

43. Straight numbering usually begins at 100.

44. Coded numbering combines numbers with letters of the alphabet.

45. Coded numbering allows files in one category to be filed together.

46. Calendar numbering inserts the month and year the file was opened as part of the file number.

47. Calendar numbering will keep all files opened in each particular year together.

48. A calendar numbering system will inform the firm how many files are opened in the year and in the month.

49. Standard numbering separates categories of numbers by a space, comma, period, or dash.

50. A standard numbering system provides the user with information by just reading the file number. It tells the user the responsible attorney, type of case, file number, and volume number.

51. A subfile is known as a volume.

52. Account numbering gives each client a permanent number, and all subsequent cases are filed with that account number.

53. All the files for one client are filed together.

54. Combination numeric numbering is a combination of the five numeric numbering systems.

55. Alphanumeric coding system is a numeric system that codes files alphabetically.

56. Files in an alphanumeric coding system are filed in alphabetical and numeric order.

57. Advantages of an alphanumeric coding system are that it can increase retrieval and filing speed up to six times, misfilings are reduced, and a cross-index is in alphabetical and numeric order.

58. A cross-index is a cross-reference of clients' files. All numeric coding systems must have an alphabetical cross-index of clients with corresponding file numbers. In a firm with many cases, it is impossible to remember the file number of each case.

59. A numeric index informs the person assigning file numbers of the next number in sequence to be assigned.

60. Color coding is used to further categorize files.

61. Color coding can convey information such as type of case, type of document, responsible attorney, branch office, area of law, or the year a file was opened.

62. A colored dot or sticker may be added to the label to add additional information.

63. When numbers are given a color, misfilings are easily spotted because a file with the contrasting color "pops out" from the rest of the files.

64. According to statistics, about 3 percent of documents are misfiled.

65. Noncompliance with retrieval procedures results in lost files.

66. In small firms, a secretary or paralegal may be responsible for file system maintenance in addition to other duties.

67. In large firms, file clerks or file coordinators, whose sole responsibility is to maintain the system, are employed.

68. An efficient system has a central person who is responsible for maintaining a system's procedures.

69. Requests for files from a centralized system are initiated by a file requisition form.

70. A written request has one important advantage over an oral request: It provides a record that the request was made.

71. Files may be in a location other than a file room for various reasons, including the following:
    i. An attorney is reviewing it.
    ii. A paralegal is working on it.
    iii. A secretary is working on it.
    iv. A law clerk, who is doing research, has it in the library.
    v. It is in the copy center having documents copied.

72. An out card is the size of a file folder, made of heavy vinyl, and has lines on the front on which to put names and dates. When a file is removed from the filing area, the responsible party inserts his or her name or initials and date on the out card. The out card is then placed in the location of the removed file.

73. Advantages to the out-card system include the following:
    i. It shows that the file is being used and has not been misplaced.
    ii. It enables a user to know the location of files at all times.
    iii. It acts as a marker to indicate the proper place for a file.

74. Problems occur with an out-card system when employees do not put their names on the out card or do not use an out card.

75. Out folders are the same as out cards, except that they allow documents to be inserted into them.

76. Law offices use bar coding as a method of managing records.

77. Automatic data collection is a data entry method used in bar code technology.

78. Symbologies are languages used in bar code technology.

79. Firms using bar codes have reported that the system provides them with more efficient document handling, an automated rather than manual master index, a more accurate index of files stored off site, and decreased retrieval time.

80. Whenever a file is removed from a central filing area, its bar code label is scanned by a portable data entry terminal that communicates its information back to the firm's computer via radio frequency.

81. As a file moves around the office, its location can be determined by using a portable bar code scanner.

82. Medium and large firms, especially, benefit from using bar code technology for their files.

83. The six benefits of using bar code technology are the following:
    i. Accuracy
    ii. Ease of use
    iii. Uniform data collection
    iv. Timely feedback
    v. Improved productivity
    vi. Increased profitability

84. Radio frequency identification is a generic term for technologies that use radio waves to identify people or objects.

85. RFID works by placing microchips, or RFID tags, in the file. The antenna in the chips transmits information to a reader, and the reader sends the information to a computer.

86. The big difference between RFID and bar codes is that a bar code is a "line-of-sight" technology. A scanner has to "see" the bar code to read it. RFID doesn't require line of sight.

87. A preclient is a person who consults an attorney but does not formally retain the services of the attorney.

88. A file is opened immediately after a client retains the firm.

89. A conflict check entails checking each new client for a possible conflict of interest.

90. A conflict-check database is maintained with clients' names and the names of all parties to a matter in which the firm was involved.

91. A conflict check is the most important aspect of file opening procedures.

92. Each time a party makes an appearance in a case, a firm's client database must be checked to determine the new party's relationship to the firm, if any.

93. If the person conducting the conflict search suspects that there may be a potential conflict with the representation, the attorney or manager must be notified immediately.

94. A file-number index is an index containing sequential file numbers and case names. It is used to indicate the next available file number.

95. A new case memorandum is used as a checklist to complete file opening procedures.

96. When a file is opened, the date on which the statute of limitations expires must be put into the firm's tickler system to monitor it.

97. When opening a file, a clerk obtains billing information from a new case memorandum.

98. The name of the person who referred the client to the firm is entered into the system so that the firm can send an acknowledgment or thank you to the referring party.

99. Type-of-case information is used by a law firm's management for statistics and marketing information.

100. In large firms, where potential conflicts are often not readily recognized, the firm will circulate a list of new clients and opposing parties to determine whether a potential conflict exists.

101. It is important that file-opening procedures and information be accurate because the information is used in timekeeping, billing, and docketing programs and because any errors at the file-opening stage will affect other programs.

102. The paralegal is responsible for maintaining clients' files in good order.

103. Now, documents consist of electronic documents, e-mails, photographs, video clips, digital images, diskettes, and CD-ROMs.

104. Rich media is image-based technology that is visual rather than text oriented.

105. The transition from text-based to image-based documents is one of the biggest changes facing records management today.

106. The first step in file maintenance is categorizing its documents within the file.

107. Correspondence is filed together in chronological order, with the most recent on top.

108. In a small case, all notes are filed together in chronological order, with the most recent on top; and pleadings are filed together in chronological order, with the most recent on top.

109. In a small case, correspondence is inserted on the left side of the folder in chronological order, with the most recent on top.

110. In a small case, pleadings are inserted on the right side in chronological order, with the most recent on top.

111. In a large case, documents are further categorized by section.

112. Case cover sheets are used to monitor the status of the case and are a synopsis of the events of the case. By looking at the case cover sheet, the attorney or paralegal can see the current status of a case.

113. The case cover sheet is put on top of the folder or documents in the file so that it can be viewed immediately on opening the file.

114. Some firms keep case cover sheets, or a copy of them, in a binder or computer so that the status of each case can be updated and available without pulling the file from the file room.

115. Indexes are used to direct the person to the document's exact location in the file.

116. Each document is given a number that is put on a tab so that it can be found quickly. The tab is then inserted on a divider sheet and protrudes so that it can be seen easily.

117. A document is inserted between each divider. A divider sheet with the document's number on the tab is inserted in front of the document so that the document can be located by lifting up the tab.

118. The number, title of document, date, and party are inserted on an index sheet, which is placed on top of the applicable section.

119. Indexes should be developed for every category of the file, except correspondence and miscellaneous notes.

120. Photographs should be taped onto a large piece of paper or put into an envelope.

121. Documents are generated in a law office in one of two ways: developed or received.

122. A document's purpose must be determined before its life cycle can be identified.

123. The three values of a document are operational, technical, and legal.

124. Operational value is determining whether a document or information is needed on a day-to-day basis.

125. A document that is referred to at least once a month has high operational value. A document that is referred to less than once a month has low operational value.

126. Technical value is determined by whether a document or information contains technical or procedural information.

127. A document has legal value if its information is covered by statute or regulation.

128. To determine the value of a document, the following questions should be asked:
    i. Why would anyone refer to this document again?
    ii. To what degree is this document needed for day-to-day business?
    iii. When will the information in this document lose its validity? Two weeks? One month?
    iv. Will this document be referred to often?
    v. Will this document be helpful information in the type of law in which I am working?
    vi. Is this document covered by a statute or regulation?
    vii. Has the statute of limitations expired on this document?

129. Keeping unnecessary documents is a waste of space and therefore costly for a firm. They also clutter files and make files less manageable.

130. To purge a file means to discard or clear it of outdated information.

131. Time management experts advise that document management decisions be made as soon as a document is received.

132. Among the documents found in a typical law office are the following:
    i. Correspondence (client correspondence, a law firm's business correspondence, promotional mail and advertisements, and miscellaneous correspondence)
    ii. Clients' case documents, such as pleadings
    iii. Interoffice memos and reports
    iv. Photocopies
    v. Meeting notes (notes from client conferences, a law firm's business meetings, and miscellaneous meetings, such as educational seminars)
    vi. Rough drafts
    vii. Articles and newspaper clippings

133. Filing experts have estimated that correspondence constitutes most of the documents received.

134. If a document was faxed, the fax cover sheet must also be saved to show the date and origin of the fax.

135. Date stamping is marking a document with the date it was received, even a fax cover sheet.

136. Date stamping correspondence when it arrives makes it easier to respond to a document in a timely manner and eliminates paper glut.

137. Envelopes need not be saved unless the correspondence was mailed certified or special delivery or unless the postmark or return address is important to a client's case.

138. The person to whom correspondence is sent is responsible for deciding whether to keep the material.

139. No document pertaining to a client's case may be discarded.

140. If a document's importance or validity to a case is unclear, the responsible attorney should be consulted.

141. All documents pertaining to employment reviews or benefits are retained.

142. If a photocopy contains notes or highlighting that makes it different from the original, it should be retained.

143. A courtesy copy is a copy of a document sent to the recipient as a courtesy or for informational purposes only.

144. A secondary recipient receives a copy of a document as a courtesy only and has no responsibility to retain the document.

145. A primary recipient is the person to whom correspondence is addressed.

146. A secondary recipient has no responsibility to retain the document.

147. Notes taken in a meeting with a client or on a client's behalf are always retained.

148. If the notetaker was in charge of the meeting, was required to report on the meeting, or was to do something as a result of the meeting, the notes are retained.

149. No rough draft of a contract is destroyed until the agreement has been fully negotiated and signed.

150. Rough drafts of correspondence or pleadings are destroyed when the final document is completed.

151. The article's source, volume number, and date of its source must be indicated on the article.

152. The files and subfiles into which electronic documents are stored must be similar in structure to the filing system for paper documents.

153. "Read only" access allows documents to be accessible to others in the firm but protects them from alteration.

154. Documents should never be removed from a file because they are likely to get lost.

155. The advantages of electronic documents are that they are stored in less space, are at your fingertips, and are easily edited.

156. The disadvantages of electronic documents are that they are difficult to manage, are easily lost without a good filing system in place, and are difficult to search and review without opening the file.

157. The functions of an automated document management system are the following:
    i. It keeps track of clients, cases, authors, keywords, and other relevant information.
    ii. A user can search the database for a document.
    iii. It can locate any document.
    iv. It calculates how much time attorneys, paralegals, and secretaries spend editing documents and automatically enters that information into the billing system.
    v. It moves seldom-used documents to remote storage.
    vi. It provides extra copies of documents in case the system fails.
    vii. It archives documents after a prearranged retention period is determined.
    viii. It keeps track of versions of documents.
    ix. It calculates the number of keystrokes typed and the number of pages printed for each document. The information is automatically transferred into a time and billing system.
    x. It makes a backup copy of the document.

158. Most automated document management packages are integrated with a firm's word processing system and can be integrated with other firm software applications, such as docketing and calendar programs, e-mail, and spreadsheet programs.

159. Once prepared, an electronic document is saved in the client's electronic file folder on the firm's network or intranet.

160. A law office must have naming and saving rules for its electronic documents.

161. Everyone in a firm should adhere to the rules; otherwise, a system will fail.

162. The characteristics of a good system for electronic documents are that it is easy to use, easy to remember, and universally accepted by all employees.

163. A popular electronic filing system that is used in some law firms contains three components: the first four or five letters of the client's name or surname, the date of the document, and a code that indicates the type of document (e.g., CMP = complaint, ANS = answer, INT = interrogatories, LTR = letter).

164. One can look at the name of the document and get an idea of the document's contents.

165. When a case is completed, the following procedures must be followed before closing the file:
    i. The file must be reviewed to make sure that all final documents have been completed.
    ii. The final bill must be paid by the client.
    iii. A disengagement letter must be sent to the client.
    iv. The file must be pruned for closing.
    v. The status of file must be changed from active to inactive.
    vi. Original documents must be returned to the client.
    vii. Electronic records must be deleted from the firm's computer system.

166. A disengagement letter promotes client relations and substantiates that the client's perception of the status of the case is the same as the attorney's.

167. Pruning a file is discarding unnecessary documents from the file.

168. A file-closing memorandum acts as a checklist for file-closing procedures.

169. A file must be reviewed to make sure that all final documents have been completed.

170. The final bill must be paid before a file is closed.

171. It is often a paralegal's responsibility to draft a disengagement letter for an attorney's signature.

172. It is often a paralegal's or secretary's responsibility to prune files.

173. Some experts recommend that the person pruning the file do so with the responsible attorney so that nothing is overlooked.

174. Other experts say that an attorney reviewing files for closing is a waste of the attorney's time and therefore too costly for a firm.

175. Changing the status changes a file from active to inactive.

176. The conflict-of-interest database should be double-checked to determine whether all parties are in it.

177. A file's retention period must be determined when a file is closed.

178. Paralegals are often responsible for determining the retention period, but other file-closing tasks are usually delegated to a secretary.

179. Original wills are stored in a safe-deposit box or other secure area.

180. Electronic documents that are stored in a client's file on the firm's computer system are deleted from the system. Before doing so, they should be reviewed to determine whether they should be put into the firm's form files and knowledge bank. The electronic documents may be put on a diskette and the diskette inserted in the closed file.

181. Inactive records should not be stored in the main filing area because they waste valuable floor and filing space.

182. A firm must employ an indexing system to locate and retrieve inactive files and records.

183. Inactive records are usually stored in filing cabinets or storage boxes outside the main storage area.

184. Each container, whether a cabinet or box, must be properly marked and labeled.

185. Storage areas include a basement, back storage room, or off-site storage facility.

186. Micrographics consists of microfilm and microform.

187. Large firms and firms that store a lot of records benefit from micrographics.

188. Smaller firms often cannot justify the expense of micrographics.

189. Imaging is when documents are scanned into a computer system and an image of the document is saved on CD-ROMs.

190. An image system consists of a control unit with a monitor, scanner and printer, CD-ROM storage unit, and software.

191. A CD-ROM will hold 250,000 documents on one disk.

192. A jukebox is a device that contains many CD-ROMs and allows retrieval of a document on request.

193. The imaging software will generate an index of all documents and identify the CD-ROM on which a document is found.

194. The best evidence rule permits the introduction of a microfilmed duplicate as evidence if the original document has been lost or destroyed, if certain conditions are met.

195. Congress has enacted two statutes that pertain to microfilmed records: the Uniform Photographic Copies of Business and Public Records as Evidence Act of 1949 (UPA) and Uniform Rules of Evidence of 1974.

196. The closed-file number and location are inserted on a closed-file index for retrieval purposes.

197. Firms that use an alphabetical coding system find that storing closed files alphabetically requires frequent reorganization.

198. Calendar numbering is the preferred method for coding closed files.

199. A closed-file index is a list of closed files.

200. The information on a closed-file index should be in alphabetical order according to the client's surname and should include the location of all files.

201. The following information should be inserted on a closed-file index:
    i. File name
    ii. Active-file number, if applicable
    iii. Closed-file number
    iv. Date file opened
    v. Date file closed
    vi. Location in storage (box or cabinet number; if microfilm, the number of the roll of film, frame on the film, and location of the film)
    vii. Short description of the disposition of the matter
    viii. Date the file may be destroyed

202. The information for a closed-file index is obtained from a closed-file index form.

203. A closed-file index form is completed by the person responsible for closing files.

204. The form is inserted in the file or taped to the front of the file folder. A copy of the form can be used as a closed-file index log.

205. Records retention is the time period during which records must be maintained by an organization because they may be needed for legal, operational, historical, or other purposes.

206. Record retention time periods are established by state and federal law.

207. Inactive records may be needed for legal, operational, historical, or other purposes.
208. Records may be destroyed after the retention period expires.
209. Research has shown that 95 percent of all references to closed files occur within the first 2 years of closing.
210. The responsibility for setting a retention period rests with management after researching legal requirements.
211. A retention schedule is a schedule of retention periods categorized according to type of document.
212. A paralegal should not rely on an automated retention schedule because a case may contain circumstances that a computer cannot analyze.
213. For business records, the following factors are considered:
    i. Statute or regulation
    ii. Future need for records
    iii. Statute of limitations
214. The future need for business records is determined by a firm's management.
215. The six considerations for retaining client records are the following:
    i. Statute or regulation
    ii. Future need for records
    iii. Statute of limitations
    iv. If minors are involved, applicable age of majority
    v. Time requirements for appeal
    vi. Malpractice and business concerns
216. The future need for records can be anticipated by the responsible attorney.
217. The statute of limitations on a minor's action does not begin until the child has reached the age of majority.
218. To ensure confidentiality, records should never be disposed of in the trash can.
219. To prepare records for shredding, all clamps, paper clips, staples, and plastic covers must be removed.
220. Witnessed records destruction is when a disposal company will haul the records off site and destroy them in the presence of a supervisor. This ensures that the confidentiality of the records is preserved.
221. For smaller shredding projects, a firm shreds the documents.
222. It is inappropriate to leave a shredder unattended because the confidentiality of the documents will not be protected.
223. Only white paper is recyclable.
224. Some state bar associations require that attorneys notify their clients by letter before destroying their files.
225. A notification letter regarding file destruction contains the following information:
    i. The date the file is scheduled for destruction
    ii. The client's right to obtain or inspect the file
    iii. Notice to the client that, if she or he chooses to preserve the file, she or he will be responsible for the cost thereof.

226. Some firms insert their file-closing and destruction policies in their retainer agreements.
227. Law firm personnel should not remove a file from the office because it may be lost or damaged while in transit from the office to home.
228. It is imperative that conflict checks be performed often.
229. If a client terminates the attorney-client relationship, the file must be returned to the client promptly so that the client can continue legal representation elsewhere.
230. Once a records retention schedule is established, it must be reviewed and approved by an attorney.
231. A file must not be destroyed until its retention period has expired because to do so would expose the firm to sanctions and/or fines.
232. Knowledge of file and records management procedures is important to the smooth operation of a law office.

Chapter 14
Law Library Organization and Management

1. Libraries are used as the background for law firm photographs and are displayed in the background of television commercials as attorneys advertise their services.
2. A library communicates a message of an attorney's expertise and knowledge of the law.
3. The two types of knowledge are knowledge we have about a subject and knowledge of where to find information about a subject.
4. The highest law in the land is the U.S. Constitution.
5. The highest law in a state is the state constitution.
6. Federal laws are enacted by Congress.
7. Each individual in the country is bound by the U.S. Constitution, state constitution, federal law, federal agency law, state law, state agency law, county ordinances, and city ordinances.
8. A paralegal must be comfortable in a library setting because success as a paralegal depends on it.
9. Acquiring knowledge of libraries is the first step in understanding a law library.
10. Gaining knowledge of the contents of a law library is the second step in understanding a law library.
11. In small and medium firms, paralegals and experienced legal secretaries act as librarians.
12. Our legal system is based on a combination of civil law and common law.
13. Civil law is based on a series of written laws.
14. Civil law was derived from Roman law.
15. In advanced countries, laws were written as early as 2100 BCE.

16. The two main sources of written law are constitutions and statutes.
17. Common law is law derived from court decisions.
18. Common law originated in England, where there were no written laws.
19. Accounts of court decisions were compiled into a series called the Yearbooks.
20. Stare decisis is the legal principle that a court will follow the decision of another court in a similar case.
21. Courts would consult the Yearbooks when making a ruling, establishing the doctrine of stare decisis.
22. Most laws of the United States originated from English common law and were codified, or arranged, into written laws.
23. *Codify* means to arrange laws by subject.
24. The classification process entails placing law into categories.
25. Classification of the law was introduced in England in 1490.
26. The Abridgment of the Yearbooks was the first legal index published.
27. Placing laws into categories helps us find them quickly.
28. Laws are categorized according to function.
29. There are 4 million case laws and 45,000 to 50,000 court decisions made each year.
30. Case law is classified according to its subject matter.
31. The four functions of law are the following:
    i. Type of legal action
    ii. Individuals involved
    iii. Nature of the law
    iv. Source of the law
32. The two types of legal actions are civil and criminal.
33. In a criminal action, the government (state or federal) is the plaintiff in the action.
34. Crimes are considered an injury to society, so they are prosecuted by the government.
35. The two types of remedies available in a civil case are monetary relief and equitable relief.
36. Monetary relief is when a party is paid money as compensation for an injury.
37. Equitable relief is when relief other than money acts as compensation for an injury (e.g., the return of a person's property that was wrongfully taken).
38. The two types of laws that apply to individuals are public laws and private laws.
39. Public laws apply to everyone.
40. Private laws apply only to individuals who fall under the jurisdiction of the law by circumstance.
41. The two natures of law are substantive and procedural.
42. Substantive laws are laws that govern society. They create, define, and regulate rights.
43. Damages are compensation for a wrong or an injury.
44. Procedural laws give direction on how to recover damages.
45. The sources of law are constitutional law, which encompasses the U.S. Constitution and the constitution of each state; federal statutory law, which encompasses laws passed by the U.S. Congress; state statutory law, which encompasses laws passed by state legislatures and local governments; and case law, which encompasses court decisions resulting from legal controversies.
46. The three classes of law are primary authority, secondary authority, and search tools.
47. Primary authority consists of constitutions, statutes, judicial opinions, court rules, and administrative regulations and decisions.
48. Primary authority consists of laws made by the three branches of government: executive, legislative, and judicial. Primary authority is given the most weight and consideration in a case.
49. The legislature also enacts procedural law.
50. The judicial branch creates laws governing the rules and procedures of the court system.
51. Local rules are rules that are created by an individual court and that apply to that court only.
52. Primary authority consists of constitutions, statutes, judicial opinions, court rules, and administrative regulations and decisions.
53. Statutes are organized according to subject matter.
54. Large libraries contain administrative rulings.
55. Annotated statutes contain historical information concerning amendments and additions to the statute, citations to judicial opinions interpreting the statute, and references to secondary sources that are relevant to the statute.
56. Unannotated statutes contain the statute, deleted repealed statutes, and all amendments and additions to the statute.
57. Annotated statutes are placed where they are most accessible.
58. Unannotated statutes are often placed in the attorney's or paralegal's office so that they are accessible whenever needed.
59. New laws are published in pocket parts.
60. A pocket part is an addition to a book that updates its contents.
61. A pocket part uses the same numbering system as the bound volume.
62. A new edition of the U.S. Code is published with supplements being incorporated into the new volumes every 5 or 6 years.
63. Pocket parts are inserted into a pocket inside the back cover of the applicable volume.
64. Pocket parts should not be allowed to accumulate because employees will not have the most recent law at their disposal.
65. Reporters contain the text of judicial opinions as they are made.
66. Reporters are numbered consecutively.
67. A series is a set of reporters numbered in numeric order.

68. When the volumes reach a high number, a publisher will name a new series and begin numbering its volumes from 1.

69. Reporters should be placed in numeric order according to series, starting with the first series.

70. Some libraries, especially small libraries, do not contain a first series because of its outdated nature and a library's limited space.

71. A slip opinion is a printed copy of a judicial opinion that is distributed soon after the decision is rendered.

72. An advance sheet is a softcover book of decisions that is circulated soon after a decision is rendered.

73. Advance sheets are sent to law libraries weekly.

74. Advance sheets are placed at the end of a reporter set.

75. Once a new volume is received, the advance sheets may be discarded and the new volume placed at the end of the set.

76. Court rules were first developed by the Judiciary Act of 1789, passed at the first session of Congress.

77. Court rules are court procedures that must be followed in cases before that court.

78. Court rules have three purposes:
    i. Aid the court in expediting the business that comes before it
    ii. Establish uniform procedures for the conduct of a court's business
    iii. Provide parties to a lawsuit with procedural information and instructions on bringing the matter before a court

79. Local rules are rules governing local courts.

80. Court rules are placed in a library where they can be retrieved quickly.

81. Court rules are updated by a publisher or the particular court.

82. Administrative agencies are established by Congress and are government entities (other than a court or legislative body) that affect the rights of people through their rules and decisions.

83. Some agencies publish their own opinions, and a few private publishers publish administrative and judicial opinions on particular subjects.

84. State agency administrative regulations and decisions are published chronologically, although some states codify their regulations. Some state administrative rulings are privately published in loose-leaf reports or by services. State administrative agency rulings are not as uniformly published as federal administrative rulings.

85. Large libraries contain administrative rulings.

86. Secondary authority is anything other than primary authority that aids a court in reaching a decision. Secondary authority is used to persuade. It is not considered in lieu of primary authority but is used in addition to primary authority.

87. Secondary authority was developed to provide aids in identifying and explaining the law.

88. Secondary authority is used to persuade.

89. Secondary authority includes treatises, periodicals, dictionaries, and encyclopedias.

90. A treatise is a legal commentary on a particular subject of law. The purpose of a treatise is to simplify and explain the law.

91. Periodicals are booklets containing articles about the law.

92. Indexes are published to provide access to all the articles published in a legal periodical.

93. The most established index service is the *Index to Legal Periodicals,* which dates back to 1908.

94. A legal dictionary is considered secondary authority and can be quoted if the meaning of a word is in dispute.

95. Encyclopedias are volumes that contain statements on principles of law and are organized alphabetically by subject matter.

96. Encyclopedias are categorized into broad topics that are subdivided into narrower topics and that act as an index and guide to the law.

97. Secondary authority is placed according to the numeric order of the volumes.

98. Dictionaries are usually placed in a central area of a library.

99. Many treatises are updated by pocket parts, restatements are rewritten, and the new material is contained in an updated series. Other treatises are updated as the law changes.

100. Search tools assist the researcher in finding primary authority.

101. Search tools are never cited as a source of law; they are tools only.

102. A digest is a collection embodying the chief matter of numerous books, articles, and court decisions.

103. A digest is usually arranged alphabetically.

104. A citator is a set of books that provide the judicial history and interpretation of reported decisions.

105. If a statute is repealed, it is abrogated, or annulled.

106. Form books assist the attorney and paralegal in drafting legal documents and following the procedures of a case.

107. The manner in which a firm's library resources are managed determines a library's organization.

108. Law libraries are described according to size.

109. Small libraries that contain only those books essential for the lawyers' needs are skeletal law libraries.

110. Skeletal libraries contain state statutes, case reporters for a specific jurisdiction in which the lawyers practice, form books, and a legal dictionary. A skeletal library may also contain a treatise in a particular area of law.

111. Libraries that contain a comprehensive collection of the laws of the country are complete law libraries. A complete law library has over 300,000 hardcover volumes, microform, and computer databases.

112. Complete law libraries are found in large law schools, some large agencies, courthouses, and major city libraries.
113. The largest complete law library in the United States is the Library of Congress in Washington, D.C. it contains 134 million items.
114. The three types of library organization are centralized, decentralized, and satellite.
115. A centralized library is found in one location that has been set aside by a firm.
116. Most large firms have a centralized library.
117. A library cooperative is a group organized to pool library resources for the benefit of the group.
118. A decentralized library is distributed throughout a firm.
119. Attorneys and paralegals use the books in their individual offices.
120. Sole practitioners and small firms have decentralized libraries.
121. A decentralized library has three advantages:
    i. The books are close to the attorneys and legal assistants using them.
    ii. The books are decorative and give the office a nice appearance.
    iii. The books act as a noise buffer, keeping an office quieter.
122. The disadvantages to a decentralized library are that books are not readily accessible when needed, are often misplaced, and are kept in offices and not returned to the shelf.
123. A satellite library is a small library maintained outside the main library area.
124. Satellite libraries are found in large firms with a large centralized library.
125. Some firms will remove specialty books from a central library and put a satellite library close to the employees using these books.
126. Tax and labor libraries are the most common satellite libraries.
127. It is important that supplement material be inserted into the proper books as soon as possible so that the attorneys and paralegals have current law at their disposal.
128. Legal publishing companies provide an update service called Advance Legislative Service.
129. Law books must be updated constantly.
130. Ninety percent of a law library's budget is spent to update law resources.
131. The three most common checkout systems used in law firm libraries are out card, bar code, and library card systems.
132. Problems arise with an out-card system when employees do not take the time to write their names on the card or the cards fall off the shelf or are out of place.
133. Some firms have bar codes placed on their books to track the books electronically.

134. Each book has a library card placed in a pocket on the inside cover of the book. A library card contains the book's name, author, and other pertinent information about the book. As the book leaves the library, the library card is placed into a card box or card holder behind the person's name taking the book. When the book is returned, the person replaces the card in the book.
135. Law libraries are getting smaller because they are implementing technology by combining it with law books. Fewer books and more technology are being purchased.
136. The five types of technology used in law libraries are the following:
    i. Online legal and nonlegal databases
    ii. Microform
    iii. CD-ROM
    iv. E-mail and telefacsimile (fax) transmission
    v. The Internet
137. An online legal database is a database of laws compiled by a publisher that charges customers to use it.
138. Computer-assisted legal research (CALR) is doing legal research on a legal database.
139. *Full text* means that the entire text of the document is displayed.
140. The two primary CALR systems are WESTLAW, from IT Thomson's West Group, and Lexis-Nexis, from Reed Elsevier, both of which provide access to full-text legal documents through a computer.
141. An abstract system does not provide the full text of a decision but instead provides an abstract, or summary, of a law.
142. A nonlegal database operates the same as a legal database but contains nonlegal information.
143. To access a database from the Internet, one needs an account and a password and must pay the requisite fees. Accessing a database from the Internet requires no specialized software (except a browser) and can be accessed from an individual computer.
144. Microform is the process of storing information photographically. It is the term used to describe any form of printing on film or paper containing miniature images of a document.
145. Microfilm is 35-millimeter film that stores a large number of pages that run continuously in sequence and that need no alteration.
146. Microfiche is a sheet of microfilm in the form of a card that is used to store a small number of pages that require updating.
147. One 100-foot roll of microfilm contains five large books.
148. Six microfiche cards are needed to photograph one book.
149. After documents have been photographed, the film is inserted into a reader/printer that enlarges the document on a screen for viewing.

150. Volumes of books are put on microfilm and stored in a small desk drawer. Many books can be stored in the same desk drawer.
151. Microfilm will last about 200 years.
152. CD-ROM stands for "compact disk read-only memory."
153. A CD-ROM can store about 300,000 manuscript pages, or 250 large law books.
154. A megabyte is a computer term used to measure data; one megabyte contains about one million characters.
155. A CD-ROM drive is needed to access material on a CD-ROM.
156. A jukebox is a CD-ROM storage device.
157. A jukebox can hold as few as six and as many as 500 CD-ROMs.
158. As laws change, a disk must be updated by its publisher. Since laws change daily, providing current material has been a challenge for legal CD-ROM publishers. Because of the time and processes needed to produce and ship them, they are often out of date when they are received.
159. A user interface is a method of operation developed by a legal publisher for its CD-ROM products.
160. The lifetime of a CD-ROM is currently 10 to 30 years—not long enough to replace microform's longevity.
161. Bar association libraries that provide library services to their members deliver materials by e-mail or fax machine. Previously, paralegals and other law firm personnel had to go to a library to copy materials.
162. According to the 2007 Technology Survey conducted by *Legal Assistant Today*, 82.4 percent of the respondents conduct legal and factual research on the Internet.
163. Access to law on the Internet is partially due to the assertive position of government agencies in placing their information on the Internet and to entrepreneurs who seek to bring viewers to their legal websites.
164. A great deal of information that lawyers and librarians need is not available on the Internet, such as secondary authority material.
165. A problem with conducting legal research over the Internet is its poor classification system, making law difficult to locate.
166. It takes longer to do research on the Internet because of its poor classification system.
167. The *Harvard Blue Book: A Uniform System of Citation* is used as a guide to legal citation.
168. The AALL recognized the need for a new citation format for electronic materials and recommended that a legal cite include the case name, year of the decision, specific court, a consecutively assigned case number, and paragraph number for the exact location of the quote.
169. In 1996, the ABA adopted the AALL's recommendation but suggested that the traditional site be included.

170. No universally accepted citation system for electronic documents exists.
171. Every law office must have an adequate supply of court forms, which are form documents used in a specific court.
172. The three methods of storing court forms are manually, on masters that are photocopied, and computer programs.
173. Court forms that are stored manually are filed in filing cabinets and are normally organized alphabetically by subject matter.
174. Photocopier-created forms are stored in three-ring binders to save space. The binders are indexed and divided into subjects. Only one copy of each form, the master form, is inserted into a binder. That form is photocopied when it is needed.
175. Computer-generated forms are software programs that provide court forms and that assist a user in completing them. They are printed after completion.
176. Some courts undertake responsibility for distributing new court forms. Most courts, however, do not want to be burdened with this responsibility and so delegate it to a printing company, court form software company, or court forms service. The legal industry supports many court form service companies that will print and distribute forms to their subscribers. They will automatically send new and updated forms when these forms become effective. Automated court forms software is updated by the publisher.
177. A knowledge bank contains samples of research and documents prepared by a firm and are used in the same manner as form books.
178. Eighty percent of work done in most law firms is not new. The work of attorneys and paralegal assistants is often similar to a previous case. If a firm can realize increased efficiencies on 80 percent of its work, it will increase productivity, resulting in increased profits. Keeping copies of briefs and research memoranda regarding an issue or subject saves employees' time in researching that issue again should a similar case arise.
179. The two types of work product retrieval systems are manual and automated.
180. A manual system is used by small firms.
181. With a manual system, documents in a knowledge bank are filed alphabetically by subject to allow searchers to locate a document quickly, like court forms.
182. A comprehensive index is required to locate a document in a manual system.
183. An index is prepared alphabetically by subject matter and contains the law or rule to which the document applies.
184. If a document has more than one subject matter, it is cross-referenced to other topics.
185. When a document is inserted into a knowledge bank, it is incorporated into the system by a research index memorandum form.

186. Automated work-product retrieval systems are used by large and medium-sized firms that have large knowledge banks.
187. A large knowledge bank must be automated to manage the high number of documents in it.
188. The four types of automated work-product retrieval system are full text, index, abstracts, and a combination of these.
189. A network or an intranet is required for a knowledge bank to be available on each person's computer terminal.
190. Without a network, a knowledge bank is found on a dedicated computer in the library.
191. The role of a law librarian is changing with the information explosion.
192. Among the duties of a law librarian are the following:
    i. Research
    ii. Collection development
    iii. Library maintenance
    iv. Indexing
    v. Establishing library policy
    vi. Organization
    vii. Training
    viii. Management
    ix. Personnel management
    x. Planning
    xi. Web maintenance
193. Some librarians have additional duties outside the library, such as managing paralegal or secretarial staff and managing a central filing area.
194. A law librarian devotes full time to a firm's library and is found in large firms with large libraries.
195. Most librarians in large firms have a master of library science degree, and some have a law degree.
196. A virtual library is an electronic library without regard to physical space or location.
197. A virtual library may include CD-ROM, Internet subscriptions, lists of annotated Web links, internal work products (such as brief banks), proprietary databases (such as Lexis-Nexis or WESTLAW), and even Web spiders or push technology that deliver targeted research to the user.

Associations for Paralegals, Legal Secretaries, and Managers

American Association for Paralegal Education (AAfPE)
19 Mantua Road
Mt. Royal, NJ 08061
856-423-2829
856-423-3420 Fax
http://www.aafpe.org
E-mail: info@aafpe.org

American Association of Law Librarians (AALL)
53 W. Jackson Blvd., #940
Chicago, IL 60604
312-939-4764
312-431-1097 Fax
http://www.aallnet.org

American Bar Association, Standing Committee on Legal Assistants
321 N. Clark St.
Chicago, IL 60611
312-988-5618
800-285-2221
http://www.abanet.org

Association of Legal Administrators (ALA)
75 Tri-State International, Ste. 222
Lincolnshire, IL 60069-4435
847-267-1252
847-267-1329 Fax
http://www.alanet.org

American Association for Justice (ATLA) (Formerly: Association of Trial Lawyers of America)
1050 31st Street, N.W.
Washington, DC 20007-4499
202-965-3500
800-424-2725
http://www.atla.org

The American Association of Law Libraries
53 W. Jackson, Suite 940
Chicago, IL 60604
312-939-4764
312-431-1097 Fax
http://www.aallnet.org

International Paralegal Management Association (IPMA) (Formerly: Legal Assistant Management Association [LAMA])
IPMA Headquarters
P.O. Box 659
Avondale Estates, GA 30002-0659
404-292-4762
404-292-2931 Fax
http://paralegalmanagement.org

Legal Marketing Association (LMA)
1926 Waukegan Rd. Ste 1
Glenview, IL 60025
847-657-6717
888-657-6819
847-657-6819 Fax
http://www.legalmarketing.org

National Association of Legal Assistants (NALA)
1516 S. Boston, Ste. 200
Tulsa, OK 74119
918-587-6828
http://www.nala.org

National Association of Legal Professionals (International) (NALS)
8159 E. 41st St.
Tulsa, OK 74145
918-582-5188
918-582-5908 Fax
http://www.nals.org

National Federation of Paralegal Associations (NFPA)
P.O. Box 2016
Edmonds, WA 98020
425-967-0045
425-771-9588 Fax
http://www.paralegals.org

National Paralegal Association
Box 406
Solebury, PA 18963
215-297-8333
215-297-8358 Fax
http://www.nationalparalegal.org

STATE AND TERRITORIAL

ALABAMA
Alabama Association of Paralegals
P.O. Box 55921
Birmingham, AL 35255
http://www.aaopi.com

ALASKA
Alaska Association of Legal Assistants
P.O. Box 101956
Anchorage, AK 99510-1956
907-646-8018
http://www.Alaska®paralegals.org

ARIZONA

Arizona Paralegal Association
P.O. Box 392
Phoenix, AZ 85001
602-258-0121
http://www.azparalegals.org

Legal Assistants of Metropolitan
Phoenix
P.O. Box 13005
Phoenix, AZ 85002
http://www.geocites.com/azlamp

ARKANSAS

Paralegal Association of Arkansas
(PAARK)
(Formerly: Arkansas Association of
Legal Assistants)
111 Center St., Ste. 1900
Little Rock, AR 72201
http://www.aala-legal.org

Central Arkansas Paralegal
Association
http://www.capainc.org

CALIFORNIA

California Alliance of Paralegal
Associations
P. O. Box 1089
San Leandro, CA 94577
http://www.caparalegal.org

California Association of Legal
Document Assistants
P.O. Box 1032
Fresno, CA 93714
http://www.calda.org

Central Coast Legal Assistant
Association
P.O. Box 93
San Luis Obispo, CA 93406

Fresno Paralegal Association
(Formerly: San Joaquin Association of
Legal Assistants)
P.O. Box 28515
Fresno, CA 93729
559-348-8939
http://www.fresnoparalegal.org

Inland Counties Paralegal
Association
P.O. Box 143
Riverside, CA 92502-0292
951-750-1071
http://www.kcpaonline.org

Kern County Paralegal Association
P.O. Box 2673
Bakersfield, CA 93303
http://www.kcponline.org

Los Angeles Paralegal Association
P.O. Box 71708
Los Angeles, CA 90071
866-626-LAPA
866-460-0506 Fax
http://www.lapa.org

Marin Association of Legal
Assistants
P.O. Box 13051
San Rafael, CA 94913-3051
415-456-6020

Orange County Paralegal
Association
P.O. Box 8512
Newport Beach, CA 92658-8512
714-744-7747
http://www.ocparalegal.org

Paralegal Association of Santa
Clara County
P.O. Box 1809
San Leandro, CA 94577-0138
408-235-0301
http://www.sccparalegal.org

Redwood Empire Legal
Assistants Association
P.O. Box 143
Santa Rosa, CA 95402
http://www.redwoodempirelegal
assistants.com

Sacramento Valley Paralegal
Association
P.O. Box 453
Sacramento, CA 95812-0453
925-941-2138
http://www.svpa.org

San Diego Paralegal Association
P.O. Box 124738
San Diego, CA 92112-4738
619-378-0076
http://www.sdparalegals.org

San Francisco Paralegal Association
985 Darlen Way
San Francisco, CA 94127
415-777-2390
415-586-6606 Fax
http://www.sfpa.com

Santa Barbara Paralegal
Association
Santa Barbara Superior Court,
Dept. 1
1100 Anacapa St.
Santa Barbara, CA 93101
805-568-2899
http://www.sbparalegals.org

Sequoia Paralegal Association
P.O. Box 2483
Visalia, CA 93279
559-733-1065
http://www.sequoiaparalegals.com

Ventura County Paralegal
Association
P.O. Box 24229
Ventura, CA 93002
http://www.vcparalegal.org

COLORADO

Association of Legal Assistants of
Colorado
5555 Tech Center Drive, #30
Colorado Springs, CO 80919
719-268-4542

Colorado Association of Professional
Paralegals and Legal Assistants
http://www.capplaweb.org

Rocky Mountain Paralegal
Association
P.O. Box 138
Denver, CO 80201-1138
303-370-9444
http://www.rockymtnparalegal.org

CONNECTICUT

Central Connecticut Paralegal
Association
P.O. Box 230594
Hartford, CT 06123-0594
http://www.ctparalegals.org

Connecticut Association of
Paralegals, Fairfield County
P.O. Box 134
Bridgeport, CT 06601-0134
http://www.paralegals.org/Connecticut

New Haven Association of
Paralegals
P.O. Box 862
New Haven, CT 06504-0862
http://www.backup.paralegals.org/
NewHaven

DELAWARE
Delaware Paralegal Association
P.O. Box 1362
Wilmington, DE 19899
302-426-1362
http://www.deparalegals.org

DISTRICT OF COLUMBIA
National Capital Area Paralegal
Association
P.O. Box 27607
Washington, DC 20038-7607
202-659-0243
http://www.ncapa.com

FLORIDA
Central Florida Paralegal
Association
P.O. Box 1107
Orlando, FL 32802-1107
407-672-6372
http://www.cfpainc.com

Gainesville Association of Florida
P.O. Box 2519
Gainesville, FL 32602
904-462-2249

Northeast Florida Paralegal
Association
221 N. Hogan St., Box 164
Jacksonville, FL 32202
http://www.nefpa.org

Northwest Florida Paralegal
Association
P.O. Box 1333
Pensacola, FL 32502
http://www.nwfpa.com

Paralegal Association of Florida
P.O. Box 7073
West Palm Beach, FL 33405
561-833-1408
http://www.pafinc.org

South Florida Paralegal
Association
P.O. Box 31-0745
Miami, FL 33231
305-944-0204
http://www.sfpa.info/site

Southwest Florida Paralegal
Association
P.O. Box 2094
Sarasota, FL 34230-2094
http://www.swfloridaparalegals.com

Tampa Bay Paralegal
Association
P.O. Box 2840
Tampa, FL 33601
813-223-7474
http://www.tbpa.org

Volusia Association of Legal
Assistants
P.O. Box 15075
Daytona Beach, FL 32115-5075
386-506-5538
http://www.volusiaparalegals.org

GEORGIA
Georgia Association
of Paralegals
3904 N. Druid Hills Rd. # 376
Decatar, GA 30033

Southeastern Association of Legal
Assistants of Georgia
2215 Bacon Park Dr.
Savannah, GA 31406
http://www.seala.org

HAWAII
Hawaii Association of Legal
Assistants
P.O. Box 674
Honolulu, HI 996809
http://www.hawaiiparalegal.org

IDAHO
Idaho Association of Legal
Assistants
P.O. Box 1254
Boise, ID 83701
http://www.idahoparalegals.org

ILLINOIS
Central Illinois Paralegal
Association
P.O. Box 1948
Bloomington, IL 61702
http://www.ciparalegal.org

Illinois Paralegal Association
P.O. Box 452
New Lenox, IL 60451-4620
815-462-4620
http://www.ipaonline.org

Peoria Paralegal Association
1308 Autumn Lane
Peoria, IL 60604

INDIANA
Indiana Legal Assistants
230 E. Ohio St., 4th Flr.
Indianapolis, IN 47204

Indiana Paralegal Association, Inc.
10 W. Market Tower, Ste. 1720
Indianapolis, IN 46204
317-464-5215
http://indianaparalegals.org

Michiana Paralegal
Association
P.O. Box 11458
South Bend, IN 46634
http://www.michianaparalegals.org

Northeast Indiana Paralegal
P.O. Box 13646
Fort Wayne, IN 46865
http://www.neindianaparalegals.org

IOWA
Iowa Association of
Legal Assistants
P.O. Box 93153
Des Moines, IA 50302-0337
http://www.ialanet.org

KANSAS
Heartland Association of Legal
Assistants
(formerly Kansas and Missouri Legal
Assistants)
P.O. Box 12413
Overland Park, KS 66282
http://www.accesskansas.org/hala

Kansas Association of Legal
Assistants
P.O. Box 47031
Wichita, KS, 67201
http://www.accesskansas.org/
kala.html

Kansas City Association of Legal
Assistants
P.O. Box 1657
Topeka, KS 66601
http://www.accesskansas.org/
ksparalegals.html

KENTUCKY
Kentucky Paralegal
Association
P.O. Box 2675
Louisville, KY 40201-2657
http://www.kypa.org

Lexington Paralegal
Association
P.O. Box 574
Lexington, KY 40586
http://www.lexingtonparalegals.org

Louisville Association of Paralegals
http://www.loupara.org

LOUISIANA

Baton Rouge Paralegal
Association
P.O. Box 306
Baton Rouge, LA 70821
http://www.brparalegals.org

Lafayette Paralegal
Association
P.O. Box 2775
Lafayette, LA 70502
337-237-2660
http://www.lpa-la.org

Louisiana State Paralegal Association
P.O. Box 56
Baton Rouge, LA 70821-0056
http://www.la-paralegals.org

New Orleans Paralegal
Association
P.O. Box 30604
New Orleans, LA 70190
504-467-3136
http://www.paralegals.org

Northwest Louisiana Paralegal
Association
333 Texas St., Ste. 717
Shreveport, LA 71101
318-227-1990

Southwest Louisiana Association
of Paralegals
P.O. Box 1143
Lake Charles, LA 70602-1143

MAINE

Maine Association of Paralegals
P.O. Box 7554
Portland, ME 04112

MARYLAND

Maryland Association of
Paralegals Inc.
550 N. Ritchie Hwy. PMB #203
Severna Park, MD 21146
410-576-2252
http://www.mdparalegals.org

MASSACHUSETTS

Central Massachusetts Paralegal
Association
P.O. Box 444
Worcester, MA 01614
E-mail: CentralMassachusetts@
paralegal.org

Massachusetts Paralegal
Association
P.O. Box 1381
Marble Head, MA 01945
800-637-4311
http://www.massparalegals.org

Western Massachusetts Paralegal
Association
P.O. Box 30005
Springfield, MA 01103-0005
http://www.wmassparalegals.org

MICHIGAN

Legal Assistants Association
of Michigan
315 S. Woodward
Royal Oak, Ml 48067
http://www.laamnet.org

Legal Assistant Section State
Bar of Michigan
306 Townsend St
Lansing, Ml 48933-2083
517-346-6300
http://www.michbar.org/
legalassistants

The Michigan Paralegal
Association Inc.
P.O. Box 1459
South Bend, IN 46634

MINNESOTA

Minnesota Paralegal
Association
1711 W. Country Rd. B #300N
Roseville, MN 55113
651-633-2778
http://www.mnparalegals.org

MISSISSIPPI

Mississippi Association of
Legal Assistants
P. O. Box 996
Jackson, MS 39205
http://www.msmala.com

MISSOURI

Heartland Association of Legal
Assistants
(formerly Kansas and Missouri Legal
Assistants)
P.O. Box 12413
Overland Park, KS 66282
http://www.accesskansas.org/hala

Kansas City Association of Legal
Assistants
P.O. Box 13223
Kansas City, MO 64199
913-381-4458

Kansas City Paralegal Association
1912 Clay St.
North Kansas City, MO 64116
816-421-0302
http://www.kcparalegals.org

Missouri Paralegal Association
P.O. Box 1016
Jefferson City, MO 65102
http://www.missouriparalegalassoc.org

MONTANA

Montana Paralegal Association
P.O. Box 693
Billings, MT 59101
http://www.malanet.org/

NEBRASKA

Nebraska Association of Legal
Assistants
http://www.neala.org

NEVADA

Nevada Paralegal Association
P.O. Box 12003
Las Vegas, NV 89112
http://www.nevadaparalegal.org

Paralegal Association of Southern Nevada
P.O. Box 1752
Las Vegas, NV 89125-1752

Sierra Nevada Association of
Paralegals
P.O. Box 2832
Reno, NV 89505
http://www.snapreno.com

NEW HAMPSHIRE

Paralegal Association of New
Hampshire
P.O. Box 728
Manchester, NH 03105
http://www.panh.org

NEW JERSEY

Legal Assistants Association
of New Jersey
P.O. Box 142
Caldwell, NJ 07006
http://www.sjparalegals.org

South Jersey Paralegal
Association
P.O. Box 355
Haddonfield, NJ 08033
http://www.sjpaparalegals.org

NEW MEXICO

Legal Assistants of New Mexico
P.O. Box 1113
Albuquerque, NM 87103-1113
505-260-7104

NEW YORK

Capitol District Paralegal
Association
P.O. Box 12562
Albany, NY 12212
E-mail: capitaldistrict@paralegals.org

Empire State Alliance of Paralegal
Associations
26F Congress St. #215
Saratoga Springs, NY 12866
E-mail: empirestateparalegals@yahoo
.com

Long Island Paralegal Association
1877 Bly Road
E. Meadow NY 11554-1158
516-357-9820
http://www.liparalegals.org

Manhattan Paralegal Association
P.O. Box 4006
Grand Central Station
New York, NY 10163
212-330-8213
E-mail: manhattan@paralegals.org

New York City Paralegal
Association
P.O. Box 4484
Grand Central Station
New York, NY 10163

Paralegal Association of Rochester
P.O. Box 40567
Rochester, NY 14604
716-234-5923
http://appwww.par.itgo.com

Southern Tier Paralegal
Association
P.O. Box 2555
Binghamton, NY 13902
716-635-8250
E-mail: southerntier@paralegals.org

Western New York Paralegal
Association
P.O. Box 207
Buffalo, NY 14202
716-635-8250
http://www. wnyparalegals.org

West/Roc Paralegal Association
Box 668
New York, NY 10956

NORTH CAROLINA

Metrolina Paralegal Association
P.O. Box 36260
Charlotte, NC 28236
704-373-8985
http://www.charlotteareaparalegals
.com

North Carolina Paralegal Association
P.O. Box 36264
Charlotte, NC 28263-6264
http://www.ncparalegal.org

NORTH DAKOTA

Red River Valley Paralegal
Association
(Formerly Red River Valley Legal
Assistants)
P.O. Box 1954
Fargo, ND 58106
http://www.rrvpa.org

Western Dakota Association of Legal
Assistants
P.O. Box 7304
Bismarck, ND 58502
http://www.wdala.org

OHIO

Cincinnati Paralegal Association
P.O. Box 1515
Cincinnati, OH 45201
513-244-1266
http://www.cincinnatiparalegals.org

Cleveland Association
of Paralegals
P.O. Box 14517
Cleveland, OH 44101
http://www.capohio.org

Greater Dayton Paralegal Association
P.O. Box 10515
Mid-City Station
Dayton, OH 45402
http://www.gdpa.org

Northeastern Ohio Paralegal
Association
P.O. Box 80068
Akron, OH 44308-0068

Paralegal Association of Central Ohio
P.O. Box 15182
Columbus, OH 43215-0812
614-470-2000
http://www.pacoparalegals.org

Toledo Association of Legal
Assistants
P.O. Box 1322
Toledo, OH 43603

OKLAHOMA

Oklahoma Paralegal Association
714 Maple Dr.
Weatherford, OK 73096
http://www.okparalegal.org

Tulsa Association of Legal
Assistants
P.O. Box 1484
Tulsa, OK 74101
http://www.tulsatala.org

OREGON

Oregon Legal Assistants
Association
P.O. Box 8523
Portland, OR 97207
503-796-1671

Oregon Paralegal Association
P.O. Box 8523
Portland, OR 97207
503-796-1671
http://www.oregonparalegal.org

Pacific Northwest Paralegal
Association
P.O. Box 1854
Portland, OR 97207
http://www.pnpa.org

PENNSYLVANIA

Central Pennsylvania Paralegal
Association
P.O. Box 11814
Harrisburg, PA 17108
717-234-4121

Chester County Paralegal Association
P.O. Box 295
West Chester, PA 19381-0295
http://www.chescoparalegal.org

Keystone Legal Assistant Association
P.O. Box 25
Enola, PA 17025
717-653-7374

Lancaster Area Paralegal Association
P.O. Box 593
Lancaster, PA 17608
717-299-7254
http://www.laparalegals.com

Lycoming County Paralegal
Association
P.O. Box 991
Williamsport, PA 17703
570-376-6555
http://www.lycolaw.org/lcpa

Montgomery County Paralegal
Association
P.O. Box 1765
Blue Bell, PA 19422
http://www.paralegals.org

Paralegal Association of
Northwestern Pennsylvania
P.O. Box 1504
Erie, PA 16507

Philadelphia Association
of Paralegals
P.O. Box 59179
Philadelphia, PA 19102-9179
215-255-8405
http://www.philaparalegals.org

Pittsburgh Paralegal Association
P.O. Box 2845
Pittsburgh, PA 15230
412-642-2345
http://www.pghparalegals.org

York County Paralegal
Association
P.O. Box 2584
York, PA 15230
717-848-4900

RHODE ISLAND

Rhode Island Paralegal
Association
P.O. Box 1003
Providence, RI 02901
http://www.paralegals.org

SOUTH CAROLINA

Charleston Association of Legal
Assistants
P.O. Box 1260
Charleston, SC 29402
http://www.charlestonlegalassistants
.org

Columbia Legal Assistant
Association
P.O. Box 11634
Columbia, SC 29211-1634

Palmetto Paralegals Association
P.O. Box 11634
Columbia, S.C. 29211-1634
803-252-0460
http://www.ppasc.org

Paralegal Association of
the Pee Dee
P.O. Box 5592
Florence, SC 29502-5592

South Carolina Upstate
Paralegal Association
http://www.scupa.org

SOUTH DAKOTA

South Dakota Paralegal Association
P.O. Box 1443
Sioux Falls, SD 57101-1443
http://www.sdparalegals.com

TENNESSEE

Greater Memphis Paralegal
Alliance
http://www.memphisparalegals.org

Memphis Paralegal Association
P.O. Box 3646
Memphis, TN 38173-0646
http://www.
memphisparalegalassociation.org

Middle Tennessee Paralegal
Association
P.O. Box 198006
Nashville, TN 37219
http://www.mtpaonline.com

Smokey Mountain Paralegal
Association
P.O. Box 445
Knoxville, TN 37901
http://www.smparalegal.org

Tennessee Paralegal Association
P.O. Box 21723
Chattanooga, TN 37424

TEXAS

Alamo Area Paralegal Association
P.O. Box 90037
San Antonio, TX 78209
http://www.alamoparalegals.org

Capital Area Paralegal Association
P.O. Box 773
Austin, TX 78767
512-505-6822
http://www.capatx.org

Dallas Area Paralegal Association
P.O. Box 12533
Dallas, TX 75225
214-991-0853
http://www.dallasparalegals.org

El Paso Paralegal Association
P.O. Box 6
El Paso, 79940
http://www.elppa.org

Fort Worth Paralegal Association
P.O. Box 17021
Fort Worth, TX 76102
817-336-3972
http://www.fwpa.org

Houston Legal Assistants Association
Lyric Centre, Ste. 900
440 Louisiana
Houston, TX 77002
713-236-7724
http://www.hlaa.net

Houston Paralegal Association
P.O. Box 61863
Houston, TX 77208
http://www.
houstonparalegalassociation.org

Legal Assistant Division State
Bar of Texas
P.O. Box 12487
Austin, TX 78711
512-463-1453

Northeast Texas Association
of Paralegals, Inc.
P.O. Box 2284
Longview, TX 75606
http://www.ntaparalegals.com

South Texas Organization of
Paralegals
P.O. Box 2486
San Antonio, TX 78299
210-554-9135
http://www.southtexasparalegals.org

Texas Panhandle Paralegal Association
http://www.texaspanhandleparalegals
.com

UTAH

Legal Assistants Association of Utah
P.O. Box 112001
Salt Lake City, UT 84147-2001
801-493-7852
http://www.laau.info

VERMONT

Vermont Paralegal Association
P.O. Box 157
Burlington, VT 05402
http://www.paralegals.org

VIRGINIA

Central Virginia Paralegal
Association
P.O. Box 143
Lynchburg, VA 24505

Fredericksburg Paralegal Association
P.O. Box 7351
Fredericksburg, VA 22404
http://www.paralegals.org/
fredericksburg.html

Virginia Peninsula Paralegal
Association
115 Freeman Dr.
Poquoson, VA 23662
http://www.vappa.org

Richmond Paralegal Association
P.O. Box 384
Richmond, VA 23218-0384
http://www.richmondparalegals.org

Roanoke Valley Paralegal Association
P.O. Box 1505
Roanoke, VA 24007-1505
703-224-8000
http://www.rvpa.org

Tidewater Association of Legal
Assistants
P.O. Box 3566
Norfolk, VA 23514
http://www.tidewaterparalegals.org

Virginia Alliance of Paralegal
Associations
2715 Huntington Ave.
Newport News, VA 23607
http://www.vaparalegalalliance.org

VIRGIN ISLANDS

Virgin Islands Paralegals
P.O. Box 6276
St. Thomas, VI 00804

WASHINGTON

Washington State Paralegal
Association
P.O. Box 58530
Seattle, WA 98138-1530
866-257-9772
http://www.wspaonline.org

WEST VIRGINIA

Association of West Virginia
Paralegals
(Fomerly: Legal Assistants
of West Virginia)
P.O. Box 1744
Clarksburg, WV 26302
http://www.awvp.org

Legal Assistants/Paralegals of
Southern West Virginia
http://www.lapswv.org

WISCONSIN

Madison Area Paralegal
Association
P.O. Box 2242
Madison, WI 53701-2242
http://www.madisonparalegal.org

Paralegal Association of
Wisconsin
P.O. Box 510892
Milwaukee, WI 53203-0151
414-272-7168
http://www.wisconsinparalegal.org

WYOMING

Legal Assistants of Wyoming
P.O. Box 155
Casper, WY 82601
http://www.lawyo.com

Definitions and Code of Ethics of National Paralegal Associations

NATIONAL ASSOCIATION OF LEGAL ASSISTANTS

PREAMBLE

A legal assistant must adhere strictly to the accepted standards of legal ethics and to the general principles of proper conduct. The performance of the duties of the legal assistant shall be governed by specific canons as defined herein so that justice will be served and goals of the profession attained (See NALA Model Standards and guidelines for Utilization of Legal Assistants, Section II).

The canons of ethics set forth hereafter are adopted by the National Association of Legal Assistants, Inc., as a general guide intended to aid legal assistants and attorneys. The enumeration of these rules does not mean there are not others of equal importance although not specifically mentioned. Court rules, agency rules, and statutes must be taken into consideration when interpreting the canons.

DEFINITION

The National Association of Legal Assistants adopted the following definition in 1984: Legal assistants, also known as paralegals, are a distinguishable group of persons who assist attorneys in the delivery of legal services. Through formal education, training, and experience, legal assistants have knowledge and expertise regarding the legal system and substantive and procedural law which qualify them to do work of a legal nature under the supervision of an attorney.

CODE OF ETHICS

CANON I

A legal assistant must not perform any of the duties that attorneys only may perform nor take any actions that attorneys may not take.

CANON II

A legal assistant may perform any task which is properly delegated and supervised by an attorney, as long as the attorney is ultimately responsible to the client, maintains a direct relationship with the client, and assumes professional responsibility for the work product.

CANON III

A legal assistant must not:

a) engage in, encourage, or contribute to any act which could constitute the unauthorized practice of law;

b) establish attorney-client relationships, set fees, give legal opinions or advice, or represent a client before a court or agency unless so authorized by that court or agency; and

c) engage in conduct or take any action which would assist or involve the attorney in a violation of professional ethics or give the appearance of professional impropriety.

CANON IV

A legal assistant must use discretion and professional judgement commensurate with knowledge and experience but must not render independent legal judgement in place of an attorney. The services of an attorney are essential in the public interest whenever such legal judgment is required.

CANON V

A legal assistant must disclose his or her status as a legal assistant at the outset of any professional relationship with a client, attorney, a court or administrative agency or personnel thereof, or a member of the general public.

A legal assistant must act prudently in determining the extent to which a client may be assisted without the presence of an attorney.

CANON VI

A legal assistant must strive to maintain integrity and a high degree of competency through education and training with respect to professional responsibility, local rules, and practice, and through continuing education in substantive areas of law to better assist the legal profession in fulfilling its duty to provide legal service.

CANON VII

A legal assistant must protect the confidences of a client and must not violate any rule or statute now in effect or hereafter enacted controlling the doctrine of privileged communications between a client and an attorney.

CANON VIII

A legal assistant must do all other things incidental, necessary, or expedient for the attainment of the ethics and responsibilities as defined by statute or rule of court.

CANON IX

A legal assistant's conduct is guided by the bar association's code of professional responsibility and rules of professional conduct.

STANDARDS AND GUIDELINES

The Guidelines represent a statement of how the legal assistant may function. The Guidelines are not intended to be a comprehensive or exhaustive list of the proper duties of a legal assistant. Rather, they are designed as guides to what may or may not be proper conduct for the legal assistant. In formulating the Guidelines, the reasoning and rules of law in many reported decisions of disciplinary cases and unauthorized practice of law cases have been analyzed and considered. In addition, the provisions of the American Bar Association's Model Rules of Professional Conduct, as well as the ethical promulgation of various state courts and bar associations, have been considered in the development of the Guidelines.

These Guidelines form a sound basis for the legal assistant and the supervising attorney to follow. This Model will serve as a comprehensive resource document and as a definitive, well-reasoned guide to those considering voluntary standards and guidelines for legal assistants.

Introduction

Proper utilization of the services of legal assistants affects the efficient delivery of legal services. Legal assistants and the legal profession should be assured that some measures exist for identifying legal assistants and their role in assisting attorneys in the delivery of legal services. Therefore, the National Association of Legal Assistants, Inc., hereby adopts these Standards and Guidelines as an educational document for the benefit of legal assistants and the legal profession.

Standards

A legal assistant should meet certain minimum qualifications. The following standards may be used to determine an individual's qualifications as a legal assistant:

1. Successful completion of the Certified Legal Assistant ("CLA") certifying examination of the National Association of Legal Assistants, Inc.;
2. Graduation from an ABA approved program of study for legal assistants;
3. Graduation from a course of study for legal assistants which is institutionally accredited but not ABA approved, and which requires not less than the equivalent of 60 semester hours of classroom study;
4. Graduation from a course of study for legal assistants, other than those set forth in (2) and (3) above, plus not less than six months of in-house training as a legal assistant;
5. A baccalaureate degree in any field, plus not less than six months in-house training as a legal assistant;
6. A minimum of three years of law-related experience under the supervision of an attorney, including at least six months of in-house training as a legal assistant; or
7. Two years of in-house training as a legal assistant.

For purposes of these Standards, "in-house training as a legal assistant" means attorney education of the employee concerning legal assistant duties and these Guidelines. In addition to review and analysis of assignments, the legal assistant should receive a reasonable amount of instruction directly related to the duties and obligations of the legal assistant.

Guidelines

These Guidelines relating to standards of performance and professional responsibility are intended to aid legal assistants and attorneys. The ultimate responsibility rests with an attorney who employs legal assistants to educate them with respect to the duties they are assigned and to supervise the manner in which such duties are accomplished.

GUIDELINE 1

Legal assistants should:

1. Disclose their status as legal assistants at the outset of any professional relationship with a client, other attorneys, a court or administrative agency or personnel thereof, or members of the general public;
2. Preserve the confidences and secrets of all clients; and
3. Understand the attorney's Code of Professional Responsibility and these Guidelines in order to avoid any action which would involve the attorney in a violation of the Rules, or give the appearance of professional impropriety.

GUIDELINE 2

Legal assistants should not:

1. Establish attorney-client relationships; set legal fees; give legal opinions or advice; or represent a client before a court; nor
2. Engage in, encourage, or contribute to any act which could constitute the unauthorized practice of law.

GUIDELINE 3

Legal assistants may perform services for an attorney in the representation of a client, provided:

1. The services performed by the legal assistant do not require the exercise of independent professional legal judgment;
2. The attorney maintains a direct relationship with the client and maintains control of all client matters;
3. The attorney supervises the legal assistant;
4. The attorney remains professionally responsible for all work on behalf of the client, including any actions taken or not taken by the legal assistant in connection therewith; and
5. The services performed supplement, merge with and become the attorney's work product.

GUIDELINE 4

In the supervision of a legal assistant, consideration should be given to:

1. Designating work assignments that correspond to the legal assistant's abilities, knowledge, training and experience;
2. Education and training the legal assistant with respect to professional responsibility, local rules and practices, and firm policies;
3. Monitoring the work and professional conduct of the legal assistant to ensure that the work is substantively correct and timely performed;
4. Providing continuing education for the legal assistant in substantive matters through courses, institutes, workshops, seminars and in-house training; and
5. Encouraging and supporting membership and active participation in professional organizations.

GUIDELINE 5

Except as otherwise provided by statute, court rule or decision, administrative rule or regulation, or the attorney's Code of Professional Responsibility, and within the preceding parameters and proscriptions, a legal assistant may perform any function delegated by an attorney, including, but not limited to, the following:

1. Conduct client interviews and maintain general contact with the client after the establishment of the attorney-client relationship, so long as the client is aware of the status and function of the legal assistant, and the client contact is under the supervision of the attorney.
2. Locate and interview witnesses, so long as the witnesses are aware of the status and function of the legal assistant.
3. Conduct investigations and statistical and documentary research for review by the attorney.
4. Conduct legal research for review by the attorney.
5. Draft legal documents for review by the attorney.
6. Draft correspondence and pleadings for review by and signature of the attorney.
7. Summarize depositions, interrogatories and testimony for review by the attorney.
8. Attend executions of wills, real estate closings, depositions, court or administrative hearings and trials with the attorney.
9. Author and sign letters providing the legal assistant's status is clearly indicated and the correspondence does not contain independent legal opinions or legal advice.

Conclusion

These Standards and Guidelines were developed from generally accepted practices. Each supervising attorney must be aware of the specific rules, decisions and statutes applicable to legal assistants within his/her jurisdiction.

NATIONAL FEDERATION OF PARALEGAL ASSOCIATIONS

DEFINITION

A paralegal/legal assistant is a person qualified through education, training or work experience to perform substantive legal work that requires knowledge of legal concepts and is customarily, but not exclusively, performed by a lawyer. This person may be retained or employed by a lawyer, law office, governmental agency or other entity or may be authorized by administrative, statutory or court authority to perform this work.

Adopted 1987

Model Code of Ethics and Professional Responsibility and Guidelines for Enforcement

PREAMBLE

The National Federation of Paralegal Associations, Inc. ("NFPA") is a professional organization comprised of paralegal associations and individual paralegals throughout the United States and Canada. Members of NFPA have varying backgrounds, experiences, education and job responsibilities that reflect the diversity of the paralegal profession. NFPA promotes the growth, development and recognition of the paralegal profession as an integral partner in the delivery of legal services.

In May 1993 NFPA adopted its Model Code of Ethics and Professional Responsibility ("Model Code") to delineate the principles for ethics and conduct to which every paralegal should aspire.

Many paralegal associations throughout the United States have endorsed the concept and content of NFPA's Model Code through the adoption of their own ethical codes. In doing so, paralegals have confirmed the profession's commitment to increase the quality and efficiency of legal services, as well as recognized its responsibilities to the public, the legal community, and colleagues.

Paralegals have recognized, and will continue to recognize, that the profession must continue to evolve to enhance their roles in the delivery of legal services. With increased levels of responsibility comes the need to define and enforce mandatory rules of professional conduct. Enforcement of codes of paralegal conduct is a logical and necessary step to enhance and ensure the confidence of the legal community and the public in the integrity and professional responsibility of paralegals.

In April 1997 NFPA adopted the Model Disciplinary Rules ("Model Rules") to make possible the enforcement of the Canons and Ethical Considerations contained in the NFPA Model Code. A concurrent determination was made that the Model Code of Ethics and Professional Responsibility, formerly aspirational in nature, should be recognized as setting forth the enforceable obligations of all paralegals.

The Model Code and Model Rules offer a framework for professional discipline, either voluntarily or through formal regulatory programs.

§1. NFPA MODEL DISCIPLINARY RULES AND ETHICAL CONSIDERATIONS

1.1 A PARALEGAL SHALL ACHIEVE AND MAINTAIN A HIGH LEVEL OF COMPETENCE.

Ethical Considerations

EC-1.1 (a): A paralegal shall achieve competency through education, training, and work experience.

EC-1.1 (b): A paralegal shall aspire to participate in a minimum of twelve (12) hours of continuing legal education, to include at least one (1) hour of ethics education, every two (2) years in order to remain current on developments in the law.

EC-1.1(c): A paralegal shall perform all assignments promptly and efficiently.

1.2 A PARALEGAL SHALL MAINTAIN A HIGH LEVEL OF PERSONAL AND PROFESSIONAL INTEGRITY.

Ethical Considerations

EC-1.2(a): A paralegal shall not engage in any ex parte communications involving the courts or any other adjudicatory body in an attempt to exert undue influence or to obtain advantage or the benefit of only one party.

EC-1.2(b): A paralegal shall not communicate, or cause another to communicate, with a party the paralegal knows to be represented by a lawyer in a pending matter without the prior consent of the lawyer representing such other party.

EC-1.2(c): A paralegal shall ensure that all time-keeping and billing records prepared by the paralegal are thorough, accurate, honest, and complete.

EC-1.2(d): A paralegal shall not knowingly engage in fraudulent billing practices. Such practices may include, but are not limited to: inflation of hours billed to a client or employer; misrepresentation of the nature of tasks performed; and/or submission of fraudulent expense and disbursement documentation.

EC-1.2(e): A paralegal shall be scrupulous, thorough and honest in the identification and maintenance of all funds, securities, and other assets of a client and shall provide accurate accounting as appropriate.

EC-1.2(f): A paralegal shall advise the proper authority of non-confidential knowledge of any dishonest or fraudulent acts by any person pertaining to the handling of the funds, securities, or other assets of a client. The authority to whom the report is made shall depend on the nature and circumstances of the possible misconduct, (e.g., ethics committees of law firms, corporations and/or paralegal associations, local or state bar associations, local prosecutors, administrative agencies, etc.). Failure to report such knowledge is in itself misconduct and shall be treated as such under these rules.

1.3 A PARALEGAL SHALL MAINTAIN A HIGH STANDARD OF PROFESSIONAL CONDUCT.

Ethical Considerations

EC-1.3(a): A paralegal shall refrain from engaging in any conduct that offends the dignity and decorum of proceedings before a court or other adjudicatory body and shall be respectful of all rules and procedures.

EC-1.3(b): A paralegal shall avoid impropriety and the appearance of impropriety and shall not engage in any conduct that would adversely affect his/her fitness to practice. Such conduct may include, but is not limited to: violence, dishonesty, interference with the administration of justice, and/or abuse of a professional position or public office.

EC-1.3(c): Should a paralegal's fitness to practice be compromised by physical or mental illness, causing that paralegal to commit an act that is in direct violation of the Model Code/Model Rules and/or the rules and/or laws governing the jurisdiction in which the paralegal practices, that paralegal may be protected from sanction upon review of the nature and circumstances of that illness.

EC-1.3(d): A paralegal shall advise the proper authority of non-confidential knowledge of any action of another legal professional that clearly demonstrates fraud, deceit, dishonesty, or misrepresentation. The authority to whom the report is made shall depend on the nature and circumstances of the possible misconduct (e.g., ethics committees of law firms, corporations and/or paralegal associations, local or state bar associations, local prosecutors, administrative agencies, etc.). Failure to report such knowledge

is in itself misconduct and shall be treated as such under these rules.

EC-1.3(e): A paralegal shall not knowingly assist any individual with the commission of an act that is in direct violation of the Model Code/Model Rules and/or the rules and/or laws governing the jurisdiction in which the paralegal practices.

EC-1.3(f): If a paralegal possesses knowledge of future criminal activity, that knowledge must be reported to the appropriate authority immediately.

1.4 A PARALEGAL SHALL SERVE THE PUBLIC INTEREST BY CONTRIBUTING TO THE IMPROVEMENT OF THE LEGAL SYSTEM AND DELIVERY OF QUALITY LEGAL SERVICES, INCLUDING PRO BONO PUBLICO SERVICES.

Ethical Considerations

EC-1.4(a): A paralegal shall be sensitive to the legal needs of the public and shall promote the development and implementation of programs that address those needs.

EC-1.4(b): A paralegal shall support efforts to improve the legal system and access thereto and shall assist in making changes.

EC-1.4(c): A paralegal shall support and participate in the delivery of Pro Bono Publico services directed toward implementing and improving access to justice, the law, the legal system or the paralegal and legal professions.

EC-1.4(d): A paralegal should aspire annually to contribute twenty-four (24) hours of Pro Bono Publico services under the supervision of an attorney or as authorized by administrative, statutory or court authority to:

1. persons of limited means; or
2. charitable, religious, civic, community, governmental and educational organizations in matters that are designed primarily to address the legal needs of persons with limited means; or
3. individuals, groups or organizations seeking to secure or protect civil rights, civil liberties or public rights. The twenty-four (24) hours of Pro Bono Publico services contributed annually by a paralegal may consist of such services as detailed in this EC-1.4(d), and/or administrative matters designed to develop and implement the attainment of this aspiration as detailed above in EC-1.4(a) B (c), or any combination of the two.

1.5 A PARALEGAL SHALL PRESERVE ALL CONFIDENTIAL INFORMATION PROVIDED BY THE CLIENT OR ACQUIRED FROM OTHER SOURCES BEFORE, DURING, AND AFTER THE COURSE OF THE PROFESSIONAL RELATIONSHIP.

Ethical Considerations

EC-1.5(a): A paralegal shall be aware of and abide by all legal authority governing confidential information in the jurisdiction in which the paralegal practices.

EC-1.5(b): A paralegal shall not use confidential information to the disadvantage of the client.

EC-1.5(c): A paralegal shall not use confidential information to the advantage of the paralegal or of a third person.

EC-1.5(d): A paralegal may reveal confidential information only after full disclosure and with the client's written consent; or, when required by law or court order; or, when necessary to prevent the client from committing an act that could result in death or serious bodily harm.

EC-1.5(e): A paralegal shall keep those individuals responsible for the legal representation of a client fully informed of any confidential information the paralegal may have pertaining to that client.

EC-1.5(f): A paralegal shall not engage in any indiscreet communications concerning clients.

1.6 A PARALEGAL SHALL AVOID CONFLICTS OF INTEREST AND SHALL DISCLOSE ANY POSSIBLE CONFLICT TO THE EMPLOYER OR CLIENT, AS WELL AS TO THE PROSPECTIVE EMPLOYERS OR CLIENTS.

Ethical Considerations

EC-1.6(a): A paralegal shall act within the bounds of the law, solely for the benefit of the client, and shall be free of compromising influences and loyalties. Neither the paralegal's personal or business interest, nor those of other clients or third persons, should compromise the paralegal's professional judgment and loyalty to the client.

EC-1.6(b): A paralegal shall avoid conflicts of interest that may arise from previous assignments, whether for a present or past employer or client.

EC-1.6(c): A paralegal shall avoid conflicts of interest that may arise from family relationships and from personal and business interests.

EC-1.6(d): In order to be able to determine whether an actual or potential conflict of interest exists, a paralegal shall create and maintain an effective recordkeeping system that identifies clients, matters, and parties with which the paralegal has worked.

EC-1.6(e): A paralegal shall reveal sufficient non-confidential information about a client or former client to reasonably ascertain if an actual or potential conflict of interest exists.

EC-1.6(f): A paralegal shall not participate in or conduct work on any matter where a conflict of interest has been identified.

EC-1.6(g): In matters where a conflict of interest has been identified and the client consents to continued representation, a paralegal shall comply fully with the implementation and maintenance of an Ethical Wall.

1.7 A PARALEGAL'S TITLE SHALL BE FULLY DISCLOSED.

Ethical Considerations

EC-1.7(a): A paralegal's title shall clearly indicate the individual's status and shall be disclosed in all business and professional communications to avoid misunderstandings and misconceptions about the paralegal's role and responsibilities.

EC-1.7(b): A paralegal's title shall be included if the paralegal's name appears on business cards, letterhead, brochures, directories, and advertisements.

EC-1.7(c): A paralegal shall not use letterhead, business cards or other promotional materials to create a fraudulent impression of his/her status or ability to practice in the jurisdiction in which the paralegal practices.

EC-1.7(d): A paralegal shall not practice under color of any record, diploma, or certificate that has been illegally or fraudulently obtained or issued or which is misrepresentative in any way.

EC-1.7(e): A paralegal shall not participate in the creation, issuance, or dissemination of fraudulent records, diplomas, or certificates.

1.8 A PARALEGAL SHALL NOT ENGAGE IN THE UNAUTHORIZED PRACTICE OF LAW.

Ethical Considerations

EC-1.8(a): A paralegal shall comply with the applicable legal authority governing the unauthorized practice of law in the jurisdiction in which the paralegal practices.

§2. NFPA GUIDELINES FOR THE ENFORCEMENT OF THE MODEL CODE OF ETHICS AND PROFESSIONAL RESPONSIBILITY

2.1 BASIS FOR DISCIPLINE

2.1(a): Disciplinary investigations and proceedings brought under authority of the Rules shall be conducted in accord with obligations imposed on the paralegal professional by the Model Code of Ethics and Professional Responsibility.

2.2 STRUCTURE OF DISCIPLINARY COMMITTEE

2.2(a): The Disciplinary Committee ("Committee") shall be made up of nine (9) members including the Chair.

2.2(b): Each member of the Committee, including any temporary replacement members, shall have demonstrated working knowledge of ethics/professional responsibility-related issues and activities.

2.2(c): The Committee shall represent a cross-section of practice areas and work experience. The following recommendations are made regarding the members of the Committee:

1) At least one paralegal with one to three years of law-related work experience.
2) At least one paralegal with five to seven years of law-related work experience.
3) At least one paralegal with over ten years of law-related work experience.
4) One paralegal educator with five to seven years of work experience; preferably in the area of ethics/professional responsibility.
5) One paralegal manager.
6) One lawyer with five to seven years of law-related work experience.
7) One lay member.

2.2(d): The Chair of the Committee shall be appointed within thirty (30) days of its members' induction. The Chair shall have no fewer than ten (10) years of law-related work experience.

2.2(e): The terms of all members of the Committee shall be staggered. Of those members initially appointed, a simple majority plus one shall be appointed to a term of one year, and the remaining members shall be appointed to a term of two years. Thereafter, all members of the Committee shall be appointed to terms of two years.

2.2(f): If for any reason the terms of a majority of the Committee will expire at the same time, members may be appointed to terms of one year to maintain continuity of the Committee.

2.2(g): The Committee shall organize from its members a three-tiered structure to investigate, prosecute and/or adjudicate charges of misconduct. The members shall be rotated among the tiers.

2.3 OPERATION OF COMMITTEE

2.3(a): The Committee shall meet on an as-needed basis to discuss, investigate, and/or adjudicate alleged violations of the Model Code/Model Rules.

2.3(b): A majority of the members of the Committee present at a meeting shall constitute a quorum.

2.3(c): A Recording Secretary shall be designated to maintain complete and accurate minutes of all Committee meetings. All such minutes shall be kept confidential until a decision has been made that the matter will be set for hearing as set forth in Section 6.1 below.

2.3(d): If any member of the Committee has a conflict of interest with the Charging Party, the Responding Party, or the allegations of misconduct, that member shall not take part in any hearing or deliberations concerning those allegations. If the absence of that member creates a lack of a quorum for the Committee, then a temporary replacement for the member shall be appointed.

2.3(e): Either the Charging Party or the Responding Party may request that, for good cause shown, any member of the Committee not participate in a hearing or deliberation. All such requests shall be honored. If the absence of a Committee member under those circumstances creates a lack of a quorum for the Committee, then a temporary replacement for that member shall be appointed.

2.3(f): All discussions and correspondence of the Committee shall be kept confidential until a decision has been made that the matter will be set for hearing as set forth in Section 6.1 below.

2.3(g): All correspondence from the Committee to the Responding Party regarding any charge of misconduct and any decisions made regarding the charge shall be mailed certified mail, return receipt requested, to the Responding Party's last known address and shall be clearly marked with a "Confidential" designation.

2.4 PROCEDURE FOR THE REPORTING OF ALLEGED VIOLATIONS OF THE MODEL CODE/DISCIPLINARY RULES

2.4(a): An individual or entity in possession of non-confidential knowledge or information concerning possible instances of misconduct shall make a confidential written report to the Committee within thirty (30) days of obtaining same. This report shall include all details of the alleged misconduct.

2.4(b): The Committee so notified shall inform the Responding Party of the allegation(s) of misconduct no later than ten (10) business days after receiving the confidential written report from the Charging Party.

2.4(c): Notification to the Responding Party shall include the identity of the Charging Party, unless, for good cause shown, the Charging Party requests anonymity.

2.4(d): The Responding Party shall reply to the allegations within ten (10) business days of notification.

2.5 PROCEDURE FOR THE INVESTIGATION OF A CHARGE OF MISCONDUCT

2.5(a): Upon receipt of a Charge of Misconduct ("Charge"), or on its own initiative, the Committee shall initiate an investigation.

2.5(b): If, upon initial or preliminary review, the Committee makes a determination that the charges are either without basis in fact or, if proven, would not constitute professional misconduct, the Committee shall dismiss the allegations of misconduct. If such determination of dismissal cannot be made, a formal investigation shall be initiated.

2.5(c): Upon the decision to conduct a formal investigation, the Committee shall:

1) mail to the Charging and Responding Parties within three (3) business days of that decision notice of the commencement of a formal investigation. That notification shall be in writing and shall contain a complete explanation of all Charge(s), as well as the reasons for a formal investigation, and shall cite the applicable codes and rules;

2) allow the Responding Party thirty (30) days to prepare and submit a confidential response to the Committee, which response shall address each charge specifically and shall be in writing; and

3) upon receipt of the response to the notification, have thirty (30) days to investigate the Charge(s). If an extension of time is deemed necessary, that extension shall not exceed ninety (90) days.

2.5(d): Upon conclusion of the investigation, the Committee may:

1) dismiss the Charge upon the finding that it has no basis in fact;

2) dismiss the Charge upon the finding that, if proven, the Charge would not constitute Misconduct;

3) refer the matter for hearing by the Tribunal; or

4) in the case of criminal activity, refer the Charge(s) and all investigation results to the appropriate authority.

2.6 PROCEDURE FOR A MISCONDUCT HEARING BEFORE A TRIBUNAL

2.6(a): Upon the decision by the Committee that a matter should be heard, all parties shall be notified and a hearing date shall be set. The hearing shall take place no more than thirty (30) days from the conclusion of the formal investigation.

2.6(b): The Responding Party shall have the right to counsel. The parties and the Tribunal shall have the right to call any witnesses and introduce any documentation that they believe will lead to the fair and reasonable resolution of the matter.

2.6(c): Upon completion of the hearing, the Tribunal shall deliberate and present a written decision to the parties in accordance with procedures as set forth by the Tribunal.

2.6(d): Notice of the decision of the Tribunal shall be appropriately published.

2.7 SANCTIONS

2.7(a): Upon a finding of the Tribunal that misconduct has occurred, any of the following sanctions, or others as may be deemed appropriate, may be imposed upon the Responding Party, either singularly or in combination:

1) letter of reprimand to the Responding Party; counseling;

2) attendance at an ethics course approved by the Tribunal;

3) suspension of license/authority to practice; revocation of license/authority to practice;

4) imposition of a fine; assessment of costs; or

5) in the instance of criminal activity, referral to the appropriate authority.

2.7(b): Upon the expiration of any period of probation, suspension, or revocation, the Responding Party may make application for reinstatement. With the application for reinstatement, the Responding Party must show proof of having complied with all aspects of the sanctions imposed by the Tribunal.

2.8 APPELLATE PROCEDURES

2.8(a): The parties shall have the right to appeal the decision of the Tribunal in accordance with the procedure as set forth by the Tribunal.

Definitions

"Appellate Body" means a body established to adjudicate an appeal to any decision made by a Tribunal or other decision-making body with respect to formally-heard Charges of Misconduct.

"Charge of Misconduct" means a written submission by any individual or entity to an ethics committee, paralegal association, bar association, law enforcement agency, judicial body, government agency, or other appropriate body or entity, that sets forth non-confidential information regarding any instance of alleged misconduct by an individual paralegal or paralegal entity.

"Charging Party" means any individual or entity who submits a Charge of Misconduct against an individual paralegal or paralegal entity.

"Competency" means the demonstration of: diligence, education, skill, and mental, emotional, and physical fitness reasonably necessary for the performance of paralegal services.

"Confidential Information" means information relating to a client, whatever its source, that is not public knowledge nor available to the public. ("Non-Confidential Information" would generally include the name of the client and the identity of the matter for which the paralegal provided services.)

"Disciplinary Hearing" means the confidential proceeding conducted by a committee or other designated body or entity concerning any instance of alleged misconduct by an individual paralegal or paralegal entity.

"Disciplinary Committee" means any committee that has been established by an entity such as a paralegal association, bar association, judicial body, or government agency to: (a) identify, define and investigate general ethical considerations and concerns with respect to paralegal practice; (b) administer and enforce the Model Code and Model Rules and; (c) disciplinary individual paralegal or paralegal entity found to be in violation of same.

"Disclose" means communication of information reasonably sufficient to permit identification of the significance of the matter in question.

"Ethical Wall" means the screening method implemented in order to protect a client from a conflict of interest. An Ethical Wall generally includes, but is not limited to, the following elements: (1) prohibit the paralegal from having any connection with the matter; (2) ban discussions with or the transfer of documents to or from the paralegal; (3) restrict access to files; and (4) educate all members of the firm, corporation, or entity as to the separation of the paralegal (both organizationally and physically) from the pending matter. For more information regarding the Ethical Wall, see the NFPA publication entitled "The Ethical Wall Its Application to Paralegals."

"Ex parte" means actions or communications conducted at the instance and for the benefit of one party only, and without notice to, or contestation by, any person adversely interested.

"Investigation" means the investigation of any charge(s) of misconduct filed against an individual paralegal or paralegal entity by a Committee.

"Letter of Reprimand" means a written notice of formal censure or other proof administered to an individual paralegal or paralegal entity for unethical or improper conduct.

"Misconduct" means the knowing or unknowing commission of an act that is in direct violation of those Canons and Ethical Considerations of any and all applicable codes and/or rules of conduct.

"Paralegal" is synonymous with "Legal Assistant" and is defined as a person qualified through education, training, or work experience to perform substantive legal work that requires knowledge of legal concepts and is customarily, but not exclusively, performed by a lawyer. This person may be retained or employed by a lawyer, law office, governmental agency, or other entity or may be authorized by administrative, statutory, or court authority to perform this work.

"Pro Bono Publico" means providing or assisting to provide quality legal services in order to enhance access to justice for persons of limited means; charitable, religious, civic, community, governmental and educational organizations in matters that are designed primarily to address the legal needs of persons with limited means; or individuals, groups or organizations seeking to secure or protect civil rights, civil liberties or public rights.

"Proper Authority" means the local paralegal association, the local or state bar association, Committee(s) of the local paralegal or bar association(s), local prosecutor, administrative agency, or other tribunal empowered to investigate or act upon an instance of alleged misconduct.

"Responding Party" means an individual paralegal or paralegal entity against whom a Charge of Misconduct has been submitted.

"Revocation" means the recision of the license, certificate or other authority to practice of an individual paralegal or paralegal entity found in violation of those Canons and Ethical Considerations of any and all applicable codes and/or rules of conduct.

"Suspension" means the suspension of the license, certificate or other authority to practice of an individual paralegal or paralegal entity found in violation of those Canons and Ethical Considerations of any and all applicable codes and/or rules of conduct.

"Tribunal" means the body designated to adjudicate allegations of misconduct.

THE AMERICAN ALLIANCE OF PARALEGALS, INC.

1. A paralegal shall not engage in the unauthorized practice of law.
2. A paralegal shall keep confidential any and all information, documents and other materials entrusted to him or her or acquired in some other way during the course of the legal representation of a client. The confidentiality shall be maintained before, during and after the legal representation unless the client has given consent or disclosure is required by law or by court order.
3. A paralegal shall avoid conflicts of interest and shall immediately disclose any potential conflicts of interest to his or her employer.
4. A paralegal shall ensure that his or her status as a paralegal is disclosed at the beginning of any professional relationship with the attorney, client, personnel of a court, or the personnel of an administrative agency.

5. A paralegal shall follow all provisions of the rules of professional conduct for a paralegal of the state in which he or she is employed. If no such specific code for paralegals exists, then a paralegal shall follow the attorney's code of ethics as it applies to paralegals within that state.

6. A paralegal shall maintain personal and professional integrity.

7. A paralegal shall attain a high degree of competency through education, training, and experience.

8. A paralegal shall maintain a high degree of competency by engaging in continuing paralegal education on an annual basis.

Glossary

A

abstract system A collection of abstracted, or summarized, documents.

accounts payable Accounts that a business owes for goods or services rendered.

actual cost True cost without consideration of mark-up for profit.

add-on A software application that can be purchased to enhance the features of another software application; also called a plug-in.

administrative microsystem A system relating to the management of a firm.

admonition A reprimand given to a lawyer.

advance To pay money before it is due; to loan money.

advance sheet A softcover book of decisions that is circulated soon after a decision is rendered.

affirm To confirm an existing judicial opinion.

aging Calculating the number of days an account has been unpaid.

amicus curiae Friend-of-the-court brief that states the position of the author relating to a case pending before the court.

annotated Referring to a publication that contains the law and other pertinent information about the law.

annual billable hours requirement The number of hours a timekeeper is required to bill in a year.

application Software that has a specific function, such as word processing, spreadsheet, or database.

arbitration The resolution of a dispute without court involvement.

attrition A reduction in workforce due to death, termination, retirement, or resignation.

autocratic Government by one person with unlimited power.

automatic data collection The data entry method used in bar code technology.

autonomous Self-governing; independent; subject to its own methods of management.

B

backup Substitute; in computer systems, a copy of a system on a different disk.

bait-and-switch A tactic used in advertising to attract customers to a sale item and switch that item with one that is not on sale.

best evidence rule The requirement that courts must admit the best evidence that is available to a party and procurable under the existing situation.

billable hour Sixty minutes of time that are billed to a client.

blawg Web logs focused on topics of interest to the legal profession.

blind insert An entry in a form document alerting the preparer to insert material; seen on the computer screen but not printed.

block billing Charging a client for services rendered in one large block of time rather than itemizing the tasks performed in that period.

blog Short for Web log. A Web log is a journal (or newsletter) that contains Internet links and is intended for public consumption and participation.

bookmarking A part of browser software that marks a website so that its URL is accessible without searching for it.

Boolean search A method of defining search criteria.

boutique A law firm that offers services in one area of law only.

brief bank A collection of documents that are used as a template to prepare new documents.

browser A software program that allows viewing and interaction with various kinds of resources available on the Internet.

buddy system Putting two employees together for training purposes.

C

capper A person who is paid to obtain cases for an attorney.

case sensitive Requiring that all letters be in a specific case. If a letter is in the wrong case, the information cannot be read.

cash payments journal Record of all checks written or cash disbursed.

cash receipts journal Record of all deposits and cash received.

CD-ROM Compact disk read-only memory. A computer disk that stores a large amount of data.

CD-ROM drive A device that is connected to the computer that reads CD-ROMs.

ceiling The maximum number of hours that may be spent on nonbillable projects.

CEMEC principle An acronym to describe employee expectations. Stands for communication, education, motivation, evaluation, and compensation.

central file control A system that documents the location of each file.

certificate of service A document appended to the end of a legal document that contains the date and place of mailing.

charging lien A lien placed on a client's proceeds or judgment for payment of an attorney's fees.

check kiting Using other clients' funds until a check clears the bank.

Chinese wall Prohibits a person from working on or discussing a case if that person has a conflict of interest.

citator A set of books that provide the judicial history and interpretation of reported decisions.

CLA Acronym meaning Certified Legal Assistant which is granted after passing an exam given by the National Association of Legal Assistants.

classification The process of separating items into categories.

client funds trust account A bank account established exclusively for clients' funds; an attorney may not use the funds for any other purpose; also called a client trust account.

client security fund A fund established to reimburse clients who have been damaged because of their attorney's fraudulent abuse of the trust account.

closed-file list A list of closed files by name, number, and closed-file number.

code of silence A construct prohibiting a person from working on or discussing a case.

codify To arrange laws by subject.

commingle Mixing one person's funds with another person's funds.

compensation expenses Employee expenses, including wages and benefits.

complete library A library containing a comprehensive collection of material.

compulsory organization An organization to which all persons of the same class must belong.

computer-assisted legal research Legal research on a legal database accessed by computer.

confirm To corroborate or verify (ratify) the ruling of a lower court.

constructive criticism Negative performance evaluation that is given for the purpose of giving instruction and direction.

consumer price index Index that determines the annual increase in the cost of living.

contingency A case in which the client pays an attorney a percentage of the amount recovered in a lawsuit.

contingency fee A fee consisting of a percentage of the possible recovery from a lawsuit.

contract attorney Attorney who works for law firms on an assignment basis, or as an independent contractor.

contract basis Working as an independent contractor on a per case or assignment basis. The person is not an employee of the firm.

controlled access The access and retrieval of a firm's files are controlled by a specific system.

controller Also called a comptroller, an employee charged with certain duties relating to the financial affairs of the business.

cost recovery system A utility program that allows data to be transferred to a billing program by copier or telephone systems.

costs Expenses of one side of a lawsuit that a judge orders the other side to reimburse; includes filing fees, service fees, and recording fees.

court rules-based calendaring software Calendaring software that has state, federal, and local court rules programmed into it.

courtesy copy A document that is sent to a person for informational purposes only.

CPA Acronym for Certified Public Accountant.

creditable nonbillable hours The time that is applied to an annual billable hours requirement.

cross-index To mark a document so that it can be easily found in a system.

cryptography The method of scrambling information so that it is unreadable except by the person who holds the key to unscramble the information.

culture Law firm working environment consisting of intangible factors such as the social environment, employee relationships, and attitudes.

cumulative Increasing by successive addition; running total of each month's services and costs.

custodial Relating to a person who has custody of another person or thing and is expected to act in its best interests.

cybercrimes Crimes committed on the Internet, including hacking and fraud.

Cyberlawyer Software that assists the public with legal issues.

cybersquatter A person who registers a trademarked domain name to extort money from the trademark holder.

cybertort Actions for damages resulting from libelous material posted on the Internet; also included is posting material that is protected by copyright or trademarks, such as magazines and photos.

D

damages Compensation for a wrong or an injury.

data validation A feature in automated docket control software that will not allow an incorrect entry.

database A collection of information for computer retrieval.

date stamp To stamp a document with the date it was received.

decrypt A way of decoding information so that it may be read.

default Failure to respond within the required time.

deponent A person whose deposition is taken.

digest A collection embodying the chief matter of numerous books, articles, court decisions, and so on, usually arranged alphabetically.

digital ID A personal ID number that is encrypted and can be read only by the extranet.

direct conflict When an attorney or firm has a relationship with a person who may be involved in the conflict or when the attorney or firm has a financial interest in an entity involved in the conflict.

direct profitability factors Factors that affect a firm's profitability in a short period of time, usually 1 year.

disbarment The taking away of a lawyer's license to practice law.

discovery The acquisition of notice or knowledge of given acts or facts; that which was previously unknown.

disengagement letter Letter informing the client that the case is closed and the representation has ceased.

dividends Distribution of a corporation's profits to shareholders.

docket An abstract or brief entry or the book or record containing such entries.

docket coordinator A person in charge of a firm's docketing process.

domain name A unique name that identifies an Internet site.

download The method by which users access and retrieve a document, software, or other files from a central computer to their computers.

downsize To reduce staff and expenses because of reduced income.

drop-down list A list of activities that are listed in an area of the screen that is visible if the list is chosen.

E

electronic mail (e-mail) An electronic message sent from one person to another through their computers.

e-mail filters Software that manages e-mail and that can be programmed to delete e-mails that contain profanity or offensive material.

emoticons Symbols used to express feelings in written e-mail communication.

encrypt A way of coding information so that if it is intercepted by a third party, it cannot be read.

engagement letter A letter summarizing the scope of representation and the fee agreement between a lawyer and a client.

equitable relief Compensation other than money for an injury.

equity Referring to the ownership of the firm and entitlement to a portion of the profits.

equity partner A partner who is entitled to a portion of the firm's profits and is responsible for a portion of the firm's losses.

ergonomics Area concerned with health factors in the workplace.

executive committee Committee comprised of heads of the various committees in a law firm.

exempt Professional status that exempts an employee from overtime compensation.

expert witness Person who testifies at trial, based on the professional expertise of the witness.

extranet A Web-based interface to a private network; used to communicate directly with clients.

extraordinary fee A fee that is awarded in addition to statutory fees and that compensates an attorney for extra work required by the circumstances of the case.

F

fee adjustment memorandum A form used by an attorney to increase or decrease a client's bill as appropriate.

fee allocation When a percentage of the bill is given to the originating or supervising attorney as compensation.

fiduciary Of, relating to, or involving great confidence and trust; a person who transacts business for another person, necessitating great confidence and trust by the second party and a high degree of good faith by the first.

file-number index An index containing sequential file numbers and case names indicating the next available file number.

File Transfer Protocol (FTP) A protocol that allows files to be transferred between computers.

firewall A protective electronic barrier constructed around a network so that unauthorized persons cannot get through.

fiscal year Annual accounting year.

flame An angry or derogatory e-mail message.

flat fee A client is charged one fee for the entire case.

floppy disks Computer diskettes as distinguished from internal hard drives.

FLSA Fair Labor Standards Act.

forecasting Planning for the future by anticipating future events.

foreclosure To shut out; a termination of all rights of the mortgagor in the property covered by the mortgage.

form files A collection of copies of form documents and frequently used documents; these documents act as a guide when developing similar documents.

formal evaluation Procedure where an employee's work performance is evaluated and rated in writing. Occurs annually or biannually.

freelance paralegal A freelance paralegal contracts his or her services out to law offices and works under the supervision of an attorney.

freeware Free software.

full text Consisting of a verbatim text that allows every word in a document to be retrieved by a researcher.

G

general counsel Attorney in charge of the corporate legal department. Often an officer of the corporation.

general ledger An accounting term used to describe the book that summarizes a business's financial accounts. Contains a separate account for every asset, liability, and expense.

general practitioner Attorney who does not specialize in a particular area of law. Accepts cases in all areas of law.

goodwill letter Letter written to create rapport and good relations.

gopher A protocol that organizes Internet information for search and retrieval.

gross income Income received before payment of expenses.

groupware Software created for and used by an intranet or extranet.

H

hard copy A copy of computer records on a sheet of paper.

hard costs Costs incurred for filing fees, service fees, deposition expenses, and so on.

hiring specifications The requirements for a position.

home page The starting point of a Web presentation that contains a table of contents for the information that is available at the website, offering direct links to the different parts of the site.

human resource audit To determine strengths and weaknesses of current employees.

hyperlinks A connection to another page or site that allows a person to navigate the Web.

Hypertext Markup Language (HTML) A software language used by documents posted on the World Wide Web.

Hypertext Transfer Protocol (HTTP) The protocol used by the World Wide Web.

I

icon A picture that symbolizes a software application or function of an application.

if clause A clause inserted in a form document alerting the preparer to insert the appropriate paragraph.

imaging The process of scanning a paper document into a computer system.

incarcerated Imprisoned; confined to a jail or penitentiary.

independent paralegal A person who does law-related work for the general public without the supervision of an attorney.

indigent Poor or needy.

indirect profitability factors Factors that affect a firm's profitability over a longer period, more than 1 year.

informal evaluation Procedure where an employee's work is evaluated verbally. Occurs in an informal manner.

in-house counsel An attorney who is an employee of a corporation and works in the corporation's legal department.

integrated software A program that combines many different software applications into one program to make it easier to use.

Internet Service Provider (ISP) A private company that provides access to the Internet for a fee.

intranet A private collection of information that is viewed by Internet Web browser software and is accessible only to authorized members of a private network; a private Internet site.

J

joint venture A grouping of two or more persons for a common goal.

jukebox A device that contains many CD-ROMs and allows retrieval of a document on request.

L

lawyer hopping Going from lawyer to lawyer for advice and representation.

legal administrator Experienced manager who is hired to manage a law firm. Has the authority of a management partner.

legal clinic Legal offices formed for the purpose of providing low-income people with free, or low-cost, legal services.

legal databases A legal database contains statutes, case law, administrative rulings, and legal memoranda.

legal document assistant An independent paralegal who has registered with his or her county and does legal work for the public.

leverage The ability to make money from the work of others.

leverage ratio A formula used to identify the number of income-producing employees per owner.

liaison A person responsible for communication between groups. Spokesperson.

library cooperative A group organized to pool library resources for the benefit of the group.

limited liability company A company formed to shield its owners and their assets from liability arising from the misconduct of other owners or employees.

listserv A group of people who exchange information about a particular topic on the Internet.

local area network (LAN) A number of computers that are connected together. If information is inserted in one computer, each computer connected to the network receives the information.

local rules Rules created by an individual court that apply in that court only.

lodestar A method of calculating an attorney's fee using the attorney's hourly rate multiplied by the number of hours worked on a case.

lurking Not responding to messages posted on a listserv.

M

manual calendar A calendar that is maintained by hand rather than by computer.

mark up To add a percentage on the cost of an item for profit.

master calendar Calendar that contains hearing and deposition dates for each attorney in the firm.

master client list A list of active clients; does not include closed files.

megabyte A computer term used to measure data; one megabyte contains about one million characters.

mega firm Firm that employs more than 1,000 attorneys and has branch offices throughout the world.

merger Union of two or more law firms to form one law firm.

microfiche Sheets of film on which documents are photographed.

microfilm Film on which documents are photographed.

microform The process of storing information photographically.

misappropriation Using funds in the trust account for personal purposes.

mitigated To make less severe; alleviation, reduction, abatement, or diminution of a penalty or punishment imposed by law.

modem A device that allows remote computers to transmit and receive data using telephone lines; short for modulator/demodulator.

modified cash basis Based on cash but including some accrual basis concepts.

monetary relief Compensation by money for an injury.

multidisciplinary practice A lawyer and a member of another profession practice together to provide both legal and nonlegal services to a client.

multipliers An amount that is added to attorney's lodestar fee to compensate for time limitations and risks.

N

netiquette An informal code of conduct that governs e-mail communication.

netvertising Advertising services on the Internet.

network Two or more computers connected to each other so they can share resources.

new case memorandum A form used to provide information about a case so that a file may be opened.

noncreditable nonbillable hours The time that is not applied to an annual billable hours requirement.

nonequity partner A partner that is not entitled to a portion of the profits and is not responsible for a portion of the losses of the firm.

nonexempt Nonprofessional status that requires payment of overtime.

nonlegal database An organized collection of nonlegal information, such as medical information, business statistics, and so on.

nonlegal subsidiary A company that is owned by a law firm but provides nonlegal services.

numeric index An index in numeric order that lists files and the date opened. The purpose is to inform the file clerk of the next number in sequence when opening files.

O

of-counsel An attorney affiliated with a firm on a part-time basis.

office manager A person hired to assist a Managing Partner or Legal Administrator with management functions of a firm.

online Connected to the Internet or the World Wide Web.

online calendaring system A service that will calculate deadlines from the Internet.

open questions Questions that require a narrative answer and cannot be answered yes or no.

operating expenses Expenses other than compensation expenses that include occupancy costs, office operating costs, costs of professional activities, and general business expenses.

ouch formula Acronym for proper interview questions. Includes objective, uniform, consistence, and have job relatedness.

outside counsel Law firm retained to do legal work for a corporate legal department.

outsourcing A firm's use of outside services for support functions.

overrule To reject or supersede an existing judicial opinion; to invalidate.

P

P.C. Acronym for professional corporation.

pad To expand in a fraudulent manner.

pathname The URL address showing the path of where a certain document may be found on a website.

per diem Latin term meaning "by the day."

permalink Permanent URLs connected to a Web log post.

per unit cost The amount of money it costs to produce a product or provide a service.

permanent associates Employed attorneys who are not eligible for partnership in or ownership of the firm.

personal calendar An individual's calendar that contains the same information as a master calendar but also includes appointment dates, follow-up, deadlines, and personal information.

Phishing Fraudulent e-mail scams that are designed to steal a person's identity.

pocket part An addition to a book that updates its contents.

portal-to-portal Of or relating to the time spent traveling from one place to another.

position description A document that describes the duties and responsibilities of a position.

positional conflict An attorney's or firm's representation of the competition of a client.

positioning Determining a firm's strengths and weaknesses in relation to those of other firms in the community.

postconviction writs A written judicial order to perform a specified act or giving authority to have it done after a criminal conviction.

potential conflict Arises when an attorney has an indirect relationship with a person who may be involved in the conflict.

precedent A court decision on a question of law that gives authority or direction on how to decide a similar question of law in a later case with similar facts.

preclient A person who consults an attorney but does not formally retain the services of the attorney.

preclient file A file containing notes of interview or consultation to be retrieved if the client retains the firm.

preliminary bill A bill prepared for an attorney's review and consideration for adjustment.

preventative law Legal information designed to avoid legal problems before they occur.

primary case name The name used to identify a case, consisting of the first-named plaintiff and the first-named defendant.

primary recipient A person to whom a document is directed or addressed.

pro bono publico Latin for "for the good"; used to describe work or services performed free of charge for indigent people. Most commonly known as pro bono.

pro se For one's own behalf; appearing for oneself in court.

probate A court procedure by which a will is proved to be valid or invalid; refers to the legal process wherein the estate of a decedent is administered.

probation A form of discipline that allows a person convicted of an offense to forego more drastic punishment under supervised conditions.

procedural law A law that defines procedures of a lawsuit.

proof of service by mail A document that informs the recipient of the date the attached document was mailed.

protocol The set of rules that two computers use to communicate with each other.

pruning To discard unnecessary documents from a file.

purge To clear or discard.

Q

quota An assigned goal.

R

radio frequency identification A generic term for technologies that use radio waves to identify people or objects.

rainmaker An attorney responsible for client development for a firm.

reader/printer A machine that accommodates microfilm and microfiche.

realization The process of turning time into cash.

realization rate The hourly rate of a timekeeper that the firm actually realizes when all accounts have been collected compared to the total amount billed.

reasonable attorney's fee The amount of an attorney's fee determined by a governing entity to be reasonable.

redline Marking a document to indicate changes made by other parties.

rehabilitation Restoration to a useful life through education and therapy.

reinstatement The restoration of a right that had ceased.

remedial Affording a remedy; giving means of obtaining redress.

repeal To abrogate or annul an existing law by the enactment of a statute that declares the former law revoked.

reporter A published volume of court decisions.

reprimand A formal rebuke; to strongly criticize.

restatement A series of volumes authored by legal scholars that describe the law, its changes, and future direction of the law.

retaining lien A lien placed on property that belongs to a client and is in the attorney's possession.

retroactive event recalculation A feature in automated docketed software programs that automatically recalculates dates in the event of a change in a corresponding date.

RFID tags Microchips encoded with a file's information.

rich media Image-based technology that is visual rather than text oriented.

S

scanned Entering text or graphics into a computer by electronically changing the characters into a computer-readable format.

school A group of persons under common influence or sharing the same belief.

scrivener A clerk or scribe; a notary.

search engine An independent company that has indexed Internet sites and categorized them so that they can be found easily.

secondary recipient A person to whom a document is sent for informational purposes only.

segregation of cash Keeping clients' funds separate from law firm funds.

series A set of reporters in numeric order.

server A large computer that contains a large amount of information and directs customers' inquiries to the Internet.

service of process Personally delivering summons, complaints, or other legal documents to a defendant or respondent.

shareware Software that is distributed without initial cost. If the user likes the software, a nominal payment is expected.

skeletal library A small library containing only essential material.

slip opinion A printed copy of a judicial opinion that is distributed soon after the decision is rendered.

snail mail The process of sending mail through the U.S. Postal Service.

soft costs Costs incurred for photocopy expense, long-distance telephone calls, fax, and so on.

sole practitioner Attorney who practices law by himself. Does not employ other attorneys.

sole proprietorship Business that has one individual owner. May employ other attorneys.

source codes The coding used by HTML to program a website's material.

spam To send unsolicited commercial e-mail messages to large numbers of people on the Internet on an indiscriminate basis.

Spoof site A fraudulent website that looks like a website from a large, reputable company.

staff attorney An employee of a law firm who has no advancement opportunities.

stare decisis The legal principle that a court will follow the decision of another court in a similar case.

static calendar program A calendaring program that requires entries to be made manually.

statute of limitations The time period after an offense within which a lawsuit must be filed.

substantive law A law that creates, defines, or regulates rights.

substantive microsystem A system of providing legal services to a client.

supra Latin term meaning "above."

suspension The temporary cessation of the right to practice law as punishment for wrongdoing.

symbology Language used in bar code technology.

T

target market A group of people a firm wants as clients.

team approach Theory of management and employees working together for the benefit of the organization.

team churning Making frequent changes in the legal team.

telefacsimile A system of transmitting documents over telephone wires.

telephone tag A situation in which someone calls a person who is unavailable and leaves a message and then is unavailable when the person returns the call.

Telnet A protocol that allows a computer to connect with a remote computer.

template A form document used as a guide to prepare new documents.

temporary restraining order An emergency judicial remedy of brief duration that may be issued only in exceptional circumstances and only until the trial court can hear arguments or evidence on the issue.

tickler system A system of controlling deadlines.

tort A legal wrong done to a person; a civil wrong that is not based on a contract.

trigger date The date of an event that starts the clock running on a deadline.

type identifier A suffix attached to a domain name that identifies the type of organization.

typosquatter Changing a letter in a trademark to circumvent the dispute resolution policy.

U

unannotated Referring to a publication that contains the text of a law only.

unbundled legal services Breaking a legal representation into tasks that are performed by a lawyer and a nonlawyer.

Uniform Resource Locator (URL) An address of a website that directs a person to the information.

unlawful detainer A statutory procedure whereby a landlord can legally evict a tenant in default on the rent.

update service A service that keeps books current.

user interface The method of operation developed by a legal publisher for its CD-ROM products.

V

value-based fee A fee that is based on the amount of value the case had for the client.

virtual library An electronic library without regard to physical space or location.

voice mail Electronic recording device that allows a person to deliver a message to another person if they are unable to answer the telephone.

W

website A collection of linked pages grouped in a certain order.

Web-based technology Internet-like software applications.

Web log Web page consisting of frequently updated, chronological entries on a particular topic.

win-lose management A form of personnel control in which the polices of management are directed totally to making profits and disregard employee needs.

write-down A decrease in the amount owed because of a discount.

write-off A credit for the total amount owed.

write-up An increase in the amount owed because of a premium.

Z

zeal Enthusiastic and diligent devotion.

Bibliography

Chapter 1

Anderson, Eugene, Randy Paar, and Joshua Gold. "Safety Net May Not Hold." *National Law Journal,* October 9, 1995.

Beardsley, Dee. "Leveling the Playing Field." @ *LAW—the NALS Magazine for Legal Professionals,* Spring 1997.

Blodgett, Nancy. "How Best to Organize a Law Firm." *Legal Management,* March/April 1995.

Brewster, Christopher. "Kids May Be Polled if Parents AreTold." *Legal Management,* December 1997.

Coburn, Jeff. "Practice Group Planning—the New Frontier." *Legal Management,* March/April 1995.

Cox, Gail Diane. "Now, It's Jacoby vs. Meyers." *National Law Journal,* July 15, 1995.

Denny, Robert. "Developing Managers." *Legal Management,* July/August 1998.

Donovan, Karen. "Should SEC Cases Await DOJ Action?" *National Law Journal,* March 24, 1997.

Editor. "An 'Eat What You Kill' Ethos Can Harm Law Firms." *National Law Journal,* June 16, 1997.

———. "First Interactive Legal Brief Filed." *Legal Management,* March/April 1997.

———. "Organizing Your Practice for Success and Avoiding Malpractice Claims." *Law Practice Management Solutions,* Autumn 1995.

———. "Paralegals Online." *Legal Assistant Today,* January/February 1998.

———. "Practice Area Growth." *Of Counsel,* April 21, 1997.

———. "Preliminary of Counsel 700 Survey Data Shows Shrewd Niche Marketing by Firms Nationwide." *Of Counsel* 16, no. 8 (April 1997).

———. "A Sample of Recent General Trends." *Law Practice Management Solutions,* Autumn 1995.

———. "What's Hot and What's Not on the Legal Profession?" *Legal Management,* September/October 2001.

Fisk, Margaret Cronin. "What Lawyers Earn." *National Law Journal,* July 15, 1996.

———. "What's Hot in the Job Market?" *National Law Journal,* August 23, 1999.

Foreman, Johnathon. "Seeking the Best, Both In-House and Outhouse." *National Law Journal,* December 2, 1996.

———. "Working out Relations with Outside Counsel." *National Law Journal,* March 24, 1997.

France, Mike. "Administrative Law Tops Earnings List." *National Law Journal,* June 27, 1995.

———. "IP's Hot, Tax Is Not, in Mid-'90s Practice." *National Law Journal,* February 26, 1996.

———. "Legal Clinics: Lights Go out for Store Fronts." *National Law Journal,* December 12, 1994.

Furi-Perry, Ursula. "The Hottest Corporate Practice Areas." *Legal Assistant Today,* November/December 2006.

Galbenski, David J. "'Tis the Season to Be in IP Law." *National Law Journal,* August 23, 1999.

Griffith, Cary. "Knowledge to the Nth Power." *Legal Management,* September/October 1996.

Hayes, Arthur S. "ABA Group: Change in the Air." *National Law Journal,* June 27, 1995.

Hazard, Geoffrey C. "The Firm's Muddy Mission." *National Law Journal,* July 15, 1995.

Hildebrant, Bradford W. "Learning from Firms That Failed." *National Law Journal,* April 25, 1994.

Hughes, Rod. "What's Driving This Market?" *Legal Assistant Today,* March/April 2001.

Ibelle, Bill. "Temp Lawyers: Should You Hire One?" *Lawyers Weekly USA,* March 10, 1997.

Jones, Leigh. "Study Shows Single-Tier Firms Do Fine." *National Law Journal,* July 24, 2006.

Jones, Leigh. "What's in a Firm Name? Not Many Commas." *National Law Journal,* September 25, 2004.

Klein, Chris. "Associate Job 1: Land Clients." *National Law Journal,* March 31, 1997.

Leibowitz, Wendy R. "Go Solo, Go High-Tech." *National Law Journal,* March 8, 1999.

Petropulos, Diane. "Choosing a Legal Specialty." *Legal Assistant Today*, May/June 1993.

———. "Paralegal Jobs beyond the Law Office." *Legal Assistant Today*, May/June 1997.

Resnick, Rosalind. "Cybertort: The New Era." *National Law Journal*, July 18, 1994.

Rovella, David E. "Non-Traditionals Surge in New Legal Market." *National Law Journal*, October 9, 1995.

Smith, William Carl. "A Sociologist's Look at Small-Firm Lawyers." *Lawyers Weekly USA*, March 10, 1997.

Smock, John. "Feeling Short Handed." *Legal Management*, January/February 1998.

Stock, Richard G. "Reaching over the Border." *Legal Management*, May/June 1996.

———. "Tools to Navigate a Firm Plan." *Legal Management*, November/December 1996.

Stoddard, Debbie. "Little Firm on the Prairie." @ *LAW— the NALS Magazine for Legal Professionals*, Spring 1997.

Thompson, Lori. "The Legal Clinic." *Legal Assistant Today*, January/February 2007.

Van Duch, Darryl L. "Some Firms Hesitate to Adopt L.L.P." *National Law Journal*, May 5, 1997.

Wesemann, H. Edward. "Culture Club." *Legal Management*, July/August 2001.

Whiteside, Frances B. "Career Alternatives for Paralegals." *Legal Assistant Today*, January/February 1993.

———. "Dinner at Dux." *The Legal Professional Career News*, Spring 1994.

———. "Paralegal Roles and Responsibilities." *National Paralegal Reporter*, Fall 1998.

Chapter 2

Anderson, Robert. "All That Glitters." *Legal Management*, January/February 1996.

Arron, Deborah. "Temping Is Big, Even for Hot-Shots." *National Law Journal*, April 12, 1999.

Astl, Catherine, CLA. "10 Ways to Stand Out and Become a Successful Paralegal." *Legal Assistant Today*, March/April, 2002.

Barge, Jeff. "Paralegals Make 'Partner.'" *Legal Assistant Today*, May/June 1996.

Beam, Vanessa. "Paralegal by Another Name." *Legal Assistant Today*, September/October 2001.

Behan, Kevin J. "Small Firms Require More." *Legal Assistant Today*, May/June 1997.

Bemiss, Randi D. "Doors Opens to Paralegals," *Legal Assistant Today*, January/February 2002.

———. "Schools Mold Programs to Meet Health Care Demands." *Legal Assistant Today*, September/October 2000.

Bill, Kriss. "Put on a Happy Face (and Mean It)." *Legal Management*, January/February 2001.

Blazek, Glenn E. "Court Reporters Now Offer a Diversity of Services." *National Law Journal*, Monday, September 22, 1997.

Blodgett, Nancy. "Back-Up Child Care Centers for Law Firms on the Rise." *Legal Management*, November/December 1993.

Blumenthal, Jeff. "Legal Secretaries: Numbers Wane, but Demand Does Not." *The Legal Intellegencer*, August 31, 2004.

Bose, Lilledashan. "2005 Predictions Are Positive." *Legal Assistant Today*, January/February 2005.

Campbell, Rachel. "High Risers: How Paralegal Managers Help Run Some of the Nation's Largest Law Firms." *Legal Assistant Today*, September/October 2004.

Carrier, Pamela Hastings. "Family and Medical Leave Act of 1993." *Orange County Paralegal Association Compendium*, July 1994.

Cazares, Leanne, and Nicole Kording. "For Love or Money." *Legal Assistant Today*, January/February 1997.

Clark, Lana J., and Dane D'Antuono. "ABA Rejects Sharing Fees with Nonlawyers." *Legal Assistant Today*, September/October 2000.

Coburn, Jeff. "The Changing Role of the Large Firm Administrator." *Legal Management*, November/December 1993.

Cohn, Steven. "California Association Proposes Specialty Exams, Certification." *Legal Assistant Today*, March/April 1994.

———. "Land of the Giants." *Legal Assistant Today*, March/April 1995.

———. "NALA Survey Shows Paralegals Changing Jobs Sooner." *Legal Assistant Today*, March/April 1994.

Conrad, Sherri L., and Ronald E. Mallen. "Legal Profession." *National Law Journal*, July 17, 1995.

Conroy, Kathleen, "Help Internal Customers Manage Their Time." *Dartnell's Quality First*, June 2001.

Conti, Al. "The Administrator as Coach: Developing a Winning Team." *Legal Management*, May/June 1997.

Coyle, Marcia. "Panic over Definition of 'Partner.'" *National Law Journal*, May 26, 1997.

Damp, Dennis. "General Schedule—White Collar/Professional/ Administative." *Internet Career Connection*, October 31, 1998.

D'Antuono, Dane. "NFPA Takes a Stand." *Legal Assistant Today*, July/August 2002.

———. "Top Paralegal Groups Draft Profession Definition." *Legal Assistant Today*, March/April 2001.

Davis, Ann. "Rainmakers Score High on Test." *National Law Journal*, September 30, 1996.

Donovan, Karen. "Firms Shed '&'s and Commas." *National Law Journal*, August 1996.

Editor. "1999–2000 Salary Survey Results." *Legal Assistant Today*, May/June 2000.

———. "ALA Announces Certification for Legal Managers." *Legal Management*, May/June 1997.

———. "The Delivery of Legal Services in the Future." *Association of Legal Administrators*, May/June 2001.

———. "E-Mail Communications." *Legal Management,* January/February 2002.

———. "E-Mail: Tool or Torment?" *Legal Management,* July/August 2001.

———. "End the Secretary Shortage by Turning Top Secretaries into Practice Managers." *Law Office Administrator,* December 1997.

———. "Firm Environment and Utilization." <http://www.nala.org/Sec.2web.htm>, August 13, 1998.

———. "Floaters Are an Alternative to Temporary Staffing." *Law Office Administrator,* September 1997.

———. "Future of Legal Administration." *Legal Management,* May/June 2001.

———. "Getting Along." *National Law Journal,* June 17, 1996.

———. *Handbook on Paralegal Utilization.* California Alliance of Paralegal Associations, July 1997.

———. "Honesty Such a Lonely Word?" *Legal Management,* May/June 2002.

———. "In the Courts." *The Legal Professional Career News,* Fall 1994.

———. "Know Your Firm's Personalities." *Legal Management,* March/April 2001.

———. "Lawsuits Filed against Paralegal Businesses." *National Federation of Paralegal Assistants Reporter,* January 1998.

———. "Lex Mundi Bolsters European and Western Pacific Membership." *Legal Management,* May/June 2001.

———. "Model Guidelines for the Utilization of Legal Assistant Services." American Bar Association Standing Committee on Legal Assistants, August 19, 1997.

———. "New ABA Definition of 'Legal Assistant.'" American Bar Association Standing Committee on Legal Assistants, August 19, 1997.

———. "New Report Details Reasons for Lateral Moves by Attorneys." *Legal Management,* May/June 2001.

———. "New York's Finest Law Firms." *Legal Assistant Today,* May/June 1996.

———. "No More Hanging Shingles." *Legal Management,* May/June 2002.

———. "Paralegal Compensation and Benefits Report." National Federation of Paralegal Associations, November 1997.

———. "Professional Service Firms: The Next Generation." *Legal Management,* May/June 2002.

———. "Retaining Client Files." *Legal Management,* January/February 2002.

———. "The Role of the Senior Administrator—Does Law Firm Size Make a Difference?" *Law Practice Management,* December 1995.

———. "Round the Industry." *Legal Management,* January/February 1998.

———. "Schaming Congratulates History's First Certified Legal Managers: 11 Pass First CLM Exam." *Legal Management,* January/February 1998.

———. "Special Report." *American Library Association News,* November/December 1996.

———. "Survey Finds Interpersonal Skills Most Important for Administrator Success." *Legal Assistant Today,* November/December 1997.

———. "Surveys Find Employees at All Levels Working More Hours." *Legal Management,* May/June 2002.

———. "The Surveys Say!" *Legal Management,* May/June 1997.

———. "Swing for Success?" *Legal Management,* May/June 2001.

———. "A Title Using the Word Assistant Is Too Often Overused and Has Lost It's Meaning as a Professional Title." *Legal Assistant Today,* November/December 2002.

———. "A Track Record of Salary Growth for Paralegals." *Legal Assistant Today,* March/April 2006.

———. "The Traditional Law Partnership Track: Does It Still Exist? Quo Vadis?" *Law Practice Management,* December 1995.

———. "Updated Study Reveals Administrators Diverse Skills." *Legal Management,* May/June 2001.

———. "Weekend Warriors: Executives Working Weekends." *Legal Management,* July/August 2001.

———. "Where Is the Profession Today?" *National Paralegal Reporter,* December 1997.

Emmons, Natasha. "ABA Paralegal Utilization Survey Reveals Trends." *Legal Assistant Today,* November/December 1998.

———. "ABA Refines Definition of Paralegal." *Legal Assistant Today,* January/February 1998.

Estrin, Chere B. "In-House vs. Law Firm Reality." *Legal Assistant Today,* May/June 2007.

———. "The $100,000 Paralegal." *Legal Assistant Today,* March/April 2007.

Evans, James. "Legal Sites: Paralegal Resources." *California Lawyer,* January 1998.

Evans, Larry. "Ten Commandments for Legal Secretaries." *The Docket,* July/August 1998.

Finkelstein, James. "MJL Founder Looks Back at Profession's Changes." *National Law Journal,* September 21, 1998.

Foonberg, Jay G. "Telephone Receptionists: Marketing's Front Line." *National Law Journal,* April 25, 1994.

Garber, Chris, Marisella Jorgenson, and Rita Madnick. "1997 OCPA Salary Survey." Orange County Paralegal Association, September 15, 1997.

Gladwell, Gina M. "The Issues Affecting Paralegals Then and Now." *Legal Assistant Today,* September/October 1997.

Goldberg, Elizabeth. "Midlevel Associates Survey: Firms Improve, but Complaints Continue." *The American Lawyer,* August 1, 2006.

Goodwin-Neuhaus, Anne. "Measure Success One Milestone at a Time." *Dartnell's Working Together,* June 2001.

Green, Matthew L. "OSHA Job Safety Rules Launched." *Legal Assistant Today,* March/April 2001.

Hawley, D. L. "ABA's Definition Attracts Another Legal Assistant Association." *Legal Assistant Today,* January/February 2002.

———. "Regional National Salary Surveys Released." *Legal Assistant Today,* May/June 2001.

Healy, Deborah J. "Are You a Paralegal? Or Are You a Banker?" *National Paralegal Reporter,* Fall 1998.

Hershkowitz, William. "Career Comparison between Paralegals/Secretaries." *Legal Assistant Today,* May/June 1998.

Hoover, Luci. "Finding the Right Job: Distinguishing between Paralegal and Legal Secretary Duties." *Legal Assistant Today,* November/December 2005.

Horowitz, Jay B., and William Kummel. "Improve Profit through Contract Legal Services." *Accounting for Law Firms* 10, no. B (August 1997).

Hughes, Rod. "Master Plan." *Legal Assistant Today,* January/February 2006.

Hunt, Stacey. "The Paralegal as Office Manager? You Bet!" *Orange County Paralegal Association Compendium,* July 1994.

Infanti, Patricia E. "Now Is the Time for All Legal Secretaries to Go Back to School." *@ LAW—the NALS Magazine for Legal Professionals,* Fall 1998.

Ip, Melody. "Scouting National Salaries." *Legal Assistant Today,* November/December 2006.

———. "Updated California Specialty Program Delayed." *Legal Assistant Today,* May/June 2007.

Johnson, Ashley. "NFPA Publishes report on Compensation." *Legal Assistant Today,* May/June 2007.

Jones, Leigh. "Law Firms Look at Closing Pay Systems." *National Law Journal,* June 26, 2006.

———. "Mentoring Plans Failing Associates." *National Law Journal,* September 18, 2006.

———. "More Firms Using Temp Attorneys." *National Law Journal,* 2006.

Kanofsky, Florence. "Legal Administrators Today: Success Strategies for a Changing Profession." *Legal Management,* September/October 1995.

Kaufman, Monty. "Outsourcing—Once a Curiosity, Now a Necessity." *Legal Management,* January/February 1995.

Klein, Chris. "Big-Firm Partners: Profession Sinking." *National Law Journal,* May 26, 1997.

Kummel, William, and Jay B. Horowitz. "Short Time Gone." *Legal Management,* September/October 1996.

Leiter, Richard. "Your Role as Librarian." *Legal Assistant Today,* January/February 1997.

Leonard, Cari A., and Charles E. Stinnett. "Legal Administrators in the New Millenium." *Legal Management,* November/December 1998.

Levy, Debra. "Oregon Associations Say No to Paralegal Definition." *Legal Assistant Today,* March/April 2001.

Lorenzo, Penny. "Distinguishing the Legal Nurse Consultant." *Legal Assistant Today,* September/October 2002.

Lurie, Sylvia. "Legal Administrators Rate Their Quality of Life." *Legal Management,* November/December 1993.

———. "The Quality of Life among Legal Administrators." *Legal Management,* September/October 1994.

Mabey, Stephen, and Michael Mabey. "The Coming of Age Story: The Individual Lawyer." *Legal Management,* September/October 2001.

Mallen, Ronald E. "Of Counsel, Affiliates May Trigger Firm Liability." *National Law Journal,* November 10, 1997.

Matsumoto, Jon. "New Paralegal Group Sets Sail." *Legal Assistant Today,* March/April 2005.

McClean, Frances M. "What Will the Legal Secretary Need to Know to Be Successful in the Year 2000?" *@ LAW—the NALS Magazine for Legal Professionals,* Fall 1996.

McGurk, John J. "California Clean-Up Bill Leaves Some Befuddled; Other's Question Need." *Legal Assistant Today,* March/April 2001.

———. "California Legislature Pulls Proposed Revisions to Paralegal Definition." *Legal Assistant Today,* July/August 2001.

Melhe, Kathy. "Visiting the Year 2005." *National Paralegal Reporter,* December 1997.

Messmer, Max. "Alleviate the Full-Time Press." *Legal Management,* September/October 1996.

Middleton, Martha. "Firms Find New Ways to Save." *National Law Journal,* January 24, 1995.

Miller, Nancy. "Administration 2000." *Legal Management,* September/October 1996.

Mitchell, Raye. "The Step Ladder to Success." *Legal Management,* January/February 2001.

Morrison, Rees W. "In-House Practice and Management." *Altman Weil,* September 2002.

Morrison, Rees W., and Al Conti. "Hitting the Mark." *Legal Management,* January/February 2000.

National Federation of Paralegal Association. "Executive Summary." *2001 Paralegal Compensation and Benefits Report,* September 2001.

———. "NFPA's Internet Connection," *The Reporter,* December 1997.

Ng, Rachel. "FLSA Face Lift Proceeds." *Legal Assistant Today,* March/April 2004.

Ng, Rachel. "Winner of Scholarship Strives for Career Advancement." *Legal Assistant Today,* March/April 2001.

Orlik, Deborah K. "A Career Alternative for Beginning Paralegals." *Legal Assistant Today,* January/February 1998.

Petropulos, Diane. "A Step in the Right Direction." *Legal Assistant Today,* January/February 1998.

Roberts, Janet. "Starting Salaries Looking Up." *Legal Assistant Today,* March/April 2006.

Rowland, Caroline. "Freelance Paralegals: Fees Upheld in California." *Paralegal Headliner,* December 1993.

Ruppenthal, R.J. "Smaller Might Be Better." *Legal Assistant Today,* July/August 2004.

Schaefer, Lyndsey. "Tailor-Made Paralegal Training." *Legal Assistant Today,* May/June 2007.

Shepherd, Ritchenya. "Law Firm Management." *National Law Journal,* October 5, 1998.

Slind-Flor, Victoria. "A Piece of the Action." *National Law Journal,* June 17, 1996.

Solomon, Robin. "No Satisfaction?" *National Paralegal Reporter,* December 1997.

Sparrow, Vince, and Ron Stratton. "Strategic Outsourcing." *Legal Management,* July/August 1995.

Sperber, Robert. "58% Paralegal Job Increase by Year 2005." *Legal Assistant Today,* May/June 1997.

———. "In-House Intellectual Property Paralegals Net Big Bucks." *Legal Assistant Today,* May/June 1997.

Stell, Camille Stucky. "North Carolina Bar Association Forms Legal Assistants Division." *Legal Assistant Today,* January/February 1998.

Stock, Richard. "A Sense of Place." *Legal Assistant Today,* March/April 1996.

Thompson, Lori. "Federal Paradigm" *Legal Assistant Today,* May/June 2007.

Wainess, Marcia Watson. "If You Build It, Will It Serve?" *Legal Management,* July/August 1998.

Walker, Bruce. "Legal Secretary Opportunities in Prosecutor's Office." *The Docket,* Spring 1996.

Weidlich, Thom. "After Slump, Paralegal Work on Rebound." *National Law Journal,* April 25, 1994.

Weston, I. Perrin. "Additional Progress Made at October Conclave Meeting." *Legal Assistant Today,* January/February 1998.

———. "Paralegal Certificate v. Bachelor Degree." *Legal Assistant Today,* January/February 1998.

———. "Paralegal Student." *Legal Assistant Today,* January/February 1998.

Widoff, Shelly G. "Working the Night Shift." *Legal Assistant Today,* January/February 1998.

Witcomb, Melanie D. "Creating Career Opportunities." *Legal Assistant Today,* March/April 2007.

———. "Leveling the Playing Field." *Legal Assistant Today,* January/February 2007.

Wood, Steven M. "Experienced Legal Secretary Salaries Reaching Higher and Higher." *The Docket,* Spring 1996.

Chapter 3

Abrahams, Sharon Meit. "Teach Your Employees Well." *Legal Management,* January/February 1998.

Atherton, Marjorie R. "What Is a Legal Administrator?" *Legal Management,* November 1986.

Baber, Brad. "The Road to In-House Training." *Legal Assistant Today,* January/February 1998.

Baldas, Tresa. "New Overtime Rules Bring Suits." *National Law Journal,* March 14, 2005.

Barnes, Fawn. "Keep Your Employees Happy." *Legal Assistant Today,* July/August 2005.

Bauer, E.G. "Are You a Good Team Player?" *Working Together,* October 1996.

Blackwell, Mary Ann. "Five Steps to Ask for a Raise." *Law Office Administrator,* July 1998.

Blodgett, Nancy. "Self-Directed Work Teams: A New Way to Operate Your Business." *Legal Management,* September/October 1995.

Boone, Norlene. "Effective Staff Benefits Are Still Possible—Even on a Tight Budget." *Law Office Administrator,* August 1997.

Brashear, Sally. "You Are Not Alone." *Legal Management,* May/June 1997.

Brimm, Jack L. "Managerial Training: Don't Leave It to Chance." American Library Association, March/April 1996.

———. "Train Your Employees to Recognize and Nurture Strengths for a Better Work Environment." *Legal Management,* March/April 2001.

Brown, James G. "Law Office Current Labor Issues." *The Docket,* September/October 1994.

Burnett, Terrill Hill. "Mediation: An Effective Tool in Law Firm Management." *Legal Management,* March/April 1995.

Calder, James. "Innovative Office Design May Feed into New, More Profitable Ways of Working." *Legal Management,* May/June 2002.

Caldwell, John. "Reasons Legal Assistants Stick-It-Out Vary from Good Pay to Cultural Fit." *Legal Assistant Today,* July/August 2000.

Carey, Theresa W., Mike Heck, and Mike Hogan. "Human Resources." *PC World,* Reader No. 660, October 1997.

Caudron, Shari. "Overtime Pay: Overrated or Making Ends Meet?" *Legal Assistant Today,* January/February 1996.

———. "Understanding Law." *Legal Assistant Today,* July/August 1995.

Delaney, Joan. "Rave Reviews." *Your Company,* Spring 1994.

DeVera, Michelle. "Survey Is Michigan's First. Flextime Competes as Most Important Benefit." *Legal Assistant Today,* September/October 2000.

Editor. "Cost per Hire Example." *Legal Management,* September/October 1996.

———. "Denver Firm Establishes Foundation to Promote Volunteerism." *Legal Management,* May/June 2002.

———. "Developing a Performance Plan." Q.\\Training\MPM\Ratt\copm.docrevised, May 22, 1997.

———. "Employees' Rights, after Hours." *Manager's Legal Bulletin,* June 1996.

———. "Factors in Setting Law Firm Goals and Objectives." *Law Practice Management,* December 1995.

———. "Firm Leadership: The Next Generation." *Legal Management,* January/February 2002.

———. "Handy Reference Guide to the Fair Labor Standards Act." U.S. Department of Labor, October 1978.

———. "Hiring Down Corporate Legal Departments; Greater Reliance on Outside Counsel Expected." *Legal Management,* January/February 2002.

———. "The HR Power Guide," Champlain, NY: William Steinberg Consultants, Inc., Fall 1994.

———. "Internet Services." *Legal Management,* January/February 2002.

———. "Is the Grass Greener? Many Non-Law Firm Attorneys Pull in Big Incomes." *Legal Management*, January/ February 2002.

———. "Large Firms Realize Increase in Presence of Woman and Attorneys of Color, but Few Part-Time Attorneys." *Legal Management*, January/February 2001.

———. "Law Department Act to Retain and Reward In-House Lawyers." *Legal Management*, November/ December 2001.

———. "Law Online: Get Used To It." *Legal Management*, July/August 2001.

———. "Legal Assistant Salary and Compensation Levels." <http://www.nala.org/Sec.4web.htm>, August 13, 1998.

———. "Let Them Know What They Do Right." *Legal Management*, July/August 2001.

———. "A Look at Hours Worked under the Fair Labor Standards Act." U.S. Department of Labor, February 1980.

———. "Nearly 1/3 of Attorneys Would Teach as Alternate Career Choice." *Legal Management*, November/December 1997.

———. "Part-Time Attorney Schedules Rarely Used by Partners, Associates." *Legal Management*, January/ February 2002.

———. "The Pryor Report." *The Pryor Report Management Newsletter* 11, no. 1a July 1996.

———. "Purchasing and Supply Management." National Association of Purchasing Management, August 1996.

———. "Show Me the Stability: Survey Identifies Key Considerations for Candidates Making a Career Move." *Legal Management*, January/February 2002.

———. "Spouses Play a Key Role When Evaluating New Job Opportunities." *Legal Management*, March/April 2002.

———. "Survey Finds Majority of Legal Professionals Seeking Greener Pastures." *Legal Management*, November/ December 2001.

———. "Survey Shows U.S. Corporations Now Widely Use Alternative Dispute Resolution over Litigation." *Legal Management*, July/August 1997.

———. "Survey Shows Yearly Performance Reviews Standard." *Legal Management*, March/April 2002.

———. "What Are the Best Methods for Recruiting and Retaining Legal Professionals?" *Legal Management*, May/ June 2002.

———. "Where Is the Profession Today?" *National Paralegal Reporter*, July 1997.

———. "You Can't Please Everyone." *Executive Female*, January/February 1997.

Ellis, Diane M. "Reviews a la Carte." *Legal Assistant Today*, September/October 1996.

Emmons, Natasha. "Military Outreach Task Force Formed." *Legal Assistant Today*, March/April 1998.

Estrin, Chere B. "Stop Bonusing Paralegals for Billable Hours, Start Rewarding for Achieving Instead." *California Alliance of Paralegal Associations*, Winter 1997.

Gurowitz, Edward M. "Flexible Leadership Styles Let You Keep Current with Firm Needs." *Legal Management*, May/June 1997.

Hale, Jill J. "What Is in Our Future?" @ *LAW—the NALS Magazine for Legal Professionals*, Fall 2002.

Haserot, Phyllis Weiss. "Relationship Management: The Primary Focus of Quality Improvement." *Legal Management*, September/October 1994.

Hayes, Arthur S. "Tough Guys Argue in Court." *National Law Journal*, September 25, 1995.

Hedrick, Alexandra Kreuger. "Ten Commandments of Personal Management." *Legal Assistant Today*, July/August 1994.

Hughes, Rod. "Working Together." *Legal Assistant Today*, November/December 2001.

Hunt, Stacey. "What Keeps Some Paralegals with Their Current Employers and What Drives Others Away." *Legal Assistant Today*, May/June 2000.

Hunt, Stacey. "Paralegals Deemed Production Workers." *Legal Assistant Today*, July/August 1996.

———. "The Paralegal 'X' Files." *Legal Assistant Today*, July/August 1997.

Hutchinson, Jennifer E. "Peer Review: A Good Way to Help Improve Law Firm Procedures." *Legal Management*, September/October 1995.

Jaffe, Leslie, and Karl Krumm. "Your Role in Post 9/11 World." *Legal Management*, November/December 2001.

Jeffries, John A. "Wage and Hour Law Applications for Paralegals." *Legal Administrator*, March/April 1988.

Kording, Nicole, and Leanne Cazares. "A Dream Job." *Legal Assistant Today*, November/December 1996.

Kornreich, Wendy L. "Quick Reference for Selected Employment Laws." @ *LAW—the NALS Magazine for Legal Professionals*, January 1998.

Kramer, Thomas J., Lori O. Lewis, and Ellen Harshman. "What's Missing from This Picture?" *Legal Management*, July/August 1999.

Lajewski, Leslie A. "The 'New' Labor Lawyer." *National Law Journal*, May 2001.

Luebke, Robert. "Designing the Effective Team in a Law Firm Environment." *Legal Management*, September/ October 1995.

Mason-Draffen, Carrie. "Sweeping Overtime Rules to Take Effect." *Newsday*, August 15, 2004.

McGurk, John J. "The Overtime Debate." *Legal Assistant Today*, July/August 2007.

McKenna, Patrick J. "Best Law Firm Management Practices." *Legal Management*, September/October 1994.

Melhuish, Gary. "Overtime Debate." *Gary Melhuish*, 2004.

Messmer, Max. "The Many Faces of Motivation." *Legal Management*, September/October 1997.

———. "The Good Ones Are Gone: Lack of Growth Opportunities Cause Top Employees to Resign." *Legal Management*, March/April 1999.

Miles, Breanda W. "Benefits and Perks in the Legal Field." @ *LAW—the NALS Magazine for Legal Professionals*, Spring 1997.

Miller, Marjorie A. "Management of People in the Legal Environment." *Legal Management,* September/October 2001.

Mullen, Deirdre. "Mentoring Programs Boost Law Firm Loyalty." *National Law Journal,* May 2001.

Natoli, Vincent J. Jr. "How Organizational Personality Affects a Firm's Human Resources." *Legal Management,* September/October 2001.

Nelson, Bob, and Peter Economy. "Managing Today Requires New Skills." *The PriceCo Connection,* March 1993.

Newman, Ruth G. "Appraising Performance: What Every Good Coach Knows." *Self Employed Professional,* May/June 1996.

Ng, Rachel. "FLSA Face Lift Proceeds." *Legal Assistant Today,* March/April 2004.

Patterson, Cynthia L. "Pricing Legal Assistant Services." *Topics in Legal Assistant Utilization,* November 1988.

Peace, Shari. "Peace Talks: Relationships That Work: How to Boost Your Productivity by Getting Along at Work!" *@ LAW—the NALS Magazine for Legal Professionals,* Summer 2002.

Petropulos, Diane. "Make Your First Count." *Legal Assistant Today,* November 1998.

Ritter, Nancy. "Where Exemption Is Concerned, Paralegals Struggle to Find the Lesser of Two Evils." *Legal Assistant Today,* July/August 2002.

Roberts, Janet. "FSLA FairPay Regulations Take Effect." *Legal Assistant Today,* September/October 2004.

Shinoda, Lyndsey. "FairPay Regulations One Year Later." *Legal Assistant Today,* September/October 2005.

Smith, Charlsye. "Brief Survey Shows What Attorneys Expect from the Paralegal Staff." *Law Office Administrator,* September 1997.

Sokolosky, Valerie. "On the Job Satisfaction." *Spirit,* November 1998.

Stewart, Patrick J. "Salaried Personnel: Are They Really Exempt from Minimum Wage and Over-time Requirements?" *Legal Management,* January/February 1990.

Stoddard, Debbie. "Get the Job Credit and the Raise with a Self-Evaluation." *Law Office Administrator,* August 1997.

Tate, John R. "Profitability Formulas and Paralegal/Associate Comparisons." *The Docket,* Spring 1997.

Ward, Frances D. "All for One." *Legal Management,* September/October 1997.

Wertheim, Lynda F., and Robert J. Berkow. "A Hot Topic in Management Committee Meetings." *Legal Assistant Today,* November/December 1987.

Williams, Monci. "The Manager as Servant." *Executive Female,* March/April 1997.

Chapter 4

Allen, Ronald J. "Dead Men Need Not Talk." *National Law Journal,* July 6, 1998.

Ballard, Mark. "The Little Ad That Changed Everything." *National Law Journal,* September 2002.

———. "A Realization About Lawyer Advertising." *National Law Review,* October 2002.

Berman, Bruce. "'Niche' Firms Can Target Other Firms." *National Law Journal,* March 10, 1997.

Blumberg, John P. "Is It Really Legal Practice?" *California Lawyer,* February 1999.

Coburn, Jeff, and Eva Ginsburg. "Create Client Satisfaction Surveys That Give You More than Useless Information." *Legal Management,* September 1998.

Cooper, Alan. "Soliciting by Mail Approved." *National Law Journal,* January 19, 1998.

Coyle, Marcia. "Ad Decision Could Spur a Rollback." *National Law Journal,* July 3, 1995.

———. "D.C. Circuit Trims Client Privilege." *National Law Journal,* September 15, 1997.

———. "Fla. Bar Asks High Court to Take a Hard Look at Ads." *National Law Journal,* January 23, 1995.

———. "High Court Eyes Client Trust Fund." *National Law Journal,* January 19, 1998.

———. "The Long Road to Changing a Controversial Ethical Rule." *National Law Journal,* February 2002.

Davis, Ann. "Calif. Offenders Can be Disbarred Permanently." *National Law Journal,* September 1996.

———. "Profit Connection: Ohio-Naples, Fla." *National Law Journal,* November 4, 1996.

DeBenedicts, Don J. "State Bar Questions Simpson Commercials." *Orange County Reporter,* March 24, 1999.

Editor. "The ABA Commission on Advertising." American Bar Association, June 4, 1995.

———. "Attorney Advertising on the Internet." <http://personal.law.miami.edu/~rappapor/internet.htm>, November 5, 1998.

———. "From the Chair." *Lawyer Advertising News* 5, no. 1 (August 1995).

———. "From the Other Side: What Should a Client Expect for a Lawyer?" *Orange County Paralegal Association Compendium,* December 1996.

———. "How Clients Hire, Fire and Spend." BTI Consulting Group, 2006.

———. "Lawyer Malpractice Claims Remain Stable." *Legal Management,* July/August 2001.

———. "Let ALA Give You a Hand!" American Library Association, October 5, 1995.

———. "Oklahoma Undue Hardship Analysis Reveals System's Inconsistencies." *Consumer Bankruptcy News,* August 1, 1996.

———. "Preparing for Layoffs: Equitable Severance Packages." *Legal Management,* July/August 2001.

———. "Round the Industry." *Legal Management,* March/April 1998.

———. "Social Security Unveils New Representing Clients' Web Site." *Legal Management,* November/December 2001.

———. "Special Supplement." *Lawyer Advertising News,* June 21, 1995.

———. "Use of Arbitration to Resolve Inter-Insurance Disputes Exceeds $1 Billion." *Legal Management,* November/December 2001.

———. "Walking a Tight Rope: Preserving the Attorney-Client Privilege." *The New York Professional Responsibility Report,* April 1998.

———. "West Group NFPA Select 2001 Scholarship Winners." *Legal Management,* September/October 2001.

———. "What Happens When the Attorney-Client Relationship Ends?" State Bar of California, 1996.

———. "What Makes a Lawyer Successful? New Study Reports How Attorneys Get Business." *Legal Management,* September/October 2001.

———. "When Their Fingers DO the Walking, Make Sure Your Firm IS Doing the Talking." *Legal Management,* January/February 2001.

———. "Yellow Pages Lawyer Advertising: An Analysis of Effective Elements." American Bar Association, May 1992.

Filip, Christine S., and Anne E. Johnston. "Misleading Message May Spark a Suit." *National Law Journal,* November 10, 1997.

Fischer, James. "When Does a Client Become a Client?" *National Law Journal,* March 10, 1997.

Gallagher, Anne, and Merry Neitlich. "Make Your Firm the First Name for Client Service and Employee Satisfaction." *Legal Management,* July/August 2001.

Gallagher, Mike. "Minimizing Internet Security Risks." *Law Technology Product News,* April 1998.

Gerstman, Sharon Stern. "Advertising a Practice Specialty." *The New York Professional Responsibility Report,* April 1998.

Graham, John R. "Redefine Your Views on Marketing." *Legal Management,* January/February 1998.

Harguindeguy, Bernard. "Wavering Attorney-Client Privilege On-Line." *Law Technology News,* January 1999.

Harned, Billie Jo. "Why Manage Risk?" American Library Association, July/August 1998.

Hazard, Geoffrey C. "It Pays to Be Alert about Unforeseen Conflicts." *National Law Journal,* February 1, 1996.

———. "More Talk of Walls to Protect Confidentiality." *National Law Journal,* August 22, 1997.

———. "The Would-Be Client II." *National Law Journal,* February 1, 1996.

Helle, Steven. "Attorney Advertising after Peel." *Illinois Bar Journal* 78, no. 11 (November 1990).

Hoffmann Elinor R., and S. Calvin Walden. "Transactions." *National Law Journal,* December 1, 1997.

Hogarth, Marie-Ann. "Firms Look Far and Wide for Marketing Chiefs," *National Law Journal,* October 25, 2004.

Hornsby, William E. "Ethics Rules for Ads May Cover Web Sites." *National Law Journal,* January 29, 1996.

Jaffe, Jay M. "Bold Ads Help Firms Position Themselves." *National Law Journal,* March 18, 1996.

Jones, Arnold W. "Withdrawal from Representation of a Client." *The Docket,* September/October 1994.

Jones, Leigh. "Law Blogs Raising Prickly Ethical Issues." *National Law Journal,* October 6, 2006.

———. "A Tough Sell." *National Law Journal,* June 4, 2007.

Kelly, John G., "Firms Must Tackle E-Commerce for the Right Reasons-Not Just Because They Can." *Legal Management,* March/April 2002.

Leibowitz, Wendy R. "Client Conflict Software: No Panacea." *National Law Journal,* July 21, 1997.

———. "Even Authorized Off-Site Parties Imperil Security." *National Law Journal,* January 12, 1998.

———. "Lawyers Find Niches in the 'Net.'" *National Law Journal,* November 23, 1998.

———. "Legal Ethics in an Electronic Age: Where No One Has Gone Before?" *National Law Journal,* March 24, 1997.

Lipsey, John S. "Shift in Focus: Keeping Clients Happy." *National Law Journal,* January 2001.

Luce, Charles F. "Confidentiality, Cell Phones and E-Mail." *Legal Ethics and the Practice of Law Online,* November 4, 1998.

———. "Ethics in Attorney Advertising and Solicitation." <http://www.mgovg.com/ethics/11advert.htm>, November 4, 1998.

McCutchon, Esq. Fredrick. "Raising the Consciousness (and conscience) of the Legal Profession." *NALS Magazine,* Fall 2005.

McDonough, Molly. "Caution Is the Keynote at ABA Gathering: Delegates Balk at Biggest Ethics Changes." *National Law Journal,* August 2001.

Meyers, Harriet S. "When Their Fingers Do the Walking; Effectively Reach Potential Clients Through Yellow Pages." *American Library Association News,* November 5, 1998.

Micheletti, Mary. "Internet Has Transformed Prepaid Legal Services." *Orange County Reporter,* March 24, 1999.

Ohringer, Mark. "Law Firms May Want to Try a Different Approach with Corporate Law Departments." *Legal Management,* November/December 2001.

Orlik, Deborah K. "What Exactly Is Confidentiality?" *Legal Assistant Today,* May/June 1992.

Parisi, Madeline. "It Takes Strategic Marketing Planning to Hook and Keep Clients." *Legal Management Today,* May/June 2002.

Perkins. "Client Trust Accounts: Disasters Waiting to Happen?" *Lawyers Weekly USA,* March 10, 1997.

Piatt, Pearl J. "Getting the Word Out." *Los Angeles Daily Journal,* October 27, 1997.

———. "Lawyer Advertising." *Orange County Reporter,* October 4, 1997.

———. "You Say You Want a Revolution?" *Los Angeles Daily Journal,* September 1997.

Pike, Robert. "Making IOLTA Voluntary May Not Affect Every State." *Orange County Reporter,* August 22, 1997.

Reinhard, Matthew. "In Document Review, It Pays to Know Privilege Law." *National Law Journal*, September, 4, 2006.

Savarino, Julie, "Getting and Keeping Clients." *Legal Management*, May/June 2001.

Schmidt, Sally. "Individual Lawyer Marketing Plans." *Memorandum*, October 23, 1998.

Shaw, B. "Court Split over IOLTA Fund Case." *Orange County Reporter*, January 15, 1998.

Shepherd, Ritchenya. "Marketers Seen Running Firms." *National Law Journal*, March 22, 1999.

———. "Why MoFo Teams with KPMG." *National Law Journal*, August 23, 1999.

Simpson, Richard A. "Legal View." *Cyberspace Lawyer* 6, no. 3 (December 1998).

Solovy, Jerold S., and Robert L. Byman. "Common Interest Privilege." *National Law Journal*, August 20, 2007.

———. "When Is Work Protectable as Work Product?" *National Law Journal*, September 21, 1998.

Spivak, Cary. "Fight over Ban on Direct Mail." *National Law Journal*, March 18, 1996.

Stiefel, David. "Cooperation Helps Publicists Polish a Firm's Image." *National Law Journal*, October 9, 1995.

Vairo, Georgene M. "Federal Jurisdiction." *National Law Journal*, March 13, 2006.

Verstegen. "Client Trust Accounting Discipline Issues." *National Law Journal*, February 6, 1996.

Weidlich, Thom. "Ten Ways to Cut Malpractice Risk." *National Law Journal*, June 3, 1994.

Zitrin, Richard A., and Carol M. Langford. "Ethics in Ashes." *California Lawyer*, November 1998.

Zwicker, Milton W. "What Clients Really Want for Their Lawyers." *Law Practice Management*, September 1994.

Chapter 5

Amon, Elizabeth. "Pro Se Litigants Are Growing in Numbers and Getting Help." *National Law Journal*, July 2002.

Anderson, Judy. "Components for Ethics for Legal Support Staff." *The Docket*, Fall 1995.

Barnes, Denise. "Educating the Public Is Far More Valuable and Proactive." *Legal Assistant Today*, November/December 2002.

Baskette, Elsbeth, Kaye Aoki, Elizabeth Jackman, and Kathleen Nevins. *Manual for the Lawyers Assistant*. St. Paul: West Publishing, 1988.

Bemiss, Randi D. "Attorney Defends Screening." *Legal Assistant Today*, May/June 2002.

———. "NFPA Delegates Affirm Controversial PACE Rule Changing Exam Deadline." *Legal Assistant Today*, March/April 2002.

———. "U.S. Trustee Prosecutes Bankruptcy Petition Preparers." *Legal Assistant Today*, September/October 2002.

Bielec, Laurel. "A Giant Leap toward Regulation." *Legal Assistant Today*, November/December 1998.

Bogen, Deborah. "Social Security Paralegal under Investigation." *Legal Assistant Today*, November/December 1998.

Brunner, Lincoln. "Georgia Looks to Overhaul Public Indigent Defense System." *Legal Assistant Today*, July/August 2002.

Caldwell, John. "Judge Upholds Ruling on UPL Case." *Legal Assistant Today*, March/April 2002.

———. "LAT Takes a Look at the future of the Paralegal Profession;" *Legal Assistant Today*, September/October 2002.

———. "LDA Law Survives First Year." *Legal Assistant Today*, March/April 2001.

Campbell, Rachel. "Oregon Pursues Legal Assistant for UPL." *Legal Assistant Today*, September/October 2004.

———. "New York Court Favors Paralegal Fees." Campbell, Rachel. *Legal Assistant Today*, November/December 2002.

Cannon, Teresa. *Ethics and Professional Responsibility for Legal Assistants*. Boston: Little, Brown, 1992.

Castillo, Brenda. "Ready for a Change." *Legal Assistant Today*, July/August 2005.

Chapman, Elwood N. From *Campus to Career Success*. New York: Pergamon, 1978.

Clas, Camille Stucky. "UPL Attacked in North Carolina." *Legal Assistant Today*, January/February 1998.

Committee on Paralegal Education and Regulation. "Law." Los Angeles Mission College Paralegal Studies Program, August 12, 1998.

———. "New Jersey Report." Los Angeles Mission College Paralegal Studies Program, August 12, 1998.

Cooper, David, and Michael Gibson. *An Introduction to Paralegal Studies*. Cincinnati: South-Western Publishing, 1994.

Council, John. "No Sale for Unlicensed CyberLawyer." <http://www.ljx.com/tech/nocyber.htm>, April 20, 1999.

Cron, Sarah K. "Certification Boosts Legal Assistant's Standing." *Legal Assistant Today*, July/August 2006.

———. "International Paralegal Survey 2005." *Legal Assistant Today*, May/June 2006.

D'Antuono, Dane. "Regulation Update." *Legal Assistant Today*, November/December 2001.

Editor. "Avoiding Conflicts of Interest." *Legal Assistant Today*, May/June 2005.

———. "Case Law." *National Paralegal Reporter*, Fall 1998.

———. "Continuing Your Ethics Education." *Legal Assistant Today*, January/February 2007.

———. "Ethical Nightmares." *Legal Assistant Today*, November/December 2006.

———. "Ethics and the Media." *Legal Assistant Today*, May/June 2007.

———. "Flying Solo." *Legal Assistant Today*, March/April 2006.

———. "Giving Advise to Friends." *Legal Assistant Today*, January/February 2005.

———. "It's Time to Tell Staff about the Little Errors That Cause Malpractice." *Law Office Management,* July 1998.

———. "A Lack of Supervision." *Legal Assistant Today,* March/April 2007.

———. "Lawsuit Filed against Paralegal Businesses." *National Federation of Paralegal Associations Reporter,* January 1998.

———. "Making News." *National Federation of Paralegal Associations Reporter,* Fall 1998.

———. "New 'Legal Document Assistants' Opposed by Paralegals." *Notary Bulletin,* December 1998.

———. "An Obligation to Delegate Work?" *Legal Assistant Today,* July/August 2007.

———. "Parabriefs." *Legal Assistant Today,* September/October 1998.

———. "Report of the Licensing of Legal Assistants Committee of the Legal Assistant Division of the Utah State Bar." Legal Assistants Committee of Utah, May 6, 1998.

———. "Temps Win Suit." *National Law Journal,* June 2002.

Emmons, Natasha. "Case against California Independents Dropped." *Legal Assistant Today,* November/December 1998.

———. "Nolo Press Wins Latest Round." *Legal Assistant Today,* November/December 1998.

Flatten, Amanda. "It's Reunion Time!" *Legal Assistant Today,* March/April 2007.

Gillis, Elizabeth A. "The Name Game." *Legal Assistant Today,* July/August 2006.

———. "Seven Ways to Lose Your Job." *Legal Assistant Today,* March/April 2006.

Grimes, Shaunta. "Washington Bar Takes Progressive Position on Nonlawyer Services." *Legal Assistant Today,* March/April 2001.

Gust, Steve. "Public Opinion Poll Underway." *Legal Assistant Today,* November/December 1998.

Hawley, D. L. "Awards for Legal Assistants." *Legal Assistant Today,* July/August 2000.

Hazard, Geoffrey C. "Erecting a Wall to Prevent Conflicts of Interest." *National Law Journal,* July 21, 1997.

Heath, Jane, "Tips for Protecting Client Confidence in the Electronic Age." *Legal Assistant Today,* November/December 2002.

Heller, Nancy B. "Paralegal Ethics." *National Paralegal Reporter,* Fall 1998.

Howery, Susan. "Hawaii Attacks Document Prep Services." *Legal Assistant Today,* May/June 1999.

Hsia, Annie. "Bank Could Not Charge Legal Fee." *National Law Journal,* August 2001.

Hughes, Rod. "The Alliance Offers Certification." *Legal Assistant Today,* July/August 2004.

———. "NoLo Wins Battle in Texas." *Legal Assistant Today,* July/August 1999.

Hunt, Stacey. "Freelance Paralegal Firms." *Legal Assistant Today,* March/April 2007.

Hunt, Stacey, and Price, Ann. "Tips to Take and Pass the Two Most Popular Paralegal Exams." *Legal Assistant Today,* January/February 2007.

Levy, Debra. "Advocates Aim Sights on Amending State Legal Assistant Definition." *Legal Assistant Today,* March/April 2001.

———. "Federal Judge Recommends Closure of Paralegal Kit Company." *Legal Assistant Today,* March/April 2002.

———. "Parent Advocate Accused of UPL." *Legal Assistant Today,* March/April 1999.

Linfield, Leslie E. "Lightning Strikes Thrice: Emerging Issues in Bankruptcy Credit Counseling." *ABI Journal,* February 2006.

Liptak, Adam. "If It Looks Like a Lawyer and Acts Like a Lawyer." *New York Times,* August 2002.

Lowell, Abbe David. "Lawyer-Client Privilege Is Absolute." *National Law Journal,* May 26, 1997.

MacLean, Pamela. "Self-Help Centers Meet Pro Se Flood." *National Law Journal,* June 26, 2006.

Martinelli, Debra. "Learn to Identify and Avoid Issues Involving Unauthorized Practice of Law." *Legal Assistant Today,* January/February 2002.

———. "More Men, Minorities Enter the Field." *Legal Assistant Today,* March/April 2002.

Matsumoto, Jon. "Calif. Couple Makes a Deal." *Legal Assistant Today,* May/June 2005.

McGurk, John J. "Examining Certification." *Legal Assistant Today,* May/June 2007.

Micheletti, Mary. "Maine Regulation Moves Ahead." *Legal Assistant Today,* July/August 1999.

Nakaahiki, Victorialei. "Hawaii Paralegals Head toward Certification through Federal Court." *National Paralegal Reporter,* Fall 1998.

Ng, Rachel. "Marketing Game Plan." *Legal Assistant Today,* March/April 2005.

———. "NALS Passes Certified Professional Paralegals." *Legal Assistant Today,* July/August 2004.

———. "N.C. State Bar Passes New Ethics Opinion." *Legal Assistant Today,* July/August 2007.

Orlik, Deborah K. *Ethics for the Legal Assistant.* Glenview, Ill.: Scott, Foresman, 1986.

———. "What Exactly Is Confidentiality?" *Legal Assistant Today,* May/June 1992.

Pareti, Tim. "Florida Supreme Court Weighs-In on UPL." *Legal Assistant Today,* September/October 2002.

———. "Minnesota May Expand Nonattorney Legal Duties in Family Courts." *Legal Assistant Today,* July/August 2002.

Penkingcarn, Lynn. "Paralegal Utilization Grows." *Legal Assistant Today,* March/April 2006.

Roberts, Janet. "UPL Alleged in Texas." *Legal Assistant Today,* March/April 2004.

Rosen, Barbara. "When Are You Giving Legal Advice?" *Legal Assistant Today,* July/August 1995.

Samborn, Hope Viner. "Defining Paralegal Ethics." *Legal Assistant Today,* January/February 1995.

Sangchompuphen, Tommy. "Inside the Computerized Criminal Mind." *Legal Assistant Today,* July/August 2007.

Simon, Stephanie. "Opting for Cut-Rate Legal Eagles." *Los Angeles Times,* June 21, 1997.

Smith, Heather. "We The People Settles FTC Case." *Legal Assistant Today,* March/April 2005.

Sperber, Robert. "NFPA Adopts Model Disciplinary Rules at Annual Meeting." *Legal Assistant Today,* July/August 1997.

———. "NFPA Issues Two Cyberspace Ethics Opinions." *Legal Assistant Today,* May/June 1997.

———. "Oregon Legislature Moves toward Licensing Independent Paralegals." *Legal Assistant Today,* July/August 1997.

Statsky, William P. *Introduction to Paralegalism, Perspectives, Problems, and Skills.* 4th ed. St. Paul: West Publishing, 1996.

Tremore, Judy. "FALAP Gets Day at Supreme Court." *Legal Assistant Today,* May/June 2002.

———. "FTC and DOJ Encourage Competition Between Lawyers, Nonlawyers." *Legal Assistant Today,* November/December 2002.

Tyo, Ann. "NALA Holds Annual Convention." *Legal Assistant Today,* September/October 2006.

Tyo, Jamie Ann. "We The People Under Fire." *Legal Assistant Today,* July/August 2005.

Vuong, Patrick. "Are You Happy as a Paralegal?" *Legal Assistant Today,* January/February 2006.

———. "Taking a Stand on Education." *Legal Assistant Today,* March/April 2006.

Wallach, Joni Mcdonald. "Where Do We Stand?" *Legal Assistant Today,* March/April 1999.

Westin, I. Perrin. "Bill Regulating Independent Paralegals Passes First Hurdle." *Legal Assistant Today,* May/June 1998.

———. "NFPA Revises Its Model Ethic Codes and Definition of Paralegalism." *Legal Assistant Today,* November/December 1997.

———. "Paralegal Defeats Ex-Firm's Efforts to Prevent Move to Competitor." *Legal Assistant Today,* January/February 1998.

Young, Gary. "Key States Scrutinize 'Captive Law Firms." *National Law Journal,* June 2002.

Chapter 6

Alexander, Karen. "Was It a 'Premium' or an Inflated Bill?" *National Law Journal,* April 6, 1998.

Allen, Rae L. "NFPA Database Covers Wide Range of Cases." *National Paralegal Reporter,* December 1997.

Altonji, Joseph B. "Calculating the Costs of Providing Legal Services." *Accounting for Law Firms Newsletter,* August 1997.

———. "Knowing the Costs of Legal Services." *National Law Journal,* December 2, 1996.

Bemiss, Randi D. "Profession Distinguished in Federal Case." *Legal Assistant Today,* March/April 2002.

Blum, Andrew. "When Getting Your Fee Gets Tough." *National Law Journal,* April 1, 1996.

Cohn, Steven. "Tow Appeals Courts Rule Paralegal Fees Recoverable at Market Rate." *Legal Assistant Today,* July/August 1994.

Cox, Gail Diane. "Cost-Cutting Targets One of Its Own." *National Law Journal,* February 17, 1997.

———. "Excessive Fees Are Attacked across the Board." *National Law Journal,* November 4, 1996.

———. "Plaintiffs Reap Payoff from Auditor's Aid." *National Law Journal,* June 30, 1997.

Davis, Ann. "No Bill to Client for Training." *National Law Journal,* August 10, 1996.

———. "Temps Use Sparks Ire in Client Ranks." *National Law Journal,* December 23, 1996.

Donovan, Karen. "Is $1,109 an Hour Too Much?" *National Law Journal,* July 21, 1997.

Dooley, Laurel Ann. "Alston Bird, Others Win Total $1.89M." *National Law Journal,* December 22, 1997.

Dresslar, Tom. "Contingency Fee Appeals Eyed." *Orange County Reporter,* May 11, 1998.

Dubin, Lawrence A. "Ethics." *National Law Journal,* December 8, 1993.

———. "Court Blasts Non-Refundable Fee." *National Law Journal,* October 1994.

Dwight, Jennifer. "How Alternative Billing Will Affect Your Firm and Your Job." *Legal Assistant Today,* May/June 1995.

Editor. "1999–2000 Salary Survey Results." *Legal Assistant Today,* May/June 2000.

———. "Alternative Fee Arrangements—Panacea or Placebo?" *Legal Management,* May/June 1994.

———. "Billing Rates: Junior to Senior Associates." *National Law Journal,* December 2000.

———. "Compensation for Associates Generally Grows with Firm Size." *National Law Journal,* November 4, 1996.

———. "Fee Changes in Effect." *California Lawyer,* March 1993.

———. "O. J. Simpson Defense." *USA Today,* August 5, 1994.

———. "Pro Bono." *National Law Journal,* March 10, 1997.

———. "Recovery of Paralegal Fees Table of Authorities." In *Handbook on Paralegal Utilization.* San Francisco, CA.: California Alliance of Paralegal Associations, 1986.

———. "Watch Out for the Billing Practices That Kill the Clients." *Law Office Administrator,* August 1997.

———. "What Can a Legal Fee Agreement Do for Me?" State Bar of California, 1997.

———. "Windy City Paralegal Rates." *Legal Assistant Today,* November/December 1998.

Eigles, Jack T. "Take It to the Bank." *Legal Administrator*, November/December 1997.

Emmons, Natasha. "Fees Reduced for Work That 'Could Have' Been Done by Paralegals." *Legal Assistant Today*, March/ April 1998.

———. "Firm Denied Recovery of Fees for Paralegals Who Crossed the Line." *Legal Assistant Today*, January/ February 1998.

———. "NFPA Releases Survey Results." *Legal Assistant Today*, January/February 1998.

Estrin, Chere B. "Looking into the Compensation Crystal Ball." *Legal Assistant Today*, May/June 1997.

Fisk, Margaret Cronin. "Corporate Firms Try Contingency." *National Law Journal*, June 20, 1996.

Harris, Andrew. "Missouri Jury Awards $118 Million." *National Law Journal*, March 2002.

Jessen, Nancy A. "The Task at Hand: Making Task-Based Billing a Working Reality in Your Firm." *Legal Management*, March/April 1996.

Kummel, William. "Things Change." *Legal Management*, May/June 1996.

Leibowitz, Wendy R. "Lawyers and Technology." *National Law Journal*, June 22, 1998.

MacLachlan, Claudia. "Court Sides with Lawyer on Expenses." *National Law Journal*, April 15, 1995.

———. "DOE in Dark on Defense Fees." *National Law Journal*, July 17, 1994.

Marshall Joseph L., and Elizabeth D. Hersey. "Take a Closer Look at Value Billing before the Compensation Does." *Legal Management*, November/December 1994.

Prohaska, Ronald R. "Are You Setting Your Fees Too Low?" *Lawyers Weekly USA*, March 10, 1997.

Samborn, Randall. "Contingent Fee Arrangements Get ABA Nod." *National Law Journal*, January 30, 1995.

Stansky, Lisa. "Firms Bills to Court Heading Skyward." *National Law Journal*, July 2002.

Statsky, Bill. "Summary-Billing for Lexis and Westlaw." *National Law Journal*, November 6, 1998.

Van Duch, Darryl. "Fee Challenged in Conn. Case." *National Law Journal*, November 6, 1995.

Van Voris, Bob. "That $10 Billion Fee." *National Law Journal*, November 30, 1998.

Weston, I. Perrin. "NY Governor Disallows Fee Recovery for Paralegal Services." *Legal Assistant Today*, January/ February 1998.

Chapter 7

Editor. "1996 Average Annual Associate Billable Hours at 10 Firms." *National Law Journal*, August 22, 1997.

———. "1996 Median Billable Hours of Lawyers Nationwide." *National Law Journal*, August 22, 1997.

———. "Billing Rates." <http://www.nala.org/Sec.3web .htm>, August 21, 1999.

———. "Do Not Squander Time." *Legal Management*, July/August 1999.

———. "Holland and Hart Foundation Finds Unexpected Rewards Through Firm-Wide Volunteerism." *Legal Management*, November/December 2001.

———. "Patterns and Practices; Measures of Law Firm Hiring, Leverage and Billable Hours." *Legal Management*, May/June 2002.

———. "Time and Billing Solutions for Legal Professionals." In *Client Success and Satisfaction*. Manual for Status Pro, Bellview, WA.: CSS, Inc., 1998.

———. "Using Paralegals as a Cost Cutting Measure Might Explain 2001's Big Increase." *Legal Assistant Today*, March/April 2002.

Goldstein, David A. "Task-Based Timekeeping: Technology's Role in Solving the Puzzle." *Legal Management*, March/April 1996.

Hunt, Stacey. "Making Time Count." *Legal Assistant Today*, May/June 1999.

Lovett, Wayne J. "It's Time Software Fit a Lawyer's Bill." *National Law Journal*, November 20, 1995.

National Association of Legal Assistants. "Legal Assistant Billing Rates." *National Association of Legal Assistants*, August 2002.

Neser, Arlin P. "Is Your Law Firm Losing the War with Time?" *Law Office Computing*, February/March 1997.

Russo, Michael A. *Timeslips Deluxe for Windows CD-ROM*. Dallas, TX.: Timeslips Corporation, 1996.

Singer, Randy B. "Macintosh OS X Time and Billing Software Options Abound." *Law Office Computing*, August/September 2002.

Thompson, Mark. "Pay Me Right, and I'll Bill You Honestly." *@ LAW—the NALS Magazine for Legal Professionals*, March, 1999.

Chapter 8

Banham, Russ. "Lawyers for Less." *CFO Magazine*, October 1, 2005.

Blodgett, Nancy. "Articulating the Values of Your Law Firm." *Legal Management*, January/February 1996.

Bollar, Robert W., and Robert D. Sheehan. "Alternative Billing Options to Keep Clients Satisfied." *Legal Management*, July/August 1994.

Burney, Brett. "E-Billing: Friend or Foe?" *Legal Assistant Today*, September/October 2005.

Cioccio, Diana Di. "No More Smoke and Mirrors." *Legal Management*, November/December 1996.

Coburn, Jeff, and Michael Preston. "Management: Survey Reveals How Firms Use Profit Centers as Strategic Tools." *Legal Management*, July/August 1997.

Correl, Bruce. "Tracking Non-Chargeables Can Keep Firm Afloat." *National Law Journal*, April 25, 1994.

Cotterman, James D. "Developing Rational Capital Structures for Law Firms."*Accounting for Law Firms* 10, no. 7 (July 1997).

Drucker, Bruce D. "Some Firms Still Vexed by Audits of Legal Bills." *National Law Journal*, July 25, 1994.

Editor. "Billable Hours." *Wall Street Journal*, May 27, 1994.

———. "Billing: The Bottom Line." *Legal Assistant Today*, March/April 2005.

———. "Don't Let Billable Time in the Library Get Written Off." *Law Office Administrator*, July 1997.

———. "Editor's In-Box." *Legal Management*, July/August 1997.

———. "55 of the Top 200 Corporate Legal Departments Use Compinfo Lawpack." *Legal Management*, November/December 1997.

———. *Getting Started with INTEGRA™*. Dawson Creek, Canada: Power Soft Innovations Corp., 1997.

———. "Have Go-Go '80s Returned?" *National Law Journal*, September 1997.

———. "Internet Law Researcher." *Legal Management*, March/April 1997.

———. "Juris Eases Compliance with Special Billing Requirements."*Legal Management*, November/December 1997.

———. "New Products." *Legal Management*, March/April 1995.

———. "Tailored Training Programs Help Some Firms Play the RFP Game." *National Law Journal*, March 3, 1997.

———. "Time & Billing Software." *National Law Journal*, December 21, 1998.

———. "U.S. Law Firms: Gross Receipts Improve, Profit Lags." *Legal Management*, November/December 1998.

———. "Watch Out for the Billing Practices That Kill the Clients." *Law Office Administrator*, 6, no. 8 (August 1997).

———. "What Lawyers Earn." *National Law Journal*, June 2, 1997.

———. "What Partners Bill Each Year." *National Law Journal*, August 22, 1997.

Eigles, Jack. "Take These Steps to Improve Your Firm's Cash Flow." *Legal Management*, May/June 2001.

Estrin, Chere B. "The Old Billable Hours Game." *Legal Assistant Today*, March/April 1997.

Ford, Chris. "Is There a Cure for the Billable-Hour Blues?" *Cyber Esq.*, Spring 1999.

Fortado, Lindsay. "Going Up Still." *Notional Law Journal*, December 12, 2005.

France, Mike. "Clock's Running on Billable Hours." *National Law Journal*, December 19, 1994.

Grunfeld, David L. "Collecting Law Firm Fees." *Legal Management*, July/August 2002.

Guynn, Jessica, and Nina Schuyler. "The Venture Law Firm Group Takes the Adventure Out of Legal Billing." *California Law Magazine*, June 1995.

Hayes, Arthur. "Uniform Task-Based Billing." *National Law Journal*, June 22, 1998.

Johnson, Kipp. "Streamline the Billing Process." @ *LAW—the NALS Magazine for Legal Professionals*, Fall 2002.

Kulpa, Bob. "10 Things—and Then One More—to Do with a Balance Sheet." *Legal Management*, January/February 1998.

Lewis, Geraldine A. "A New Era in Billing Practices." *California Lawyer*, September 1998.

Neath, James J. "Task-Based Billing—the Way of the Future." *Legal Management*, March/April 1995.

Nilsson, David S. "There Must Be 60 Ways to Lead Your Finances." *Legal Management*, July/August 1997.

Orlik, Deborah K. "A Question of Billing." *Compendium*, December 1995.

———. "Those Elusive Billable Hours." *Legal Assistant Today*, May/June 1995.

Poll, Edward. "These Win/Win Tips will Keep Your Firm's Cash Flowing." *Legal Management*, September/October 2001.

Preston, Michael. "Managing Partners Voice Their Views on Profit Center Measurement." *Legal Management*, September/October 1997.

Pritchard, Grant, and John R. Tate. Law Office Economics & Management Manual. *Orientation to Law Firm Accounting*. Deerfield, IL.: Callaghan & Co., 1991.

Schley, Sandra G. "Don't Stop Thinking about Tomorrow." *Legal Management*, November/December 1996.

Singleton, Ruth. "How Billing Rates React to the Larger Economy." *National Law Journal*, December 8, 1997.

Slind, Victoria. "'Grown-Up' Lawyers Do Non-Billables." *National Law Journal*, November 13, 1995.

Smith, Colin. "Grow Your Own Way." *Legal Management*, November/December 1996.

Snyder, Theda. "Complaints about Legal Billing Practices." *Law Practice Management*, April 1999.

Sturgill, Stephen J. "New System Offers Easier and More Exact Billing." *National Law Journal*, October 17, 1994.

Turnbow, Richard B. "Be Proactive—Explain Your Law Firm's Billing Practices to Clients." *Legal Management*, July/August 1995.

———. "Revising Your Billing Practices Can Fund Your Tech Upgrades." *Law Technology News*, March 1999.

Van Duch, Darryl. "Test Case for Insurers' Billing Rules." *National Law Journal*, January 25, 1999.

———. "Troubled Firms Must Act Fast." *National Law Journal*, September 22, 1997.

Wilke, John T. "Know What to Look for When Analyzing Income Trends." *Legal Management*, July/August 1997.

Yost, Sandra L. "Alternative Billing Strategies—New Wave or Passing Fad." *Legal Management*, March/April 1994.

Chapter 9

Coyle, Marcia. "Critics of Mandatory IOLTA Have Their Day." *National Law Journal,* June 2002.

———. "Critics: Now We'll See Where IOLTA Funds Go." *National Law Journal,* June 29, 1998.

Editor. Accounting for Law Firms 10, no. 6 (June 1997).

———. "Brief Accounting." <http://www.briefaccounting.com/pages/trust.htm>, August 21, 1999.

———. *The Case for Integra™.* Dawson Creek, Canada: Power Soft Innovations Corp., 1998.

———. "In Texas, IOLTA Survives Round Two." *National Law Journal,* February 2001.

———. "Trust Accounting." <http://www.stilegal.com/trustacc.htm>, August 21, 1999.

Hsia, Annie. "No Taking Found in IOLTA Plan." *National Law Journal,* December 3, 2001.

Oster, Patrick. "IOLTA Redux." *National Law Journal,* June 29, 1998.

Thomas, Richard. "IOLTA Funds Are Clients." *National Law Journal,* September 30, 1996.

Thorne, Deborah, L. "Check-Kiting Schemes." *ABLI Journal,* October 2002.

Chapter 10

Alberts, Alan. "The Integrated Desktop: Budgeting and Strategic Planning for Your Next Upgrade." *Legal Management,* March/April 1997.

Alizadeh, Steve. "Predictions from an Expert." *Legal Management,* November/December 1998.

Ambrogi, Robert J. "Finding Ethics via the World Wide Web." *Law Technology Product News,* December 1998.

Ballon, Ian C. *Selected Issues in the Emerging Law of the Internet.* Legal Works 98. Little Falls, N.J.: Glasser Legal Works, 1998.

Bathija, Sandhya. "Blogging May Be Tcket to a Job." *National Law Journal,* July 9, 2007.

Bemiss, Randi D. "Nonlawyer Screens Are Legal." *Legal Assistant Today,* July/August 2002.

Bendell, Adam S. *State-of-the-Art Document Management.* Legal Works 97. Little Falls, N.J.: Glasser Legal Works, 1997.

Berg, Martin. "Lawyers in Federal Court Say They're Tickled by Elmo." *Cyber Esq.,* Spring 1999.

Bernstein, David S. "A 64-Year-Old Litigator Gets with the Tech Program and Outshines Opponents." *National Law Journal,* July 2002.

Biddle, Brad. "Public Key Infrastructure and 'Digital Signature' Legislation: Ten Public Policy Questions." *Cyberspace Lawyer* 2, no. 2 (1997).

Brewer, John. "35 + Vital Sites: Seven Experts Offer Up Their Valuable Web Resources." *Legal Assistant Today,* November/December 2002.

———. "Seven Expert Attorneys Offer Up Their Most Valuable Web Resources." *Law Office Computing,* October/November 2002.

Burrows, Jennifer. "Searching for Answers." *WebSite Journal* 2, no. 26 (June 30, 1999).

Bush, Christopher E. "Can Technology Revolutionize How Firms Educate Their Staff?" *Legal Management,* July/August 2001.

———. "Hone Your Communication Skills When Using E-Mail. The Web." *Legal Management,* May/June 2002.

Butler, Charles. "Knowledge Is Power." *Legal Management,* March/April 1999.

Caddell, Douglas D. "Bridge the Gap." *Legal Management,* March/April 1999.

Caldwell, John. "Appeals Court Says E-Mail Service Acceptable Method." *Legal Assistant Today,* July/August 2002.

———. "Safeguarding Your Data." *Law Office Computing.* August/September 2002.

Calhoun, Richard A. "Automation Requirements for the Year 2000." *Legal Management,* May/June 1995.

Campbell, Rachel. "Emerging Technologies and the Legal World." *Legal Assistant Today,* November/December 2002.

———. "The Numbers Are in for the 2001 ABA Legal Technology Survey." *Law Office Computing,* October/November 2002.

Canfield, Curt A. "Dismiss Groupware at Your Own Peril." *Law Technology Product News,* March 1998.

Casali, Harold O. "From Word Processing to the Office of the Future." *Legal Management,* March/April 2001.

Cohen, Steve. *Maintaining a Secure Legal Extranet.* Legal Works 98. Little Falls, N.J.: Glasser Legal Works, 1998.

Curreri, Michael. *Networking Counsel Efforts: Extranets for Litigation and Matter Management.* Legal Works 98. Little Falls, N.J.: Glasser Legal Works, 1998.

Davis, Susan E. "Duty to Surf." *California Lawyer,* November 1998.

Dean, Martin L. "The Portable Lawyer." *California Lawyer,* November 1998.

Diboise, James. "E-Mail Security, Section 998 Offers, and Clean Air Act Liability." *California Lawyer,* August 1998.

Dimstead, John W. Jr., MBA. "Coach Your Firm Staff Members for Better Performance." *Legal Management,* March/April 2001.

Dhamija, Tina. "Take it Back." *Legal Assistant Today,* March/April 2005.

Donahue, Robert J., and Joseph M. Hartley. "Dangerous but Irresistible: 2003 Legal Technology Predictions." *Law Office Computing,* October/November 2002.

Editor. "1997 Survey Shows Internet Is Hot." American Bar Association, July 1997.

———. "2001 Technology Survey Demonstrates That Paralegals Haven't Been Scared Off by the Millennium Bug, and Are Instead, Continuing to Embrace Technology." *Legal Assistant Today,* March/April 2001.

———. "2002 Legal Technology Directory." *Legal Assistant Today,* May/June 2002.

———. "Accessibility and Distribution of Information on the Web." <http://www.wwwmetrics.com/>, August 20, 1999.

———. "Advanced Web Searching Techniques." <http://www.learnthenet.com/english/html/77advance.htm>, April 11, 1999.

———. "All about News Groups." <http://www.learnthenet.com>, April 5, 1999.

———. "Anatomy of an E-Mail Message." <http://www.learnthenet.com/english/html/21e_anat.htm>, April 5, 1999.

———. "Avoiding Technology Traps." *Legal Assistant Today,* May/June 2006.

———. "Best of the Web." @ *LAW—the NALS Magazine for Legal Professionals,* Fall–Winter 1998.

———. "Beware Workplace E-Mail: Reduce Risk and Avoid Court Dates." *Legal Management,* September/October 2001.

———. "The Buzz about Blogging." *Legal Assistant Today,* May/June 2006.

———. "Case Management Software." *Legal Assistant Today,* March/April 1997.

———. "Caught on the Net." *Legal Management,* March/April 2001.

———. "Communications Without Borders." *Future Law Office,* August 2002.

———. "Dataviz Debuts Web Buddy 1.1." *Legal Management,* June 1997.

———. "Direct Contact with Prospective Clients." ABA Professional Conduct on the Internet White Paper, July 1998.

———. "eGems Provides Superior Interface for Collecting Electronic Information." *Law Office Computing,* August/September 2002.

———. "Electronic Communications." <http://www.learnthenet.com>, April 5, 1999.

———. "Eliminate Lengthy Online Searches." *Legal Assistant Today,* July/August 2000.

———. "Expanded Reach of Technology." *Future Law Office,* August 2002.

———. "Florida Firm Uses E-Mail to Solve Phone Problems." *Law Office Administrator,* July 1998.

———. "Frequently Asked Questions." <http://www.learnthenet.com/english/toolbar/faq.htm>, March 29, 1999.

———. "How E-Mail Works." <http//www.learnthenet.com/english/html/20how.htm>, March 28,1999.

———. "How to Find People's E-Mail Addresses." <http://www.cis.ohiostate.edu/hypertext/faq/usenet/finding-addresses/faq.htm>, April 5, 1999.

———. "How Law Firms Use the Internet." *California Lawyer,* July 1997.

———. "The Internet and the Practice of Law." *Web Counsel.* LLC. March 20, 1998.

———. "Internet Survey Results." *Cyber Esq./California Lawyer,* Spring 1998.

———. "Interview: The ILPN Talks with Will Hornsby about Internet Ethics." *National Law Journal,* November 18, 1996.

———. "IOMA Site." *Law Technology Product News,* mid-April 1998.

———. "The Law Firm Intranet." *Internet Law Researcher,* March 1998.

———. "Law Women Anticipate Their Employer Three Years Earlier Than Men." *Legal Management,* March/April 2001.

———. "Lawyers Average Nearly 50 E-mail Messages Daily." *Legal Management,* March/April 2002.

———. "Lawyers Reluctant to Use Internet for Confidential Correspondence." *Legal Management,* May/June 1998.

———. "Legal Software Directory." *Legal Assistant Today,* September/October 1997.

———. "Legal Software Directory." *Legal Assistant Today,* November/December 1998.

———. "Legal Technology Purchasing Guide." *Daily Journal,* June 21, 1998.

———. "Mailing Lists." <http://www.learnthenet.com/english/html/24mlists.htm>, April 5, 1999.

———. "Needles." *Legal Assistant Today,* March/April 2005.

———. "One Firm's New Policy." *Legal Management,* March/April 1998.

———. "Organizing Your Virtual Desktop." *Home Based Working Moms,* March 2002.

———. "Penetrating the U.S. Market." *Legal Integrations, USA,* May 1999.

———. "Practice Management." *Practice Management,* February 2002.

———. "Practice Management Software." *Law Office Computing,* August/September 2002.

———. "Practice-Specific Domain Names Are Not Common." *National Law Journal,* April 2000.

———. "Products and Services for the Legal Community." *Legal Assistant Today,* May/June 1997.

———. "Real Legal Practice Manager." *Real Legal,* July 2002.

———. "Recent Technology Survey Provides New Information." *National Federation of Paralegal Associations Reporter,* January 1998.

———. "Research Identifies Technology Advances, Work-Life Issues and Enhanced Client Service Among Factors Expected to Shape Law Office and Careers." *Legal Management,* September/October 2001.

———. "Small Law Firms Find Advantages as Technology Trendsetters." *Legal Management,* September/October 2001.

———. "Smileys." <http://www.learnthenet.com/english/html/25smile.htm>, April 5, 1999.

———. "Starting Salaries for Legal Support Professionals Will Rise in 1999, Survey Says." *Legal Management,* March/April 1999.

———. "State Developments." *Cyberspace Lawyer* 2, no. 2 (1997).

———. "Subscribing." <http://www.learnthenet.com/english/html/28subscr.htm>, April 5, 1999.

———. "Technology: House Panel Approves Web Domain for Children." *The Times*, July 2002.

———. "Tips for Improving Your E-mail Style." *LegalAssistant Today*, September/October 2001.

———. "Tips and Timesavers." *Legal Assistant Today*, July/August 1998.

———. "21st Century Lawyer—Case and Trial Management in the Same Program." *Law Office Technology Solutions*, March 1997.

———. "Understanding E-Mail Addresses." <http://www.learnthenet.com/english/html/22email.htm>, April 5, 1999.

———. "Web Stop." *Legal Assistant Today*, November/December 1998.

Efquist, David J., Esq. "Encryption Of-Mail: Paradigm or Paranoia?" *@ LAW—the NALS Magazine for Legal Professionals*, Fall 2002.

Eppers, Julie, A. "The Web's Business Presence Hits Five Years. How Do Firms Measure Up?" *Legal Management*, March/April 2001.

Estrin, Chere B., and Kevin J. Behan. "Enter the Net." *Legal Assistant Today*, July/August 1999.

Evans, Cheryl D. "Legal Sites: Findlaw." *California Lawyer*, May 1998.

———. "Legal Sites: Know Your Bill." *California Lawyer*, July 1998.

Feather, Kathryn. "Law Firm Goes the Extra Mile." *Legal Assistant Today*, July/August 2005.

Feather, Kathryn. "What's New." *Legal Assistant Today*, March/April 2005.

Fleischer, Matt. "Portland Paradise May Not Last Long." *National Law Journal*, June 2001.

Flynn, Nancy. "New Book Offers an Outline for Your Firm's E-Policies." *Legal Management*, March/April 2001.

Forrest, Elizabeth. "What's the Word." *Legal Management*, March/April 1999.

Fox, John C. "Electronic Lawyers Assist Employers." *National Law Journal*, November 20, 1995.

Freeling, Kenneth A., and Ronald E. Wiggings. "States Develop Rules for Using Digital Signatures." *National Law Journal*, October 20, 1997.

George, Molly. *Electronic Discovery Litigation's Newest Challenge to Corporate Records*. Legal Works 97. Little Falls, N.J.: Glasser Legal Works, 1997.

Gillis, Elizabeth A. "Overcome Information Chaos." *Legal Assistant Today*," September/October 2001.

Glickenhaus, Lee H. *Extranets Merge Virtues of Internet and Intranets*. Legal Works 99. Little Falls, N.J.: Glasser Legal Works, 1999.

———. "Knowledge." *Law Practice Management*, March 1999.

———. "Untangling the Web: Secure Extranets as a Legal Management and Collaboration Tool." *Legal Assistant Today*, November/December 1998.

Goldhaber, Michael. "Work Aplenty for Seattle Tech Firms." *National Law Journal*, April 2000.

Goldsborough, Reid. "Internet Information May Warrant a Double Check." *Inside the Internet*, Winter 1997.

Gonzalez, Sandra. "If You Build It Right, They Will Come." *Law Technology Product News*, mid-September 1998.

Gottesman, Ben Z. "The Web Workplace." *PC Magazine*, June 22, 1999.

Griffith, Cary. "Lawyers Can't Afford Not to Automate Case Management." *U.S. Business Litigation*, March 1997.

———. "Put the Web to Work." *Legal Management*, November/December 1997.

Hawley, D. L. "Tips for Improving Your E-Mail Style." *Legal Assistant Today*, September/October 2001.

Hobbs, Allen. "The Internet Offers Expanded Alternatives for Law Firm Marketing." *National Law Journal*, April 3, 1995.

Hornsby, William E. "The Regulation of Technology-Based Lawyer Advertising and Internet Use Policies." *Legal Management*, July 1998.

Hughes, Paul. "E-Mail Wiretapping Has Arrived." *Legal Assistant Today*, July/August 2001.

Johnson, Amy. "Courtroom of the Future Gets Raves from Lawyers." *Lawyers Weekly USA*, March 10, 1997.

Johnson, Ashley. "Technology Budgets Increase." *Legal Assistant Today*, May/June 2007.

Jones, Leigh. "Want to Poach Associates? Good Luck." *National Law Journal*, September, 2006.

Jucovy, Esq. Timothy, and Matthew Kudzin. "Employee Blogging." *Facts & Findings*, August 2007.

Kahan, Steven. "Don't Wait to Start Building Your Human Firewall." *Legal Management*, March/April 2002.

Kaplan, Ari. "The Extranet Revolution." *Legal Assistant Today*, November/December 2006.

Kashi, Joseph L. *How to Conduct On-Premises Discovery of Computer Records*. Legal Works 98. Little Falls, N.J.: Glasser Legal Works, 1998.

———. *Upgrading Older Computers: What's New, Smart and Cost-Effective?* Legal Works 98. Little Falls, N.J.: Glasser Legal Works, 1998.

Kennedy, Dennis. "It's A Jungle Out There." *Legal Assistant Today*, September/October 2004.

Kennedy, Dennis M. "Prepare Your Firm with These Key Legal Technology Predictions." *Legal Management*, March/April 2002.

———. "Prepare Your Firm with These Key Legal Technology Predictions." *Legal Management*, January/February 2002.

———. "Watch for These 2001-Give or Take Technology Trends in 2001." *Legal Management*, March/April 2001.

Klau, Richard P. *Litigation Management through the Use of Secure Internet-Based Networks*. Legal Works 99. Little Falls, N.J.: Glasser Legal Works, 1999.

Kohlmann, Susan. *Internet: Domain Name System To Be Restructured*. Legal Works 98. Little Falls, N.J.: Glasser Legal Works, 1998.

Kohn, Lawrence M., and Lisa Ellis. "Market the Megabyte$." *Legal Management,* March/April 1999.

Kozlowski, Ken. "Around the Legal Web Sites." *Internet Law Researcher* 3, no. 11 (February 1999).

Krager, Dwayne E. "E-Discovery Is Silently Becoming the Norm." *Legal Assistant Today,* September/October 2002.

———. "Some Simple Electronic Tools Can Keep You Organized In and Out of the Office." *Legal Assistant Today,* November/December, 2002.

———. "Today's Paralegals Need to Master Computer Software and Hardware Used to Prepare and Try a Case." *Legal Assistant Today,* January/February 2001.

———. "Users Guide to Choosing Among Popular Litigation Support Programs." *Legal Assistant Today,* July/August 2001.

Krakaur, Peter. *Intranets and Extranets: Using Internet Technology to Enhance the Practice of Law.* Legal Works 97. Little Falls, N.J.: Glasser Legal Works, 1997.

Lake, Matt. "Journey to the Ends of the Search Tools and Prevail." *PC World,* June 1999.

Landry, Robert J. "Federal Bankruptcy Practice Exception to the State Bar Examination: Not Exactly!" *ABI Journal,* October 2002.

Leibowitz, Wendy R. "E-Mail Policy on Trial." *National Law Journal,* November 9, 1998.

———. "Future Law Tech. Visions." *National Law Journal,* September 13, 1999.

———. "Lawyers and Technology." *Law Technology Center,* March 3, 1999.

———. "Is Every Web Store a Law Breaker?" *National Law Journal,* August 23, 1999.

Levin, Carol. "Little Devices Will Think." *PC Magazine,* June 22, 1999.

Lewis, Shari Claire. "Beware the Unauthorized Practice of Law in Cyberspace." *New York Law Journal,* June 6, 2007.

Loundy, David. "E-Law: Rising Awareness Shown in Three New Encryption Bills." *Cyberspace Lawyer* 2, no. 2 (1997).

Lovett, Wayne J. "Document Software Called to Assembly." *National Law Journal,* June 26, 1995.

MacLean, Pamela A. "Erasing E-mails Brings Liabilities." *National Law Journal,* March 20, 2006.

Macleod, Don. *Legal Research and the Internet.* Legal Works 97. Little Falls, N.J.: Glasser Legal Works, 1997.

Mattiano, Paul. "Get the Skinny on Thin-Client-Server Computing." *Legal Management,* July/August 1999.

Maw, Cynthia. "Electronic Discovery 101." *@ Law—the NALS Magazine for Legal Professionals,* Spring 2007.

McCullum, Kenya. "You've Got IMs" *Legal Assistant Today,* January/February 2007.

McGuire, David. "New Internet Domains a Year or More Away." *Tech News,* July 2002.

McKenzie, Diana. "Business in Cyberspace Calls for Cautious Dealings." *National Law Journal,* June 26, 1995.

McQueen, Howard, and Jean E. DeMatteo. "A CIO's Perspective on Intranet Development." *Internet Professional,* no. 4 (November/December 1998).

Middlehurst, Carl. *Intranets for Legal Departments.* Legal Works 97. Little Falls, N.J.: Glasser Legal Works, 1997.

Miller, Michael J. "Also on the Horizon." *PC Magazine,* June 22, 1999.

———. "Computers Will Be More Human." *PC Magazine,* June 22, 1999.

Nadler, David M. "New Encryption Export Rules: Two Views." *Cyberspace Lawyer* 3, no. 10 (1999).

Nagel, Rebecca Thompson. "ABA Tech Survey Released." *Legal Assistant Today,* November/December 1998.

———. "Bonnie Hill's Web Picks." *Legal Assistant Today,* March/April 1998.

Overly, Michael R. "E-eek!" *Legal Management,* November/December 1998.

Ozolin, Peter J. "Leveraging the Internet to Better Serve Clients." *Law Technology Product News,* April 1998.

Pacifici, Sabrina. *Law Firms Intranets: Harnessing the Power of Knowledge Resources.* Legal Works 98. Little Falls, N.J.: Glasser Legal Works, 1998.

Piatt, Pearl J. "Greedy Lawyers on Line." *Cyber Esq.,* Spring 1999.

Plonsky, Kim. "Communication in Today's Hi-Tech World." *Legal Assistant Today,* September/October 2007.

Plonsky, Kim. "Turning the Tables." *Legal Assistant Today,* November/December 2005.

Putnam, Melanie. "The Internet Guide to Reference Resources." *Internet Law Researcher* 3, no. 11 (February 1999).

Rich, Tracey R. "Advanced Internet Searching." *National Law Journal,* July 9, 2007.

Rinaldi, Arlene. "Lister VS/Mailing Lists/Discussion Groups." *The Net: Users Guidelines and Netiquette,* April 5, 1999.

Robson, Gary D. "Cybercasts Pose Alternatives to Videoconferencing." *National Law Journal,* July 1997.

Robson, Ken "Layering: The Best Way to Keep the Hackers Out?" *@ LAW—the NALS Magazine for Legal Professionals,* Summer 2002.

Rogers, James. "Space Odyssey: Law Offices for the 21st Century." *National Law Journal,* January 30, 1995.

Rosch, Mark, and Carole Levitt, J.D., M.L.S. "Extranets for Small Firms and Solos." *Law Office Computing,* October/November 2002.

Rosenberg, Geanne. "Anderson Legal Goes High Tech to Better Compete with Law Firms." *National Law Journal,* August 2000.

Ross, Susan B. "Balance Your Practice, the Internet and Ethics." *Legal Management,* November/December 1997.

Rothbart, George. *Designing, Building and Maintaining a Web Site.* Legal Works 99. Little Falls, N.J.: Glasser Legal Works, 1999.

Rovner, Jeffery S. "Law Firm Extranets: The New Kid on the Block." *Legal Works '98.* Little Falls, N.J.: Glasser Legal Works.

———. "Three Benefits of a Law Firm Intranet." *Law Technology News*, September 1998.

Rupley, Sebastian. "The Web Will Be Smart." *PC Magazine*, June 22, 1999.

Santella, Chris. "Firm Managers and Marketers Should Read All About 'Em." *Legal Management*, September/October 2000.

Saxon, Steve. "Voice Recognition Software Makes You George Jetson." *Legal Management*, March/April 1999.

Sevy, Monica. *Live Demonstration III Word 97 and Word Perfect 7.0*. Legal Works 97. Little Falls, N.J.: Glasser Legal Works, 1997.

Shanghai-Beech, Hannah. "Living It Up in the Illicit Internet Underground." *Time*, July 2002.

Skeels, William H. "Web-Based Management Facilities for the Law Practice." *Legal Management*, May/June 2001.

Snider, Anna. "Web Photos Pulled." *National Law Journal*, March 8, 1999.

Socha, George. *Processing the Electronic Ore: Reconstructing and Analyzing the Other Side's Electronic Evidence*. Legal Works 97. Little Falls, N.J.: Glasser Legal Works, 1997.

Sommers, Robert L. *Client Development on the Internet*. Legal Works 98. Little Falls, N.J.: Glasser Legal Works, 1998.

———. "If Operating Systems Ran the Airlines." *The Internet*, BillStatsky@Delmar.com, August 20, 1999.

———. *Surf Rider*. Legal Works 98. Little Falls, N.J.: Glasser Legal Works, 1998. Statsky, Bill. "Websites and UPL's." *New York Opinion*, October 24, 1998.

Steele, Eric H., and Thomas Scharbach. "Efficiently Set up an Intranet/Extranet?" *Law Technology News*, January, 1999.

Steinberg, Marty. "Why Extranets Are Gaining Litigators' Trust." *Law Technology Product News*, mid-September 1998.

Stoddard, Sonia Von Mott. "E-Mail Etiquette." *Legal Assistant Today*, March/April 1998.

Suni, Ellen Yankiver. "Ethics & Technology: Preserving Confidentiality in a High Tech World." *@ Law—the NALS Magazine for Legal Professionals*, Spring 2007.

Templeton, Denise. "Sending and Receiving Information in a Technology-Based World." *Legal Assistant Today*, March/April 2002.

Teshima, Daryl. "Eight Predictions for 1998." *Legal Assistant Today*, March/April 1998.

Thompson, Kathryn A. "The Worlds of Ethics." *Legal Assistant Today*, September/October 2005.

Twibell, Scott, and Marie Monte. "Administrators Hope ASPs Answer Their Tech Problems." *Legal Management*, March/April 2001.

Tyburski, Genie. "Judging Information on the World Wide Web." *Legal Assistant Today*, March/April 2001.

———. "Tips and Tricks for Finding What Your Need on the Web." *Legal Assistant Today*, July/August 2001.

Van Duch, Darryl. "Allstate Again Under the Gun: Low-Cost Defense Via the Internet Is Fraud, a New Suit Claims." *National Law Journal*, July 2001.

Voorhees, Mark. "Surf's Up: Guide to the Best Web Sites for Lawyers." *National Law Journal, April 2000*.

Vuong, Patrick. "Studies Show Improvements in e-Government." *Legal Assistant Today*, January/February 2006.

———. "Top 200 Firms Stay Connected." *Legal Assistant Today*, March/April 2006.

———. "The Internet Serves Up an Array of Legal Specialty Choices." *Legal Management*, July/August 2001.

Wallach, McDonald J. "Bookmarking Basics." *Legal Assistant Today*, July/August 1998.

Walter, Skip. "Plantiffs' Law Firms No Longer as Disadvantaged." *National Law Journal*, July 5, 2004.

Wright, Benjamin. "Electronic Commerce Litigation: Frequently Asked Questions." *Cyberspace Lawyer* 2, no. 2 (1997).

Yelin, Andrea B. "Staying Professionally Connected." *Legal Assistant Today*, January/February 1998.

Young, Rufus. "E-Etiquette for E-Mailers." *National Law Review*, August 2002.

Chapter 11

Adkins, Andrew Z. "Case Management Might Be Exactly What Your Firm Needs." *Legal Assistant Today*, May/June 2002.

Dodge, John A. "Outside Your Windows." *Wall Street Journal*, April 19, 1999.

Gillis, Elizabeth. "Managing Processes for Increased Productivity." *Legal Assistant Today*, May/June 2002.

Grimes, Linda A. "Teamwork Is Essential in Systems Management." *National Law Journal*, January 30, 1995.

Editor. "Paralegals Online." *Legal Assistant Today*, May/June 1998.

———. "What Corporate Clients Think of Outside Counsel Billings." *National Law Journal*, January 30, 1995.

Hunt, Stacey. "NALA Announces 1998 Member Exchange Presentations." *Legal Assistant Today*, March/April 1998.

Messmer, Max. "The Human Side of New Technology in Law Firms." *@ LAW—the NALS Magazine for Legal Professionals*, Fall–Winter 1998.

Meyers, Harriet S. "Everybody's Gone Surfing." *Legal Management*, September/October 1997.

Nagel, Rebecca Thompson, "Plugged in and on Top." *Legal Assistant Today*, March/April 1998.

Schlein, Carol L. "Those Who Don't Learn from Their Past Are Destined to Buy the Wrong System Again." *Legal Management*, July/August 2001.

Stauble, Gary. "Implement Systems to Keep Top Talent with Your Firm." *Legal Management*, July/August 2000.

Chapter 12

Davis, Susan E. "Docket Science." *CompuLaw*, October 1998.

Dean, Martin L. "Software Guaranteed to Save Money." *California Lawyer*, November 1989.

Dodge, John A. "Outside Your Windows." *Wall Street Journal*, April 19, 1999.

Editor. "Insurance Discounts." *CompuLaw*, September 1998.

———. "Paralegals Online." *Legal Assistant Today*, May/June 1998.

———. "Pays for Itself." *CompuLaw*, September 1998.

———. "Polk Research." *CompuLaw*, October 1998.

———. "What Corporate Clients Think of Outside Counsel Billings." *National Law Journal*, January 30, 1995.

Grier, John. "It's on the Calendar!" *Legal Management*, November/December 1996.

Grimes, Linda A. "Teamwork Is Essential in Systems Management." *National Law Journal*, January 30, 1995.

Hunt, Deborah M. "Court Rules Databases are Key When Choosing Calendaring Software." *@ LAW—the NALS Magazine for Legal Professionals*, Summer 2005.

Hunt, Stacey. "NALA Announces 1998 Member Exchange Presentations." *Legal Assistant Today*, March/April 1998.

———. "Ten Tips for Implementing a Case Management System." *Legal Assistant Today*, November/December 1997.

Kaplan, Ronald E. "Reaping the Benefits of a Computerized Calendar System." *CompuLaw*, October 1998.

Messmer, Max. "The Human Side of New Technology in Law Firms." *@ LAW—the NALS Magazine for Legal Professionals*, Fall–Winter 1998.

Meyers, Harriet S. "Everybody's Gone Surfing." *Legal Management*, September/October 1997.

Murai, Ray. "Bringing Hi-Tech Docket Calendaring to the Nation's Premier Hi-Tech Law Firm." *@ LAW—the NALS Magazine for Legal Professionals*, July 1996.

Nagel, Rebecca Thompson. "Plugged in and on Top." *Legal Assistant Today*, March/April 1998.

Schilling, Joan. "Law Office Management: Calendaring Is Critical." *California Lawyer*, January 1998.

Scott, Joseph, Attorney. "Online Calendaring." *Facts & Findings*, May 2005.

Yellen, Howard. "Risk Reduction." *CompuLaw*, October 1998.

Chapter 13

Baldwin, Merri A., and Pamela Phillips. "Client Files: Handle with Care." *California Lawyer*, May 1998.

Barr, Jean G. "Computers Are the Future for Keeping Track of Files. But First You Have to Get Ready." *Legal Assistant Today*, November/December 1993.

Bemiss, Randi. "DAPA Makes Move to Define Paralegals in Texas." *Legal Assistant Today*, January/February 2001.

Bodine Larry. "It Really Is Who You Know (and What You Know, Too)." *Legal Management*, January/February 2001.

Bendell, Adam S. "State-of-the-Art Document Management." *American Law Technology*, Spring 1997.

Colloway, Jim. "Management Assistance Program." *Oklahoma Bar Journal*, August 4, 2007.

Davis, Susan. "Getting Down to Cases." *California Lawyer*, June 1996.

Dietel, Edwin. "Effective Information and Records Management: Why Is It Important to Lawyers? *The Metropolitan Corporate Counsel*, October/December 2001.

Dwight, Jennifer. "The Nuts and Bolts of Civil Case Organization." *Legal Assistant Today*, March/April 1995.

Editor. "1999 Legal Products and Services Directory." *Legal Assistant Today*, May/June 1999.

———. "About Bar Coding." <http://www.learnthenet.com>, May 15, 1999.

———. "Ask ETHICSearch." <http://www.learnthenet.com>, February 26, 1999.

———. "Bridging the Document Management Gap." *Law Office Computing*, August/September 2002.

———. "DFS-General Information." Applied Engineering Management Corporation. May 8, 1999.

———. "Document Management." *Law Technology News*, June 1999.

———. "Effective Record Management." *The Docket*, July/August 1993.

———. "Is That New Client Bringing the Firm a Malpractice Risk?" *Legal Office Administrator*, 7, no. 7 (July 1998).

———. "Large Firms." *Law Technology Product News*, August 1998.

———. "Mobil Shelving Helps New York Firm Add Years of Records Storage." *Legal Management*, November/December 2001.

———. "Slow Down the Paper Chase by Making Full Use of the Record System." *Law Office Administrator*, August 1997.

———. "Twelve Steps in Automating Your Files." *The Docket*, July/August 1993.

———. "Watch Out for the Risks in the Client Engagement Letter." *Legal Office Administrator*, 7, no. 4 (April 1998).

Emmons, Natasha. "The Specialty Star." *Legal Assistant Today*, May/June 1999.

Fienman, Harvey B. "Trends in Automated Litigation Document Management." <http://.lib.polyu.edu.hk/electdb/DATAPRO/57579-1.htm>, May 7, 1999.

Foonberg, Jay G. "When and How to Close a File." *Lexisone*, December 2002.

Ford, Chris. "Bank on It." *Cyber Esq.*, Spring 1999.

Gable, Julie. "Records Management in Electronic Document Management." <http://.lib.polyu.edu.hk/electdb/DATAPRO/ 57529-1.htm>, September 9, 1998.

Gierke, Oliver M. "Preparing Privilege Logs." *Legal Assistant Today,* May/June 2007.

Glanell, Barry. "A Solo Creates Defacto Document Management." *Law Technology News,* May 1999.

Gold, Gloria. "Set the Records Straight." *Legal Management,* March/April 1999.

Greenwald, David, and Guy Wiggins. "Document Management Shootout." *Law Office Computing,* June/July 1997.

Jones, Nancy B. "Risk Management." *The Docket,* March/April 1994.

Kanofsky, Florence. "The Automated Office—Technical Skills for Legal Secretaries." *The Docket,* September/October 1994.

Katz, Stanley. "For the Record." *Legal Management,* January/February 1996.

Kazemi, Dana L. "Tips and Timesavers." *Legal Assistant Today,* July/August 1994.

Kodner, Ross L. "Small Law Office Calendaring: A Quick Survey." *LexisOne,* December 2002.

Levy, Debra. "New York Students Pair Up with Mentors in the Legal Field to Explore Career Options." *Legal Management,* January/February 2001.

Micheletti, Mary. "Paralegals and the Document Management Programs They Use." *Legal Assistant Today,* March/April 2000.

Morgan, Barbara D. "Transfer: Breaking Boundaries with Web-Based Networks." *Law Practice Management,* March 1999.

Myers, Gini. "Law Office Technology: Systems Filing." *@ LAW—the NALS Magazine for Legal Professionals,* July 1996.

Plonsky, Kim. "Exploring Electronic Medical Records." *Legal Assistant Today,* January/February 2006.

———. "The File Factor." *Legal Assistant Today,* November/December 2006.

———. "Taking a Stab at the Numbers." *Legal Assistant Today,* September/October 2005.

Polisar, Lisa. "Converting a Large Firm to Automated Imaging." *Law Technology Product News,* August 1998.

Pollan, Lynne E. "Every Law Office Needs a Good Filing System." *National Law Journal,* October 17, 1994.

Reed, Richard C. "The Lawyer: Brain Power vs. Computer Power." *Law Practice Management,* March 1999.

Salmons, Phyllis A. "Web Site Offers a Multitude of Corporate Resources and Promise Future Expansion." *Legal Assistant Today,* January/February 2001.

Sell, Lois. "As Knowledge Management Evolves, Corporate Legal Department Use of KM Must As Well." *Legal Management,* January/February 2001.

Shill, Rhonda. "Beyond Search and Retrieval." *Law Technology Product News,* March 1998.

Simon, Roy. "Do I Have to Keep These Old Files?" *The New York Professional Responsibility Report,* April 1998.

Skupsky, Donald S. "Records Retention Programs for Law Firms." *Legal Management,* January/February 1995.

Solomon, Barry. *Choosing a Relationship Management System.* Legal Works 98. Little Falls, N.J.: Glasser Legal Works, 1998.

Zaben, Alan S. "Managing Electronic Documents, Including E-mail." <http://www.learnthenet.com>, May 5, 1999.

Chapter 14

Aarons, Anthony. "From Free to Fee." *Cyber Esq.,* July 1998.

Baker, Brian L. "Librarians Might Get Entangled in the Web." *National Law Journal,* October 2, 1995.

Beyer, Robin. "Controlling Costs in the Law Library." *Legal Management,* January/February 1994.

Biberman, Thor Kamban. "Technology Brings About the Incredible Shrinking Law Office." *San Diego Source, Daily Transcript,* April 30, 2007.

Bohill, Ruth. "Electronic Citation Guide for Legal Materials." <http://law.anu.edu.au/nglrw/lr3.htm>, May 28, 1999.

Davis, Ann. "Swapping Books for 'Jukebox.'" *National Law Journal,* November 6, 1995.

Davis, Susan E. "Books versus Bytes." *California Lawyer,* July 1998.

Editor. "2002 Legal Technology Directory." *Legal Assistant Today,* May/June 2002.

———. "Inmagic® Tech Flash." <http://www.learnthenet.com>, May 25, 1999.

———. "MLA Style." <http://www.learnthenet.com>, May 28, 1999.

———. "Query Help." <http://www.learnthenet.com>, May 28, 1999.

———. "Recent Technology Surveys." <http://www.learnthenet.com>, April 15, 1999.

———. "Technology Survey: 6th Annual." *Legal Assistant Today,* May/June 2007.

Emrick, Nicholas. "Storehouse of Legal Expertise." *The Docket,* July/August 1993.

Estes, Mark. "Try These Eight Tactics to Cut the Cost of Library Subscriptions." *Law Office Administrator,* July 1997.

Freriks, David. "Library of Progress." *Legal Management,* March/April 1997.

Gediman, Mark A. "Books vs. Bytes." *Legal Assistant Today,* May/June 2005.

Giangrande, Mark. "Research Tools for Today." *National Law Journal,* July 17, 1995.

Glickenhaus, Lee H. *Knowledge.* Legal Works 99. Little Falls, N.J.: Glasser Legal Works, 1998.

Kinglsy, Martin. "Show Me the Money—Measuring the Return on Knowledge Management," <http://www.llrx.com>, May, 2007.

Leibowitz, Wendy R. "Big-Firm Librarians to Publishers: Get Your CD-ROM Acts Together." *National Law Journal,* October 20, 1997.

Leiter, Richard A. "The Five Laws of Library Science." *Legal Assistant Today,* November/December 1996.

Mingo, Michael. "Developing Your Own Online Research Strategy." *Law Technology News,* April 1999.

Orlik, Deborah K. "Technology and the Law." *Legal Assistant Today,* May/June 1996.

Platt, Nina. "Managing a (High-Tech) Library Effectively." *Law Technology Product News,* October 1997.

Plonsky, Kim. "Building a Knowledge Bank." *Legal Assistant Today,* March/April 2006.

————. "Free Internet Tools for Paralegals." *Legal Assistant Today,* January/February 2007.

————. "Making Paralegal Work Easier." *Legal Assistant Today,* March/April 2007.

Relles, George, and Richard C. Solomon. "Law Office Management, Charging for Online Research and CD-ROM." *California Lawyer,* April 1998.

Scarbrough, Bill. "The Library 'Space' Race." *Legal Management,* March/April 1999.

Schorr, Morriss E. "Will CD-ROMs Replace Books in Law Libraries?" *Law Technology Product News,* April 1999.

Shimpock-Vieweg, Kathy. "Library Cost Control: Trimming the Fat." *Legal Assistant Today,* July/August 1994.

————. "Work Product Retrieval: Design and Implementation." *Legal Assistant Today,* March/April 1994.

Stathis Andrew L. "Technology Offers Incentive to Downsize Law Libraries." *National Law Journal,* October 2, 1995.

Sternfeld, Donald O. "Facilitating Document Retrieval." *National Law Journal,* March 21, 1994.

Teshima, Daryl. "The Challenge: Westlaw.com and Lexis-Nexis Xchange." *Legal Assistant Today,* July/August 1998.

————. "Finding Needles in Digital Haystacks." *Legal Assistant Today,* January/February 1998.

Voorhees, Mark, and Lovett, Wayne. "Surf's Up: Guide to the Best Web Sites for Lawyers." *National Law Journal,* April 3, 2000.

Index